LINUX
DESKTOP STARTER KIT

Linux Desktop Starter Kit

John Lathrop

McGraw-Hill
New York   San Francisco   Washington, D.C.
Auckland   Bogotá   Caracas   Lisbon   London
Madrid   Mexico City   Milan   Montreal   New Delhi
San Juan   Singapore   Sydney   Tokyo   Toronto

Library of Congress Cataloging-in-Publication Data

Lathrop, John P.
    Linux desktop starter kit / John P. Lathrop.
        p.   cm.
    ISBN 0-07-212283-8
    1. Linux. 2. Operating systems (Computers) I. Title.
  QA76.76.O63 L3676   2000
  005.4′469—dc21

                                     99-088660
                                         CIP

McGraw-Hill

*A Division of The **McGraw·Hill** Companies*

P/N 0-07-212281-1
PART OF ISBN 0-07-212283-8

The sponsoring editors for this book were Simon Yates and Sharon Linsenbach, and the production supervisor was Claire Stanley. It was set in New Century Schoolbook by V&M Graphics, Inc.

Printed and bound by Quebecor/Martinsburg.

 This book is printed on recycled, acid-free paper containing a minimum of 50% recycled, de-inked fiber.

To

Dr. Ayşen Akpınar

For her encouragement and hospitality, over several
computers, in Silver Towers, Cyprus, Istanbul.

UNIX is strictly old hat—it's been around for two decades. But it's still used—now, as Linux, on the PC. It's stable, a known quantity, and it works. Sometimes the old solutions work the best. Look at fire. Look at the wheel.

Patrick Lathrop, Computing Services, San Francisco State University

CONTENTS

Contents

PREFACE

Who Should Read This Book?

This book is for people who want to do practical work in Linux; it is not for the UNIX computer guru. It is for computer users who know little or nothing about Linux, or about UNIX, but who either have to or want to work—wordprocess, produce spreadsheets or presentations, or use the Internet for e-mail and the Web—in the Linux operating system.

The purpose of this book is to show everyday Microsoft Windows users how to install, configure, and productively use Linux, side by side on the same computer with Windows.

How This Book Is Organized

Part 1: Installation.   Installing Linux is much easier than it used to be, but there can still be hurdles to overcome. This part will get you over them. Four major distributions are covered: Red Hat, Caldera, TurboLinux, and SuSE. Special attention is given to configuring a Windows machine to run both Windows and Linux—without destroying the present configuration. If you are already running a Linux machine, jump to Part 2.

Part 2: Under the Hood: Linux at the Command Line.   In this part, basic configuration and command line tools are presented in an easy, step-by-step, tutorial approach.

Part 3: X Window.   This part covers X Window—Linux's answer to Microsoft Windows. More stable, more configurable, and with a different 'desktop' for each distribution, this feature-rich workplace will strike the new user as both reassuringly familiar—and interestingly different.

Part 4: Productivity.   Back to the mouse. From the Linux Windows environment, to the Internet, to an MS Office look-alike, this part shows how to get serious work done in a familiar, Windows-like, mouse-driven environment, using many of the same programs you probably use now.

Part 5: Guru Status. This part covers laptops, system management, kernel re-compiles, DOS emulation and home networking.

What Is Linux?

Linux is a computer operating system, an alternative to Microsoft Windows, originally invented by a Finnish computer student named Linus Torvalds. The system has been under constant development by hundreds of unpaid programmers, an effort still broadly overseen by Torvalds. It was originally built to run on the IBM PC, but now runs not only on the PC, but on several other "platforms"—other types of computers—as well.

How do you pronounce "Linux"? The operating system itself will tell you in Part Two.

What About Application Programs?

There's both good news and bad news. The good news is that for standard applications such as word processing, spreadsheets, presentations, graphics, Web browsing, and e-mail, Linux now has applications every bit as good as Microsoft Windows. There's more good news: many Linux applications are so similar to their Windows counterparts that there's virtually no learning curve when switching over to the new operating system. Some programs are even the same: Netscape's browser and e-mail software run on both systems.

The bad news is that there are still missing applications. Commonly used financial software, such as Quicken, is not yet available. And there is still no database as useful on the desktop as Access, although far more powerful (and complex) databases are available.

Every month, however, more software and hardware companies are announcing their plans to start supporting Linux—companies as big as IBM, Oracle, Sun, and Corel. For the desktop basics, everything's already there.

Why Use Linux?

There are several reasons why you might need to, or want to, use Linux:

Performance and Cost. Linux has a reputation for speed and stability that Microsoft Windows cannot match. The windows environment in Linux is faster than Microsoft's product, and even large programs, like StarOffice, an MS Office look-alike, are faster. In addition, you can virtually forget about operating system crashes, hangs, and general protection faults. If an application program (such as Netscape) does hang—application programs sometimes do go awry, on any operating system—it won't take the whole computer down with it. You can just close the application down and restart it, without rebooting the whole machine, running scandisk, etc. This is a fast, stable, solid operating system.

On top of that, Linux is incredibly inexpensive. A complete Linux productivity solution—the operating system, internet programs, and a powerful office suite that rivals MS Office—is available as a package from several different distributors for from $25 to $80. The operating system alone can be bought on CD, without documentation, for $1.79. All major applications are also available as free downloads from the Web.

Virus-Free! Say goodbye to Microsoft viruses—they can't touch a Linux system. The UNIX/Linux system is traditionally virus-free.

Adoption by Business and Universities. Many businesses run Linux as print and file servers; more and more businesses are using Linux as the backbone of their networks. Naturally, the operating system migrates to the corporate desktop. You may soon be running it on yours!

Linux is taking over academia. Many academic institutions are switching completely, abandoning Microsoft. If this is the case in your institution, you may have to run Linux at work, and you may want to run it at home.

Being in the Vanguard Rather Than the Rear. Although it's riskier being ahead of the rest of the pack, it's also more interesting—and in today's increasingly information technology driven–world, it can be fatal to fall behind.

Run Both Operating Systems. Although you cannot run Windows and Linux on the same computer simultaneously, you can switch easily from one to another. You do it with a boot manager, a small program that gives you the choice of which operating system to use when you turn the machine on. You can run whichever operating system you wish. You switch from one to the other simply by turning the machine off and then on again, and selecting the other operating system. It's easy to pass files from Windows to Linux and back again. At the moment you probably use Windows. By using both operating systems, you can try out Linux while keeping your current system intact. You can go back to Windows whenever you want to, and when you feel like it, go forward to Linux.

Commercial Distributors

There are several commercial distributors of Linux, the two largest (in the United States) being Red Hat Software, Inc., of Durham, North Carolina, and Caldera, Inc., of Orem, Utah. In Japan the most popular is TurboLinux, and the Germans prefer SuSE. Both the Japanese and the German distributions have beachheads in the United States, from which they are expanding their operations and gaining market share.

Each Linux distribution has its own installation procedure—some more automated than others—and each has chosen a slightly different desktop look. However, under the hood they are all basically the same.

Why This Book?

There are a growing number of Linux books on the market, divided roughly into books for the novice and books for the UNIX expert. The books for the UNIX expert are quite good and undoubtedly give the UNIX expert a smooth and thorough introduction to the more arcane aspects of Linux administration. Unfortunately, the books for the novice are usually also written by UNIX experts—who can have a hard time understanding that the vast majority of computer users today are completely mouse- and icon-oriented and have never heard of or used the command line.

It is true that the command line has its charms. It is fast. It is reliable. It is uniquely useful for solving configuration problems. And, through consistent use, it enhances the operator's typing ability. I have devoted an entire part (Part 2) of this book to it.

However, the major orientation of this book is to working in Linux in exactly the same way as you would work in Windows. This book was written to make Linux as easily accessible as possible to the average computer user.

ACKNOWLEDGEMENTS

First, I would like to thank the people from the major commercial distributors who helped me with this book. At Caldera Systems, Inc., Debi Cunningham, Director of Human Resources/Legal, obtained for me a significant level of staff support. Dean Zimmerman of Product Marketing was more than helpful, he was proactive, in providing prepublished documentation, news of upcoming bug fixes, files, and screen shots.

At TurboLinux, Lonn Johnston, Vice President, was very encouraging, and Justin Ryan proved to be a wizard in generating the images I needed.

Andy Dickens, Red Hat's Sales Director in Europe, pushed through a channel to Edward Bailey, who broke all records in the support of this book.

Second, I would like to thank two individuals who offered different kinds of help: my brother, a UNIX guru, who helped me with some of the more arcane aspects of system management, and my wife, Mariann Befus, who never lost her patience during months of Linuxing.

—JOHN LATHROP
<linuxjl@attglobal.net>

## PART 1

Installation

This is the first and biggest hurdle to overcome: getting the operating system on and working. The good news is that most of the major distributors have made huge strides in simplifying the installation process. Linux is now much easier to install than it used to be even a little while ago. The bad news is that Linux will usually not automatically detect as much of your computer's hardware as Microsoft Windows. This means that a little preliminary detective work may be a good idea before installation.

For users who want to run both Linux and Windows on the same machine—and most probably will—there is one potential complication. To prepare a dual-operating system machine, you should use a modern, easy-to-use, and safe disk partitioning program (more on this later). Unfortunately, only one distribution as of this writing—Caldera's—comes with such a program. So if you aren't installing Caldera, you probably have additional software to buy.

This part starts with Red Hat's installation procedures, and then goes on to Caldera, TurboLinux, and SuSE. There are a variety of network installation methods, but I leave those to the system manager, who would be in charge of them in any case. The installation method described in this part is that used by the typical desktop computer user.

## CHAPTER 1

Preparing for the Installation

Purpose of Chapter: Create Space for the Linux Installation, and Gather System Information

You should probably buy a separate program called PartitionMagic if you are installing Red Hat, TurboLinux, or SuSE on a Windows computer. You have to create free space on your hard drive for the Linux installation, and only Caldera's OpenLinux does this automatically.

Linux will not always automatically detect your graphics adapter, so it's a good idea to get this information in Windows, before starting the Linux installation.

Disk Space Requirements

You need at least 700 Mbytes to install a workstation system—a setup that will enable you to do in Linux what you now do in Windows. You'd be better off with 1 Gbyte, but if you're installing Linux as the second operating system on the same hard drive as your current Windows configuration, of course, you'll need more free space. It's doubtful that you'll switch completely to Linux as soon as you install it. You'll go back and forth between the two systems for some time, so you'll need adequate free space on your old Windows partition for new files, new programs, etc.

A good minimum is1.5 Gbytes: 1 Gbyte for Linux, and 500 Mbytes free space left for Windows.

Do I Have to Buy a Separate Program?

The simple answer is: if you want to run a dual Windows/Linux machine, and you aren't going to use Caldera's OpenLinux, then you probably should buy a separate disk partitioning program.

Creating free space on your hard drive can be an automatic or a manual operation, depending on which Linux distribution you decide to load. Table 1-1 shows the different partitioning capabilities of the different distributions.

What is a Partition?

A partition is simply a part of your hard disk that has been magnetically prepared to load and run a computer program: an operating system like

TABLE 1-1

Automatic
Repartition
Features, by
Distribution

Distribution	Create Space by Automatically Resizing the Windows Partition	Automatically Create New Linux Partitions from Free Space
Red Hat Linux 6.1	No	Yes
Caldera OpenLinux 2.3	Yes	Yes
TurboLinux 3.6	No	No
SuSE Linux 6.1	No	No

Windows or Linux or an application like Word or Excel. Most computers come with their hard drives magnetically arranged in just one large partition. That's all that Windows needs. But Linux and Windows use different file systems, and the different file systems need separate partitions. Linux needs at least two partitions of its own.

Why Does Linux Need Two Partitions?

One is for your main Linux program, and one is for the swap file.

Your computer has two different kinds of memory: RAM, or thinking memory, and hard disk storage memory. Sometimes there's a lot of program code or data in RAM that doesn't really need to be there. To make more thinking memory available, Linux temporarily swaps the code or data out of RAM, and writes it to a special file on the hard disk—the swap file.

The swap file is constantly growing and shrinking, so in Linux it's put on a separate partition so it won't interfere with the rest of the program.

PartitionMagic

PartitionMagic is a disk partitioning program that magnetically resizes your current partition, thereby making room for Linux. There are several old-fashioned programs of this kind around. Fdisk is an example, used in UNIX, Linux, DOS, and even Microsoft Windows. All the distributions of Linux come with a partitioning program called FIPS. These old programs are typically complicated for the novice to use, unforgiving, and can even destroy the data on a hard disk. Modern programs are graphical, mouse-driven, and don't destroy anything.

The average user should not fiddle around with Fdisk, FIPS, or any of the other old partitioning programs. They are too complex and dangerous. There are several modern disk partitioning programs available on the market, but since this is a critical issue, and a critical program, I suggest you go for the most established and market-tested: PartitionMagic by PowerQuest.

Preparing Your Disk with PartitionMagic

There are several steps to take: install Windows if it's not already on; back up your data; install PartitionMagic; and finally, create free space for Linux.

IMPORTANT: Caldera's OpenLinux comes complete with a stripped-down but automated version of this program. If you are installing Caldera's product, then skip forward to Step 5, Gathering Information on Your Graphics Chip and Monitor.

Step 1: Installing Windows

Install Microsoft Windows, if you don't already have it on your machine and you want both operating systems. This is the basic rule: when running another operating system on the same computer as Microsoft Windows, always install Windows first.

Step 2: Backup

Back up your data, and as many of your programs as you think you should, if the very worst happened and you lost everything. It is very unlikely that anything is going to happen—this is just a precaution.

Step 3: Loading PartitionMagic

PartitionMagic is a typical easy-to-use and easy-to-load Windows program. Most users will only have to insert the CD into their CD-ROM drive. The installation procedure will automatically start up. If it doesn't, click on the Start button, then the Run button, and type:

```
d:setup
```

where d is the letter for your CD-ROM drive.

When the initial installation screen comes up, click on Install Partition-Magic. Just below you will see another button, Install BootMagic. Do not click on this. Installation after that is a breeze—just accept all defaults.

Why Not Install BootMagic? BootMagic is a small program called a *boot manager*. It displays a small menu that pops up as the first thing you see when you start your machine, and lets you manually choose which operating system you want to use. Modern partition programs typically come with a number of such add-on programs: boot managers, drive mappers, etc. Some of these additional programs are more stable than others. I advise you to avoid them. Linux comes with its own boot manager, and it has a number of advantages over its competition:

1. It is free.
2. It is small and does not need its own partition.
3. It is automatically configured and is relatively easy to reconfigure.
4. It will not take over your entire machine—it does its job unobtrusively.
5. It is stable.

I advise you to use the Linux boot manager.

Step 4: Creating Free Space for Linux

Use PartitionMagic to create at least 700 Mbytes of free space.

> NOTE: You should use PartitionMagic once: to shrink your Windows partition. After that it's best to leave the program alone. Although it won't disturb your Windows configuration, repeated use can complicate the Linux installation procedure, and can also cause the Linux boot manager to fail.

You will probably have to reduce the size of your Windows partition to make room for Linux. Don't reduce your Windows partition as far as you can: you'll still need room on it for new data and programs. But reduce it enough, if possible, so that you have at least 700 Mbytes of free space on your hard disk—preferably 1 Gbyte.

There are many different partitioning scenarios, depending on whether or not you already have free space on your disk, whether or not you already have more than one partition, and so on. But most users will probably fall under one of the three most common scenarios below. If you're not sure of your current configuration, don't worry: PartitionMagic will show you graphically.

Partitioning Scenario 1   The most common scenario is that you have one hard drive and on it one large Windows partition. There is little or no free space on the disk. Figure 1-1 shows what this situation looks like in PartitionMagic. You will have to use PartitionMagic to make space for Linux by shrinking your current Windows partition.

1. Start the program and place the mouse pointer on the drive representation—the long green bar with the letter C in the middle—and click once with your right mouse button.

2. Click on Resize / Move. You now see something similar to Figure 1-2. The dark green area on the left of the bar represents the minimum size of the partition if you shrank it as far as it would go. This size will vary on your machine, depending on how much data you have on it.

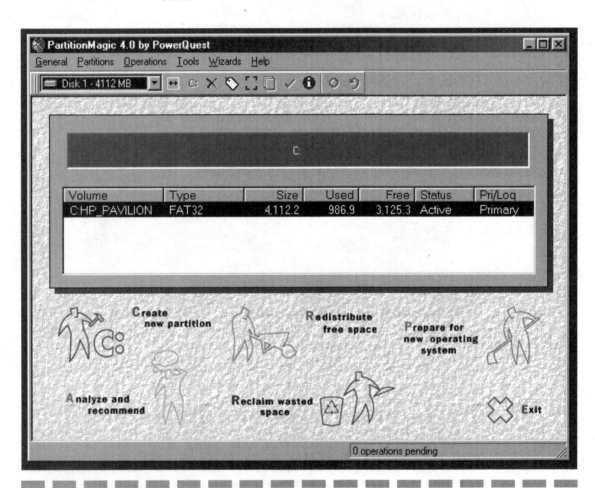

Figure 1-1 PartitionMagic. The Most Typical Scenario: One Hard Drive and One Large Windows Partition

Figure 1-2
The Minimum Size

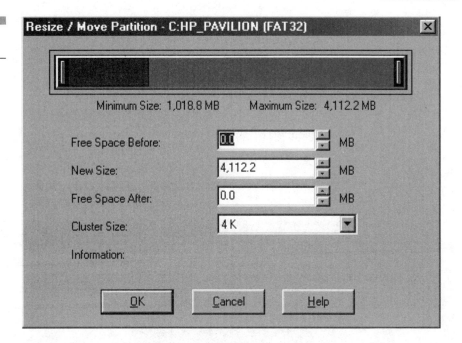

Figure 1-3
Resized to Half the
Original

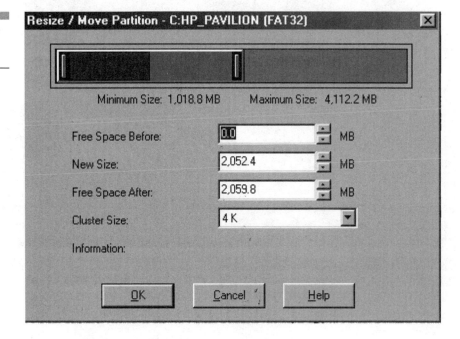

3. Place your mouse pointer on the right-hand side of the bar, until the pointer changes shape to a double-arrow.

4. Hold down the mouse button, and slide it toward the left about halfway (Figure 1-3). Notice that the figures for New Size and Free Space After are almost exactly the same.

5. Now click on the OK button. The PartitionMagic screen shows clearly (Figure 1-4) that you have shrunk your original partition to only one-half the size of your hard disk, freeing up, in this case,

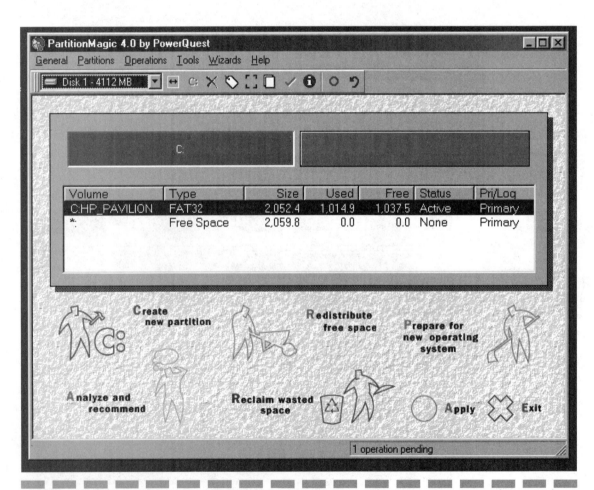

Figure 1-4 The Result: 2 Gbytes Free Space for Linux

Figure 1-5

Scenario One: From
One Partition to a
Partition and
Free Space

From:

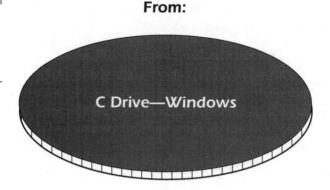

To:

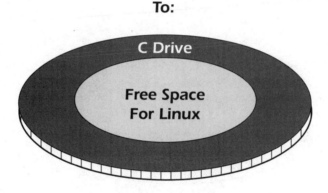

2 Gbytes of hard disk real estate for Linux. However, you haven't actually done anything yet! None of these changes take place until you click on the Apply button.

6. Click on the Apply button. The computer will reboot into MS-DOS mode, shrink the partition, and then reboot back into Windows automatically.

The diagram in Figure 1-5 shows what's been done in this scenario.

Partitioning Scenario 2. You have one hard drive and on it one large Windows partition. But in this case you do have some free space already

Figure 1-6
Scenario Two:
Increasing the
Amount of
Free Space

From:

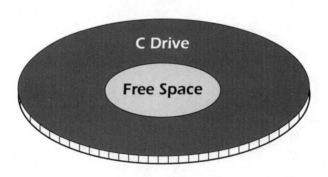

To:

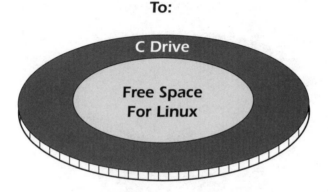

available—just not enough. You have to follow the same procedure as above, to increase the amount of free space on your disk (Figure 1-6).

Partitioning Scenario 3. You already have two partitions on your hard drive. C is your Windows partition, and your applications, or perhaps your data, are kept on partition D. (Note how partitions in Windows follow your drive letters.) In this case you have three steps to follow:

1. Shrink the C partition, as before.
2. Move the D partition next to C.
3. Shrink the D partition, freeing up disk space for Linux (Figure 1-7).

Figure 1-7
Scenario Three:
Shrinking and
Moving Two
Partitions to Make
Free Space

From:

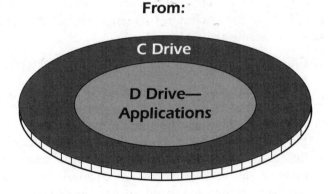

To:

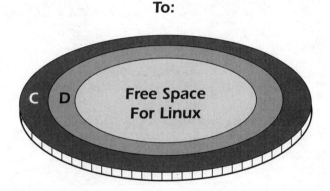

Partitioning Scenario 4.   You have two hard drives. If you want to, you can install Linux on the second drive, but part of Linux may have to reside on your first drive. I advise you to install Linux on your first hard drive, if possible.

Step 5: Gathering Information on Your Graphics Chip and Monitor

If you are sure you already know the manufacturer and model number of your graphics chip, and the manufacturer, model number, and resolution of your monitor, then skip to this chapter's last paragraph. Otherwise read on.

Linux is getting better at automatically detecting this kind of information, but it's not perfect yet. Fortunately, all the information you need should be easily available in Windows.

1. Click anywhere on any blank area of the desktop with your right mouse button.

2. Go down to the bottom of the floating menu and click on Properties.

3. The Display Properties window appears (Figure 1-8). Click on the Settings tab. Study Figure 1-9 carefully. There's quite a lot of information here. It tells us that the actual monitor is a Compaq Presario 150, and we can verify this information simply by checking out the monitor itself—that information is generally on the front of

Figure 1-8
Display Properties
Window

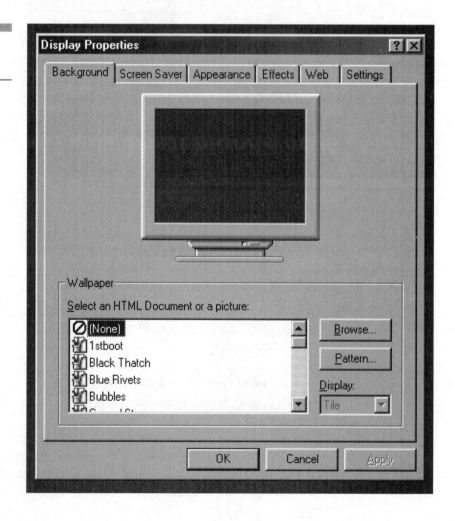

Figure 1-9
Display Properties
Settings—Monitor,
Color Depth, and
Screen Area
Information

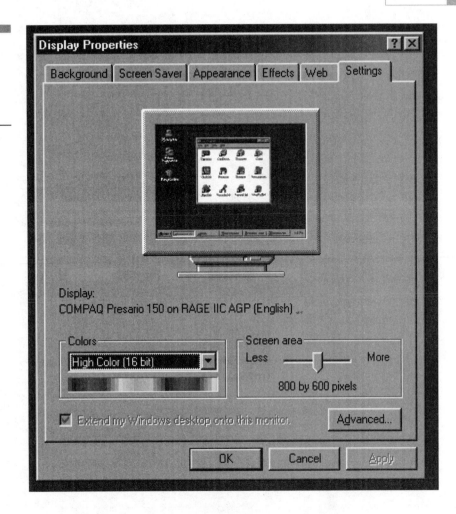

the instrument. It also tells us that the graphics adapter is a
RAGE IIC AGP. The color depth is 16 bits (this is normally in units
of bits per pixel, or bpp), and the screen area is 800 by 600 pixels.
Make notes.

4. Next click on the Advanced button, and then on the Adapter tab.
Figure 1-10 shows us more detailed information. It turns out that
RAGE IIC AGP is just an adapter marketing label, hiding the
information we really need: the actual chip type. It's a Mach64GT.
The manufacturer is also important: ATI Tech. Make another note.
Sometimes the adapter and the chip will have the same name, and
sometimes the same chip will be marketed under several different
adapter names. The chip name is what you want.

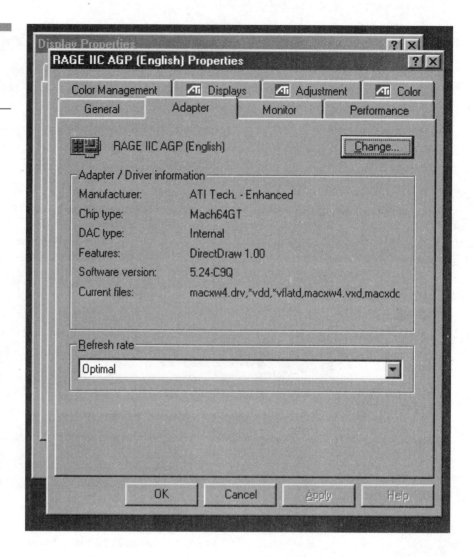

Figure 1-10
The Adapter
Window—and the
Real Adapter
Information

5. Next click on the Adjustment tab. Under Monitor Mode you'll see the vertical and horizontal frequency of your monitor—in this case, 60 Hz and 37.79 kHz (Figure 1-11). Make another note.

6. Finally, click on the Refresh Rate button near the bottom of the menu. Make a final note of the highest rate listed. (NOTE: Not all of this information will be available on some machines. If it's missing on yours, try to find it in your computer's documentation.)

Figure 1-11
The Adjustment
Window, Showing
the Monitor's Vertical
and Horizontal
Frequencies

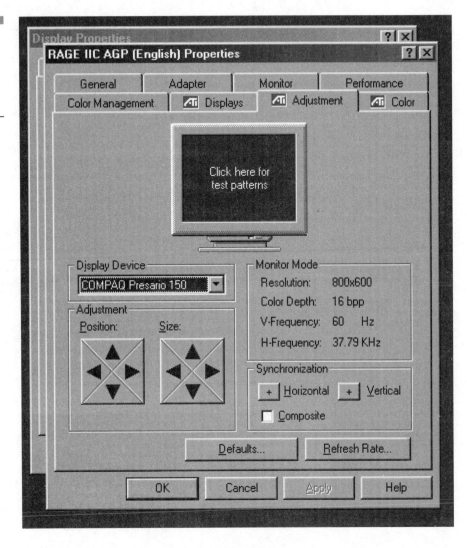

That's all the preparation you need to do. The next step is to proceed to the installation chapters themselves. The list below shows you where to go, depending on which distribution you're installing:

Red Hat Linux: Chapter 2

Caldera OpenLinux: Chapter 4

TurboLinux: Chapter 6

SuSE Linux: Chapter 7

Installing Red Hat Linux

Purpose of Chapter: Install Red Hat Linux on a Typical PC Using the Workstation Configuration

Red Hat Linux, like all distributions, has its installation strengths and weaknesses. Although it will not create space on the hard drive—you have to do that yourself with PartitionMagic—it will automatically create its own partitions, and will even automatically set up the Linux boot manager to dual-boot both Windows and Linux.

Red Hat's latest installation routine is a great improvement on its previous versions and will even automatically detect your graphics adapter. But don't throw away the information you gathered in Chapter 1. There's a lot there you'll still need.

The fastest and simplest way to install Red Hat Linux is by booting up your computer with the Linux CD. Most modern machines will be able to use this method. However, if your machine is unable to boot from the CD, then you'll have to start the installation process with a 3½-inch Linux boot diskette. All the major distributors supply boot disks, but if you are using the CDs that come with this book, you will have to make your own. Instructions are in the Appendix.

Installing the Operating System

1. Insert your Linux CD, and shut down your machine. Then turn it back on. You'll see the Welcome To Red Hat Linux! screen.

2. Type:

   ```
   text
   ```

   and hit the Enter key.

   (NOTE: Why am I suggesting that you use a text instead of a graphical installation mode? Because it's the least buggy, and most likely to succeed. Just hitting Enter will probably work just fine on your computer—but if you want to keep your chances of failure to a minimum, follow my instructions.)

3. The first screen (Figure 2-1) is Language Selection: you're prompted to choose a language. The default is English. Your

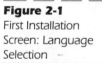

Figure 2-1
First Installation
Screen: Language
Selection

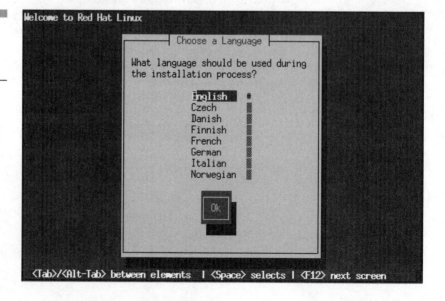

mouse at this stage of the installation routine won't yet work. You can scroll up or down the list, if you want to, with the arrow keys. If English is your language, hit Enter again.

4. You're prompted for a keyboard type. It defaults to US. This is a standard choice for American keyboards. Hit Enter again.

5. Another welcome screen. Hit Enter.

6. The next screen, Installation Type (Figure 2-2), is critical. You are given five choices:

   - Install GNOME Workstation.
   - Install KDE Workstation.
   - Install Server System.
   - Install Custom System.
   - Upgrade Existing System.

   The two workstation installations both automatically select the Linux programs you are likely to need, and will automatically create Linux partitions from the free space you've make on your hard drive. The only major difference between the two is that one will setup the Gnome desktop, and the other will setup the KDE desktop. Generally speaking, the KDE desktop is a little more refined, while the Gnome desktop is a little more configurable. A lot boils down to looks—functionality is about the same. Gnome is Red Hat's specialty—why not try it? You can always reload later.

Figure 2-2
The Installation Type
Screen

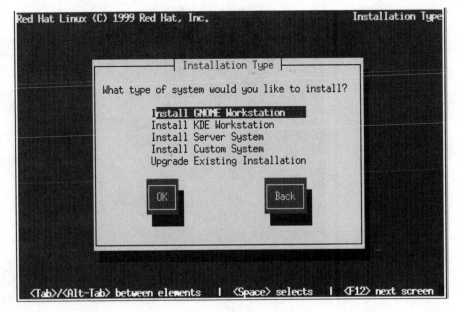

The Server installation type is just that—unless you intend to configure you Linux machine as a dedicated server, stay away from this choice—especially since it will reformat your entire hard disk!

Custom is for experts. Unless you know exactly what you're doing in the partition department, avoid it.

When you've made your selection, tab to the OK button, and Hit Enter.

7. The Automatic Partitioning warning screen comes up. Make sure that "Continue" is highlighted, and hit Enter.

8. The next screen is network related: if your are on a network, ask your administrator what your computer's hostname is, and type it in. Otherwise, type:

```
localhost
```

and hit Enter to reach the OK button, then Enter again.

9. Next is the Mouse Selection screen. For some reason, on every machine I've loaded this distribution on, Red Hat has selected the Generic 3 Button Mouse (PS/2)—despite the fact that I've never used such a mouse. Most people are likely to be using a generic 2 button serial mouse. Select yours, make sure to check the "Emulate 3 Buttons" box, tab to the OK button and hit Enter.

10. The Time Zone Selection window appears. Use the arrow keys to choose your time zone, tab to the OK button, and press Enter.

11. The Root Password screen appears (Figure 2-3).

Figure 2-3
The Root Password
Screen

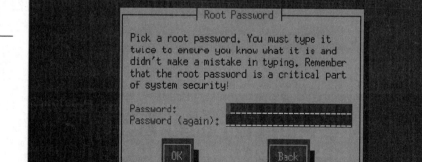

You have to log into Linux every time you start it, using a user name and a password. You don't choose your first user name, it is given to you: "root"—in UNIX-speak, you are the root user, or system administrator. You do have to choose a password.

Take a moment to consider this before typing anything. There are two restrictions to your password: it must be at least 6 characters long, and it will be case-sensitive. In other words, the password "Sesame" is different from "sesame."

Choose a password you can memorize. Type it in, hit the Tab key, and type it again. Then tab to the OK button and hit Enter.

12. Next is the Add User screen. This prompts you to add another user account—another way to log on to your computer.

Why do you need two different account names and passwords to log on to your own computer?

When you log on as "root," you can do the same sort of system administration tasks that you have always done on your old Windows system: delete files, directories, etc. When you log on as a regular user, such activities will be restricted. Linux users traditionally come from the UNIX community of industrial-strength network management, or, more recently, from the proprietors of web-sites. In both cases, many users log on to the same system, and security is a paramount concern. If, however, you are loading Linux on your home computer, then security for you under Linux will be no more important than it always has been under Windows, or whatever operating system you've been using.

If you want to add an additional account name and password here (if not for yourself, perhaps for your spouse, or children), then do so. Otherwise, just tab down to the OK button, and hit Enter.

13. The X probe results screen shows you your video card—hopefully the information is correct. If it isn't, don't worry: in any case there's nothing to do about it now. Hit Enter, and at the next screen, "Installation to begin," hit Enter again.

The Package Installation screen comes up. On my machine, this told me that a total of 397 packages, totaling 563 MB were being installed over an estimated period of about 12 minutes. Why so many software packages? Linux itself is just an operating system, and the absolute fundamental center of it, called the kernel, is only one file. But there are many other files and programs necessary to run Linux productively.

Have a cup of coffee. Step outside and get a breath of fresh air.

Graphics Configuration

Once file installation is complete, the installation routine will attempt to configure Linux to run X Window properly on your computer's graphics adapter and monitor. This is where you can use the information you made a note of earlier, in Microsoft Windows. If you don't have Windows on your machine, then you may be able to find the information you need on your graphics adapter card, etc., either in the documentation that came with your computer, or on the manufacturer's website.

Windows in Linux

Like Microsoft's product, Linux has its own windows environment, which is called the X Window System. In this book I'll refer to Microsoft's graphic environment as "Windows," and to the Linux graphic environment as "X Window."

1. The Monitor Setup screen (Figure 2-4) gives you a long list of different monitor makes and models. If you want, you can scroll down the list and try to find your model. Choosing it could possibly lead to a successful graphics setup. Or it could lead to a very complicated mess.

Figure 2-4
Monitor Setup

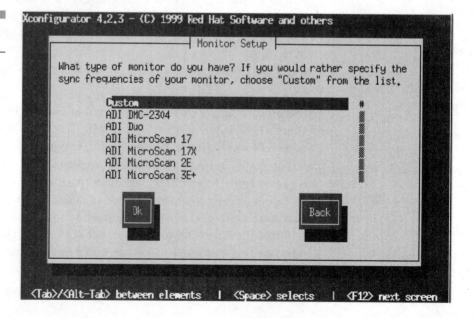

I advise you to choose "Custom," and press Enter, and at the next screen, press Enter again.

2. At the screen titled, "Custom Monitor Setup (Continued)," ignore the text at the top of the page regarding your monitor's horizontal sync range—"horizontal" is here a Red Hat typo. Instead, choose the monitor description that best matches your screen size— probably either 800×600 or 1024×768—along with the vertical frequency which you noted in chapter one, probably somewhere between 56 and 74 HZ. Then hit Enter.

3. The next screen, confusingly, has exactly the same title as the previous one. This screen too has to do with vertical sync frequency. Highlight the first choice that includes yours—for most people, the default will do. Press Enter, and Enter again at the "Probing to begin" screen.

4. If everything has gone correctly, your screen will blink two or three times, then you will see the "Probing finished" screen. Inspect carefully the color depth and resolution figures that Red Hat has come up with. If they match the figures you made a note of in Chapter One, then choose the "Use Default" button, and hit Enter. However, if they differ, then tab to the "Let Me Choose" button.

5. If you override the default, you get to the Select Video Modes screen (Figure 2-5). Tab to the correct selection—choose only the

Figure 2-5
Select Video Modes

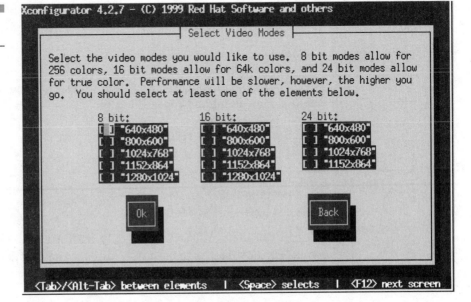

depth (mode) and screen area that you noted in chapter one. Then tab to the OK button and hit Enter.

6. IMPORTANT! At the next window, "Starting X," tab to the Skip button and hit Enter. It is quite possible that you have successfully configured X Window, but there is no point in checking it yet. Skip it for now.

That's it. Press the Enter key at the congratulations screen (well-earned), and eject your CD. This is an important point: if you don't eject your CD, you will go through the whole installation process over again!

First Boot and X Window Test

Upon rebooting, you'll see the following prompt:

```
LILO boot:
```

For now, just hit Enter. A seemingly interminable list of loading messages—all of them Greek to you—will scroll up the screen. Eventually, you'll see:

```
Red Hat Linux release 6.1 (Cartman)
Kernel 2.2.12-20 on an i686

localhost login:
```

At this point, type:

```
root
```

hit Enter, type in your password and press Enter again. Your screen should now look like this:

```
Red Hat Linux release 6.1 (Cartman)
Kernel 2.2.12-20 on an i686

localhost login: root
Password:
[root@localhost /root]#
```

Congratulations! You're in! Not only in, but at the dreaded command prompt. The next step is to try out X Window, and, if it doesn't work, to configure it properly.

To start X Window, type:

```
startx
```

and hit Enter.

Something very similar to Figure 13-1 (skip ahead to look) should appear. In the middle of the screen a small window titled "Warning" pops up, telling you that you are running the GNOME File Manager as root. With your mouse, click on the OK button in the window's lower-right hand corner.

The details on how to navigate in and operate your new desktop are in Chapter 13. For now, if everything looks OK, just click your mouse on the footprint in the lower-left hand corner of the screen, click on Log Out, and hit Enter.

You're back at the command prompt.

If it worked, skip the next section, and go on to Reboot into Windows.

If It Doesn't Work

If you typed in `startx`, and hit Enter, and either X Window didn't start up, or if the screen was garbled, then you will have to run the X Window setup utility.

NOTE: If X Window starts garbled, or if for any reason you are unable to normally close it down, just press and hold down the Ctrl + Alt + Backspace keys. That will immediately shutdown X Window, and return you to the command prompt.

Type:

```
setup
```

and hit Enter.

The Text Mode Setup Utility screen appears (Figure 2-6). With the arrow key, move down to X configuration, and press Enter, and Enter again at the welcome screen.

The utility will attempt to probe and identify your adapter card. Press Enter at the identification screen.

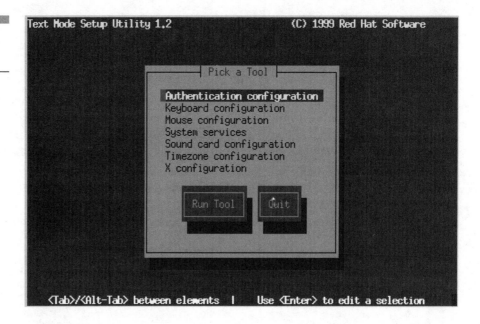

Figure 2-6
Text Mode Setup
Utility

Once again, the Monitor Setup screen (previous Figure 2-4) appears. It may be time to do things a bit differently. Scroll down and try to find your make and model of monitor. It is not always necessary to find an exact match, although it certainly helps. If you can find it, choose it and press Enter.

The next window asks you if you want the utility program to automatically probe your graphic adapter card. It's quite possible that the utility will successfully probe your card—it's also quite possible that it won't. Why take the chance? Choose Don't Probe, and hit Enter.

Using your arrow key, select the correct amount of video memory (modern computers usually have between 4 and 8 MB—this is not system RAM!), tab to the OK button and hit Enter. (This information should be in your computer's documentation; it can also be found within Windows—see Chapter 1).

At the next screen, Clockchip Configuration, simply go along with the default choice and press Enter.

Once again you are presented with the Select Video Modes screen (previous Figure 2-6). As before, select the same settings you made a note of in Chapter 1, tab to the OK button, and press the Enter key. At the prompt, hit OK to test your new configuration.

If successful, you will see a very small window asking you to click on the Yes button if you see the message. Do so. Next, you will see a similarly small window asking you if you want X to automatically start upon booting. This is a very poor idea. Click on the No button, then the OK button.

If there is a problem, you will be prompted to go back to Monitor Setup and start again. Continue at it. A successful configuration can generally be achieved. If you simply can't get it to work, more help can be found in Chapter 12.

If X Window does seem to be working, exit the text mode setup utility by clicking on the Quit button.

Rebooting into Windows

Before doing anything else, I advise you to reboot back into Windows.

1. Type:

```
reboot
```

and Press Enter. The computer will restart. The moment you see:

```
LILO boot
```

2. Type:

```
dos
```

and hit the Enter key.

Welcome back to Windows! Reentering your familiar environment after the first Linux installation is usually a great morale booster. It reassures you that you haven't, after all, destroyed your computer. It's all still there.

You can easily reset LILO so that Windows starts up automatically, if you want to. Details appear later.

It's Too Weird! I Want to Get Out!

If, after getting back into Windows, panic overcomes you, and you decide to destroy the monster you have created (while keeping your Windows installation safe), nothing is simpler. Follow this procedure:

1. From within Windows, start up your partition program. You will see that Linux has actually added three new partitions to what was your empty space. Two of the new partitions are quite small, and one is large. You want to delete all of them—all of the new Linux partitions, that is. This is as simple as clicking on them with your right mouse button, and choosing delete from the subsequent menu.

After you've deleted your Linux partitions, there is still one important step remaining: you have to get rid of LILO, the boot manager. That resides on what is called your Master Boot Record (MBR). Follow this procedure:

2. Reboot your computer, by clicking on Start, then on Shut Down, and then by choosing Restart in MS-DOS mode. You'll see LILO again.

3. Type:

```
dos
```

and hit Enter. This will take you to the DOS prompt:

```
C:\WINDOWS>.
```

4. Type exactly as follows:

```
fdisk /mbr
```

and press Enter.

5. Then type:

```
win
```

and hit Enter again. (NOTE: Follow this procedure only if you lose your nerve!)

If you keep Linux on your system, and you want to effectively use both operating systems together, you'll have to edit one small file. Go on to Chapter 3 for instructions.

If you're running Red Hat Linux alone, go straight to Part 2, Configuration.

Configuring Red Hat Linux for Windows

Purpose of Chapter: Configure Red Hat Linux to Read and Write to the Windows Partition

You can now boot up to either Windows or Linux, as you like. But Linux cannot yet read the Windows partition. Enabling this will allow you to pass files back and forth from one operating system to another, greatly enhancing your ability to start doing productive work in Linux.

Enable Linux to Mount the Windows Partition

At this stage, Linux is completely unaware that Windows is even on your machine—just as Windows is unaware of Linux. By "mounting" a partition, we mean being able "see" it—and to read data from it. We need to enable Linux to mount the Windows partition. This is a three-step procedure:

1. Boot up Linux.
2. Discover which Linux device number the Windows partition is assigned to.
3. Add one line to a Linux file named `fstab`.

Boot up Linux

1. From Windows, reboot your computer. When you see:

   ```
   LILO boot:
   ```

   do nothing at all. In five seconds Linux will boot up. A great number of system messages will fly by on the screen. Eventually, the scrolling will stop, and you will see these three lines:

   ```
   Red Hat Linux release 6.1 (Cartman)
   Kernel 2.2.12-20 on an i686

   localhost login:
   ```

2. You must always login with Linux. Type:

   ```
   root
   ```

   and press Enter. (NOTE: Linux is case-sensitive. That means that "root" is not the same as "Root" or "ROOT." You have to be absolutely accurate at the command line.)

Why "root"?

Linux was designed as a multiuser, networked operating system, and so you always have to login—there's no way to defeat this—and the system administrator's login name is always "root." As the system administrator, you have certain privileges that other users normally don't: creating and deleting files, directories, etc.

3. You're prompted for a password. Type in your password, and press Enter again. You should see a line something like this:

```
[root@localhost /root]#
```

Congratulations! You're in.

Identifying the Windows Device

In Linux, every disk partition and every port is given a device name and number. Examples are in Table 3-1. We are only interested in the Windows partition device. It will almost certainly be hda1—the first primary partition on your first hard disk. But to make sure, you should check it out with the fdisk program.

Using **fdisk**

Follow these instructions exactly. It is possible when manipulating the fdisk program to destroy every bit of data on your hard drive. But you aren't going to manipulate fdisk. You're simply going to start it, take a look at the hard drive, and then immediately close the program down.

1. Type:

```
fdisk/dev/hda
```

and press Enter. (NOTE: Remember: Linux is case-sensitive. In other words, "fdisk" is not the same as "Fdisk" or "FDISK." You

TABLE 3-1

Partition and Device Identification in Linux

Hard Disk Partitions	Linux Device
First primary partition of first hard disk	hda1
Second primary partition of first hard disk	hda2
First primary partition of second hard disk	hdb1
Ports	
First floppy disk drive	fd0
First serial port (typically for a mouse)	cua0
Second serial port (typically for a modem)	cua1
First parallel port (typically for a printer)	lp0

have to be exact at the Linux command line.) You will see the following line:

```
Command (m for help):
```

2. Type:

```
p
```

and press Enter. You should see something like Figure 3-1. (NOTE: In this example, the hard disk is 4 Gbytes and is divided equally between one Windows 95 partition and three Linux partitions clustered together in an extended partition.)

We're only interested in the Device column (far left) and the System column (far right). Locate Win95 under the System column. The device we want will be in the same row, in the Device column. In our example, above, the Windows device is: /dev/hda1.

3. First, make a note of the Windows device on your machine.

4. Then type:

```
q
```

and press Enter. You should be back at the command line.

Editing the `fstab` File with the Vi Editor

The Vi editor will be covered in Part 2. For now, we are only interested in adding one line to one file. Vi is a command-line editor, so everything will be keyboard-based—no mouse involvement, no mice allowed.

IMPORTANT! If you think you're getting into deep water and may have fouled up the file you're working on, don't panic! You can always back out of the editor, and the file, without causing any damage at all, by pressing:

Figure 3-1
fdisk: The Device
and Partition List

```
Disk /dev/hda: 240 head, 63 sectors, 557 cylinders
Units = cylinders of 15120 * 512 bytes

    Device Boot      Start      End      Blocks      ID     System
   /dev/hda1    *        1      278     2101648+    b      Win95 FAT32
   /dev/hda2            279      557     2109240     5      Extended
   /dev/hda5            279      281       22648+   83      Linux
   /dev/hda6            282      548     2018488    83      Linux
   /dev/hda7            549      557       68008    82      Linux swap
```

the Escape key
then the colon (:) key
then the "q" key
then the exclamation mark
and then Enter.

This will exit the editor without saving a thing, so your file should not be damaged.)

The `fstab` file determines which partitions, and which devices like floppies and CD-ROMS, are mounted in Linux. The file resides in a directory called "etc." (For Windows users, a directory is the older name for a "folder.")

First, we'll move to the correct directory, then open the file, then edit it, and finally save it and reboot.

1. Type:

   ```
   cd /etc
   ```

   and press Enter.

2. Next type:

   ```
   vi fstab
   ```

   and press Enter. You'll now see the `fstab` file (Figure 3-2). Our job is to add one line at the very beginning of this file.

3. Hit the Escape key. You should hear a little beep.

4. Now type:

   ```
   i
   ```

   You should see the word INSERT at the lower left of the screen.

5. Hit the Enter key.

6. Hit the up arrow key.

7. Type:

   ```
   /dev/hda1   /C   vfat   noauto   0 0
   ```

Figure 3-2
The `fstab` File

```
/dev/hda5     /boot           ext2       defaults      1  1
/dev/hda6     /               ext2       defaults      1  2
/dev/hda7     swap            swap       defaults      0  0
/dev/fd0      /mnt/floppy     ext2       noauto        0  0
/dev/cdrom    /mnt/cdrom      iso9660    noauto,ro     0  0
none          /proc           proc       defaults      0  0
none          /dev/pts        devpts     mode=0622     0  0
```

Figure 3-3
The Edited
fstab File

```
/dev/hda1      /C              vfat        noauto      0  0
/dev/hda5      /boot           ext2        defaults    1  1
/dev/hda6      /               ext2        defaults    1  2
/dev/hda7      swap            swap        defaults    0  0
/dev/fd0       /mnt/floppy     ext2        noauto      0  0
/dev/cdrom     /mnt/cdrom      iso9660     noauto,ro   0  0
none           /proc           proc        defaults    0  0
none           /dev/pts        devpts      mode=0622   0  0
```

In our example above, when you are finished adding the line, your fstab file should look like Figure 3-3. If you make a typing mistake, use the Backspace key to erase the error. If you make a real hash of it, hit the Escape key and type :, then q, then !, and press Enter, and start over again.

What does it all mean? Simply that /dev/hda1 is our Windows partition, it will be mounted as "C" (just as it's called in Windows and DOS), and the type of file system is vfat—meaning Windows 95 and above.

Now, let's save it and exit the Vi editor.

8. Hit the Escape key again.

9. Type the colon key.

10. Type:

    w

    and press Enter.

11. Type the colon (:) key again.

12. Type:

    q

    and press Enter.

That's it! Now reboot for your changes to take effect, and go on to Part 2, Configuration.

4

Installing Caldera OpenLinux

Purpose of Chapter: Install Caldera OpenLinux on a Typical PC Using the Commercial Configuration

Caldera = Automated

The Caldera OpenLinux 2.3 distribution has two advantages over the other distributions on the market:

1. It is exceptionally automated, so that very little prior knowledge of your computer's internals is necessary for a successful installation.

2. It comes complete with a stripped-down, semiautomated version of PartitionMagic. As a result, you can install Caldera's OpenLinux as your second operating system on your current Windows machine with little difficulty or preparation, and without having to buy an expensive extra program.

Caldera's product installs directly from Microsoft Windows, and automatically creates both free space for the installation and its own Linux partitions. It has the fastest and most automatic installation routine of any Linux distribution.

Creating Linux Partitions

1. Start up Microsoft Windows.

2. Insert the Windows Tools and Commercial Packages CD. The installation routine should start automatically. If it doesn't, double-click on the My Computer icon, and then on the OpenLinux icon. The opening installation screen appears. Click on the first line: Install Products.

3. A second installation screen with four options appears (Figure 4-1). It is only necessary to click on the first line: Install PartitionMagic CE. PartitionMagic is a program by PowerQuest that easily and nondestructively partitions your hard disk for a Linux install. Caldera is the only Linux distributor so far to bundle this program—albeit a stripped-down version of it—with their product. Its automated features help make a Caldera Linux installation much more user-friendly than most.

4. Four PartitionMagic install screens come up, asking you to sign off on their license, etc. Click Yes to all. The program installs itself on your hard disk in a matter of seconds. Click on the Finish button.

5. At this point you are asked to eject the CD and click on the OK button. This is an important step. The computer then reboots in MS-DOS mode, and the PartitionMagic Caldera Edition screen comes up (Figure 4-2).

Determining the Size of the Main Linux Partition

The important part of Figure 4-2 is under "Linux partition size." You may be given several choices for the size of your Linux partition, depending on how much space PartitionMagic can find to free up. The first option is likely to be 300 or 350 Mbytes; the second or third will be a larger amount, depending on your amount of free space available; and the last choice will be Maximum.

Figure 4-1 Caldera OpenLinux Installation Options

If you can, you should choose as close to 1 Gbyte as you can get, while leaving several hundred megabytes free on your Windows partition. Remember: your goal is to load and use both operating systems on the same computer.

1. Select your Linux partition size option, and click on the OK button.

2. Press Enter at the next screen. PartitionMagic will now shrink your Windows partition and create two new Linux partitions in the free space created. This should take less than 5 minutes.

3. At the Partition Creation Complete screen, insert your Linux Kernel and Installation CD.

4. Press Enter. The machine will reboot.

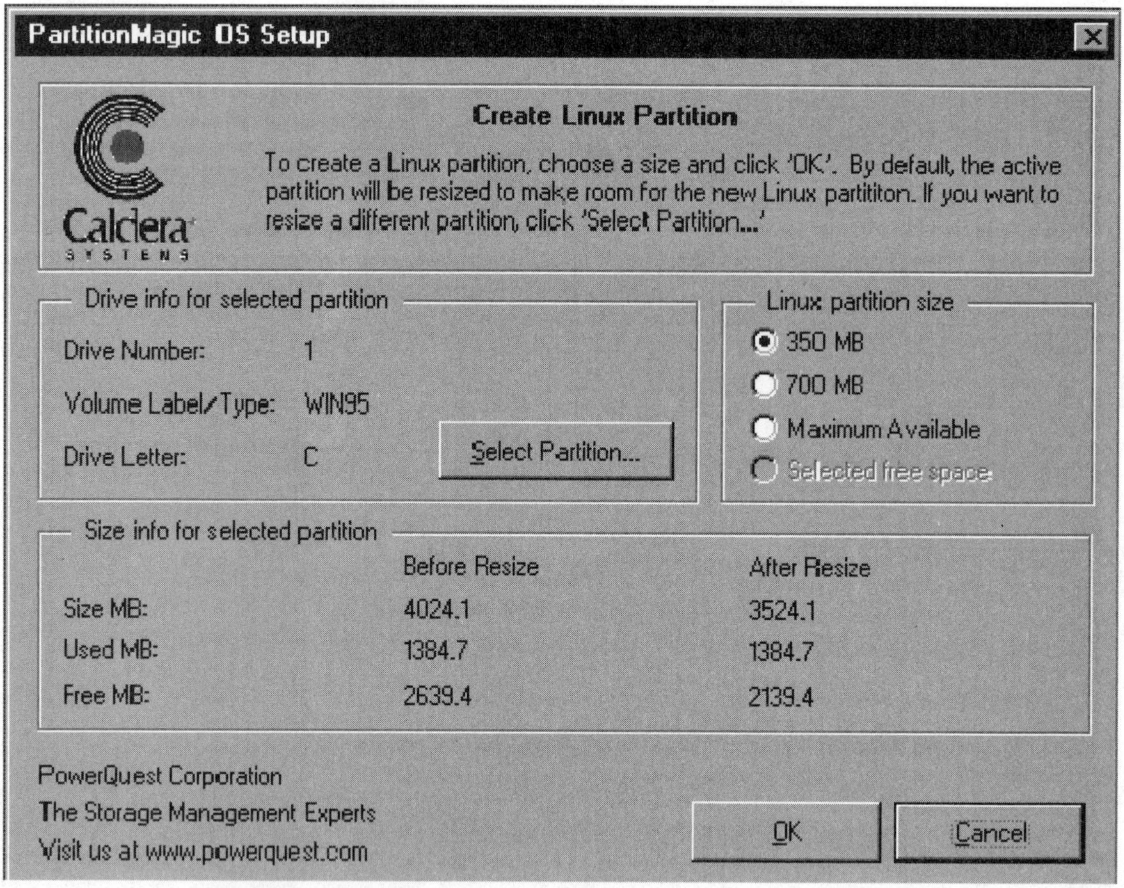

PartitionMagic OS Setup ⊠

Create Linux Partition

To create a Linux partition, choose a size and click 'OK'. By default, the active partition will be resized to make room for the new Linux partititon. If you want to resize a different partition, click 'Select Partition...'

Caldera
SYSTEMS

— Drive info for selected partition —

Drive Number: 1

Volume Label/Type: WIN95

Drive Letter: C   Select Partition...

— Linux partition size —

◉ 350 MB
○ 700 MB
○ Maximum Available
○ Selected free space

— Size info for selected partition —

	Before Resize	After Resize
Size MB:	4024.1	3524.1
Used MB:	1384.7	1384.7
Free MB:	2639.4	2139.4

PowerQuest Corporation
The Storage Management Experts
Visit us at www.powerquest.com

OK   Cancel

Figure 4-2 PartitionMagic Caldera Edition

Installing the Operating System

1. The system startup screen appears, as the program probes your computer. A collage of Caldera logos come and go. The first screen that asks for your input is the Language Selection screen (Figure 4-3).

2. Select the language you prefer, and then click on the Next button.

3. Choose your mouse, and click on the Next button. If you mess around with this screen, the program may lose its connection with your mouse; if that happens, use the Tab key to make your selection, and after highlighting the Next button, press Enter.

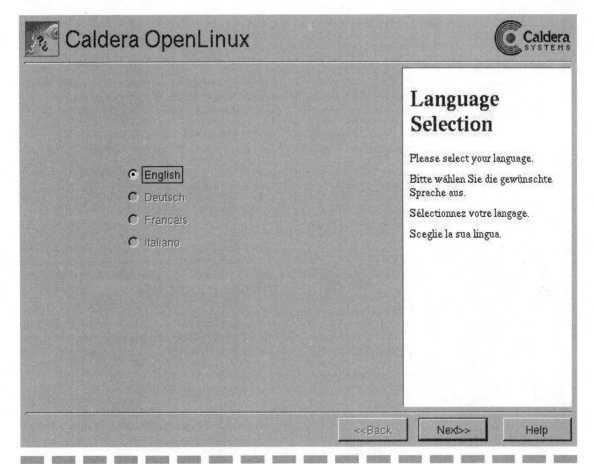

Figure 4-3 Language Selection

4. Select your keyboard type and language, and hit Enter.

The following three sections all configure X Window to run properly on your computer.

Windows in Linux

Like Microsoft's product, Linux has its own windows environment, which is called the X Window System. In this book I refer to Microsoft's graphic environment as Windows, and to the Linux graphic environment as X Window.

Configuring Graphics

1. The next screen, Select Video Card (Figure 4-4), should show you your video card—unlike other distributions, Caldera's identifies it automatically. You can check on this by consulting your notes (in the unlikely case that a mistake was made, you can correct it later). Click on the Probe button—this will identify your card's details further. When probing is finished, click on the Next button.

2. You must select your own monitor (Figure 4-5). The make and model can generally be found on the front of the instrument. On the screen, simply scroll down to the manufacturer's name, click on

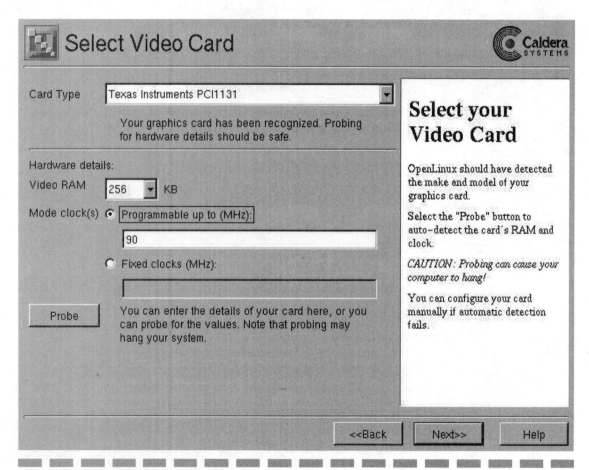

Figure 4-4 Select Video Card

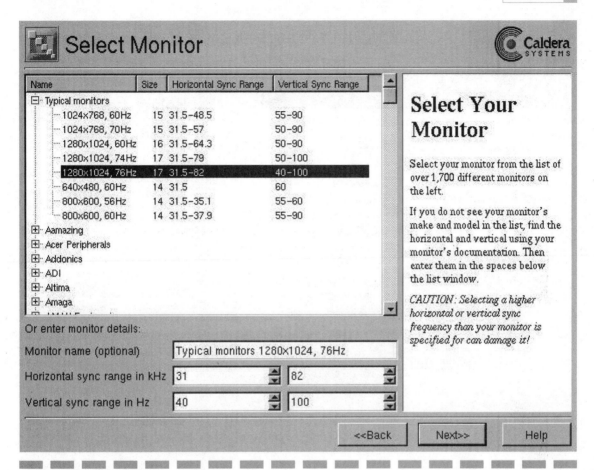

Figure 4-5 Select Monitor

the plus sign, and select the model. If your model isn't listed, then you have the option of choosing one of the "Typical Monitors" at the top of the list. The important things are 1) not to choose a resolution greater than you were using in Windows, and 2) the vertical and horizontal frequency sync ranges, at the bottom of the screen, should encompass the frequencies you noted down earlier in Windows. When you're finished, click on the Next button.

3. In the Select Video Mode screen (Figure 4-6), you should select the same resolution and refresh rate that you were using in Windows. You can test your choice by clicking on the Test This Mode button. When you are finished, click on the Next button.

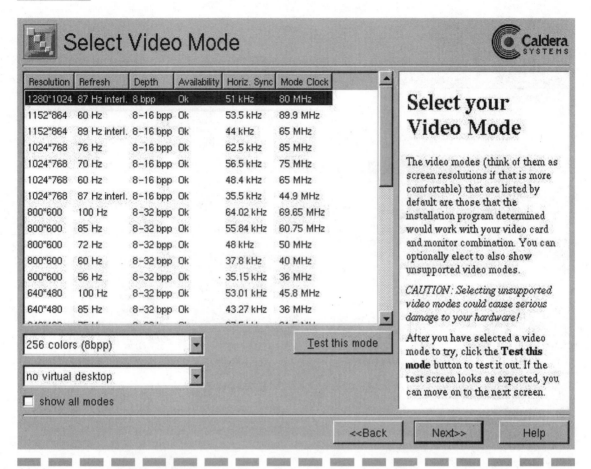

Figure 4-6   Select Video Mode

Partitions, Packages, and Passwords

1. At the next screen, Installation Target, choose Prepared Partitions, and click on the Next button.

2. The Select Root Partition simply confirms the previous automatic selection. Hit Enter.

3. At the next screen, Partition Information (Figure 4-7), simply click on the Format Chosen Partitions button, and after a few moments, click on the Next button.

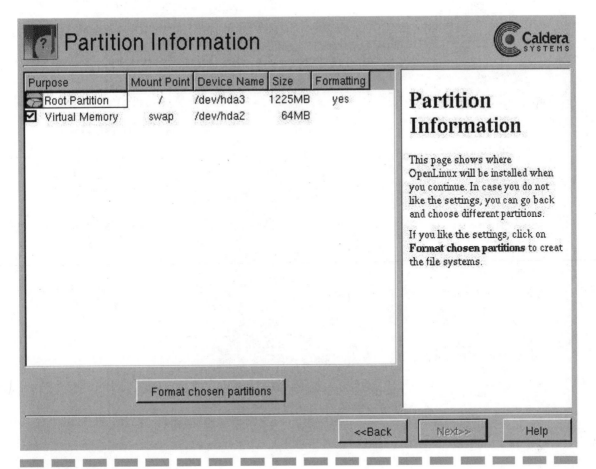

Figure 4-7 Partition Information

4. The following screen, Select Installation (Figure 4-8), gives you a choice of preselected packages for the number and type of programs you want to load, based on the type of work you are likely to do. Most people who intend to use Linux as a desktop replacement will choose either Business Workstation or Home Computer. Choose your option and then hit the Enter key.

5. You may or may not see a screen titled Test Sound Card. If you do, you are lucky: Linux has automatically detected, and probably configured, your sound card. Test it out using the buttons available, and then click on the Next button.

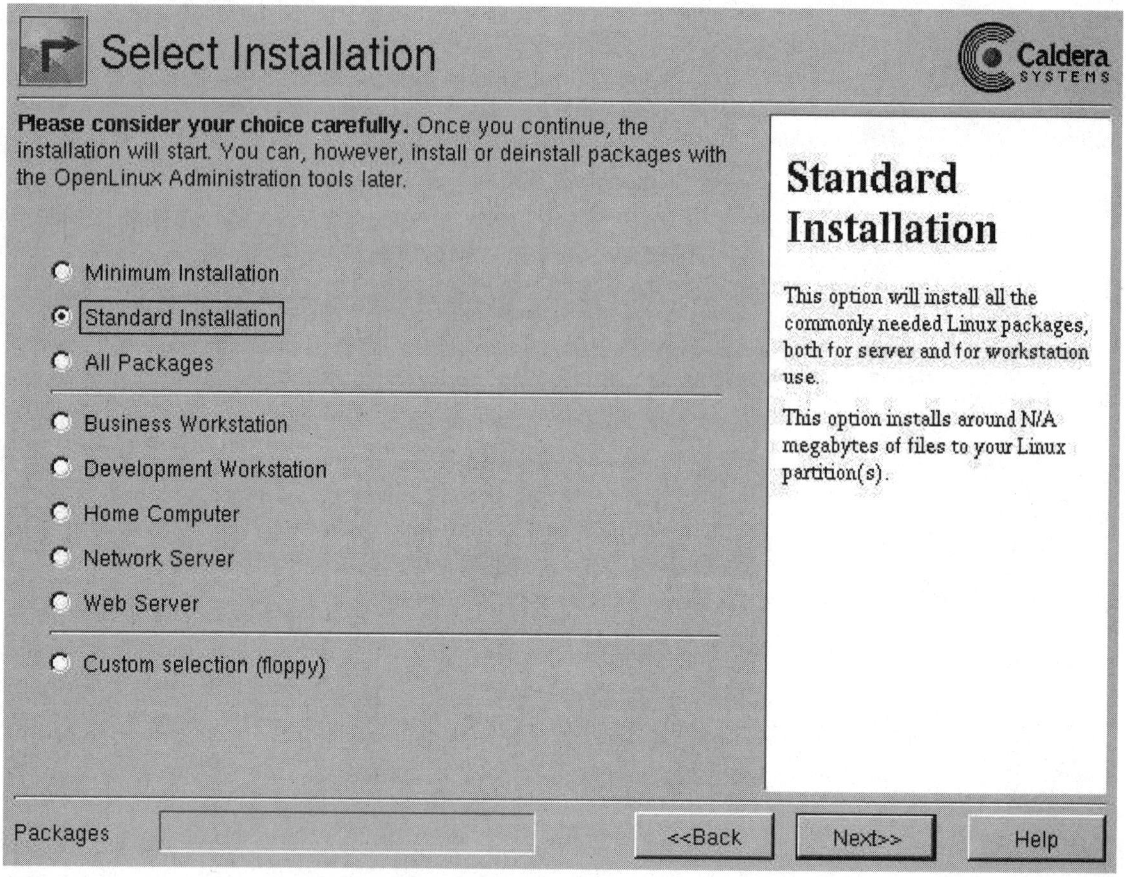

Figure 4-8 Select Installation

6. The next screen asks you for your password. Linux needs a password—this is not an optional step. "Root" means the chief administrator, sometimes called the *superuser* (you, in other words). That will be your initial logon name. The most important thing to remember about your password is that it is case-sensitive—in other words, a lower-case letter cannot be substituted for an upper-case letter. This means, for instance, that "George" is not the same as "george." So choose a password that you can remember easily, and remember how you type it in as well. I recommend all lower-case. When you're finished, click the Next button.

7. Caldera insists you add another user's name and password at the Set Login Name screen. It can be anything you like. After filling in the blanks, click on the Add User button, and then the Next button.

8. On the Set Up Networking screen, simply select No Ethernet if you are on a stand-alone machine, connecting to the Internet via a modem. Otherwise, call your system administrator. Click on the Next button.

9. The Linux Loader screen (Figure 4-9) is critical. Although Caldera OpenLinux comes complete with BootMagic, I advise you to use the Linux Loader (sometimes called LILO, or the boot manager) instead.

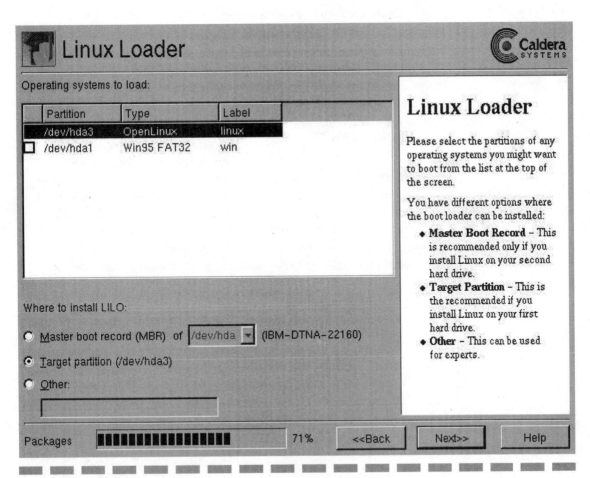

Figure 4-9 Linux Loader Screen

Although Caldera recommends that you install LILO on your target partition, I suggest you install it instead on your Master Boot Record. Just check the Master Boot Record (MBR) box in the lower half of the screen.

You also need to add your Windows partition to the LILO menu. Do this by clicking on the empty box next to:

```
/dev/hda1     Win95 FAT32       win
```

near the top of the screen. Some details may be different on your machine, but you should see something that identifies your Windows partition. There will be no check box next to your Linux partition, because that is automatically included in the LILO menu.

Finally, click on the Next button.

10. The Choose Time Zone screen is an interesting geographical exhibit. By moving the cursor around the map, you can try and locate your region, possibly even your city. The port city of Aden is listed, in case you are living in Yemen, near the southern tip of the Arabian peninsula; so is the settlement of Swift Current, up in Saskatchewan. Once you have found your region, simply click on it, and then on the Next button .

11. If you've been fairly prompt in going through all the screens, you will have reached the end while Linux is still loading. If that's the case, you can play the game that is furnished for your amusement. Most of us at this stage are more likely to want a breath of fresh air or perhaps a cup of coffee or a cigarette to calm our nerves while the process finishes. When the progress bar at the bottom of the screen reads Postinstall 100%, click on the Finish button.

At this point your computer starts Linux for the first time. But your work isn't finished yet. Caldera OpenLinux is installed, but there are two or three serious configuration issues to resolve. While your machine reboots, turn the page to Chapter 5.

5

Configuring Caldera OpenLinux for Windows

Purpose of Chapter:
1. **Configure OpenLinux to Boot to the Command Line, Not to X Window**
2. **Configure the LILO Boot Manager to Boot Either Linux or Windows**
3. **Configure OpenLinux to be Able to Read and Write to the Windows Partition**

Although Caldera's installation procedure is simpler, more automatic, and shorter than Red Hat's, its initial post-installation configuration is a little more challenging.

Configuring OpenLinux to boot to the command line is not necessary, but is in my opinion a good idea.

Although the LILO boot manager should have been configured during installation, it's a good idea to make sure—this is an area where bugs abound.

Finally, the ability to pass files to and from one operating system to another will greatly enhance your ability to start doing productive work in Linux.

Reconfiguring OpenLinux

Your system is now configured to boot right into X Window—the graphical interface similar to Microsoft's product—as soon as you logon. Although this behavior is becoming more and more popular as a default configuration (because after all a Windows-style interface is more user-friendly than a command line), it is not really a good idea. It is better to boot first to a command prompt. For one thing, although Caldera has made great strides in ensuring that X Window is configured correctly during installation, it is still possible that it may fail at startup. In that case the machine could boot to a hopelessly garbled screen. The command prompt is the place to begin.

The command line is practical in many ways. Although the novice will almost certainly at first hate it, eventually the new user may grow, if not to love, at least to appreciate it. Certainly, users should not be aggressively cut off from the command line, protected from it, as if it were a bogey, ready to bite.

Next, we need to make sure that Windows is added to the boot manager.

Finally, we have to enable Linux to read to and write from the Windows partition.

Getting to the Command Line

At the end of the last chapter, Linux was just booting up for the first time. The Caldera OpenLinux login screen (Figure 5-1) appears (NOTE: Yours will look slightly different).

1. Click on the Shutdown button on the lower right-hand corner of the window.
2. Click on Console mode, and on the OK button.
3. Hit Enter.

    You have reached the command line login prompt. There will be four or five lines of apparent nonsense on the screen, ending in the word login.

4. Type:

    ```
    root
    ```

    and press Enter.

5. You are prompted for a password. Type in yours, and press Enter again.

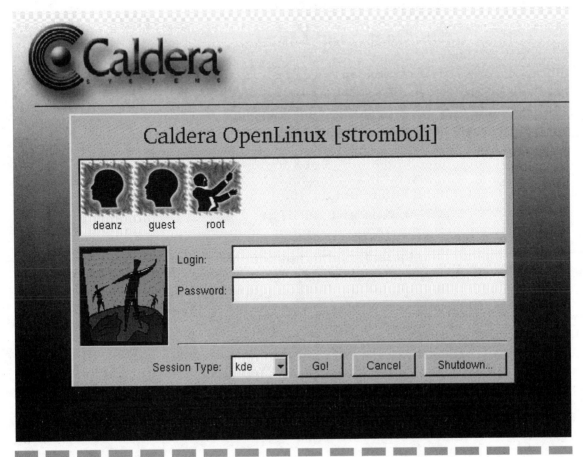

Figure 5-1 Caldera OpenLinux Login Screen

6. Type, exactly as below, with no capital letters:

```
clear
```

and press Enter again. Your screen will now be black and blank, except for the upper left-hand corner, where you will see a line something like this:

```
[root@noname /root]#
```

You are now at the Linux command line. Part 2 of this book goes into the command line in detail. Here, we are only interested in getting one command line job done. Just follow the instructions below exactly. Remember: Linux is case-sensitive. If I ask you to type cd, don't type Cd. It won't work.

Editing the `inittab` File to Boot to the Command Line

This is not as bad as it will look. You only have to change one character in one line in one file. But the file itself is pretty horrifying to the novice.

1. First, we'll move to the correct directory. Type:

   ```
   cd /etc
   ```

   and press Enter. Please note the importance of typing everything accurately. For instance, in the line above, there is a single space between `cd` and `/`.

2. Now, we'll open the file. Type:

   ```
   vi inittab
   ```

   and press Enter. The horrifying file now appears. On a typical screen, it will look like Figure 5-2, although there may be more lines visible on a higher-resolution monitor.

```
#
# inittab       This file describes how the INIT process should set up
#               the system in a certain run-level.
#
# Author:       Miquel van Smoorenburg, <miquels@drinkel.nl.mugnet.org>
#               Modified for RHS Linux by Marc Ewing and Donnie Barnes
#               Modified for COL by Raymund Will
#


# The runlevels used by COL are:
#       0 - halt (Do NOT set initdefault to this)
#       1 - Single user mode (including initialization of network interfaces,
#           if you do have networking)
#       2 - Multiuser,  (without NFS-Server and some such)
#           (basically the same as 3, if you do not have networking)
#       3 - Full multiuser mode
#       4 - unused
#           (should be equal to 3, for now)
#       5 - X11
#       6 - reboot (Do NOT set initdefault to this)


#
# Default runlevel.
Id:5:initdefault:

# System initialization.
```

Figure 5-2 `inittab` File

Don't let this file throw you—there is only one small change to make.

1. Hit the Esc key in the upper left-hand corner of your keyboard. You will probably hear a beep.

2. Now press the letter "i" key once. You will see the word INSERT appear at the bottom of the screen.

3. Use the down arrow key to move the cursor to this line near the bottom of the screen: `id:5:initdefault:`

4. Use the right arrow key to move the cursor directly over the number 5 in that line.

5. Hit the Delete key once, to delete the number 5, and then press the 3 key once, to insert that number in its place. The line should now read: `id:3:initdefault:`

6. Hit the Escape key once more, and then the colon (:) key.

7. A colon appears at the lower left corner of the screen. Press the "w" key, then the "q" key, and then hit Enter.

Congratulations! You have edited your first Linux file! If you are running Linux by itself, on a computer without Windows installed, skip the rest of this chapter and go ahead to Part 2. Otherwise, read on.

Installing and Configuring the Boot Manager

Configuring LILO, the boot manager, is easy—Caldera has a special program to simplify the procedure—but it is a multiple-step procedure. Read carefully, and follow the instructions.

1. Making sure not to use any capital letters, type:

   ```
   lisa
   ```

   and press Enter. LISA is Caldera's older program for system installation and maintenance. It is still very useful. Unfortunately, the mouse will not work in LISA, so you will have to navigate with the up and down arrow keys and the Tab key.

2. Use the arrow keys to highlight System Configuration, and then hit Enter. The System Configuration screen (Figure 5-3) appears.

3. Now down arrow to Configure Boot Manager, and press Enter.

4. Simply hit Enter at the next screen, Boot Setup Analysis.

Figure 5-3
System Configuration
(LISA screen)

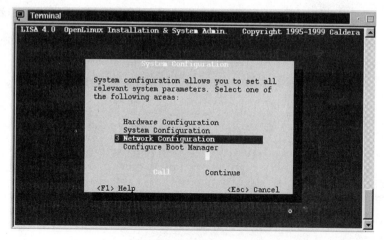

5. At the next screen, LILO Boot Manager Installation, use the arrow key to highlight selection 1: The first IDE hard disk. (The MBR of /dev/hda). Then hit Enter.

6. Now you have to choose which operating system you want to boot up by default. I advise you to choose Windows. When experimenting with a brand new operating system, it's reassuring to know that your old one will boot up by itself, just as before. You can always change this later if you want to.

7. Use the arrow keys to highlight the line that has Win95 on it. This line will probably start with /dev/hda1. Make a note of that line—it will come in handy in the next section—and hit Enter.

8. LISA suggests dos as the label for the Windows entry in the boot manager menu. Accept it for now. Tab to the OK button, and press Enter.

9. Now add Linux to the boot manager. Use the arrow keys to highlight the line: /boot/vmlinuz-2.2.10-modular (Linux Kernel Image), and hit Enter.

10. LISA again prompts you for a label. Accept linux, tab to the OK button, and press Enter.

11. At the LILO Boot Parameters screen, simply tab to the OK button and press Enter.

12. At the next screen make sure that the line No further entries to add to LILO is highlighted, and press Enter.

13. LISA shows you the configuration file. It will mean nothing to you. Hit Enter again.
14. A small menu asks you if you're certain that you want to install LILO—the Linux boot manager—as configured. Hit Enter, and then Enter again at the success message.

Enabling Linux to Mount the Windows Partition

By "mounting" a partition, we mean being able to read to and write from it. At this stage in the install, Linux is completely unaware that Windows is on your machine—just as Windows is unaware of Linux. We need to enable Linux to "see" the Windows partition. LISA will help us do it.

1. You should be at LISA's System Configuration screen. Use the up arrow key to highlight System Configuration (choice 2), and hit Enter.
2. Another System Configuration screen appears. Move down to Configure Mount Table, and press Enter.
3. Move down to Add a new entry to the mount table, and press Enter.
4. Now consult the notes you made in step 7, above. Type:

   `/dev/hda1`

   and hit Enter. (hda1 is the typical value, and my example, but the value could be different for you; consult the note you made in step 7, above.)
5. At the next screen, Mount Point Definition, type:

   `/C`

   and hit Enter.
6. Move the arrow down to Make access read-write, and press Enter again.
7. Press Enter again at the Info Box.
8. Hit the Escape key four times, or until you return to the command line.
9. That's it! Make sure to remove your CD, and then type:

   `reboot`

   and hit the Enter key. You'll see a number of "stopping" messages, and your machine will reboot. Presently the OpenLinux System

Startup screen will appear, with the logo on the right (the three shaky figures astride the earth), and to the left, under `Boot checkpoint`, the prompt:

```
boot:
```

10. Hit the Tab key. You should see:

```
dos     linux
```

Congratulations! This means you've succeeded in adding Linux to your boot manager, and can start up either one. For now, let's calm our beating heart, and boot back into Windows.

11. Type:

```
dos
```

and hit Enter.

Now go on to Part 2, where you'll boot into Linux again, take a quick look at X Window, and begin to get down to the serious business of configuration.

6

Installing TurboLinux Workstation 3.6

Purpose of Chapter: Install TurboLinux on a Typical PC

The TurboLinux installation routine is one of the longest and most manual—and also most automated and most thorough—of the bunch.

On the manual side, the necessity to configure Linux partitions will be off-putting to many—although it does give the user a very high degree of control over the process.

All users will appreciate the automatic detection and configuration of the graphics adapter. This is a big plus, as are the prompts to mount the Windows partition, and install and configure LILO, the Linux boot loader, so that you have a choice to boot up either Linux or Windows immediately after the installation.

The TurboLinux installation is so thorough there is no need for an extra chapter just for command line configuration. The basics are all done during the first install.

The fastest and simplest way to install TurboLinux Workstation 3.6 is by booting up your computer with the Linux CD. Most modern machines will be able to use this method. However, if your machine is unable to boot from the CD then you'll have to start the installation process with a 3½-inch Linux boot diskette. All the major distributors supply boot disks, but if you are using the CDs that come with this book, you will have to make your own. Instructions are in Appendix A.

Installing the Operating System

1. Insert your TurboLinux CD, and shut down your machine. Then turn it back on. You'll see a screen like Figure 6-1.

2. Unless you have a 17-inch or larger monitor, I advise you to type:

   ```
   install25
   ```

   and press Enter.

3. The next screen asks if you have a color display, thus suggesting the original age of the installation routine. Just hit Enter.

4. The first welcome screen comes up. Hit Enter again.

5. You're prompted for a keyboard type. It defaults to US. This is a standard choice for American keyboards. Your mouse at this stage in the installation routine won't yet work, so if you have to choose a different keyboard, use the arrow keys. Then hit Enter.

6. The PCMCIA support screen is next. Even if you are a laptop user, with a PCM card, do not choose Yes, unless you are installing TurboLinux over a network connection through your PCM card. In other words, practically everyone will just hit Enter.

Figure 6-1
Initial TurboLinux
Installation Prompt

```
TurboLinux 3.6 (Miami)—May, 1999
© 1999 TurboLinux, Inc.  http://www.turbolinux.com/

    <ENTER> to start the installation in 50-line VGA mode.
  'install25' to start the installation in 25-line VGA mode.



boot:
```

7. At the TurboProbe screen, press the Enter key.

8. It is very unlikely that you will need to choose Yes at the Parallel Port IDE screen. An example of this kind of hardware would be if you were installing TurboLinux from an external CD-ROM drive attached to your parallel printer port. Make sure the No button is selected, and press Enter.

9. If you have neither a network card, nor an SCSI drive, you will see the No Modules Loaded screen. Just press Enter.

10. The Installation Method screen (Figure 6-2) is next. Make sure the CD-ROM Drive is selected—the default—and press Enter.

11. Since you already have the CD inserted, hit Enter again.

12. At the Set Installer Preferences screen, it's a good idea to choose Extended Verbosity. Press the Tab key and then the down arrow key to select Extended Verbosity, and then hit the Enter key.

13. The System/Module Configuration screen (Figure 6-3) comes up next. Using your Tab key to move around, and your space bar to

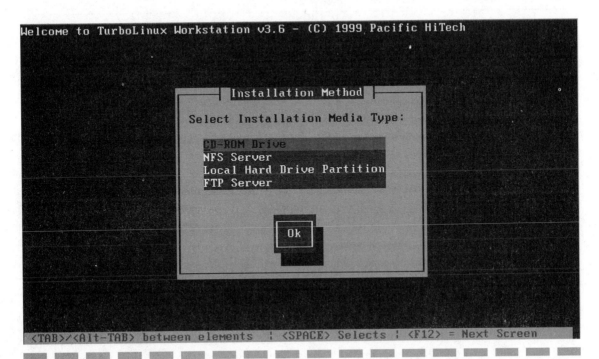

Figure 6-2 Installation Method Screen

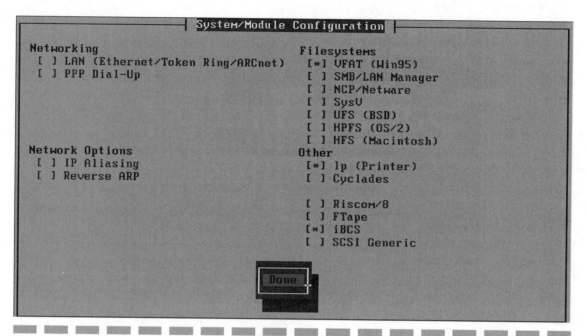

Figure 6-3   System/Module Configuration Screen

mark, select PPP Dial-Up under Networking, and any other modules you may want to load at start-up. On a non-networked, stand-
alone PC running Windows, you would want VFAT under
Filesystems, and lp (Printer) under Other selected. When you're
finished, hit the Enter key.

14. If you have an SCSI, now is the time to verify that it's working
correctly. Otherwise make that that the No button is selected, and
press Enter.

Making Linux Partitions

TurboLinux will not automatically create your Linux partitions. It will create
them from the free space you have already created on your hard disk with
PartitionMagic, but first you have to decide how large the new partitions
will be.

The installation program gives you two choices of partitioning programs
to select from: FDISK and CFDISK. Neither are particularly user-friendly.
CFDISK is somewhat easier for the novice user, and that method is presented here.

1. Tab to the CFDISK button and press Enter. You will see a screen much like Figure 6-4. The screen is divided into two main parts: the part just beneath the long dashed line, which shows the different partitions and free space on the computer's hard drive; and the menu section at the bottom. In our example, the partitions section shows that we have a single hard drive (the hda1) which has a primary partition with a Windows95 file system of 2,052 Mbytes, or about 2 Gbytes. The other half of the hard drive is free space. Your job is to create two Linux partitions in the free space. Unfortunately, the method of moving around the screen and the menu is not especially intuitive. You have to use the arrow keys. The right and the left arrow keys move through the menu items at the bottom of the screen, while the up and down arrow keys move between the partitions and free space above. Experimenting with this, you will notice that a partition has a different menu at the bottom than does free space.

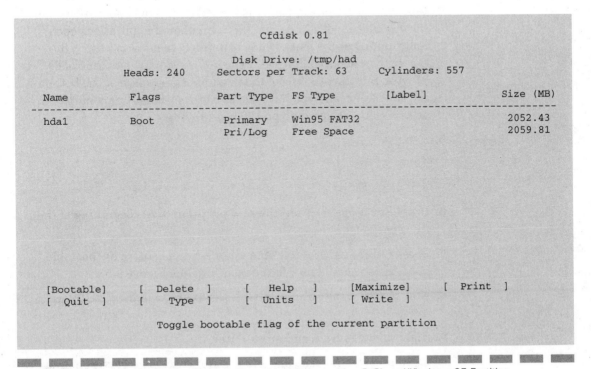

Figure 6-4 CFDISK Screen, Showing a 4-Gbyte Hard Drive, with a 2-Gbyte Windows 95 Partition

2. Use the down arrow key to highlight the Free Space line. The menu at the bottom of the screen changes to:

```
[ Help ]    [ New ]    [ Print ]    [ Quit ]    [ Units ]
                    Print help screen
```

3. Use the right arrow key to highlight New on the bottom menu, and hit Enter.

4. Use the right arrow key to highlight Logical on the bottom menu, and hit Enter.

   At this point you have to determine the size of your main Linux partition. The two factors to consider are the amount of free space, which is shown you at the bottom of the screen, and the amount of free space you want to reserve for the swap file partition. The most desirable size of a Linux swap file partition is a matter of some dispute. Twice the size of system RAM has been suggested, although this was more common in the days when 16 Mbytes of RAM was something to be proud of. The prospective load also has to be taken into account. My own experience indicates that a stand-alone system with 64 Mbytes of RAM, dedicated to desktop applications and heavily multitasked (i.e., that has a number of applications open and running at the same time), is unlikely to develop a swap file larger than about 32 Mbytes. I suggest a swap file partition of 64 Mbytes. Subtract that from the amount of free space at the bottom of your screen, and you have the size of your main Linux partition. In this example, it would be 1995.81 Mbytes.

5. Type in:

   ```
   1995
   ```

   and press Enter.

6. Press Enter again to add the new partition to the beginning of the free space.

7. Press Enter again to "flag" the main Linux partition as "bootable." Your screen should now look something like Figure 6-5.

8. Now to create the swap partition. Down arrow to the Free Space line.

9. Right arrow to New, and press Enter.

10. Right arrow to Logical, and press Enter twice. The Partition area at the top of the screen should now look like this:

```
                              Cfdisk 0.81

                         Disk Drive: /tmp/had
                 Heads: 240   Sectors per Track: 63     Cylinders: 557

     Name          Flags          Part Type   FS Type       [Label]           Size (MB)
    ----------------------------------------------------------------------------------
     hda1          Boot           Primary     Win95 FAT32                       2052.43
     hda5          Boot           Logical     Linux                            1993.36
                                  Pri/Log     Free Space                         66.45




     [Bootable]      [  Delete  ]     [  Help  ]    [Maximize]    [  Print  ]
     [  Quit  ]      [   Type   ]     [  Units ]    [ Write  ]

              Toggle bootable flag of the current partition
```

Figure 6-5 CFDISK Screen, Showing the Same Hard Drive with a 1993-Mbyte Linux Partition and 66 Mbytes of Free Space

```
     Name   Flags   Part Type   FS Type    [Label]   Size (MB)
    ---------------------------------------------------------
     hda1   Boot    Primary     Win95 FAT3            2052.43
     hda5   Boot    Logical     Linux                1993.36
     hda6           Logical     Linux                  66.45
```

You now have two Linux partitions, but your job isn't done yet. A Linux swap partition is a different kind of partition than a regular Linux partition. We have to change the type of the last 66-Mbyte partition to Linux Swap.

11. Make sure that the 66-Mbyte partition is highlighted, and right arrow to Type in the menu section. Press Enter.

12. Type:

    82

    and press Enter. The Partition area at the top of the screen should now look like this:

Name	Flags	Part Type	FS Type	[Label]	Size (MB)
hda1	Boot	Primary	Win95 FAT3		2052.43
hda5	Boot	Logical	Linux		1993.36
hda6		Logical	Linux Swap		66.45

The change is small, but significant. You will see Linux Swap under FS Type on the last line. Make a note of the Name of the swap partition—hda6, for instance. Now you have to write your changes to disk.

13. Use the right arrow key to highlight Write on the bottom menu, and press Enter.

14. Type:

    yes

    and press Enter.

15. Use the right arrow key to highlight Quit, and press Enter.

16. At the Partition Disks screen, make sure that the Done button is highlighted, and press Enter.

17. The Activate Swap Space screen is next. Make sure that the swap partition device name is the same as the note you made in step 12, above. If it is, tab to the OK button, and press Enter.

Adding Windows to the Mount Table

By "mounting" a partition, we mean, in Linux, being able to read to and write from it. If you complete the installation as is, Linux will be unaware that Windows is on your machine. Enabling Linux to read and write your Windows files can greatly increase your productivity. You enable this by editing the mount table shown in the Edit Mount Table screen. Here is an example of the two most important lines:

Device	Size	Partition Type	Mount Point
/dev/hda1	2101648	Win95 FAT32	
/dev/hda5	2041168	Linux Native	/

A "mount point" is like a directory in DOS. In this example the main Linux partition is mounted under /. That is standard. But the Windows partition is not mounted at all—Linux will not be able to see a single Windows file.

Mount the Windows partition using this procedure:

1. With the up and down arrow keys, make sure that the Win95 FAT32 line is highlighted.

2. Tab to the Edit button, and press Enter.

3. Type:

```
/C
```

Tab to the OK button, and press Enter. That's it. The two lines in the above example would now look like this:

```
Device        Size    Partition Type    Mount Point
/dev/hda1    2101648   Win95 FAT32       /C
/dev/hda5    2041168   Linux Native      /
```

5. Tab to the OK button again, and press Enter.

6. At the Format Partitions screen, tab to the OK button and hit Enter.

Networking

Several screens may come up for LAN networking or for a PPP connection. If you're connected to a LAN, call your system administrator for the required information to fill in. Otherwise, tab to the OK button, and press Enter. Press Enter again at the Install Log screen.

Installing Packages

1. Hit Enter at the Welcome screen. The next screen, Installation Type (Figure 6-6), gives the choice of choosing either a preselected choice of programs, or choosing your own customized set. I advise you to select the Workstation choice.

2. Use the down arrow key to select Workstation.

3. Tab to the Install button, and press Enter.

4. At the Confirm Selection screen, hit Enter.
   At this point take a cigarette or coffee break. According to the Installation Status screen, it will take several minutes to finish loading all programs. It informs us that a total of 386 software packages are being installed, for a total of 489 Mbytes. On my computer this took about 7 minutes. Why so many software packages? Linux itself is just an operating system, and the absolute fundamental center of it, called the kernel, is only one file. But there are many other files necessary to run Linux productively.

5. After all files have been loaded, you are prompted to select a kernel. If you have a regular desktop PC, accept the default and press

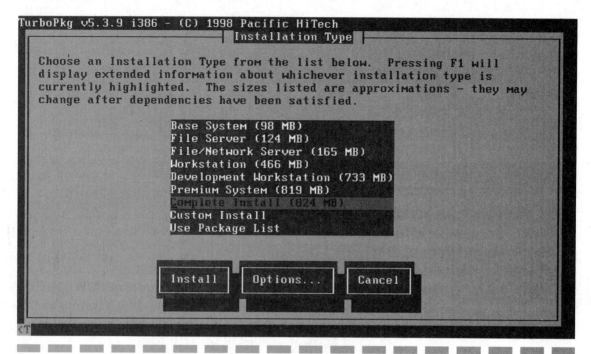

Figure 6-6 Installation Type Screen

Enter. If your computer has Advanced Power Management (APM) support—all modern laptops and many newer PCs have this—down arrow to that choice, and press Enter.

Installing and Configuring the Boot Manager

LILO is the Linux boot manager, or boot loader, enabling you to boot up either Linux or Windows at will.

1. The LILO Installation screen (Figure 6-7), asks you where you want to install LILO. Accept the default, the Master Boot Record, and press Enter.

2. At the next screen simply press Enter again.

3. The next screen, Bootable Partitions, is very important. You should have at least two lines in the middle of this screen, representing two partitions—Linux and Windows—looking something like this:

```
/dev/hda1      Win95 FAT32
/dev/hda5      Linux native      Linux
```

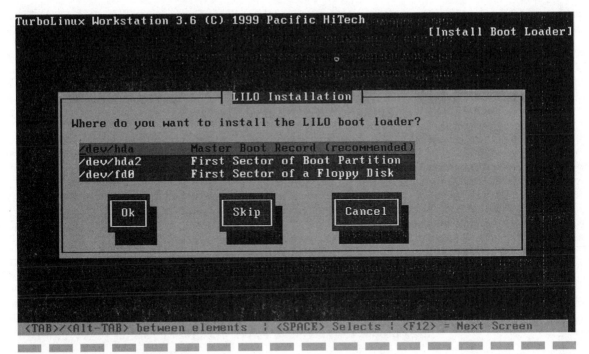

Figure 6-7 LILO Installation Screen

4. You need to add a label to your Windows partition entry. Make sure that the Win95 line is highlighted, then tab to the Edit button.

5. At the Edit Boot Label screen, type:

   dos

   and tab to the OK button. Hit Enter.

6. Your Bootable Partitions screen should now look like this:

   ```
   /dev/hda1      Win95 FAT32     dos
   /dev/hda5      Linux native    Linux
   ```

7. Tab to the OK button, and press Enter.

The Graphics Adapter

Up to now the installation routine has been almost completely manual. However, TurboLinux does have the capability to automatically detect your graphics adapter. Just to make sure the results are accurate, take out the notes you made in Chapter 1.

1. At the Probe Video Card screen, hit Enter.

2. The Probe Results screen (Figure 6-8 is an example) should give you a good deal of information. Check the Chipset—it should be very similar to your own notes. Press the Enter key.

3. You're asked to accept the probed values, or configure your graphics adapter manually. If the results were satisfactory, highlight the Use Probed Values button, and press Enter.

Configuring X Window

The next section starts with the console keyboard, but after that goes on to configure a number of things—monitors, fonts, etc.—for use in X Window.

1. At the Welcome to Turboxcfg screen, press Enter.

2. At the Configure Console Keyboard screen, choose your keyboard—the default, US, is adequate for most American keyboards—and press Enter.

3. Next select a keyboard for use within the X Window system. For most people, the default will work fine. After choosing, press Enter.

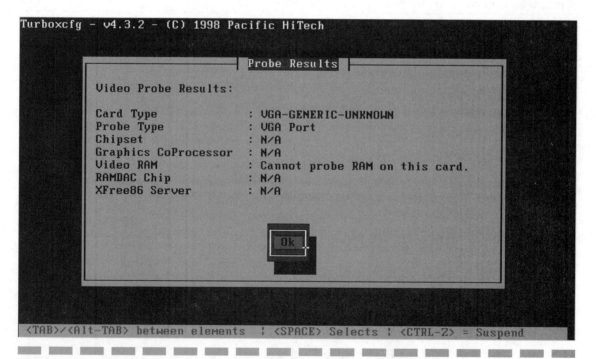

Figure 6-8   Probe Results Screen

Windows in Linux

Like Microsoft's product, Linux has its own windows environment, which is called the X Window System. In this book I refer to Microsoft's graphic environment as Windows, and to the Linux graphic environment as X Window.

4. The mouse. Choose yours, and tab to the OK button. Press Enter.

5. Mouse buttons. Make the correct choice, tab to the OK button, and press Enter.

6. The Select Monitor screen appears. The list is not really very large. If yours is there, you're in luck. Otherwise, choose Default Monitor, tab to the OK button, and hit Enter.

7. At the Default Color Depth screen (Figure 6-9) you will need the information you gathered in Chapter 1. Choose the correct number in bits per pixel (bpp) and tab to the OK button. Press Enter.

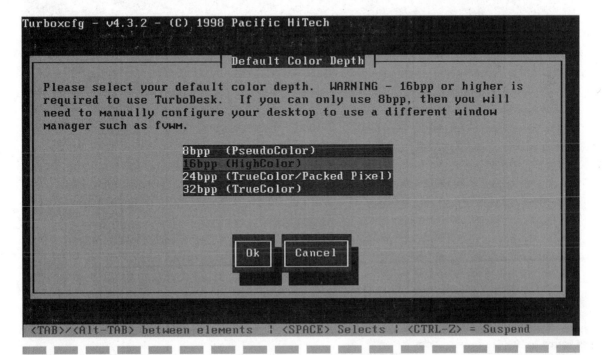

Figure 6-9 Default Color Depth

8. The Select Resolutions screen (Figure 6-10) may give you one value, or several. To be on the safe side, choose the one you made a note of in Chapter 1. Your value will probably be either 800×600 or 1024×768 (in Windows this was the screen area, in pixels). Then tab to the OK button, and press Enter.

9. At the Refresh Rates screen, accept the default—configure automatically—and press Enter.

10. At the Font Resolution screen, accept the default, and press Enter.

11. Now for the test. Hit the Enter key. The entire screen should turn gray, and then a black box with yellow lettering should appear in the upper-left hand corner (Figure 6-11). If you can read the text, your system is properly configured. If not, you will have to hit the Ctrl, the Alt, and the Backspace keys together, holding them all down for a moment, to get back to the installation screen. If the setup fails, you will be given a chance to try again. If need be, you can tweak every setting until you get it right.

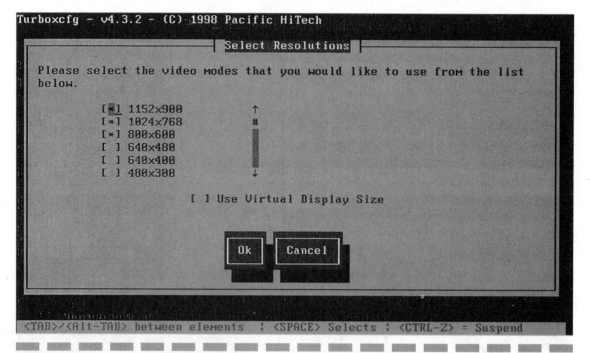

Figure 6-10   Select Resolutions Screen

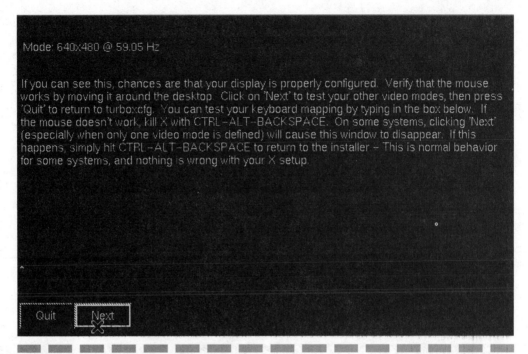

Mode: 640x480 @ 59.05 Hz

If you can see this, chances are that your display is properly configured. Verify that the mouse works by moving it around the desktop. Click on 'Next' to test your other video modes, then press 'Quit' to return to turboxcfg. You can test your keyboard mapping by typing in the box below. If the mouse doesn't work, kill X with CTRL-ALT-BACKSPACE. On some systems, clicking 'Next' (especially when only one video mode is defined) will cause this window to disappear. If this happens, simply hit CTRL-ALT-BACKSPACE to return to the installer – This is normal behavior for some systems, and nothing is wrong with your X setup.

Quit   Next

Figure 6-11   Example of X Configuration Test Screen

12. Clicking on the Quit button takes you to the Test Results screen. If there are problems, tab to the No button, and go back for reconfiguration. If everything went well, hit Enter at the Yes button.

13. At the Select Login Method screen, tab to the Text-Based Login screen, and press Enter. Press Enter again at the Success screen.

Final Configuration

1. At the Configure Timezone screen, hit the spacebar to select GMT, and tab down to your time zone. Then tab to the OK button, and press Enter.

2. At the Configure Printers screen, tab to the Add button, and hit Enter.

3. If you have a standard desktop system, with a local printer, hit Enter.

4. Hit Enter twice at the Printer Queue screen.

5. Only two settings should have to be edited at the Edit Printer Settings screen (Figure 6-12). They are the Printer Type and Resolution. Just tab to the <Configure...> areas to the right of Type and Resolution, hit Enter, and choose the correct value. The resolution you can gather from your printer documentation. When you're finished, tab to the OK button, and hit Enter.

6. Back at the Configure Printers screen, tab to the Save & Exit button, and press Enter.

7. At Configure ISA PnP Devices, hit Enter. At the PnP Setup Complete screen, hit Enter again.

8. You may or may not now be prompted to set up your PPP Internet connection. I advise against it at this time. Escape to the next screen.

9. At the Service Status Board, simply select Close by pressing the Escape key and then Enter.

10. At the next screen, Select Windowmanager, just hit Enter.

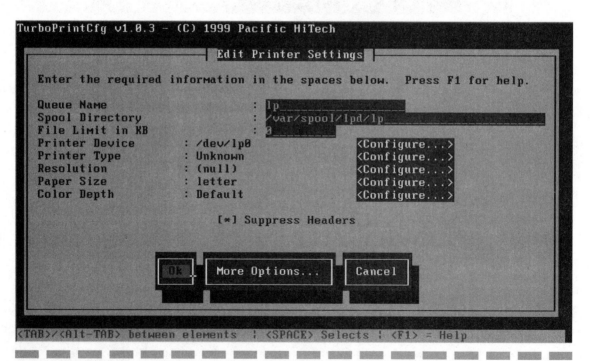

Figure 6-12 Edit Printer Settings

11. The Root Password screen comes up. You have to log into Linux every time you start it, using a username and a password. Your first username will be "root"—it means the system administrator—and you have to choose a password. Take a moment to consider this before typing anything. There are two restrictions to your password: it must be at least 6 characters long, and it will be case-sensitive. In other words, the password "Sesame" is different from "sesame."

    Linux users traditionally come from the UNIX community of industrial-strength computer users, or, more recently, from the proprietors of Web sites. In both cases, security is a paramount concern. If, however, you are loading Linux on your home computer, then security for you under Linux will be no more important that it always has been under Windows, or whatever operating system you've been using.

    Choose a password you can memorize. Type it in, hit the Tab key, and type it again. Then tab to the OK button, and hit Enter.

12. You're now asked to define a "normal user account." Choose whatever username and password you like for this, or just tab to the Cancel button, and press Enter.

That's it. You'll see the Complete screen and the Finish button at the bottom. But don't hit it yet!

Rebooting into Windows

When you press Enter for the last time (not yet!) the machine will reboot—restart. If you loaded Linux onto a machine with no other operating system installed, Linux will immediately boot up. But if you loaded it onto a machine with Windows already installed, then the first thing you will see is the Linux boot manager prompt:

```
LILO boot:
```

When you see this you'll have 5 seconds to decide whether you want to boot into Linux, or back into Windows. If you do nothing, then in 5 seconds Linux will start up automatically—that's the default. I advise you to reboot back into Windows first.

1. Press Enter. The computer will restart. As soon as you can, take out the Linux CD. The moment you see:

```
LILO boot:
```

2. Type:

```
dos
```

and hit the Enter key.

Welcome back to Windows! Reentering your familiar environment after a long, tedious, and often nerve-wracking Linux installation is usually a great morale booster. It reassures you that you haven't, after all, destroyed your computer. It's all still there.

You can easily reset LILO so that Windows starts up automatically, if you want to. Details appear later.

It's Too Weird! I Want to Get Out!

If, after getting back into Windows, you are overcome with panic and want to destroy the monster you have created (while keeping your Windows installation safe), nothing is simpler. NOTE: Follow this procedure only if you lose your nerve! It will mean having to reinstall Linux from scratch!

1. From within Windows, start up your partition program. You will see that Linux has actually added three new partitions to what was your empty space. Two of the new partitions are quite small, and one is large. You want to delete all of them—all of the new Linux partitions, that is. This is as simple as clicking on them with your right mouse button, and choosing delete from the subsequent menu.

   After you've deleted your Linux partitions, there is still one important step remaining: you have to get rid of LILO, the boot manager. That resides on what is called your Master Boot Record (MBR). Follow this procedure:

2. Reboot your computer, by clicking on Start, then on Shut Down, and then by choosing Restart in MS-DOS mode. You'll see LILO again.

3. Type:

```
dos
```

and hit Enter. This will take you to the DOS prompt:

```
C:\WINDOWS>
```

4. Type exactly as follows:

```
fdisk /mbr
```

and press Enter.

5. Then type:

```
win
```

and hit Enter again.

Hopefully, you will not succumb to the temptation to destroy your Linux installation. If you care to proceed, move on to Part 2.

## CHAPTER 7

Installing SuSE Linux 6.1

Purpose of Chapter:
Install SuSE Linux on a Typical PC

SuSE is a German distribution that has gained some market share in the States. The installation can be a trial for the novice. The overall feel is far from intuitive, and the SuSE installation manual focuses more on German thoroughness than on easy usability.

However, there are some excellent automatic features built in—such as the ability to automatically detect and configure your graphics adapter card—that come as pleasant surprises in a very comprehensive installation routine.

The fastest and simplest way to install SuSE Linux 6.1 is by booting up
your computer with the Linux CD. Most modern machines will be able to
use this method. However, if your machine is unable to boot from the CD,
then you'll have to start the installation process with a 3½-inch Linux
boot diskette. All the major distributors supply boot disks, but if you are
using the CDs that come with this book, you will have to make your own.
Instructions are in Appendix A.

Installing the Operating System

1. Insert your SuSE Linux CD, and shut down your machine. Then
   turn it back on. You'll see a brief welcome screen, showing the
   company's American and German addresses, and then the language screen. The default is Deutsche—German.
   The mouse doesn't work at this stage, so use the down arrow key
   to move to English, and hit Enter.

2. The next screen asks if you have a color display, thus suggesting
   the original age of the installation routine. Just hit Enter.

3. The keyboard map screen is next. As you did with the language
   screen, choose the language of your keyboard, and hit Enter.

4. At the next screen, make sure `Start installation / system`
   is highlighted, and press Enter.

5. At the following screen, make sure `Start installation` is
   highlighted, and press Enter.

6. You are asked to choose the source media. `CD-ROM` should be highlighted. Just hit Enter.

7. The CD fires up, and the Type of Installation screen comes up.
   `Install Linux from scratch` should be highlighted. Just hit
   Enter.

8. At the Partition Harddrives screen, use the Tab key to move to the
   Partitioning button, and hit Enter.

9. The installation routine automatically picks up the free space you
   created on your machine in Chapter 1. Make sure the Yes button
   is highlighted, and press Enter.
   At this point the SuSE installation creates both your main
   Linux partition and your Linux swap partition. This takes a
   minute or two. Upon finishing, a very confusing Package

Installation screen comes up. It has several menu items. The first is Load configuration, and the last is Main menu.

Ignore all of these menu items but one.

10. Down arrow to the Start installation menu item, and press Enter.

Program installation begins, loading up SuSE's default package of Linux programs. (The default is quite large: over 700 Mbytes). This takes some time, and unlike the other distributions, you can't very well go out and take a coffee or cigarette break: SuSE uses a multi-CD process, and you will be prompted to insert several CDs as the install proceeds. At the end of it all, you're presented with the Package Installation screen again. Down arrow to Main menu, and hit Enter.

11. You're asked to make sure that CD number 1 is installed. Hit Enter.

12. The Select Kernel screen comes up. Make sure the first line is highlighted—the one that says recommended and supported— and press Enter.

13. The Kernel Release screen—it will probably be titled something like Rel 2.2.7 recommended and supported—looks very complex, but isn't really. If you have a normal CD-ROM, just hit Enter. If you have a SCSI drive (if you have one, you will likely know it), choose yours from the list and hit Enter.

14. The next screen asks you if you want to create a boot disk for use if your system becomes so corrupt it won't boot correctly. There is, however, relatively little chance of successfully salvaging a corrupt Linux system with a boot disk. The best way to guard against system corruption is to regularly back up your data. Tab to the No button, and hit Enter.

15. At the small Confirmation screen for LILO, press Enter.

Configuring the Boot Manager (LILO)

SuSE's LILO configuration screen is important. It is absolutely critical that LILO be configured correctly, for this is the boot manger that will allow you to boot up either Linux or Windows, as you like. The procedure demands a lot of user input, and looks complex. However, it is actually semiautomated, and simpler than it first appears.

1. Hit the F4 key at the top of your keyboard.

2. At the next screen, LILO Boot Configuration, enter the configuration data for Windows first. Type:

```
dos
```

and tab to the next window.

3. Use the down arrow key to highlight the Boot DOS/Win choice, and press Enter again. The three central lines in the screen should now look like this:

```
Configuration name               :dos  :
Which operating system           [Boot DOS/Win      ]
(Root-) partition to boot        :/dev/hda1      :
```

Note that the last line—/dev/hda1—is an example only. It is, however, the most typical setting.

4. Tab once to the Continue button, and press Enter.

5. Now configure the Linux entries. Hit the F4 key again.

6. Type:

```
linux
```

and tab to the next window.

7. The Boot Linux choice should be highlighted. Press Enter. The three central lines in the screen should now look like this:

```
Configuration name               :linux :
Which operating system           [Boot Linux        ]
(Root-) partition to boot        :/dev/hda2      :
```

Note that the last line—/dev/hda2—is again only an example only. It is, however, the most typical setting.

8. Tab once to the Continue button, and press Enter.

9. That's it. In the square at the lower right you should have two entries: dos and linux. Tab to Continue at the bottom of the screen, and hit Enter.

10. Hit Enter at the Confirmation screen.

Final Configuration

1. At the Time Zone Configuration screen, choose yours and hit Enter.

2. Choose GMT or local time, and hit Enter.

3. You are forced to enter a Hostname at the next screen. If you are on a LAN, contact your system administrator. If not, I suggest you enter the word "local" in both the Hostname and Domain name space.

4. Tab to Continue, and press Enter.

5. At the next screen, just press Enter if you are not on a network. If you are on a network, choose Real network, hit Enter, and consult your system administrator.

6. At the screen informing you that your network is configured, hit Enter.

7. Sendmail is a UNIX standard for e-mail. You are very unlikely to use it, unless you are connected to a UNIX network. If that is the case, consult your system administrator. Otherwise, down arrow to Do not install, and press Enter.

8. Press Enter again at the OUTPUT of SuSEconfig screen.

9. Press Enter again upon being informed that the base system has been successfully installed.

10. Linux now starts up on your machine. The installation routine prompts you for a password. You have to log into Linux every time you start it, using a username and a password. Your first user-name will be "root"—it means the system administrator—and you have to choose a password. Take a moment to consider this before typing anything. There are two restrictions to your password: it must be at least 5 and no more than 8 characters long, and it will be case-sensitive. In other words, the password "Sesame" is different from "sesame." Linux users traditionally come from the UNIX community of industrial-strength computer users, or, more recently, from the proprietors of Web sites. In both cases, security is a paramount concern. If, however, you are loading Linux on your home computer, then security for you under Linux will be no more important that it always has been under Windows, or whatever operating system you've been using.

11. Choose a password you can memorize. Type it in, and hit the Enter key. Re-enter it, and hit the Enter key again.

12. You're asked if you want to create an example user. You can do this later if you want. Tab to No, and hit Enter.

13. Hit Enter when asked if you want to set up your modem.

14. Most PC modems are set to communications port 2—com2. At the Modem Configuration screen, tab down to the line that reads:

    TtyS1—com2: under DOS

    and press Enter.

15. Hit Enter when asked if you want to set up your mouse.

16. Choose your mouse as best you can from the Mouse Configuration screen, and hit Enter.

17. Most PC mice are set to com1. At the Mouse Configuration screen, just hit Enter.

18. Hit Enter at the next screen, which asks if you want to run GPM—the General Purpose Mouse.

19. At the TEST GPM screen, see if your mouse works. If it doesn't, go back and choose another mouse or another port (consult your computer documentation if you're at a loss). If the mouse is working, choose Keep, and hit Enter.

20. Hit Enter at the Information screen, confirming that all packages are installed.

Logging in for the First Time

At the prompt to press Return, press the Enter key. The system will start up, and you have to login. When you see:

    Login:

1. Type:

    Root

    and press Enter.

2. At:

    Password:

    type your password, and hit Enter. You will be presented with a prompt similar to the one below ("root" is an example of the host-name you entered in step 3, above):

    Root:/#

Configuring X Window

Like Microsoft's product, Linux has its own windows environment, which is called the X Window System. In this book I refer to Microsoft's graphic environment as Windows, and to the Linux graphic environment as X Window.

SuSE is different than every other distribution in insisting that you configure X Window after booting up the main operating system. Fortunately the process is largely automatic once started. In particular, it should find and automatically configure your graphics adapter.

1. Type:

   sax

   and hit Enter. The first screen that comes up is devoted to your mouse. If it was working in step 19, above, it should be working now.

2. Use your mouse to click on the Apply button at the bottom of the screen, and then the OK button.

3. The SaX Mouse screen is next. Since this has already been configured, click on the Next button in the lower right-hand corner.

4. Your keyboard should also be configured by now. Click on the Next button again.

5. Your card should be autodetected. Click on the Next button again.

6. At the SaX Monitor screen select your monitor's vendor in the column on the left, and the model name on the right. The most important information is in the Info box. The horizontal and vertical sync rates that you made a note of in Chapter 1 should be within the range listed on the screen. When you're finished, click on the Next button again.

7. At the SaX Desktop screen select the color value and resolution that you made a note of in Chapter 1. Then click the Next button again, and the Yes button.

Your screen should go into graphics mode at this point, showing you two boxes. The box in the upper left of the screen tells you the screen's size and resolution. The larger box in the middle lets you adjust the size and position of the screen image.

IMPORTANT: If something goes wrong—the screen, for instance, goes blank and stays that way, or flickers uncontrollably—just hit the Ctrl, Alt, and Backspace keys simultaneously. You will be returned to the previous setup screen to adjust your settings.

When you have the screen looking as you want it, click on the Save button at the lower right. You will be returned to the command prompt.

Rebooting into Windows

1. Type:

   ```
   Reboot
   ```

   and press Enter.

2. Your computer will reboot, and show you the boot manager prompt:

   ```
   LILO boot:
   ```

3. If you want to boot up Linux, type:

   ```
   Linux
   ```

   and press Enter.

4. If you want to boot up Windows, then do nothing at all, and in a few seconds your familiar Windows will boot up as normal.

It's Too Weird! I Want to Get Out!

If, after getting back into Windows, you are overcome with panic and want to destroy the monster you have created (while keeping your Windows installation safe), nothing is simpler. NOTE: Follow this procedure only if you lose your nerve! It will mean having to reinstall Linux from scratch!

1. From within Windows, start up your partition program. You will see that Linux has actually converted your empty space into two new partitions, one large and one small. You want to delete both of them—the new Linux partitions, that is. This is as simple as clicking on them with your right mouse button, and choosing delete from the subsequent menu.

   After you've deleted your Linux partitions, there is still one important step remaining: you have to get rid of LILO, the boot manager. That resides on what is called your Master Boot Record (MBR). Follow this procedure:

2. Reboot your computer, by clicking on Start, then on Shut Down, and then by choosing Restart in MS-DOS mode. You'll see LILO again.

3. Type:

```
dos
```

and hit Enter. This will take you to the DOS prompt:

```
C:\WINDOWS>
```

4. Type exactly as follows:

```
fdisk /mbr
```

and press Enter.

5. Then type:

```
win
```

and hit Enter again.

Hopefully, you will not succumb to the temptation to destroy your Linux installation. If you care to proceed, move on to Part 2.

2

Under the Hood: Linux at the Command Line

From the 1940s to the 1970s, the automobile made America the most mechanically literate nation on the face of the earth. It was the used car that did the trick, the very used car—the old banger. Dad bought it for nothing and gave it to his son, and often enough his daughter, who then proceeded to spend an entire summer learning about automobile mechanics in the most practical and efficient way there was: wrench in hand, under the hood.

The command line is the computer equivalent of under the hood.

The modern Windows user may reply that practically no one does serious work on their own car any more (cars are now too complicated, for one thing). Why should we learn this old command line stuff? Can't we do it all by pointing and clicking a mouse in X Window?

The answer is that you can do quite a lot of it in X Window. But not all yet. And the command line has a number of advantages:

1. *Speed*. Many operations, such as editing configuration files, and even moving and copying files, are done faster at the command line than within a text editor or file manager in X Window.

2. *Convenience*. Some things, like mounting a Microsoft Windows partition, are just plain easier at the command line.

3. *Configuration and maintenance*. What if you can't get X Window to work on your machine? You'll have to rerun the setup routine from the command prompt. What if the X Window program to set up your internet connection fails to do the job (good chance it will fail, with most distributions)? Editing the necessary files at the command prompt is a simple and sure way to get connected.

4. *Troubleshooting*. You'll have a better chance of fixing your system when something goes wrong, if you have at least a slight idea of what's going on under the hood.

Part 2 is divided into five chapters.

Chapter 8 is devoted to the most basic operations: logging on and off, and exploring the system.

Chapter 9 shows how to read and edit text configuration files.

Chapter 10 is devoted to basic manipulation, from accessing CD-ROM drives and floppies to copying files.

Chapter 11 shows how to set up a dial-up Internet connection.

Chapter 12 presents each distribution's main command line setup programs.

All chapters are deliberately presented for the Windows user who has little or no experience with the command line. If you're a novice, I urge you to read them. Even if you don't enjoy grease, you'll learn the satisfaction of every mechanic—including the amateur—upon successfully tuning or fixing a machine with his or her own bare hands.

## CHAPTER 8

Command Line Basics

Purpose of Chapter:
To Use Command Line Basics to:
1. Log On and Off
2. Explore the System
3. Get Help

Logging on and off in Linux is traditionally a command line function—although both Red Hat and Caldera have included this in their latest graphical desktops.

Every Linux user should know the basics of how to get around and explore his or her system using the command line. The cd, ls, and locate commands are still the fastest—and most fundamental—way to investigate and navigate your system. Basics of directory structure are also covered in this chapter. Finally, command line help via the man pages is covered.

This chapter and the following two chapters are presented in the form of lessons and exercises. A primer on command line operations lends itself well to such a presentation.

Unlike Windows, where it can be turned on or off, you *always* have to log on to Linux, and in the beginning you log on as "root."

Linux was designed from the beginning as a networked operating system, and as a result when you first log on, you log on as the system administrator. That is the root account. From there, if you want to, you can create separate user accounts, each with their own password. These user accounts have fewer privileges than the root account; for instance, they may not be able to create or delete directories, or even run executable files. For a networked operating system, for any situation where security is important in a multi-user environment, this makes sense.

For a stand-alone system, it is not obviously necessary.

UNIX writers on this subject will insist that it is necessary. They will insist that the first thing you should do is to create your own user account, as a way to protect your system against yourself. They will point out that as the root user—the system administrator—you have a complete set of permissions to do anything you like: to create and to remove files, to remove directories, to even destroy the whole setup, partition-by-partition.

All that is very true. But how is that different from the user of a stand-alone PC running Windows? The fact is, PC users have always been used to total control over their own machines. They have always been their own system administrators. And there's no reason they shouldn't continue to be under Linux.

Lesson 1: Starting Linux and Logging on as Root

There are three steps:

1. Boot up Linux.
2. Log on as root.
3. Type in your password.

REMEMBER: Linux is case-sensitive. "Root" is not the same as "root." Everything you type in at the command prompt has to be exact—even your password.

Starting from the top:

1. First, start up the computer, or restart from Windows. When you see this prompt:

   `LILO boot:`

   boot up Linux by typing:

   `linux`

   and pressing Enter.

2. When you see the login prompt:

   `localhost login:`

   type:

   `root`

   and press Enter. You'll see the password prompt.

3. Type your password and press Enter. That's it. You're in.

All four distributions have similar login screens, but all four also have differences. Examples of all four distributions are as follows: Red Hat (Figure 8-1), Caldera (Figure 8-2), TurboLinux (Figure 8-3), and SuSE (Figure 8-4).

Figure 8-1
Red Hat Command Line Login

```
Red Hat Linux release 6.1 (Cartman)
Kernel 2.2.12-20 on an i686

localhost login: root
Password:
Last login: Fri Oct 15 08:47:03 on tty1
[root@localhost /root]#
```

Figure 8-2
Caldera Command Line Login (with the inittab file modified as described in Chapter 5)

```
Caldera OpenLinux (TM)
Version  2.3
Copyright 1996-1999 Caldera Systems, Inc.

noname.nodomain.nowhere login:  root
Password:
Last login: Tue Aug 10 14:29:02 1999 on tty1

Welcome to your OpenLinux system!

You can start KDE with 'kde' or plain X11 with 'startx'.

[root@noname /root]#
```

Figure 8-3
TurboLinux
Command Line Login

```
TurboLinux release 3.6 (Miami)
Kernel 2.2.5-15 on an i686 (localhost.localdomain)
VC: tty1

localhost login: root
Password:
Last login: Tue Aug 10 01:41:35 from :0.0
[root@localhost /root]#
```

Figure 8-4
SuSE Command Line
Login

```
Welcome to SuSE Linux 6.1 (i386) - Kernel 2.2.5-15 (tty1).

root login: root
Password:
Have a lot of fun...
Last login: Mon Aug 9 20:03:21 on tty1.
You have new mail.
root:~ #
```

Lesson 2: Shutting Down Linux

There are three good ways of doing this, depending on whether or not you want to reboot. The simplest is the `halt` command. If you want to automatically reboot, there is the `reboot` command. Slightly more complicated is the `shutdown` command. And in the extremely unlikely situation that the whole system freezes—hangs—there is always the emergency method: Ctrl, Alt, and Delete.

LINUX ETIQUETTE: Never, never just turn your computer off when running Linux. The operating system keeps a number of files open and running all the time in the background, and needs to close these down in an orderly way. Linux has ways to automatically recover from an improper shutdown, but why push it? Turn your computer off properly, and lengthen the life of your configuration.

Halt

This is the simplest method to shut down the operating system and turn off your computer simultaneously.

Type:

```
halt
```

and press Enter.

Reboot

This is the method to use when you want to reboot your machine, i.e., when you want the computer to start back up again automatically, either into Windows or Linux.

Type:

```
reboot
```

and hit Enter. Your computer will now give you a large number of shutdown messages, and finally reboot.

Shutdown

This method is slightly more complex, but also more versatile. Like many Linux commands, it depends on flags or arguments that follow the actual command. To reboot, type:

```
shutdown -r now
```

and hit Enter. This does exactly the same thing as the reboot command. However, suppose you don't want to reboot your computer, but only want to turn it off? In that case you use the shutdown command with the -h flag—h for halt. Type:

```
shutdown -h now
```

and hit Enter. The usual messages will stream by, and the system will shut itself down.

Exercise 1   Cycle your computer through reboot and shutdown by using the reboot and shutdown commands. Finish by rebooting again into Linux.

Lesson 3: Using `updatedb` and `locate` to Locate Files

Once Linux is up and running, probably the first thing you want to do is run the `updatedb` command. This command, as its name suggests, updates a database of every single file on your system. You search the database by using the `locate` command.

First, create the database. Type:

```
updatedb
```

and hit Enter. The hard drive will whirl for a minute or two. One or two messages may or may not come up on the screen. When the hard drive activity stops and the command prompt returns, the database is updated.

Now, try it out. Suppose you want to locate a file called XF86Config. This is in fact the main configuration file for your X server, or in other words, the file that determines whether or not X Window is going to operate properly on your computer. But where is it? Type:

```
locate XF86Config
```

and press Enter. In Red Hat, you will see several lines looking something like this:

```
/etc/X11/XF86Config
/usr/X11R6/lib/X11/XF86Config
/usr/X11R6/lib/X11/XF86Config.eg
/usr/X11R6/man/man5/XF86Config.5x
```

In Caldera, the output will be slightly different but still similar:

```
/etc/XF86Config
/etc/XF86Config.vga16
/usr/X11R6/lib/X11/XF86Config.eg
/usr/X11R6/man/man5/XF86Config.5x.gz
```

In SuSE:

```
/etc/XF86Config
/usr/X11R6/lib/X11/XF86Config.eg
/usr/X11R6/man/man5/XF86Config.5x.gz
```

XF86Config is an extremely important file, and as you can see, all three distributions give us very similar, if slightly different, results (the `locate` command is not included in the TurboLinux distribution). In Red Hat, we can find the file in `/etc/X11`. In Caldera and SuSE, it is in `/etc`. The meaning of these letters and slashes is covered next.

A Primer on Linux Directories

Despite a couple of differences, the Linux directory system looks and even behaves like the DOS and Windows directory system. In Windows, of course, a directory is called a *folder*, but this is only a semantic difference.

Figure 8-5
Example of Directory
Structure

```
/  (root)
|
/etc
    |
    /X11
        |
            XF86Config
```

A directory, like a Windows folder, is simply a magnetic address for files, and perhaps other directories. It's similar to the drawers of a desk, or of a file cabinet. After all, any computer system is made up of hundreds, perhaps thousands, of files, and just as you wouldn't keep hundreds of files in stacks on top of your desk, so you don't keep hundreds of files without any organization on your hard drive.

The operating system puts the files in directories. Figure 8-5 gives a graphical representation of directory structure, starting at the "top"—like the top of a desk—and going down to a subdirectory called X11, and a file within it that we've seen before, called XF86Config. In this representation, / is the symbol for the root—that is, the very top of the desk. The other two directories, or subdirectories, are beneath it—the subdirectory X11 is rather like a drawer within a drawer, and the file XF86Config is a file within it.

An example of a much deeper directory tree is the long list of subdirectories necessary to drill down through to reach a text file that you would be interested in reading, if you were running Linux on a laptop with a graphics chip made by Chip and Technologies (Figure 8-6). In this example, we have to go down through five directories to find README.chips, a useful text file for many laptop owners.

Figure 8-6
Example of Directory
Structure: Drilling
Down to
README.chips

```
/  (root)
|
/usr
    |
    /X11R6
        |
        /lib
            |
            /X11
                |
                /doc
                    |
                        README.chips
```

Exercise 2   Use the `locate` command to find the file `pap-secrets`. This is an important file for Chapter 11: Hooking Up to the Internet.

Lesson 4: Getting Around with `cd` and Checking Location with `pwd`

`cd` stands for Change Directory, and `pwd` is short for Print Working Directory. Both commands are used lowercase.

At the moment, you are logged in as the root user—the system administrator—and your prompt probably looks something like this:

```
[root@localhost /root]#
```

No matter which distribution you're using, the last word you see will be root. That is in fact a directory—the home, or personal directory of the root user. Let's use the `cd` command to get above it, to the actual root of the directory structure.

> The word "root" has three different meanings in Linux. The root user—you—means the system administrator, the user with the most privileges in terms of deleting and creating files, etc. Second, your home directory is named for you (`root`), and that directory is where your system will start every time you log in. Finally, the system's root directory is the very top of the directory tree, the point at which all directories are below it. That root directory is shown as the single slash (/). Your own personal root directory is one level beneath it: `/root`.

`cd`

The `cd` command has several different usages. The simplest is used to move directly to the top—the root—of the directory structure, from wherever you happen to be. Type:

```
cd /
```

and press Enter. Notice that there is a space between the `cd` and the /. At the Linux command prompt, you have to be exact. Your prompt should now look something like this:

```
[root@localhost /]#
```

The word "root" has disappeared from the end of the prompt, because we have left that directory—like closing a drawer.

Now let's use cd a different way. Instead of getting to the top, let's use it to go down one level, to the etc directory. Type:

```
cd etc
```

and press Enter. Your prompt should now look something like this:

```
[root@localhost /etc]#
```

The etc at the end shows that we're now one level down, at the etc directory. Let's go one level lower. Type:

```
cd X11
```

and press Enter. (Notice that the letter X is capitalized in this directory name.) Your prompt should now look something like this:

```
[root@localhost X11]#
```

Two things have changed. First, etc has been replaced by X11. Second, the / has disappeared, indicating to us that we are more than one level below the root of the directory structure.

Next, let's suppose that you want to go right back to the top. Nothing simpler. Type:

```
cd /
```

and hit Enter. The root command line prompt appears once again.

Now suppose you want to get back to /etc/X11, but you want to do it in one step, instead of two. This is not a problem. Type:

```
cd /etc/X11
```

and hit Enter; you can see from the prompt that you're back again at the X11 subdirectory.

Another twist. You want to go back up just one level, to /etc. Type:

```
cd ..
```

and hit Enter (notice the space between cd and ..). The slash in front of the etc at the new prompt tells you that you're just one level below the root.

To repeat one example: suppose you want to get directly to a rather remote directory, /usr/X11R6/bin. Type:

```
cd /usr/X11R6/bin
```

and press Enter. From this rather remote directory, suppose you want to go up two directories. Type:

```
cd ../..
```

and press Enter. The prompt should now read:

```
[root@localhost /usr]#
```

Finally, you want to go down two levels from the current directory, back to /X11R6/bin. Type:

```
cd X11R6/bin
```

and hit Enter. So, the simple syntax for the cd command is shown in Figure 8-7.

pwd

Suppose that you come back to your computer after some hours away and are faced with the /bin prompt. You've completely forgotten where in the directory structure bin actually is. You need to know. Type:

```
pwd
```

and hit Enter. You should see the following line print out on the screen:

```
/usr/X11R6/bin
```

with the command line reappearing beneath it. This is an excellent method of checking where you are.

Figure 8-7
Syntax of cd
Command

```
cd /       =   go up all the way to the root directory.
cd X       =   go down one level at a time, to directory X.
cd X/X     =   go down two levels from the current directory
               (or more).
cd ..      =   go up one level at a time.
cd ../..   =   go up two levels from the current directory
               (or more).
cd /X/X    =   change directory to /X/X, or /X/X/X, etc.,
               above or below the current directory—as long as
               the first slash represents the directory root.
```

Exercise 3   Use the `cd` and `pwd` commands to:

1. Move to the top of the directory tree in one command.
2. Move down one level to the `etc` directory.
3. Move down two more levels—`/rc.d/init.d`—with one command.
4. Use `pwd` to check your location.
5. Move back up to the `etc` directory with one command.
6. Return to the top of the directory tree.

Lesson 5: Listing Files with `ls`; Using **alias**; `ls` Continued: Files, Directories, and Wildcards; and Clearing the Screen with **clear**

The `ls` command is equivalent to the old DOS `dir` command. It lists files and directories, can be used with wildcards, and can be "colorized" to make it more meaningful. `alias` is a handy command used to customize other commands. Finally, `clear` does just what you would think: it clears the screen.

ls

You should now be at the root or top-level directory. Use the `ls` command to list all the top-level directories and files. Type:

```
ls
```

and press Enter. You should see something like this:

```
C     boot   etc    lib          mnt   proc   sbin   usr
bin   dev    home   lost+found   opt   root   tmp    var
```

With the exception of the C, these are the standard top-level directories in most Linux systems.

There are usually no files at this level. So let's open the `etc` directory, and inspect the files and subdirectories there. Type:

```
cd etc
```

and press Enter. Now use the `ls` command again.

You should see dozens of files and directories—in fact, the entire screen should fill up with four columns of them. But now we come to a problem: how can we tell which of these names are files, and which are directories?

In DOS it was quite simple. The convention there was to capitalize all directories and file names, but directories all had a <DIR> tag next to them for identification. But in Linux there are no identifying tags. The convention is for directories to be lowercase, unless the directory name is the same as a file which has uppercase letters (and in fact, the convention is very loosely applied). As for files—although again the convention is lowercase, in fact they can be anything they like. Even a mix, as in the file XF86Setup—which is also the name of a directory!

Color is the solution. Although some Linux distributions come with color already activated at the command prompt, neither Red Hat nor Caldera do. So let's add it. Type:

```
ls --color
```

and press Enter. Directories are identified by the color blue; ordinary files are white.

But now run ls again. The color disappears. So we need a way to permanently colorize the ls command. We'll do that in the next chapter. For now, there's a way to colorize the ls command for the length of this session—that it, until you reboot your computer.

alias

The alias command lets you customize any command. Its use is quite simple, and its syntax, that is, the rules that govern how a command should be entered, are also quite simple. Type:

```
alias ls="ls --color"
```

and hit Enter. The files and directories are colorized again, and will remain so until reboot. This simply means that from now on—during this session—when you type ls, the computer will consider it, ls --color.

ls Continued: Files, Directories, and Wildcards

The ls command can be used to easily check the existence of a single file in a crowded directory, by simply typing the file's name after the command. Make sure you're in the etc directory. Type:

```
ls fstab
```

and press Enter. The command returns the one line: `fstab`. This means that the `fstab` file is in fact in that directory.

In addition, `ls` can be used to check the contents of a subdirectory of the current directory, without the necessity of drilling down to it first with the `cd` command. For instance, one of the subdirectories in `etc` is `ppp`. Instead of changing directory to `ppp`, we can just use the `ls` command. Type:

```
ls ppp
```

and hit Enter, and you can see the several files and subdirectories within `ppp`.

Finally, wildcard characters can be used. The concept of the wildcard will be familiar to older DOS users. The wildcard is usually a star (*) and is used to represent any character or number, uppercase or lowercase. The concept and usage are best shown by examples. Make sure you're at the `etc` directory. Type:

```
ls f*
```

and press Enter. You should have an output of at least three files, all of which begin with the letter "f." Another example is to type:

```
ls *.conf
```

and press Enter. You now have an instant listing of all the configuration files in the `etc` directory. Finally, the wildcard can also be used to simultaneously list files of a certain description in the current directory, as well as subdirectories fitting that description and the files within them. Type:

```
ls p*
```

and hit Enter. Not only do we have a listing of all the files in `etc` that start with "p," but we also have four subdirectories that start with "p," and a listing of all the files in them.

clear

The final command in this lesson is `clear`. After the last command, you have in front of you a screenful of files and directories. Suppose you want to get back to a simple, blank screen? This is easy. Type:

```
clear
```

and press Enter. The screen is wiped clean, and the command prompt returns to the top.

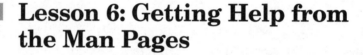

Lesson 6: Getting Help from the Man Pages

The on-line manual pages are the basic help resource for command line commands and configuration files. They are usually just called the "man" pages, from the command used to display them: man.

Suppose, for instance, you have forgotten how to colorize the ls command. In that case, the simplest thing to do is to display the on-line manual page for ls. Type:

```
man ls
```

and hit Enter. You'll see a screen similar to Figure 8-8.

Admittedly, this looks pretty obscure. No one can accuse the writers of man pages of trying for clarity above all else. However, it can be figured out. The command's name is given, and what it stands for. The Synopsis tells how it's used, in this case, the command first, followed by any options, and also by file name. The Description gives us a little more information, and is followed by a long list of options.

Figure 8-8
Beginning of On-Line Manual for the ls Command

```
LS (1)                          FSF                          LS (1)

NAME
       ls - list directory contents


SYNOPSIS
       ls [OPTION]... [FILE]...


DESCRIPTION
       List information about the FILEs (the current directory
       by default). Sort entries alphabetically if none of
       -cftuSUX nor --sort.

       -a,   --all
              do not hide entries starting with .

       -A,   --almost-all
              do not list implied . and ..

       -b,   --escape
              print octal escapes for nongraphic characters.

       --block-size=SIZE
              use SIZE-byte blocks.
```

In this case, you are looking for the option that controls color. There are many options for the `ls` command; you can scroll up and down the page by using either the up and down arrow keys, or the page up and page down keys. Use the down arrow key to find the listing that reads:

```
--color [=WHEN]
        control whether color is used to distinguish
        file types. WHEN may be 'never', 'always', or
        'auto'
```

Exit the manual by typing the single, lower-case letter, "q."

Exercise 4   Use the `cd`, `ls`, `man`, and `reboot` commands to:

1. Change to the `/usr/src` directory.
2. List the contents of the `/usr/src` directory.
3. List all subdirectories beginning with the letter "l," and their files.

   A symbolic link is a file (or directory) that is actually a pointer to another file (or directory). In this case, we have two directories that appear to have identical sets of files.
4. Find out what the `-l` option for the list command does, by looking that option up in the `ls` man page.
5. Now run `ls` again, with the `-l` option. Which directory appears to be "pointing" to another? Which directory is just a symbolic link to another? What color signifies a symbolic link?
6. Reboot the computer.

## CHAPTER 9

Reading and Editing Configuration Files

Purpose of Chapter: To Use `less` and `vi` to Read and Edit Text Configuration Files

All the different Linux distributions are now rich with a variety of semiautomated setup programs and graphical X Window programs, the main purpose of which is to shield you from ever having to manually edit a text configuration file. However, the fact is that not all of these programs do a very good job, and sometimes it's just faster—and more accurate—to do it yourself.

The `less` program is a command line text file reader. It's very, very easy to use. The `vi` program is a text file editor. `vi` comes from the dark ages of computing, and is quite different from any kind of word processor the typical Windows user is likely to have used. However, with just a little practice, you'll find it both easy and fast. This chapter, like the last, is presented as lessons and exercises.

One of the earliest and most central tenets of UNIX, adopted by Linux, is that the user should be able to customize almost every feature of the program by editing a simple text file. What's a text file? It's simply a computer file that is designed to be read at the console—that is, at the command prompt. Since the file is in English, it can be easily read, understood, and edited.

less is a text file reader, and vi is a text file editor. The basic usage for starting both is the same: you simply type the command, either less or vi, followed by the name of the file you want to either read or edit.

Lesson 1: Using less to Read the XF86Config File

1. Boot up and login to linux.

2. Use the locate command to find the file XF86Config. (NOTE: On some distributions, this file will be in /etc, and in others it will be in /etc/X11.)

3. Use the cd command to move to the directory that XF86Config is located in.

Figure 9-1
First Page of
XF86Config File

```
#   File generated by XConfigurator.

#   *********************************************************************
#   Refer to the XF86Config (4/5) man page for details about the
#   format of this file.
#   *********************************************************************

#   *********************************************************************
#   Files sections. This allows default font and rgb paths to
#   be set
#   *********************************************************************

#   Section "Files"

#   The location of the RGB database. Note: this is the name of
#   the file minus the extension (like ".txt" or ".db"). There is
#   normally no need to change the default.

        RgbPath        "/usr/X11R6/lib/X11/rgb"

#   Multiple FontPath entries are allowed (they are concatenated
#   together)
#   By default, Red Hat 6.0 and later now use a font server
#   independent of the X server to render fonts.
```

4. Check that you're in the right directory by using the `ls` command.

5. Type:

```
less XF86Config
```

and press Enter. You should see a screen something like Figure 9-1.

Use the arrow keys to move down the file and back up again. I've purposely chosen the `XF86Config` file, because it's likely to be somewhat long. If you want to read it quickly, page by page, simply use the Page Up and Page Down keys. Exiting `less` is even faster and easier than starting it. Type:

```
q
```

The command prompt appears once again.

Exercise 1 First use `locate` to find the `bashrc` file, then change to its directory and use `less` to read it.

Lesson 2: Using the `vi` editor to Edit the `bashrc` File

The `vi` editor has been used by the older generation of UNIX gurus as one of the two word processors of choice for many years. At least one well-known Linux author, a scion of the UNIX world, even wrote a whole Linux book using `vi`.

No convert coming to Linux from the Windows world is ever going to use `vi` unless they absolutely have to, and they certainly won't use it for word processing. However, for editing text configuration files, it is still very useful, and that's how I present it in this book: as a first-class configuration file editor.

The `bashrc` file is one of two (the other is the `profile` file) that contains environmental settings. It is read at system startup, and again whenever a new console or terminal is started (see A Taste of the Guru Status, at the end of this chapter).

If you insert in `bashrc` an `alias` command to enable color, then every time you start up Linux, the `ls` command will automatically return a color display. This is much more convenient than having to type in the `alias` command every time you start the computer. (NOTE: Red Hat Linux and Caldera's OpenLinux both start up without color enabled, but TurboLinux's and SuSE's distributions already have it enabled by default.)

In Red Hat, `bashrc` is found in the `etc` directory. In Caldera, it is found in the root directory (`/root`) and has a period before it. If you run the `locate` command in Caldera, looking for `bashrc`, the last line will look like this:

```
/root/.bashrc
```

What does the period mean?

HIDDEN FILES: In Linux, whenever a file is preceded by a dot or period, that means it is a hidden file. The `ls` command will not display hidden files—unless you use the `-a` option. However, you can read them with `less` and edit them with `vi`. The purpose of a hidden file is security, to keep them hidden away from prying eyes.

The `vi` editor is started just like `less`.

1. Use the `cd` command to move to the appropriate directory—`/etc` for Red Hat, `/root` for Caldera.

2. Type:

```
vi bashrc
```

and press Enter. (Note: Caldera users will type `vi .bashrc`)

The result, in Red Hat, will look like Figure 9-2 (it is longer and more complex in Caldera).

Figure 9-2
The `bashrc` File
(Red Hat Version)

```
# /etc/bashrc

# System wide functions and aliases
# Environmental stuff goes in /etc/profile

# For some unknown reason bash refuses to inherit
# PS1 in some circumstances that I can't figure out.
# Putting PS1 here ensures that it gets loaded every time.
PS1="[\u@\h \W]\\$"
~
~
~
~
~
~
"bashrc" 9 lines, 276 characters.
```

There is only one line of actual code in this file. Everything that begins with # is simply a comment. If you read the comments in Red Hat's bashrc carefully, you will see that even professional Linux programmers are sometimes confused, and are reduced to doing something a certain way simply because it works—why, they don't know. If you spend any time around programmers, you'll find that this is actually quite a common phenomena. Programmers are people too—and like most of us, they seldom have all the answers.

Our job is to add a new bottom line to the bashrc file, the alias line. The first thing to do is to put the editor into command mode.

1. Press the Esc key once. You should hear your computer give a small beep. Now, put the editor into insert mode.

2. Type:

```
i
```

You should see the word INSERT appear at the bottom left-hand corner of the screen. Now you can insert your new text.

3. Use the down arrow key to move the cursor to the PS1 line.

4. Use the right arrow key to move the cursor to the end of that line.

5. Hit Enter.

6. Type:

```
alias ls="ls --color"
```

Now, write the edited file to the disk.

7. Hit the Escape key again.

8. Type:

```
:wq
```

and hit Enter. A line indicating that the new line has been written appears at the bottom of the screen, and then below it, the command prompt.

Congratulations! You have just edited your first file in Linux.

A little analysis of the operation above show that vi operates in two "modes": input and command. Pressing the Escape key puts it into input mode. There are many input commands, the most common being i, for insert, x, for delete a single character, dd for delete a line, and u for reverse the last change. Hitting the Escape key followed by the colon puts the editor into command mode. The most common commands are w, for write, and q, for quit, or exit. The exclamation mark has a special meaning. If you think you've made a mess and want to get out of the editor, without saving the file, type q! A short command summary is shown in Table 9-1.

Lesson 3: Using the `vi` Editor to Edit the `lilo.conf` File

The `lilo.conf` file configures LILO—the Linux boot loader—the program that enables you to boot up either Windows or Linux when you turn on your computer. And it should be working just fine on your computer. So, why change it?

Right now it is likely that LILO is configured to boot up Linux by default, a few seconds after you see the boot loader prompt. Of course, you can boot up Windows instead just by typing `dos` and hitting Enter. But since you probably still do most of your work in Windows, and will continue that way for awhile—at least until you get a little more adept in Linux—perhaps you'd like your machine to boot Windows by default.

1. Use the `locate` command to find `lilo.conf`. It should be in the `/etc` directory.

2. Use the `cd` command to move to the correct directory.

3. Type:

   `vi lilo.conf`

   and press Enter. The `lilo.conf` should look something like Figure 9-3.

TABLE 9-1

`vi` Text File Editor Command Summary

Action	Command
Start Editor and Open File	`vi file`
Enter Input Mode	Escape key
Insert Text	`i`
Delete Text	`x`
Delete a Line	`dd`
Reverse Change	`u`
Enter Command Mode	Escape key + :
Write File	`w`
Exit	`q`
Insist on Exiting without Saving	`q!`

Figure 9-3

The `lilo.conf` File

```
boot=/dev/hda
map=/boot/map
install=/boot/boot.b
prompt
timeout=50
image=/boot/vmlinuz-2.2.5-15
        label=linux
        root=/dev/hda6
        read-only
other=/dev/hda1
        label=dos
        table=/dev/hda
```

You don't have to understand everything about this file. The most important elements right now are the lines that begin with the word "label" appearing under the lines that begin with the words "image" and "other." In my example, you'll see that the first label is set equal to `linux`, and the second is equal to `dos`. That means that `linux` will boot up default, unless you override it by typing in `dos`.

To change this behavior, all you have to do is insert one line. TurboLinux may already have this line in the file. In that case, it just has to be edited. The line is `default=dos`.

1. Enter input mode by hitting the Escape key.
2. Type:

   `i`

3. Use the down arrow key to move the cursor down to the word "image."
4. Press the Enter key. A blank line should appear above the cursor.
5. Use the up arrow key to move the cursor to the blank line.
6. Type:

   `default=dos`

   (NOTE: If there is a `default=linux` line already there, place the cursor at the beginning of the word `linux`, hit the Delete key until it disappears, and then type in `dos`.)

7. Enter command mode by pressing the Escape key and typing:

   `:`

8. Then write the edited file to the disk and exit by typing:

   `wq`

   and hitting Enter. (Remember: if you think you've messed up the file, simply type `q!` and hit Enter, and you'll exit the editor without writing any changes to the file.)

One last thing: whenever you've made a change to the `lilo.conf` file, you must run the program to set the change. Type:

```
lilo
```

and press Enter. Now reboot, and test your changes. If you do nothing whatsoever, the computer should boot by itself into Windows. To boot up Linux, simply type: `linux` and hit Enter at the LILO prompt.

Lesson 4: Using the `vi` Editor to Edit the `fstab` File

The `fstab` file determines which partitions and devices (your floppy disk drive or CD-ROM) Linux can access, or "mount." You want your Windows partition to be in that file, because you want to be able to read your Windows data files—your MS Word, Excel, and PowerPoint files—within Linux. But is it a good idea to always have your Windows partition visible in Linux?

No, it isn't. It's not a good idea because, at the Linux command line, it is possible for the root user to type in a single command that will wipe clean the Linux partitions, and any other partitions that Linux is able to read. That command is `rm * -f -r`. It means: forcibly remove every file and directory from this point down through the directory tree. It is an excellent command for quickly cleaning up unwanted files and directories, but it is also very dangerous to use. If used at the root of the directory tree, it will destroy every directory and every file on every partition it sees.

So, just to be on the safe side, you should make sure that Linux only reads your Windows partition when you want it to—when you're actually using it. To make sure of that, you probably have to edit your `fstab` file.

1. Use the `cd` command to maneuver to the `/etc` directory. Use `ls` to make sure `fstab` is there.

2. Type:

```
vi fstab
```

and hit Enter. The `fstab` file should look something like Figure 9-4.
     The file has five columns; we're interested in the first four only. The first column lists the partitions and devices which Linux can access. The second gives their mount points. A mount point, for a

partition, is like a directory. For instance, /dev/hda1 is the Windows partition, and it can be accessed within Linux from the directory /C. The third column indicates the file system type for each partition or device. vfat stands for a Microsoft Windows 95 or 98 file system, and ext2 is the standard Linux file system. msdos (which is probably not present) stands for a DOS file system. Finally, the fourth column indicates how and when the partition should be mounted, or accessed. defaults means that the partition is mounted at system startup.

You need to change two things. You need to make sure that your Windows partition is not mounted at startup, and you need to change your floppy drive's file system type to DOS.

3. Enter input mode by hitting the Escape key.

4. Type:

   i

5. Use the right arrow key to move the cursor to the fourth column, so that it's under the d of defaults.

6. Hit the Delete key until defaults is deleted.

7. Type:

   noauto

   That line should now read:

   /dev/hda1   /C   vfat   noauto   0 0

8. Now use the down arrow and left arrow keys to move the cursor to the first letter of ext2, on the same line as /dev/fd0 and /mnt/floppy.

Figure 9-4
The fstab File

```
/dev/hda1      /C              vfat      defaults      0 0
/dev/hda6      /               ext2      defaults      1 1
/dev/hda5      /boot           ext2      defaults      1 2
/dev/hda7      swap            ext2      defaults      0 0
/dev/fd0       /mnt/floppy     ext2      noauto        0 0
/dev/cdrom     /mnt/cdrom      iso9660   noauto,ro     0 0
none           /proc           proc      defaults      0 0
none           /dev/pts        devpts    mode=0622     0 0
```

9. Use the Delete key to delete `ext2`, and replace it with:

   `msdos`

   That line should now read:

   `/dev/fd0      /mnt/floppy      msdos      noauto      0 0`

10. You have finished editing the file. Enter command mode by pressing the Escape key and typing:

    `:`

11. Write the edited file to the disk and exit by typing:

    `wq`

    and hitting Enter.

Now, when you next reboot your computer and login to Linux, your Windows partition will be safely hidden from view—until you need it. Then you will have to manually mount it. That process, as well as basic techniques of manipulating files, is in the next chapter.

A Taste of the Guru Status

Virtual Consoles

Looking at the command prompt, you are staring at one screen—a console. But in Linux, you can have several consoles open at one time. Why on earth, you may ask, would anyone want to do that? Well, what if you need to edit a text file, but you want to have the man page for the file right in front of you? One answer is to edit the file in one console, and keep the man page open in another.

You can have up to six consoles open at one time. The consoles are identified and accessed by the first six function keys at the top of your keyboard, F1 through F6. When your computer starts up, you are always at the F1 console. Suppose you want to switch to console F2. Press down the following keys in succession: Ctrl + Alt + F2 (this means that you press and hold down the Ctrl key, then the Alt key, and then the F2 key, holding them down all together). Then release all three keys.

You are at another login prompt! Type:

`root`

and press Enter, then your password and Enter again. You're now logged in at the second console. If you want to go back to the first, simply press down Ctrl + Alt + F1. You can see how easy it is to switch from one console to another.

You can have all six consoles going at once. By itself, each console takes little memory to run. Of course, if you have too many open at the same time, you are apt to fall into confusion, but having two or three open can be very convenient.

10

Accessing Drives and Manipulating Files

Purpose of Chapter:
To Use the Command Line to Access Drives and Manipulate Files

Accessing or mounting partitions is a simple matter in Linux, but CD-ROMs and floppy disk drives behave differently than they do in Windows. Although they are easier to manipulate in X Window than at the command line, understanding how to manipulate them at the command line will be a great help if troubleshooting becomes necessary.

File manipulation at the command line is one of the most basic and handy skills that you can have, and it's easy to learn. This chapter, like the last, is presented as lessons and exercises.

Accessing Drives at the Command Line

By "drive," I mean a hard drive, a partition, or a device such as a CD-ROM or floppy disk drive. You use the same command to mount or access all these devices, but there are additional considerations for CD-ROMs and floppies.

Lesson 1: Using the mount Command to Mount Your Windows Partition

Your Windows partition should not be mounted by default—you have to manually mount it when you want to access it within Linux. At the command line you do this with the `mount` command.

1. Change your directory to the root of the file system, by typing:

   ```
   cd /
   ```

   and pressing Enter.

2. Now use the `ls` command to check that you have your Windows mount point. You should see a C directory. You need a mount point, both in your `fstab` file, and also in your directory structure. You made sure of the `fstab` file in the last chapter, and you should already have the C mount point for your Windows partition. If you don't, just type `mkdir C`.

3. Mount the Windows partition by typing:

   ```
   mount C
   ```

   and pressing Enter. Now, check that it's worked by changing directory to C, and using the `ls` command.

4. Type:

   ```
   cd /C
   ```

   and press Enter.

5. Type:

   ```
   ls
   ```

   and press Enter. You should see a long list of your Windows directories and files.

Lesson 2: Using the umount Command to Unmount Your Windows Partition

As I mentioned, for safety you should only access your Windows partition when you absolutely have to. So, shortly after you mount it, you'll probably want to unmount it. You do that with the umount command.

1. First you have to back out of the C directory. Type:

   ```
   cd /
   ```

   and press Enter.

2. Now, unmount the Windows partition by typing:

   ```
   umount /C
   ```

   and pressing Enter.

3. Check to make sure the command has worked by typing:

   ```
   ls /C
   ```

   and pressing Enter. Nothing should be returned.

Lesson 3: Using the mount Command to Mount the CD-ROM

The simple rule to follow is: insert and eject the CD with the CD-ROM unmounted. In other words, insert the CD and mount the player, and when you're finished, unmount the player and then eject the CD. This procedure is necessary because in Linux the CD-ROM will not eject as long as it is mounted. (NOTE: This procedure is automated in X Window, when playing the CD audio player. All you have to do then is point and click to eject and play.)

1. Use the cd command to move to the directory /mnt.

2. Use the ls command to make sure that the two device mount points, cdrom and floppy, are both there.

3. Insert a CD with computer files on it, such as your Linux CD.

4. Type:

   ```
   mount cdrom
   ```

   and press Enter.

5. Type:

```
cd cdrom
```

and press Enter.

6. Use the `ls` command to view the CD's contents.

Lesson 4: Using the `umount` Command to Unmount the CD-ROM

1. Go back to the `/mnt` directory by typing:

```
cd ..
```

and hitting Enter. Remember to put a space between the `d` and the two dots.

2. Type:

```
umount cdrom
```

and press Enter.

3. Now eject your CD.

Exercise 1: Mounting, Reading, and Unmounting Your Floppy Drive   The floppy drive unit is mounted and unmounted in exactly the same way as the CD-ROM unit, with exactly the same limitations. The mount point is `/mnt/floppy`. Make sure you use a floppy with some files on it, so that you can test your mount.

Basic File Manipulation

Manipulating files at the command line in Linux is very similar to DOS, so the older readers of this book should feel fairly at home. One difference is that Linux commands typically have far more options that their DOS counterparts did. Here I'll cover the basics.

Lesson 1: Using the `mkdir` and `rmdir` Commands to Create and Remove Directories

1. Move back to the root of the file system with `cd /`.

2. Create a new directory called LETTERS, by typing:

```
mkdir LETTERS
```

and hitting Enter.

3. Check to see if it worked by using the `ls` command. Make sure it's the right color for a directory.

NOTE: Directory names are just like files names in Linux (to be exact, in Linux a directory is just another file)—they are case-sensitive. Many people find it a useful personal convention to capitalize the directories they create, although it is certainly not a requirement. Occasionally a Linux program will even fail to identify a directory if it is upper-case: the first release version of StarOffice version 5.1 would not recognize `C` as a directory, although it would recognize `c`!

4. Now let's test it out further. Change to the directory you have just created by typing:

```
cd LETTERS
```

and hitting Enter. Your command prompt should look something like this:

```
[root@localhost /LETTERS#
```

The `rmdir` command—remove directory—is used in exactly the same way, but to remove or delete a directory.

Exercise 1: Making and Removing a Directory Using the `mkdir` and `rmdir` Commands At the `/LETTERS` directory, create a subdirectory called `PERSONAL`. Then use the `rmdir` command to remove it. Use the `ls` command at the `/LETTERS` directory to make sure it's gone.

Lesson 2: Using the > Operator to Create a File

In a previous chapter you learned how to use the man pages to find help. However, as you saw from the man page for the `ls` command, they can be quite long and difficult to interpret. A sort of digest can often be found by typing the command, followed by `--help`. Try this now. Type:

```
ls --help
```

and hit Enter. But there is a problem! It is evident that part of the help display has just scrolled right up over the screen! What can we do about it?

We can use the redirect operator (>) to create a file, and then use `less` to read it.

The > operator is typically used to redirect the output of a command to a file. That isn't as confused as it sounds. In this example, if we type `ls --help`, the output of that command is sent to the screen. But if we type `ls --help > lshelp`, then the output is "redirected" to a brand new file named `lshelp`. Let's try it.

1. Type:

   ```
   ls --help > lshelp
   ```

   and press Enter. (Note: the new file name doesn't have to be `lshelp`. It can be anything you like.)

2. Now make sure you have in fact created the new file with the `ls` command.

3. Read it by using the `less` command.

Lesson 3: Using the `cp` Command to Copy a File

One of the more straightforward commands is `cp`. It's usage is quite simple. You simply type the command, then the filename, followed by the directory you want to copy it to. For instance, in order to copy the file you just made to /, perform these steps. Type:

```
cp lshelp /
```

and press Enter. Now `cd` back to the root, and use `ls` to check for the file. There it is. The original is still in /LETTERS.

Copying a file to a subdirectory—or your Windows partition or a floppy—is as simple as just including the subdirectory in the copy command's destination. For instance, type:

```
cp lshelp /etc
```

and press Enter. Of course, if you want to copy a file to or from your floppy or your Windows partition, you'll have to first mount the floppy or Windows partition.

Exercise 2: Using the `cp` Command to Copy a File   Copy the `lshelp` file to the /etc/X11 subdirectory, maneuver there using the `cd` command, and check that it's there using `ls`.

Lesson 4: Using the mv Command to Move and Rename a File

The difference between copying and moving a file is that, when copying, the original file is left in place, but when moving, the file is deleted from the original directory. The method of using the mv command is exactly the same as with the cp command.

You should be in the /etc/X11 directory. Type:

```
mv lshelp /home
```

and press Enter. Now move to the /home directory and look for the lshelp file with the ls command. Then go back to /etc/X11, and look there. It should be gone.

The mv command can also rename a file. The syntax of the command is nearly the same, except of course you have to include the file's new name. Let's try an example:

1. First use the cd command to move back to the /home directory.
2. Type:

```
mv lshelp test
```

and hit Enter. Now use the ls command to check your work. The lshelp file should be renamed test.

If you want to, you can move and simultaneously rename a file. Type:

```
mv test /etc/X11/testmv
```

and hit Enter. Now type ls. The file should be gone. Use the cd command to change directory to /etc/X11, and check it out. You should find the testmv file. You moved and simultaneously renamed the file.

Exercise 3: Using the mv Command to Simultaneously Move and Rename a File Use the mv command to move the testmv file from /etc/X11 to / and simultaneously rename it to movetest.

Lesson 5: Using the rm Command to Remove a File

Removing a file is the same as deleting it. However, in Linux, at the command prompt, once you've deleted a file, that's it: there is no going back. It's gone for good. The same is true in Windows, if you are working at the

DOS command prompt, but there are third-party programs that will allow you to "undelete" files—even if they were deleted in DOS. No such third-party programs as yet exist in the Linux world. So it's extremely important that you use the rm command sparingly and carefully.

The rm command, when used in its simple form, only deletes files, not directories. However, it is possible to use it to remove directories, and it is even possible to remove your entire directory structure, including every file you have on every Linux-readable partition. In other words, you can use this simple command to trash your computer.

Let's use it to get rid of a single file:

1. Change to the /LETTERS directory. Type:

   ```
   rm lshelp
   ```

   and hit Enter.

2. You will see this line: `rm: remove 'lshelp'?`

3. Type:

   ```
   y
   ```

   and press Enter. Now check your work with ls. The /LETTERS directory should be empty.

Lesson 6: Using Wildcard Characters

Wildcards, introduced in Chapter 8, can be used for all the basic Linux commands. Let's try an example using the rm command with the wildcard character *. (First make sure to unmount any Windows partitions!)

1. To move back to the root, type:

   ```
   cd /
   ```

   and press Enter.

2. You should have two files in the root directory, ishelp and movetest. Use the ls command to make sure.

3. Delete both by typing:

   ```
   rm *
   ```

   and pressing Enter. You'll be prompted for each file. Type y and hit Enter for the two files you want to delete; if you're prompted for a file you want to keep, type n and hit Enter.

A useful option for removing large numbers of files is -f, typed after the asterisk. It means "force", and tells the remove command to delete every file without prompting you.

Exercise 4: Basic File Manipulation   In this multipart exercise, you'll try out some of the skills you've learned in this chapter.

1. Mount your Windows partition by using the mount /C command.

2. Change to the /C directory, and use the ls command to check that the Windows partition is mounted.

3. Insert a floppy disk into the floppy drive and mount it using the mount /mnt/floppy command.

4. Use the cp command to copy the config.sys file from /C to your floppy disk.

5. Change the directory back to the root (/), and unmount the Windows partition by using the umount /C command.

6. Move the config.sys file from your floppy to the /LETTERS directory.

7. Unmount your floppy.

8. Change to the /LETTERS directory, and create a new directory with the mkdir command, called PERSONAL.

9. Move and simultaneously rename the config.sys file to /LETTERS/PERSONAL/configuration.

10. Now, one last lesson. Make *absolutely sure* that you're in the LETTERS directory. Use the * wildcard and the -f and -r options to remove all directories, and their files, from /LETTERS.

> NOTE: -r stands for "recursive." It simply means repetitive: repeat the action. In the case of rm * -f -r, it means: remove forcibly every file and every directory from this point down the directory tree.

11. Type:

    ```
    rm * -f -r
    ```

    and hit Enter.

12. Use the ls command to see what's happened. Move back to the root, and use the rmdir command to delete /LETTERS.

What do you think would have happened if you had used the rm * -f -r command at the root of the directory system?

A Taste of the Guru Status

Easy File and Floppy Manipulation with Mtools.

With mtools you can easily copy files to and from a floppy disk, without having to mount it first. Mtools is a set of programs that allow you to use traditional DOS commands—prefixed with an 'm'—to manipulate files, and even format floppies. The only catch is that the commands only work on DOS filesystems. However, since every pre-formatted PC floppy sold is formatted with a DOS filesystem, that's not much of a restriction.

For instance, suppose you wanted to see what was on a floppy disk. Traditionally, you would first mount the floppy, then use the `ls` command. But with mtools, it's much easier:

Type:

```
mdir a:
```

and hit Enter.

To copy a file called linux.doc from the floppy to the root directory (/): Type:

```
mcopy a:linux.doc /
```

and hit Enter.

Note that the mtools are not as particular about certain conventions as the old DOS commands were. For instance, all three of the following commands will do exactly the same thing:

```
mcopy a:linux.doc /
mcopy a:/linux.doc /
mcopy a:\linux.doc /
```

Some of the most useful mtools commands are:

mcopy	Copies files to and from DOS and Linux filesystems.
mdel	Deletes DOS files.
mdeltree	Removes a directory and all the files and subdirectories it contains.
mdir	Displays a directory's contents.
mformat	Formats a floppy disk.

11

Hooking Up to the Internet

Purpose of Chapter:
To Establish an Internet Connection via Your Current ISP—in Linux

The vast majority of home and small business users depend on modems and dial-up connections to access the Internet. But establishing such a connection from Linux has traditionally been close to rocket science. Many Linux books simply avoid the subject. Others give instructions that manage to be both complex and vague.

It's actually quite simple. For most users, there are only four very small text configuration files to create, that will allow you to easily logon and logoff the Internet, using the same ISP you now use in Windows.

One day soon most ISPs will ship automated connection programs to their Linux customers. That day hasn't yet arrived. Most Linux distributions do have some sort of "fill in the blanks" program to set up a dial-up account. Sometimes these programs work. More usually they do not.

The surest way to configure Linux for the Internet is still by the command line. This chapter shows you how. Instead of lessons and exercises, this chapter gives you several concrete examples, using real files that connect to real ISPs.

Modems, Windows, Linux, and Configuration Files

Configuring a dial-up Internet connection requires a working modem, information on your ISP connection that you can obtain from Windows, and four to five simple text configuration files.

Step 1: Modems

The first thing to learn is that not all modems work with Linux. The so-called "winmodems" will not work in Linux, period. These are very cheap modems designed to work only with Microsoft Windows. A normal modem comes complete with software on a chip that enables it to function in several different operating systems, from DOS to Windows 3.1, to Windows 95/98, to Linux. Winmodems, on the other hand, are manufactured without that software—they rely on Windows 95/98 to provide the necessary software to work.

Although the vast majority of normal, Hayes-compatible, external and internal modems will work with Linux, some will not. Not all PCI modems, especially dual-use modems—fax and speakerphone modems, for instance—are as yet supported. On the other hand, Linux does support a large number of PCMCIA card modems. For special instructions on these, see Chapter 24, Laptops.

Using Minicom to Check Your Modem   Before the World Wide Web, it was common for computer enthusiasts to use their modems to dial up bulletin boards and download files. There was nothing graphical about bulletin boards, and the Web has killed them dead. In those days of the dim past (not yet a decade ago), people used modem communication programs that were then ubiquitous, but which are now completely forgotten.

One such program in the UNIX world was Minicom. It is still included in most Linux distributions, and it still works—if you can find a bulletin board to log onto. The great use of this program today is as a modem checker.

To check whether your modem is working in Linux, follow this procedure:

1. Login to Linux as root.
2. Type:

    ```
    minicom -c on
    ```

    and hit Enter (-c on tells it to start up using color).

You should go directly to the Minicom screen—most of which will be black. If instead you are given a small menu box titled `configuration`, use your down arrow key to highlight the menu item `Exit`, and press Enter. This will take you to the main Minicom screen. There will be a red bar at the bottom of your screen, and a few lines of text at the top. The text at the top should look something like Figure 11-1. The important lines here are 5 and 6. Line 5 may well look different, but it's important that something be there. And it's crucial that the last line—`OK`—be there as well.

`OK` tells you that Linux is communicating with your modem. You're in good shape, and can go on to step 2. If Linux is having trouble communicating with your modem, don't panic yet. There are a few simple procedures to follow which could put you back on track. First, though, exit Minicom:

1. Press the Ctrl and the A key together for a moment.

2. Then hit the X key and press Enter.

If your modem is working, go to step 2. If it's not, also go to step 2, unless you're running Red Hat. If you're running Red Hat and the modem is not working, continue on below.

Using `ls` to Check the Modem File and Link   Minicom, like other communication programs, accesses your modem by addressing a file symbolically linked to the serial port your modem is attached to. This is not straightforward, but is not really complex. In Minicom's case, the program "talks" to your modem by addressing a file called, appropriately, `modem`. This file has a symbolic link to the device file `ttyS1`, which is the serial port the actual modem is attached to. Both files are in the `/dev` directory.

The only distribution I've seen that doesn't always make the modem file and the link automatically during installation, is Red Hat. However, Red Hat does have a very simple and easy-to-use graphical tool that can be

Figure 11-1
The Minicom Screen

```
Welcome to minicom 1.82

OPTIONS: History Buffer, F-key Macros, Search History Buffer, I18n
Complied on Mar 21 1999, 21:10:56.

Press CTRL-A Z for help on special keys

AT S7=45 S0=0 L1 V1 X4 &c1 E1 Q0
OK
```

used to make the modem file, and also to change the link to a different serial port at any time.

First, check to make sure you have these files and links, by changing to the /dev directory, and typing:

```
ls modem -l
```

You should see a line like this:

```
lrwxrwxrwx  1 root  root  5 Sep 2 16:56 modem -> /dev/ttyS1
```

The important part of this line is at the very end: modem -> /dev/ttyS1. If you're running Red Hat and the modem file isn't there, the following Red Hat solution will fix it.

A Red Hat Solution   You will have to have X Window properly configured. If you don't, see the next chapter.

1. Type:

```
startx
```

and press Enter. You'll see Gnome startup—the desktop used by Red Hat's version of X Window.

2. When you see a box warning you that you're running Gnome as root, just click on the OK button.

3. In the lower left-hand corner of the screen, you'll see a footprint. Click on it with your mouse.

4. A Windows-style menu appears. Move the mouse pointer to the menu item, System.

5. The System menu appears to the right. Move the mouse over and down to Control Panel. Click on it.

6. You'll see the control panel, a vertical strip graphic with square buttons (Figure 11-2).

7. Click on the bottom button, showing a telephone. The Configure Modem tool appears (Figure 11-3).

The text at the top of the graphic says it all. This tool will both create your modem file, and create the link to the serial port you choose. For most users, this will be ttyS1—the same as COM2 in Windows and DOS. All you have to do is click once on the correct choice.

Once you've finished with the modem tool, logout of X Window.

Figure 11-2
Gnome Control Panel

Figure 11-3
Configure
Modem Tool

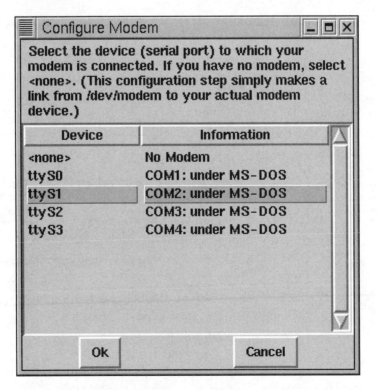

1. Click on the OK button, click on the footprint again, and on Log out.

2. When prompted, simply click on the Yes button to close down X Window.

Now rerun Minicom. See if the OK appears. If this doesn't solve your problem, chances are that your modem file is set to the wrong com port, or there's an interrupt conflict (this is most likely with a PCMCIA modem), or your modem is simply unsupported in Linux.

If it didn't work, there's still hope. Continue with the following section.

Step 2: Gathering Information in Windows

Reboot from Linux and boot back into Windows. The information you gather on your modem from within Windows may help you if your modem isn't working. You will also need that information, and the information you obtain from Dial-Up Networking, to produce the files necessary to connect to the Internet in Linux.

Obtain Information on Your Modem   The information you need to obtain is:

1. The modem COM port number (probably 2).

2. The modem Interrupt (IRQ) number.

3. The modem's maximum speed.

All this information is easily available in Windows. Follow this procedure:

1. Click on the Start button.

2. Move the mouse pointer to Settings, and to the right to Control Panel. Click the mouse.

3. In the Control Panel box, double-click on Modems—the telephone icon. The Modem Properties window appears (Figure 11-4).

4. Click on the Diagnostics tab. You'll see a screen something like Figure 11-5.

5. Click on the COM port number that has a modem description next to it—in this example, COM2.

6. Click on the More Info button.

7. After a moment you should see the More Info screen (Figure 11-6). Make a note of the COM port number (in this example, and for most people, COM2); the Interrupt number (in this example, 10); and the Highest Speed

Figure 11-4
Modem Properties
in Windows

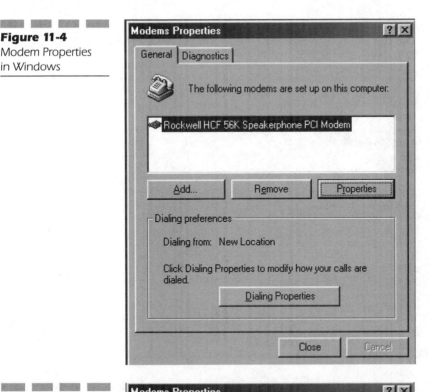

Figure 11-5
Modem Diagnostics
Window

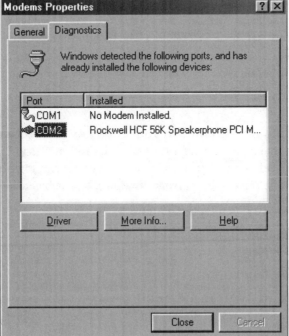

Figure 11-6
More Info Window

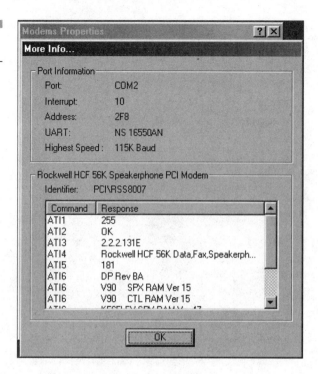

number (in this example, 115K). Also take a close look at the modem's description. In this example, you'll see that the modem is listed as a Speakerphone PCI Modem. The PCI is an immediate red flag—it might work in Linux, it might not. Try to see also on your machine if the modem is described as a winmodem. If it is, the chances are quite good that it will not work in Linux.

Obtain Information on Your Internet Connection   This information is required to write your Internet configuration files in Linux. You could get this information directly from your Internet Service Provider, but there is an easier way. You can get it from Windows. The information you need to obtain is:

1. Your ISP's telephone number.
2. Your ISP's primary and secondary Domain Name Server (DNS) addresses.
3. Your user name.

The software that your ISP gave you to set up your Internet connection worked by configuring a small application, or applet, called Windows Dial-Up Networking. All you have to do is read the information you need from that applet.

1. Double-click on the My Computer icon.

2. Double-click on the Dial-Up Networking icon. The Dial-Up Networking window appears. You will see at least two icons; one titled Make New Connection, and another with the name of your own ISP.

3. Click on your ISP's icon with your right mouse button.

4. A small menu appears. Click on the bottom choice: Properties. Your ISP's properties window appears (Figure 11-7). Start making notes. First take down the telephone number you used to connect to your ISP.

5. Now click on the Server Types tab. Go down to the bottom of that window and click on the TCP/IP Settings button. The TCP/IP

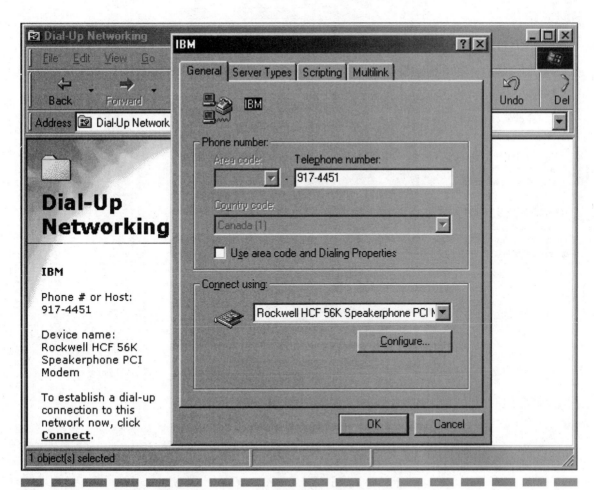

Figure 11-7 Your ISP's Properties Window in Windows Dial-Up Networking

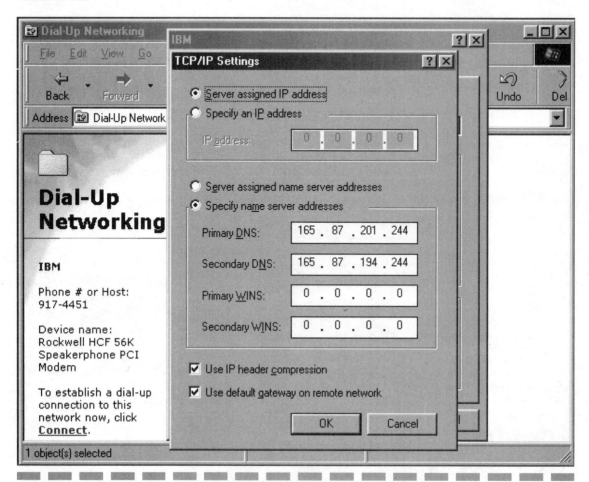

Figure 11-8   TCP/IP Settings Window

Settings window (Figure 11-8), is divided into three sections. You're interested in the middle section. Make a note of the Primary DNS address and the Secondary DNS address. In the example shown in Figure 11-8, your notes would read:

Primary   165.87.201.244

Secondary   165.87.194.244

6. To obtain your user name, click on the Cancel buttons twice, until you're back at the Dial-Up Networking window.

7. Double-click on the your ISP icon. The Connect To window will open (Figure 11-9). Make a note of the user name.

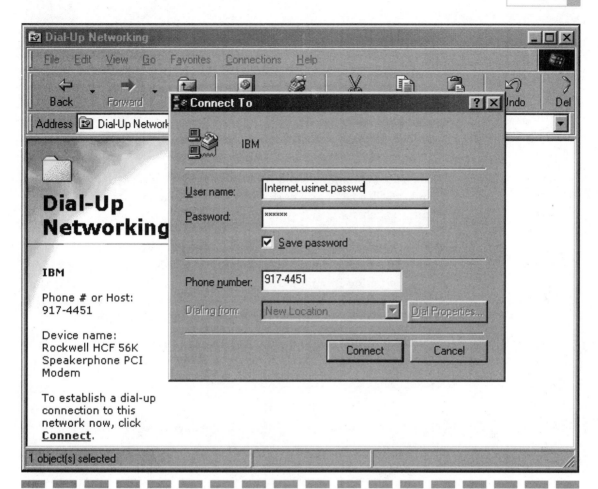

Figure 11-9 The Connect To Windows, Showing User Name, in Windows Dial-Up Networking

That's it. If your modem was working in Linux, you're ready to move on to step 4. If your modem wasn't working, continue below to step 3. Exit Windows, and reboot into Linux.

Step 3: Back to Linux: Trying Different Serial Ports with the ln Command

If your modem wasn't working in Linux, it's possible that your modem wasn't linked to the correct serial port. From the notes you made above, you should now know which serial port your modem is on.

First, move to the /dev directory, and use the ls command to check the serial port your modem is linked to in Linux. Type:

```
ls modem -l
```

and press Enter. The far right end of the line that appears should look something like this:

```
modem -> /dev/ttyS1
```

The method of naming COM ports in Linux is different from the method in Windows. The comparison chart in Table 11-1 shows the naming conventions in each operating system.

The second COM port, COM 2 in Windows and ttyS1 in Linux, is the standard COM port for modems. But there are plenty of exceptions. If your modem in Windows is set to a different port, and it's not working in Linux, then try switching it. Follow this procedure (this example assumes that you're in the /dev directory, that your modem is mistakenly set to COM port 2, and that you're going to try switching to COM port 3):

1. First, remove the current symbolic link, by removing the modem file. Type:

```
rm -f modem
```

   and hit Enter.

2. Next, create a new symbolic link—and a new modem file—to ttyS2. Type:

```
ln -s ttyS2 modem
```

   and hit Enter.

3. Now check to see if it's worked. Type:

```
ls modem -l
```

TABLE 11-1

Comparison of Windows and Linux COM Port Numbering Systems

Windows 95/98	Linux
COM 1	ttyS0
COM 2	ttyS1
COM 3	ttyS2
COM 4	ttyS3

and hit Enter. You should see a line that ends with the following:

```
modem -> /dev/ttyS2
```

Now re-run Minicom. See if the OK appears. If this doesn't solve your problem, try connecting to the other COM ports in turn. If none of them appear to work, then reconnect the modem to the COM port it uses in Windows. There's a slight chance that the modem is in fact working, but that Minicom is not. However, the chances are better that your modem is either unsupported in Linux, or that there's an interrupt conflict. This is most likely with a PCMCIA modem. If you're running a laptop with a PCMCIA modem, consult Chapter 24. If your modem is internal, borrow or buy an external modem, and try connecting with that.

Continue on to step 4

Step 4: Writing the Configuration Files

Linux is a networking operating system. Linux can connect to the Internet through any Internet service provider—although some of them don't appear to know it yet. Although several quite small ISPs will be happy to provide you with the support necessary to connect via Linux, at least one quite large ISP insists that their "system" doesn't support Linux! That's nonsense. You can connect through any service provider.

There are three ways to configure Linux to work with your ISP:

1. Use the ISP's own Linux configuration program. This is the preferred method. It is virtually or completely automatic, and is almost certain to work. Unfortunately, most ISPs don't yet offer configuration programs for Linux.

2. Use your Linux distribution's own Internet configuration program. Sometimes these programs work. Usually they don't.

3. Write your own configuration files. This method definitely works—if you know what you're doing. This is the method described below.

PPPD is the name of the Linux program that handles dial-up Internet connections. There are a number of configuration files, or scripts, available to PPPD, and for any one Internet connection, there are many variations of files that would work. This is a very flexible program, but that doesn't necessarily make life easier—it can make it more complex.

To make this section useful, I'm giving real files from working Internet connections with three different ISPs (except for passwords and names, which are changed). To keep it simple, I'm concentrating only on the most common types of Internet connections. For instance, there are two different Internet protocols, PPP and SLIP. Although some ISPs still use SLIP, and some use both protocols, almost all now use only PPP—the SLIP protocol is becoming obsolete. I use only PPP in the sample files that follow. Similarly, there are two authentication protocols, PAP and CHAP. I use only the most common: PAP.

There are five files that need to be written. Their file names and directories are:

1. /etc/resolv.conf
2. /etc/ppp/options
3. /etc/ppp/pap-secrets
4. /usr/sbin/ppp-on
5. /usr/sbin/ppp-off

(NOTE: It is essential that you create your files *exactly* according to the examples shown below. The smallest error will keep you from making a connection. It is also essential that each file be in its correct directory.)

The `resolv.conf` File   This file includes your primary and secondary DNS addresses. You found this information from Windows, in the step shown in Figure 11-8. The example below is from an IBM Global Network connection. Use the `vi` editor to make your file, using the following procedure:

1. Move to the /etc/ directory.
2. Type:

   vi resolv.conf

   and hit Enter.
3. Press the Escape key.
4. Type:

   i
5. Type:

   domain ibm.net
   nameserver 165.87.194.244
   nameserver 165.87.201.244
6. At the end of the last line, hit the Escape key again.
7. Type:

   :qw

   and hit Enter.

8. To check your work, type:

```
less resolv.conf
```

and hit Enter. You should see the text you just typed. Leave the `less` reader by hitting q.

The options File   This file includes your modem speed and your user name for logging in. You found this information from Windows, in the steps shown in Figures 11-6 and 11-9. The example below is from the same IBM Global Network connection. Use the `vi` editor to make your file, using the previous procedure. Note: the `options` file is in the `/etc/ppp` directory, and may already exist; if it does, just edit it.

```
115200
name Internet.usinet.passwd
noauth
defaultroute
noipdefault
```

The pap-secrets File   This file includes your user name for logging in, just as above, and your password. You found this information from Windows, in the step shown in Figure 11-9. The example below is from the same IBM Global Network connection. Use the `vi` editor to make your file, using the previous procedure. Note that the `pap-secrets` file is in the `/etc/ppp` directory, and may already exist; if it does, just edit it.

```
"Internet.usinet.passwd"   *   "passwd"
```

The ppp-on File   This file includes your modem port—the serial port your modem is connected to (but using the Linux naming convention: COM 2 is equal to ttyS1)—and your ISP's telephone number. You found this information from Windows, in the steps shown in Figures 11-5 and 11-9. The example below is from the same IBM Global Network connection. Use the `vi` editor to make your file, using the previous procedure. Note that the `ppp-on` file is in the `/usr/sbin` directory.

```
pppd /dev/ttyS1 connect 'chat -v "" atdt9174451 "CONNECT"'
```

The ppp-off File   This file includes no information whatever from Windows—it is simply a script file that kills the Internet connection. The example below is from the same IBM Global Network connection. Use the `vi` editor to make your file, using the previous procedure. Note that the `ppp-off` file is in the `/usr/sbin` directory.

```
DEVICE=ppp0
if [ -r /var/run/$DEVICE.pid ]; then
 kill -INT 'cat /var/run/$DEVICE.pid'
fi
```

Note the slanting apostrophes (') on the third line of this file. On most keyboards, this character will be on the upper left hand corner of the keyboard, just above the Tab key.

Setting File Permissions with chmod   Right now, if you just typed ppp-on, you might connect to the Internet—or you might get a message saying, "Permission denied."

Every file in Linux has a set of "permissions" that controls who can read the file, write to the file, or execute the file. You have to make sure that your two executable files, ppp-on and ppp-off, have the permissions you need. You set a file's permissions with the chmod command. Follow this procedure:

1. At the /usr/sbin directory, type:

```
chmod a=rwx ppp-on
```

2. Hit Enter. This sets the file so that all (a) users have read (r), write (w), and execute (x) permission. Do exactly the same for the ppp-off file.

Other ISP Examples   Your ppp-off file will be exactly the same no matter which ISP you use; your ppp-on file will only differ from the example above in your ISP's telephone number, and possibly in your COM port—if your modem does not use the standard ttyS1.

Below are examples of the other three files; resolv.conf, options, and pap-secrets, from two other actual connections with two other ISPs. I've tested these and others. They work. I've changed only the names and passwords.

TELUS   This is a Canadian telecom and ISP located in Alberta. The resolv.conf file:

```
nameserver 199.185.220.36
nameserver 198.80.55.1
```

The `options` file:

```
115200
name jdoe
noauth
defaultroute
noipdefault
```

The `pap-secrets` file:

```
"jdoe"    *       "passwd"
```

EARTHLINK   This is an American ISP headquartered in California.

The `resolv.conf` file:

```
nameserver    207.217.126.81
nameserver    207.217.120.83
```

The `options` file:

```
115200
name ELN/jdoe
noauth
defaultroute
noipdefault
```

The `pap-secrets` file:

```
"ELN/jdoe"     *      "passwd"
```

Connecting and Checking It Out with Separate Consoles and `tail`

Try your scripts out on one console, while checking your login and logout messages on a second "virtual" console. You can do this by using the `tail` command.

The concept of virtual consoles was covered at the end of Chapter 9. To recap: you have up to six different virtual consoles on one machine, and you access them by pressing and holding the Ctrl key along with the Alt key, and by pressing the function keys, F2 to F6. To get back to the original console, just press Ctrl + Alt + F1.

Keeping a second console open can be helpful in several ways. In this case, you can keep tabs on how your Internet connection is doing on console 2, while logging on, downloading, and logging off on console 1.

Follow this procedure:

1. Move to console 2 by pressing Ctrl + Alt, and hitting the F2 key.

2. Log in. There is a file called messages in your /var/log directory, which is automatically updated by Linux whenever an Internet connection is established or ended. The tail command prints the end of this file to the screen, and the -f option keeps printing it to the screen. In this way you can keep track of your connection.

3. Type:

   tail -f /var/log/messages

   and press Enter.

4. Now go back to console 1, by pressing Ctrl + Alt and hitting the F1 key.

5. Enter your /usr/sbin directory, and start your Internet connection by typing:

   ppp-on

   and hitting Enter. Nothing appears to happen. You're simply back at the command prompt. After a moment or two, you should hear your modem dialing. But you won't see a thing.

6. Now switch to console 2, and check your messages. If everything worked, you'll see a variety of connection messages scroll by on console 2. They may well look something like Figure 11-10.

   Disconnecting is just as easy.

1. Switch back to console number 1.

2. Type:

   ppp-off

Figure 11-10

Typical Internet Connection Message

```
pppd 2.3.7 startd by root, uid 0
expect (CONNECT)
send (atdt917-4451 ^M)
Serial connection established.
Using interface ppp0
Connect:  ppp0  <-->/dev/ttyS1
CONNECT
--got it
local   IP address 129.37.157.206
remote  IP address 129.37.152.16
```

Figure 11-11
Typical Internet
Disconnect Message

```
Terminating on signal 2.
Hangup  (SIGHUP)
Modem hangup
Connection terminated.
Connect time 0.4 minutes.
Sent 203 bytes, received 183 bytes.
```

3. Hit Enter. If you switch back to console number 2, you should see a few new lines at the bottom of the message file, something like Figure 11-11:

Step 5: Troubleshooting

Of course, if everything's working just fine, you won't need this step. But there are a number of things that can go wrong:

1. Typos are the most common reason for failure. Connection scripts are notoriously demanding: they really do have to be written just right. There is no room for error. Check both the information that you gathered from Windows, and the Linux scripts themselves. Proofread them character by character, space by space.

2. It is possible, although increasingly unlikely, that your ISP uses the SLIP protocol instead of PPP. In that case, the method shown above definitely will not work—you need a special SLIP connection script that only your ISP can provide.

3. It is possible, although increasingly unlikely, that your ISP uses the CHAP authentication protocol, instead of PAP. This will involve more information from your ISP, and another script.

If all fails, then you have two choices. You can try using your distribution's own utility programs for establishing an Internet connection. All distributions now have these programs, and occasionally they work.

Your other option is to contact your ISP, and ask for their help. There are tiny ISPs that will give you enormous help, and tiny ISPs that will give you none whatever. Similarly, there are huge global ISPs that will give you terrific help, and global ISPs that will give you none.

The only certainty is the trendline: more and more ISPs all the time are coming on board, and giving serious support to Linux.

12

X Window and Sound Configuration

Purpose of Chapter: Reconfiguring X Window and Configuring the Sound Card

This chapter is divided into two parts: reconfiguration of X Window, and configuration of the sound card.

With any luck, you won't have to use the first part of this chapter. However, even though Linux installation routines are much better—more automated and more accurate—than they used to be, occasionally there are still problems with X Window. Most of the time you can solve these problems by re-running the distributor's own X Window configuration program—the one that ran during installation. But in some cases it may still be necessary to try one of the older programs designed to configure X Window—or even, *in extremis*, to try and configure it by hand.

Sound was never a priority in Linux, but support is getting better. If your card is compatible with any of those supported, then configuration is usually straightforward.

Reconfiguring X Window

You will need to reconfigure X Window if the installation routine was unable to get it working, or if you are unhappy about its performance. It is a fact that Linux does not as yet support as wide a combination of graphics adapters and monitors as Microsoft's product. However, you can usually get X Window to work just as well on your computer as Microsoft Windows—if not better.

Do You Need to Reconfigure?

Type:

```
startx
```

and hit Enter. (Note: in Caldera, type: kde, and hit Enter.) If X Window comes up clearly, without distortion or waviness, if the colors are clear and the icons the correct size, then you probably don't need to reconfigure. Save yourself some trouble, and skip ahead to the second part of this chapter: sound configuration.

Keep in mind, however, that the need may not at first be apparent. For instance, you might be running at 24 bpp in Windows 95/98, but 16 bpp—a lower color saturation—in Linux. You may notice the lower color saturation only after some time, and want to reconfigure then.

In X Window, there are two things to configure: the server and the desktop. Configuring the desktop simply means configuring the way X Window looks and behaves once it's up and running. That is covered in Part 3. But configuring the server determines whether or not X Window is going to work at all, as well as the most basic appearance issues such as color depth and resolution.

Choices in Semiautomatically Reconfiguring X Window

All the distributions covered in this book let you rerun their own, often proprietary, installation routine's configuration program. This is the best place to start. These programs are usually the most up-to-date, and the easiest to use. To run the original configuration program at the command line, simply type in the program name (being careful with capitalization, as always), and hit Enter.

If the original configuration program doesn't work, all four distributions have two additional configuration programs to try before manual editing becomes necessary. Your choice is summed up in Table 12-1.

Step-by-step instructions on each distributor's own installation programs are given in Part One of this book. Instructions for the two additional programs follow.

XF86Setup The XF86Setup program predates the distributors' own X Window configuration programs, but it can still be quite useful—and it will often result in a far shorter configuration file. It is graphical and mouse-enabled, and thus is fairly easy to use. To run it, first get together again all the information on your graphics adapter and monitor that you obtained in Chapter 1, and then type:

```
XF86Setup
```

and hit Enter. The program asks you if you want to accept the existing XF86Config file for defaults. If you only want to make a small adjustment, then you might as well choose y for yes. Otherwise type:

```
n
```

and hit Enter, then Enter again. This takes you to the introduction screen of the program.

xf86config This also predates the distributors' own configuration programs, but it is not as easy to use as either the distributors' programs or as XF86Setup. It does, however, have one great advantage. Since it is completely text-based, you can use it to build an XF86Config file even if you are unable to enter graphics mode on your computer. To run it, first get

TABLE 12-1

X Window Re-Configuration Programs, by Distribution

Distribution	Configuration Program from Installation	Additional Configuration Program	Additional Configuration Program
Red Hat	Xconfigurator	XF86Setup	xf86config
Caldera	lizardx	XF86Setup	xf86config
TurboLinux	turboxcfg	XF86Setup	xf86config
SuSE	sax	XF86Setup	xf86config

together again all the information on your graphics adapter and monitor
that you obtained in Chapter 1, and then type:

```
xf86config
```

and hit Enter.

Manually Configuring X Window

One file configures the server: XF86Config. It is usually found in either
/etc or /etc/X11. Figure 12-1 is an example of this file, configured and
optimized for a Toshiba Tecra laptop.

Figure 12-1
Example of the
XF86Config File

```
# XF86Config auto-generated by XF86Setup
#
# Copyright (c) 1996 by The XFree86 Project, Inc.
#
# See 'man XF86Config' for info on the format of this file

Section "Files"
    RgbPath      "/usr/X11R6/lib/X11/rgb"
    FontPath     "/usr/X11R6/lib/X11/fonts/local"
    FontPath     "/usr/X11R6/lib/X11/fonts/misc:unscaled"
    FontPath     "/usr/X11R6/lib/X11/fonts/75dpi:unscaled"
    FontPath     "/usr/X11R6/lib/X11/fonts/100dpi:unscaled"
    FontPath     "/usr/X11R6/lib/X11/fonts/Type1"
    FontPath     "/usr/X11R6/lib/X11/fonts/Speedo"
    FontPath     "/usr/X11R6/lib/X11/fonts/misc"
    FontPath     "/usr/X11R6/lib/X11/fonts/75dpi"
    FontPath     "/usr/X11R6/lib/X11/fonts/100dpi"
    FontPath     "unix/:-1"
EndSection

Section "ServerFlags"
EndSection

Section "Keyboard"
    Protocol        "Standard"
    XkbRules        "xfree86"
    XkbModel        "pc101"
    XkbLayout       "us"
    XkbOptions      "ctrl:ctrl_aa"
EndSection

Section "Pointer"
    Protocol        "PS/2"
    Device          "/dev/mouse"
EndSection
```

■■ ■■ ■■ ■■

Figure 12-1

Example of the
XF86Config File
(Continued)

```
Section "Monitor"
    Identifier      "Primary Monitor"
    VendorName      "Unknown"
    ModelName       "Unknown"
    HorizSync       35.464-68.8
    VertRefresh     60-87
    Modeline    "800x600"  53.197 800 856 976 1040 600 637 643 666
+hsync +vsync
    Modeline    "640x480"  35.464 640 696 752 832 480 481 484 509
-hsync -vsync
EndSection

Section "Device"
    Identifier      "Primary Card"
    VendorName      "Unknown"
    BoardName       "None"
    Chipset         "ct65550"
    VideoRam        2048
    Option              "no_bitblt"
EndSection

Section "Screen"
    Driver          "SVGA"
    Device          "Primary Card"
    Monitor         "Primary Monitor"
    DefaultColorDepth 16
    SubSection "Display"
        Depth       8
        Modes       "800x600" "640x480"
    EndSubSection
    SubSection "Display"
        Depth       16
        Modes       "800x600" "640x480"
    EndSubSection
    SubSection "Display"
        Depth       24
        Modes       "800x600" "640x480"
    EndSubSection
EndSection
```

Editing this file, although not exactly enjoyable for most people, need
not be as painful as it looks. The file is broken up into digestible sections.
The usual sections are:

Files (file pathnames for fonts)

Keyboard (keyboard configuration)

Pointer (pointer configuration)

Monitor (monitor description and specifications)

Device (defines your graphics adapter)

Screen (specifies which graphics adapter and which monitors are to be
used together, in which configuration)

The Monitor, Device and Screen sections are the ones you will likely need to concentrate on. Before opening this file up in vi, you will first want to get as much information on your computer as you can—from Windows 95/98, and also from your computer's documentation. In addition, you will want to read the README.config file and any special Linux text files that may exist for your adapter card. All these files will be in:

```
/usr/X11R6/lib/X11/doc
```

This is a ways to drill down, but the results will probably be worth it. Examples of files in this directory that offer configuration advice for specific adapter cards are:

README.chips for Chips & Technologies adapter cards

README.ati for ATI adapter cards

README.WstDig for Western Digital cards

This directory contains a number of other very useful documents for the person taking on the manual configuration of an X Window server.

However, with a total of six different configuration programs spread over four distributions, for most people manually editing the XF86Config file will not be an issue.

Configuring Sound in Linux

Sound card configuration suffers from the same problems in Linux that modems do: a lack of drivers, particularly for PnP and PCI cards. With a nonsupported modem card, this is easy to rectify: simply buy the most generic Hayes-compatible external modem you can find, and plug it into a serial port. However, a nonsupported sound card is not that simple to fix.

Fortunately, if your sound card is Sound Blaster–compatible (and most are), then there is a fairly good chance that the installation routine will set it up automatically. However, if that fails, you may still have an option left. Two distributions—RedHat and TurboLinux—have sound card setup utility programs that you can run after installation, at the command line. But to use them successfully, you will first have to get some information about the resources your sound card uses in Windows.

The easiest way to do this is to boot into Windows, click on the Start button, go up to Settings, and then over to Control Panel. Click on Control Panel.

1. Click on the System icon.
2. You'll see the System Properties window. Click on the Device Manager tab.
3. Click on the + sign next to Sound, video and game controllers. Your screen should look something like Figure 12-2.

Something similar, but not identical. The trick is to find which of these "controllers" actually have the information you need: the resources being used by your sound card. The answer in this example is fairly simple. We aren't configuring a gameport joystick, so we can ignore that one. The two entries for modems look doubtful, and if you check their properties, you'll see that they include none of the information we're looking for:

Interrupt Requests (IRQs),
Input/Output Ranges, and
Direct Memory Access settings.

However, if you click on Crystal PnP Audio System, then on the Properties button, and finally on the Resources tab, you'll see something similar to

Figure 12-2
Device Manager Box in Windows, Showing Sound, Video, and Game Controllers

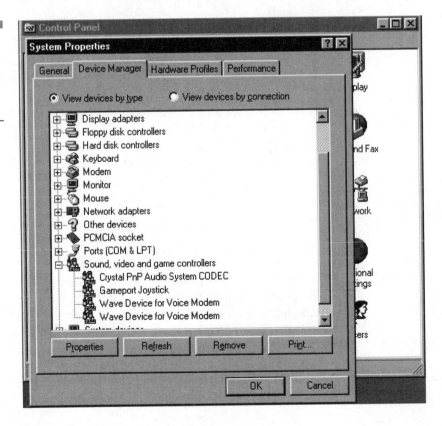

Figure 12-3

Example of Sound
Card Resources in
Windows Device
Manager

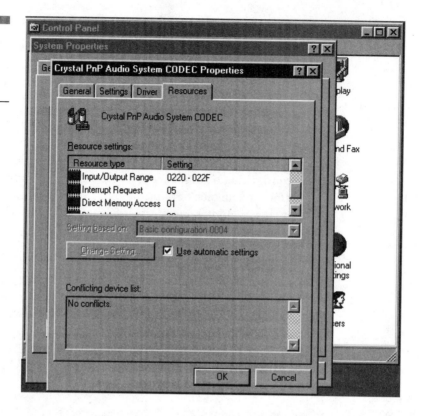

Figure 12-3. This gives us the information we're looking for, and that we
can probably use in Linux.

Redhat's and TurboLinux's sound card utility programs are almost identical, but their names are different. In Redhat, type:

```
sndconfig
```

and hit Enter. In TurboLinux, type:

```
turbosoundcfg
```

and hit Enter. Both programs will first try to probe your sound cards.
When that fails, they then present you with a list of sound cards to choose
from and to manually configure. If your card isn't listed, I suggest you try
one of the Sound Blaster cards. Many nonsupported cards are compatible
with the Sound Blaster standards, and you may be able to get yours to
work with them.

If you do succeed, and you are running RedHat, then you will find out
from the horse's mouth how to pronounce "Linux."

X Window

X Window is the term for the graphical user environment in Linux— an environment similar to Microsoft Windows. Anyone who uses Microsoft's product will feel right at home using X Window in Red Hat or Caldera. They may have a slightly harder time, however, in TurboLinux. That is because X Window, unlike MS Windows, is capable of running different "desktops."

Most Linux distributions, in an effort to distinguish themselves from their competition, have adopted a different look and feel to their version of X Window. Red Hat runs a desktop called Gnome; Caldera a desktop called KDE; and TurboLinux another desktop, called TurboDesk. SuSE defaults to yet another desktop, but lets you change to KDE if you wish.

All have approximately the same set of major features, most of which work in approximately the same way. But their appearance is significantly different. In addition, the set of minor features is different, and the methods of customizing the look and feel of feature sets can be very different from desktop to desktop.

None of this changes the fact, however, that if you use Microsoft Windows now, you can start to use X Window immediately. And Linux has the advantage that X Window, by both performance and design, is better suited to multitasking and is more stable.

13

Using Red Hat's Gnome Desktop

Purpose of Chapter: To Introduce the Gnome Desktop

Since Red Hat has the biggest market share of commercial Linux distributions in the United States (as of this writing), it follows that the Gnome desktop will be the default desktop of most Linux purchasers.

Gnome is often said to be less refined than its main rival, Caldera's KDE. There is something to that—KDE does have a slightly crisper feel. However, in terms of functionality the two desktops are almost identical. Which is best? It mainly depends on personal taste. I like the Gnome appearance, and look forward to future refinements.

The bottom line is: if you are proficient in Microsoft Windows, you will almost immediately be proficient in X Window, and Gnome.

Start up X Window in Red Hat by typing:

```
startx
```

and hitting Enter. You will see a warning that you are running as "root." Click on the OK button. At first the desktop appears to be a confusing jumble of windows. Before going any further, let's simplify the picture. Click on the X—the close window button—on each window's upper right hand corner. Your screen should now resemble Figure 13-1.

Similarities and Differences

With two exceptions the main features of Gnome's default desktop are identical to Microsoft Windows. First, the similarities.

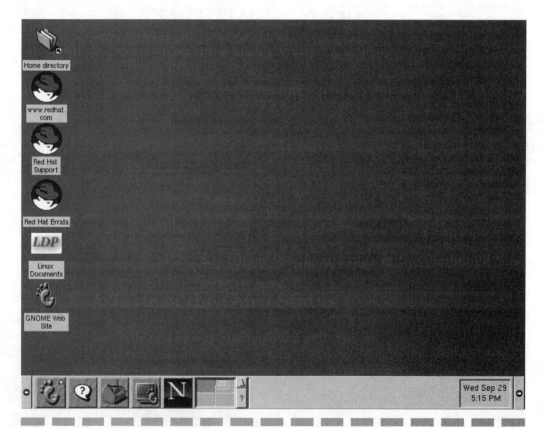

Figure 13-1   Initial Gnome Desktop

On the left hand side of the screen is a vertical row of icons. Desktop icons act in Gnome exactly as they do in Windows: double-clicking them opens up whatever they are linked to, an applet, a program, a program file, or a Web page.

At the bottom left hand corner is a square icon displaying a footprint. Gnome people call this absurd icon the Main Menu button, but we may as well call a spade a spade, and refer to it as the Start button. Clicking it brings up the main menu. From here you can navigate to programs in sub-menus, such as applications, graphics, the Internet, etc.

The two main differences are the toolbar, called the *panel*, stretching across the bottom of the screen, and the icon on the panel called the *pager*, which is usually to the right of the Netscape icon. The pager is divided into quarters, with a small up arrow at the upper right corner. The pager is one of the most useful features of the X Window system.

The Panel

The default appearance is shown in Figure 13-2. Most icons are self-explanatory. If you click on the Netscape icon, Netscape Navigator will start. If you click on the terminal emulation program icon next to it, a terminal, or command-line, window will open. If you click on the aptly designed toolbox icon, a configuration tool called the *control center* will appear. If you click on the question mark, a help window will appear. The Start button leads to the main menu.

The panel is highly configurable, and can also be moved out of the way. Click on the tiny left arrow at the panel's far left hand side. It moves right off the screen, leaving only a small right arrow. Click on the arrow to restore the panel. The usefulness of this behavior will become evident a bit later on.

The Pager

The pager allows you to work at your computer exactly as you do at your desk. For the first time, a computer desktop resembles an actual desktop. A simple demonstration will show how this works.

Figure 13-2   Initial Gnome Panel

1. Click on the Start button. The main menu appears.

2. Click on the File Manager menu item, and then on the OK button. The Gnome file manager appears—very similar to the Windows Explorer.

3. Now, go down to the pager and click on the lower left quarter. The file manger disappears.

4. Click on the Start button again, go up to Internet, and over and down to Netscape Communicator. Click on Netscape.

5. Click on the Accept button for the license agreement, and then on the Maximize button—the small square on the upper right hand corner of the Netscape window. Netscape fills the screen.

6. Go down to the pager again, and click on the lower right hand quarter. Click on the Terminal Emulation Program icon on the panel at the bottom of the screen. A terminal window appears.

7. Now click on all four quarters of the pager in turn.

The pager is your real desktop. Using the pager in this way, you can work in X Window exactly as if you had your work arranged on separate areas of your real desk—if your real desk were big enough.

There are three ways to move from one area of the desktop to another. One is to simply click on different parts of the pager, as you've been doing. Another is to click on the tiny up arrow in the pager's corner, and then click on one of the programs in the list—you're immediately switched to that section of the pager. The third is to simply move the mouse pointer to the border of the section you want to move to, but that feature first has to be configured.

Now move to the section of the desktop where you have Netscape running. You'll notice that the panel hides the bottom of the browser window. Simply click on the left or right arrow at the ends of the panel to move it out of the way.

Customizing the Desktop

Gnome is almost infinitely customizable—a decent-sized book could easily be written on the subject. However, a quick walk through of some of the basics can get you up and running, and show you how to customize the desktop further to suit your own needs and tastes.

Adding Drive Mount Applets to the Panel

The latest version of Gnome mounts a CD-ROM as soon as you insert the CD. However, that still leaves the default behavior of Linux unchanged when you want to eject the CD: you have to first unmount the drive. Adding a drive mount applet to the panel simplifies this procedure.

1. Click on the Start button.

2. Go up to Panel, and over and up to Add Applet, and over and down to Utility, and finally over to Drive Mount.

3. Click on Drive Mount. You'll see that a very small drive icon has now been added to the panel, right next to the Start button. If you inspect it closely, you'll see that it is in fact an icon for a floppy drive.

4. Position the mouse pointer over the drive icon, and click on the right mouse button.

5. Click on Properties.

6. The Drive Mount Settings window appears. Click on the Floppy bar, and choose CD-ROM. Then, in the section labeled Mount point: type in:

   /mnt/cdrom

7. The window should now look like Figure 13-3. Click on the Apply, and then on the Close buttons.

The drive icon on the panel now resembles a CD-ROM. Check it out by inserting a CD. The file manager should immediately come up on the screen, with the left panel showing the /mnt/cdrom directory selected, and the right panel showing the folders and files on the CD (Figure 13-4).

To eject the CD, first close the file manager (the CD can't be unmounted while it is being accessed), then just click once on the drive icon. To immediately mount it again, and bring up the file manager, just click again on the icon. This is a very considerable improvement over having to enter mount /mnt/cdrom at the command line.

You can also add to the panel a drive mount icon for your Windows partition. Go through exactly the same procedure, but change the Drive Mount Settings window for the new mount to Figure 13-5. Finally, if you care to, you can add a drive mount icon for your floppy in the same way.

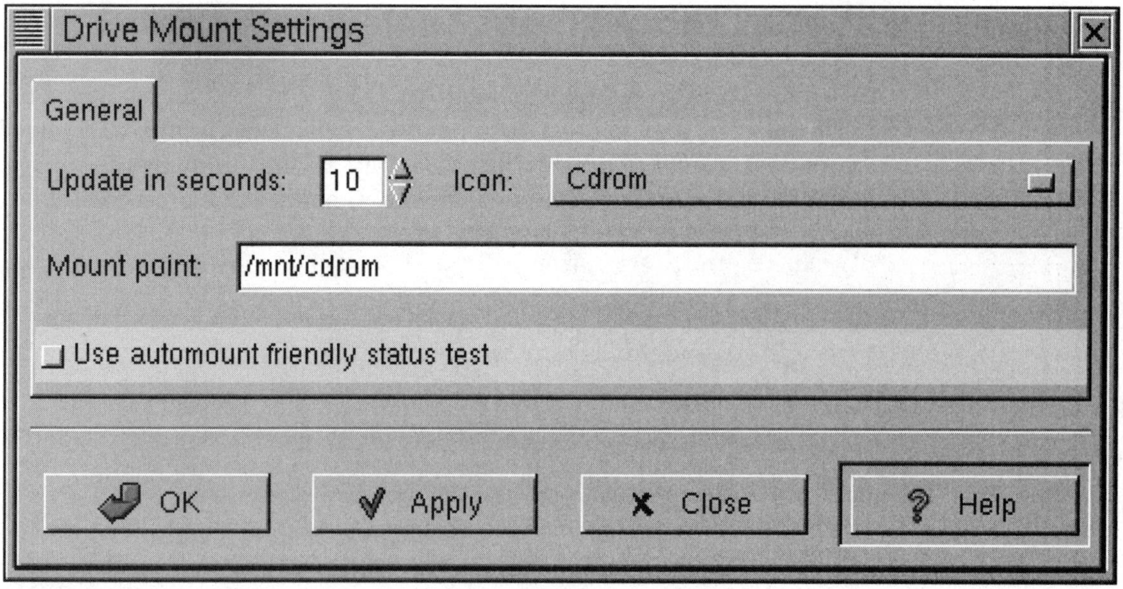

Figure 13-3 Drive Mount Settings for a CD-ROM

Configuring the Pager

Once you get used to the idea of multitasking—keeping more than one program open at a time, without having to worry about excessive memory use or the whole system crashing—you may want to expand the pager. It is not a difficult procedure.

1. Click on the toolbox icon on the panel.
2. In the Control Center window that appears, choose Window Manager (Figure 13-6).
3. Click on the bar titled Run Configuration Tool for Enlightenment.
4. The Enlightenment Configuration Editor window appears. Click on Desktops in the left hand panel.
5. Under Size of Virtual Screen, there are four squares. By sliding the horizontal and vertical sliders with your mouse (hold down the left button), you can change the pager's appearance as you wish. Figure 13-7 shows the pager configured for six virtual screens, two down and three across.

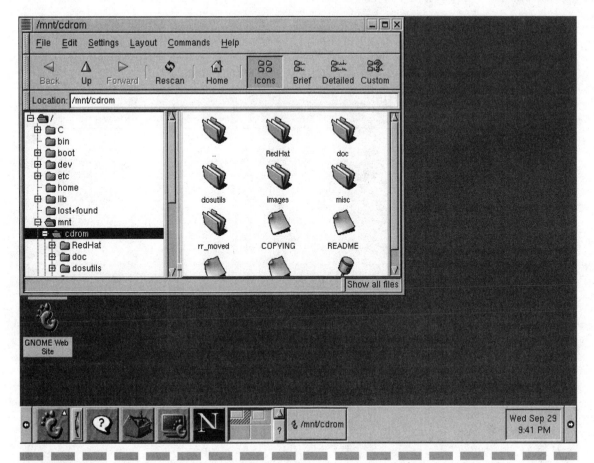

Figure 13-4 File Manager Showing CD-ROM Mounted

6. I advise you to also move the Edge Flip Resistance slider on the same screen to about a 50 setting. This will allow you to move from one virtual screen to another by simply sliding the mouse in the correct direction, but will enable enough delay to keep you from accidentally switching screens.

7. Click on the Apply and OK buttons.

Configuring Desktop Behavior

1. Go through steps 1 through 3 above to reach the Enlightenment Configuration Editor again.

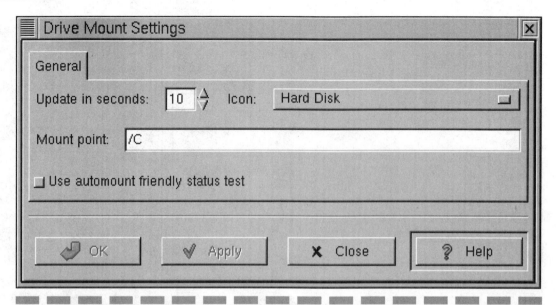

Figure 13-5   Drive Mount Settings for the Windows Partition

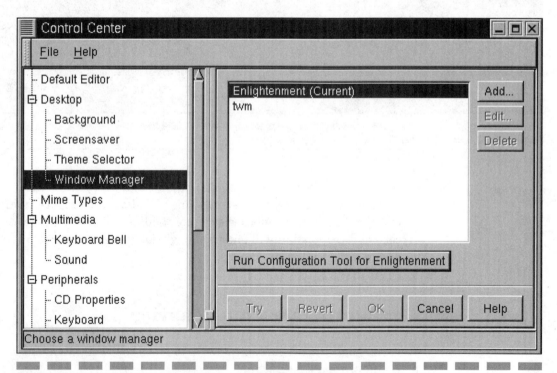

Figure 13-6   Control Center with Window Manager Selected

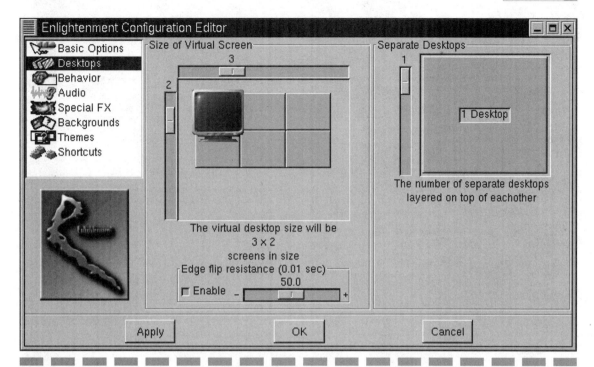

Figure 13-7 Pager Configuration in the Enlightenment Configuration Editor

2. This time click on Basic Options in the left panel (Figure 13-8). In order to avoid having to click on each new window to activate it, click on the Keyboard focus follows Mouse Pointer button.

3. Now, to make sure that each new window automatically gets the keyboard focus, click on Behavior in the left panel, and to the right, check All new windows that appear get the keyboard focus.

4. Click on the Apply and the OK buttons.

Configuring the Screen Saver

In the Control Center, click on Screensaver on the left panel. The default setting is random. You can try out all the settings under Screensaver, and preview them in the window to the right. You can adjust the amount of time to elapse before the screen saver comes up, and whether or not to use power management.

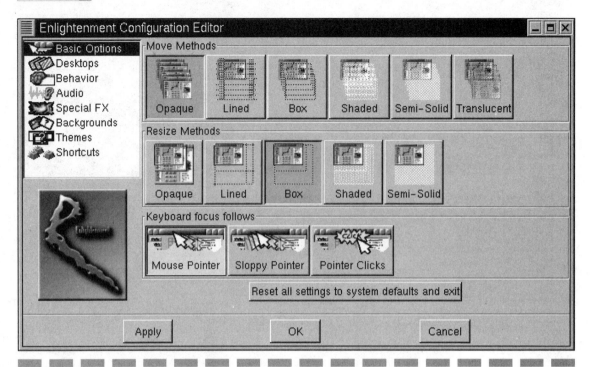

Figure 13-8 Basic Options and Keyboard Focus

Adding to and Deleting Program Icons from the Desktop

Deleting an icon from the desktop is as simple as clicking on it with the right mouse button, and choosing `delete` from the pop-up menu.

There are at least two ways to add an icon to the desktop. The first is simply to right click anywhere on the desktop, and choose New and Launcher. The Desktop Entry Properties window comes up. As an example, if you wanted to add a Netscape icon to the desktop, you would fill in the blanks as shown in Figure 13-9, and then click on the Apply and Close buttons. Alternatively, if you already have a menu entry, you can just hold the left mouse button down on it, and drag it to the desktop, creating an instant copy.

Adding Internet Icons to the Desktop

Three very useful icons to have on your desktop are Internet On, Off, and Connection Status. If you're using the Internet connection scripts you learned in Chapter 11, then you can create the icons using the Desktop

Figure 13-9
Desktop Entry
Properties, Showing
Entries for Netscape

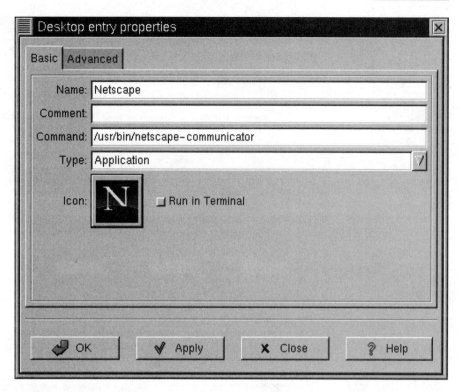

Entry Properties shown in Figures 13-10, 13-11, and 13-12. Note in Figure 13-12 to make sure to check the Run in Terminal box. The icon graphics shown are completely optional.

Connecting to the Internet

The killer applet that so many Linux users have been waiting for is the applet that, after prompting you for basic information, automatically and accurately configures dial-up networking. One day we will have that applet.

Until then, you can experiment with the Red Hat PPP Dialer (Start, Internet, RH PPP Dialer), which may even work for you. Almost certainly, the day will come when this applet works reliably. That day has not yet arrived.

The best way so far to connect via a PPP dial-up account within Gnome is to create the scripts in Chapter 11, and then the desktop icons (or menu items) in the Adding Internet Icons to the Desktop section, above.

Figure 13-10
Desktop Entry
Properties for
Internet On Icon

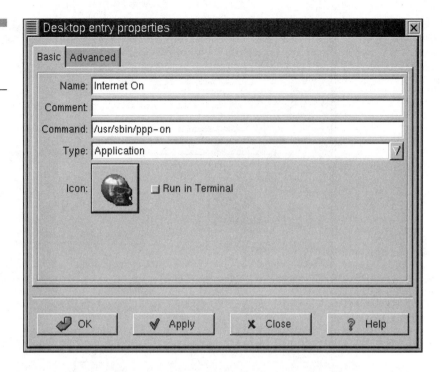

Figure 13-11
Desktop Entry
Properties for
Internet Off Icon

Figure 13-12
Desktop Entry
Properties for
Connection Status
Icon

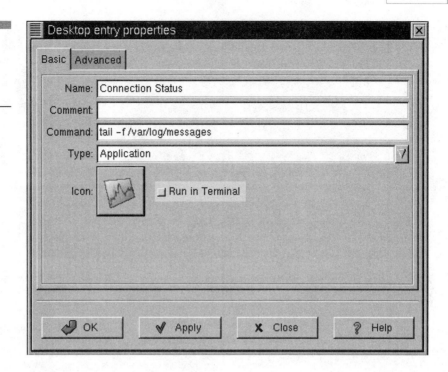

Desktop entry properties

Basic | Advanced

Name: Connection Status

Comment:

Command: tail –f /var/log/messages

Type: Application

Icon: ☐ Run in Terminal

OK   Apply   Close   Help

Before connecting, double-click on the Connection Status icon to start up the "tail" program in a terminal emulation window. Then click on the Internet On icon. The status window will show you the progress of your connection and when it's established (Figure 13-13—note that the icon titles in the figure differ).

Setting Up the Printer

In the previous versions of Red Hat Linux, the printer was set up in a lengthy routine during installation. That has been eliminated—how many people still print at the command line? The Gnome setup routine is far simpler.

1. Click on the Start button, go up to System, and over and down to Control Panel. Once the control panel appears, click on the printer icon, the third one from the top.

2. If Linux prompts you that ncpfs and/or samba are not installed, just click on the OK buttons.

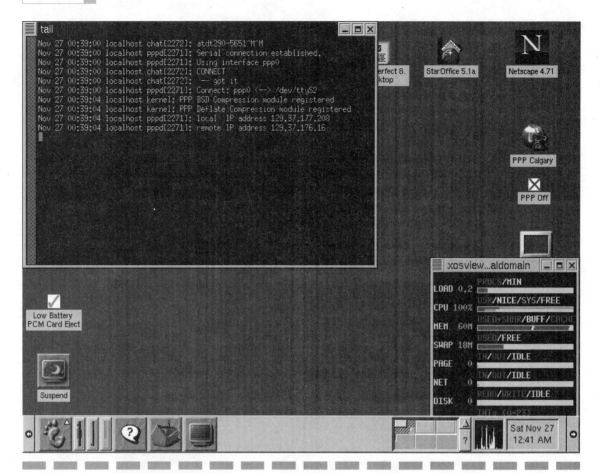

Figure 13-13   Connecting to the Internet in Gnome

3. At the Red Hat Linux Print System Manager (Figure 13-14), click on the Add button, and choose Local Printer (unless you're on a network—if so, consult your system administrator). Click on the OK button.

4. In the next box there should be a Detected message next to one of the printer ports, generally next to /dev/lp0. If for some reason this isn't working, make sure your computer is connected to your printer, turn it on, and try rebooting. Hit the OK button.

5. At the Edit Local Printer Entry window, click on the Select button.

6. The Configure Filter window (Figure 13-15) is where you actually choose your printer. Find either your model or one very similar to

Figure 13-14
Adding a Printer
Entry

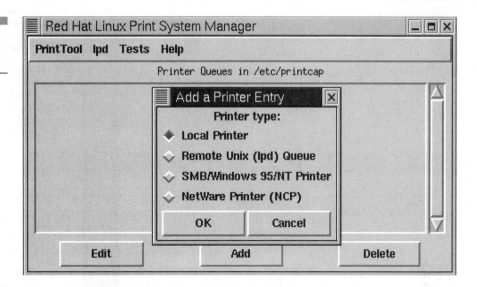

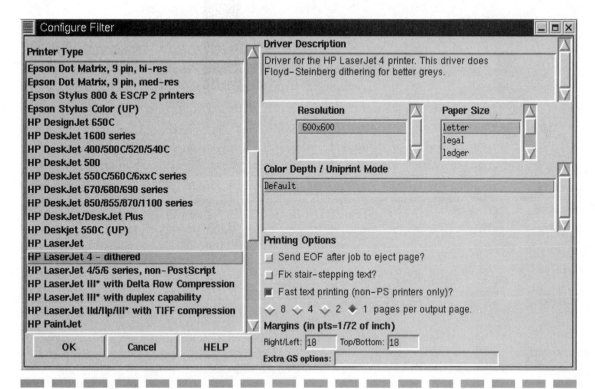

Figure 13-15 Choosing a Printer

it on the left, making sure that the Resolution and Paper Size on the right are correct. Then click on OK, and on the next OK button as well.

7. Try printing a test page. Don't worry if it seems to take a little longer than usual—that's normal.

Using the File Manager

The file manager can be accessed either by the Home Directory icon on the desktop, or from the main menu. It will give you the familiar warning that you're accessing it as the "root" user—just click on the OK button.

Gnome's file manager has complete drag-and-drop capability. However, if you are using a two-button mouse, it is first necessary for you to activate the three-button emulation. If you haven't done it already, then run the Setup program at a command prompt, choose Mouse Configuration, and make sure that the Emulate 3 Buttons box is checked.

To move a file from the right panel to any directory on the left, just hold down the left mouse button. In order to copy it, however, press down both buttons simultaneously and move the mouse pointer to the new location. When you release the mouse, you'll be given a choice of whether to move or copy the file.

You can also open a file simply by double-clicking on its icon—the file will be opened by the program you select. You can configure this by right-clicking on a file, and choosing the application you prefer.

An obvious and useful file manager configuration would be to mount your Windows partition, right-click on one of your Word document files, and choose StarOffice as your preferred application to open it in Linux.

The similarity of Gnome's file manager to Windows Explorer will ensure an easy transition for the new Linux user.

Exiting Gnome

To close down Gnome and get back to the command line:

1. Click on the Start button.
2. Click on Log Out.

3. Under Action, you have three choices. Choose which you prefer—Logout to return to the command line.

4. Click on the Yes button.

At the end of your first X Window session, make sure to check Save Current Setup when you log off.

14

Using Caldera's KDE Desktop

Purpose of Chapter: To Introduce the KDE Desktop

Caldera has been neck-and-neck with Red Hat for some time, and Caldera's X Window desktop, KDE, is generally considered to be more refined than Red Hat's Gnome. KDE is a mature desktop environment, with the same basic feature set of Microsoft Windows. Any current user of Windows will feel right at home.

At the command line, start up X Window in Caldera by typing:

```
kde
```

and hitting Enter. KDE will initially start up with two open windows. Kill the smaller one by double-clicking on its upper left hand corner. Next, move the panel that stretches along the bottom of the screen out of the way by clicking once on the left arrow at the panel's far left side. Your screen should now look like Figure 14-1—the major part of it is taken up by the KDE Setup Wizard.

Figure 14-1   Initial KDE Desktop

Initial Setup

This application is the first thing on your screen, and the first program to run.

1. Click on the Next button.
2. Click on the KDE Default Theme button, and then on the Next button again.
3. Click on the Floppy Disk and CD-ROM icons, and then on the Next button again.
4. Click on the Printer icon, and on Next.
5. Choose which of the offered Websites you want on your desktop, and click on the OK button.

Printer Setup

Caldera does not automatically set up a printer during installation, but it's quite easy to do it within KDE.

1. Click on the Start button (with a large K on it) at the lower left hand corner of the screen.
2. Go up to COAS, over and down to Peripherals, and over to Printer. Click once. Click again on the OK button.
3. At the Printer Configuration window, click on the Printer button, and on Add.
4. Find your printer, or a similar model, and click on it. Then click again on the OK button.
5. You should not need to modify the attributes. Click on the OK button, and on Save.
6. When prompted to create the printer queue, click on OK and then on Done.
7. Back at the Printer Configuration window, you can edit the printer's properties to you heart's content by clicking on Printer and then on Edit. When you're finished, click on OK.

You're now returned to your configured desktop (Figure 14-2).

Figure 14-2 The Configured KDE Desktop

Similarities and Differences

With two exceptions the main features of the KDE desktop are identical to Microsoft Windows. First, the similarities. A vertical row of icons stretches up the left hand side of the screen. Desktop icons act in KDE exactly as they do in Windows: double-clicking them opens up whatever they are linked to: an applet, a program, a program file, or a Webpage. At the bottom left hand corner is a square icon displaying a capital K and a gear—the Start button. Clicking it brings up the main menu. From here you can navigate to programs in submenus, such as applications, graphics, the Internet, etc. At the top of the screen is the taskbar—you are probably used to seeing it at the bottom.

The two main differences are the toolbar, called the *panel*, stretching across the bottom of the screen, and the icon in the middle of the panel, called the *pager*, divided into four numbered rectangles. The pager is one of the most useful features of the X Window system.

The Panel

The panel is shown in Figure 14-3. Most icons are self-explanatory. If you click on the Netscape icon, Netscape Navigator will start. If you click on the terminal emulation icon, a terminal, or command-line, window will open. The file manager—similar to Windows Explorer—is represented by the file folder icon. Two very important panel icons are the Caldera Open Administration System (COAS) icon and the KDE Control Center icon. The Start button leads to the main menu.

The Pager

The pager allows you to work at your computer exactly as you do at your desk. For the first time, a computer desktop resembles an actual desktop. A simple demonstration will show how this works.

1. Click on the folder next to the Netscape icon on the panel. The File Manager window fills the screen.

2. Now go down to the pager and click on the lower left quarter, labeled Two. The file manger disappears, and the screen background changes from deep blue to black.

3. Click on the Netscape Communicator icon on the panel.

4. Click on the Accept button for the license agreement, and then on the Maximize button—the small square on the upper right hand corner of the Netscape window. Netscape fills the screen.

5. Go down to the pager again, and click on the lower right hand quarter. Click on the Terminal Emulation icon on the panel. A terminal window appears.

6. Now click on all four quarters of the pager in turn.

Figure 14-3   The KDE Panel

The pager is your real desktop. Using the pager in this way, you can work in X Window exactly as if you had your work arranged on separate areas of your real desk—if your real desk were big enough.

There are two ways to move from one area of the desktop to another. One is to simply click on different parts of the pager, as you've been doing. The other is to click on alternative program buttons on the toolbar at the top of the screen.

You will discover that in Linux the ability to do practical multitasking— to keep more than one program open and going at a time—is far greater than in Microsoft Windows. Linux uses both RAM and Swap memory more sparingly. And it never seems to get memory areas mixed up—the cause of the ubiquitous general protection fault, or page fault, under Windows.

Customizing the Desktop

KDE is highly customizable—an entire book has been written on the subject. But a quick walk through of some of the basics can get you up and running and show you how to customize the desktop further to suit your own needs and tastes.

Configuring the Pager

Once you get used to the idea of multitasking—keeping more than one program open at a time without having to worry about excessive memory use or the whole system crashing—you may want to expand the pager. It is not a difficult procedure.

1. Click on the KDE Control Center icon on the panel.
2. Click on the + sign next to Applications, and then on Panel.
3. Click on the Desktops tab.
4. To expand the number of virtual desktops, slide the Visible slider bar to the right.
5. Click on Apply and on OK.

Configuring Panel and Toolbar Behavior

Both the panel and the toolbar take up screen real estate and sometimes hide parts of application windows (like Navigator) you want to see. If you want, you can automatically hide them, making them reappear when you place your mouse pointer on the side of the screen.

1. Go through steps 1 and 2, above, to reach the panel option in the KDE Control Center.

2. Click on the Options tab.

3. Now under Visuals check the Auto Hide Panel and Taskbar boxes.

4. This feature works best if you move the sliders for Delay all the way to the left, and the sliders for Speed all the way to the right (Figure 14-4).

5. Click on Apply and OK.

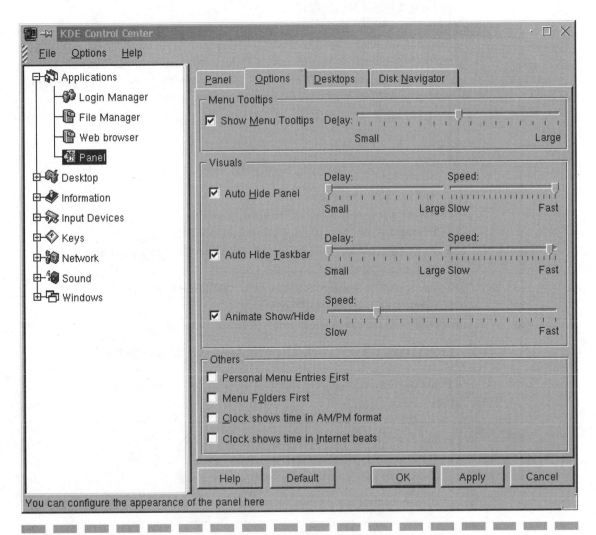

Figure 14-4   Options Tab in the Panel Section of the KDE Control Center

Configuring the Screensaver

Start up the KDE Control Center as before. Click on Desktop, and on Screensaver.

The default setting is none. You can try out all the settings under Screensaver, and preview them in the window above. You can also adjust the amount of time to elapse before the screen saver comes up.

Adding to and Deleting Program Icons from the Desktop

Deleting an icon from the desktop is as simple as clicking on it with the right mouse button, and choosing Delete from the pop-up menu.

Adding an icon to the desktop is almost as simple. As an example, suppose you wanted to add a Netscape program icon to the desktop.

1. Right click anywhere on the desktop, and choose New, and Application.
2. In the small box that comes up, type:

   `Netscape.kdelnk`

   and click on the OK button.
3. The window that appears is similar to Gnome's Desktop Entry Properties window. Click on the Execute tab.
4. Fill in the blank under Execute with the directory path and name of the program (Figure 14-5).
5. Click on the Icon button and find a suitable example.
6. Finally, click on the OK button.

Adding Internet Icons to the Desktop

Three very useful icons to have on your desktop are Internet On, Off, and Connection Status. If you're using the Internet connection scripts you learned in Chapter 11, then you can create the icons using the same method as in the section above. The entries for each icon under the Execute tab would be:

Internet On: `/usr/sbin/ppp-on`

Internet Off: `/usr/sbin/ppp-off`

Connection Status: `tail -f /var/log/messages`

The choice of graphics for the icons is your own.

Figure 14-5
Execute Tab Showing
Netscape Entry for
Desktop Program
Icon

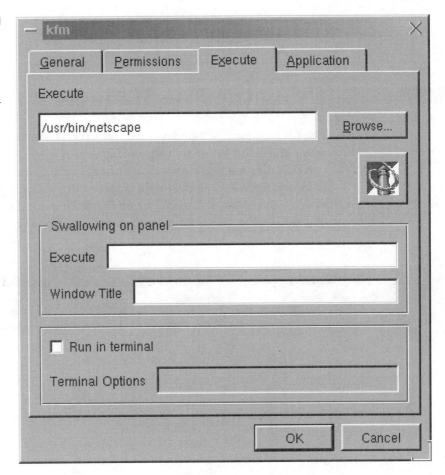

Connecting to the Internet

The killer applet that so many Linux users have been waiting for is the applet that, after prompting you for basic information, automatically and accurately configures dial-up networking. One day we will have that applet.

Until then, you can experiment with Kppp, the Internet Dial-Up Tool (Start, Internet, Kppp), which may even work for you. Almost certainly, the day will come when this applet works reliably. That day has not yet arrived.

The best way so far to connect via a PPP dial-up account within KDE is to create the scripts in Chapter 11, and then the desktop icons (or menu items) in the Adding Internet Icons to the Desktop section, above.

Before connecting, double-click on the Connection Status icon to start up the "tail" program in a terminal emulation window. Then click on the

Internet On icon. The status window will show you the progress of your connection and when it's established.

Using the File Manager

The file manager can be accessed from the Home Directory on the main menu or the file folder icon on the panel.

KDE's file manager does not at first particularly resemble Windows Explorer, but a couple of simple adjustments will get you there. Click on View on the Menu Bar, and click on Show Tree and Long View. The result (Figure 14-6) is very similar to the familiar Explorer.

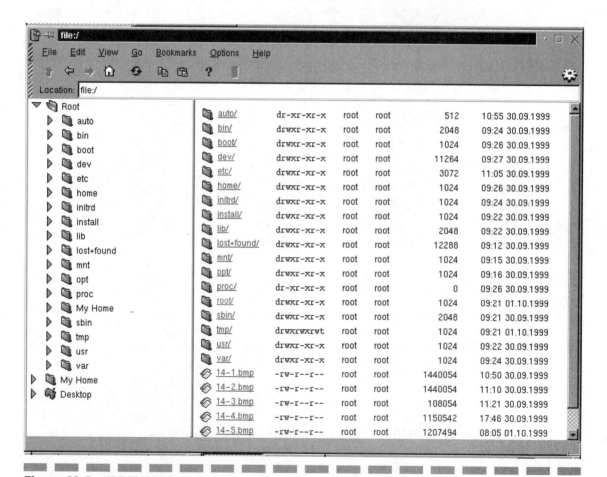

Figure 14-6 KDE File Manager

The file manager has complete drag-and-drop capability. To move a file from the right panel to any directory on the left, just hold down the left mouse button and drag it over. You will be prompted to either copy or move it to the new location.

You can also open a file simply by double-clicking on its icon—the file will be opened by the program you select. You can configure this by double-clicking on the file, clicking on the Browser button, and choosing the application you prefer.

The similarity of KDE's file manager to Windows Explorer will ensure an easy transition for the new Linux user.

Exiting KDE

To close down KDE and get back to the command line:

1. Click on the Start button.
2. Click on Logout.
3. Click on the Logout button.

15

Using TurboLinux's TurboDesk

Purpose of Chapter: To Introduce TurboDesk

TurboDesk is TurboLinux's development of a previous desktop called AfterStep. TurboLinux has deliberately produced a somewhat different looking desktop from its two major rivals, Red Hat and Caldera.

The result is colorful, crisp, and classy looking. However, it is not at the same stage of development as its main competition. It does not have quite as many functions and is not as easy to customize. And if you want a Windows 98 look-alike, you will almost certainly be more comfortable with Gnome or KDE.

Despite these shortcomings, however, TurboDesk is, like every X Window desktop, a better multitasker and more stable than MS Windows.

Start up X Window in TurboLinux by typing:

```
startx
```

and hitting Enter. Your screen should now resemble Figure 15-1.

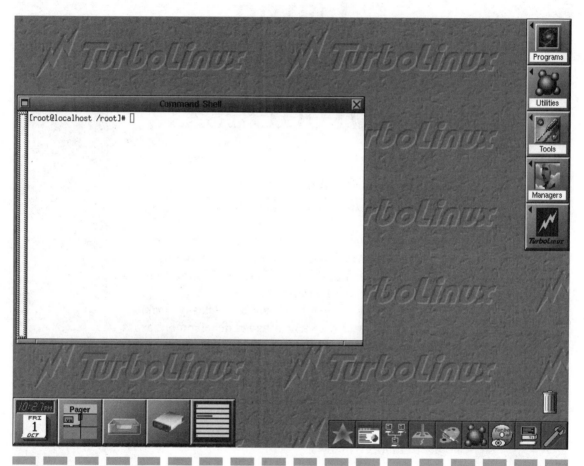

Figure 15-1 Initial TurboDesk Desktop

Differences and Similarities

Unlike Gnome and KDE, TurboDesk has more differences from than similarities to Windows.

There is no Start button, nor is there a taskbar. On the other hand, if you click once and hold down the left mouse button in any blank area of the screen (outside of the command shell), you will see the Desktop Menu, which in terms of functionality is identical to the Main Menu of Windows.

Three strips of buttons line two sides of the screen. The button bar along the upper right hand side is called the Wharf. The one along the lower right of the screen is the Application Launcher. Finally, there's the so-called Dwarf along the lower left.

A command shell, or terminal emulation window (similar to Windows' MS-DOS Prompt), is open by default in the middle of the screen.

The Wharf

This is an interactive button bar: when you click once on an icon or button, a string of buttons representing programs, utilities, tools, or "managers" shoots out. A single click on one of these buttons opens its program, or utility, or whatever.

The Wharf is not easily configurable, but it can be hidden: middle-click (or double-click) on the Program button to hide the entire toolbar; to reveal it again, click on it once more.

The Application Launcher

The Application Launcher is basically the same as the Wharf, except that it uses menus to choose programs and is more configurable. Clicking on one of the Launcher's buttons gives you a menu of programs; just double-click on the program name to start it up.

If you click anywhere on the Launcher with the right mouse button, you can choose Configure to change its location, or Close to make it disappear.

To restore it, simply click on the Programs button on the Wharf, and then on the AppLnchr button.

Adding a Program to the Application Launcher

You can add, edit, or remove programs to any of the Launcher menus. To add a program:

1. Click on the button to open the menu.
2. Right-click anywhere on the menu.
3. Click on Add New App, type in the name of the new program, and click on the OK button.
4. Now just fill in the blanks of the Edit App Setting window. An example, set up for Netscape Navigator, is shown in Figure 15-2.

The Dwarf

This oddly named button bar is devoted to system utilities. It can be closed or reopened in the same way as the Wharf, by middle-clicking (or double-clicking) on it.

It contains a date and time button; an in-basket button for e-mail, which, however, only works if you are using Pine, a UNIX mail client; a modem indicator that may work; and a system monitor that does work, although as an icon it is so small and unlabelled as to be practically use-

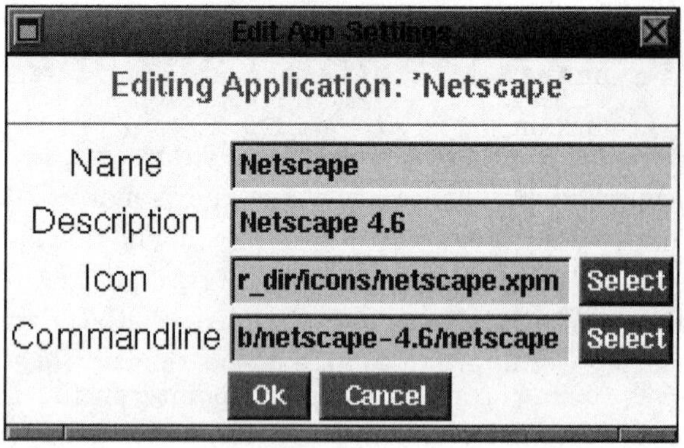

Figure 15-2
Netscape Navigator
Settings in the Edit
App Settings Window

less (double-clicking on it opens a huge system monitor that suffers from the opposite flaw).

However, the Dwarf also contains the pager, the button divided into quarters, which is one of the most useful parts of the desktop.

The Pager

The pager allows you to work at your computer exactly as you do at your desk. For the first time, a computer desktop resembles an actual desktop. A simple demonstration will show how this works.

1. You already have one application running on your desktop: the Command Shell. Now, go down to the pager and click on the lower left quarter. The Command Shell disappears.

2. Open the Desktop Menu by clicking on a blank area of the desktop and holding down the left mouse button. Go down to Utilities, and over and down to File Manager (FileRunner). TurboDesk FileRunner appears—a program with many of the functions of Windows Explorer.

3. Now, go down to the pager and click on the lower right quarter. The file manager disappears.

4. Click on Wharf's Program button again, and on the Netscape icon.

5. In order to click on the Accept button for the license agreement, you may have to minimize the Dwarf. Once you accept the license, Netscape fills the screen.

6. Maximize the Dwarf, and click on the upper right quarter of the pager.

7. Click on the Wharf's Utilities button, and on the CD Player icon.

8. Now click on all four quarters of the pager in turn.

The pager is your real desktop. Using the pager in this way, you can work in X Window exactly as if you had your work arranged on separate areas of your real desk—if your real desk were big enough.

There are two ways to move from one area of the desktop to another. One is to click on different parts of the pager, as you've been doing. The other is to simply move the mouse pointer in the direction of the area of desktop you want to move to, and continue on past the border.

Figure 15-3
Internet On Settings
in Edit App Settings
Window

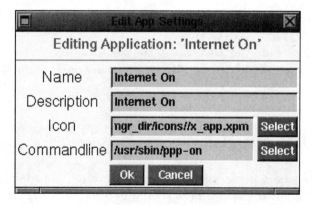

Adding Internet Menu Items to the Application Launcher

Two very useful menu items to have in your Application Launcher are Internet On and Internet Off. If you're using the Internet connection scripts you learned in Chapter 11, then you can create the menu items using the Edit App Settings shown in Figures 15-3 and 15-4.

Figure 15-4
Internet Off Settings
in Edit App Settings
Window

Edit App Settings

Editing Application: 'Internet Off'

Name	Internet Off
Description	Internet Off
Icon	ngr_dir/icons//x_app.xpm Select
Commandline	/usr/sbin/ppp-off Select

Ok   Cancel

File Managers

TurboDesk has two file managers—one very simple to use but somewhat limited, and the other function-rich but complex.

To access the simple file manager, click on the Utilities button on Wharf, and then on the File Manager button. The program that comes up (Figure 15-5) has the basic functionality needed for copy and paste jobs, and to open files by automatically activating the necessary application programs.

To access the more complex file manager, click on the desktop and bring up the Desktop Menu, and then go down to Utilities and over and down to File Manager (FileRunner).

Figure 15-5
Window of
TurboLinux's Simple
File Manager

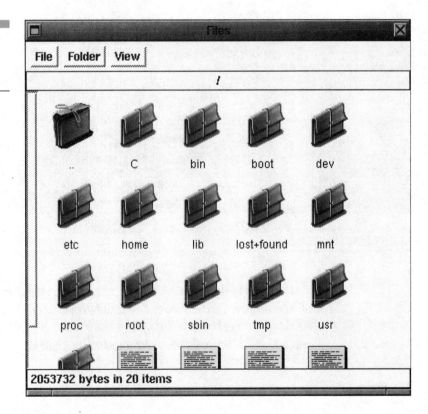

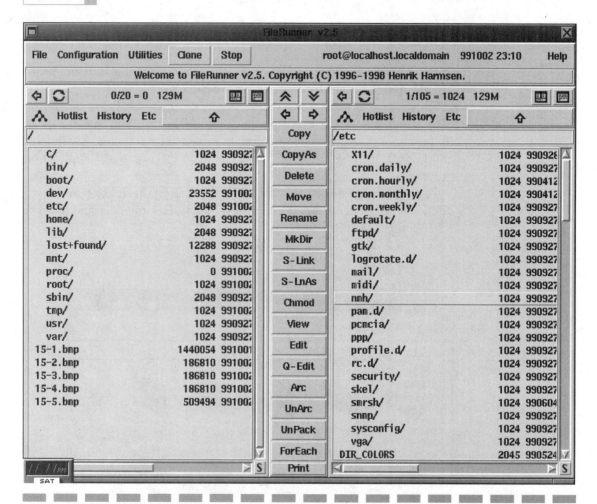

Figure 15-6   FileRunner Window

FileRunner (Figure 15-6) is the richest, most interesting, and most complex file manager in the Linux X Window repertory. It is perhaps slightly over-rich for some, but will repay the time spent learning its operation.

Log out of TurboDesk by bringing up the Desktop Menu, and moving over to Quit from TurboLinux.

Productivity: E-Mail and the Web; Office Suites and Graphics

This is the crux of the matter: getting work done in Linux in about the same way you do in Windows—but without the lockups, general protection faults, out of memory messages, etc.

For current users of Netscape for Web browsing and e-mail: good news! The same program is available in Linux, and works just as well—without bringing down the operating system, as it does too often in Windows.

For current users of MS Office—good news as well. StarOffice is a serious contender, boasting a Word-style word processor, Excel-style spreadsheet program, and PowerPoint-style presentation program—for free! It has filters that support the import and export of Microsoft files. And, with its recent purchase by Sun Microsystems, it has the financial, programming, and marketing muscle of a giant behind it, to ensure further development. Finally, Corel has ported its Windows word processor, Word Perfect—a very refined product—to Linux.

The material in Chapters 18 through 20, devoted to StarOffice, is conceived as one large learning unit, the point being to not only demonstrate how to use each program, but how to use all three together.

## CHAPTER 16

E-Mail and the Web: Netscape Configuration and Use

Purpose of Chapter: To Configure and Use Netscape for E-Mail

The two major web browsers, Netscape Navigator and Windows Explorer, may still be doing battle in Windows, but in Linux there's only one contender: Netscape. As anyone who has used both will know, there is little practical difference between the two—except that Netscape comes complete with an e-mail client that is faster and more intuitive to use than Outlook.

Since all Linux distributions now come complete with the latest version of Netscape preinstalled, we are spared an installation chapter. E-mail configuration, fortunately, is also quite simple—it is in fact identical to configuring Netscape in Windows.

Configuring Netscape for E-Mail

This operation is exactly the same in Linux as it is in Windows—and the information you need to do it is the same, as well. I advise you to first boot up to Windows, and obtain from your e-mail client there—Netscape, Outlook, Eudora, whatever—the information you'll need.

Required Information

You should first obtain the following information:

1. Your incoming mail server. This will probably start with pop.
2. Your outgoing mail server. This will probably start with smtp.
3. Your user name.
4. Your e-mail address.
5. Your e-mail password.

Configuring Communicator

1. First, start up Netscape by clicking on its menu item.
2. Accept the license provisions, etc.
3. The opening screen will be different depending on the distribution you are using; Figure 16-1 shows the opening screen in Red Hat. The first screen you see may or may not be maximized, and when you do maximize it, it may not fit the screen very well. I advise you to first maximize it, and then, using the handles at the bottom right or left corners, reduce its size slightly.
4. Now click on Edit on the Menu Bar, and on Preferences. You should see a screen very similar to Figure 16-2.
5. In the left panel, click on the small triangle next to Mail & Newsgroups, and then on Identity. You have only to fill in the Your name and Email address sections, as in Figure 16-3. Then click on Mail Servers, just below Identity in the left panel.
6. Under Incoming Mail Servers in the center panel, click on pop, and then click on the Edit button.

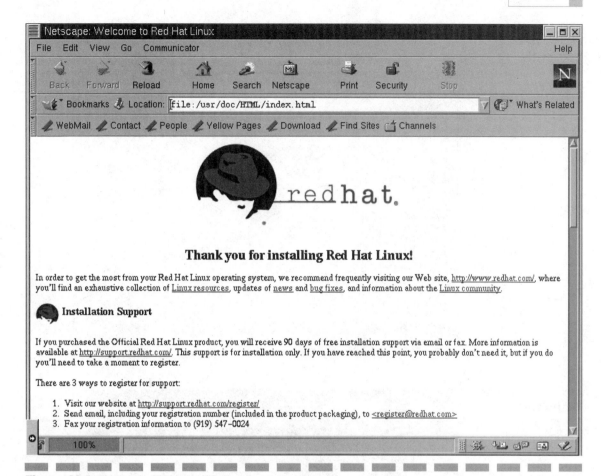

Figure 16-1 Netscape Welcome Window

7. In the window that appears, type in your pop incoming server name, and below it your user name. Make sure to check the Remember password box. An example of how to fill out this window is in Figure 16-4, but your settings, of course, will be different.

8. When you're finished, click on the OK button, and then again on the OK button in the lower left.

And that's it for configuring your e-mail in Netscape. It's a pretty straightforward process.

Figure 16-2
Preferences
Window—
Appearance

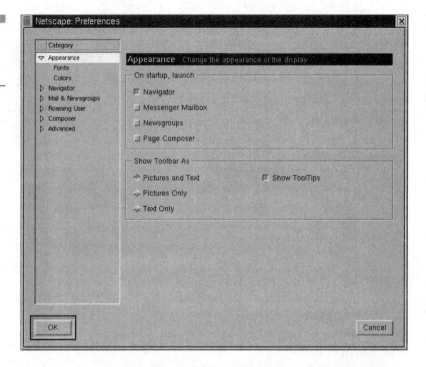

Figure 16-3
Preferences
Window—Identity

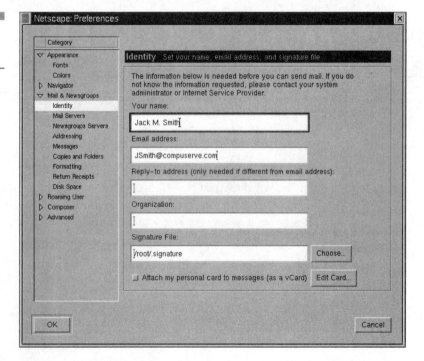

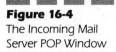

Figure 16-4
The Incoming Mail
Server POP Window

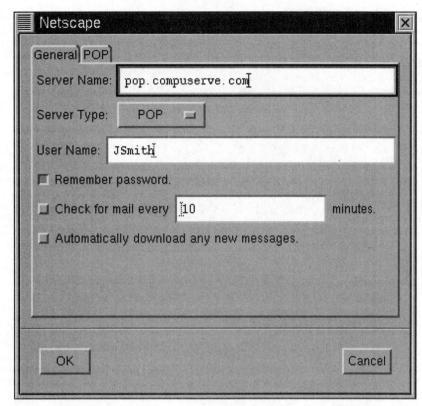

Downloading Mail

1. Log on to the Internet, using the script you wrote in Chapter 11, and the icon you made in Part 3.

2. Click either on the letter-slot icon in the lower right hand side of the main Netscape window, or Communicator on the Menu Bar, and then on Messenger.

3. Click on the Get Msg icon on the Tool Bar. Since this is the first time you have used Netscape Messenger in Linux, you get a password prompt box. Type in your e-mail password (Figure 16-5).

4. Click on the OK button.

5. Netscape proceeds to download your mail

But what about all your old addresses, and even your old mail, back in Windows? Do you have to laboriously enter in all those addresses?

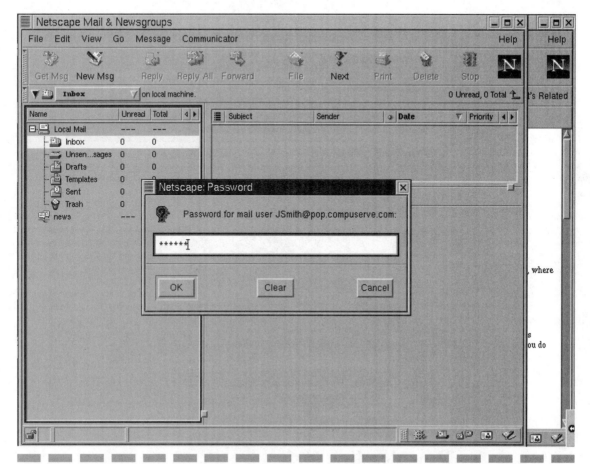

Figure 16-5   Prompting for a Password

You may not have to. As long as you were using Netscape in Windows, you can copy over both your addresses and your old mail.

Importing Mail from Windows

1. First, logout of Linux and reboot into Windows.
2. Open up Windows Explorer.
3. Burrow down on your main Windows partition to: Program Files/Netscape/Users/YourName/Mail. In this subdirectory, you'll see a list of files similar to Figure 16-6. Your mail is composed of every file *without* an extension.

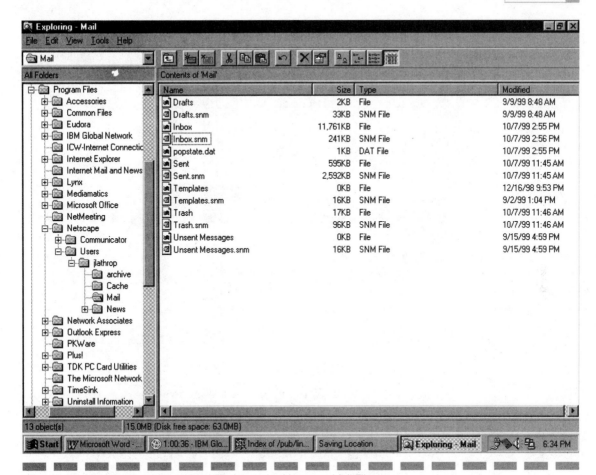

Figure 16-6   Exploring Mail within Windows: the Netscape Mail Files

4. Now, reboot into Linux.

5. Mount your C partition (or whichever mountpoint your Windows partition is on).

6. Change directory to your Windows partition, and drill down to the same subdirectory you were in with Explorer.

7. Copy each file without an extension to the `/root/nsmail` directory.

That's it. Open up Netscape Messenger again, and click, one by one, on Inbox, Unsent Messages, Drafts, etc. They will all come up on your window.

Figure 16-7
Exporting an Address
Book: Netscape in
Windows

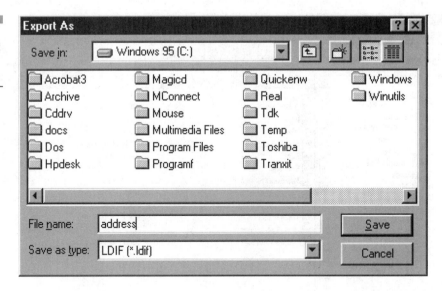

Importing Your Address Book from Windows

This is also quite simple—as long as you were using Netscape in Windows.

1. First, logout of Linux and reboot into Windows.

2. Open up Netscape Navigator in Windows, click on Communicator in the Menu Bar, and on Address Book.

3. Now, click on File on the Menu Bar, and on Export. An Export As window appears.

4. Navigate up the directory tree until you reach the C drive. In the File Name blank, type:

   `address`

   and hit the Save button (Figure 16-7).

5. Now, reboot into Linux, and mount your Windows partition.

6. Open up Netscape Navigator, click on Communicator in the Menu Bar, and on Address Book.

7. Click on File on the Menu Bar, and on Import.

8. Find the file `address.ldif`, select it, and hit the OK button.

You've just migrated your entire address book.

17

StarOffice Installation and Configuration

Purpose of Chapter: Installing and Configuring the StarOffice Applications Suite

StarOffice is the office productivity suite, including a word processor, a spreadsheet program, a presentation program, and even an e-mail client, that enables most people to be as productive in Linux as they normally are in Windows. This is a major package, both rivaling its competitor, MS Office, and also compatible with it; file transfers, through Star's converters, are the best in the business. Should you move to Linux, you will probably wind up spending most of your time in Star.

The suite is available through three channels: as a free and very large download, bundled free with a distribution, or bought with a support package and documentation from the manufacturer.

This chapter is divided into three parts: installation, covering the methods used when installing from a bundled CD and from the manufacturer's CD; setup; and configuration.

StarOffice Installation

All major distributions except TurboLinux 3.6 come with StarOffice bundled on a separate CD. The installation routines are straightforward and differ only slightly. I'll first cover the bundled routines and then installation via the manufacturer's CD.

Installing StarOffice in Red Hat Linux

In the latest Red Hat (6.1), StarOffice is now included on its own CD, with the logo of Sun Microsystems. The installation procedure is now much simpler than before.

1. First, start up X Window.

2. Second, insert the Sun CD into the CD-ROM. With the latest version of Gnome, the CD-ROM is automatically mounted as soon as you insert a CD. At the same time, the File Manager will come up on the screen (Figure 17-1).

3. Next, in the File Manager, click on the + sign next to the mnt folder, then next to the cdrom folder, then the + sign next to the linux folder, and finally click on the office51 folder.

4. In the right pane of the File Manager, scroll down until you come to the icon of a piston, titled, setup (Figure 17-2).

5. Double click on the setup icon.

6. Sit back while the installation starts. It may take several moments.

Now skip ahead to step 5 of the StarOffice Setup section, on page 211.

Installing StarOffice in Caldera

In Caldera, StarOffice is on the Windows Tools & Commercial Packages CD. Caldera has its own installation method, which may not work—it is somewhat buggy. I'll first give Caldera's suggested installation method, then an alternative.

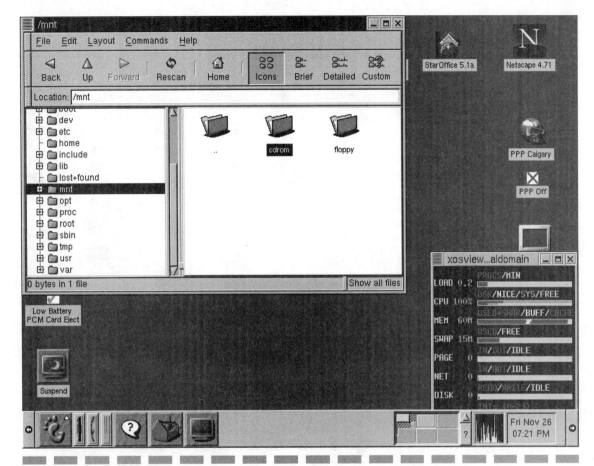

Figure 17-1 Gnome File Manager

Caldera's Suggested Method

1. Start up X Window in Caldera by typing:

   kde

   and pressing Enter.

2. Click on the Start button (the icon with the large K), go up to COAS, and over and down. Click on Commercial Products. A screen similar to Figure 17-3 appears.

3. Follow the directions. Insert the CD and click on the link.

4. Select the StarOffice 5.1 office suite, the language, etc. When you get to the kpackage window, click on Install.

Figure 17-2
StarOffice Setup Icon

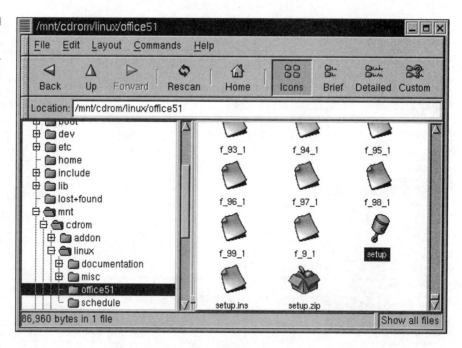

Figure 17-3
Commercial Products Unit

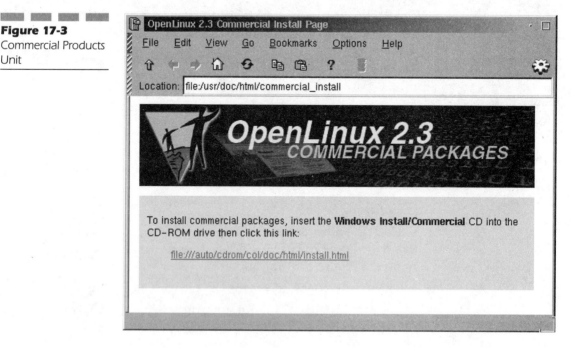

This is the recommended method. However, when you click on the link in Figure 17-3, it may give you an error message instead of installation instructions. In that case, you will have to install it using the alternative method below.

Alternative Method

1. Click on the Terminal Emulation icon at the bottom of the screen.
2. In the terminal window, type:

   ```
   mount /mnt/cdrom
   ```

   and press Enter.
3. Click on the file folder icon at the bottom of the screen.
4. Click on the up arrow icon on the toolbar, until you see folders for the usual root-level directories. Double-click on the mnt and the cdrom folders.
5. Double-click on the Packages folder, and then on the RPMS folder. You should now see a display of icons for several different commercial packages, including several different language versions of StarOffice (Figure 17-4).

Figure 17-4
StarOffice Icons in Caldera

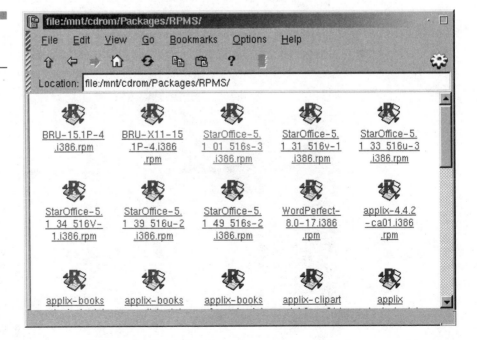

6. The different language versions are not clearly identified. The English version is the first icon reading from the left: `StarOffice-5.1_01_516s-3`. Click on it once. The `kpackage` window will appear (Figure 17-5).

7. Click on the Install button at the lower left.

Once the installation is finished, close down all windows. The program is installed, but it still needs to be set up. Skip ahead to the StarOffice Setup and Configuration sections.

Installing StarOffice via the StarOffice CD

This is the method used if you're running a distribution that doesn't come with the program bundled, or if you buy a more current version from the manufacturer. (NOTE: The instructions below cover the latest CD manufactured by StarDivision. Sun Microsystems recently bought Star. Sun is still offering free downloads, as well as selling the CD version—for a lower price, as of now, than the former owner! The following installation instructions are current as of going to press.)

Figure 17-5

kpackage Window, Showing StarOffice 5.1 Package Information

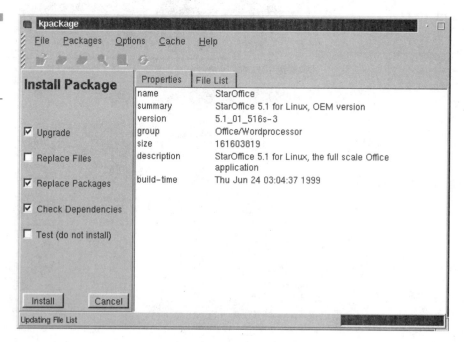

1. Insert the Star CD.
2. Start up X Window, and open a terminal window.
3. In the terminal window, mount the CD-ROM.
4. Change directory to:

   `/mnt/cdrom/linux/office51`

5. Type:

   `./setup`

   and press Enter.

The rest of the installation routine is identical to the following setup routine. Start at step 5 in the StarOffice Setup section, below.

StarOffice Setup

The setup procedure is identical in all distributions.

1. Begin the setup by opening a terminal window within X Window.
2. Within the terminal window, change directory to `/opt/Office51/bin` by typing:

   `cd /opt/Office51/bin`

   and hitting Enter.
3. Now, type:

   `ls`

   and hit Enter.
4. You'll see a number of files and directories that the StarOffice installation routine added. You're interested in the `setup` file. Type:

   `./setup`

   and hit Enter (Figure 17-6).
5. The Welcome to the Installation Program screen comes up (Figure 17-7). Click on the Next button.
6. The Enter the Key Code screen comes up (Figure 17-8). Your key could be on the cover of your application CD slipcover, or inside the front cover of your Linux documentation. If you're installing this at work, your system administrator will probably give it to you. Enter it in the blank, and click on Next.

Figure 17-6
Entering the
./setup Command
at the Terminal
Window

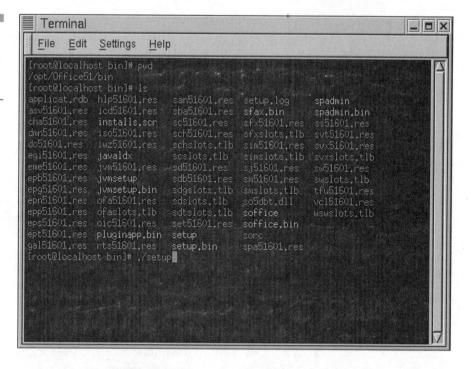

Figure 17-7
The Installation
Welcome Screen

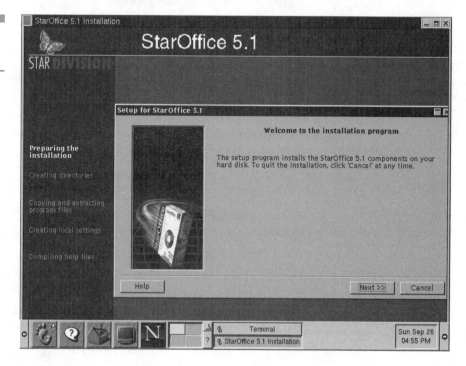

Figure 17-8
The Enter Key Code
Screen

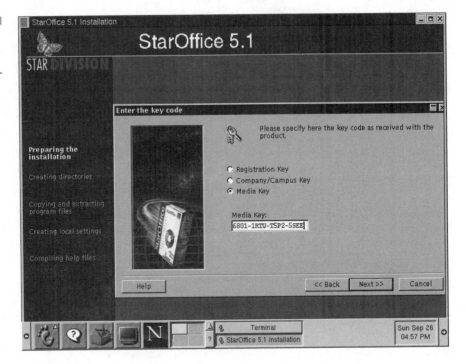

7. The Enter User Data screen comes up. This is the data that will be used to register your copy of the software. Fill in the blanks, and click on Next. A number of license screens and so forth appear. Accept them all.

8. The Select Installation Type appears (Figure 17-9). Since you are installing this on your hard drive, make sure to choose Standard Installation (local), and click on Next again.

9. The Select Installation Directory comes up. You can accept the default directory, /root/Office51, or choose to create another. Just make sure you don't choose the current directory—the installation would fail. When you're finished, click on the Next button.

10. Click on the Complete button, on the OK button at the JAVA window, and sit back and let the setup program work. When it's finished, click on the various OK and Complete buttons, and you'll be back at the terminal window.

11. Restart your desktop—note that you do not have to restart your operating system! This isn't Windows!

Figure 17-9
Select Installation
Type

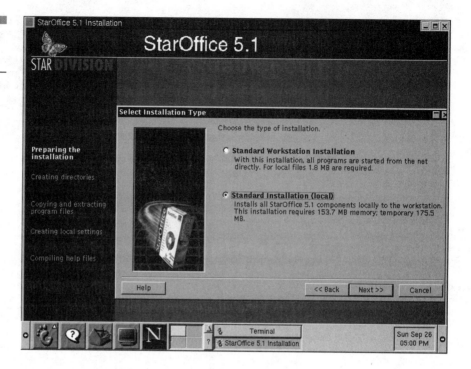

StarOffice Configuration

Configuring StarOffice proceeds in four steps: adding Star icons to the start menus and desktops (if desired); first startup and Internet configuration; registration; and finally, initial configuration of the Star environment.

Adding Icons to the Menus and Desktop

Caldera's KDE desktop automatically adds icons for Star to the Personal Menu. However, users of other distributions will have to manually add a Star icon to their menus and desktops (not a difficult procedure).

Inserting StarOffice in Red Hat's Applications Menu

1. Click on the Start button (the footprint icon), go up to Settings, over and down, and click on the Menu editor.
2. The Menu editor will open up. Click on the Applications folder in the left panel, and then on the New Item icon on the toolbar.

3. Fill in the Name and Command blanks according to Figure 17-10.

4. Now click on the Icon button in the middle of the window.

5. Click on the Browse button in the upper right hand corner of the Icon window.

6. In the Choose an Icon window, double-click on the `..`/ symbol in the Directories panel, until you get up to the `root` directory. Then click on `opt`, and then on `so51`.

7. Use the vertical scrollbar on the right hand side of the Files panel to get to the bottom of the file list, and click on `s_office.xpm`. You'll see a very small icon somewhat resembling a house with a high-pitched roof. This is the StarOffice icon.

8. Click on the OK button.

9. Now click on the Save button, and close the Gnome Menu Editor.

Inserting a StarOffice Icon on Red Hat's Desktop   This is a very simple procedure.

Figure 17-10
StarOffice Settings in the Gnome Menu Editor's New Item Window

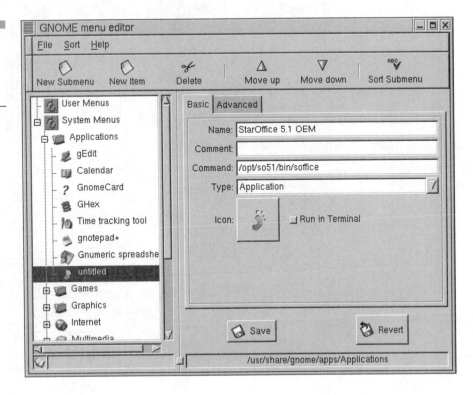

1. Click on the Start button, go up to Applications, and over and down to the StarOffice 5.1 icon.

2. Holding the left mouse button down on the StarOffice icon, move it to the region of the desktop where you'd like it to appear.

3. Release the mouse button. The icon appears. Unfortunately, the picture is tiny—we have to insert the larger one.

4. Click on the icon with your right mouse button, and on the Properties menu item.

5. Click on the Options tab, and on the Icon button.

6. Double-click on the larger of the two icons. Your screen should now resemble Figure 17-11.

7. Click on the OK button.

Figure 17-11
StarOffice Desktop
Properties Window,
with Large Icon

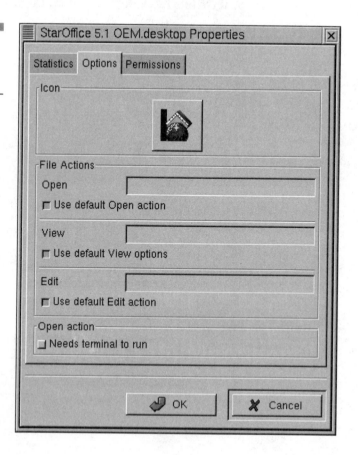

Inserting StarOffice into TurboLinux's Desktop Menu

1. Bring up the desktop menu by placing the mouse pointer in the middle of the screen and holding down the left button.

2. Highlight TurboLinux, and move over and down to TurboDesk Control panel.

3. Click on TurboDesk Control panel.

4. Click on User Tools. The TurboDesk Control panel should now look like Figure 17-12.

5. Double-click on the arrow next to Pull-Down Menu Editor.

6. You'll see a directory tree for the Desktop Menu. Double-click on Applications.

7. The Edit Pull-Down Menu window appears. Click on the Add Element bar.

8. The Add Menu Element window now appears. Click on the Command Line button, and fill in the blanks as shown in Figure 17-13. Then click on the OK button.

9. Double-click on Save & Exit, and close down the various windows.

10. Restart X Window. You will find StarOffice under Applications in the Desktop Menu.

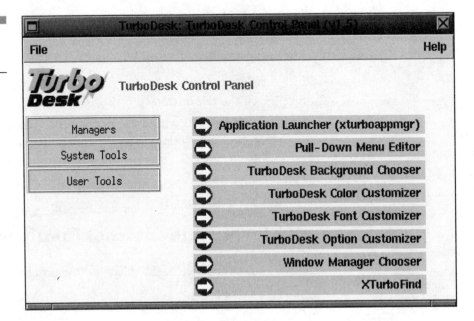

Figure 17-12
TurboDesk
Control Panel

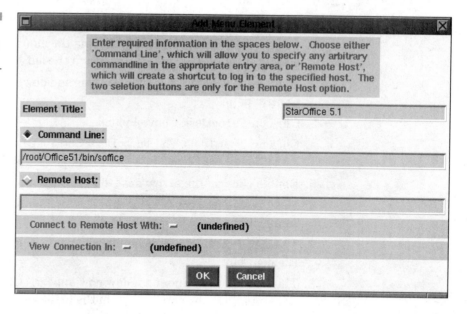

Figure 17-13
Add Menu Item, with
Entries for StarOffice

Inserting StarOffice into TurboLinux's Applications Launcher

1. Click on the Applications button of the Applications Launcher.
2. With the mouse pointer anywhere in the pop-up menu, click with the right mouse button.
3. Click on Add New App.
4. Type in the blank:

   `StarOffice 5.1`

   and click on the OK button.
5. The Edit App Settings window appears. Enter the information in the Command Line section, as in Figure 17-14. Then double-click the OK button.

StarOffice is now added to the Applications Launcher.

First Startup and Internet Configuration

1. Click on the StarOffice desktop icon or menu item—whichever your distribution has.

Figure 17-14
Command Line
Settings in the Edit
App Settings Window

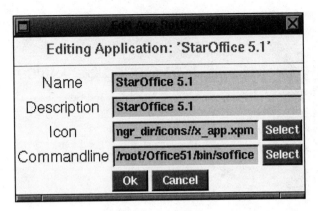

Figure 17-14
Command Line
Settings in the Edit
App Settings Window

2. The first thing that starts is the Internet Setup Pilot. This has nothing to do with the operating system, or with Netscape Communicator. However, it will make registering your software (absolutely necessary with StarOffice) much easier. Click on the Next button.

3. Ignore the proxy server (unless you have one). Click on Next again.

4. The e-mail settings are important. Type in your receiving (POP) server name and your sending server (SMTP) name. Include your user name and password. Enter the same information that you used to configure your e-mail in Netscape. Continue clicking on the Next and Create buttons until the Setup Pilot is finished.

5. When you have finished, the StarOffice desktop will fill the screen, with a welcome message in the lower panel. To eliminate this bottom window, check the Don't display tips box in the lower left hand corner and then click on the small down arrow button on the upper left hand side of the panel's border.

Registration

This is absolutely necessary! Even if you bought your copy, it will expire in 30 days without registration.

1. Click on Help on the Menu bar, then on Registration. The initial registration screen appears (Figure 17-15). Online registration is the simplest and fastest method. Connect to the Internet, and then click on the underlined Online Registration.

Figure 17-15
Initial Registration
Screen

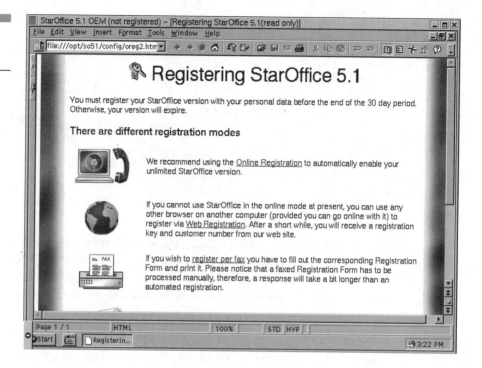

2. You'll be taken to a screen showing all the personal information you earlier entered. Click on the Submit Data button.

3. Presently, your first e-mail message will appear on the screen—from StarDivision—informing you that you have successfully registered the product. If you ever need to read this message again, it will be in StarOffice's Inbox.

Initial Configuration of the Star Environment

The initial desktop, after registration and closing out the welcome windows, will appear similar to Figure 17-16. StarOffice is capable of almost endless customization. However, to begin with, the printer, user data, saving, and paths are the most important elements to configure.

The Printer   Click on the Printer Setup icon on the Star desktop. The Printer Installation window (Figure 17-17) will appear.

Printing is Star's one great weak spot. StarOffice uses its own printer drivers, but every one of them up to now is for a PostScript printer. The

Figure 17-16
Initial StarOffice
Desktop

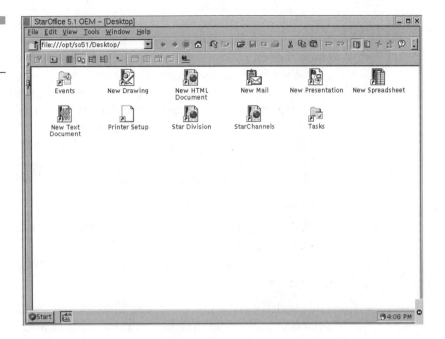

Figure 17-17
Printer Installation
Window

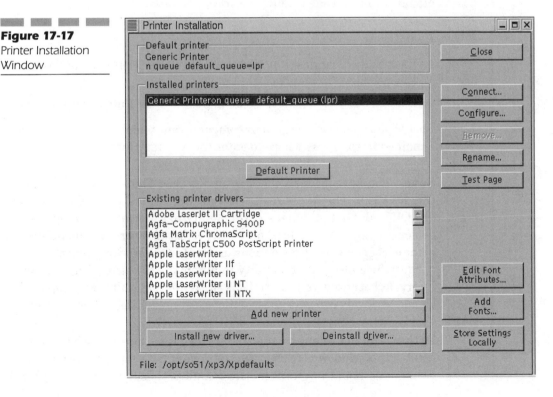

vast majority of printers on the market, however, are not PostScript. Linux gets around this by using a converter program called GhostScript to print these files on unsupported printers. This process is completely transparent—there's no setup required. But as a result of this conversion step, printing in Star, most of the time, is slower than printing in Windows.

If you have a printer listed in the Existing Printer Drivers panel (Figure 17-17), you should choose it and test it out. But if your printer is not included, you should probably stick with the default driver in the panel under Installed Drivers.

First check the configuration, and then test the driver.

1. Click on the Configure button.

2. Make sure that Paper Size, Orientation, and Resolution match your own printer.

3. Click on the OK button, and then on the Test Page button. Save your settings when prompted.

The resulting test sheet is self-explanatory and should be acceptable. The default printer driver—a generic driver—should work. If it doesn't, try others until you find one that does work.

User Data

1. Back at the Star desktop, click on Tools on the Menu bar, and then on Options.

2. Click on the + sign next to General, then on User Data (Figure 17-18).

Should you move or change your company, your telephone number, or your e-mail address, this is where to enter the new information.

Save The next item on the tree under User Data is Save. Click on it (Figure 17-19). One of the really convenient features of StarOffice—which MS Office doesn't yet offer—is the ability to automatically reopen every document you were working on when restarting Star. You should make a point of checking all three options under Restore Working View.

StarOffice also has the ability to automatically save your work at an interval chosen by you, as well as make automatic backup copies. You should seriously consider these options, especially the automatic save.

Paths The next item on the tree under User Data is Paths. The main point of this window is to change your default path for opening and saving documents should you want to. The default path is the subdirectory work,

Figure 17-18
User Data, under
Tools, Options,
General

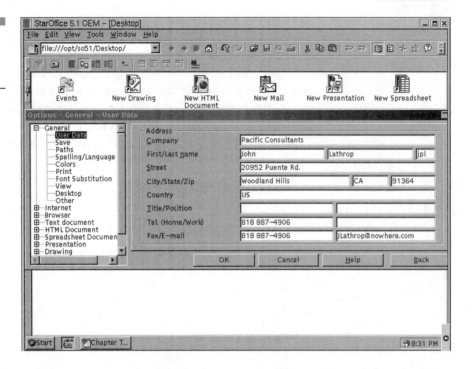

Figure 17-19
Save Options

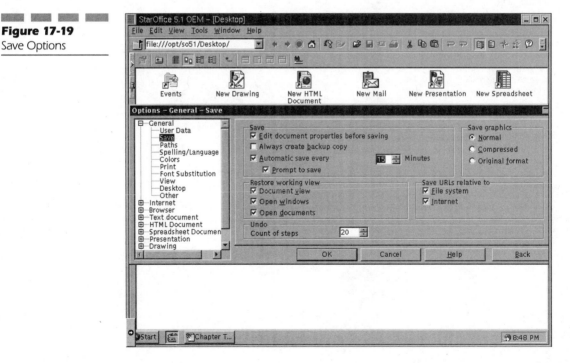

under the main StarOffice program directory. In other words, if the program were installed into /opt/so51, your default directory for opening and saving documents would be /opt/so51/work—quite a ways to drill down should you want to quickly reach a document outside of the program.

You can simplify this by scrolling down to the last directory in the Default panel, and changing the path of the Work Folder to something more accessible—perhaps, /My Documents.

Now, to begin the StarOffice tutorial, turn to Chapter 18.

Word Processing with StarWriter

Purpose of Chapter:
To Create Professional Quality Documents Using StarWriter

The word processor from StarDivision is very close in feel and in basic feature set to its main competitor from Microsoft. The fundamental "paradigms" are identical, even many minor points are practically identical, and editing in StarWriter is actually faster than in Word. Compatibility with MS Word is assured through some of the best conversion filters in the business.

This chapter is divided into three major sections:

1. A Familiar Environment

2. Fundamentals

3. Proficiency

Sections 2 and 3 are presented in the form of lessons and exercises.

A Familiar Environment: StarWriter's Desktop

The StarWriter environment, from the appearance of most tool and menu bars, to the mechanics of document creation, editing, and formatting, to advanced features, is familiar to any user of Word. Although some features are in slightly different places, nearly all the old familiar things are there—and immediately recognizable.

A Tour of StarWriter

Open the program by double-clicking on the New Text Document icon on the StarOffice desktop. Figure 18-1 shows the text editing screen as it will typically appear after installation—notice that the X Window toolbar, or panel, at the bottom of the screen, has been moved out of the way.

This standard or default environment has all the features you would expect in a Windows word processor. At the top of the screen is a horizontal

Figure 18-1
Initial New
Document Text
Editing Screen

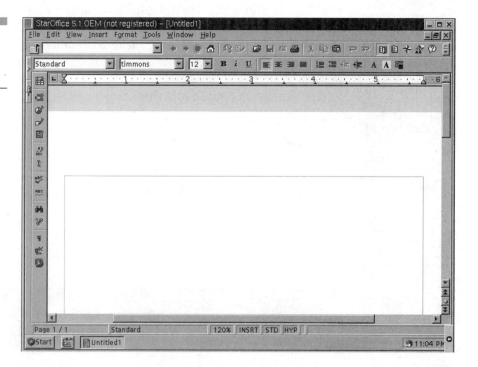

ruler; above that appears the Formatting Toolbar (called the Object Bar in StarWriter—the Windows name is better), and above that the Standard Toolbar (called the Function Bar in Star). The Menu Bar and the Title Bar take up their usual places at the top of the screen.

Along the left side of the screen is a third bar, called in Star the Main Toolbar. Some of its icons are familiar, such as the Speller, but in general most of the icons we see on the Main Toolbar would be in either menus or other toolbars in Word. Vertical and horizontal scrollbars surround the other two sides of the screen.

Most of the icons on the top two toolbars are sufficiently like their counterparts in other word processors to need no explanation. However, the icons and their behavior on the Main Toolbar deserve a little of our attention.

The Main Toolbar   Several of the icons on the Main Toolbar would be more familiar to us if they were up on the Standard Toolbar (the long Load URL box on Star's Standard Toolbar is the interloper that has stolen these icons' usual territory).

Starting from the bottom, the most commonly useful icons are:

1. The Search On/Off icon. Clicking on this brings up the familiar Search & Replace.
2. The Spelling icon. Clicking on this starts up the Speller.
3. The Show Draw Functions icon. Note that clicking on this brings up the Drawing Toolbar (in place of the Formatting Toolbar), and holding down the left mouse button on this icon brings out a new drawing toolbar, from which you can choose the shape or type of line that you want to draw.
4. The Insert Fields icon. Clicking on this brings up a new menu, with standard fields such as Date, Time, Page Numbers, etc.
5. The Insert icon. Clicking on this brings up a new toolbar, with such insert items as Frames, Pictures, Tables, and Columns.

All of these functions are also available from the drop-down menus of the Menu Bar at the top of the screen.

Different Desktop Configurations

The two things to consider when deciding on a desktop configuration are: the number of toolbars and other "shortcut" items that you want available, and how many nonprinting characters and fields you want visible on the editing screen.

Two schools of thought conflict. One, older and declining in influence, urges a clean, uncluttered editing area. The other wants every possible shortcut tool and toolbar surrounding an increasingly marginalized editing window. It is to Star's credit that there are limits to how far you can take the second approach within their word processor.

Two example of desktops are shown in Figures 18-2 (cluttered), and 18-3 (clean). The clean example can be carried to its logical extreme by clicking on View on the Menu Bar, and on Full Screen. Should you try this experiment, you can return the menu bars, etc., simply by clicking on the icon in the upper left hand corner of the screen.

By checking the appropriate items on the View Menu, you can change the number of fields and nonprinting characters that appear on the screen.

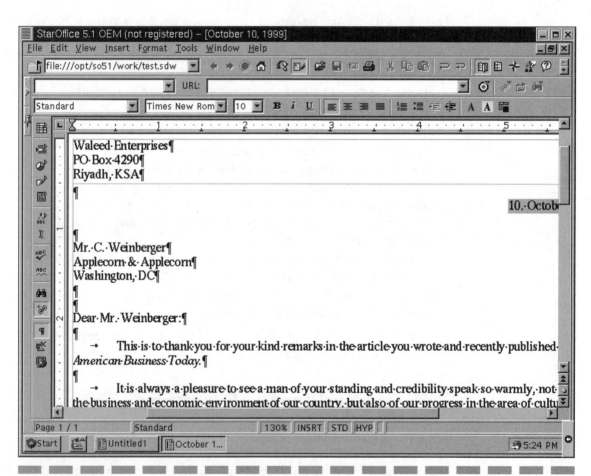

Figure 18-2   A Graphically Enabled (Cluttered) Desktop

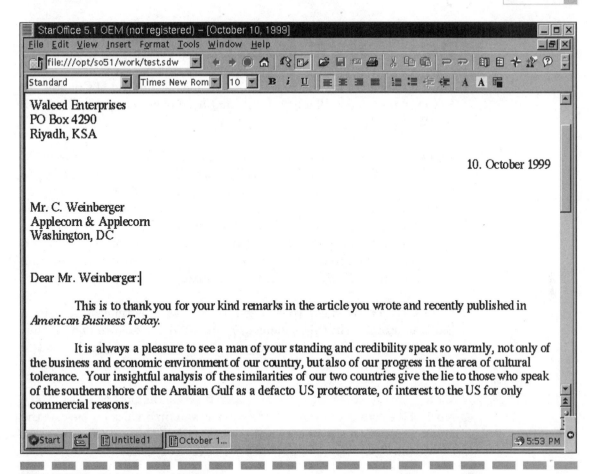

Figure 18-3 An Uncluttered Desktop

By clicking on Toolbars in the same menu, you choose which toolbars to make visible.

You can increase the number of rulers and scroll bars and boundary lines by choosing Tools on the Menu Bar, Options, and Layout under Text Document.

Fundamentals

These are the basics—from printer setup and page layout to importing graphics—that everyone needs to know to get going.

Lesson 1: Basic Configuration—Printer Setup, Page Layout, View, and Options

Most of the basic setup in StarOffice was done at the end of Chapter 17. However, there are still a few things that need to be set up specifically in StarWriter.

Printer Setup   Although the printer was set up at the StarOffice desktop shortly after installation, not all the settings may have migrated to StarWriter. Click on File on the Menu Bar, and on Printer Setup. The printer name shown in the Printer Setup window should be the same as the one you set up before. Click on the Properties bar.

The Printer Settings window (Figure 18-4) pops up next. Make sure you have the paper set to Letter if you're in the United States or Canada, and A4 in the United Kingdom. When you're finished, click on the OK button.

Page Layout   To check your page layout, click on Format on the Menu Bar, and on Page. In this window (Figure 18-5), make sure (again) that your printer settings are correct, and also that your margins are set to your preference.

View   This refers to the familiar "zoom" function that lets you decide how much of the screen you want on the window at a time. Click on View on the Menu Bar, and on Zoom. From the window that appears (Figure 18-6), choose the figure you're happy with—it pays to experiment.

Figure 18-4
The Printer Settings Window

Printer Settings	
Printer properties	
Paper	Letter
Orientation	PORTRAIT
Paper tray	Autotray
Duplex printing	<default>
Postscript Level	2
Scale	100
Editing Bitmaps	
Color	Color
Depth	24
	☐ Compress

OK   Cancel

Figure 18-5
Page Layout

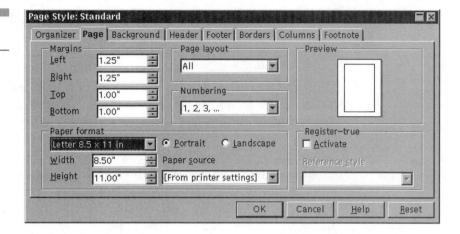

Figure 18-5
Page Layout

Text Document Options It's also a good idea to check your text-specific options by clicking on Tools on the Menu Bar, on Options, and Text Document. Layout is a good place to check tab stops and measurement units, as well as some additional nonprinting characters mentioned earlier. Further down, clicking on Standard Fonts lets you choose the default selection you prefer—Times for Standard and Helvetica for Headings are safe choices.

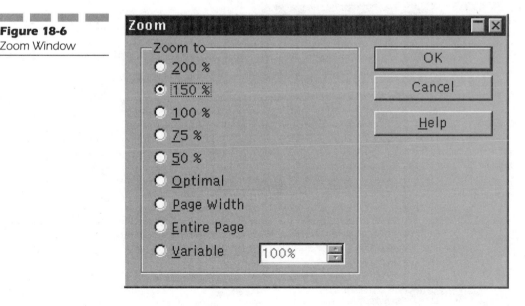

Figure 18-6
Zoom Window

Lesson 2: Document Creation and Saving

Every time you open up StarWriter by clicking on the New Text Document icon on the StarOffice desktop, you automatically open up a new document. The StarOffice desktop icon is always visible in the lower left hand corner of the screen; clicking on it takes you back to the desktop, and clicking again on the New Text icon will open up a new window—and a new document.

Alternatively, you can click on StarOffice's Start button on the lower left hand corner of the screen—if the Gnome or KDE panel is moved out of the way. Clicking on the Start button brings up StarOffice's own Start Menu (Figure 18-7). At the top, click on Text Document, or click on File on the Menu Bar, on New, and press the t key.

Any way you do it, you will notice not one but two document buttons on the bottom of your screen, Untitled1 and Untitled2. More on this presently.

But, have you really created a new document? Not really. You have created a new document editing window. Technically, a new document is not created until you save the contents of that window as a file—a document. To try this out, type a few words, and then click on the Save Document icon—the familiar floppy disk—on the Main Toolbar.

The Save As window comes up the first time you save any document. Click on the Save button. Alternatively, click on File on the Menu Bar, and

Figure 18-7
StarOffice Start Menu

on Save. For subsequent saves of the same document, the Save As window will not appear unless you purposely choose it from the Menu Bar.

Lesson 3: Document Retrieving and Printing

The fastest way to open a document is by clicking on the Open File icon (the open folder) on the Toolbar. This brings up the Open window—identical to the Save As window. Click on the file you wish to retrieve, and then on the Open Bar. Alternatively, you can use the Menu Bar and click on Open there.

Other methods are to click on the recently opened files list at the bottom of the File menu, or on the Load URL button on the Toolbar.

To print your file, simply click on the printer icon on the Toolbar. Alternatively, click on File on the Menu Bar, on Print, and on OK. This second method gives you a number of choices: whether to print the whole document, a range of pages, or only certain pages; the number of copies; and other options.

Lesson 4: File Manipulation: Renaming, Deleting, and Changing Locations

StarOffice, through its Desktop and Explorer features, offers a variety of ways to manipulate files—it is, in fact, its own file manager. However, there is little point in reinventing the wheel. Concentrating on StarWriter alone, there are very simple and very familiar ways to rename, delete, and change the save and retrieve locations.

Renaming and Deleting Files To rename a file, click either on the Open icon on the Toolbar, or choose Save As under File on the Menu Bar. In both cases, the same window comes up—just with a different name. Click with your right hand mouse button on your file, and then on either Rename or Delete (when you have finished typing in the new name, hit the Enter key).

Saving to a Different Location The three buttons on the right of the Open and Save As windows let you navigate to wherever you'd care to go in the file system. Two of the buttons work in a slightly different way from what you might expect. By clicking on the Up One Level button, you do go up one level, and the files and directories on view in the center window

change accordingly. However, if you click and hold the mouse button down
for just a moment, upon release another menu comes up, showing the
directories directly above the current path, as well as a complete picture of
primary directories available at the root level (Figure 18-8).

The Default Directory button, when clicked, takes you back to the
default save directory—a handy, time-saving device. However, when you
click and hold the mouse down for just a moment, as before, you can actually change the default save or open directory—although the change lasts
only during the current session.

The Create New Directory button lets you do just that, doing away
with the necessity of entering the StarOffice Desktop, the Explorer, the
Linux file manager, or the command line.

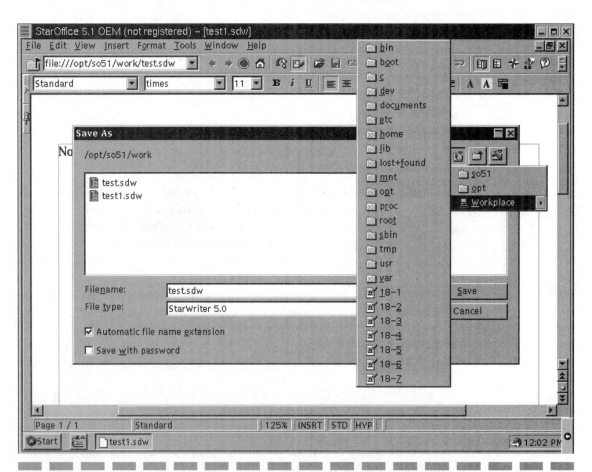

Figure 18-8   *The Up One Level Button Depressed, Showing Directory Tree and Root Level Directories*

Exercise 1: Creating, Saving, and Manipulating a File   Close down StarOffice. Reopen it, and open a new document. Type in your name, and save the document as test in the default directory. Type in your address under your name. Access the Save As window, and rename the file to Address. Resave it, this time in the /tmp directory.

Lesson 5: Star's Multiple Document Paradigm; Multiple Saving

Star's paradigm for working with multiple documents open at the same time is both more flexible than Word's, and also fundamentally different in one respect. In Star, you can both cascade and tile multiple documents horizontally or vertically through choosing the options under Window on the Menu Bar (Figure 18-9). But the major difference is that the documents are also listed as icons on the Task Bar at the very bottom of the screen. You can switch from one document to the other by simply clicking on the document's icon. This is a simple yet very useful innovation.

The Save All function is a handy timesaver. To save every open document you're working on, just click on File on the Menu Bar, and on Save All.

Lesson 6: Navigation and Editing; Copying and Pasting; Formatting and Tools

Navigation and editing techniques are identical to Star's two major competitors. In this case, as in so many others, proficiency or even ability in one leads to ability in all.

Navigation and Editing   You may scroll up or down a document by using the arrow keys, the Page Up and Page Down keys, or the scroll bars. You may jump to a variety of objects within a document by using the tiny Navigation button in the lower right hand corner of the screen.

Editing is accomplished by the usual backspace and delete methods, and also by selecting text with the mouse and applying to it the options found on the Formatting Toolbar. To replace a section or entire paragraph with new text, simply select it with the mouse, and type in the new text. If a multipage document must be changed in its entirety, use Edit on the Menu Bar to reach Select All.

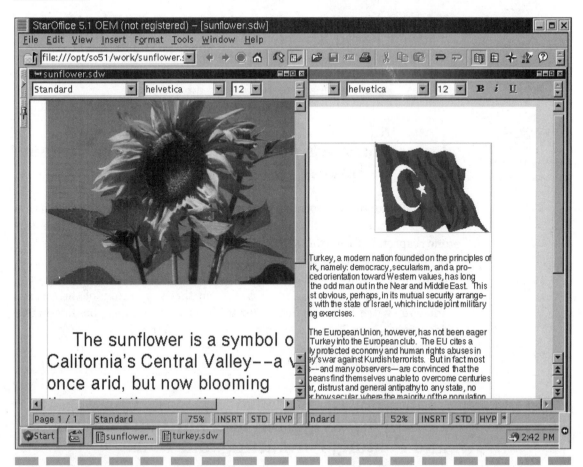

Figure 18-9 Multitasking: Vertical Tiling in StarWriter

Copying and Pasting A leading competitor recently remarked in a press release that Linux suffered from its applications not being linked together in an integral code by the same manufacturer. However, using the usual copy and paste techniques—even the usual copy and paste icons—you can cut or copy and paste text from and to StarWriter, and a Linux text editor such as gnotepad+, another word processor, such as Corel Word Perfect, or even your e-mail client, such as Netscape Messenger.

Formatting and Tools The standard formatting tools found on the Formatting Toolbar are augmented in the Character menu, under Format on the Menu Bar (Figure 18-10). A long list of paragraph formatting options, including indents and line spacing, alignment, and tabs and drop caps, are found in the Paragraph menu, also under Format.

Clicking on Tools on the Menu Bar gives three important writing and proofing tools: Spelling (including a manual and automatic spellchecker), a Thesaurus, and automatic Hyphenation.

Lesson 7: Insertions: Headers and Pictures

To insert a header, click on Insert on the Menu Bar, and then on Header. If you have the Text Boundaries option enabled, you will be able to see both the header boundaries and the text boundaries.

The formatting of headers is a little different in Star. To achieve a successful result, both the headers and the page margins—the top margin—must be formatted together. Fortunately, the controls for doing that are together in the Page Style window under Format on the Menu Bar.

You can insert a variety of clipart or photographs, or even a scanned image, into your document. Inserting charts, etc., is generally better done through the copy and paste method from StarCalc and StarImpress.

To insert a picture, click on Insert on the Menu Bar, on Picture, and then choose either From File or Scan. If you choose From File, you will be taken to the Insert Picture Window, which will open to /opt/so51/gallery. The subdirectories here contain everything from bullets to maps to a variety

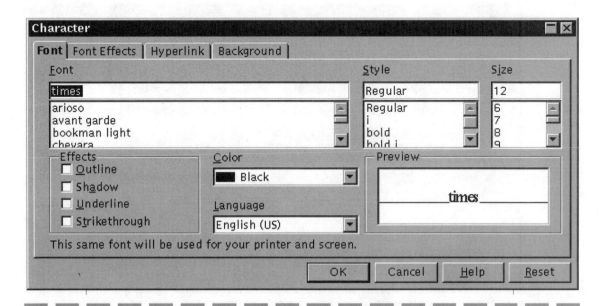

Figure 18-10 Character Format Window

of high-quality scenic photographs. For a sample, click on the maps directory, choose Italy, and check the Preview button (Figure 18-11).

Exercise 2: Creating an Invitation with Formatting and Graphics
Try to recreate an invitation like Figure 18-12. A photograph of green apples has been inserted into a header to produce the logo—tip: resize the picture with the corner resizing arrows, and click on it with your right mouse button. Choose Wrap and Page Wrap.

Proficiency—Templates and Working with Word

The first item in this section is a handy way to speed up your work and make it a little classier; the second item, however, is absolutely necessary

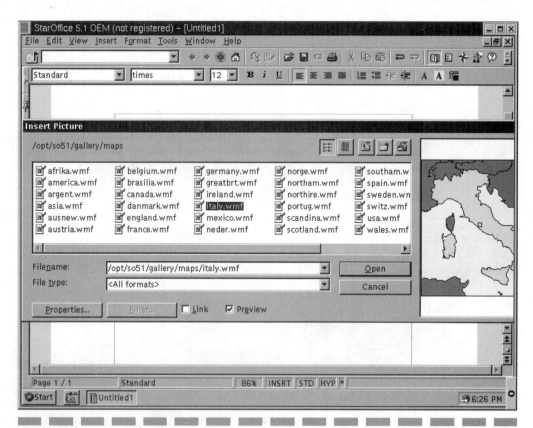

Figure 18-11   Italy

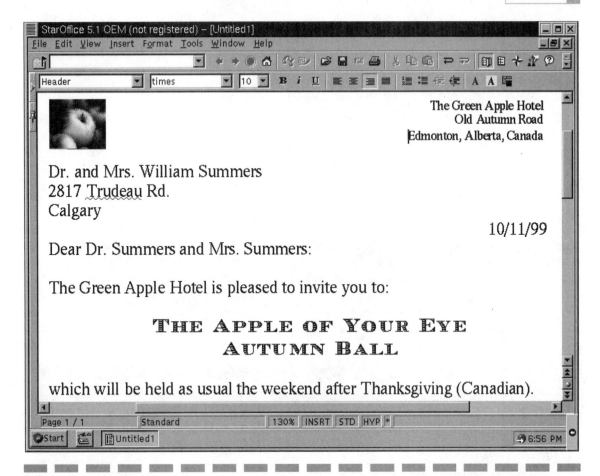

Figure 18-12   Photo Imported into Invitation

for the user who wants to pass files back and forth from StarWriter to Microsoft Word.

Lesson 8: Using Document Templates

There are two advantages to using templates:

1. They are faster than having to constantly produce the same format over again.

2. They are consistent.

Depending on your ability, there may be one more advantage: they may simply be more attractive than anything you're likely to produce yourself.

There are two ways to start a document template.

1. Start from the StarOffice desktop by clicking on the Start button, and choosing More and From Template.

2. Start from any open document by pressing Ctrl + n.

In both cases you are taken to the Template window. Choose the category you're interested in and a template belonging to that category. Then click on the More button, and check the Preview box. This will give you an idea of what the template looks like (Figure 18-13). Choose Business Correspondence and Contemporary Business Letter, and click on the OK button.

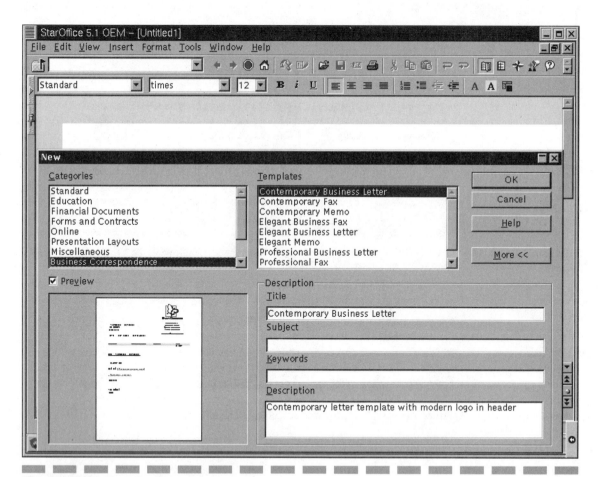

Figure 18-13 Template Preview

The template opens into a new window, with the StarOffice address book open above it. To insert a name and address from the address book to the template, first select an entry by clicking on the square to the left of the name—in this case, click on the square to the left of Ms. Patricia Fisher—and then click on the Data to Fields icon, which should be just above the Company field in the address book. Immediately the address fields in the template are filled by the data from the fields above (Figure 18-14).

(NOTE: The address book is a useful feature in StarOffice, taking the place of a similar table in a desktop database. It can be edited and added to by clicking on Edit and on Address Book.)

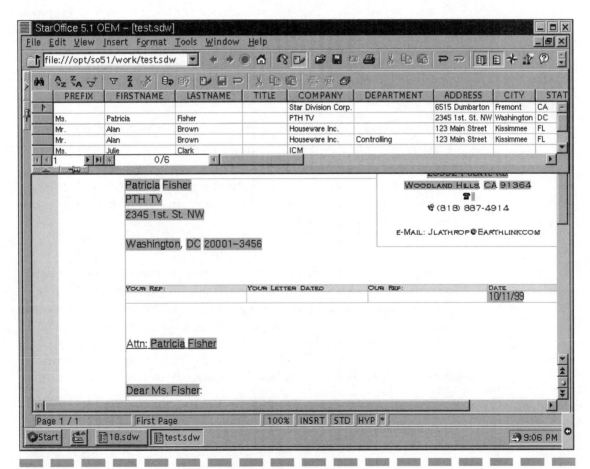

Figure 18-14 Template with Address Fields Automatically Filled In

Now close the address book by clicking on the small up-arrow button beneath it, and proceed to complete your letter. It can be saved and printed in the normal way.

Lesson 9: Customizing Document Templates

It is possible, of course, that you may not like the picture of the butterfly on your business correspondence. In short, you may wish to customize these templates. That is not a problem.

Exercise Three: Customizing a Template   Open the template closest to the one you would like to customize. Change what you will: graphics, fonts, fields, etc. Produce a template you can live with. When you are finished customizing it, click on File on the Menu Bar, and on Templates. Under Categories, choose where your new template is going to go, and under New Template, type in the name you prefer. Click on OK.

Lesson 10: Ménage à Deux—Transferring Documents to and from Word

It is very unlikely that anyone who has been using MS Office will simply abandon Windows and MS Office overnight. They have too much invested—too many files, for one thing.

So, how to you make the switch without leaving all that behind?

The answer is simple: by taking it with you.

StarOffice has some of the finest converters in the business. It is possible to import a Word file from your Windows partition, work on it in StarWriter without even converting it to a StarWriter file, and export it back to Windows when you're finished. And, of course, it's possible to import all your Word files and convert them into StarWriter format.

Notice that all the work is done in Linux. Linux can read and write to a Windows partition. Windows, however, will never be able to even recognize your Linux partition.

A word must be said about conversion. The perfect converter has yet to be manufactured—by anyone. The old rule of conversion still applies: the more heavily formatted the original document, the more likely it is that something will be lost in the conversion.

However, for your average document, conversion should be no problem.

A Two-Step Procedure

The first step is to mount your Windows partition. Chapter 10 should refresh your memory on this. Quite simply, you should open up a terminal, and type:

```
mount /c
```

and hit Enter. Note that I have used a small c—the reason for this is that the latest version of StarOffice, version 5.1, will not recognize capitalized directory mounts.

The second step is simply to open the Word file. Click on File on StarWriter's Menu Bar, and on Open. Click on the Up One Level button until you reach the directory on your Windows partition that holds your Word files. Select the file you want to work on, and click on Open. (Note: Figure 18-15 shows this operation on my own machine. I am within StarWriter, opening the Word document acknowledgements.doc, from /e/msoffice/win-word/linux. Note the small w next to every chapter name.)

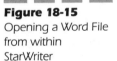

Figure 18-15
Opening a Word File
from within
StarWriter

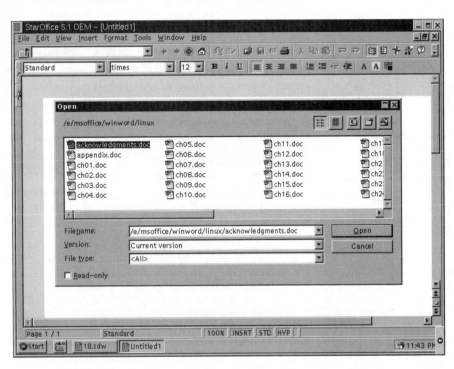

Figure 18-16

Saving a StarWriter
File as a Word File

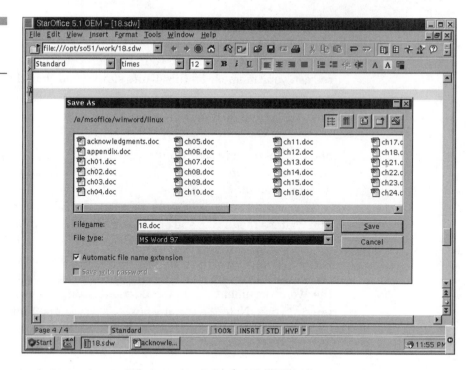

Exporting a StarWriter file to Windows is just as easy. Mount your Windows partition as before. Choose File on the Menu Bar, and Save As. Navigate up until you're at the directory you want to save your file into. Make sure that the Automatic File Name Extension box is checked, and that you have chosen MS Word 97 next to File Type. Then click on Save (Figure 18-16).

It's transparent and safe, with little reformatting required: Windows and Linux on the same machine, Word and StarWriter exchanging files. It works.

19

Spreadsheets with StarCalc

Purpose of Chapter: To Create Spreadsheets Using StarCalc

The spreadsheet program from StarDivision is, like its companion, StarWriter, very close in feel and in basic feature set to its own main competitor from Microsoft. The fundamental "paradigms" in every spreadsheet program are identical, and even many minor points in StarCalc are identical to those in Excel.

StarCalc's file conversion module supports even more file types than StarWriter's. You should have little trouble importing your spreadsheets into StarCalc.

This chapter is divided into three major sections:

1. A Familiar Environment
2. Fundamentals
3. Proficiency

The various techniques used are presented by building up, step-by-step, a sample spreadsheet.

A Familiar Environment: StarCalc's Desktop

The StarCalc environment, from the appearance of most tool and menu bars, to the mechanics of spreadsheet creation using data, functions, formulas, and labels, to formatting, charting, and working with other programs, is familiar to any user of Excel. Although some features are in slightly different places, nearly all the old familiar things are there—and immediately recognizable.

A Tour of StarCalc

Open the program by double-clicking on the New Spreadsheet icon on the StarOffice desktop. Figure 19-1 shows the screen as it will typically appear after installation—notice that the X Window Toolbar, or panel, at the bottom of the screen, has been moved out of the way.

This standard or default environment has all the features you would expect in a Windows spreadsheet. The screen is divided into columns and

Figure 19-1
Initial New
Spreadsheet Screen

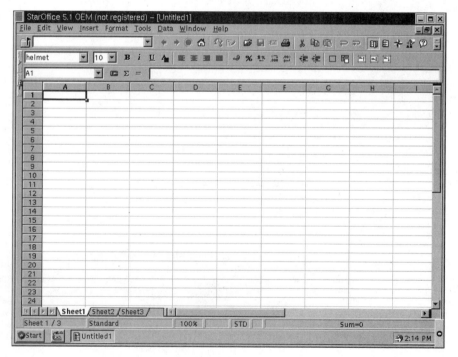

rows, with row numbers at the left, and column letters across the top. Above that is the Input Line and a Formatting and Standard Toolbar. The Menu Bar and the Title Bar take up their usual places at the top of the screen. Nearly all the menus and toolbar icons are immediately familiar.

Along the left bottom of the screen are three sheet tabs—we are used to more, but more can easily be inserted. A horizontal scrollbar fills the rest of the screen's bottom, and a vertical scrollbar frames the screen on the right.

A Main Toolbar, similar to StarWriter's, is available from View and Toolbars on the Menu Bar. If selected, it occupies the same space on the left as it does in StarWriter. It is not visible by default, and the screen is cleaner without it.

Fundamentals

These are the basics—from printer setup to data, label, and formula entry, to formatting and charting—that everyone needs to know to get going.

Lesson 1: Printer Setup and Zoom

Basic printer setup was done in StarOffice at the end of Chapter 17. However, it's a good idea to check it in StarCalc—settings that should be global sometimes don't behave internationally.

Click on File on the Menu Bar, and on Printer Setup. The printer name shown in the Printer Setup window should be the same as the one you set up before. Click on the Properties Bar.

The Printer Settings window pops up next. Make sure you have the paper set to Letter if you're in the United States or Canada, and A4 in the United Kingdom. When you're finished, click on the OK button.

The Zoom function works the same as in StarWriter: click on View on the Menu Bar and on Zoom. For this chapter, I'd suggest 150 percent.

Lesson 2: Data and Label Entry

The three major components of a spreadsheet are data, labels, and formulas and functions. Data usually refers to numbers, and labels usually refer to descriptive text that is not intended to be calculated. To enter either, simply type the number or text in the cell, and then hit Enter or one of the arrow keys.

Enter the labels shown in Figure 19-2. Notice that the years are also labels—we have no intention of calculating them. Notice also that the entire label "Income Statement for Years 1996 to 1999" is typed in one cell: A3. Three of the labels extend into adjacent cells; the moment you actually type something in the adjacent cells, the label is truncated.

Now place your mouse pointer on the lower right hand side of cell B5, hold down the left mouse button, and drag it to E5. Release. You should see the arrow become a + sign. At this point, hold the left mouse button down, and drag it over to cell E5. The additional years are created automatically.

Enter the data shown in Figure 19-3. Notice the two truncated labels.

Lesson 3: Cutting and Pasting

It occurs to you that you would like the Income Statement line up higher, next to Linux Solutions, Inc. Select cell A3 with your mouse, and click in it with your right mouse button. In the menu that comes up, choose Cut. Now select cell C1, click in it with your right mouse button, and choose Insert.

Figure 19-2

Labels Alone for Struggling Linux Solutions, Inc.

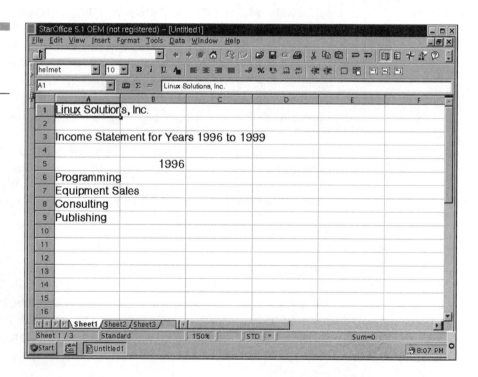

Figure 19-3

A Fuller Picture, with Data

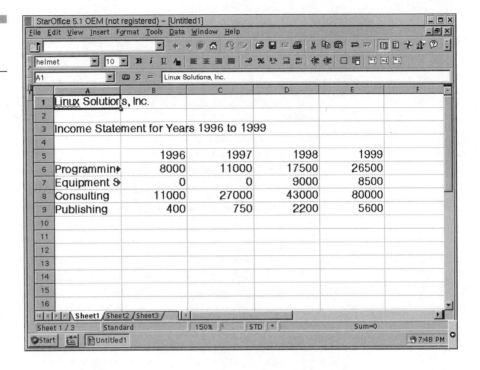

Another look at your developing spreadsheet convinces you that the bulk of it should be moved up one row. Select the range A5 to E9. With your mouse pointer inside that area, click on the right mouse button, and choose Cut. Now click into cell A3, bring up the same menu as before, and choose Insert.

You're still not happy. You want an empty row between the years and the data. Move the range A4 to E7 down one row.

An entire range needs to be selected only once, during the copying or cutting stage—not during the pasting or inserting stage.

Lesson 4: Basic Calculations

Click into cell B9. If you wanted to, you could type:

```
=b5+b6+b7+b8
```

However, there is a considerably easier way. Type instead:

```
=S
```

and press Enter. The rest of the simple "sum" formula, without the cell range, appears automatically. Simply type:

```
b5:b8
```

and press Enter. The result is =sum(b5:b8), and the actual number should be 19,400. (NOTE: In one respect Excel takes the palm: StarCalc is not as backward-compatible as Excel. If you try to enter an old DOS Lotus 1-2-3 command, such as @sum(b5..b8), in Star, it turns up its nose and treats it like a label. Excel still accepts the older program's command.)

A simpler way to enter this formula is from the Sum button—Σ—next to the Input Line. Click once in to cell C9, then click on Σ. Now click on the little green accept check mark. Once you have a formula, you can drag and copy it to the next two cells. Put your mouse pointer directly on the lower right hand corner of C9, hold down the left mouse button, and drag it to cell E9. Now, click into cell F5, and use the Sum button to add the range B5 to E5. Then copy the formula down to F8.

As an idea of how you've done overall, you'd like an average of your annual income over the past four years. If you wanted, you could use a mathematical formula—something quite simple, like =(sum(b9:e9))/4. Or, you could use the Average formula by clicking into cell B12, and typing:

```
=a
```

and hitting Enter. All you have to do now is type b9:e9 and hit Enter. The result should be 62,612.5. Give it a label by typing Average Annual Income: into cell A11. Type in another label, TOTAL, into cell A9, and copy it into cell F4. The screen should now look something like Figure 19-4.

Lesson 5: Sorting

Before you format your spreadsheet, make sure the data is arranged in the most telling pattern. In this case, it would make sense to have the consultancy's most important income source at the top, with the rest arranged in descending order. You could do this manually, but there's a faster way.

Select range A5 to F9, click on Data on the Menu Bar, and on Sort. In the window that appears, click on the Descending box, and choose column F—our column showing totaled income by source. The range selected is automatically sorted.

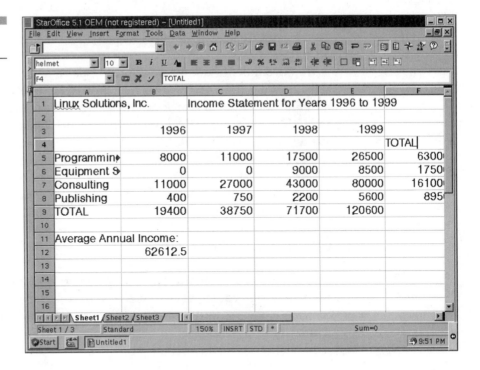

Lesson 6: Formatting

Start by adding commas to all numbers, and then currency signs to the totals. First, select A5 to F12—every number in the spreadsheet (not including year labels). With your mouse anywhere in the selection, click on the right button, and choose Format Cells.

The Numbers tab is the only one that need concern us here. Under Options to the right, check the two boxes, Negative Numbers Red, and Thousands Separator. The Preview window beneath shows you the result. Click on the OK button.

Add currency signs to the totals by first selecting one Total range, then, while holding down the Ctrl key, selecting the other Total range and the Average Annual Income cell. Thus are nonadjacent ranges selected. Click on the Number Format: Currency icon on the Formatting Toolbar. Eliminate the two decimal points by clicking on the Number Format: Delete Decimal icon.

The result is coming close to a nicely formatted spreadsheet, although we have yet to add color. This is often the downfall of the deadline, and for this reason we resort to the AutoFormat feature.

Select range A3 to F9, click on Format on the Menu Bar, and on AutoFormat. To keep it simple, I suggest choosing Standard. Click on the OK button.

We have a definite improvement, but as so often with automatic formatting, it has left us with some new problems. To restore column B to an optimum width, double-click on the border between the column labels B and C. Manually narrow column C to 0.59 inch by positioning the mouse pointer between the C and D labels, holding down the left button, and dragging. Now reformat the numbers and totals.

Our formatted spreadsheet has expanded; change the Zoom to a variable width of 135 percent. You should have something similar to Figure 19-5.

Lesson 7: Charting

A picture is worth a thousand words. The charting capabilities of StarCalc are both advanced and easy to use. The first and most important step is knowing what you want to chart, and what range of data to select to obtain the desired result.

Figure 19-5
The Formatted Spreadsheet, Ready for Printing or Exporting

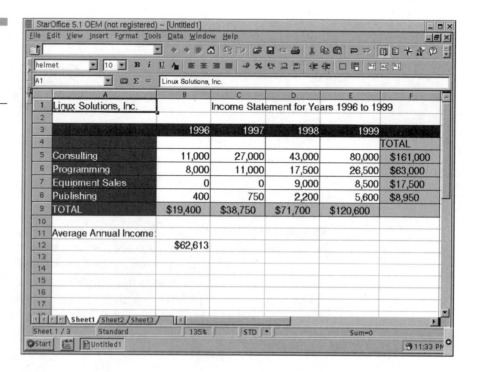

There are many ways to chart even the simplest spreadsheet. Let's use a simple line chart, designed to chart each income source's yearly total, over the period of the spreadsheet.

To do this we have to select nonadjacent ranges, because it would be fatal to select a superfluous row or column. So select range A3 to E3, and then, holding down the Ctrl key, range A5 to E8. Next, click on Insert on the Menu Bar, and on Chart. In the AutoFormat Chart that then appears, make sure that both the First Row as Label, and First Column as Label boxes are checked, and select Sheet2 under Chart Results in worksheet. Then click on Next.

The following window (Figure 19-6) is where you choose your basic chart type. You can experiment. Make sure to check the Show Text Elements. . . box, and then switch between Rows and Columns. The best choice will soon be evident. Click on Next. In the following window, choose the Symbols variant.

In window 4 of AutoFormat Chart, type in a main title—something descriptive, and not too dry—add other titles as you see fit, and click on the Create button. You are taken immediately to Sheet 2. Your chart will almost certainly need resizing. I advise you first to move it into the upper left hand corner, so that you have a kind of baseline, and to resize it gently—you don't want to deform the text. The data lines may be too narrow; double-click on one, then double-click again. In the window that appears, increase the width very gently, in small increments—perhaps to 0.03 inch. Do the same with the others.

The result (Figure 19-7) is at a standard business presentation level. Now save your work by clicking on the Save icon on the toolbar—both sheets are part of the same file and don't have to be saved separately.

Figure 19-6
Different Chart Types

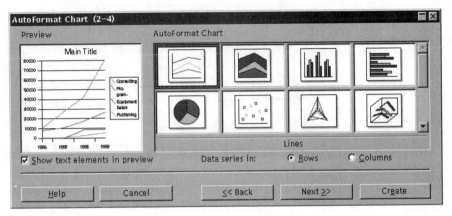

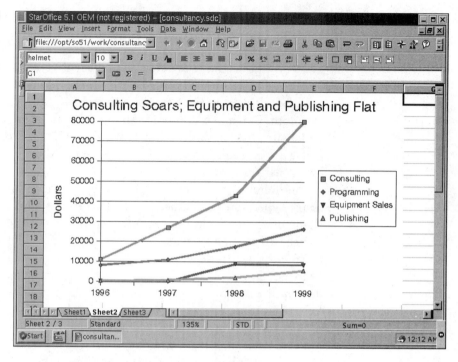

Proficiency—Exporting to StarWriter, and Working with Excel

Why export to StarWriter? Doesn't the word processor have its own charting and table modules? Yes, it does, but they are not primarily for calculations. Serious spreadsheets and the charts derived from them should be done in StarCalc and then imported into your text document. This follows the rule that each program should be used for what it does best.

Transferring spreadsheets to and from Excel from StarCalc is exactly like doing the same transfer between Windows and StarOffice word processors. It's quite simple and generally works quite well. And it will be necessary for the Windows user thinking of migrating to Star.

Lesson 8: Exporting to StarWriter

First open a StarWriter template by pressing Ctrl+n and choosing Business Correspondence and Contemporary Business Letter (or choose the template you modified in the last chapter). You should now have two files open at the same time in StarOffice: a spreadsheet and a text document, both identified by separate buttons at the bottom of the page. Switch from one to the other simply by clicking on the buttons. If you haven't already done it, save your spreadsheet.

Now, select your chart by clicking anywhere on it once. Then, choose Edit on the Menu Bar, and Copy. Switch back to your text document. Position your cursor at the point (presumably beneath the text you've written) where you'd like the chart, and go up to Edit on the Menu Bar, and Paste Special.

The Paste Special window comes up, giving you several choices of file type to import (Figure 19-8). My experience is that the simple Chart type results in better printer output. Click on the OK button to bring it in (Figure 19-9). The chart can now be moved or resized using the normal methods.

The spreadsheet itself can be imported in exactly the same way, with just one difference: the range you wish to import should be selected with the mouse before copying. You will have an even larger selection of file types to import—I suggest you stick to the original file type, as before. The result (Figure 19-10—shown in Full Screen View) will be quite satisfactory.

Lesson 9: Ménage à Deux—Transferring Spreadsheets to and from Excel

You can move from Excel to StarCalc almost effortlessly. But what about those files you left behind? Take them with you.

Figure 19-8
Paste Special
Window

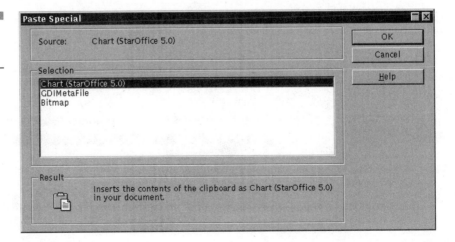

Figure 19-9

StarWriter Document from Template with Imported StarCalc Chart

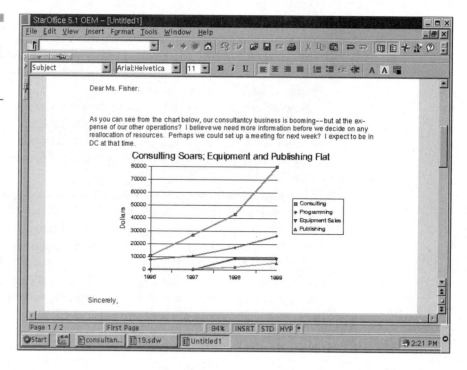

Figure 19-10

StarWriter Document with Imported StarCalc Spreadsheet

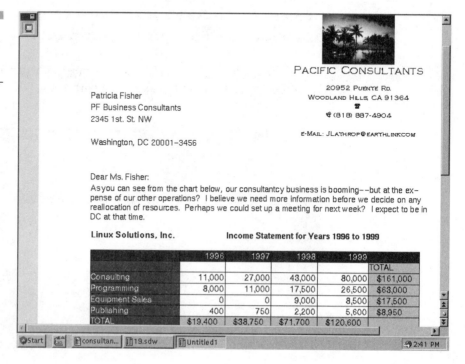

StarCalc will open most Excel 97 spreadsheets with no problem. The automatic conversion is not always perfect—as with all converters, the more highly formatted the original, the more reformatting may have to be done. However, all the data, and for nearly all common spreadsheets, all formulas, should be intact.

To import an Excel spreadsheet, first mount the Window partition, and then simply open the file. You can save it as either a native Excel file, or as a StarCalc file. To export a StarCalc file to Excel format, choose File on the Menu Bar and Save As. Choose Excel 97 or 95.

Windows and Linux on the same machine, with Excel and StarCalc exchanging files: it works.

20

Presentations with StarImpress

Purpose of Chapter: To Create Professional Quality Presentations with StarImpress

The presentations program from StarDivision is, like all modern presentation programs, capable of automatically producing outlines for professional presentations of several kinds, on a variety of subjects. It is also provided with a wide range of effects and animations, and breaks new ground in user-friendliness.

However, an automatic presentation is only the starting point. What sets yours off from the rest will always be the special content you provide, both in text, and in imported materials such as spreadsheets and charts from StarCalc.

Creating Automatically Generated Presentations in StarImpress

There are two basic methods of starting a new presentation in StarImpress: opening a template or opening a blank presentation. Both allow you to pre-select a range of "looks" and effects, but the template method also provides a range of sample outlines.

Lesson 1: Using Templates

At the StarOffice desktop, double-click on the New Presentation icon. The first page of the AutoPilot Presentation appears. Under Type, check From Template. Choose Presentations beneath that, and, as an example, choose Company Introduction (Figure 20-1). Make sure the Preview box is checked, and then click on Next. (Don't worry about the graphics in the preview—you can change that next.)

In page 2 of the AutoPilot, you get to choose a page style and a presentation medium. On style, a quick hint: it pays to keep it simple. I'm using the Triangles style, in order not to draw attention from the message—the medium is a lot, but it's not everything.

Click on Next again, and you get page 3, with transition types and speeds. Experiment with the transition types—they can be a lot of fun, and generally they don't hijack the viewer's attention as much as other other effects or animations.

On page 4 you get to enter the information that will be included on your title slide—in this case, the company's name and the scope of the presentation. Once again, don't worry too much about this—like the decorative elements, you can always change the text later.

The real work begins on the next page. Here you get to take a look at the suggested outline and to prune the pages you don't think you'll need. To take a look at each page's suggested text, click on the small + signs; to eliminate a page, remove the check mark on the page's icon. When you're finished, highlight the first (top) page, and click on the Create button.

Lesson 2: Different Views

The screen that appears next shows you the title slide surrounded by all the paraphernalia of the editing apparatus. At the bottom of the screen are slide tabs, allowing you to switch from one slide to the next; at the top is

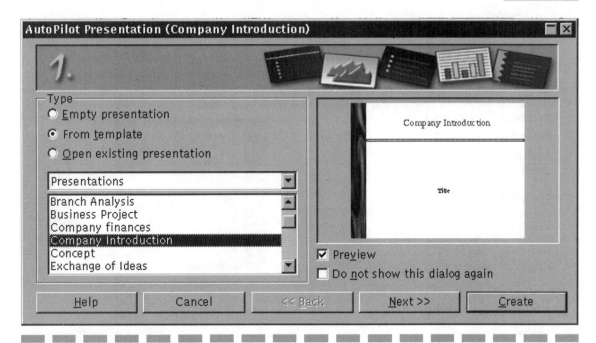

Figure 20-1 StarImpress Autopilot

the usual Standard Toolbar and Menu Bar. Along the upper right hand corner of the editing screen is the View Bar, giving icons for five different views: Drawing, Outline, Slide Sort, Notes, and Handout, as well as starting the slide show.

Each view has a different purpose. The Drawing view, the default, is primarily for changing the appearance either of the design as a whole, individual slides, or elements of individual slides. The Outline view is primarily for entering text. Star's Preview window is a useful feature—you don't have to switch away to see how the text is going to look on the finished slide. (You will probably want to adjust the zoom setting to see more of the outline, as in Figure 20-2.)

The Slide Sort view is of use should you wish to rearrange your slides; the Notes and Handout views are more useful—notes in pariticular can come in handy during a long presentation, and a combination of notes and handouts will prove excellent insurance should the higher-tech elements of the presentation suddenly fail, as they have been known to do.

The last icon on the strip is for previewing the slide show on your own screen. Simply click the mouse to go from one slide to another—hitting the Escape key takes you back to the editing screen.

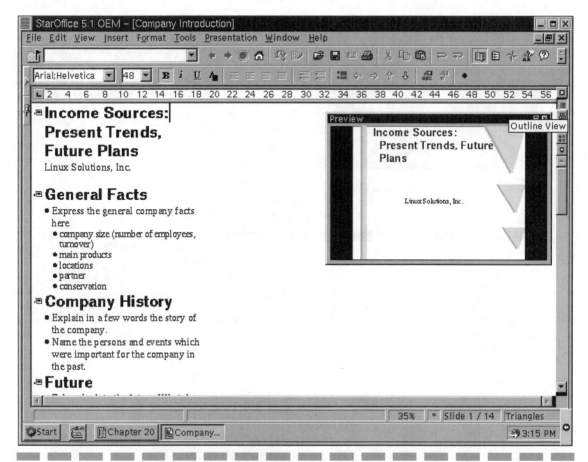

Figure 20-2 Outline View

Lesson 3: Importing Spreadsheets and Charts from StarCalc

Software should always be used for the purpose for which it is designed—the results will not only be better, a great deal of time will be saved by "using the correct tool." For this reason, there is very little point is producing charts and tables and so on in StarWriter or StarImpress—such items, unless they are merely decorative and without a numerical foundation, should be produced in StarCalc and then imported.

To insert the spreadsheet you made in the previous chapter into your current presentation, first make sure you're in Drawing view, and insert a new slide by clicking on the Insert Slide button in the Presentation box. Type in a name to identify the slide—this name won't actually appear on the slide itself, just on the slide's tab below—and choose an autolayout. I suggest a plain title layout.

Now double-click on the new slide's title box, and type in something like:

```
Company Income History...'96-'99
```

Open up the spreadsheet file you made in the last lesson. Once it's open, you should have three buttons on the bar at the very bottom of the screen, one for each program. With your mouse select the part of the spreadsheet you want to import, and click on the Copy icon on the Menu Bar.

Now move into StarImpress. Click on the Paste icon on the Menu Bar. Your spreadsheet should come in with no difficulty. You will most likely have to resize and move it, using your mouse.

Use exactly the same technique to bring in your chart (Figure 20-3). Note that any changes you want to make in the chart, perhaps to make it

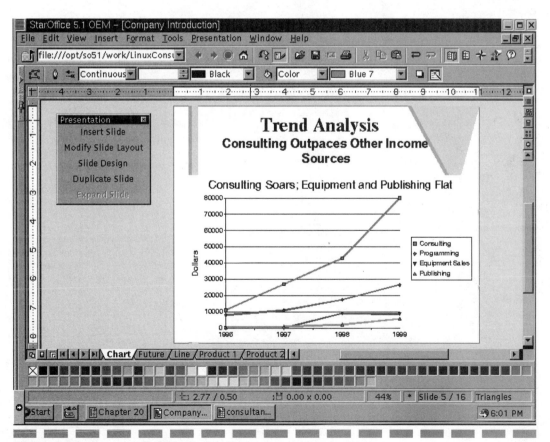

Figure 20-3 Imported StarCalc Chart in StarImpress

more easily readable at the smaller size inside a slide, should be done back in StarCalc.

To sum up, the ease of use and range of features in StarImpress should ensure that anyone who has worked in other presentation programs and decides to migrate will feel right at home—and perhaps even pleasantly surprised.

## CHAPTER 21

Office Suites: The Promise of Corel

Purpose of Chapter: To Install, Configure and Use Corel WordPerfect

Corel Corporation has announced its intention not only to port its entire suite of office applications to Linux, but to do so as part of its own Linux distribution. This distribution may well be on the streets as you buy this book.

The ability to run Corel's office suite would be a major boost to Linux's viability as a desktop replacement. For although StarOffice is more of an MS Office look-alike than Corel's product, Corel's office suite, previously running under Windows, is definitely the more refined.

For now, we have Corel WordPerfect, the flagship word processor that, in its salad days—several years ago—ruled the DOS desktop world. It still has a Windows presence today, but its future is in Linux.

Installing and Configuring Corel WordPerfect

Although it's possible to download this program as a single large file from Corel's Web site, the usual method is either to buy the CD from Corel or to load a trial version from a distributor's commercial CD. As you would expect from such a long-established firm, the installation routine is as easy, user-friendly, and straightforward as the program itself.

Installation

If you are installing a version from a distributor's CD, it is probably in rpm format. Insert the CD, mount it, and type:

```
rpm -ivh WordPerfect*
```

and hit Enter. The program should install to the /opt/wp8/wpbin direc-tory. Start X Window, open a terminal window, change to the WordPerfect directory, and type:

```
./xwp
```

and hit Enter.

If you are installing from the Corel WordPerfect 8 CD, follow the instructions below:

1. Insert the Corel WordPerfect CD and mount the CD-ROM.

2. Start X Window. Open a terminal window within X Window, and change the directory to /mnt/cdrom.

3. Type:

   ```
   ./install.wp
   ```

   and press Enter. The initial Install Configuration screen (Figure 21-1) comes up.

4. Click on the OK button, and accept the license terms by clicking on the Accept button.

5. The next screen asks you for an installation directory. It can be anything you like. Since I've put StarOffice in /opt/so51, I'm going to suggest /opt/wp for Corel. Type it into the blank, and hit the OK button.

Figure 21-1
Initial Corel
Installation Window

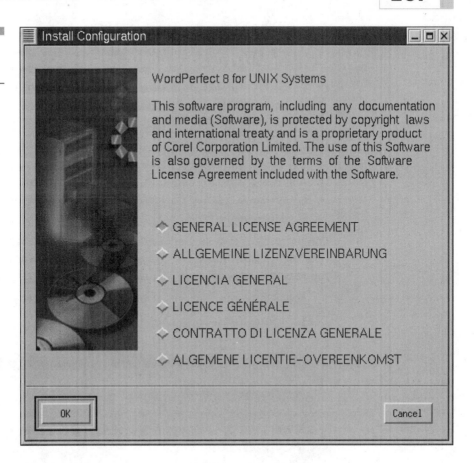

6. Choose which installation size you prefer—if you have the room,
   I suggest the Full installation—and hit the OK button.

7. Since you don't have a previous installation of the program, simply hit OK here.

8. At the registration screen, enter your registration number, which
   should have come with the program. Then hit the usual OK.

9. Click on Update, and hit the OK button.

10. Select your language, and hit OK.

11. A blast from the past! WordPerfect supports a much greater range
    of printers than does either native Linux or StarOffice. Select
    yours, and hit OK.

12. In the next configuration window (Figure 21-2), click on the Assign button, choose lp, and then OK. This is simply to direct the printer driver to the correct port. Then click on OK.

13. In the Optional Installation Features window, the only useful choice out of the three is the online manual. If you want it, check the box, and hit OK.

14. A final window offers to let you review your selections. If you're happy with them, hit the OK button.

15. A series of feature windows blinks by as the program loads. When it's finished, a README review window comes up. Just click on the Done button.

The program is now loaded, and you're back at the terminal window in X Window. Change to the /opt/wp/wpbin directory (or the directory where you installed the program, followed by /wpbin), and type:

    ./xwp

and hit Enter. The opening windows of WordPerfect appear (Figure 21-3).

Figure 21-2
Printer Driver
Destination Window

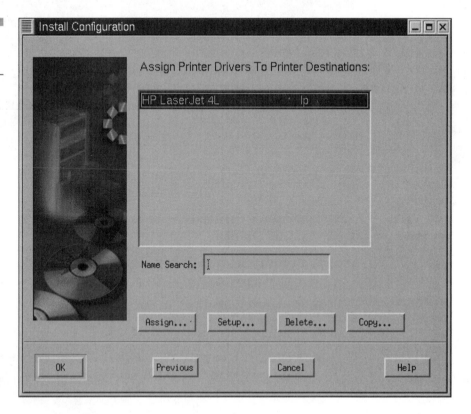

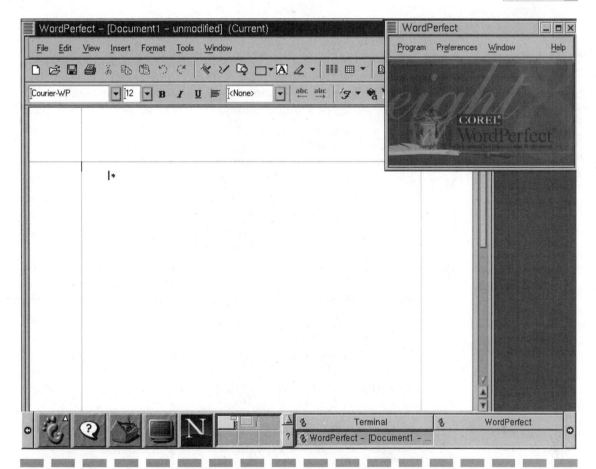

Figure 21-3 Initial WordPerfect Editing and Control Screens

You may add a menu item to either the applications menu or the desktop of Gnome by following the directions in Chapter 13; a fairly decent icon to use is `/opt/wp/wpgraphics/pictures/business/document.bmp`.

Configuring Default Preferences

These preferences are in place every time the program is started and are set in the small WordPerfect control window. This window, shown in the upper right-hand corner of Figure 21-3, is always the first to open and is generally in the background. Closing the control window will immediately close down the entire program. With two major exceptions, most of the window's functions are repeated in the Menu Bar of the main editing window. One major exception is the simple but extremely useful command Save All, which is under Programs on the Menu Bar. The other exception is actually the entire Menu Bar selection of Preferences.

Selecting Preferences gives you the window shown in Figure 21-4. The settings in Preferences are and become the defaults each time you open WordPerfect. Two especially useful areas are Environment and Files. Click first on the Environment button.

The Environment Preferences window, shown in Figure 21-5, has one very useful setting which you change: Save Workspace. Check either the Always or Prompt on Exit button. This is a most useful feature. The purpose of this feature is not to protect you from disasters, but rather to automatically reopen the documents you're working on when next you start up WordPerfect. Click on the OK button when you've finished. You can test this feature by typing anything in the editing window, and then clicking on the Close Window button (the X in the upper right-hand corner) of the control window. You are first prompted to save your file—do so—and then the program closes. When next you start WordPerfect, the document you just saved is automatically opened.

The Files Preferences window, shown in Figure 21-6, has two important features: the Default Directory and Timed Document Backup. The Default Directory is where your documents will be automatically saved, and where

Figure 21-4
Preferences Window

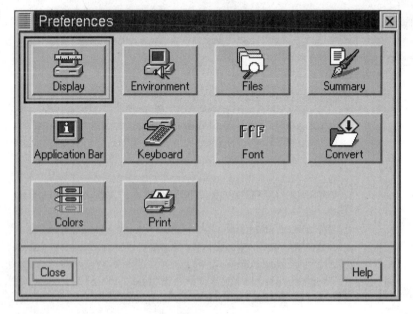

Figure 21-5
Environment
Preferences Window

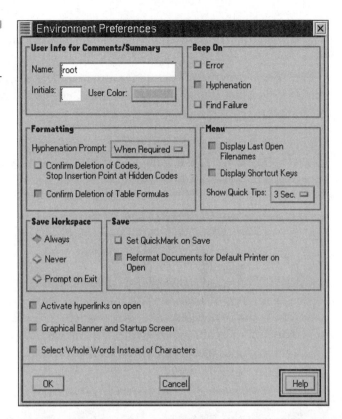

Figure 21-5
Environment
Preferences Window

Figure 21-6
Files
Preferences Window

the program will automatically look first when you click on the file open icon. You can type in whatever you like here, but the directory does have to exist—WordPerfect won't create it for you.

The Timed Document Backup feature is by default checked for every 10 minutes—you can change this as you like. Click on the Close button to exit Preferences.

Configuring Document Preferences (Formatting)

Document preferences can be set either document by document, or a default style can be set. To change the default document style:

1. Click on File on the Menu Bar.
2. Click on Document, move over and down, and click on Current Document Style. This opens up the Style Editor. Suppose, for instance, that you disliked having courier as a default font—Times is more common and more attractive. You would change it by:
3. Clicking on Format on the Menu Bar.
4. Clicking on Font.
5. Under Font Face, choosing CG Times.
6. Clicking on the OK button.
   A slightly obscure but very useful feature to have always turned on is Widow and Orphan protection—a feature that prevents the first and last lines of a paragraph from becoming separated on adjacent pages. To turn this on:
7. Click again on Format on the Menu Bar, and then on Keep Text Together.
8. Check the box beneath Widow/Orphan, and then click on the OK button.
9. Click on the small Use as Default button in the lower center of the window.

Note in Figure 21-7 how the settings we have just made, Font: CG Times and Wid/Orph: On, appear in the Contents box. This box lists all of the changes we have made to the new default style. Now click on the OK button. If you close down WordPerfect and then reopen it, the new font will be CG Times.

Document-by-document formatting is done through Page Setup under File on the Menu Bar, and in several items under Format on the Menu Bar.

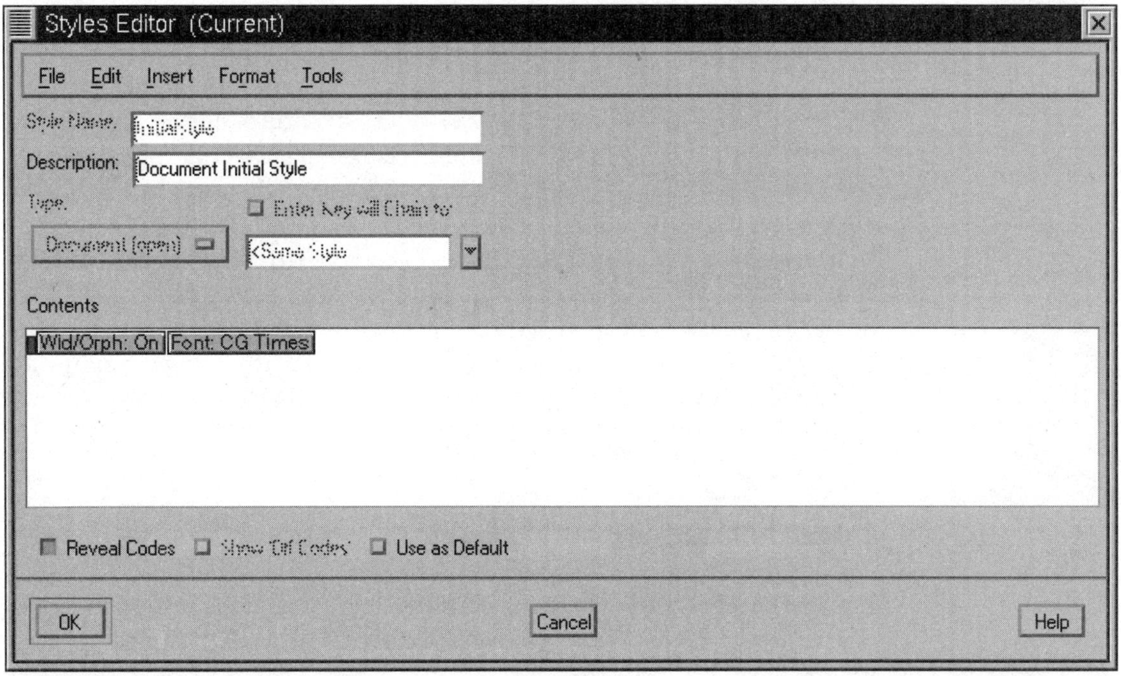

Figure 21-7 Styles Editor Window

Using Corel WordPerfect

The good news: WordPerfect includes every major and most minor functions of its competitors. The bad news: the Tool Bar icons and Menu Bar items in WordPerfect are not as close to MS Office style as are StarOffice's icons and menus. However, a Windows wordprocessor is a Windows wordprocessor—whether you're working in Microsoft or Linux. Anyone who is even somewhat proficient in Word will soon be proficient in WordPerfect.

Creating, Saving and Retrieving Files

When you first start up WordPerfect, both the small control window and the large editing window appear. A file is not created until it is saved, and saving files is identical to the procedure in Star or Word: simply click on the floppy drive icon on the Tool Bar, or click on File on the Menu Bar, and then on Save. Note, that if you have enabled the Summary feature (using the Summary button under Preferences, in the control window), then as soon as you click on Save, the Document Summary window will appear (Figure 21-8). This is a very old WordPerfect feature, dating back to the DOS days, when it was a way of adding a long document name to an old 8.3 file name. Now, however, it has been greatly expanded, as you can see by clicking on first the Configure, then the Options buttons.

Retrieving a file is just as straightforward. With your mouse, click on the open file icon on the menu bar. The Open window appears, with a list of files on the left, and a list of directories on the right. By clicking on a particular file name, and then on the View button beneath, you get a snapshot of your file's first page (Figure 21-9)—a handy feature, when you're not sure if you've got the name right, or not.

Formatting

Fundamental text formatting is done in exactly the same way as in either StarOffice or Word. However, WordPerfect offers both refinements and unique advanced features.

Figure 21-8
Document Summary
Window

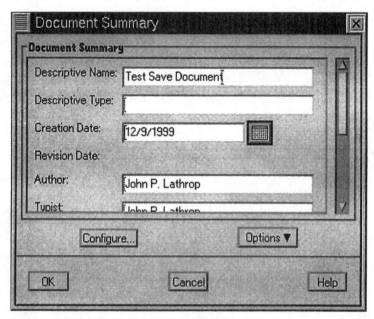

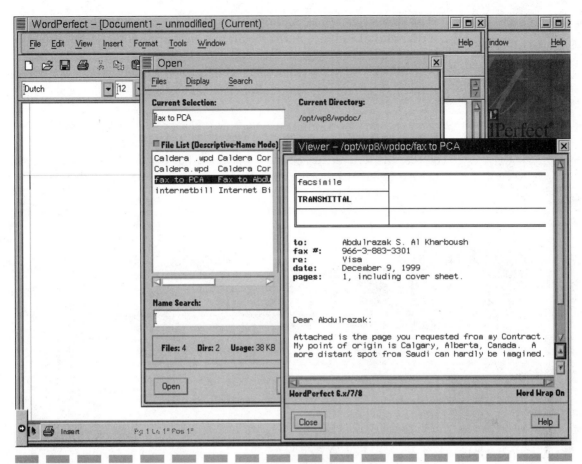

Figure 21-9 The Right Document? Viewing Before Opening

ExpressDocs—WordPerfect Templates In WordPerfect, templates are called ExpressDocs. To use them, simply click on File on the Menu Bar, and then on ExpressDocs. Before choosing one to experiment with, click first on the User Info button, and enter your name, address, etc. This information will be automatically merged into the new document.

The range of templates offered is unexampled in other wordprocessors—possibly because WordPerfect has been around longer than any of its surviving competition. You can choose from business cards, to fax cover sheets, to quarterly cash flows, to a variety of plain old letters. As an example, scroll down using the vertical slider until you reach one of the letter templates. Click on the Select button.

The new letter opens in a new document window, with your name and address and other personal information already merged. The program then prompts you to insert the recipient's name, address, etc. (Figure 21-10). When you're finished, the new document appears with everything but the body of the text already inserted and formatted.

Envelopes and Labels   Although Star does offer these features, most American users will find them better implemented within WordPerfect. The reasons for this are Star's reliance on Postscript printer support, its more European orientation, and, it must be said, WordPerfect's generally more polished support.

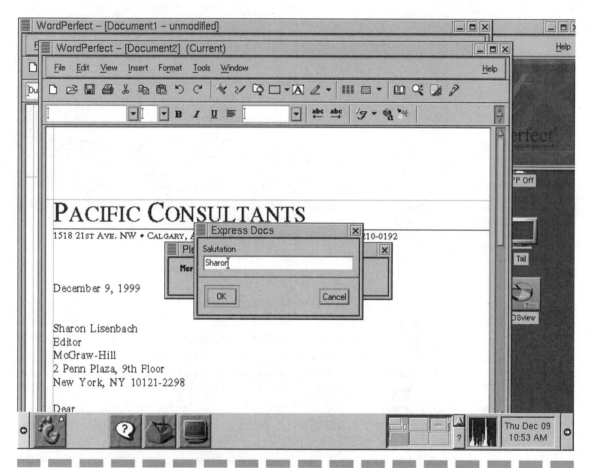

Figure 21-10   Express Docs: The Program Prompts You

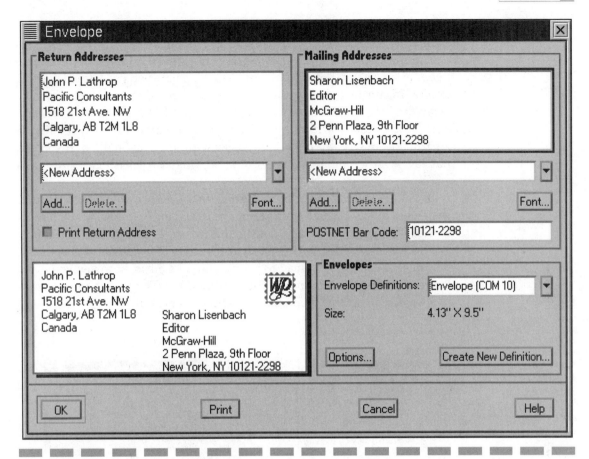

Figure 21-11　Automatic Envelope Creation

To automatically create an envelope for the previous letter, choose Format, then Envelope. In the Envelope box that then opens, you must type in—just once, the first time—your own complete return address. It will always subsequently be available. The recipient's mailing address is automatically inserted, including the postnet bar code. At this point you can choose from a variety of different envelopes, or even create you own envelope definition. The completed box will look similar to Figure 21-11. When finished, click on either print, or OK to include the envelope as the last page in your document.

Typesetting and Fonts　WordPerfect has certain typesetting features which are usually reserved for far more expensive document creation packages than a standard wordprocessor. Two of these can be found under Format on the Menu Bar, and then in Typesetting.

The Word Spacing and Letterspacing box (Figure 21-12), lets you enable automatic kerning: the adjustment of spacing between predefined pairs of letters. It is a fact that some letters look better if they are placed very slightly closer to certain other letters in a word. This is the kind of thing that people notice without noticing: without knowing why, reading a lengthy document will be a little easier with kerning enabled. If you are putting together publishable documents, this is a good feature to have working.

If you are publishing serious manuscript, I advise you to play around with word spacing and letterspacing. You may, for instance, find a noticeable difference in legibility simply by increasing letterspacing to 108%.

Finally, WordPerfect lets you install a variety of fonts that will both display on screen and download to your printer. To do so, however, you must first be running the program as the administrator. You can set the program to always start in this mode, or only when you need it.

Figure 21-12
Advanced
Typesetting Features

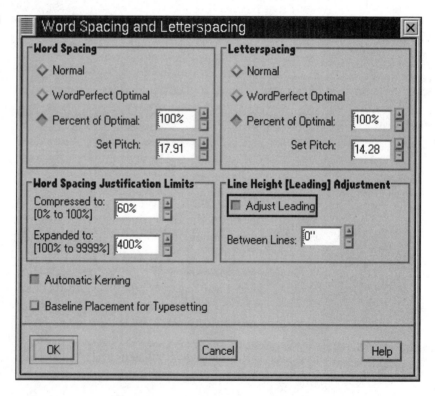

To start up WordPerfect as the administrator, open a terminal window within X Windows, and type:

```
/opt/wp8/wpbin/xwp \adm
```

Then hit Enter. (To start the program every time in administrator mode, simply edit the menu entry.)

To install fonts, click on Format on the Menu Bar, then on Font, and then on the Install Fonts button. In the Select Font Type windows, check either Type 1, or HP LaserJet. In the next window, select the correct directory where your new fonts are located, and then install them.

Charting

The charting modules in most wordprocessors are somewhat poor. They may have a decent graphics capability, but usually they lack any obvious tie-in with the data they are supposed to graphically display. For that reason I generally advise users to produce charts in their spreadsheet program, and then import them into their wordprocessor. However, the situation in WordPerfect is different: its charting capabilities are not only extensive, they are tied into customized examples of data presented in easy-to-read tables, that make clear not only how to use each kind of chart, but also which kind of chart is best suited for different types of data.

To inspect WordPerfect's charting capabilities, click on Insert on the Menu Bar, then go down to Graphics and over and down to Chart. The WordPerfect Draw module opens with an example of an overlapped, 3D bar chart. There are six different types of charts to choose from, with several varieties of each chart. The sample data in the table changes to reflect the type of chart displayed (Figure 21-13).

Reveal Codes

Users of WordPerfect gain certain advantages that Microsoft Word never had—or perhaps that Word for some reason dropped somewhere along the way. Reveal Codes, for instance. How many times have Word users been irritated at the difficulty of overriding some format option, particularly at the end of a highly formatted paragraph? In WordPerfect, you simply track it down and eliminate it—visually.

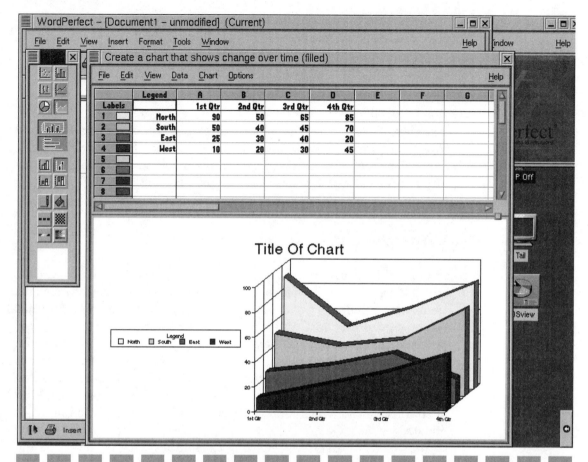

Figure 21-13 WordPerfect Charting Example/Tutorial

To see exactly where your formatting codes are in your document, click on View on the Menu Bar, and on Reveal Codes. An example of what appears is shown in figure 21-14 (an excerpt of an interview by The New York Times' Philip Shenon with Burma's Aung San Suu Kyi). The panel below reveals every formatting code—and its position—in the document. To eliminate a code, simply click on one of the format tabs and delete it with the Delete key.

To sum up: WordPerfect is one of the most developed and refined word-processors available today. It is well-integrated into Linux—you can cut or copy and paste from WordPerfect into a Linux wordprocessor or Netscape,

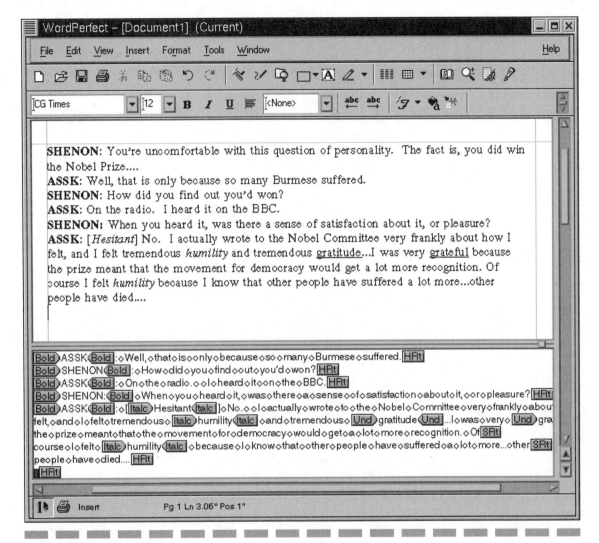

Figure 21-14   Reveal Codes

and vice-versa. It is easily networked—switching to a network printer in WordPerfect is a graphical operation; in Star you need to know the command prompt routine. It has unrivaled document conversion capability. WordPerfect started in the early days of DOS, is enjoying a resurgence of interest from within the Windows environment, and will soon boast of its very own Linux distribution. This is a wordprocessor that will around for some time to come.

## CHAPTER 22

Graphics and Multimedia

Purpose of Chapter:
To Explore Linux Graphics and Multimedia Programs

Although multimedia is not yet richly supported in Linux, graphics are. StarOffice has its own drawing module, and there are several stand-alone X Window graphics programs of varying ambitions and capabilities. The programs presented here (with the exception of StarOffice if used for business purposes) are all noncommercial software.

Graphics and Multimedia in Linux

With the exception of StarDraw, all the programs in this chapter are available in every major commercial distribution of Linux. Graphics programs in Linux come in a bewildering variety of sizes and capabilities. I have included two, GIMP and GQview, as unusually refined examples from both ends of the size and capability spectrum. GIMP is enormous and enormously capable; GQview is a perfect example of a program that does one thing, but does it very, very well.

StarDraw

StarOffice has its own graphics program, called StarDraw. It is a typical office suite drawing package. Access it by starting up StarOffice and clicking on the New Drawing icon on the Desktop. You'll see that the editing screen is almost identical to the presentations module, StarImpress.

The Main Toolbar on the left has a standard set of icons for selecting objects, changing views, and inserting text, as well as for object creation from lines to 3-D objects. If a toolbar icon has a small triangle, holding down the mouse button on that icon for a moment will reveal an extended, or floating, toolbar offering you several choices.

As a simple example of how to use this program, click on the 3-D Objects icon on the Main Toolbar, and choose the pyramid. Move your mouse pointer to the editing window and, holding down the left mouse button, draw a rectangle of perhaps a third of a page wide, and a little less high. Once it is drawn, you may resize it by the green editing handles and move it by simply positioning the mouse within the drawing and holding down the left mouse button.

The default color is blue, but Egyptian pyramids are generally brown, so click on the brown color square (orange 3 was good on my monitor) at the bottom of the screen. The object changes color accordingly.

Now, click on any blank area of the screen and then on the Text icon on the Main Toolbar. Choose Text to Size, and draw a box at the top of the pyramid. Within it, type:

```
The Apex.
```

Choose the Text icon again, but this time plain text, and click beneath the pyramid. Go up to the Text Size button on the Formatting Toolbar, and choose 32. Also on the Formatting Toolbar, click on Center. Now, type:

```
Strategies for Success
in the
Egyptian Tourist Industry
```

Move around and resize the various elements until you're satisfied with them. At a 50 percent zoom (click on View on the Menu Bar, and Zoom), this simple cover idea for a tourism strategy report or presentation would look something like Figure 22-1.

The GIMP

The GNU Image Manipulation Program is the major free graphics program in Linux. It is an extremely full-featured graphics editor. Any user

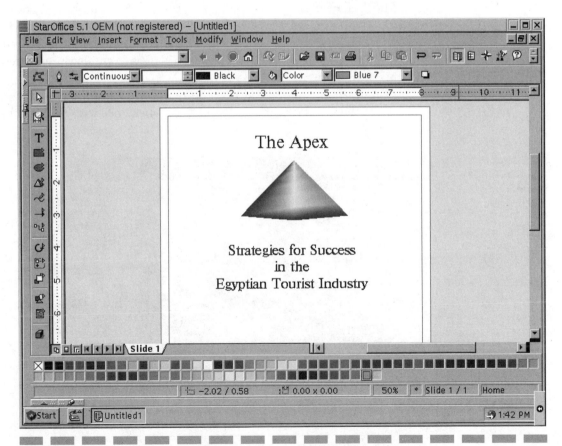

Figure 22-1   The Apex: A Simple Example of Drawing in StarDraw

with a graphics background will immediately appreciate the GIMP's capabilities.

As a very simple beginning lesson on how to use the GIMP to grab a screenshot, select by color, recolor and save, first start the program by clicking on the GIMP icon in your distribution's menu or toolbar. An installation screen will appear if this is the first time you've tried opening the program. After installing, the GIMP startup screen appears (Figure 22-2), along with a tips screen which you may want to get rid of. The three column GIMP Control Window floats on its own, usually off to the upper left (Figure 22-3).

Next, open up Netscape Navigator. The distributor's logo will probably appear as the home page (in my example, it's Red Hat). Use the resize arrows at the corners of the screen to reduce the Netscape window to perhaps two thirds of the screen.

Now, use the GIMP to grab a screen shot of the Netscape Window. On the GIMP Menu Bar, click on Xtns, and then on Screen Shot. Make sure that the Grab a single window box is checked, and click on the Grab button. Position your mouse pointer over the Netscape window, and click once. Two beeps and the deed is done—the Netscape window is enclosed is a GIMP frame (Figure 22-4).

To change both the red hat and the red text to, say, a yellow hat and text, place the mouse pointer in the hat, and click once with the right but-

Figure 22-2
The Startup
GIMP Screen

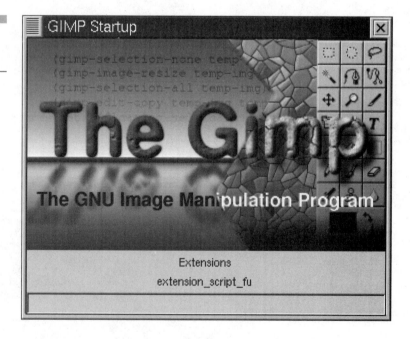

Figure 22-3
The GIMP
Control Window

Figure 22-4
A GIMP Screen Shot
of Netscape

ton. The right button brings up the full GIMP menus. Go down to Select, and move right and down all the way to By Color.

The By Color Selection window appears. Move it to one corner of the screen, and click once anywhere in the red color area of the red hat in the captured Navigator window. A moving dashed line will appear around the hat and the text logo.

Now move to the left, to the bottom of the GIMP's Control window. Click on the `black square to white square` transformation icon at the window's very bottom. In the Color Selection window that appears, click on the narrow yellow band in the vertical color bar, and then click in the far upper right-hand corner of the color transition square. Next, click on the Close button.

Back on the GIMP's Control window, click on the paint can icon, and then on the red hat. Presto. You now have a yellow hat and text logo. To save this image, click on the Select Rectangular Regions icon on the Control window, and select the new Yellow Hat logo. Use the right mouse button to bring up the main menu, and go to Edit and Cut.

Close out the capture frame and the Netscape window beneath it.

On the Control window's Menu Bar, click on File and New. Replace the Width and Height numbers in the New Image window to about 400 each. Click on the OK button. In the new, blank window, click outside of the new logo (you must deselect it), and then with the right mouse button, bring up the main menu, and go to Edit and to Paste. Save the new logo (Figure 22-5).

Figure 22-5
New, Red Hat Logo
(Yours Should be
Yellow)

This is only the most miniscule example of the ability of this program to transform images. To find the manual, click on Xtns on the Menu Bar, down to Web Browser, and over to GIMP Manual. Make sure you're connected to the Internet and ready to download.

GQview

This program is what its name implies—a good image viewer. It will view files of the following types: JPG/JPEG; XPM; TIF/TIFF; GIF; PNG; PPM; PGM; PCX; BMP.

GQview's ease of use is remarkable. Simply use the standard menu to browse through your file system until you find the graphic file you want to view (Figure 22-6). If you want to edit the picture, you can choose your editor without leaving the current program—just click on Edit on the Menu Bar.

CD Player

The CD Player (Figure 22-7) works quite well in Linux—as long as you've managed to get your sound card working. The player is simplicity itself,

Figure 22-6
Sunset in GQview

Figure 22-7
CD Player

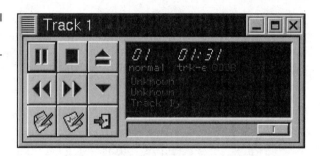

and you can, through the Preferences button on the player, configure it to automatically start when you insert a CD and to automatically eject the CD when it stops.

One word of warning: the CD Player does take over your CD-ROM when it's up on the screen. The normal eject, mount and umount commands may no longer work as long as you're playing music with CD Player.

## PART 5

Guru Status

A nyone using Linux can read with profit the first chapter of the final part of this book. The second, third and fourth chapters are more specialized.

The very term 'System Management' has a guru ring about it, but in fact it is a topic everyone can benefit from, for it is the lack of even rudimentary system management that causes the most problems with computers. An ounce of prevention is worth a pound of cure.

Laptops have always been a special case with Linux, and although support is much better now than it was in the past, there are still a few special things to learn to make laptop life easier.

For the real (or wannabe) guru, Chapter 25 presents FTP, DOS, and kernel recompiles.

Finally, the last chapter shows how to integrate Linux into your home LAN, one of the fastest growing features of home computing.

23

System Management

Purpose of Chapter:
To Make Sure Your Own Computer
is Running Optimally in Linux

Just as you keep your eye on the speedometer, tachometer, and gas gauge in your car, so should you keep your eye on a handful of important indicators in Linux. The purpose is to enhance your system's performance and to catch and correct any performance problems. In addition, knowing your system's resources and how it's using them can help you to avoid problems in the future.

System Management: The Four Major Indicators—and Constraints

The four major areas of system resources and activity are:

1. Hard disk usage
2. RAM usage
3. Swap file usage
4. CPU activity

With the correct tools, most of these systems can be not only monitored, but controlled.

Tools for System Management

The tools listed below have been familiar to the UNIX world for years. True to their roots, they do not have user-friendly displays (although `top` does have a revamped X Window version). You shouldn't let that intimidate you. The most important information these tools offer is easy to read—once you know where to look.

All these system management tools can be run at any command line, including a virtual terminal in X Window.

Disk Free—the `df` Command   In any terminal, type:

```
df
```

and hit Enter. This tool shows you hard disk usage on any currently mounted partition—except for the swap partition. A typical readout is in Figure 23-1. From the left to the right this shows that two partitions are mounted. One is close to 1 Gbyte in size, whereas the other is very small. Approximately 650 Kbytes of the first partition is used; that is, the space is already taken up with files, whereas the second partition has hardly more than 3 Kbytes of information stored on it. The next field shows space available on each partition, followed by the percentage used. Finally, the mount points of each partition are given, and from these we can see that the first is our main Linux partition, and the second is our boot partition.

Although this is not an interactive tool, and will not itself adjust anything, it is the most basic and important of the bunch—without adequate disk space, no other resource is going to matter.

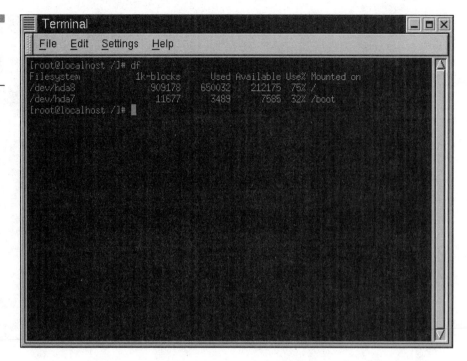

Figure 23-1

Output of the df Command, Showing Disk Usage

```
[root@localhost /]# df
Filesystem          1k-blocks        Used Available Use% Mounted on
/dev/hda8             909178      650032    212175  75% /
/dev/hda7              11677        3489      7585  32% /boot
[root@localhost /]#
```

Free Memory—the free Command   In any terminal, type:

```
free
```

and hit Enter. This tool shows you the amount of Random Access Memory (RAM) you have on your system, and how it's being used; it also shows how large a partition you have for your swap file, and the current size of your swap file. A typical readout is in Figure 23-2.

From the left, the upper line shows that this Linux machine has approximately 64 Mbytes of RAM, and that it is apparently all used—if I didn't look further, I'd be getting alarmed. However, read on to the right. It appears that over half this "used" memory is cached—and cache memory can be dynamically reallocated as free and thus is able to be used—by the operating system as it sees fit.

It's the second line that really gives us a good idea of memory usage—and how much we have left. Under "used" is 27864, which is the amount of RAM memory used, in kilobytes, minus both buffers and cache. It's evident that in fact we have over half our RAM memory still able to allocated, which is confirmed by the next number, 35532, which is the RAM nominally free, but with buffers and cache added.

Figure 23-2
Output of the free
Command, Showing
RAM Usage

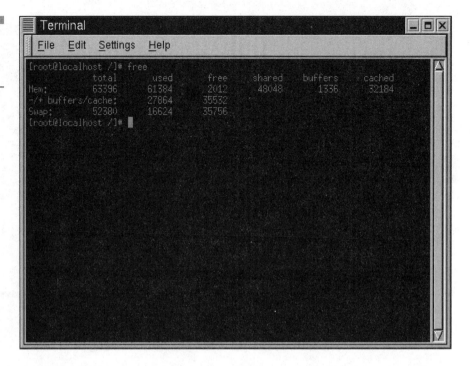

The third line is devoted to our swap partition and the swap file on it. It is not difficult to read. The first number, reading from the left, is the size in kilobytes of the partition devoted to the swap file; the second number is the current size of the swap file, and the third is free space.

Processes—the ps Command   In any terminal, type:

```
ps
```

and hit Enter.

The ps command gives you a snapshot of the active processes on your machine. Figure 23-3 shows the output of the ps command in a terminal window within X Window. The two main columns are PID and CMD. The first gives you the process ID number of that running program or process. The second gives you its name.

As an example, you can see that PID 101 belongs to apmd, which is the automatic power management program running in the background. Programs are listed in the order they started from top to bottom.

ps is useful in that it shows you what's running, and what PID it has. It sometimes happens that a program gets out of control and can't be stopped by normal means. In that case, you have to use the kill command.

Figure 23-3

Output of the ps Command, Showing Process IDs and Names

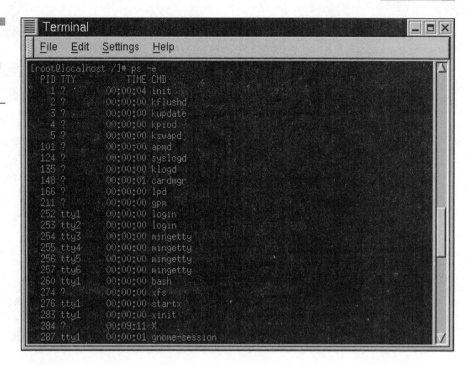

Thinning the Herd with kill The kill command does just what it implies: it kills a running process, a running program. Suppose, for instance, that while running Netscape, it suddenly locks up on you. You can't do anything with it. You can't even close it down using normal methods. You could run ps, get the PID for Netscape (in this example, 387), and kill it by typing, in a terminal window:

```
kill pid 387
```

and hitting Enter.

Netscape should vanish from the screen. If it does not, then try the command again with the -s 9 option:

```
kill -s 9 pid 387
```

This is a more drastic—more violent—method of killing the process. Sometimes it is necessary; errant processes can be hard to kill.

Top In any terminal, type:

```
top
```

and hit Enter.

Figure 23-4

Output of the top
Command, Showing
CPU and Memory
Usage

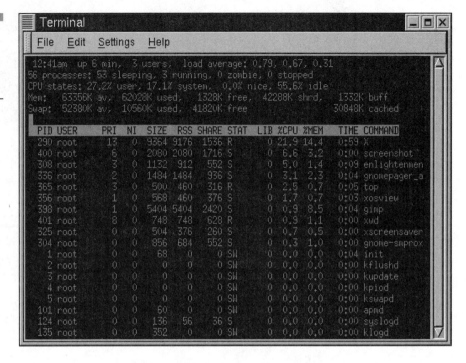

The result of this command is shown in Figure 23-4. It does not at first look appealing, but it might help if you regard it as a sort of enhanced, interactive, real-time, constantly updated version of ps.

The column on the left is familiar: PID. The two most important columns are to the right: %CPU and %MEM. All the way to the right is the actual name of the process.

The default behavior of top is to sort processes by CPU usage, with the most processor-hungry program at the top. However, you can sort programs by memory usage by pressing Shift + m. Return it to the default by pressing Shift + p.

top is your most useful program for monitoring programs' usage of resources, and for killing them off should the need occur. Simply type k and the PID, and then hit Enter. It's gone.

Two examples of how this program can be useful:

1. A program suddenly goes wacko, freezes and ties up all resources. You check top, and sure enough, the program's cpu usage is through the roof. Kill it off.

2. A program seems to shutdown normally, but won't start up again. You check top, and discover that in fact the program has left 'orphaned' processes hanging around. Kill them off. Restart the program.

Figure 23-5
The Gnome System Manager, Showing Resident Memory Usage

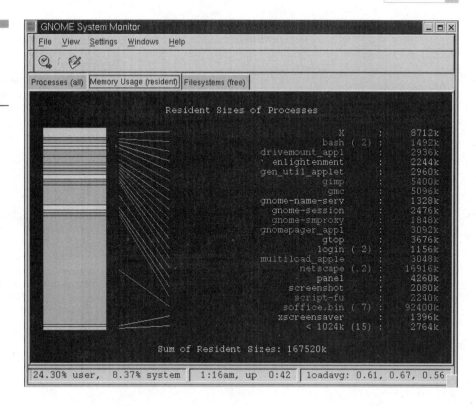

A very full-featured version of `top` for X Window is `Gtop`, or the Gnome System Monitor, found in the Utilities menu in Red Hat's Gnome. This extraordinary development of `top` is practically the ultimate system manager. Although it has the normal `top` readout—quite enhanced—it also provides graphic readout of memory and disk usage. Figure 23-5 shows its memory picture. In this example, StarOffice is clearly the single largest user of RAM.

Figure 23-6
Xosview

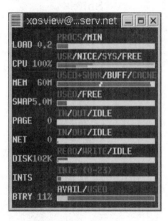

xosview This excellent X Window utility is really the ultimate Linux dashboard. Its bar graphs keep track of every major system. The example shown in Figure 23-6 is somewhat customized from the default; the configuration file is `/usr/X11R6/lib/X11/app-defaults/xosview`. Read the main page for this program—it's highly configurable.

24

Laptops

Purpose of Chapter:
To Explore Special Issues and
Programs for Users of Linux
on Laptops

Linux has had a reputation for being particularly difficult
to run successfully on laptops. However, several companies
now offer laptops with Linux pre-installed, and there is ample
evidence, on the web and elsewhere, that Linux is very configurable for most laptops on the market.

This book was written in Linux, on a Toshiba Tecra.

But laptops are special, and anyone thinking of running
Linux on theirs should be aware of certain issues, and certain programs that are particular to the laptop world.

Laptops: Issues and Programs

The downside is that there are issues that every Linux laptop user should know about, which potentially constrain performance. The upside is that the most important issue—the display—is highly configurable, and that there are excellent Linux utility programs designed particularly for the laptop user.

You will find on the web a host of third-party utility programs to help you with your laptop needs. A word of warning: although the hackers who write these programs are well-intentioned, you should consider these products as alpha software, untested, perhaps unsuitable, and possibly even dangerous to your hardware. Be careful. The programs you can count on are in your distribution—and are described in the next few pages.

The Power Management Issue

Although automatic power management is available, and works well on the whole—suspend and resume features, for instance, may work better in Linux than in Windows—there is a problem with powering down the hard disk.

It is common in Windows to power down the hard disk while on battery power. This is an excellent power conservation feature. And, the moment you go on battery power in Linux, the hard disk will in fact power down. The problem is that it may not stay down: it will usually start back up intermittently on a far more frequent basis than in Windows.

There are ways around this, but the most direct way: powering the hard disk down with the hdparm command, will usually not by itself work for more than a few moments. If you want to try this for yourself, type:

```
hdparm -Y/dev/hda
```

and hit Enter.

This problem is caused by the fact that Linux is constantly running a variety of programs that regularly access the hard disk. Some of these programs may not be strictly necessary on the typical desktop environment.

Possible Solutions

Try turning off, or at least slowing down, some of the programs which may be constantly accessing your hard disk. One of these programs is the update daemon (a 'daemon' is a program that runs and provides services in the background). Check your /etc/inittab file. If you have a line in it like this:

```
ud::once:/sbin/update
```

Change it to:

```
ud::once:/sbin/update —s3600 —f3600
```

That should slow that program down to once-an-hour access. Please note, however, that if your system crashes, it may return in a more unstable state.

The hdparm program can be used to power down your disk automatically. At the command line, type:

```
hdparm —S 120/dev/hda
```

This will set it to power down every ten minutes.

Another tip: when in X Window, avoid using utility programs that access the hard disk regularly, like top, or xosview.

Finally, try using your laptops keyboard controls for blanking the display, and turning off the hard disk. You may find that they still work quite well in the Linux environment.

On the Linux laptop home page you will find many documents that give detailed suggestions on living with Linux. Just remember: use the hacked programs on offer with care.

The Display Issue

Laptops frequently use display adapters that have been "tweaked" particularly for that machine. This means that sometimes the XF86Config file in /etc or /etc/X11 may have to be tweaked as well. Laptop Linux users are likely to become extremely familiar with their XF86Config file. Once again, the Linux laptop home page if full of useful information, including lists of both specific computers and of specific display adapters.The documents to be found in the /usr/X11R6/lib/X11/doc directory can also be very useful in this regard. If you wind up manually editing your XF86Config file, you should take particular care with the horizontal and vertical frequencies, with the dot clock settings, and also over the various options available to include.

Remember: the text-based program to configure your X Window display is xf86config.

The PCMCIA Issue

PCM cards are generally very well supported in Linux—the `cardmgr` program that detects these cards and runs them is excellent and getting better every year. However, it is possible that this program will grab an interrupt for the PCM card that the BIOS has reserved for another piece of hardware, for instance, an internal modem.

If you think this may be happening, try editing the `config.opts` file in `/etc/pcmcia`. Simply revise the "include" and "exclude" settings. An example of this file is below (Figure 24-1):

Figure 24-1
PCMCIA config.opts
File, Showing
Inclusion and
Exclusion of IRQs

```
#
# Local PCMCIA Configuration File
#
# System resources available for PCMCIA devices
#
include port 0x100-0x3ff, memory 0xc0000-0xfffff
# PCMCIA controller
## include port 0x3e0-0x3e1, memory 0xd1000-0xd1fff
# TDK PCM modem
# include port 0x2e8-0x2ef, memory 0xd0000-0xd0fff
include irq 10
#
# Extra port range for IBM Token Ring
#
include port 0xa00-0xaff
#
# Resources we should not use, even if they appear to be available
#
# First built-in serial port
exclude irq 4
# Second built-in serial port
exclude irq 3
# First built-in parallel port
exclude irq 7
# Soundblaster port
exclude irq 5
# Options for loadable modules
#
# To fix sluggish network with IBM Ethernet adapter...
#module "pcnet_cs" opts "mem_speed=600"
#
# Options for Xircom Netwave driver...
#module "netwave_cs" opts "domain=0x100 scramble_key=0x0"
```

Linux Utility Programs for Laptops

There are two of particular interest: `cardctl`, for controlling PCM cards at the command line, and `apm`, which suspends the computer.

cardctl   This utility not only identifies which PCM cards you have, and their resources, it can also electronically "eject" them, and reinsert them. To see the status of your PCM cards, type:

```
cardctl ident
```

and hit Enter.

To eject them—electronically turn them off—type:

```
cardctl eject
```

and hit Enter.

To re-insert them, type:

```
cardctl insert
```

and hit Enter.

Besides showing exactly what resources these cards are using, it is usually a very good idea to eject your PCM cards before suspending them. More on that in the next section, below.

apm   To use this program to send your laptop into suspend mode, type:

```
apm -s
```

and hit Enter.

You will probably be astonished at how fast it goes under. This program can safely be run from within a terminal in X Window and is generally more stable, and leads to more successful suspend/resumes, than its Windows counterparts.

If you have one or more PCM cards, then it is a good idea to make a small executable file that uses first the `cardctl` utility, then apm. An example:

```
cardctl eject
apm -s
```

This simple two-line file will, when run from a terminal, first electronically eject your PCM cards, then suspend your machine. The cards will be automatically re-inserted upon resuming operation.

Web Support

There is an amazing amount of it. Not only are lots of people using Linux on Laptops, they are writing about it, too. Start at the Linux laptop home page, at `www.cs.utexas.edu/users/kharker/linux-laptop`. This site is a treasure trove for laptops users. It includes information on specific laptop models, specific laptop issues and programs, as well as general information on the subject. The PCMCIA home page is also a good place to visit: `www.pc-card.com`. Bookmark both addresses.

## CHAPTER 25

FTP, DOS, and Kernel Recompiles

Purpose of Chapter: To Introduce Internet File Transfers at the Command Line, DOS Emulation, and Kernel Recompiles

This chapter is divided into three distinct sections:

1. FTP
2. DOS
3. Kernel Recompiles

The File Transport Protocol (FTP) was one of the earliest ways of transferring files across a network. In terms of efficiency, it is still the best.

If you've been into computers for more than six or seven years, you probably remember DOS. It's quite common for people who once used that operating system to still use a couple of DOS programs in Windows—they're used to them, and the slowest DOS program runs faster than the fastest Windows equivalent.

Finally, kernel recompiles. I've seen at least one distribution, after a very standard installation, refuse to recognize Windows file systems. In that case, the kernel would have to be recompiled, with that support turned on. Fortunately, the need for kernel recompiles decreases as distributors produce better installation routines and Linux matures.

Using the File Transport Protocol (FTP)

Command-line FTP is a common and efficient way to send or receive a file across the Internet or even a LAN—as long as you know exactly where you're sending the file to, or where it's coming from.

Specific examples of when you might want to use FTP to send or receive a file include:

1. Downloading the executable of the latest office application suite from the company LAN

2. Uploading your latest sales, production, or maintenance report to your division headquarters

3. Downloading the latest bug fix for your Linux machine

4. Uploading a recently completed chapter from your book to your publisher

In all cases, FTP is a simple, swift, efficient command-line solution that will happily run in the background while you get on with your work.

A Sample FTP Session

Suppose you wanted to download a file named xsnow.rpm from an FTP site called sunsite.unc.edu/pub/linux/games. First you would connect

What's an RPM File?

A file with the extension of rpm is a "Red Hat package management file," in other words, a Linux program file that is compressed and prepackaged to install itself correctly and automatically. This is a considerable improvement over the traditional method of downloading a file that is a consolidated and compressed set of "source" files. Such a file first has to be uncompressed, then unconsolidated, and finally compiled. When downloading Linux program files, you will often be given the choice of an rpm file, or a file with an extension such as tar, or tzp. Take my advice, and choose the rpm file.

To install an rpm file, for instance, dosemu.rpm, simply type:

```
rpm -ivh dosemu.rpm
```

and hit Enter.

to your ISP—perhaps with the script you learned in Chapter 11. Then, in your login terminal, one of the full screen virtual terminals, or in an X Window terminal, access the FTP site by typing the following:

```
ftp sunsite.unc.edu
```

and hitting Enter. Presently you'll see a message that you are connected, and a line asking you for your name. Login as anonymous, by typing the word and hitting Enter. You'll then be asked to enter your complete e-mail address in lieu of a password. Enter it, and hit Enter again. At this point you'll probably see four lines on your screen:

```
Logged in anonymously.
Remote system type is UNIX.
Using binary mode to transfer files.
ftp>
```

You're in.

Your next job is to navigate to the directory your file is in. You use the same command-line commands that you learned in Chapter 8. In this case, type:

```
cd /pub/linux/games
```

and hit Enter. Now, to make sure the file you want is there, use the ls command to list the files in the directory—if there are quite a few, you may want to try ls xsnow.rpm.

Once you verify that your file is there, you want to download it. There are two modes for downloading files, depending on whether they are ASCII (text) or binary. We'll assume that xsnow is a binary file, so make sure that the binary mode is turned on by typing:

```
bin
```

and hitting Enter. Now, to download the file, type:

```
get xsnow.rpm
```

and hit Enter. The file will download. The remote system will inform you when download is completed. The next step is to log off. To do this, simply type:

```
bye
```

and press Enter.

Some Tips

Before logging on, it's a good idea to make sure that you are at the directory you want to download the file into. Although it's quite simple to change your local directory after connecting, it's an easy thing to forget to do. If you are uploading or downloading several files at a time, start the FTP session with `ftp -i`. This turns off prompting, which can be a real pain if you have several large files. Use wildcard characters. A good example of how useful they can be is if you wanted to upload every single file in a local directory. The command `mput *` would take care of it.

Summary of Useful Commands

There are dozens of FTP commands. Those listed in Table 25-1 are only the most common and most useful.

TABLE 25-1

Common FTP
Commands

Command	Function
`ftp` (FTP address)	Logs in
`ftp -i` (FTP address)	Logs in without prompting for multiple file up or downloads
`bin`	Changes to binary mode
`asc`	Changes to ASCII (text) mode
`ls`	Lists contents of directories
`pwd`	Displays the working directory of the remote system
`lcd`	Displays the working directory of the local system
`lcd` (directory)	Changes the working directory of the local system
`cd` (directory)	Changes the directory on the remote system
`get`	Downloads a file
`mget`	Downloads several files
`put`	Uploads a file
`mput`	Uploads several files
`bye`	Terminates the FTP session

■ ■ ■ DOS

The Linux DOS emulator has been around for quite a few years, and it is still undergoing development and refinement—proof that in Linux, nothing ever dies.

Obtaining the DOS Emulator

Most distributions come with the DOS emulator included, and on some of them it even works the first time you try it. However, the emulator is a moving target—like so much in Linux—and you may as well benefit from running the latest version. The latest version can be downloaded from the FTP site at `ftp.dosemu.org`. Follow these directions:

1. Start up your Internet connection.

2. To connect to the site and start your FTP session, type:

   ```
   ftp ftp.dosemu.org
   ```

   and hit Enter.

3. Now log on as anonymous, and give your e-mail address as a password.

4. `Cd to dosemu`. The start message will tell you which is the latest stable version of `dosemu` (as of this writing, the latest stable version was 0.98.8).

Linux More Backward-Compatible on Microsoft Products Than Microsoft

Microsoft has recently announced that in order to enhance the stability of the latest version of its operating system, Windows 2000, it will no longer permit the loading or running of some older software designed for DOS (Microsoft's own product) and even for earlier versions of Windows. Linux, on the other hand, not only supports many older DOS programs, it also supports an increasing number of Windows programs as well, through the WINE project—without sacrificing stability.

5. Look for all versions of the latest stable version by typing:

   ```
   ls dosemu-0.98*
   ```

   Look for an rpm version—one that ends with the rpm extension. This will be much more likely to load properly and include X Window support.

6. Make sure you're in binary mode by typing:

   ```
   bin
   ```

   and hitting Enter.

7. Download the file by typing:

   ```
   get dosemu-0.98.8-1.i386.rpm
   ```

   and hitting Enter.

8. The latest version is a not inconsiderable 1.4 Mbytes, even in rpm format, so the download will take a little while. Once it's finished, type:

   ```
   bye
   ```

   and hit Enter to close the connection. Now log off the Internet.

Installing the DOS Emulator

If you have downloaded the rpm file, installation should be a breeze. At the command prompt and the directory where you downloaded the file, simply type:

```
rpm -ivh —force dosemu*
```

and hit Enter. (The options stand for: I = install; v = verbose; h = use hash marks to mark the progress of the installation; and force = forcibly install the package, even if another version or the same version is already installed.)

Setup and Configuration

To begin with, the program files necessary to set up the DOS emulator are in the /var/lib/dosemu directory. The ASCII document files that tell you how to set up and configure the emulator are in the /usr/doc/dosemu directory.

Setup and configuration of the DOS emulator can be quite simple, or quite difficult, depending on the circumstances. There are several things to consider. For instance, where are the DOS programs that you want to run? On your C drive? On a typically set up computer, that will become your D drive in the DOS emulator, and that may end up confusing your DOS programs—you may have to reconfigure them.

I have come to the conclusion that if you are serious about running DOS programs in Linux, it is a good idea to divide your hard disk into three major partitions: a primary, C drive for Windows; another primary C drive for the DOS operating system; and an extended partition, the first logical drive of which is D, for your DOS applications (the remainder of the extended partition would be given up to Linux). Because only one primary partition is every visible at a time on a PC, this setup allows you to run your DOS programs, without any reconfiguration, in Windows, in DOS, and in Linux via the DOS emulator. It is important to remember that whether you have your DOS programs on your Window partition or a separate primary partition, that partition must be in your `fstab` file, and mounted on your file system.

First, make a DOS boot disk. This is not necessary if you are running an older version of DOS on a mounted partition, but it is necessary on some computers running recent versions of Windows. I'll use this as the default method to get started.

1. Boot up Windows, and immediately hit F8 and choose to boot up to the command prompt only.

2. Insert a blank, formatted floppy, and type:

   ```
   sys a:
   ```

   and hit Enter.

3. This will transfer the basic DOS files you need to the floppy. Remove the floppy and reboot into Linux.

4. Start up X Window.

5. Open a virtual terminal.

6. Within the terminal, change the directory to `/var/lib/dosemu`.

7. Type:

   ```
   ./setup-dosemu
   ```

   and hit Enter. The DOSEMU Run-Time Configuration window appears (Figure 25-1). This is an interactive program to set up your DOS emulator configuration file.

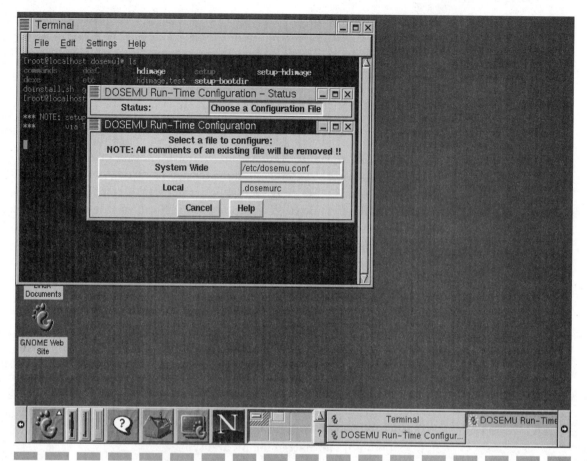

Figure 25-1   DOSEMU Run-Time Configuration Window

8. Click on the System Wide bar. The Main Menu appears (Figure 25-2).

9. Click on the Keyboard bar. The Keyboard interrupts box is already checked, but the Bypass normal keyboard input box has a warning that checking it might be dangerous. I have found, however, that it definitely helps WordPerfect. I advise checking it.

10. Click on the Serial Ports & Mice bar, and then on the Serial bar.

11. This section of the setup is useful primarily for setting up an internal or external modem. Yours is likely to be on COM2. If it is, then click in the blank next to COM2, and type:

```
/dev/ttyS1
```

Figure 25-2
Main Menu for
DOSEMU
Configuration

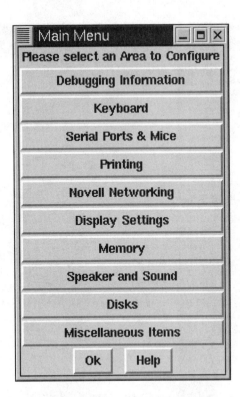

12. Then click on the OK button (for a complete list of DOS and Linux serial port IDs, consult Table 11-1).

13. Now click on the Mouse bar. The Mouse Configuration window comes up (Figure 25-3). Check the box next to the type of mouse you have. Usually, it will be a PS/2. Next, in the blank next to Device - com1, com2, etc., type in the port your mouse is connected to. Usually you can simply type /dev/mouse.

14. Click on the OK button, and then again on the next OK button to get back to the Main Menu.

15. You generally don't have to worry about Printing. But click on the Display Settings bar. The X Window and Terminal will generally be set correctly. However, do click on the General Video bar.

16. Click on the Video Chipset bar, and choose your adapter type, if it's listed. Then click on the OK button.

17. Make sure that the first three boxes beneath the Video Chipset bar are checked, and then click on Video Bios Details. If you know these settings on your computer, make sure the entries are correct.

Figure 25-3

Mouse Menu for
DOSEMU
Configuration

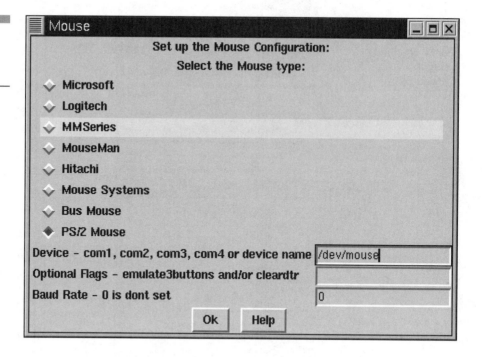

18. Click on the OK buttons until you get back to the Main Menu.

19. Click on the Memory bar. The normal settings are fine for late DOS programs. Earlier DOS programs used EMS memory. If you want to set this up, type in 2048 next to Amount of EMS. Click on the OK button.

20. Click on the Speaker and Sound bar. Click on the Speaker bar, and check the Emulated box. Click on OK.

21. Click on the Sound Card Emulation bar. At this time, only Sound Blaster–compatible cards are supported. If yours is a compatible card, check the box and make sure the settings are correct. Click on the OK button.

22. The Disks settings are critical. Click on the Disks button.

23. Your floppy drive is probably set up correctly, but you should click on the blank next to Hard Drives and type in the following (as in Figure 25-4):

```
hdimage.first /dev/hda1
```

and then hit the OK button.

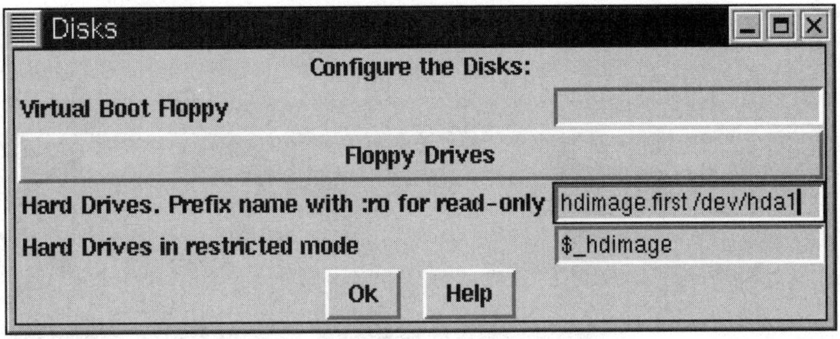

Figure 25-4
Disk Menu for
DOSEMU
Configuration

Figure 25-4
Disk Menu for
DOSEMU
Configuration

24. Note that this will enable the emulator to read your Windows partition—which I assume is where your current DOS programs are. However, if your DOS programs are on a second primary partition, then you should include that partition instead.

25. And that's it. Click on the Main Menu's OK button, check Replace Existing File, and click on the OK button once more. Your configuration file is written—for those interested, it is `/etc/dosemu.conf`.

26. You're returned to the terminal window. Type:

    `./setup-hdimage`

    and hit Enter.

27. A message appears that there don't seem to be any bootable DOS partitions. Reinsert your bootable floppy disk, and type:

    `/dev/fd0`

    and hit Enter twice.

28. Hit Enter again, twice.

29. When your terminal window looks like Figure 25-5, type:

    `wq`

    and hit Enter.

30. Type the same thing and hit Enter again at the next screen.

That's it. You've finished—if you're lucky! Try it out by typing:

    `xdos`

and pressing Enter. You should see a screen something like Figure 25-6.

Figure 25-5

Config.sys File
Screen in Last Stage
of DOS Configuration

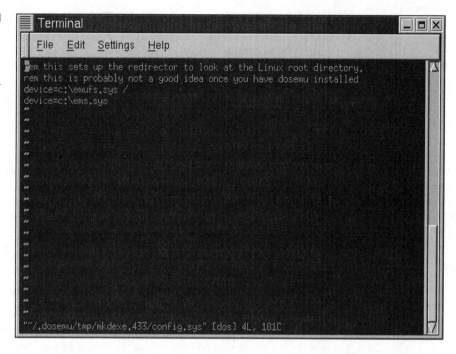

Figure 25-6

Initial Xdos Screen

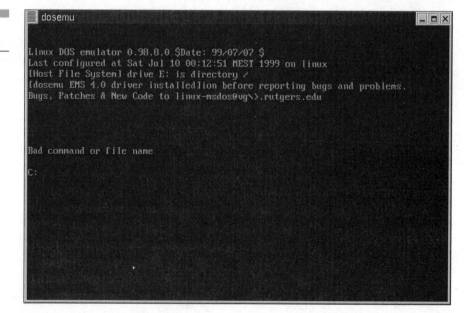

The emulator is started at the command line by typing dos and hitting Enter, and in X Window by opening a terminal window and typing xdos. Quit the emulator by typing exitemu.

If the emulator doesn't start, you should check the following:

1. Is the C partition mounted? It shouldn't be. The emulator will read it by itself, without you mounting it in Linux.

2. Is the video card information configured correctly? Graphics are still poorly supported in the emulator. You may have to turn the graphics off entirely.

You can run the setup-dosemu program as many times as you want to try and change or simplify setting. However, if it's getting you nowhere, then you had best remove the contents of the /var/lib/dosemu directory, and start over by reinstalling the rpm file. This time, skip the setup-dosemu program entirely, and only run setup-hdimage. The default configuration that results should get you up and running.

Kernel Recompiles

Recompiling your kernel is much easier than installing the DOS emulator—it is also much more serious, and more dangerous. Misconfiguring a DOS emulator is nothing. Doing the same to your kernel can easily destroy your system.

This is something that, unless you are an inveterate tweaker, it is better to leave alone if you can. And there is less and less need for it. At one time it was often necessary to recompile because the installation program failed to discover all of your hardware. It was also often necessary when you added a new bit of hardware to your system. But in both cases Linux has now grown more sophisticated, and the necessity of recompiling is becoming, if not rare, at least less likely.

The main reasons to recompile your kernel are:

1. To add functionality in order to get something to work

2. To lessen unneeded functionality in order to reduce the kernel's size and memory requirements.

3. To upgrade to a more recent kernel

The first and second reasons are fine. The third is becoming less and less reasonable because of the subsidiary requirements. With each new version of the Linux kernel, the latest versions of hosts of other programs are needed. The kernel, after all, is just what it sounds like: the center, or heart, of the operating system. It needs many other programs to drive a modern PC productively. The hassle of making sure that every single peripheral file or resource or program is also up-to-date is something best left to the commercial distributors. Buy a CD. Stay away from recompiling for the hell of it unless you have the leisure to struggle and fiddle for hours.

Recompilation

The steps necessary are neither very many, nor very difficult. There is, however, one primary, cardinal rule: only change one thing at a time! The temptation to change a number of things at once can be hard to resist, especially when you discover how long a recompile can take. But it should be resisted. Changing one small thing in a kernel, even something apparently quite harmless, can lead to unforeseen consequences. If you make several changes, it may be almost impossible to successfully troubleshoot the problem and get things back to normal.

1. First, start up X Window.

2. Next, open a terminal window.

3. `cd` to `/usr/src/`.

4. Do an `ls` and see what you've got in that directory. You should have three directories:

   `linux`   `linux-2.2.12`   `redhat`

   You need at least the linux directories. They contain the source files that actually build the new kernel. However, you'll also need a host of other files—dependencies of various sorts—to get the source files to actually work. If the `linux` directories aren't there, your best bet is to reinstall Linux, making sure you choose the kernel development package—probably in a "custom," or "expert" install.

5. If the Linux directories are there, `cd` to `linux-2.2.12` (either Linux directory would do—one is a link to the other).

6. Now type:

   `make xconfig`

   and hit Enter.

7. Presently, the Linux Kernel Configuration window will appear (Figure 25-7). This is where it's essential that you really do have an idea of what you're doing—or at least of what you want. As an example, suppose you have recently added a sound card and want to load the sound module that may make it work. Or, you've recently added a new Ethernet card and want to load that support. These are examples of concrete needs—which, unless you have a great deal of leisure time, are the only justification for going through this. And remember: only change one thing at a time.

8. Click on the section you're interested in, and choose the driver that appears to have the functionality you're looking for. When you're finished, click on the Save and Exit bar.

9. Click on the OK button.

10. Now, back in the terminal, type:

    ```
    make dep
    ```

    and hit Enter.

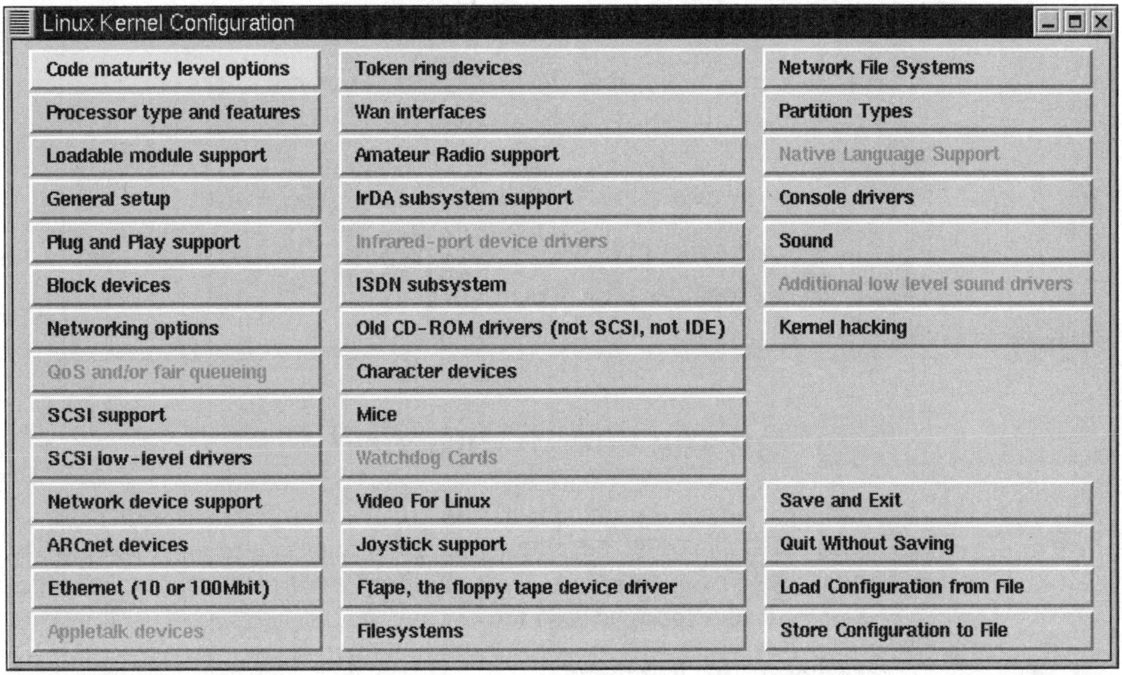

Linux Kernel Configuration		
Code maturity level options	Token ring devices	Network File Systems
Processor type and features	Wan interfaces	Partition Types
Loadable module support	Amateur Radio support	Native Language Support
General setup	IrDA subsystem support	Console drivers
Plug and Play support	Infrared-port device drivers	Sound
Block devices	ISDN subsystem	Additional low level sound drivers
Networking options	Old CD-ROM drivers (not SCSI, not IDE)	Kernel hacking
QoS and/or fair queueing	Character devices	
SCSI support	Mice	
SCSI low-level drivers	Watchdog Cards	
Network device support	Video For Linux	Save and Exit
ARCnet devices	Joystick support	Quit Without Saving
Ethernet (10 or 100Mbit)	Ftape, the floppy tape device driver	Load Configuration from File
Appletalk devices	Filesystems	Store Configuration to File

Figure 25-7   Linux Kernel Configuration Window

11. When it has finished making dependencies, type:

    ```
    make zImage
    ```

    and hit Enter (note the unusual capitalization of `zImage`). `zImage` is the compressed kernel `image`. Making this is likely to take some time. Sit back and relax.

12. If you get an error message saying that your system is too large, type:

    ```
    make bzImage
    ```

    and hit Enter.

13. When that's finished, the next step is to move the new kernel image to your boot directory. Type:

    ```
    cd arch/i386/boot
    ```

    and hit Enter (this will take you to the `/usr/src/linux/arch/i386/boot` directory).

    Type:

    ```
    mv bzImage /boot
    ```

    and hit Enter.

14. Next, make your modules. First change directory back to `/usr/src/linux-2.2.12`. Then type:

    ```
    make modules
    ```

    and hit Enter.

15. When that is finished—it will take some time—type:

    ```
    make modules_install
    ```

    and hit Enter (note the underline between modules and install).

Configuring and Running LILO

Although the new kernel is made, and its modules made as well, the boot loader, LILO, is so far unaware of it. If you reboot right now, chances are you won't see any difference at all. You first have to add the new kernel to the boot loader configuration file `lilo.conf`.

1. Change directory to `/etc`

2. Type:

    ```
    vi lilo.conf
    ```

Figure 25-8
lilo.conf

```
boot=/dev/hda
map=/boot/map
install=/boot/boot.b
prompt
timeout=50
image=/boot/vmlinuz-2.2.12
      label=linux
      root=/dev/hda6
      read-only
other=/dev/hda1
      label=dos
      table=/dev/hda
```

and hit Enter. You will probably see something like Figure 25-8.
Use the editing skills you learned in Chapter 9 to add the two lines
shown in Figure 25-9:

3. Now, the final step. Type:

lilo

and hit Enter.

You should be given a message, probably consisting of three lines, that all
three images have been added.

Cross your fingers and reboot. When you get to the LILO prompt, hit the
Tab key. Type the label you've given to the new kernel image.

Good luck!

Figure 25-9
Edited lilo.conf,
with New Kernel
Added

```
boot=/dev/hda
map=/boot/map
install=/boot/boot.b
prompt
timeout=50
image=/boot/vmlinuz-2.2.12
      label=linux
      root=/dev/hda6
      read-only
image=/boot/bzImage
      label=new
other=/dev/hda1
      label=dos
      table=/dev/hda
```

26

Home Networking with Linux

Purpose of Chapter:
To Show How to Share Resources with Multiple PCs in a Home LAN

A recent market survey indicated that the number of home LANs will increase fourfold during the next three years. But that survey was for Windows only computers—what if you want to share your LAN with your Linux PC?

This chapter will show you how, in a mixed Windows/Linux environment, you can share:

- Files
- Printers
- Network connections

In this chapter I take it for granted that you access the internet through a dial-up modem connection, and already have either:

1. a home LAN running, using Windows and Ethernet cabling, or

2. at the least, you have network interface cards (NICs) already installed in your computers, and the Windows drivers, cabling and hub are also connected.

The Home LAN and Linux

Sharing printers and sharing an internet connection are the two most popular reasons for setting up a local area network (LAN) in your home.

Setting up a home LAN with Microsoft Windows is now, especially with the profusion of home networking kits on the market, as simple as falling off a log. It is not yet quite that simple for the beginner to network Linux into a Windows dominated LAN—although system administrators have been doing it and relying on it for years in corporations around the world. However, setting up such a LAN is getting easier, particularly with some of the newer X Window tools available in RedHat and Caldera. It is definitely not beyond the range of the home enthusiast.

The difficulty with setting up a mixed Linux/Windows network is that the two operating systems speak different networking languages—their basic 'protocols' are different. Linux uses TCP/IP to connect with other Linux machines—the same protocol that it uses in a regular Internet connection. Windows however uses a completely different protocol called SMB to connect with other Windows machines.

The answer? Samba—a program designed to enable the two different operating systems to network together.

Practically speaking this simply means a little more setup. On the Windows side, it is all point-and-click. On the Linux side, it is also mostly point-and-click—but there is also a little bit of text file editing still to do.

Sharing Files

To setup file sharing between your Linux machine and your Windows machines, you need to:

1. Make sure that your Windows computers are setup for TCP/IP networking on their Ethernet adapter, and are setup for Windows file and print sharing (easy).

2. Make sure that both computers are setup for the same LAN.

3. Enable Samba support on the Linux computer.

Setting Up Your Windows Computers for TCP/IP Networking

This is the first and undoubtedly the easiest part of the undertaking. There are only a few steps involved. The instructions below hold good for both Windows 95 and 98.

1. Click on Start, navigate to Settings, and Control Panel. Now double-click on the Network icon.

   If you already have a Windows LAN working, then you have quite a list of network components in the Configuration window (Figure 26-1). Although you should already have both Client for Microsoft Networks, and NetBEUI installed, it doesn't hurt to check, or even to install them again.

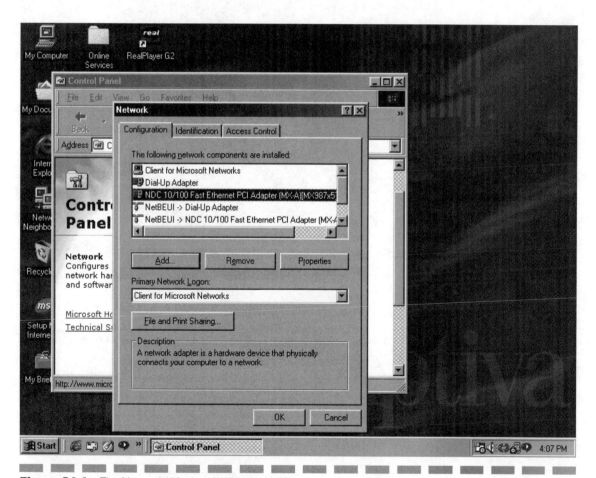

Figure 26-1 The Network Window in Windows 98

1. Click once on the line showing your Ethernet adapter card, and then click on the Add button. In the Select Network Component Type window, click on Protocol, and on the Add button.

2. The next window to appear, Select Network Protocol, has a number of choices. In the left pane, under Manufacturers, click on Microsoft. Then, in the right pane, under Network Protocols, scroll down to TCP/IP (Figure 26-2). Select it with your mouse, and click on the OK button.

Figure 26-2
Adding TCP/IP

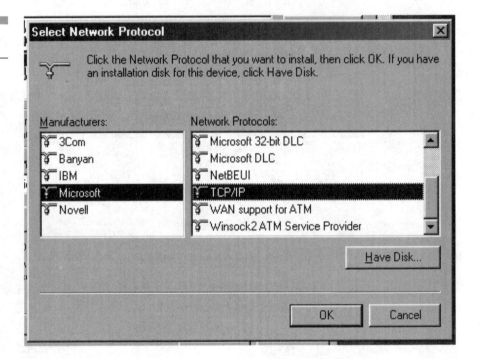

3. Now do precisely the same thing over again, but instead of adding TCP/IP, add NetBEUI.

4. Next, a step you've probably already done if you set up a Windows LAN: click on the Add button again, and then select Service. Click on that window's Add button, and in the Select Network Service window choose File and printer sharing for Microsoft Networks (Figure 26-3). Click on the OK button.

Figure 26-3

Adding File and
Printer Sharing for
Microsoft Networks

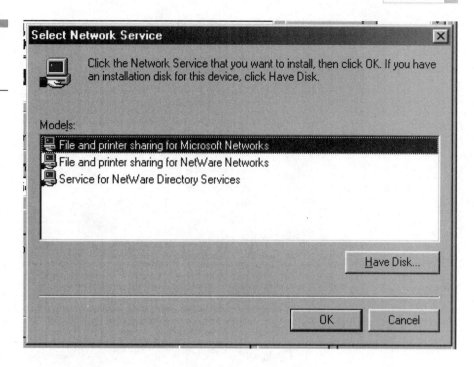

Figure 26-3

Adding File and
Printer Sharing for
Microsoft Networks

5. Back in the Network window, click on the File and Print Sharing
button, and check both boxes in the small window that appears
(Figure 26-4).

6. Finally, repeat another Windows LAN step: double-click on the My
Computer icon on the desktop, right-click once on the C drive icon,
and click on Share. Click on the Sharing tab. Check the Shared As
button, and in the Share Name box, type in an obvious name for the
C drive—such as 'C', for instance. Under Access Type, check Full,
and leave the Password box at the bottom blank (Figure 26-5).

Make Sure That Both Computers Are Setup
for the Same LAN

This is a bit more complex, but not impossibly so—we should start first
with some brief examples of domain names and IP addresses, and then
move on to configuring first your Windows machines, and then your Linux
machine.

Figure 26-4
Enabling File and
Print Sharing

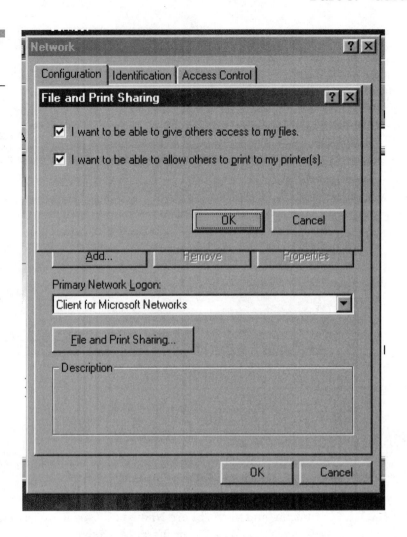

Domain names are how people identify their own and other computers on the internet. The term, 'domain name', as generally used, is actually short for 'fully qualified domain name', or FQDN. Each FQDN is made up of a hostname, and at least one level of domain name. Some examples:

Hostname	Subdomain	Subdomain	Domain	= FQDN
pbs			org	= pbs.org
peter	telus		net	= peter.telus.net
wangyi	hr	motorola	com	= wangyi.hr.motorola.com
commons	parliament	gov	uk	= commons.parliament.gov.uk

That's how people identify computers. But how do computers identify themselves and others? Not through such easy-to-read names. Rather

Figure 26-5
Enabling Sharing
on a Windows
Hard Drive

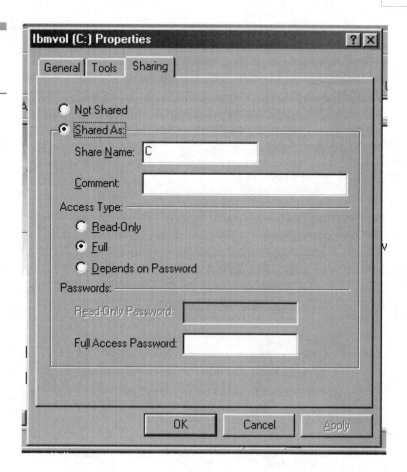

through Internet Protocol (or IP), addresses. A program called a name resolver converts human-readable domain names to machine-readable IP names.

Does My Computer Need an IP Address? For the dial-up modem connection, don't worry about it. Your ISP probably gives you an IP address automatically each time you dial in. And in a pure Windows home LAN, computer addresses are handled by the operating system. All you need to supply are specific computer names and a Windows workgroup.

Linux, however, uses TCP/IP—the same protocol that the Internet uses—to connect the computers on a LAN together. So, yes, even if you have a dial-up connection, and even if you are currently networked through Windows—yes, you do need to give each computer its own IP address if you want to connect them in a Linux LAN.

Assigning Names and Addresses on a Home LAN Basically, for a home LAN whose computers use a dial-up modem connection to connect to the Internet, you can usually assign your computers any name or address you want. When they're connected to the Internet, they'll use the address your ISP gives them. When they talk via Ethernet among themselves, they'll use the address you provide.

But you might as well do things right. It so happens that there are whole ranges of IP addresses that are reserved especially for intranets. I shall use one of these ranges in the examples in this chapter.

Consider how you want to choose your host and domain names. One plan is to use your family name, or your initials, as your domain name (remember: this is only for your internal, home LAN). Such a solution may be banal, but it is at least easy to remember. In this example, I'll use my initials, jpl, for my domain name—common across all the computers on my network—and, since each computer is from a different manufacturer, I shall use their manufacturers' initials as their hostnames. Therefore the three computers belonging to this home LAN are named:

```
toshiba.jpl
ibm.jpl
hp.jpl     (hp for Hewlett Packard)
```

The IP addresses are from one of the ranges mentioned above. The computers' domain names and their corresponding IP addresses are below:

```
toshiba.jpl   192.168.0.1
ibm.jpl       192.168.0.2
hp.jpl        192.168.0.3
```

Once again, I could assign any name and address I wanted, since this is just an internal LAN. But it is just as well to assign names and addresses that make sense, and are easy to recall.

Assigning Names and Addresses in Windows

1. Go back to the Network window which you reached earlier in this chapter, and click on the Identification tab. (This step may not be absolutely necessary, but it will help harmonize your Windows and Linux settings.) In the Computer Name blank, type in the computer's hostname. In the Workgroup blank, type in the domain name you have decided on (Figure 26-6).

2. Now click on the Access Control tab, right next to the Identification tab, and check the small 'Share-level Access Control' button.

Figure 26-6
Identifying
Your Networked
Computers

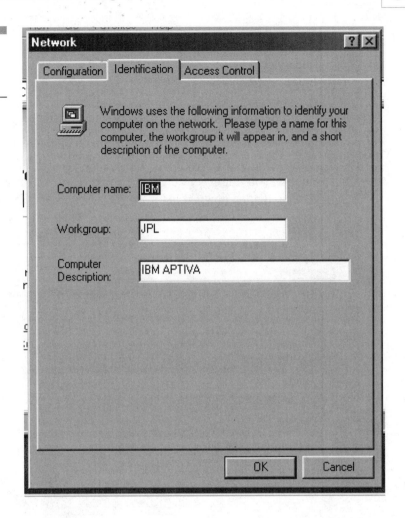

3. Go back to the Configuration tab. Scroll down the window until you see a line that begins with: TCP/IP, and includes the specific manufacturer and model of your Ethernet adapter. An example would be:

```
TCP/IP -> NDC 10/100 Fast Ethernet PCI Adapter
(MX-A)[MX987x5]
```

4. Highlight this line and click on the Properties button below it. The TCP/IP Properties window will open.

5. Click on the IP Address tab, and check the 'Specify an IP Address' button. Then fill in the IP Address line below, with the address of that particular computer. Beneath it, fill in the Subnet Mask line

as shown in Figure 26-7. (Note: for a more thorough but still basic discussion of IP addresses, etc., see the NET3-4-HOWTO.txt file in the appendix.)

6. Next, click on the DNS Configuration tab, and check the Enable DNS button.

7. In the Host and Domain boxes, type in the hostname and domain name that you have assigned your machine. See Figure 26-8.

8. Although the next section is not strictly needed until later in this chapter, you might as well do it at this point, since you've already drilled down this far. In the DNS Server Search Order box, type in the same nameserver addresses that you entered in the /etc/resolv.conf file on your Linux machine (see chapter 11),

Figure 26-7
Filling in the IP
Address and
Subnet Mask

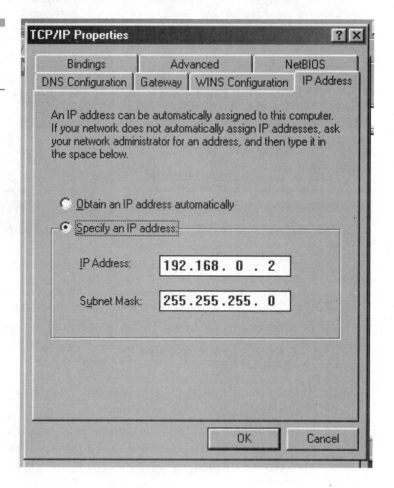

and click on the Add button to get them in the lower box. Finally, under Domain Suffix Search Order, type in the domain name of your ISP, and the domain name you assigned your home LAN (Figure 26-8).

Assigning Names and Addresses in Linux   There are two ways to go here: use your X Window's graphical system to edit the necessary files, or do it manually. The only system I've found that sets up everything properly and consistently is Redhat's Network Configurator, in Gnome. I shall first walk you through that graphical system, then list the files that have to be edited, if you want to do it manually instead.

Figure 26-8
DNS Configuration

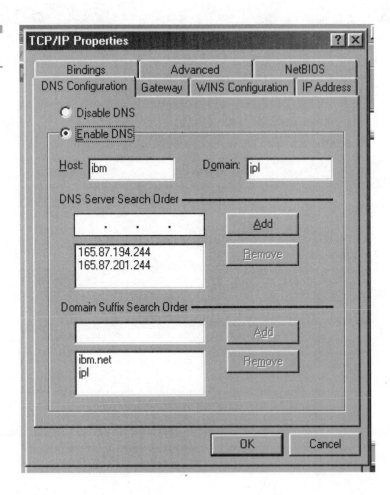

1. In Gnome, click on the Start button (that footprint), then up to System, and over and down to Control Panel. Click on Control Panel.

2. When you place your mouse pointer over the fourth icon from the top, it should say, Network Configuration. Click on that icon.

3. The Network Configurator program appears (Figure 26-9). Notice in the Names window that I have written in the name of my Linux machine in the Hostname section, and my local domain beneath. In the area below, I have written in my ISP's domain name (ibm.net). Beneath that are my ISP's nameservers. All of this information comes from and goes into your /etc/resolv.conf file.

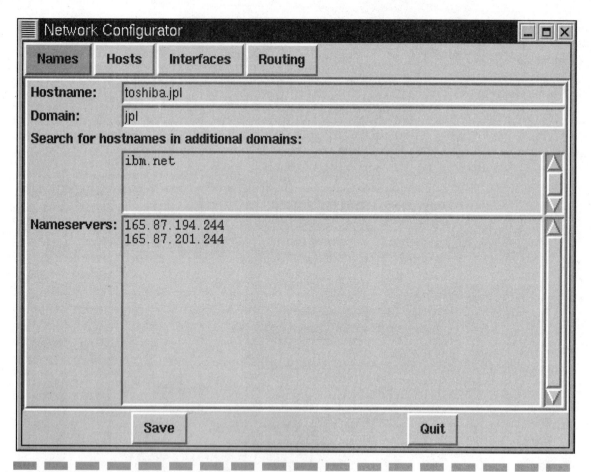

Figure 26-9　Assigning a Hostnames, Domains, and Nameservers in Red Hat Linux

4. Click on the Hosts button (Figure 26-10). This information is from
your /etc/hosts file. Basically, your machine looks in here to
resolve host names, before going into the resolv.conf file.
Entering your various machines' local host names and local ISP
addresses in here just speeds up the process of finding them. The
first line, the 'localhost', is always included.

5. Next, click on the Interfaces button to open up that window. This
configures your Ethernet card. Select your card, and click on the
Edit button at the bottom. Your screen should now look something
like Figure 26-11. Notice the similarities between this screen and
Windows' IP Address screen, in the Network-TCP/IP section. In the

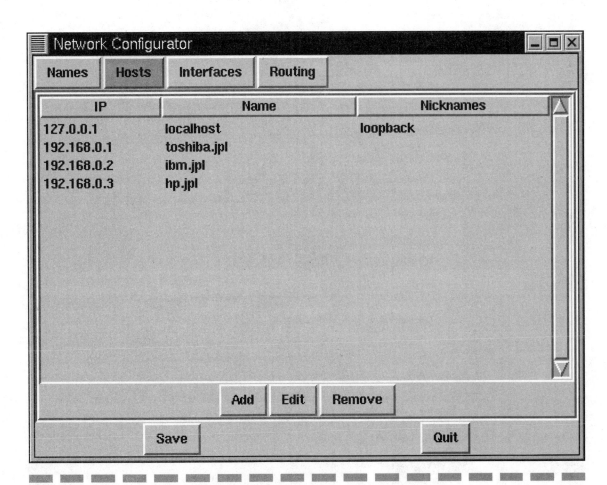

Figure 26-10 IP Addresses and Names (From the /etc/hosts File)

example shown in Figure 26-11, I have entered the IP address for the Linux machine on my local LAN. In addition, I have configured the interface to be active at boot.

6. Finally, click on the Routing button. Strictly speaking, this is not needed for this section of the chapter; this actually configures sharing an internet connection. However, since you're here, you might as well configure it now. Make sure that Default Gateway shows your Linux machine's IP address, and that Network Packet Forwarding is checked (Figure 26-12).

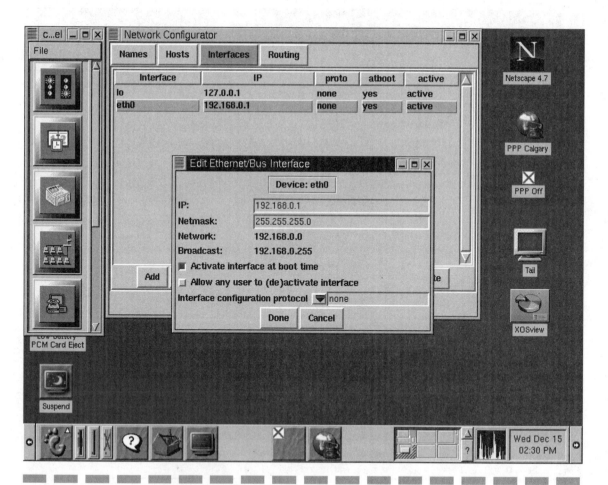

Figure 26-11   Editing the Ethernet Interface

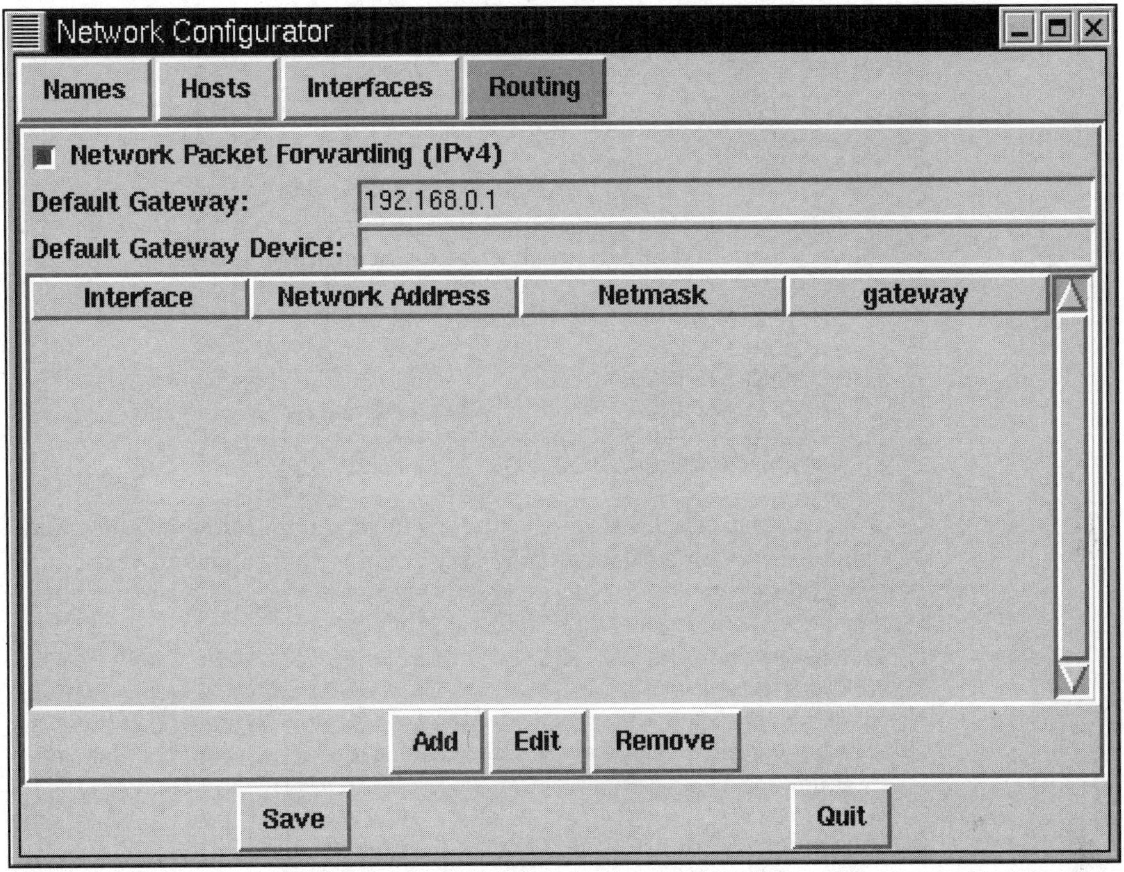

Figure 26-12 Network Packet Forwarding (for Your Linux Internet Server)

If you have a different distribution, and want to edit the necessary files manually, or just check up on them, here they are, in the order in which they were edited in the steps above:

```
/etc/resolv.conf
/etc/hosts
/etc/sysconfig/network-scripts/ifcfg-eth0
/etc/sysconfig/network
```

An example of the /etc/resolv.conf file:

```
search jpl ibm.net
nameserver 165.87.194.244
nameserver 165.87.201.244
```

An example of the /etc/hosts file:

```
127.0.0.1      localhost      loopback
192.168.0.1    toshiba.jpl
192.168.0.2    ibm.jpl
192.168.0.3    hp.jpl
```

The /etc/sysconfig/network-scripts/ifcfg-eth0 file is likely to be very long. Just make sure that the following lines—examples—are in it:

```
DEVICE=eth0
IPADDR=192.168.0.1
NETMASK=255.255.255.0
GATEWAY=192.168.0.1
BROADCAST=192.168.0.255
NETWORK=192.168.0.0
```

Note: instead of editing this file directly (if you aren't running RedHat, and can't use Gnome's Control Panel), try running this command at the command line:

```
ifconfig eth0 192.168.0.1 netmask 255.255.255.0 up
```

Also, Caldera has a pretty good KDE tool for setting up Ethernet cards. Simply choose COAS/Network/Ethernet Interfaces from the KDE main menu.

An example of the /etc/sysconfig/network file:

```
NETWORKING=yes
FORWARD_IPV4=yes
HOSTNAME=toshiba.jpl
GATEWAY=192.168.0.1
```

Enable Samba support on the Linux computer

The last step to sharing files between Linux and Windows computers is setting up Samba—the program that allows Linux and Windows to network effectively. Fortunately, Samba is already setup and running by default in most Linux distributions. All you have to do is slightly edit the Samba configuration file, and provide Samba passwords.

Editing the smb.conf **file** You probably already have a smb.conf file, either in /etc or, if you're using Caldera, a sample version in /etc/samba.d.

1. Only if you're using Caldera, copy the file: /etc/samba.d/smb.conf.sample to /etc/samba.d/smb.conf, with these commands:

   ```
   cd /etc/samba.d

   cp smb.conf.sample smb.conf
   ```

2. For everyone, edit the /etc/smb.conf file so that the workgroup name at the top of the file is the same as the workgroup name you have given your computers. As an example, I have given my computers the workgroup name: jpl. So the first entry (not including remarks), in my smb.conf file is:

   ```
   workgroup = jpl
   ```

3. You will notice that most lines in the smb.conf are preceded with a #, or a ;. The first indicates a remark, and the second indicates a configuration line that has been temporarily disabled by the semicolon. The smb.conf file supplied is already setup pretty well for sharing printers. However, for sharing files, you need to make sure that certain configuration lines are enabled, by deleting the semicolon in front of them. For later versions of Windows 95, and all versions of Windows 98 and NT, make sure that the following lines are enabled in the file:

   ```
   encrypt passwords = yes
   smb passwd file = /etc/passwd
   ```

4. For all Windows versions, type in the following lines under the remark line that suggests enabling a 'specific roving profile share':

   ```
   [your name, or your computer's name]
   path = /
   browseable = yes
   guest ok = yes
   public = yes
   writeable = yes
   ```

Passwords Samba requires a password for a Windows user to log on to the Linux machine successfully. The Caldera distribution comes with a program called mksmbpasswd, that allows you simply to create a new

Samba password file from your current Linux password file. To use it, run the following command at the Linux prompt:

```
cat /etc/passwd | mksmbpasswd > /etc/samba.d/smbpasswd
```

If you are running a different distribution, use the `smbpasswd` command, as below:

```
smbpasswd username
```

where `username` is the name you use to log on to your Windows machine. When prompted for a password, use the same password you use on Windows. Afterwards, restart Samba with this simple command:

```
samba restart
```

From Windows: Bringing in Linux Files

1. From your Windows machine, double-click on the Network Neighborhood icon on the desktop.
2. When prompted, type in the password you entered above.
3. You should see an icon for your Linux system, identified by the hostname you gave it in your `hosts` file. Simply double-click on the icon to browse your Linux drive and directories.

You can also map your Linux server to a network drive on Windows. Log on to Windows using the same user name and password that you used with Linux, and make sure that your Samba username and password are also identical. Then double-click in Network Neighborhood on the Linux machine's icon. The screen that comes up will show a folder with the name you entered in the `smb.conf` file, above, under `roving profile share`.

Right click on that folder, and then click on Map Network Drive (Figure 26-13). You have now mapped your Linux computer to a networked Windows drive, and can very easily transfer files, using Windows Explorer or other standard methods, from Linux to Windows.

From Linux: Bringing in Windows Files

The best way of doing this is by using a Samba program called `smbmount`. This program mounts Windows network drives onto a directory you choose on your Linux system.

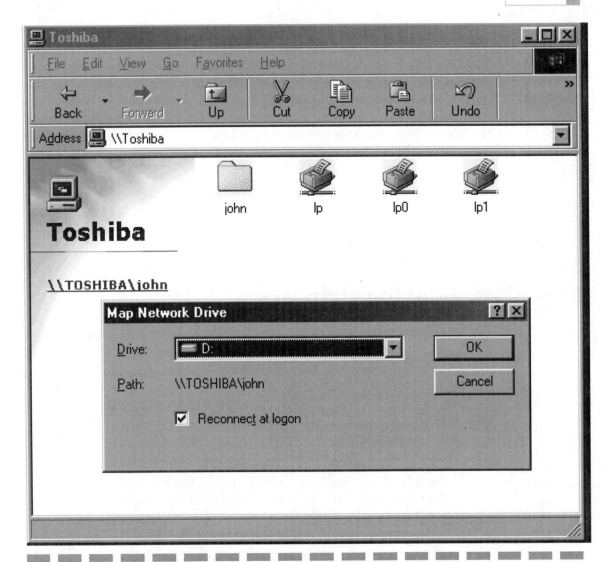

Figure 26-13 Mapping your Linux Computer to a Networked Drive in Windows

In this example, I have created, using the mkdir command, a directory called /IBM on my Linux computer. From the command prompt, I then type in:

```
smbmount  //ibm/c/  IBM
```

and hit Enter. (Please notice the double slashes—//) Then enter the Windows password when prompted.

With this simple command you have mounted your Windows drive C onto your Linux machine, and can browse it at the command prompt as if it were part of your own computer. Or, go into X Window, open your file manager, and browse the Windows C drive graphically (Figure 26-14).

Please note that although the smbmount program works, it does have its bugs. Although it will not harm your files, it is liable to the occasional breakdown—making a reboot necessary. For this reason, I recommend using it when necessary, and then turning it off. As an example, I would unmount the drive above by simply typing in:

```
smbumount /IBM
```

and hitting Enter.

Sharing Printers

Sharing a Windows printer with a Linux machine works quite well in practice, but it can be a terrible thing to set up manually. The Windows end is no problem—it's the Linux end that can be problematical. I therefore suggest that in Linux you use your X Window printer setup tool. It should do the job at least semi-automatically. The best tool for this purpose I've seen so far is RedHat's, and I use their distribution and their Gnome desktop in the example below.
First, though, the Windows end.

1. Double-click on the My Computer icon on the Windows desktop, and then on the Printers folder. You should see a list of printers available on that computer.

2. Right-click on the printer that you want to share with your Linux machine. In the small menu box that opens, click on 'Sharing'.

3. In the properties windows that opens up, click on the Sharing tab, check 'Shared As', and type in a brief descriptive name for the printer in the Share Name box. Leave the Comment and Password boxes empty (Figure 26-15).

Now the Linux end.

1. Click on the start button, and then navigate up to System, and over and down to Control Panel. Click on the printer icon, the third down from the bottom. The Print System Manager window opens up.

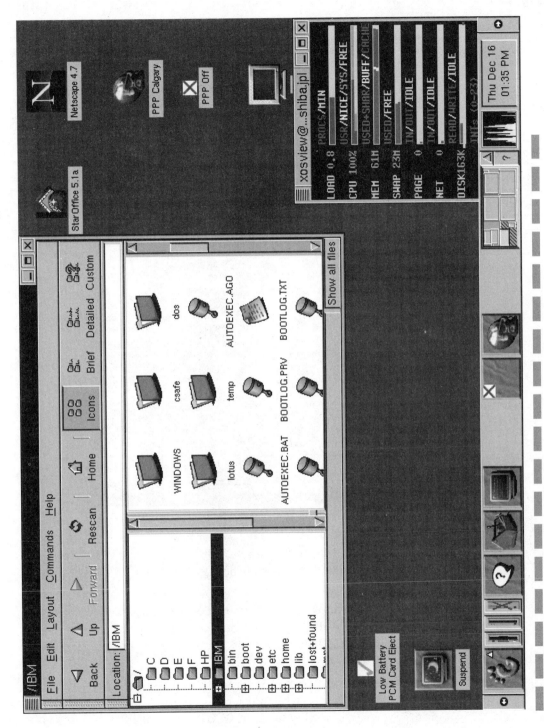

Figure 26-14 Browsing a Mapped Windows Drive From Within Windows

Figure 26-15
Setting Up Printer
Sharing From
Within Windows

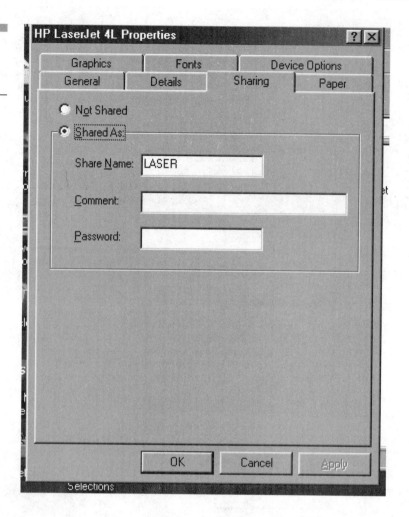

Figure 26-15
Setting Up Printer
Sharing From
Within Windows

2. Click on the Add button. The Add a Printer Entry appears. Check the SMB/Windows 95/NT Printer box (Figure 26-16). Then click on the OK button.

3. In the window that opens, the first three entries are made for you. The rest you must fill in yourself, but fortunately it is pretty straightforward. Below, in Table 26-1, are explanations of the entries in Figure 26-17:

4. After filling in the entries—except for the last—hit the Select button, and select the printer definition that most closely matches the printer you're connecting to. I run an HP 1100 LaserJet, but this is a fairly recent model and there is as yet no printer definition for it.

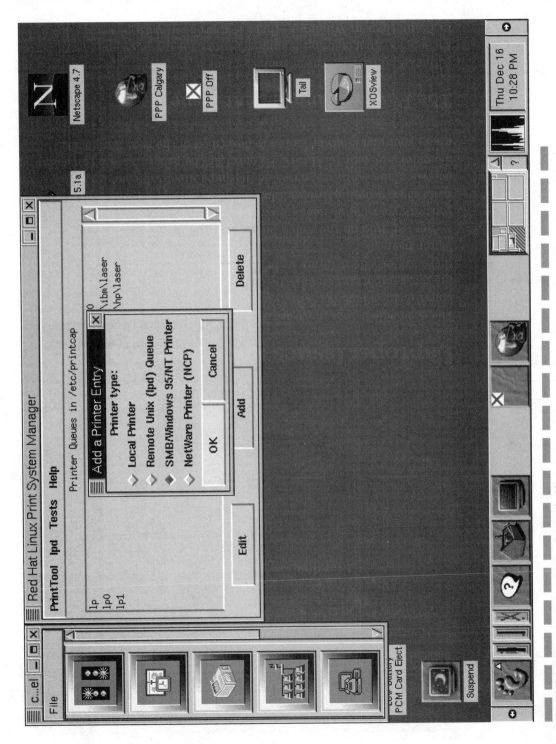

Figure 26-16 Adding a Samba Printer in Linux

TABLE 26-1

Explanations of
Sample Entries for
a Samba Printer

Hostname of Printer Server	hp	The hostname of the Windows machine the printer is attached to.
IP Number of Server	192.168.0.3	The local LAN IP address of the Windows machine.
Printer Name	laser	The name you gave the printer in the previous step, above, in Windows.
User	Mariann	The network logon name for the hp.
Password	******	Mariann's logon password
Workgroup	JPL	The LAN workgroup name, entered in Windows networking.
Input Filter	*Auto*— LaserJet4dither	The printer name you select after pressing the Select button.

Figure 26-17
Typical Printer Entries
for a Samba Printer

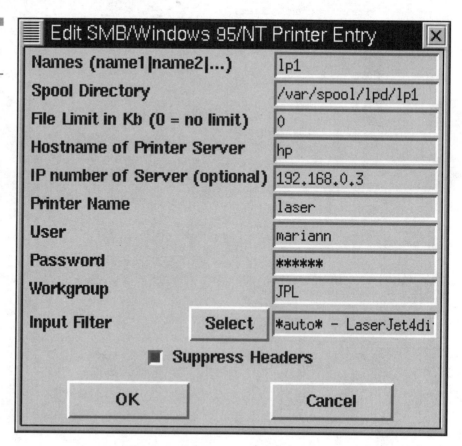

So I just select the LaserJet 4L. The driver is practically identical, and works just fine at the correct resolution.

You're finished—except for the testing. In the Print System Manager click on Tests, and try printing out a Postscript page. If things don't work properly the first time, don't lose heart. Sometimes, if there are still unprinted jobs in the local print queue, the printer program won't run the network job. If it's practical, hook up your printer cable directly to your Linux computer, and see if anything starts printing. Or, just delete your local printer print queue: `/var/spool/lpd/lp`. Then restart `lpd` (there's a menu bar item for this in the Print System Manager), and try printing again through the network.

Of course, you will still have to set up your applications—StarOffice, WordPerfect, etc.—to print to the new printer you've created. But that will be easy. The new printer port will show up on all of your applications—all you have to do is set up a printer on that port.

Sharing an Internet Connection

Linux is designed as a network server, and it will happily serve a network connection to as many computers on a LAN as required. But what exactly does 'sharing an Internet connection' mean?

It means that you can dial up an Internet connection once, from your Linux machine, and immediately all the other computers on your home LAN will have access to the World Wide Web and E-mail. This feature has the interesting technical name of 'IP Masquerading'. In a typical home environment, the main advantage of this is that every computer can use the Internet simultaneously on a single telephone line, although of course speed will be somewhat degraded if a number of people are actively browsing at the same time.

In my experience, however, speed degradation is not a noticeable problem on a good quality home telephone line, with 56K modems and a 100MBPS Ethernet connection linking up to three computers.

Unfortunately, setting this up can be a challenge. For one thing, it involves recompiling the kernel, since commercially distributed kernels do not typically come with this feature enabled. And since kernel options change on every release of a new kernel version, it is impossible for a book such as this to keep up with them. By the time this is published, a new kernel will be out, with new options.

The options in Table 26-2 should by treated as a guide. If, when recompiling your kernel, you see these, enable or disable them as indicated.

TABLE 26-2

Kernel Recompile
Options for IP
Masquerading

Prompt for development and/or incomplete code/drivers	Yes
Enable loadable module support	Yes
Networking support	Yes
Packet socket	Yes
Kernel/User netlink socket	Yes
Routing messages	No
Network firewalls	Yes
TCP/IP networking	Yes
IP: Advanced router	No
IP: verbose route monitoring	Yes
IP: firewalling	Yes
IP: firewall packet netlink device	Yes
IP: always defragment	Yes
IP: masquerading	Yes
IP: ICMP masquerading	Yes
IP: masquerading special modules support	Yes
IP: ipautofw masq support	No
IP: ipportfw masq support	Yes
IP: ip fwmark masq-forwarding support	No
IP: optimize as router not host	Yes
IP: GRE tunnels over IP	No
IP: TCP syncookie support	Yes
Network device support	Yes
Dummy net driver support	Yes
/proc filesystem support	Yes

If you followed my suggestions in the earlier part of this chapter, regarding setting your machines' IP addresses, then there should only be one more job to do: writing the `rc.firewall` file.

Use the vi editor to prepare this file, which should read as follows:

```
echo "1" > /proc/sys/net/ipv4/ip_forward
echo "1" > /proc/sys/net/ipv4/ip_dynaddr
/sbin/ipchains -M -S 7200 10 160
/sbin/ipchains -P forward DENY
/sbin/ipchains -A forward -s 192.168.0.2/32 -j MASQ
/sbin/ipchains -A forward -s 192.168.0.3/32 -j MASQ
```

Please note that this example takes it for granted that you have used my suggested scheme for assigning IP addresses, and also that there are three machines on your network, with the Linux machine, as 192.168.0.1, as your Internet server. Once saved, make the file executable with: `chmod a=rwx /etc/rc.d/rc.firewall`.

Finally, open up your `/etc/rc.d/rc.local` file with the vi editor, and add the following line to the very end:

```
/etc/rc.d/rc.firewall
```

This last step will fire up your rc.firewall script every time the Linux computer boots.

Reboot your Linux machine, dial up your ISP, and then try opening up a browser on another machine on the network. It should work. If it doesn't, I advise you to read the `ipmasq-HOWTO` file in the Appendix.

This rather long but very complete and clear HOWTO will be your most up-to-date source on IP masquerading. It should give you all the information you need (and more!), including exhaustive trouble-shooting techniques, to set up Internet sharing on your Linux/Windows LAN.

Installing Linux by Booting from a Floppy Disk

The preferred method of booting Linux from a bootable CDROM may not always be available. Some older computers won't boot from a CD, and on others where the possibility exists, but is not yet configured, the user may not have the expertise or the time to make the necessary adjustments.

In such cases, booting from a floppy disk will be necessary.

However, before giving up on the CD, see if your computer can read the Linux CD from a command prompt. If it can, you don't need the floppy.

A command prompt from within Windows won't work: you have to boot up to a command prompt. This is quite simple. As soon as you turn your computer on, and the boot process begins, press the F8 key. If you wait until the Windows logo comes up on the screen, you've probably waited too long, and will have to reboot and try again

When you press F8 at the right moment, the Microsoft Windows Startup Menu appears. Choose the Command Prompt Only option, and hit Enter. At this point your Windows machine will boot to the command prompt: C:\>.

Check to make sure that your computer is reading the CDROM drive. It may not be. If it isn't, it's probably because the device driver lines have been omitted or remarked out. In that case, you have two options:

1. Check the config.sys and autoexec.bat files. If the driver lines are there, but have been remarked out, delete the 'rems'.

2. Use the Linux boot disk that came with your machine, or make one following the manufacturer's instructions, or the instructions on the next page.

Assuming that your machine can read the CD-ROM, insert the Linux CD (if you haven't already), move to the CD drive, and type:

```
dir
```

and hit Enter.

You should see a short list of directories and files. You want to get into the DOSUTILS directory, so, type:

```
cd dosutils
```

and hit Enter.

Now, type:

```
autoboot
```

and hit Enter.

And that should do it!

If You Really Do Have to Use a Floppy

Boot from the Linux boot diskette which comes with every distribution. If you are using the CDs that came with this book, then you will have to make a boot diskette. Nothing could be simpler.

1. To make a boot diskette, start up a DOS window in Windows 95 or 98.

2. Insert into your diskette drive a blank, formatted floppy, and into your CD-ROM drive insert your Linux CD.

3. At the DOS prompt, type:

```
g: (or whatever your CD-ROM drive is)
cd dosutils
rawrite - f g:\images\boot.img -d a:
```

This will write a 'bootable image' to your floppy. Now, exit Windows and reboot.

Resource
Appendix

Introduction to Resource Appendix

There is always more to write, more to include. But overloading a beginners' Linux book would be fatal: there are already too many unedited, disorganized 800 page Linux 'bibles' on the market. This book is meant to target the typical professional Windows user, and to present the issues, problems and fixes which they are most likely to need.

However, there are still many pitfalls in Linux, even in getting it basically installed. There are bound to be readers who need to know more to get their systems working. And, I hope that readers will eventually be interested enough to look further into networking, the subject for which Linux has up to now been most famous.

The documents in the Resource Appendix are all Open Source, and are all on the web. Although some sections of some documents have been left out—because they would not have been of interest to most readers of this book—the documents have not been otherwise edited.

LIST OF DOCUMENTS:

BootPrompt-HOWTO

A useful guide to the kernel options you can type in at boot time.

The Linux Modem-HOWTO

Selecting, connecting, configuring, trouble-shooting modems.

Linux-Modem

From the online document, "Winmodems are not Modems." They aren't! Find out before you buy whether the new computer is going to be able to connect to the internet. A list of all known modems up to December of 1999 which do work, might work, and definitely do not work with Linux.

Sound-HOWTO

How to configure sound in Linux—if your distribution didn't do it automatically.

NET3-4-HOWTO

An excellent introduction to networking concepts from the Linux perspective.

Linux IP Masquerade HOWTO

Everything you wanted to know, and quite up-to-date, about IP Masquerading—the technique of using your Linux computer as an internet server for your home LAN.

Diagnosing Your Samba Server

Samba is an excellent tool for networking Linux amongst Windows machines. But it can be challenging to set up. If yours doesn't work, try following the simple steps in this document. An excellent diagnostic.

Acknowledgements

Section A: Copyright © 1995–1999 by Dr. P. Gortmaker.

Section B: Copyright © 1998–1999 by David S. Lawyer.

Section C: Courtesy of Rob Clark <gromitkc@o2.net>. Copyright © 1998.

Section D: Copyright © 1995–1999 by Jeff Tranter.

Section E: Reprinted with permission of the author, Joshua Drake, and LinuxPorts.Com. Copyright © 1999.

Section F: Copyright by David A. Ranch and Ambrose Au.

Section G: Taken from the following website: <http://usl.samba.org/samba/docs.DIAGNOSIS.html> Contents by contributor Andrew Tridgell.

SECTION

BootPrompt-HOWTO

This is the BootPrompt-HOWTO, which is a compilation of all the possible boot time arguments that can be passed to the Linux kernel at boot time. This includes all kernel and device parameters. A discussion of how the kernel sorts boot time arguments, along with an overview of some of the popular software used to boot Linux kernels is also included.

Introduction

The kernel has a limited capability to accept information at boot in the form of a `command line`, similar to an argument list you would give to a program. In general this is used to supply the kernel with information about hardware parameters that the kernel would not be able to determine on its own, or to avoid/override the values that the kernel would otherwise detect.

However, if you just copy a kernel image directly to a floppy, (e.g., `cp zImage /dev/fd0`) then you are not given a chance to specify any arguments to that kernel. So most Linux users will use software like LILO or loadlin that takes care of handing these arguments to the kernel, and then booting it.

This present revision covers kernels up to and including v2.2.9. Some features that are unique to development/testing kernels up to v2.3.2 are also documented.

The BootPrompt-HowTo is by: Dr. P. Gortmaker, <p_gortmaker @yahoo.com.>

Disclaimer and Copyright

This document is Copyright © 1995–1999 by Dr. P. Gortmaker. Please see the Disclaimer and Copying information at the end of this document ("copyright") for information about redistribution of this document and the usual 'we are not responsible for what you manage to break . . .' type legal stuff.

Intended Audience and Applicability

Most Linux users should never have to even look at this document. Linux does an exceptionally good job at detecting most hardware and picking reasonable default settings for most parameters. The information in this document is aimed at users who might want to change some of the default settings to optimize the kernel to their particular machine, or to a user who has 'rolled their own' kernel to support a not so common piece of hardware for which automatic detection is currently not available.

IMPORTANT NOTE: Driver related boot prompt arguments only apply to hardware drivers that are compiled directly into the kernel. They have no effect on drivers that are loaded as modules. Most Linux distributions come with a basic 'bare-bones' kernel, and the drivers are small modules that are loaded after the kernel has initialized. If you are unsure if you are using modules then look at `man depmod` and `man modprobe` along with the contents of your `/etc/conf.modules`.

Related Documentation

The most up-to-date documentation will always be the kernel source itself. Hold on! Don't get scared. You don't need to know any programming to read the comments in the source files. For example, if you were looking for what arguments could be passed to the AHA1542 SCSI driver, then you would go to the `linux/drivers/scsi` directory, and look at the file `aha1542.c`—and within the first 100 lines, you would find a plain english description of the boot time arguments that the 1542 driver accepts.

The linux directory is usually found in `/usr/src/` for most distributions. All references in this document to files that come with the kernel will have their pathname abbreviated to start with linux—you will have to append the `/usr/src/` or whatever is appropriate for your system. (If you can't find the file in question, then make use of the find and locate commands.)

The next best thing will be any documentation files that are distributed with the kernel itself. There are now quite a few of these, and most of them can be found in the directory `linux/Documentation` and subdirectories from there. Sometimes there will be `README.foo` files that can be found in the related driver directory (e.g. `linux/drivers/???/`, where examples of `???` could be `scsi`, `char`, or `net`).

If you have figured out what boot-args you intend to use, and now want to know how to get that information to the kernel, then look at the documentation that comes with the software that you use to boot the kernel (e.g. LILO or loadlin). A brief overview is given below, but it is no substitute for the documentation that comes with the booting software.

The Linux Newsgroups

If you have questions about passing boot arguments to the kernel, please check this document first. If this and the related documentation mentioned above does not answer your question(s) then you can try the Linux newsgroups. General questions on how to configure your system should be directed to the comp.os.linux.setup newsgroup. We ask that you please respect this general guideline for content, and don't cross-post your request to other groups.

Of course you should try checking the group before blindly posting your question, as it may even be a Frequently Asked Question (a FAQ). A quick browse of the Linux FAQ before posting is a good idea. You should be able to find the FAQ somewhere close to where you found this document. If it is not a FAQ then use newsgroup archives, such as those at <http://www.dejanews.com> to quickly search years worth of postings for your topic. Chances are someone else has already asked (and another person answered!) the question that you now have.

New Versions of this Document

New versions of this document can be retrieved via anonymous FTP from most Linux FTP sites in the directory /pub/Linux/docs/HOWTO/. Updates will be made as new information and/or drivers becomes available. If this copy that you are presently reading is more than six months old, then you should probably check to see if a newer copy exists. I would recommend viewing this via a WWW browser or in the Postscript/dvi format. Both of these contain cross-references that are lost in a simple plain text version.

If you want to get the official copy, here is URL.

BootPrompt-HOWTO
<http://metalab.unc.edu/mdw/HOWTO/BootPromptHOWTO.html>

Overview of Boot Prompt Arguments

This section gives some examples of software that can be used to pass kernel boot-time arguments to the kernel itself. It also gives you an idea of how the arguments are processed, what limitations there are on the boot args, and how they filter down to each appropriate device that they are intended for.

It is important to note that spaces should not be used in a boot argument, but only between separate arguments. A list of values that are for a single argument are to be separated with a comma between the values, and again without any spaces. See the following examples below.

```
ether=9,0x300,0xd0000,0xd4000,eth0 root=/dev/hda1
   *RIGHT*
ether = 9, 0x300, 0xd0000, 0xd4000, eth0 root =
   /dev/hda1   *WRONG*
```

Once the Linux kernel is up and running, one can view the command line arguments that were in place at boot by simply typing `cat/proc/cmdline` at a shell prompt.

LILO (LInux LOader)

The LILO program (LInux LOader) written by Werner Almesberger is the most commonly used. It has the ability to boot various kernels, and stores the configuration information in a plain text file. Most distributions ship with LILO as the default boot-loader. LILO can boot DOS, OS/2, Linux, FreeBSD, etc. without any difficulties, and is quite flexible.

A typical configuration will have LILO stop and print LILO: shortly after you turn on your computer. It will then wait for a few seconds for any optional input from the user, and failing that it will then boot the default system. Typical system labels that people use in the LILO configuration files are linux and backup and msdos. If you want to type in a boot argument, you type it in here, after typing in the system label that you want LILO to boot from, as shown in the example below.

```
LILO: linux root=/dev/hda1
```

LILO comes with excellent documentation, and for the purposes of boot args discussed here, the LILO append= command is of significant importance when one wants to add a boot time argument as a permanent addition to the LILO config file. You simply add something like `append = foo=bar` to the `/etc/lilo.conf` file. It can either be added at the top of the config file, making it apply to all sections, or to a single system section by adding it inside an image= section. Please see the LILO documentation for a more complete description.

LoadLin

The other commonly used Linux loader is `LoadLin` which is a DOS program that has the capability to launch a Linux kernel from the DOS prompt (with `boot-args`) assuming that certain resources are available. This is good for people that use DOS and want to launch into Linux from DOS.

It is also very useful if you have certain hardware which relies on the supplied DOS driver to put the hardware into a known state. A common example is 'SoundBlaster Compatible' sound cards that require the DOS driver to set a few proprietary registers to put the card into a SB compatible mode. Booting DOS with the supplied driver, and then loading Linux from the DOS prompt with `LOADLIN.EXE` avoids the reset of the card that happens if one rebooted instead. Thus the card is left in a SB compatible mode and hence is useable under Linux.

There are also other programs that can be used to boot Linux. For a complete list, please look at the programs available on your local Linux ftp mirror, under `system/Linux-boot/`.

The `rdev` Utility

There are a few of the kernel boot parameters that have their default values stored in various bytes in the kernel image itself. There is a utility called `rdev` that is installed on most systems that knows where these values are, and how to change them. It can also change things that have no kernel boot argument equivalent, such as the default video mode used.

The rdev utility is usually also aliased to swapdev, ramsize, vidmode and rootflags. These are the five things that rdev can change, those being the root device, the swap device, the RAM disk parameters, the default video mode, and the readonly/readwrite setting of root device.

More information on rdev can be found by typing `rdev  -h` or by reading the supplied man page (man rdev).

How the Kernel Sorts the Arguments

Most of the boot args take the form of:

```
name[=value_1][,value_2]...[,value_11]
```

where `name` is a unique keyword that is used to identify what part of the kernel the associated values (if any) are to be given to. Multiple boot args are just a space separated list of the above format. Note the limit of 11 is real, as the present code only handles 11 comma separated parameters per keyword. (However, you can re-use the same keyword with up to an additional 11 parameters in unusually complicated situations, assuming the setup function supports it.) Also note that the kernel splits the list into a maximum of ten integer arguments, and a following string, so you can't really supply 11 integers unless you convert the 11th arg from a string to an int in the driver itself.

Most of the sorting goes on in `linux/init/main.c`. First, the kernel checks to see if the argument is any of the special arguments `root=`, `ro`, `rw`, or `debug`. The meaning of these special arguments is described further on in the document.

Then it walks a list of setup functions (contained in the bootsetups array) to see if the specified argument string (such as `foo`) has been associated with a setup function (`foo_setup()`) for a particular device or part of the kernel. If you passed the kernel the line `foo=3,4,5,6,bar` then the kernel would search the bootsetups array to see if `foo` was registered. If it was, then it would call the setup function associated with `foo` (`foo_setup()`) and hand it the integer arguments 3, 4, 5 and 6 as given on the kernel command line, and also hand it the string argument bar.

Setting Environment Variables

Anything of the form 'foo=bar' that is not accepted as a setup function as described above is then interpreted as an environment variable to be set. An example would be to use `TERM=vt100` or `BOOT_IMAGE=vmlinuz.bak` as a boot argument. These environment variables are typically tested for in the initialization scripts to enable or disable a wide range of things.

Passing Arguments to the `init` Program

Any remaining arguments that were not picked up by the kernel and were not interpreted as environment variables are then passed onto process one, which is usually the init program. The most common argument that is passed to the init process is the word single which instructs init to boot the computer in single user mode, and not launch all the usual daemons. Check the manual page for the version of init installed on your system to see what arguments it accepts.

General Non-Device Specific Boot Args

These are the boot arguments that are not related to any specific device or peripheral. They are instead related to certain internal kernel parameters, such as memory handling, ramdisk handling, root file system handling and others.

Root Filesystem Options

The following options all pertain to how the kernel selects and handles the root filesystem.

The root= Argument   This argument tells the kernel what device is to be used as the root filesystem while booting. The default of this setting is the value of the root device of the system that the kernel was built on. For example, if the kernel in question was built on a system that used /dev/hda1 as the root partition, then the default root device would be /dev/hda1. To override this default value, and select the second floppy drive as the root device, one would use root=/dev/fd1.

Valid root devices are any of the following devices:

1. /dev/hdaN to /dev/hddN, which is partition N on ST-506 compatible disk 'a to d'.

2. /dev/sdaN to /dev/sdeN, which is partition N on SCSI compatible disk 'a to e'.

3. /dev/xdaN to /dev/xdbN, which is partition N on XT compatible disk 'a to b'.

4. /dev/fdN, which is floppy disk drive number N. Having N=0 would be the DOS 'A:' drive, and N=1 would be 'B:'.

5. /dev/nfs, which is not really a device, but rather a flag to tell the kernel to get the root fs via the network.

The more awkward and less portable numeric specification of the above possible disk devices in major/minor format is also accepted. (e.g., /dev/sda3 is major 8, minor 3, so you could use root=0x803 as an alternative.)

This is one of the few kernel boot arguments that has its default stored in the kernel image, and which can thus be altered with the rdev utility.

The ro Argument   When the kernel boots, it needs a root filesystem to read basic things off of. This is the root filesystem that is mounted at boot. However, if the root filesystem is mounted with write access, you can not reliably check the filesystem integrity with half-written files in progress. The ro option tells the kernel to mount the root filesystem as readonly so that any filesystem consistency check programs (fsck) can safely assume that there are no half-written files in progress while performing the check. No programs or processes can write to files on the filesystem in question until it is 'remounted' as read/write capable.

This is one of the few kernel boot arguments that has its default stored in the kernel image, and which can thus be altered with the rdev utility.

The rw Argument   This is the exact opposite of the above, in that it tells the kernel to mount the root filesystem as read/write. The default is to mount the root filesystem as read/write anyway. Do not run any fsck type programs on a filesystem that is mounted read/write.

The same value stored in the image file mentioned above is also used for this parameter, accessible via rdev.

Options Relating to RAM Disk Management

The following options all relate to how the kernel handles the RAM disk device, which is usually used for bootstrapping machines during the install phase, or for machines with modular drivers that need to be installed to access the root filesystem.

The ramdisk_start= Argument   To allow a kernel image to reside on a floppy disk along with a compressed ramdisk image, the ramdisk_start=<offset> command was added. The kernel can't be included into the compressed ramdisk filesystem image, because it needs to be stored starting at block zero so that the BIOS can load the bootsector and then the kernel can bootstrap itself to get going.

Note: If you are using an uncompressed ramdisk image, then the kernel can be a part of the filesystem image that is being loaded into the ramdisk, and the floppy can be booted with LILO, or the two can be separate as is done for the compressed images.

If you are using a two-disk boot/root setup (kernel on disk 1, ramdisk image on disk 2) then the ramdisk would start at block zero, and an offset of zero would be used. Since this is the default value, you would not need to actually use the command at all.

The load_ramdisk= Argument   This parameter tells the kernel whether it is to try to load a ramdisk image or not. Specifying load_ramdisk=1 will tell the kernel to load a floppy into the ramdisk. The default value is zero, meaning that the kernel should not try to load a ramdisk.

Please see the file linux/Documentation/ramdisk.txt for a complete description of the new boot time arguments, and how to use them. A description of how this parameter can be set and stored in the kernel image via rdev is also described.

The `prompt_ramdisk=` Argument   This parameter tells the kernel whether or not to give you a prompt asking you to insert the floppy containing the ramdisk image. In a single floppy configuration the ramdisk image is on the same floppy as the kernel that just finished loading/ booting and so a prompt is not needed. In this case one can use `prompt_ramdisk=0`. In a two floppy configuration, you will need the chance to switch disks, and thus `prompt_ramdisk=1` can be used. Since this is the default value, it doesn't really need to be specified. (Historical note: Sneaky people used to use the `vga=ask` LILO option to temporarily pause the boot process and allow a chance to switch from boot to root floppy.)

Please see the file `linux/Documentation/ramdisk.txt` for a complete description of the new boot time arguments, and how to use them. A description of how this parameter can be set and stored in the kernel image via `rdev` is also described.

The `ramdisk_size=` Argument   While it is true that the ramdisk grows dynamically as required, there is an upper bound on its size so that it doesn't consume all available RAM and leave you in a mess. The default is 4096 (i.e. 4MB) which should be large enough for most needs. You can override the default to a bigger or smaller size with this boot argument.

Please see the file `linux/Documentation/ramdisk.txt` for a complete description of the new boot time arguments, and how to use them. A description of how this parameter can be set and stored in the kernel image via `rdev` is also described.

The `ramdisk=` Argument (obsolete)   (Note: This argument is obsolete, and should not be used except on kernels v1.3.47 and older. The commands that should be used for the ramdisk device are documented above.)

This specifies the size in kB of the RAM disk device. For example, if one wished to have a root filesystem on a 1.44MB floppy loaded into the RAM disk device, they would use:

```
ramdisk=1440
```

This is one of the few kernel boot arguments that has its default stored in the kernel image, and which can thus be altered with the rdev utility.

The `noinitrd` (initial RAM disk) Argument   The v2.x and newer kernels have a feature where the root filesystem can be initially a RAM disk, and the kernel executes `/linuxrc` on that RAM image. This feature is typically used to allow loading of modules needed to mount the real root filesystem (e.g. load the SCSI driver modules stored in the RAM disk image, and then mount the real root filesystem on a SCSI disk.)

The actual `noinitrd` argument determines what happens to the `initrd` data after the kernel has booted. When specified, instead of converting it to a RAM disk, it is accessible via `/dev/initrd`, which can be read once before the RAM is released back to the system. For full details on using the initial RAM disk, please consult `linux/Documentation/initrd.txt`. In addition, the most recent versions of LILO and LOADLIN should have additional useful information.

Boot Arguments Related to Memory Handling

The following arguments alter how Linux detects or handles the physical and virtual memory of your system.

The `mem=` Argument   This argument has two purposes: The original purpose was to specify the amount of installed memory (or a value less than that if you wanted to limit the amount of memory available to linux). The second (and hardly used) purpose is to specify `mem=nopentium` which tells the Linux kernel to not use the 4MB page table performance feature.

The original BIOS call defined in the PC specification that returns the amount of installed memory was only designed to be able to report up to 64MB. (Yes, another lack of foresight, just like the 1024 cylinder disks . . . sigh.) Linux uses this BIOS call at boot to determine how much memory is installed. If you have more than 64MB of RAM installed, you can use this boot argument to tell Linux how much memory you have. Here is a quote from Linus on the usage of the `mem=` parameter.

"The kernel will accept any `mem=xx` parameter you give it, and if it turns out that you lied to it, it will crash horribly sooner or later. The parameter indicates the highest addressable RAM address, so `mem=0x1000000` means you have 16MB of memory, for example. For a 96MB machine this would be `mem=0x6000000`. If you tell Linux that it has more memory than it actually does have, bad things will happen: maybe not at once, but surely eventually."

Note that the argument does not have to be in hex, and the suffixes 'k' and 'M' (case insensitive) can be used to specify kilobytes and Megabytes, respectively. (A 'k' will cause a 10 bit shift on your value, and a 'M' will cause a 20 bit shift.) A typical example for a 128MB machine would be `mem=128m`.

The `swap=` Argument   This allows the user to tune some of the virtual memory (VM) parameters that are related to swapping to disk. It accepts the following eight parameters:

```
MAX_PAGE_AGE
PAGE_ADVANCE
PAGE_DECLINE
PAGE_INITIAL_AGE
AGE_CLUSTER_FRACT
AGE_CLUSTER_MIN
PAGEOUT_WEIGHT
BUFFEROUT_WEIGHT
```

Interested hackers are advised to have a read of `linux/mm/swap.c` and also make note of the goodies in `/proc/sys/vm`. Kernels come with some useful documentation on this in the `linux/Documentation/vm/directory`.

The `buff=` Argument   Similar to the `swap=` argument, this allows the user to tune some of the parameters related to buffer memory management. It accepts the following six parameters:

```
MAX_BUFF_AGE
BUFF_ADVANCE
BUFF_DECLINE
BUFF_INITIAL_AGE
BUFFEROUT_WEIGHT
BUFFERMEM_GRACE
```

Interested hackers are advised to have a read of `linux/mm/swap.c` and also make note of the goodies in `/proc/sys/vm`. Kernels come with some useful documentation on this in the `linux/Documentation/vm/directory`.

Boot Arguments for NFS Root Filesystem

Linux supports systems such as diskless workstations via having their root filesystem as NFS (Network FileSystem). These arguments are used to tell the diskless workstation which machine it is to get its system from. Also note that the argument `root=/dev/nfs` is required. Detailed information on using an NFS root fs is in the file `linux/Documentation/nfsroot.txt`. You should read that file, as the following is only a quick summary taken directly from that file.

The `nfsroot=` Argument This argument tells the kernel which machine, what directory and what NFS options to use for the root filesystem. The form of the argument is as follows:

```
nfsroot=[<server-ip>:]<root-dir>[,<nfs-options>]
```

If the nfsroot parameter is not given on the command line, the default `/tftpboot/%s` will be used. The other options are as follows:

> `<server-ip>`—Specifies the IP address of the NFS server. If this field is not given, the default address as determined by the `nfsaddrs` variable (see below) is used. One use of this parameter is for example to allow using different servers for RARP and NFS. Usually you can leave this blank.

> `<root-dir>`—Name of the directory on the server to mount as root. If there is a `%s` token in the string, the token will be replaced by the ASCII-representation of the client's IP address.

> `<nfs-options>`—Standard NFS options. All options are separated by commas. If the options field is not given, the following defaults will be used:

```
port        = as given by server portmap daemon
rsize       = 1024
wsize       = 1024
timeo       = 7
retrans     = 3
acregmin    = 3
acregmax    = 60
acdirmin    = 30
acdirmax    = 60
flags       = hard, nointr, noposix, cto, ac
```

The `nfsaddrs=` Argument This boot argument sets up the various network interface addresses that are required to communicate over the network. If this argument is not given, then the kernel tries to use RARP and/or BOOTP to figure out these parameters. The form is as follows:

```
nfsaddrs=<my-ip>:<serv-ip>:<gw-ip>:<netmask>:<name>:
  <dev>:<auto>
```

> `<my-ip>`—IP address of the client. If empty, the address will either be determined by RARP or BOOTP. What protocol is used depends on what has been enabled during kernel configuration and on the `<auto>` parameter. If this parameter is not empty, neither RARP nor BOOTP will be used.

<serv-ip>—IP address of the NFS server. If RARP is used to determine the client address and this parameter is NOT empty only replies from the specified server are accepted. To use different RARP and NFS server, specify your RARP server here (or leave it blank), and specify your NFS server in the nfsroot parameter (see above). If this entry is blank the address of the server is used which answered the RARP or BOOTP request.

<gw-ip>—IP address of a gateway if the server in on a different subnet. If this entry is empty no gateway is used and the server is assumed to be on the local network, unless a value has been received by BOOTP.

<netmask>—Netmask for local network interface. If this is empty, the netmask is derived from the client IP address, unless a value has been received by BOOTP.

<name>—Name of the client. If empty, the client IP address is used in ASCII-notation, or the value received by BOOTP.

<dev>—Name of network device to use. If this is empty, all devices are used for RARP requests, and the first one found for BOOTP. For NFS the device is used on which either RARP or BOOTP replies have been received. If you only have one device you can safely leave this blank.

<auto>—Method to use for autoconfiguration. If this is either rarp or bootp the specified protocol is being used. If the value is both or empty, both protocols are used so far as they have been enabled during kernel configuration Using none means no autoconfiguration. In this case you have to specify all necessary values in the fields before.

The <auto> parameter can appear alone as the value to the nfsaddrs parameter (without all the : characters before) in which case autoconfiguration is used. However, the none value is not available in that case.

Other Misc. Kernel Boot Arguments

These various boot arguments let the user tune certain internal kernel parameters.

The debug Argument   The kernel communicates important (and not-so important) messages to the operator via the printk() function. If the message is considered important, the printk() function will put a copy on the present console as well as handing it off to the klogd() facility so that it gets logged to disk. The reason for printing important messages to the console as well as logging them to disk is because under unfortunate circumstances (e.g. a disk failure) the message won't make it to disk and will be lost.

The threshold for what is and what isn't considered important is set by the console_loglevel variable. The default is to log anything more important than DEBUG (level 7) to the console. (These levels are defined in the include file kernel.h) Specifying debug as a boot argument will set the console loglevel to 10, so that all kernel messages appear on the console.

The console loglevel can usually also be set at run time via an option to the klogd() program. Check the man page for the version installed on your system to see how to do this.

The init= Argument   The kernel defaults to starting the 'init' program at boot, which then takes care of setting up the computer for users via launching getty programs, running rc scripts and the like. The kernel first looks for /sbin/init, then /etc/init (depreciated), and as a last resort, it will try to use /bin/sh (possibly on /etc/rc). If for example, your init program got corrupted and thus stopped you from being able to boot, you could simply use the boot prompt init=/bin/sh which would drop you directly into a shell at boot, allowing you to replace the corrupted program.

The kbd-reset Argument   Normally on i386 based machines, the Linux kernel does not reset the keyboard controller at boot, since the BIOS is supposed to do this. But as usual, not all machines do what they should. Supplying this option may help if you are having problems with your keyboard behaviour. It simply forces a reset at initialization time. (Some have argued that this should be the default behaviour anyways.)

The maxcpus= Argument   The number given with this argument limits the maximum number of CPUs activated in SMP mode. Using a value of 0 is equivalent to the nosmp option.

The mca-pentium Argument   The IBM model 95 Microchannel machines seem to lock up on the test that Linux usually does to detect the type of math chip coupling. Since all Pentium chips have a built in math processor, this test (and the lock up problem) can be avoided by using this boot option.

The md= Argument   If your root filesystem is on a Multiple Device then you can use this (assuming you compiled in boot support) to tell the kernel the multiple device layout. The format (from the file `linux/Documentation/md.txt`) is:

```
md=md_device_num,raid_level,chunk_size_factor,fault_le
vel,dev0,dev1,...,devN
```

Where md_device_num is the number of the md device, i.e. 0 means md0, 1 means md1, etc. For raid_level, use -1 for linear mode and 0 for striped mode. Other modes are currently unsupported. The chunk_size_factor is for raid-0 and raid-1 only and sets the chunk size as PAGE_SIZE shifted left the specified amount. The fault_level is only for raid-1 and sets the maximum fault number to the specified number. (Currently unsupported due to lack of boot support for raid1.) The dev0-devN are a comma sepa-rated list of the devices that make up the individual md device: e.g. `/dev/hda1,/dev/hdc1,/dev/sda1`

The no387 Argument   Some i387 coprocessor chips have bugs that show up when used in 32 bit protected mode. For example, some of the early ULSI-387 chips would cause solid lockups while performing floating point calculations, apparently due to a bug in the `FRSAV/FRRESTOR` instructions. Using the `no387` boot argument causes Linux to ignore the math coprocessor even if you have one. Of course you must then have your kernel compiled with math emulation support! This may also be useful if you have one of those really old 386 machines that could use an 80287 FPU, as Linux can't use an 80287.

The no-hlt Argument   The i386 (and successors thereof) family of CPUs have a `hlt` instruction which tells the CPU that nothing is going to happen until an external device (keyboard, modem, disk, etc.) calls upon the CPU to do a task. This allows the CPU to enter a 'low-power' mode where it sits like a zombie until an external device wakes it up (usually via an interrupt). Some of the early i486DX-100 chips had a problem with the `hlt` instruction, in that they couldn't reliably return to operating mode after this instruction was used. Using the `no-hlt` instruction tells Linux to just run an infinite loop when there is nothing else to do, and to not halt your CPU when there is no activity. This allows people with these broken chips to use Linux, although they would be well advised to seek a replacement through a war-ranty where possible.

The `no-scroll` Argument Using this argument at boot disables scrolling features that make it difficult to use Braille terminals.

The `noapic` Argument Using this option tells a SMP kernel to not use some of the advanced features of the interrupt controller on multi processor machines. See linux/Documentation/IO-APIC.txt for more information.

The `nosmp` Argument Use of this option will tell a SMP kernel on a SMP machine to operate single processor. Typically only used for debugging and determining if a particular problem is SMP related.

The `panic=` Argument In the unlikely event of a kernel panic (i.e. an internal error that has been detected by the kernel, and which the kernel decides is serious enough to moan loudly and then halt everything), the default behaviour is to just sit there until someone comes along and notices the panic message on the screen and reboots the machine. However if a machine is running unattended in an isolated location it may be desirable for it to automatically reset itself so that the machine comes back on line. For example, using `panic=30` at boot would cause the kernel to try and reboot itself 30 seconds after the kernel panic happened. A value of zero gives the default behaviour, which is to wait forever.

Note that this timeout value can also be read and set via the `/proc/sys/kernel/panic sysctl interface`.

The `pci=` Argument

The `pirq=` Argument Using this option tells a SMP kernel information on the PCI slot versus IRQ settings for SMP motherboards which are unknown (or known to be blacklisted). See linux/Documentation/IO-APIC.txt for more information.

The `profile=` Argument Kernel developers can enable an option that allows them to profile how and where the kernel is spending its CPU cycles in an effort to maximize efficiency and performance. This option lets you set the profile shift count at boot. Typically it is set to two. You can also compile your kernel with profiling enabled by default. In either case, you need a tool such as `readprofile.c` that can make use of the `/proc/profile` output.

The reboot= Argument   This option controls the type of reboot that Linux will do when it resets the computer (typically via /sbin/init handling a Control-Alt- Delete). The default as of v2.0 kernels is to do a 'cold' reboot (i.e. full reset, BIOS does memory check, etc.) instead of a 'warm' reboot (i.e. no full reset, no memory check). It was changed to be cold by default since that tends to work on cheap/broken hardware that fails to reboot when a warm reboot is requested. To get the old behaviour (i.e. warm reboots) use reboot=w or in fact any word that starts with w will work.

Why would you bother? Some disk controllers with cache memory on board can sense a warm reboot, and flush any cached data to disk. Upon a cold boot, the card may be reset and the write-back data in your cache card's memory is lost. Others have reported systems that take a long time to go through the memory check, and/or SCSI BIOSes that take longer to initialize on a cold boot as a good reason to use warm reboots.

The reserve= Argument   This is used to protect I/O port regions from probes. The form of the command is:

```
reserve=iobase,extent[,iobase,extent]
```

In some machines it may be necessary to prevent device drivers from checking for devices (auto-probing) in a specific region. This may be because of poorly designed hardware that causes the boot to freeze (such as some ethercards), hardware that is mistakenly identified, hardware whose state is changed by an earlier probe, or merely hardware you don't want the kernel to initialize.

The reserve boot-time argument addresses this problem by specifying an I/O port region that shouldn't be probed. That region is reserved in the kernel's port registration table as if a device has already been found in that region (with the name reserved). Note that this mechanism shouldn't be necessary on most machines. Only when there is a problem or special case would it be necessary to use this. The I/O ports in the specified region are protected against device probes that do a check_region() prior to probing blindly into a region of I/O space. This was put in to be used when some driver was hanging on a NE2000, or misidentifying some other device as its own. A correct device driver shouldn't probe a reserved region, unless another boot argument explicitly specifies that it do so. This implies that reserve will most often be used with some other boot argument. Hence if you specify a reserve region to protect a specific device, you must generally specify an explicit probe for that device. Most drivers ignore the port registration table if they are given an explicit address.

For example, the boot line

```
reserve=0x300,32 blah=0x300
```

keeps all device drivers except the driver for `blah` from probing 0x300-0x31f.

As usual with boot-time specifiers there is an 11 parameter limit, thus you can only specify 5 reserved regions per reserve keyword. Multiple reserve specifiers will work if you have an unusually complicated request.

The vga= Argument Note that this is not really a boot argument. It is an option that is interpreted by LILO and not by the kernel like all the other boot arguments are. However its use has become so common that it deserves a mention here. It can also be set via using `rdev -v` or equivalently `vidmode` on the `vmlinuz` file. This allows the setup code to use the video BIOS to change the default display mode before actually booting the Linux kernel. Typical modes are 80x50, 132x44 and so on. The best way to use this option is to start with `vga=ask` which will prompt you with a list of various modes that you can use with your video adapter before booting the kernel. Once you have the number from the above list that you want to use, you can later put it in place of the `ask`. For more information, please see the file `linux/Documentation/svga.txt` that comes with all recent kernel versions.

Note that newer kernels (v2.1 and up) have the setup code that changes the video mode as an option, listed as Video mode selection support so you need to enable this option if you want to use this feature.

Boot Arguments to Control PCI Bus Behaviour (pci=)

The `pci=` argument (not avail. in v2.0 kernels) can be used to change the behaviour of PCI bus device probing and device behaviour. Firstly the file linux/drivers/pci/pci.c checks for architecture independent `pci=` options. The remaining allowed arguments are handled in linux/arch/???/kernel/bios32.c and are listed below for ???=i386.

The pci=bios and pci=nobios Arguments These are used to set/clear the flag indicating that the PCI probing is to take place via the PCI BIOS. The default is to use the BIOS.

The `pci=conf1` and `pci=conf2` Arguments   If PCI direct mode is enabled, the use of these enables either configuration Type 1 or Type 2. These implicitly clear the PCI BIOS probe flag (i.e. `pci=nobios`) too.

The `pci=io=` Argument   If you get a message like PCI: Unassigned IO space for . . . / then you may need to supply an I/O value with this option. From the source:

"Several BIOS'es forget to assign addresses to I/O ranges. We try to fix it here, expecting there are free addresses starting with 0x5800. Ugly, but until we come with better resource management, it's the only simple solution."

The `pci=nopeer` Argument   This disables the default peer bridge fixup, which according to the source does the following:

"In case there are peer host bridges, scan bus behind each of them. Although several sources claim that the host bridges should have header type 1 and be assigned a bus number as for PCI2PCI bridges, the reality doesn't pass this test and the bus number is usually set by BIOS to the first free value."

The `pci=nosort` Argument   Using this argument instructs the kernel to not sort the PCI devices during the probing phase.

The `pci=off` Argument   Using this option disables all PCI bus probing. Any device drivers that make use of PCI functions to find and initialize hardware will most likely fail to work.

The `pci=reverse` Argument   This option will reverse the ordering of the PCI devices on that PCI bus.

Boot Arguments for Video Frame Buffer Drivers

The `video=` argument (not avail. in v2.0 kernels) is used when the frame buffer device abstraction layer is built into the kernel. If that sounds complicated, well it isn't really too bad. It basically means that instead of having a different video program (the X11R6 server) for each brand of video card (e.g. XF86_S3, XF86_SVGA, . . .), the kernel would have a built in driver available for each video card and export a single interface for the video program so that only one X11R6 server (XF86_FBDev) would be required. This is similar to how networking is now—the kernel has drivers available for each brand of network card and exports a single network interface so that just one version of a network program (like Netscape) will work for all systems, regardless of the underlying brand of network card.

The typical format of this argument is `video=name:option1, option2,...` where name is the name of a generic option or of a frame buffer driver. The `video=` option is passed from `linux/init/main.c` into `linux/drivers/video/fbmem.c` for further processing. Here it is checked for some generic options before trying to match to a known driver name. Once a driver name match is made, the comma separated option list is then passed into that particular driver for final processing. The list of valid driver names can be found by reading down the fb_drivers array in the `file fbmem.c` mentioned above.

Information on the options that each driver supports will eventually be found in `linux/Documentation/fb/` but currently (v2.2) only a few are described there. Unfortunately the number of video drivers and the number of options for each one is content for another document itself and hence too much to list here.

If there is no Documentation file for your card, you will have to get the option information directly from the driver. Go to `linux/drivers/video/` and look in the appropriate `???fb.c` file (the ??? will be based on the card name). In there, search for a function with _setup in its name and you should see what options the driver tries to match, such as font or mode or ...

The `video=map:...` Argument   This option is used to set/override the console to frame buffer device mapping. A comma separated list of numbers sets the mapping, with the value of option N taken to be the frame buffer device number for console N.

The `video=scrollback:...` Argument   A number after the colon will set the size of memory allocated for the scrollback buffer. (Use Shift and Page Up or Page Down keys to scroll.) A suffix of 'k' or 'K' after the number will indicate that the number is to be interpreted as kilobytes instead of bytes.

The `video=vc:...` Argument   A number, or a range of numbers (e.g. `video=vc:2-5`) will specify the first, or the first and last frame buffer virtual console(s). The use of this option also has the effect of setting the frame buffer console to not be the default console.

Boot Arguments for SCSI Peripherals

This section contains the descriptions of the boot args that are used for passing information about the installed SCSI host adapters, and SCSI devices.

Arguments for Mid-level Drivers

The mid level drivers handle things like disks, CD-ROMs and tapes without getting into host adapter specifics.

Maximum Probed LUNs (`max_scsi_luns=`) Each SCSI device can have a number of 'sub-devices' contained within itself. The most common example is any of the SCSI CD-ROMs that handle more than one disk at a time. Each CD is addressed as a 'Logical Unit Number' (LUN) of that particular device. But most devices, such as hard disks, tape drives and such are only one device, and will be assigned to LUN zero.

The problem arises with single LUN devices with bad firmware. Some poorly designed SCSI devices (old and unfortunately new) can not handle being probed for LUNs not equal to zero. They will respond by locking up, and possibly taking the whole SCSI bus down with them.

The kernel has a configuration option that allows you to set the maximum number of probed LUNs. The default is to only probe LUN zero, to avoid the problem described above.

To specify the number of probed LUNs at boot, one enters `max_scsi_luns=n` as a boot arg, where n is a number between one and eight. To avoid problems as described above, one would use n=1 to avoid upsetting such broken devices

SCSI Logging (`scsi_logging=`) Supplying a non-zero value to this boot argument turns on logging of all SCSI events (error, scan, mlqueue, mlcomplete, llqueue, llcomplete, hlqueue, hlcomplete). Note that better control of which events are logged can be obtained via the `/proc/scsi/scsi` interface if you aren't interested in the events that take place at boot before the `/proc/ filesystem` is accessible.

Parameters for the SCSI Tape Driver (`st=`) Some boot time configuration of the SCSI tape driver can be achieved by using the following:

```
st=buf_size[,write_threshold[,max_bufs]]
```

The first two numbers are specified in units of kB. The default buf_size is 32kB, and the maximum size that can be specified is a ridiculous 16384kB. The `write_threshold` is the value at which the buffer is committed to tape, with a default value of 30kB. The maximum number of buffers varies with the number of drives detected, and has a default of two. An example usage would be:

```
st=32,30,2
```

Full details can be found in the README.st file that is in the scsi directory of the kernel source tree.

Arguments for SCSI Host Adapters

General notation for this section:

iobase—the first I/O port that the SCSI host occupies. These are specified in hexidecimal notation, and usually lie in the range from 0x200 to 0x3ff.

irq—the hardware interrupt that the card is configured to use. Valid values will be dependent on the card in question, but will usually be 5, 7, 9, 10, 11, 12, and 15. The other values are usually used for common peripherals like IDE hard disks, floppies, serial ports, etc.

dma—the DMA (Direct Memory Access) channel that the card uses. Typically only applies to bus-mastering cards. PCI and VLB cards are native bus-masters, and do not require and ISA DMA channel.

scsi-id—the ID that the host adapter uses to identify itself on the SCSI bus. Only some host adapters allow you to change this value, as most have it permanently specified internally. The usual default value is seven, but the Seagate and Future Domain TMC-950 boards use six.

parity—whether the SCSI host adapter expects the attached devices to supply a parity value with all information exchanges. Specifying a one indicates parity checking is enabled, and a zero disables parity checking. Again, not all adapters will support selection of parity behaviour as a boot argument.

Adaptec aha151x, aha152x, aic6260, aic6360, SB16-SCSI (aha152x=)
The aha numbers refer to cards and the aic numbers refer to the actual SCSI chip on these type of cards, including the Soundblaster-16 SCSI.

The probe code for these SCSI hosts looks for an installed BIOS, and if none is present, the probe will not find your card. Then you will have to use a boot argument of the form:

```
aha152x=iobase[,irq[,scsi-id[,reconnect[,parity]]]]
```

Note that if the driver was compiled with debugging enabled, a sixth value can be specified to set the debug level.

All the parameters are as described at the top of this section, and the reconnect value will allow device disconnect/reconnect if a non-zero value is used. An example usage is as follows:

```
aha152x=0x340,11,7,1
```

Note that the parameters must be specified in order, meaning that if you want to specify a parity setting, then you will have to specify an iobase, irq, scsi-id and reconnect value as well.

Adaptec aha154x (aha1542=)   These are the aha154x series cards. The aha1542 series cards have an i82077 floppy controller onboard, while the aha1540 series cards do not. These are busmastering cards, and have parameters to set the "fairness" that is used to share the bus with other devices. The boot argument looks like the following.

```
aha1542=iobase[,buson,busoff[,dmaspeed]
```

Valid iobase values are usually one of: 0x130, 0x134, 0x230, 0x234, 0x330, 0x334. Clone cards may permit other values.

The buson, busoff values refer to the number of microseconds that the card dominates the ISA bus. The defaults are 11us on, and 4us off, so that other cards (such as an ISA LANCE Ethernet card) have a chance to get access to the ISA bus.

The dmaspeed value refers to the rate (in MB/s) at which the DMA (Direct Memory Access) transfers proceed at. The default is 5MB/s. Newer revision cards allow you to select this value as part of the soft-configuration, older cards use jumpers. You can use values up to 10MB/s assuming that your motherboard is capable of handling it. Experiment with caution if using values over 5MB/s.

Adaptec aha274x, aha284x, aic7xxx (aic7xxx=)   These boards can accept an argument of the form:

```
aic7xxx=extended,no_reset
```

The extended value, if non-zero, indicates that extended translation for large disks is enabled. The no_reset value, if non-zero, tells the driver not to reset the SCSI bus when setting up the host adaptor at boot.

AdvanSys SCSI Host Adaptors (`advansys=`) The AdvanSys driver can accept up to four i/o addresses that will be probed for an AdvanSys SCSI card. Note that these values (if used) do not effect EISA or PCI probing in any way. They are only used for probing ISA and VLB cards. In addition, if the driver has been compiled with debugging enabled, the level of debugging output can be set by adding an 0xdeb[0-f] parameter. The 0-f allows setting the level of the debugging messages to any of 16 levels of verbosity.

Always IN2000 Host Adaptor (`in2000=`) Unlike other SCSI host boot arguments, the IN2000 driver uses ASCII string prefixes for most of its integer arguments. Here is a list of the supported arguments:

`ioport:addr`—Where addr is IO address of a (usually ROM-less) card.

`noreset`—No optional args. Prevents SCSI bus reset at boot time.

`nosync:x`—x is a bitmask where the 1st 7 bits correspond with the 7 possible SCSI devices (bit 0 for device #0, etc). Set a bit to PREVENT sync negotiation on that device. The driver default is sync DISABLED on all devices.

`period:ns`—ns is the minimum # of nanoseconds in a SCSI data transfer period. Default is 500; acceptable values are 250 to 1000.

`disconnect:x`—x = 0 to never allow disconnects, 2 to always allow them. x = 1 does 'adaptive' disconnects, which is the default and generally the best choice.

`debug:x`—If DEBUGGING_ON is defined, x is a bitmask that causes various types of debug output to printed—see the DB_xxx defines in in2000.h

`proc:x`—If PROC_INTERFACE is defined, x is a bitmask that determines how the /proc interface works and what it does—see the PR_xxx defines in in2000.h

Some example usages are listed below:

```
in2000=ioport:0x220,noreset
in2000=period:250,disconnect:2,nosync:0x03
in2000=debug:0x1e
in2000=proc:3
```

AMD AM53C974 based hardware (AM53C974=) Unlike other drivers, this one does not use boot parameters to communicate i/o, IRQ or DMA channels. (Since the AM53C974 is a PCI device, there shouldn't be a need to do so.) Instead, the parameters are used to communicate the transfer modes and rates that are to be used between the host and the target device. This is best described with an example:

```
AM53C974=7,2,8,15
```

This would be interpreted as follows: 'For communication between the controller with SCSI-ID 7 and the device with SCSI-ID 2, a transfer rate of 8MHz in synchronous mode with max. 15 bytes offset should be negotiated.' More details can be found in the file `linux/drivers/scsi/README.AM53C974`.

BusLogic SCSI Hosts with v1.2 kernels (buslogic=) In older kernels, the buslogic driver accepts only one parameter, that being the I/O base. It expects that to be one of the following valid values: 0x130, 0x134, 0x230, 0x234, 0x330, 0x334.

BusLogic SCSI Hosts with v2.x kernels (BusLogic=) With v2.x kernels, the BusLogic driver accepts many parameters. (Note the case in the above; upper case B and L!!!). There are simply too many to list here. A complete description is tucked away in the middle of the driver linux/ drivers/scsi/BusLogic.c and searching for the string BusLogic= will put you right on it.

EATA SCSI Cards (eata=) As of late v2.0 kernels, the EATA drivers will accept a boot argument to specify the i/o base(s) to be probed. It is of the form:

```
eata=iobase1[,iobase2][,iobase3]...[,iobaseN]
```

The driver will probe the addresses in the order that they are listed.

Future Domain TMC-8xx, TMC-950 (tmc8xx=) The probe code for these SCSI hosts looks for an installed BIOS, and if none is present, the probe will not find your card. Or, if the signature string of your BIOS is not recognized then it will also not be found. In either case, you will then have to use a boot argument of the form:

```
tmc8xx=mem_base,irq
```

The mem_base value is the value of the memory mapped I/O region that the card uses. This will usually be one of the following values: 0xc8000, 0xca000, 0xcc000, 0xce000, 0xdc000, 0xde000.

Future Domain TMC-16xx, TMC-3260, AHA-2920 (`fdomain=`)   The driver detects these cards according to a list of known BIOS ROM signatures. For a full list of known BIOS revisions, please see `linux/drivers /scsi/fdomain.c` as it has a lot of information at the top of that file. If your BIOS is not known to the driver, you can use an override of the form:

```
fdomain=iobase,irq[,scsi_id]
```

IOMEGA Parallel Port / ZIP drive (`ppa=`)   This driver is for the IOMEGA Parallel Port SCSI adapter which is embedded into the IOMEGA ZIP drives. It may also work with the original IOMEGA PPA3 device. The boot argument for this driver is of the form:

```
ppa=iobase,speed_high,speed_low,nybble
```

with all but iobase being optionally specified values. If you wish to alter any of the three optional parameters, you are advised to read `linux/ drivers/scsi/README.ppa` for details of what they control.

NCR5380 based controllers (`ncr5380=`)   Depending on your board, the 5380 can be either i/o mapped or memory mapped. (An address below 0x400 usually implies i/o mapping, but PCI and EISA hardware use i/o addresses above 0x3ff.) In either case, you specify the address, the IRQ value and the DMA channel value. An example for an i/o mapped card would be: `ncr5380=0x350,5,3`. If the card doesn't use interrupts, then an IRQ value of 255 (0xff) will disable interrupts. An IRQ value of 254 means to autoprobe. More details can be found in the file `linux/ drivers- /scsi/README.g_NCR5380`

NCR53c400 based controllers (`ncr53c400=`)   The generic 53c400 support is done with the same driver as the generic 5380 support mentioned above. The boot argument is identical to the above with the exception that no DMA channel is used by the 53c400.

NCR53c406a based controllers (`ncr53c406a=`)   This driver uses a boot argument of the form:

```
ncr53c406a=PORTBASE,IRQ,FASTPIO
```

where the IRQ and FASTPIO parameters are optional. An interrupt value of zero disables the use of interrupts. Using a value of one for the FASTPIO parameter enables the use of `insl` and `outsl` instructions instead of the single-byte `inb` and `outb` instructions. The driver can also use DMA as a compile-time option.

Pro Audio Spectrum (`pas16=`)   The PAS16 uses a NCR5380 SCSI chip, and newer models support jumper- less configuration. The boot argument is of the form:

```
pas16=iobase,irq
```

The only difference is that you can specify an IRQ value of 255, which will tell the driver to work without using interrupts, albeit at a performance loss. The iobase is usually 0x388.

Seagate ST-0x (`st0x=`)   The probe code for these SCSI hosts looks for an installed BIOS, and if none is present, the probe will not find your card. Or, if the signature string of your BIOS is not recognized then it will also not be found. In either case, you will then have to use a boot argument of the form:

```
st0x=mem_base,irq
```

The mem_base value is the value of the memory mapped I/O region that the card uses. This will usually be one of the following values: 0xc8000, 0xca000, 0xcc000, 0xce000, 0xdc000, 0xde000.

Trantor T128 (`t128=`)   These cards are also based on the NCR5380 chip, and accept the following options:

```
t128=mem_base,irq
```

The valid values for mem_base are as follows: 0xcc000, 0xc8000, 0xdc000, 0xd8000.

Ultrastor SCSI cards (`u14-34f=`)   Note that there appears to be two independent drivers for this card, namely `CONFIG_SCSI_U14_34F` that uses u14-34f.c and `CONFIG_SCSI_ULTRASTOR` that uses ultrastor.c. It is the u14-34f one that (as of late v2.0 kernels) accepts a boot argument of the form:

```
u14-34f=iobase1[,iobase2][,iobase3]...[,iobaseN]
```

The driver will probe the addresses in the order that they are listed.

Western Digital WD7000 cards (wd7000=)   The driver probe for the wd7000 looks for a known BIOS ROM string and knows about a few standard configuration settings. If it doesn't come up with the correct values for your card, or you have an unrecognized BIOS version, you can use a boot argument of the form:

```
wd7000=irq,dma,iobase
```

SCSI Host Adapters that Don't Accept Boot Args

At present, the following SCSI cards do not make use of any boot-time parameters. In some cases, you can hard-wire values by directly editing the driver itself, if required.

Adaptec aha1740 (EISA probing),

NCR53c7xx,8xx (PCI, both drivers)

Qlogic Fast (0x230, 0x330)

Qlogic ISP (PCI)

Hard Disks

This section lists all the boot args associated with standard MFM/RLL, ST-506, XT, and IDE disk drive devices. Note that both the IDE and the generic ST-506 HD driver both accept the hd= option.

IDE Disk/CD-ROM Driver Parameters

The IDE driver accepts a number of parameters, which range from disk geometry specifications, to support for advanced or broken controller chips. The following is a summary of all the possible boot arguments. For full details, you really should consult the file ide.txt in the linux/ Documentation directory, from which this summary was extracted.

"hdx=" is recognized for all "x" from "a" to "h", such as "hdc".
"idex=" is recognized for all "x" from "0" to "3", such as "ide1".

"hdx=noprobe"	: drive may be present, but do not probe for it
"hdx=none"	: drive is NOT present, ignore cmos and do not probe
"hdx=nowerr"	: ignore the WRERR_STAT bit on this drive
"hdx=cdrom"	: drive is present, and is a cdrom drive
"hdx=cyl,head,sect"	: disk drive is present, with specified geometry
"hdx=autotune"	: driver will attempt to tune interface speed to the fastest PIO mode supported, if possible for this drive only. Not fully supported by all chipset types, and quite likely to cause trouble with older/odd IDE drives.
"idex=noprobe"	: do not attempt to access/use this interface
"idex=base"	: probe for an interface at the addr specified, where "base" is usually 0x1f0 or 0x170 and "ctl" is assumed to be "base"+0x206
"idex=base,ctl"	: specify both base and ctl
"idex=base,ctl,irq"	: specify base, ctl, and irq number
"idex=autotune"	: driver will attempt to tune interface speed to the fastest PIO mode supported, for all drives on this interface. Not fully supported by all chipset types, and quite likely to cause trouble with older/odd IDE drives.
"idex=noautotune"	: driver will NOT attempt to tune interface speed This is the default for most chipsets, except the cmd640.
"idex=serialize"	: do not overlap operations on idex and ide(x^1)

The following are valid ONLY on ide0, and the defaults for the base,ctl ports must not be altered.

`"ide0=dtc2278"`	: probe/support DTC2278 interface
`"ide0=ht6560b"`	: probe/support HT6560B interface
`"ide0=cmd640_vlb"`	: *REQUIRED* for VLB cards with the CMD640 chip (not for PCI — automatically detected)
`"ide0=qd6580"`	: probe/support qd6580 interface
`"ide0=ali14xx"`	: probe/support ali14xx chipsets (ALI M1439/M1445)
`"ide0=umc8672"`	: probe/support umc8672 chipsets

Everything else is rejected with a BAD OPTION message.

Standard ST-506 Disk Driver Options (hd=)

The standard disk driver can accept geometry arguments for the disks similar to the IDE driver. Note however that it only expects three values (C/H/S) — any more or any less and it will silently ignore you. Also, it only accepts hd= as an argument, i.e. hda=, hdb= and so on are not valid here. The format is as follows:

```
hd=cyls,heads,sects
```

If there are two disks installed, the above is repeated with the geometry parameters of the second disk.

XT Disk Driver Options (xd=)

If you are unfortunate enough to be using one of these old 8 bit cards that move data at a whopping 125kB/s then here is the scoop. The probe code for these cards looks for an installed BIOS, and if none is present, the probe will not find your card. Or, if the signature string of your BIOS is not recognized then it will also not be found. In either case, you will then have to use a boot argument of the form:

```
xd=type,irq,iobase,dma_chan
```

The type value specifies the particular manufacturer of the card, and are as follows: 0=generic; 1=DTC; 2,3,4=Western Digital, 5,6,7=Seagate; 8=OMTI. The only difference between multiple types from the same manufacturer is the BIOS string used for detection, which is not used if the type is specified.

The `xd_setup()` function does no checking on the values, and assumes that you entered all four values. Don't disappoint it. Here is an example usage for a WD1002 controller with the BIOS disabled/removed, using the 'default' XT controller parameters:

```
xd=2,5,0x320,3
```

CD-ROMs (Non-SCSI/ATAPI/IDE)

This section lists all the possible boot args pertaining to CD-ROM devices. Note that this does not include SCSI or IDE/ATAPI CD-ROMs. See the appropriate section(s) for those types of CD-ROMs.

Note that most of these CD-ROMs have documentation files that you should read, and they are all in one handy place: `linux/Documentation/cdrom`.

The Aztech Interface (`aztcd=`)

The syntax for this type of card is:

```
aztcd=obase[,magic_number]
```

If you set the `magic_number` to 0x79 then the driver will try and run anyway in the event of an unknown firmware version. All other values are ignored.

The CDU-31A and CDU-33A Sony Interface (`cdu31a=`)

This CD-ROM interface is found on some of the Pro Audio Spectrum sound cards, and other Sony supplied interface cards. The syntax is as follows:

```
cdu31a=iobase,[irq[,is_pas_card]]
```

Specifying an IRQ value of zero tells the driver that hardware interrupts aren't supported (as on some PAS cards). If your card supports interrupts, you should use them as it cuts down on the CPU usage of the driver.

The is_pas_card should be entered as PAS if using a Pro Audio Spectrum card, and otherwise it should not be specified at all.

The CDU-535 Sony Interface (sonycd535=)

The syntax for this CD-ROM interface is:

```
sonycd535=iobase[,irq]
```

A zero can be used for the I/O base as a 'placeholder' if one wishes to specify an IRQ value.

The GoldStar Interface (gscd=)

The syntax for this CD-ROM interface is:

```
gscd=iobase
```

The ISP16 Interface (isp16=)

The syntax for this CD-ROM interface is:

```
isp16=[port[,irq[,dma]]][[,]drive_type]
```

Using a zero for irq or dma means that they are not used. The allowable values for drive_type are noisp16, Sanyo, Panasonic, Sony, and Mitsumi. Using noisp16 disables the driver altogether.

The Mitsumi Standard Interface (mcd=)

The syntax for this CD-ROM interface is:

```
mcd=iobase,[irq[,wait_value]]
```

The wait_value is used as an internal timeout value for people who are having problems with their drive, and may or may not be implemented depending on a compile time DEFINE.

The Mitsumi XA/MultiSession Interface (mcdx=)

At present this 'experimental' driver has a setup function, but no parameters are implemented yet (as of 1.3.15). This is for the same hardware as above, but the driver has extended features.

The Optics Storage Interface (optcd=)

The syntax for this type of card is:

```
optcd=iobase
```

The Phillips CM206 Interface (cm206=)

The syntax for this type of card is:

```
cm206=[iobase][,irq]
```

The driver assumes numbers between 3 and 11 are IRQ values, and numbers between 0x300 and 0x370 are I/O ports, so you can specify one, or both numbers, in any order. It also accepts cm206=auto to enable autoprobing.

The Sanyo Interface (sjcd=)

The syntax for this type of card is:

```
sjcd=iobase[,irq[,dma_channel]]
```

The SoundBlaster Pro Interface (sbpcd=)

The syntax for this type of card is:

```
sbpcd=iobase,type
```

where type is one of the following (case sensitive) strings: 'SoundBlaster', 'LaserMate', or 'SPEA'. The I/O base is that of the CD-ROM interface, and not that of the sound portion of the card.

Serial and ISDN Drivers

The ICN ISDN driver (`icn=`)

This ISDN driver expects a boot argument of the form:

```
icn=iobase,membase,icn_id1,icn_id2
```

where iobase is the i/o port address of the card, membase is the shared memory base address of the card, and the two icn_id are unique ASCII string identifiers.

The PCBIT ISDN driver (`pcbit=`)

This boot argument takes integer pair arguments of the form:

```
pcbit=membase1,irq1[,membase2,irq2]
```

where membaseN is the shared memory base of the Nth card, and irqN is the interrupt setting of the Nth card. The default is IRQ 5 and membase 0xD0000.

The Teles ISDN driver (`teles=`)

This ISDN driver expects a boot argument of the form:

```
teles=iobase,irq,membase,protocol,teles_id
```

where iobase is the i/o port address of the card, membase is the shared memory base address of the card, irq is the interrupt channel the card uses, and teles_id is the unique ASCII string identifier.

The DigiBoard Driver (`digi=`)

The DigiBoard driver accepts a string of six comma separated identifiers or integers. The 6 values in order are:

Enable/Disable this card

Type of card: PC/Xi(0), PC/Xe(1), PC/Xeve(2), PC/Xem(3)

Enable/Disable alternate pin arrangement

Number of ports on this card

I/O Port where card is configured (in HEX if using string identifiers)
    Base of memory window (in HEX if using string identifiers)

An example of a correct boot prompt argument (in both identifier and integer form) is:

```
digi=E,PC/Xi,D,16,200,D0000
digi=1,0,0,16,512,851968
```

Note that the driver defaults to an i/o of 0x200 and a shared memory base of 0xD0000 in the absence of a digi= boot argument. There is no auto-probing performed. More details can be found in the file linux/ Documentation/digiboard.txt.

The RISCom/8 Multiport Serial Driver (`riscom8=`)

Up to four boards can be supported by supplying four unique i/o port values for each individual board installed. Other details can be found in the file linux/Documentation/riscom8.txt.

The Baycom Serial/Parallel Radio Modem (`baycom=`)

The format of the boot argument for these devices is:

```
baycom=modem,io,irq,options[,modem,io,irq,options]
```

Using modem=1 means you have the ser12 device, modem=2 means you have the par96 device. Using options=0 means use hardware DCD, and options=1 means use software DCD. The io and irq are the i/o port base and interrupt settings as usual. There is more details in the file README.baycom which is currently in the `/linux/ drivers/ char/`

Other Hardware Devices

Any other devices that didn't fit into any of the above categories got lumped together here.

Ethernet Devices (`ether=`)

Different drivers make use of different parameters, but they all at least share having an IRQ, an I/O port base value, and a name. In its most generic form, it looks something like this:

```
ether=irq,iobase[,param_1[,param_2,...param_8]]],name
```

The first non-numeric argument is taken as the name. The `param_n` values (if applicable) usually have different meanings for each different card/driver. Typical `param_n` values are used to specify things like shared memory address, interface selection, DMA channel and the like.

The most common use of this parameter is to force probing for a second ethercard, as the default is to only probe for one. This can be accomplished with a simple:

```
ether=0,0,eth1
```

Note that the values of zero for the IRQ and I/O base in the above example tell the driver(s) to autoprobe.

IMPORTANT NOTE TO MODULE USERS: The above will not force a probe for a second card if you are using the driver(s) as run time loadable modules (instead of having them complied into the kernel). Most Linux distributions use a bare bones kernel combined with a large selection of modular drivers. The ether= only applies to drivers compiled directly into the kernel.

The Ethernet-HowTo has complete and extensive documentation on using multiple cards and on the card/driver specific implementation of the param_n values where used. Interested readers should refer to the section in that document on their particular card for more complete information. Ethernet-HowTo <http://metalab.unc.edu/mdw/HOWTO/EthernetHOW-TO.html>

The Floppy Disk Driver (`floppy=`)

There are many floppy driver options, and they are all listed in README.fd in linux/drivers/block. There are too many options in that file to list here. Instead, only those options that may be required to get a Linux install to proceed on less than normal hardware are reprinted here.

floppy=0,daring Tells the floppy driver that your floppy controller should be used with caution (disables all daring operations).

floppy=thinkpad Tells the floppy driver that you have a Thinkpad. Thinkpads use an inverted convention for the disk change line.

floppy=nodma Tells the floppy driver not to use DMA for data transfers. This is needed on HP Omnibooks, which don't have a workable DMA channel for the floppy driver. This option is also useful if you frequently get "Unable to allocate DMA memory" messages. Use of 'nodma' is not recommended if you have a FDC without a FIFO (8272A or 82072). 82072A and later are OK). The FDC model is reported at boot. You also need at least a 486 to use nodma.

floppy=nofifo Disables the FIFO entirely. This is needed if you get 'Bus master arbitration error' messages from your Ethernet card (or from other devices) while accessing the floppy.

floppy=broken_dcl Don't use the disk change line, but assume that the disk was changed whenever the device node is reopened. Needed on some boxes where the disk change line is broken or unsupported. This should be regarded as a stopgap measure, indeed it makes floppy operation less efficient due to unneeded cache flushings, and slightly more unreliable. Please verify your cable connection and jumper settings if you have any DCL problems. However, some older drives, and also some Laptops are known not to have a DCL.

floppy=debug Print (additional) debugging messages.

floppy=messages Print informational messages for some operations (disk change notifications, warnings about over and under-
runs, and about autodetection).

The Sound Driver (sound=)

The sound driver can also accept boot args to override the compiled in
values. This is not recommended, as it is rather complex and the documentation for it in the kernel mysteriously vanished (a hint). You are better off to use sound as a module, or compile in your own values.

If you choose to use it regardless, then processing of the argument takes
place in the file dev_table.c in linux/drivers/sound. It accepts a
boot arg of the form:

```
sound=device1[,device2[,device3...[,device11]]]
```

where each deviceN value is of the following format 0xDTaaaId and the
bytes are used as follows:

D—second DMA channel (zero if not applicable)

T—device type: 1=FM, 2=3B, 3=PAS, 4=GUS, 5=MPU401, 6=SB16,
7=SB16-MIDI, . . . The listing of soundcard types up to 26 (don't forget to convert back to hex for command line use) are listed in the
file linux/include/linux/soundcard.h and 27 to 999 (newer models)
can be found in the file linux/drivers/sound/dev_table.h.

aaa—I/O address in hex.

I—interrupt line in hex (i.e 10=a, 11=b, . . .)

d—First DMA channel.

As you can see it gets pretty messy, and you really are better off to use
a modular driver or compile in your own personal values as recommended. Using a boot arg of sound=0 will disable the sound driver
entirely.

The Bus Mouse Driver (bmouse=)

The busmouse driver only accepts one parameter, that being the hardware
IRQ value to be used.

The MS Bus Mouse Driver (`msmouse=`)

The MS mouse driver only accepts one parameter, that being the hardware IRQ value to be used.

The Printer Driver (`lp=`)

With this boot argument you can tell the printer driver what ports to use and what ports not to use. The latter comes in handy if you don't want the printer driver to claim all available parallel ports, so that other drivers (e.g., PLIP, PPA) can use them instead.

The format of the argument is multiple i/o, IRQ pairs. For example, lp=0x3bc,0,0x378,7 would use the port at 0x3bc in IRQ-less (polling) mode, and use IRQ 7 for the port at 0x378. The port at 0x278 (if any) would not be probed, since autoprobing only takes place in the absence of a lp= argument. To disable the printer driver entirely, one can use lp=0.

Copying, Translations, Closing, etc.

Hey, you made it to the end! (Phew. . .) Now just the legal stuff.

Copyright and Disclaimer

Closing

If you have found any glaring typos, or outdated info in this document, please let me know. It is easy to overlook stuff, as the kernel (and the number of drivers) is huge compared to what it was when I started this. Thanks,

Paul Gortmaker, p_gortmaker@yahoo.com

The Linux Modem-HOWTO

Help with selecting, connecting, configuring, trouble-shooting, and understanding modems for a PC. See Serial-HOWTO for multiport serial boards.

Introduction

DSL, Cable, and ISDN Modems in Other HOWTOs

This HOWTO covers conventional modems for PCs, mainly modems on the ISA bus (although much of this should also apply to the PCI bus).

- DSL modems: see the mini-howto: ADSL

- Cable-Modems-HOWTO (was once a LDP mini-Howto)
  <http://www.cs.unm.edu/~vuksan/linux/Cable-Modem.html>

- ISDN Howto (not a LDP Howto)
  <http://sdb.suse.de/sdb/en/html/isdn.html>: drivers for ISDN "Modems". Much related info on this is in German. For a tutorial on ISDN see <http://public.swbell.net/ISDN/overview.html>

See also "Addendum D: Other Types of Modems".

Also Not Covered: PCMCIA Modems, PPP

For modems on the PCMCIA bus see the PCMCIA-HOWTO: PCMCIA serial and modem devices. This HOWTO doesn't cover PPP (used to connect to the Internet via a modem) or communication programs. Except it does show how to use communication programs to test that your modem works OK and can make phone calls. If you want to use a modem to connect to the Internet then you need to set up PPP. There's a lot of documentation for PPP (including a PPP-HOWTO which is being revised). Some of it might be found in `/usr/doc/ppp` or the like.

Copyright, Disclaimer, Trademarks, & Credits

Copyright   Copyright © 1998–1999 by David S. Lawyer

Please freely copy and distribute (sell or give away) this document in any format. Forward any corrections and comments to the document maintainer. You may create a derivative work and distribute it provided that you:

1. Send your derivative work (in the most suitable format such as sgml) to the LDP (Linux Documentation Project) or the like for posting on the Internet. If not the LDP, then let the LDP know

where it is available. Except for a translation, send a copy to the previous maintainer's url as shown in the latest version.

2. License the derivative work in the spirit of this license or use GPL. Include a copyright notice and at least a pointer to the license used.

3. Give due credit to previous authors and major contributors.

If you're considering making a derived work other than a translation, it's requested that you discuss your plans with the current maintainer.

Disclaimer While I haven't intentionally tried to mislead you, there are likely a number of errors in this document. Please let me know about them. Since this is free documentation, it should be obvious that I cannot be held legally responsible for any errors.

Trademarks If certain words are trademarks, the context should make it clear to whom they belong. For example "MS Windows" (or just "Windows") implies that "Windows" belongs to Microsoft (MS). "Hayes" is a trademark of Microcomputer Products Inc. I use "winmodem" to mean any modem which requires MS-Windows and not in the trademark sense.

Credits The following is only a rough approximation of how version 0.0 of this document was created: About 1/3 of the material here was lifted directly from Serial-HOWTO v. 1.11 by Greg Hankins. <mailto:gregh@cc.gatech.edu> (with his permission). About another 1/3 was taken from that Serial-HOWTO and revised. The remaining 1/3 is newly created by the author: David S. Lawyer <mailto:dave@lafn.org>.

Contacting the Author

Please don't email me asking which modem to buy or asking if a certain modem will work under Linux. Look at the huge list at "Software (Internal) Modems." Also, please don't ask me how to configure a modem unless you've looked over this HOWTO and still can't do it.

Please let me know of any errors in facts, opinions, logic, spelling, grammar, clarity, links, etc. But first, if the date is over a month old, check to see that you have the latest version. Please send me any other info that you think belongs in this document.

New Versions of this HOWTO

New versions of this Modem-HOWTO come out every month or so since modem situation is rapidly changing (and since I'm still learning). Your problem might be solved in the latest version. It will be available to browse and/or download at LDP mirror sites. For a list of such sites see: <http://metalab.unc.edu/LDP/mirrors.html>. If you only want to quickly check the date of the latest version go to <http://metalab.unc.edu/LDP/ HOWTO/Modem-HOWTO.html> and compare it to the version you are currently reading: v0.08, 1 Jan. 2000.

What is a Modem?

A modem is a device that lets one send digital signals over ordinary telephone lines not designed for digital signals. If telephone lines were all digital then you wouldn't need a modem. It permits your computer to connect to and communicate with the rest of the world. When you use a modem, you normally use a communication program or web browser (which includes such a program) to utilize the modem and dial-out on a telephone line. Advanced modem users can set things up so that others may phone in to them and use their computer. This is called "dial-in".

There are two basic types of modems for a PC: external and internal. The external sets on your desk outside the PC while the internal is not visible since it's inside the PC. The external modem plugs into a connector on the back of the PC known as a "serial port". The internal modem is a card that is inserted inside the computer and has an (invisible) serial port built into it. For a more detailed comparison see "External vs. Internal". Thus when you get an internal modem, you also get a dedicated serial port (which can only be used with the modem and not with anything else such as another modem or a printer). In Linux, the serial ports are named ttyS0, ttyS1, etc. (usually corresponding respectively to COM1, COM2, etc. in DOS/Windows).

The serial port is not to be confused with the "Universal Serial Bus" (USB) which uses a special modular connector and may be used with modems in the future. See "Modem & Serial Port Basics" for more details on modems and serial ports.

Modems often include the ability to send Faxes (Fax Modems). See "Fax" for a list of fax software. "Voice" modems can work like an automatic answering machine and handle voicemail. See "Voicemail".

Quick Install

External Modem Install With a straight-thru or modem cable, connect the modem to an unused serial port on the PC. Make sure you know the name of the serial port: in most cases COM1 is ttyS0, COM2 is ttyS1, etc. You may need to check the BIOS setup menu to determine this. Plug in the power cord to provide power to the modem. See "All Modems" for further instructions.

Internal Modems (on ISA bus) (For the PCI bus see "PCI Bus Not Yet Supported" and "PCI Modems".) If the modem says it will only work under MS Windows, you are out of luck. If you already have 2 serial ports, make the modem the 3rd serial port (ttyS2 = COM3). Find an unused IRQ number to use. In the past IRQ 5 was often used but today IRQ 5 is also used for sound cards. Then set the jumpers (or the like) on the internal modem to the unused IRQ and IO address 3E8 (ttyS2).

"Or the like" (in the previous sentence) may be a bit tricky. If the modem is a Plug and Play (PnP) for the ISA bus, the equivalent probably can be done using the isapnp program which comes with isapnptools. See man isapnp or the FAQ for it. See also "Plug- and-Play-HOWTO". With a PnP-BIOS you may be able to tell the CMOS setup menu that you don't have a PnP OS and then the BIOS may set a suitable IRQ and IO address in the modem card. If you want to "force" the BIOS to set a certain IRQ and/or IO then you may be able to do this using Window9x on the same PC. It can set them into the PnP BIOS's flash memory where they will be used to configure for Linux as well as Windows. See "Plug-and-Play-HOWTO" and search for "forced" (occurs in several places). For Windows 3.x you can do the same thing using the ICU under Windows 3.x. There may even be a way to disable PnP using software (under Windows) that came with the modem.

Finally you must also find the file where setserial is run and add a line something like: setserial /dev/ttyS2 irq5. Except for setserial v2.15 and later you may (if you distribution lets you) just run setserial on the command line and the results are saved to a configuration file. See "What is Setserial" for more info. See the next subsection "All Modems" for further instructions on quick installation.

All Modems Plug the modem into a telephone line. Then start up a communication program such as minicom and go to the configuration menu for the serial port. Assign it a high baud rate a few times higher than the bit rate of your modem. See "Speed Table" for the "best" speeds to use.

Tell it the full name of your serial port such as /dev/ttyS1. Set hardware flow control (RTS/CTS). Now you need to save these settings and exit minicom. Then start minicom again, type AT to see if your modem is there and responds with OK. Then go to the dial directory (or menu) and dial a number.

Modems for a Linux PC

External vs. Internal

A modem for a PC may be either internal or external. The internal one is installed inside of your PC (you must remove screws, etc., to install it) and the external one just plugs into a serial port connector on a PC. Internal modems are less expensive, are less likely to to suffer data loss due to buffer overrun, usually use less electricity, and use up no space on your desk.

External modems are much easier to install and require less configuration. They have lights which may give you a clue as to what is happening and aid in troubleshooting. The fact that the serial port and modem can be physically separated also aids in troubleshooting. External modems are easy to move to another computer.

Unfortunately most external modems have no switch to turn off the power supply when not in use and thus are likely to consume a little electricity even when turned off (unless you unplug the power supply from the wall). Each watt they draw costs you about $1/yr. Another possible disadvantage of an external is that you will be forced to use an existing serial port which may not support a speed of over 115,200 k (although as of late 1998 most new internal modems don't either—but some do). If a new internal modem had a 16650 UART it would put less load on the CPU (but almost none do as of late 1998).

Internal modems present a special problem for Linux, but will work just as well as external modems provided you avoid the high percentage of them that will work only for MS Windows, and also provided that you spend time (sometimes a lot of time) to configure them correctly. Some of the modems which will work only under MS Windows are, unfortunately, not labeled as such. If you buy a new one, make sure that you can return it for a refund if it will not work under Linux.

While most new modems are plug-and-play you have various ways to deal with them:

■ Use the isapnp program

■ Have a PnP BIOS do the configuring

■ Patch the kernel to create a PnP Linux (not currently available)

Each of the above has shortcomings. Isapnp documentation is difficult to understand although reading the Plug-and-Play-HOWTO (at present incomplete) will aid in understanding it. If you want the PnP BIOS to do the configuring, all you need to do is to make sure that it knows you don't have a PnP operating system. But it may not do it correctly. To find out what it's done see "What is set in my serial port hardware?". Patching the kernel has worked in the past but no patch seems to be currently available. Check out the website for it.

There are many Linux users that say that it's a lot simpler just to get an external modem and plug it in. But since new peripherals are mostly PnP today, you may eventually need to deal with it, so why delay the inevitable? Still, the most expedient (and expensive) solution is an external modem (if you have a free serial port).

External Modems

PnP External Modems   Many external modems are labeled "Plug and Play" (PnP) but they should all work fine as non-PnP modems. Since you usually plug the modem into a serial port which has its own IRQ number and IO address, the modem needs no PnP features to set these up. However, the serial port itself may need to be configured (IRQ number and IO address) unless the default configuration is OK.

How can an external modem be called PnP since it can't be configured by PnP? Well, it has a special PnP identification built into it that can be read (thru the serial port) by a PnP operating system. Such an operating system would then know that you have a modem on a certain port and would also know the model number. Then you might not need to configure application programs by telling them what port the modem is on (such as /dev/ttyS2 or COM3). But since you don't have such a PnP operating system you will need to configure your application program manually by giving it the /dev id (such as /dev/ttyS2).

Cabling & Installation   Connecting an external modem is simple compared to connecting most other devices to a serial port that require various types of "null modem" cables. Modems use straight through cable, with no pins crossed over. Most computer stores should have these. Make sure you get the correct gender. If you are using the DB9 or DB25 serial port at your computer, it will always be male which means that the connector on the cable should be female. Hook up your modem to one of your serial ports. If you are willing to accept the default IRQ and IO address of the port you connect it to, then you are ready to start your communication program and configure the modem itself.

What the Lights (LEDs) Mean

- TM Test Modem
- AA Auto Answer (If on, your modem will answer an incoming call)
- RD Receive Data line = RxD
- SD Send Data line = TxD
- TR data Terminal Ready = DTR (set by your PC)
- RI Ring Indicator (If on, someone is "ringing" your modem)
- OH Off Hook (If off, your modem has hung up the phone line)
- MR Modem Ready = DSR ??
- EC Error Correction
- DC Data Compression
- HS High Speed (for this modem)

Internal Modems

An internal modem is installed in a PC by taking off the cover of the PC and inserting the modem card into a vacant slot on the motherboard. There are modems for the ISA slots and others for the PCI slots. While external modems plug into the serial port (via a short cable) the internal modems have the serial port built into the modem. In other words, the modem card is both a serial port and a modem.

Setting the IO address and IRQ for a serial port was formerly done by jumpers on the card. These are little black rectangular "cubes" about 5x4x2 mm in size which push in over pins on the card. Plug-and-Play modems (actually the serial port part of the modems) don't use jumpers for setting these but instead are configured by sending configuration commands to them (via IO address space on the ISA bus inside the computer). Such configuration commands can be sent by a PnP BIOS, the `isapnp` program (for the ISA bus only) or by a PnP operating system. The configuring of them is built into Windows 95/98 OSs. Under Linux you have a choice of ways (none of which is always easy) to io-irq configure them:

1. Use isapnp which may be run automatically at every boot-time
2. Use a PnP BIOS alone (which runs at every boot-time)
3. Patch Linux to make it a PnP operating system

Software (Internal) Modems (Mostly winmodems)

Software modems turn over much (or even almost all) of the work of the modem to the main processor (CPU) chip of your computer (such as a Pentium chip). Complex proprietary software programs (drivers) do this work on the CPU. A majority of internal modems made after about mid-1998 don't work with Linux since they are software modems which only work under Windows and are often called "winmodems". Although a few volunteers were willing to try writing Linux drivers for these modems, specs were not made available so this couldn't be done. Prior to about 2000, no software modem could be used with Linux due to no drivers for them under Linux.

Then finally in late 1999 two software modems appeared that could work under Linux. Lucent Technologies supplied a Linux binary-only code to support it's PCI software modems, but bugs were reported in the first version. PC-TEL introduced a new software modem for Linux. Will other companies follow these leads and thus create "linmodems"? For a list of modems which work/don't_work under Linux see modem list <http://www.o2.net/~gromitkc/winmodem.html> A project to get winmodems to work under linux is at <http://linmodems.org>.

If code is made available to operate a "winmodem" under Linux, then one may call it a "linmodem". Is it still a "winmodem"? Perhaps it is since it also works under MS Windows. The term "Winmodem" is a trademark for a certain type of "winmodem".

Here is some more precise terminology regarding software modems. HSP (Host Signal Processor) means that the host processor (your CPU chip) creates the code needed to produce the electrical signal on the phone line. The modem itself just creates whatever electrical waveshape the CPU tells it to. In contrast to this, a "controllerless" modem can create the waveshapes on its own (but can't control the modem). It contains no facilities to deal with bytes being sent and received. It can't compress strings of bytes; it can't check for errors; it can't put them into packets. In other words it can't control the modem but instead has the CPU do all this work using software. The Rockwell HCF (Host Controlled Family) does this. If the software that does all this could be ported to Linux and then there wouldn't be this problem. Besides the above, a modem which doesn't simulate a serial port will not work under Linux.

How do you determine if an internal modem will work under Linux? First see if the name or description of it indicates it's a software modem: HSP, HCF, HSF, controllerless, host-controlled, host-based, and soft-. . . modem. If it's a software modem it will only work for the rare cases (so far) where a Linux driver is available. If you don't know the model of the modem and you also have Windows on your Linux PC, click on the "Modem" icon in the "Control Panel". Then check out the modem list on the Web mentioned 4 paragraphs above. If the above doesn't work (or isn't feasible), you can look at the package it came in (or a manual) find the section on the package that says something like "Minimum System Requirements" or just "System Requirements". It may be in fine print. Read it closely. If Windows is listed as one of the requirements then it will likely not work under Linux.

Otherwise, it may work under Linux if it fails to state explicitly that you must have Windows. By saying it's "designed for Windows" it may only mean that it fully supports Microsoft's plug-and-play which is OK since Linux uses the same plug-and-play specs (but it's harder to configure under Linux). Being "designed for Windows" thus gives no clue as to whether or not it will work under Linux. You might check the Website of the manufacturer or inquire via email. I once saw a web-page that specifically stated that one model worked under Linux while implying that another model didn't.

Besides the problems of getting a driver, what are the pros and cons of software modems. Since the software modem uses the CPU to do much of its work, the software modem requires less on-board electronics and thus costs less. At the same time, the CPU is heavily loaded by the modem which may result in slower operation. This is especially true if other CPU-intensive tasks are running at the same time. Of course when you're not using the software modem there is no degradation in performance at all. Is the cost savings worth it? In some cases yes, especially if you seldom use the modem or are not running any other CPU intensive tasks when the modem is in use. Thus there are cases where use of a software modem is economically justified. The savings in modem cost could be used for a better CPU which would speed things up a little. But the on-board electronics of a modem can do the job more efficiently than a general purpose CPU. So if you use the modem most of the time it's probably better to avoid software modems (and then you can use a less powerful CPU :-).

PCI Modems

A PCI modem card is one which inserts into a PCI-bus slot on the motherboard of a PC. Unfortunately, it seems that most PCI modems will not work under Linux but efforts are underway to support some of them. See "PCI Bus Yet Supported".

Which Internal Modems Might Not Work with Linux

- "Software (Internal) Modems" only work in rare cases where a Linux driver is available.

- "PCI Modems" seldom work under Linux

- "MWave and DSP Modems" might work, but only if you first start Windows/Dos each time you power on your PC

- Modems with "RPI (Rockwell)" drivers work but with reduced performance

MWave and DSP Modems Such modems use DSPs (Digital Signal Processors) which are programmed by algorithms which must be downloaded from the hard disk to the DSP's memory just before using the modem. Unfortunately, the downloading is done by DOS/Windows programs so one can't do it from Linux. Ordinary modems that work with Linux often have a DSP too (and may mention this on the packaging), but the program that runs it is stored inside the modem. This is not a "DSP modem" in the sense of this section and should work OK under Linux. An example of a DSP modem is IBM's Aptiva MWAVE.

If a DSP modem modem simulates a serial port, then it is usable with Linux which communicates with modems via the serial port. If you also have DOS/Windows on the same PC you may be able to use the modem: You first install the driver under DOS (using DOS and not Window drivers).

Then start DOS/Windows (make sure the modem gets initialized) and without turning off the computer, go into Linux. One way to get to Linux is to use `loadlin.exe` which is a DOS program that will boot Linux from DOS (See Config-HOWTO). Another way is to just press CTRL- ALT-DEL. The modem remains on the same com port (same IO address) that it used under DOS.

Rockwell (RPI) Drivers   Modems that require Rockwell RPI (Rockwell Protocol Interface) drivers can still be used with Linux even thought the driver software works only under Windows. This is because the Windows software which you don't have does only compression and error correction. If you are willing to operate the modem without compression and error correction then it's feasible to use it with Linux. To do this you will need to disable RPI by sending the modem (via the initialization string) a `RPI disable` command each time you power on your modem. On my modem this command is `+H0`. Not having data compression available may not be much of a handicap since most long files which you download from the Internet are already compressed and attempts at further compression may only slow things down a bit.

Multiport Modem Cards

These are internal modems, but there is more that one per card. 8 modems/ card is common. You will need these if you want to have several people simultaneously dial in/out to your computer. Note that these modems are not digital modems and will thus not be able to use 56k for people who dial-in. So they are not suitable for ISPs. The cards listed claim to work with Linux and the websites should point you to a driver for them.

- MultiModemISI by Multi-Tech Systems. 56K or 33.6K, PCI or ISA, 4 or 8 ports. ISDN/56K hybrids.
  <http://www.multitech.com/products/>

- RAStel by Moreton Bay Products. 56K PCI or ISA, 4 or 8 ports. Also 2 modems + 2 vacant serial ports.
  <http://www.moretonbay.com.au/MBWEB/product/rastel/rastel.htm>

- RocketModem by Comtrol. ISA 33.6K, 4 or 8 port.
  <http://www.comtrol.com/SALES/SPECS/Rmodem.htm>

- AccelePort (RAS Family) by Digi.
  <http://www.dgii.com/digi.cfm?p=940564.pi.prd.00000046>

The use of modems by ISPs is not covered in this HOWTO since it's become somewhat complex due to the introduction of 56k modems which require a digital connection to the phone company. See "What Do I Need to Be An ISP?". Cyclades promotes their own products here so please do comparison shopping before buying anything. Also bear in mind that one may turn a PC into a "remote access server" by buying expensive specialized PCI cards containing digital modems, etc.

Basics Modem & Serial Port

You don't have to understand the basics to use and install a modem. But understanding it may help to determine what is wrong if you run into problems. After reading this section, if you want to understand it even better you may want to see "How Modems Work" in this document (not yet complete). More details on the serial port (including much of this section) will be found in Serial-HOWTO.

Modem Converts Digital to Analog (and Conversely)

Most all telephone main lines are digital already but the lines leading to your house (or business) are usually analog which means that they were designed to transmit a voltage wave which is an exact replica of the sound wave coming out of your mouth. Such a voltage wave is called "analog". If viewed on an oscilloscope it looks like a sine wave of varying frequency and amplitude. A digital signal is like a square wave. For example 3 v (volts) might be a 1-bit and 0 v could be a 0-bit. For most serial ports (used by external modems) +12 v is a 0-bit and −12 v is a 1-bit (some are + or − 5 v).

To send data from your computer over the phone line, the modem takes the digital signal from your computer and converts it to "analog." It does this by both creating an analog sine wave and then "MODulating" it. Since the result still represents digital data, it could also be called a digital signal instead of analog. But it looks something like an analog signal and almost everyone calls it analog. At the other end of the phone line another modem "DEModulates" this signal and the pure digital signal is recovered. Put together the "mod" and "dem" parts of the two words above and you get "modem" (if you drop one of the two d's). A "modem" is thus a MODulator-

DEModulator. Just what modulation is may be found in the section "Modulation Details".

What is a Serial Port?

Intro to Serial   The serial port is an I/O (Input/Output) device. Since modems have a serial port between them and the computer, it's necessary to understand the serial port as well as the modem.

Most PCs have one or two serial ports. Each has a 9-pin connector (sometimes 25-pin) on the back of the computer. Computer programs can send data (bytes) to the transmit pin (output) and receive bytes from the receive pin (input). The other pins are for control purposes and ground.

The serial port is much more than just a connector. It converts the data from parallel to serial and changes the electrical representation of the data. Inside the computer, data bits flow in parallel (using many wires at the same time). Serial flow is a stream of bits over a single wire (such as on the transmit or receive pin of the serial connector). For the serial port to create such a flow, it must convert data from parallel (inside the computer) to serial on the transmit pin (and conversely).

Most of the electronics of the serial port is found in a computer chip (or a section of a chip) known as a UART. For more details on UARTs see the section "What Are UARTs? How Do They Affect Performance?". But you may want to finish this section first so that you will hopefully understand how the UART fits into the overall scheme of things.

Pins and Wires   Old PCs used 25 pin connectors but only about 9 pins were actually used so today most connectors are only 9-pin. Each of the 9 pins usually connects to a wire. Besides the two wires used for transmitting and receiving data, another pin (wire) is signal ground. The voltage on any wire is measured with respect to this ground. Thus the minimum number of wires to use for 2-way transmission of data is 3. Except that it has been known to work with no signal ground wire but with degraded performance and sometimes with errors.

There are still more wires which are for control purposes (signalling) only and not for sending bytes. All of these signals could have been shared on a single wire, but instead, there is a separate dedicated wire for every type of signal. Some (or all) of these control wires are called "modem control lines". Modem control wires are either in the asserted state (on) of +12 volts or in the negated state (off) of −12 volts. One of these wires is to signal the computer to stop sending bytes out the serial port cable.

Conversely, another wire signals the device attached to the serial port to stop sending bytes to the computer. If the attached device is a modem, other wires may tell the modem to hang up the telephone line or tell the computer that a connection has been made or that the telephone line is ringing (someone is attempting to call in). See the Serial-HOWTO: Pinout and Signals for more details.

Internal Modem Contains Serial Port   For an internal modem there is no 9-pin connector but the behavior is almost exactly as if the above mentioned cable wires existed. Instead of a 12 volt signal in a wire giving the state of a modem control line, the internal modem may just use a status bit in its own memory (a register) to determine the state of this non-existent "wire". The internal modem's serial port looks just like a real serial port to the computer. It even includes the speed limits that one may set at ordinary serial ports such as 115200 bits/sec. Unfortunately for Linux, many internal modems today don't work exactly this way but instead use software (running on the CPU) to do much of the modem's work. Unfortunately, such software is often only available for the MS Windows OS (it hasn't been ported to Linux). Thus you can't use most of these modems with Linux. See "Software (Internal) Modems".

IO Address & IRQ

Since the computer needs to communicate with each serial port, the operating system must know that each serial port exists and where it is (its I/O address). It also needs to know which wire (IRQ number) the serial port must use to request service from the computer's CPU. It requests service by sending an interrupt on this wire. Thus every serial port device must store in its non-volatile memory both its I/O address and its Interrupt ReQuest number: IRQ. See "Interrupts". For the PCI bus it doesn't work exactly this way since the PCI bus has its own system of interrupts. But since the PCI-aware BIOS sets up chips to map these PCI interrupts to IRQs, it seemingly behaves just as described above except that sharing of interrupts is allowed (2 or more devices may use the same IRQ number).

I/O addresses are not the same as memory addresses. When an I/O addresses is put onto the computer's address bus, another wire is energized. This both tells main memory to ignore the address and tells all devices which have I/O addresses (such as the serial port) to listen to the address to see if it matches the device's. If the address matches, then the I/O device reads the data on the data bus.

Names: ttyS0, ttyS1, etc.

The serial ports are named ttyS0, ttyS1, etc. (and usually correspond respectively to COM1, COM2, etc. in DOS/Windows). The /dev directory has a special file for each port. Type `ls /dev/ttyS*` to see them. Just because there may be (for example) a `ttyS3` file, doesn't necessarily mean that there exists a physical serial port there.

Which one of these names (ttyS0, ttyS1, etc.) refers to which physical serial port is determined as follows. The serial driver (software) maintains a table showing which I/O address corresponds to which ttyS. This mapping of names (such as ttyS1) to I/O addresses (and IRQs) may be both set and viewed by the `setserial` command. See "What is `setserial`". This does not set the I/O address and IRQ in the hardware itself (which is set by jumpers or by plug-and-play software). Thus what physical port corresponds to say ttyS1 depends both on what the serial driver thinks (per `setserial`) and what is set in the hardware. If a mistake has been made, the physical port may not correspond to any name (such as ttyS2) and thus it can't be used. See "Serial Port Devices `/dev/ttyS2`, etc." for more details.

Interrupts

Bytes come in over the phone line to the modem, are converted from analog to digital by the modem and passed along to the serial port on their way to their destination inside your computer. When the serial port receives a number of bytes (may be set to 1, 4, 8, or 14) into its FIFO buffer, it signals the CPU to fetch them by sending an electrical signal known as an interrupt on a certain wire normally used only by that port. Thus the FIFO waits for a number of bytes and then issues an interrupt.

However, this interrupt will also be sent if there is an unexpected delay while waiting for the next byte to arrive (known as a timeout). Thus if the bytes are being received slowly (such as someone typing on a terminal keyboard) there may be an interrupt issued for every byte received. For some UART chips the rule is like this: If 4 bytes in a row could have been received, but none of these 4 show up, then the port gives up waiting for more bytes and issues an interrupt to fetch the bytes currently in the FIFO. Of course, if the FIFO is empty, no interrupt will be issued.

Each interrupt conductor (inside the computer) has a number (IRQ) and the serial port must know which conductor to use to signal on. For example, ttyS0 normally uses IRQ number 4 known as IRQ4 (or IRQ 4). A list of them and more will be found in "man `setserial`" (search for "Configuring Serial Ports"). Interrupts are issued whenever the serial port needs to get the CPU's attention. It's important to do this in a timely manner since the buffer inside the serial port can hold only 16 (1 in old serial ports) incoming bytes. If the CPU fails to remove such received bytes promptly, then there will not be any space left for any more incoming bytes and the small buffer may overflow (overrun) resulting in a loss of data bytes.

For an external modem, there is no way (such as flow control) to stop the flow rapidly enough to prevent this. For an internal modem the 16-byte FIFO buffer is on the same card and a good modem will not write to it if it's full. Thus a good internal modem will not overrun the 16-byte buffers but it may need to use "Modem-to-Modem Flow Control" to prevent the modem itself from being overrun. This is one advantage of an internal modem over an external.

Interrupts are also issued when the serial port has just sent out all 16 of its bytes from its small transmit buffer out the external cable. It then has space for 16 more outgoing bytes. The interrupt is to notify the CPU of that fact so that it may put more bytes in the small transmit buffer to be transmitted. Also, when a modem control line changes state an interrupt is issued.

The buffers mentioned above are all hardware buffers. The serial port also has large buffers in main memory. This will be explained later.

Interrupts convey a lot of information but only indirectly. The interrupt itself just tells a chip called the interrupt controller that a certain serial port needs attention. The interrupt controller then signals the CPU. The CPU runs a special program to service the serial port. That program is called an interrupt service routine (part of the serial driver software). It tries to find out what has happened at the serial port and then deals with the problem such a transferring bytes from (or to) the serial port's hardware buffer. This program can easily find out what has happened since the serial port has registers at IO addresses known to the the serial driver software. These registers contain status information about the serial port. The software reads these registers and by inspecting the contents, finds out what has happened and takes appropriate action.

Data Compression (by the Modem)

Before continuing with the basics of the serial port, one needs to understand about something done by the modem: data compression. In some cases this task is actually done by software run on the computer's CPU but unfortunately at present, such software only works for MS Windows. The discussion here will be for the case where the modem itself does the compression since this is what must happen in order for the modem to work under Linux.

In order to send data faster over the phone line, one may compress (encode it) using a custom encoding scheme which itself depends on the data. The encoded data is smaller than the original (less bytes) and can be sent over the Internet in less time. This process is called "data compression".

If you download files from the Internet, they are likely already compressed and it is not feasible for the modem to try to compress them further. Your modem may sense that what is passing thru has already been compressed and refrain from trying a compress it any more. If you are receiving data which has been compressed by the other modem, your modem will decompress it and create many more bytes than were sent over the phone line. Thus the flow of data from your modem into your computer will be higher than the flow over the phone line to you. The ratio of this flow is called the compression ratio. Compression ratios as high as 4 are possible, but not very likely.

Error Correction

Similar to data compression, modems may be set to do error correction. While there is some overhead cost involved which slows down the byte/sec flow rate, the fact that error correction strips off start and stop bits actually increases the data byte/sec flow rate.

For the serial port's interface with the external world, each 8-bit byte has 2 extra bits added to it: a start-bit and a stop-bit. Without error correction, these extra start and stop bits usually go right thru the modem and out over the phone lines. But when error correction is enabled, these extra bits are stripped off and the 8-bit bytes are put into packets. This is more efficient and results in higher byte/sec flow in spite of the fact that there are a few more bytes added for packet headers and error correction purposes.

Data Flow (Speeds)

Data (bytes representing letters, pictures, etc.) flows from your computer to your modem and then out on the telephone line (and conversely). Flow rates (such as 56k [56000] bits/sec) are (incorrectly) called "speed". But almost everyone says "speed" instead of "flow rate". If there were no data compression the flow rate from the computer to the modem would be about the same as the flow rate over the telephone line.

Actually there are two different speeds to consider at your end of the phone line:

- The speed on the phone line itself (DCE speed) modem-to-modem
- The speed from your computer's serial port to your modem (DTE speed)

When you dial out and connect to another modem on the other end of the phone line, your modem often sends you a message like "CONNECT 28800" or "CONNECT 115200". What do these mean? Well, its either the DCE speed or the DTE speed. If it's higher than the advertised modem speed it must be the DTE modem-to-computer speed. This is the case for the 115200 speed shown above. The 28800 must be a DCE (modem-to-modem) speed since the serial port has no such speed. One may configure the modem to report either speed. Some modems report both speeds and report the modem-to-modem speed as (for example): CARRIER 28800.

If you have an internal modem you would not expect that there would be any speed limit on the DTE speed from your modem to your computer since you modem is inside your computer and is almost part of your computer. But there is since the modem contains a dedicated serial port within it.

It's important to understand that the average speed is often less than the specified speed, especially on the short DTE computer-to-modem line. Waits (or idle time) result in a lower average speed. These waits may include long waits of perhaps a second due to "Flow Control". At the other extreme there may be very short waits (idle time) of several micro-seconds separating the end of one byte and the start of the next byte. In addition, modems will fall-back to lower speeds if the telephone line conditions are less than pristine.

For a discussion of what DTE speed is best to use see section "What Speed Should I Use?".

Flow Control

Flow control means the ability to stop the flow of bytes in a wire. It also includes provisions to restart the flow without any loss of bytes. Flow control is needed for modems to allow a jump in instantaneous flow rates.

Example of Flow Control   For example, consider the case where you connect a 36.6k external modem via a short cable to your serial port. The modem sends and receives bytes over the phone line at 36.6k bits per second (bps). It's not doing any data compression or error correction. You have set the serial port speed to 115,200 bits/sec (bps), and you are sending data from your computer to the phone line. Then the flow from the your computer to your modem over the short cable is at 115.2K bps. However the flow from your modem out the phone line is only 33.6K bps. Since a faster flow (115.2K) is going into your modem than is coming out of it, the modem is storing the excess flow (115.2K − 33.6K = 81.6K bps) in one of its buffers. This buffer would eventually overrun (run out of free storage space) unless the 115.2K flow is stopped.

But now flow control comes to the rescue. When the modem's buffer is almost full, the modem sends a stop signal to the serial port. The serial port passes on the stop signal on to the device driver and the 115.2K bps flow is halted. Then the modem continues to send out data at 33.6K bps drawing on the data it previous accumulated in its buffer. Since nothing is coming into the buffer, the level of bytes in it starts to drop. When almost no bytes are left in the buffer, the modem sends a start signal to the serial port and the 115.2K flow from the computer to the modem resumes. In effect, flow control creates an average flow rate in the short cable (in this case 33.6K) which is significantly less than the "on" flow rate of 115.2K bps. This is "start-stop" flow control.

The above is a simple example of flow control for flow from the computer to a modem, but there is also flow control which is used for the opposite direction of flow: from a modem (or other device) to a computer. Each direction of flow involve 3 buffers:

1. In the modem
2. In the UART chip (called FIFOs)
3. In main memory managed by the serial driver.

Flow control protects certain buffers from overflowing. The small UART FIFO buffers are not protected in this way but rely instead on a fast response to the interrupts they issue. FIFO stand for "First In, First Out" which is the way it handles bytes. All the 3 buffers use the FIFO rule but only one of them also uses it as a name. This is the essence of flow control but there are still some more details.

You don't often need flow control in the direction from the modem to a PC. For complex example of a case where it's needed see "Complex Flow Control Example" in the Serial-HOWTO. But if you don't have a high enough speed set between the modem and the computer (serial port speed) then you do need to slow down the flow from the modem to the PC. To do this you must stop the incoming flow of bytes over the telephone line. Your modem must tell the other modem to stop sending. See "Modem-to-Modem Flow Control".

Hardware vs. Software Flow Control   If feasible it's best to use "hardware" flow control that uses two dedicated "modem control" wires to send the "stop" and "start" signals. Modern modems almost always use hardware flow control between the modem and the serial port.

Software flow control uses the main receive and transmit wires to send the start and stop signals. It uses the ASCII control characters DC1 (start) and DC3 (stop) for this purpose. They are just inserted into the regular stream of data. Software flow control is not only slower in reacting but also does not allow the sending of binary data unless special precautions are taken. Since binary data will likely contain DC1 and DC3, special means must be taken to distinguish between a DC3 that means a flow control stop and a DC3 that is part of the binary code. Likewise for DC1. To get software flow control to work for binary data requires both modem (hardware) and software support.

Symptoms of No Flow Control   Understanding flow-control theory can be of practical use. For example I used my modem to access the Internet and it seemed to work fine. But after a few months I tried to send long files from my PC to an ISP and a huge amount of retries and errors resulted (but eventually Kermit could send a long file after many retries). Receiving in the other direction (from my ISP to me) worked fine. The problem turned out to be a hardware defect in my modem that had resulted in disabling flow control. My modem's buffer was overflowing (overrunning) on long outgoing files since no "stop" signal was ever sent to the computer to halt sending to the modem. There was no problem in the direction from the modem to my computer since the capacity (say 115.2K) was always higher than the flow over the telephone line. The fix was to enable flow control by putting into the init string an enable-flow-control command for the modem (It should have been enabled by default but something was wrong).

Modem-to-Modem Flow Control   This is the flow control of the data sent over the telephone lines between two modems. Practically speaking, it only exists when you have error correction enabled. Actually, even without error correction it's possible to enable software flow control between modems but it may interfere with sending binary data so it's not often used.

Data Flow Path; Buffers

Although much has been explained about this including flow control, a pair of 16-byte FIFO buffers (in the hardware), and a pair of larger buffers inside a modem there is still another pair of buffers. These are large buffers (perhaps 8K) in main memory also known as serial port buffers. When an application program sends bytes to the serial port (and modem) they first get stashed in the the transmit serial port buffer in main memory. The pair consists of both this transmit buffer and a receive buffer for the opposite direction of byte-flow.

The serial device driver takes out say 16 bytes from this transmit buffer, one byte at a time and puts them into the 16-byte transmit buffer in the serial hardware for transmission. Once in that transmit buffer, there is no way to stop them from being transmitted. They are then transmitted to the modem which also has a fair sized (say 1K) buffer. When the device driver (on orders from flow control) stops the flow of outgoing bytes from the computer, what it actually stops is the flow of outgoing bytes from the large transmit buffer in main memory. Even after this has happened and the flow to the modem has stopped, an application program may keep sending bytes to the 8K transmit buffer until it becomes fill.

When it gets fill, the application program can't send any more bytes to it (a "write" statement in a C_ program blocks) and the application program temporarily stops running and waits until some buffer space becomes available. Thus a flow control "stop" is ultimately able to stop the program that is sending the bytes. Even though this program stops, the computer does not necessarily stop computing. It may switch to running other processes while it's waiting at a flow control stop. The above was a little oversimplified since there is another alternative of having the application program itself do something else while it is waiting to "write".

Modem Commands

Commands to the modem are sent to it from the communication software over the same conductor as used to send data. The commands are short ASCII strings. Examples are AT&K3 for enabling hardware flow control (RTS/CTS) between your computer and modem; and ATDT5393401 for Dialing the number 5393401. Note all commands are prefaced by AT. Some commands such as enabling flow control help configure the modem. Other commands such as dialing a number actually do something. There are about a hundred or so different possible commands. When your communication software starts running, it first sends an init string of commands to the modem to configure it. All commands are sent on the ordinary data line before the modem dials (or receives a call).

Once the modem is connected to another modem (on-line mode), everything that is sent from your computer to your modem goes directly to the other modem and is not interpreted by the modem as a command. There is a way to "escape" from this mode of operation and go back to command mode where everything sent to the modem will be interpreted as a command. The computer just sends +++ with a specified time spacing before and after it. If this time spacing is correct, the modem reverts to command mode. Another way to do this is by a signal on a certain modem control line.

There are a number of lists of modem commands on the Internet. The section "Web Sites" has links to a couple of such web sites. Different models and brands of modems do not use exactly the same set of such commands. So what works for one modem might not work for another. Some common command (not guaranteed to work on all modems) are listed in this HOWTO in the section "Modem Configuration".

Serial Software: Device Driver Module

The device driver for the serial port is the software that operates the serial port. It is now provided as a serial module. This module will normally get loaded automatically if it's needed. The kernel 2.2 + will do this. In earlier kernels, you had to have kerneld running in order to do auto-load modules on demand. Otherwise the serial module needed to be explicitly listed in /etc/modules. Before modules became popular with Linux, the serial driver was usually built into the kernel. If it's still built into the kernel (you might have selected this when you compiled the kernel) don't let the serial module load. If you do and wind up with two drivers, it's reported that you can't use the serial ports and get an I/O error if an attempt is made to open them.

When the serial module is loaded it displays a message on the screen about the existing serial ports (often showing a wrong IRQ). But once the module is used by setserial to tell the device driver the (hopefully) correct IRQ then you should see a second display with the correct IRQ, etc. See "What is Setserial" for more info on setserial.)

One may modify the driver by editing the kernel source code. Much of the serial driver is found in the file serial.c. For details regarding writing of programs for the serial port see Serial- Programming-HOWTO (currently being revised by Vern Hoxie).

Configuring Overview

If you want to use a modem only for MS Windows/DOS, then you can just install almost any modem and it will work OK. With a Linux PC it's not usually this easy unless you use an external modem. All external modems should work OK (even if they are labeled "Plug and Play") But most new internal modems are Plug-and-Play (PnP) and have PnP serial ports. If it's a ISA modem may need to use the Linux `isapnp` program to configure these PnP serial ports. See the Plug-and-Play-HOWTO for more information.

Since each modem has an associated serial port there are two parts to configuring a modem:

- Configuring the modem itself: Done by the communication program
- Configuring the modem's serial port: Done only *partly* by the communication program

Most of the above configuring (but not necessarily most of the effort) is done by the communication program that you use with the modem such as minicom or seyon, wvdial (for PPP). If you use the modem for dial-in, then the `getty` program which you use to present outsiders with a login-prompt, will help configure. Thus to configure the modem (and much of the serial port) you need to configure the communication program (such as the PPP dialer or `getty`).

Unfortunately the above configuring doesn't do the low-level configuring of the serial port: setting its IO address and IRQ in both the hardware and the driver. If you are lucky, this will happen automatically when you boot Linux. Setting these in the hardware was formerly done by jumpers but today it's done by "Plug-and-Play" software.

But there's a serious problem: Linux (as of late 1999) is not a Plug- and-Play operating system but it does have Plug-and-Play tools which you may use to set up the configuration although they are not always very user friendly. This may create a difficult problem for you. The next section will go into this in much more detail.

Configuring the Serial Port

PCI Bus Not Yet Supported

The kernel 2.2 serial driver contains no support for the PCI bus. But kernels 2.3 and 2.4 will eventually support some PCI serial cards (and modem cards). Most PCI cards need special support in the driver. The driver will read the id number digitally stored on the card to determine how (or if) to support the card. If you have a PCI card which you are convinced is not a winmodem but it will not work, you can help in attempting to create a driver for it. To do this you'll need to contact the maintainer of the serial driver, Theodore (Ted) Y. Ts'o.

You will need to email him a copy of the output of `lspci -vv` with full information about the model and manufacturer of the PCI modem (or serial port). Then he will try to point you to a test driver which might work for it. You will then need to get it, compile it and possibly recompile your kernel. Then you will test the driver to see if it works OK for you and report the results to Ted Ts'o. If you are willing to do all the above (and this is the latest version of this HOWTO) then email the needed info to him at: <mailto:tytso@mit.edu>.

PCI modems are not well standardized. Some use main memory for I/O with the PC (ISA ones use the I/O address space for this). Some require special enabling of the IRQ. The output of `lspci` can help determine if one can be supported. If the details are not too complex I may find them and put them here in a future revision.

Configuring Overview

In many cases, configuring will happen automatically and you have nothing to do. But sometimes you need to configure (or just want to check out the configuration). If so, first you need to know about the two parts to configuring the serial port under Linux:

The first part (low-level configuring) is assigning it an IO address, IRQ, and name (such as ttyS2). This IO-IRQ pair must be set in both the hardware and told to the serial driver. We might just call this `io-irq` configuring for short. The setserial is used to tell the driver. PnP methods, jumpers, etc., are used to set the hardware. Details will be supplied later. If you need to configure but don't understand certain details it's easy to get into trouble.

The second part (high-level configuring) is assigning it a speed (such as 38.4K bits/sec), selecting flow control, etc. This is often done by communication programs such as `PPP`, `minicom`, or by `getty` (which you may run on the port so that others may log into your computer). This high-level configuring may also be done with the `stty` program. `stty` is also useful to view the current status if you're having problems. However you will need to tell these programs what speed you want, etc. by using a menu or a configuration file. See also the Serial-HOWTO section: `stty`. When Linux starts, some effort is made to detect and configure (low-level) a few serial ports. Exactly what happens depends on your BIOS, hardware, Linux distribution, etc. If the serial ports work OK, there may be no need for you to do any configuring. Application programs often do the high-level configuring but you may need to supply them with the required information. With Plug-and-Play serial ports (often built into an internal modem), the situation has become more complex. Here are cases when you need to do low-level configuring (set IRQ and IO addresses):

- Plan to use more than 2 serial ports
- Installing a new serial port (such as an internal modem)
- Having problems with serial port(s)

For kernel 2.2+ you may be able to use more that 2 serial ports without low-level configuring by sharing interrupts. This only works if the serial hardware supports it and this may be no easier than low-level configuring. See "Interrupt sharing and Kernels 2.2+".

The low-level configuring (setting the IRQ and IO address) seems to cause people more trouble (than high-level), although for many it's fully automatic and there is no configuring to be done. Thus most all of this section is on that topic. Until the serial driver knows the correct IRQ and IO address the port will probably not work at all. It may not even be found by Linux. Even if it can be found, it may work extremely slow if the IRQ is wrong. See "Extremely Slow: Text appears on the screen slowly after long delays".

In the Wintel world, the IO address and IRQ are called "resources" and we are thus configuring certain resources. But there are many other types of "resources" so the term has many other meanings. In review, the low-level configuring consists of putting two values (an IRQ number and IO address) into two places:

1. The device driver (often by running `setserial` at boot-time)
2. Memory registers of the serial port hardware itself

You may watch the start-up (= boot-time) messages. They are usually correct. But if you're having problems, there's a good chance that some of these messages don't show the true configuration of the hardware (and they are not supposed to). See "I/O Address & IRQ: Boot-time Messages".

Common Mistakes Made re Low-Level Configuring

Here are some common mistakes people make:

- `setserial` command: They run it (without the `autoconfig` option) and think it has checked out the hardware (it hasn't).

- `setserial` messages: They see them displayed on the screen at boot-time, and erroneously think that the result shows how their hardware is actually configured.

- `/proc/interrupts`: When their serial device isn't in use they don't see its interrupt there, and erroneously conclude that their serial port can't be found (or doesn't have an interrupt set).

- `/proc/ioports`: People think this shows the hardware configuration when it only shows about the same data (possibly erroneous) as `setserial`.

I/O Address & IRQ: Boot-time Messages

In many cases your ports will automatically get low-level configured at boot-time (but not always correctly). To see what is happening, look at the start-up messages on the screen. Don't neglect to check the messages from the BIOS before Linux is loaded (no examples shown here). These BIOS messages may be frozen by pressing the Pause key. Use Shift-PageUp to go back to all the messages after they have flash by. Shift-PageDown will scroll in the opposite direction. The dmesg command may be used at any time to view some of the messages but it often misses important ones. Here's an example of the start-up messages (as of mid 1999). Note that `ttyS00` is the same as `/dev/ttyS0`.

At first you see what was detected (but the irq is only a wild guess):

Serial driver version 4.27 with no serial options enabled

`ttyS00` at 0x03f8 (irq = 4) is a 16550A

`ttyS01` at 0x02f8 (irq = 3) is a 16550A

`ttyS02` at 0x03e8 (irq = 4) is a 16550A

Later you see what was saved, but it's not necessarily correct either:

Loading the saved-state of the serial devices . . .

`/dev/ttyS0` at 0x03f8 (irq = 4) is a 16550A

`/dev/ttyS1` at 0x02f8 (irq = 3) is a 16550A

`/dev/ttyS2` at 0x03e8 (irq = 5) is a 16550A

Note that there is a slight disagreement: The first message shows `ttyS2` at `irq=4` while the second shows it at `irq=5`. You may only have the first message. In most cases the last message is the correct one. But if you're having trouble it may be misleading. Before reading the explanation of all of this complexity in the rest of this section, you might just try using your serial port and see if it works OK. If so it may not be essential to read further.

The second message is from the `setserial` program being run at boot-time. It shows what the device driver thinks is the correct configuration. But this too could be wrong. For example, the irq could actually be set to `irq=8` in the hardware (both messages wrong). The `irq=5` is there because someone incorrectly put this into a configuration file (or the like). The fact that Linux sometimes gets IRQs wrong is because it doesn't probe for IRQs. It just assumes the "standard" ones (first message) or accepts what you told it when you configured it (second message). Neither of these is necessarily correct. If the serial driver has the wrong IRQ the serial port is very slow or doesn't seem to work at all.

The first message is a result of Linux probing the serial ports. If a port shows up here it exists but the irq may be wrong. Linux doesn't check IRQs because doing so is not foolproof. It just assumes the IRQs are as shown because they are the "standard" values. You may check them manually with `setserial` using the `autoconfig` and `auto_irq` options but this isn't guaranteed to be correct.

The data shown by the BIOS messages (which you see at first) is what is set in the hardware. If your serial port is Plug-and-Play PnP then it's possible that the `isapnp` will run and change these settings. Look for messages about this after Linux starts. The last serial port message shown in the example above should agree with the BIOS messages (as possibly modified by `isapnp`). If they don't agree then you either need to change the setting in the port hardware or use `setserial` to tell the driver what is actually set in the hardware.

Also, if you have Plug-and-Play (PnP) serial ports, Linux will not find them unless the IRQ and IO has been set inside the hardware by Plug-and-Play software. This is a common reason why the start-up messages do not show a serial port that physically exists. The PC hardware (a PnP BIOS) may automatically low-level configure this. PnP configuring will be explained later.

What is the Current IO Address and IRQ of My Serial Port?

The previous section indicated how to attempt to do this by looking at the start-up messages. If they give you sufficient info then you may not need to read this section. If they don't then there are some other ways to look into this.

There are really two answers to the question "What is my IO and IRQ?"

1. What the device driver thinks has been set (This is what `setserial` usually sets and shows).
2. What is actually set in the hardware.

They both should be the same. If they're not it spells trouble since the driver has incorrect info on the physical serial port. If the driver has the wrong IO address it will try to send data to a non-existing serial port—or even worse, to an actual device that is not a serial port. If it has the wrong IRQ the driver will not get interrupt service requests from the serial port, resulting in a very slow or no response. See "Extremely Slow: Text Appears on the Screen Slowly After Long Delays". If it has the wrong model of UART there is also apt to be trouble. To determine if both I0-IRQ pairs are identical you must find out how they are set in both the driver and the hardware.

What Does the Device Driver Think?   This is easy to find out. Just look at the start-up messages or type `setserial -g /dev/ttyS*`. If everything works OK then what it tells you is likely also set in the hardware. There are some other ways to find this info by looking at `files` in the `/proc` directory. An important reason for understanding these other ways is to warn you that they only show what the device driver thinks. Some people view certain `files` in the `/proc` directory and erroneously think that what they see is set in the hardware but "it ain't necessarily so".

`/proc/ioports` will show the IO addresses that the drivers are using. `/proc/interrupts` shows the IRQs that are used by drivers of currently running processes (that have devices open). Note that in both cases above you are only seeing what the driver thinks and not necessarily what is actually set in the hardware. `/proc/interrupts` also shows how many interrupts have been issued (often thousands) for each device. You can get a clue from this because if you see a large number of interrupts that have been issued it means that there is a piece of hardware somewhere that is using that interrupt. Sometimes a showing of just a few interrupts doesn't mean that that interrupt is actually being physically generated by any serial port. Thus if you see almost no interrupts for a port that you're trying to use, that interrupt might not be set in the hardware and it implies that the driver is using the wrong interrupt. To view `/proc/interrupts` to check on a program that you're currently running (such as `minicom`) you need to keep the program running while you view it. To do this, try to jump to a shell without exiting the program.

What is Set in My Serial Port Hardware?   How do you find out what IO address and IRQ are actually set in the device hardware? Perhaps the BIOS messages will tell you some info before Linux starts booting. Use the Shift-PageUp key to step back thru the boot-time messages and look at the very first ones which are from the BIOS. This is how it was before Linux started. Setserial can't change it but isapnp or pciutils can.

One crude method is try probing with setserial using the auto-config option. You'll need to guess the addresses to probe at. See "What is Setserial". For a PCI serial port, use the lspci command (for kernels <2.2 look at /proc/pci). If your serial port is is Plug-and-Play see the next two subsections.

For a port set with jumpers, its how the jumpers were set. If the port is not Plug-and-Play (PnP) but has been setup by using a DOS program then it's set at whatever the person who ran that program set it to.

What is Set in My PnP Serial Port Hardware?   PnP ports don't store their configuration in the hardware when the power is turned off. This is in contrast to Jumpers (non-PnP) which remain the same with the power off. If you have an ISA PnP port, it can reach a state where it doesn't have any IO address or IRQ and is in effect disabled. It should still be possible to find the port using the pnpdump program.

For Plug-and-Play (PnP) on the ISA bus one may try the pnpdump program (part of isapnptools). If you use the—dumpregs option then it should tell you the actual IO address and IRQ set in the port. The address it "trys" is not the device's IO address, but a special.

For PnP ports checking on how it's configured under DOS/Windows may not be of much help. Windows stores its configuration info in its Registry which is not used by Linux. It may supply the BIOS's non-volatile memory with some info but it may not be kept in sync with the current Window configuration in the Registry ?? If you let a PnP BIOS automatically do the configuring when you start Linux (and have told the BIOS that you don't have a PnP operating system when running Linux) then Linux should use whatever configuration is in the BIOS's non-volatile memory.

Choosing Serial IRQs

If you have a true Plug-and-Play set up where either the OS or a PnP BIOS configures all your devices, then you don't choose your IRQs. PnP determines what it thinks is best and assigns them. But if you use the tools in Linux for Plug-and-Play (`isapnp` and `pcitools`) then you have to choose. If you already know what IRQ you want to use you could skip this section except that you may want to know that IRQ 0 has a special use (see the following paragraph).

IRQ 0 is Not an IRQ   While IRQ 0 is actually the timer (in hardware) it has a special meaning for setting a serial port with `setserial`. It tells the driver that there is no interrupt for the port and the driver then will use polling methods. This is quite inefficient but can be tried if there is an interrupt conflict or mis-set interrupt. The advantage of assigning this is that you don't need to know what interrupt is set in the hardware. It should be used only as a temporary expedient until you are able to find a real interrupt to use.

Interrupt Sharing and Kernels 2.2+   The general rule is that every device should use a unique IRQ and not share them. But there are situations where sharing is permitted such as with most multi-port boards. Even when it is permitted, it may not be as efficient since every time a shared interrupt is given a check must be made to determine where it came from. Thus if it's feasible, it's nice to allocate every device it's own interrupt.

Prior to kernel 2.2, serial IRQs could be shared with each other only for most multiport boards. Starting with kernel 2.2 serial IRQs may be sometimes shared between all serial ports. In order for sharing to work in 2.2 the kernel must have been compiled with `CONFIG_SERIAL_SHARE_IRQ`, and the serial port hardware must support sharing (so that if two serial cards put different voltages on the same interrupt wire, only the voltage that means `this is an interrupt` will prevail). Thus even if you have 2.2, it may be best to avoid sharing.

What IRQs to Choose?   The serial hardware often has only a limited number of IRQs it can be set at. Also you don't want IRQ conflicts. So there may not be much of a choice. Your PC may normally come with `ttyS0` and `ttyS2` at IRQ 4, and `ttyS1` and `ttyS3` at IRQ 3. Looking at `/proc/interrupts` will show which IRQs are being used by programs currently running. You likely don't want to use one of these. Before IRQ 5 was used for sound cards, it was often used for a serial port.

Here is how Greg (original author of Serial-HOWTO) set his up in `/etc/rc.d/rc.serial`. `rc.serial` is a file (shell script) which runs at start-up (it may have a different name of location). For versions of setserial after 2.15 it's not always done this way anymore but this example does show the choice of IRQs.

```
/sbin/setserial /dev/ttyS0 irq 3  # my serial mouse
/sbin/setserial /dev/ttyS1 irq 4  # my Wyse dumb
                                     terminal
/sbin/setserial /dev/ttyS2 irq 5  # my Zoom modem
/sbin/setserial /dev/ttyS3 irq 9  # my USR modem
```

Standard IRQ assignments:

IRQ 0   Timer channel 0 (May mean "no interrupt".
        See below.)

IRQ 1   Keyboard

IRQ 2   Cascade for controller 2

IRQ 3   Serial port 2

IRQ 4   Serial port 1

IRQ 5   Parallel port 2, Sound card

IRQ 6   Floppy diskette

IRQ 7   Parallel port 1

IRQ 8   Real-time clock

IRQ 9   Redirected to IRQ2

IRQ 10 not assigned

IRQ 11 not assigned

IRQ 12 not assigned

IRQ 13 Math coprocessor

IRQ 14 Hard disk controller 1

IRQ 15 Hard disk controller 2

There is really no Right Thing to do when choosing interrupts. Just make sure it isn't being used by the motherboard, or any other boards. 2, 3, 4, 5, 7, 10, 11, 12 or 15 are possible choices. Note that IRQ 2 is the same as IRQ 9. You can call it either 2 or 9, the serial driver is very understanding. If you have a very old serial board it may not be able to use IRQs 8 and above.

Make sure you don't use IRQs 1, 6, 8, 13 or 14! These are used by your motherboard. You will make her very unhappy by taking her IRQs. When you are done, double-check /proc/interrupts when programs that use interrupts are being run and make sure there are no conflicts.

Choosing Addresses—Video Card Conflict with `ttyS3`

The IO address of the IBM 8514 video board (and others like it) is allegedly 0x?2e8 where ? is 2, 4, 8, or 9. This may conflict (but shouldn't if the serial port is well designed) with the IO address of `ttyS3` at 0x02e8 if the serial port ignores the leading 0 hex digit (many do). That is bad news if you try to use `ttyS3` at this IO address.

In most cases you should use the default addresses if feasible. Addresses shown represent the first address of an 8-byte range. For example 3f8 is really the range 3f8-3ff. Each serial device (as well as other types of devices that use IO addresses) needs its own unique address range. There should be no overlaps (conflicts). Here are the default addresses for the serial ports:

```
ttyS0  address  0x3f8
ttyS1  address  0x2f8
ttyS2  address  0x3e8
ttyS3  address  0x2e8
```

Set IO Address & IRQ in the Hardware (Mostly for PnP)

After it's set in the hardware don't forget to insure that it also gets set in the driver by using `setserial`. For non-PnP serial ports they are either set in hardware by jumpers or by running a DOS program ("jumperless") to set them (it may disable PnP). The rest of this subsection is only for PnP serial ports. Here's a list of the possible methods of configuring PnP serial ports:

- Using a PnP BIOS CMOS setup menu [usually only for external modems on `ttyS0` (Com1) and `ttyS1` (Com2)]
- Letting a PnP BIOS automatically configure a PnP serial port. See "Using a PnP BIOS to IO-IRQ Configure"
- Doing nothing if you have both a PnP serial port and a PnP Linux operating system (see Plug-and-Play-HOWTO).
- Using `isapnp` for a PnP serial port non-PCI)
- Using `pciutils` (`pcitools`) for the PCI bus

The IO address and IRQ must be set (by PnP) in their registers each time the system is powered on since PnP hardware doesn't remember how it was set when the power is shut off. A simple way to do this is to let a PnP BIOS know that you don't have a PnP OS and the BIOS will automatically do this each time you start. This might cause problems in Windows (which is a PnP OS) if you start Windows with the BIOS thinking that Windows is not a PnP OS. See Plug-and-Play-HOWTO.

Plug-and-Play was designed to automate this io-irq configuring, but for Linux at present, it has made life more complicated. The standard kernels for Linux don't support plug-and-play very well. If you use a patch to the Linux kernel to covert it to a plug-and-play operating system, then all of the above should be handled automatically by the OS. But when you want to use this to automate configuring devices other that the serial port, you may find that you'll still have to configure the drivers manually since many Linux drivers are not written to support a Linux PnP OS. If you use `isapnptools` or the BIOS for configuring plug-and-play this will only put the two values into the registers of the serial port section of the modem card and you will likely still need to set up `setserial`. None of this is easy or very well documented as of early 1999. See Plug-and-Play-HOWTO and the `isapnptools` FAQ.

Using a PnP BIOS to I0-IRQ Configure While the explanation of how to use a PnP OS or isapnp for io-irq configuring should come with such software, this is not the case if you want to let a PnP BIOS do such configuring. Not all PnP BIOS can do this. The BIOS usually has a CMOS menu for setting up the first two serial ports. This menu may be hard to find and for an "Award" BIOS it was found under `chipset features setup`. There is often little to choose from. Unless otherwise indicated in a menu, these first two ports normally get set at the standard IO addresses and IRQs. See "Serial Port Device Names & Numbers".

Whether you like it or not, when you start up a PC a PnP BIOS starts to do PnP (io-irq) configuring of hardware devices. It may do the job partially and turn the rest over to a PnP OS (which you probably don't have) or if thinks you don't have a PnP OS it may fully configure all the PnP devices but not configure the device drivers. This is what you want but it's not always easy to figure out exactly what the PnP BIOS has done.

If you tell the BIOS that you don't have a PnP OS, then the PnP BIOS should do the configuring of all PnP serial ports—not just the first two. An indirect way to control what the BIOS does (if you have Windows 9x on the same PC) is to "force" a configuration under Windows. See Plug-and-Play-HOWTO and search for "forced". It's easier to use the CMOS BIOS menu which may override what you "forced" under Windows. There could be a BIOS option that can set or disable this "override" capability.

If you add a new PnP device, the BIOS should change its PnP configuration to accommodate it. It could even change the io-irq of existing devices if required to avoid any conflicts. For this purpose, it keeps a list of non-PnP devices provided that you have told the BIOS how these non-PnP devices are io-irq configured. One way to tell the BIOS this is by running a program called ICU under DOS/Windows.

But how do you find out what the BIOS has done so that you set up the device drivers with this info? The BIOS itself may provide some info, either in it's setup menus of via messages on the screen when you turn on your computer. See "What is Set in My Serial Port Hardware?"

Giving the IRQ and IO Address to `setserial`

Once you've set the IRQ and IO address in the hardware (or arranged for it to be done by PnP) you also need to insure that the `setserial` command is run each time you start Linux. See the subsection "Boot-time Configuration".

Other Configuring

Configuring Hardware Flow Control (RTS/CTS)   See "Flow Control" for an explanation of it. You should always use hardware flow control if possible. Your communication program or `getty` should have an option for setting it (and if you're in luck it might be enabled by default). It needs to be set both inside your modem (by an init string or default) and in the device driver. Your communication program should set both of these (if you configure it right).

If none of the above will fully enable hardware flow control. Then you must do it yourself. For the modem, make sure that it's either done by the init string or is on by default. If you need to tell the device driver to do it is best done on startup by putting a file that runs at boot-time. See the subsection "Boot-time Configuration." You need to add the following to such a file for each serial port (example is ttyS2) you want to enable hardware flow control on:

```
stty crtscts < /dev/ttyS2
```

If you want to see if flow control is enabled do the following: In minicom (or the like) type AT&V to see how the modem is configured and look for &K3 which means hardware flow control. Then see if the device driver knows about it by typing: stty -a < /dev/ttyS2. Look for crtscts (without a disabling minus sign).

Modem Configuration (excluding the Serial Port)

Finding Your Modem

Before spending a lot of time configuring your modem, you need to make sure it can be found and that AT commands and the like can be sent to it. So I suggest you first give it a very simple configuration using the communication program you will be using on the port and see it it works. If so, then it's been found. If not then see "My Modem is Physically There but Can't be Found". A winmodem may be hard to find and will not work under Linux.

AT Commands

While the serial port on which a modem resides requires configuring, so does the modem itself. The modem is configured by sending AT commands (or the like) to it on the same serial line that is used to send data.

Most modems use an AT command set. These are cryptic and short ASCII commands where all command strings are prefaced by the letters AT. For example: ATZ&K3 There are two commands here Z and &K3. Unfortunately there are many different variations of the AT command set so that what works for one modem may or may not work for another modem. Thus there is no guarantee that the AT commands given in this section will work on your modem. Another point is that to get the modem to act on the AT command string, a return character must be sent at the end of the string.

Such command strings are either automatically sent to the modem by communication programs or are sent directly by you. Most communication programs provide a screen where you can type commands directly to your modem. This is good for setting up the modem as you can have it remember how it was set even after its powered off.

If you have a manual for your modem you can likely look up the AT command set in it. Otherwise, you may try to find it on the Internet. One may use a search engine and include some actual commands in the search terms to avoid finding sites that just talk about such commands but fail to list them. You might also try a few of the sites listed in the subsection "Web Sites."

Init Strings: Saving and Recalling

The examples given in this subsection are from the Hayes AT modem command set. All command strings must be prefaced by the two letters AT (for example: AT&C1&D3). When a modem is powered on, it automatically configures itself with one of the configurations it has stored in its non-volatile memory. If this configuration is satisfactory there is nothing further to do.

If it's not satisfactory, then one may either alter the stored configuration or configure the modem each time you use it by sending it a string of commands known as an init string (= initialization string). Normally a a communication program does this. What it sends will depend on how you configured the communications program or what script you wrote for it if you use Kermit. You can usually edit the init string your communication program uses and change it to whatever you want. Sometimes the communications program will let you select the model of your modem and then it will use an init string that it thinks is best for that modem.

The configuration of the modem uses when it's first powered on could be expressed by an init string. You might think of this as the default "string" (called a profile). If your communications program sends the modem another string (the init string), then this string will modify the default configuration. For example, if the init string only contains two commands, then only those two items will be changed. However, some commands will recall a stored profile from inside the modem so a single such command in the init string can thereby change everything in the configuration.

Modern modems have a few different stored profiles to choose from that are stored in the modem's non-volatile memory (it's still there when you turn it off). In my modem there are two factory profiles (0 and 1, neither of which you can change) and two user defined profiles (0 and 1) that the user may set and store. Your modem may have more. Which one of these user-defined profiles is used at power-up depends on another item stored in the profile. If the command &Y0 is given then in the future profile 0 will be used at power-on. If it's a 1 instead of a 0 then profile 1 will be used at power-on.

There are also commands to recall (use it now) any of the 4 stored profiles. One may put such a command in an init string. Of course if it recalls the same profile as was automatically loaded at power-up, nothing is changed unless the active profile has been modified since power-up. Since it could have been modified, it's a good idea to use some kind of an init string even if it does nothing more than recalling a stored profile.

Recalling a saved profile (use 1 instead of 0 for profile 1): Z0 recalls user-defined profile 0 and resets (hangs up, etc.) &F0 recalls factory profile 0.

Once you have sent commands to the modem to configure it the way you want (including recalling a factory profile and modifying it a little) you may save this as a user-defined profile: &W0 saves the current configuration to user-profile 0.

Many people don't bother saving a good configuration in their modem, but instead, send the modem a longer init string each time the modem is used. Another method is to restore the factory default at the start of the init string and then modify it a little by adding a few other commands to the end of the init string. By doing it this way no one can cause problems by modifying the user-defined profile which is loaded at power-on.

You may pick an init string supplied by someone else that they think is right for your modem. Some communication programs have a library of init strings to select from. The most difficult method (and one which will teach you the most about modems) is to study the modem manual and write one yourself. You could save this configuration inside the modem so that you don't need an init string. A third alternative is to start with an init string someone else wrote, but modify it to suit your purposes.

Now if you look at init strings used by communication programs you may see symbols which are not valid modem commands. These symbols are commands to the communication program itself (such as meaning to pause briefly) and will not be sent to the modem.

Other Modem Commands

Future editions of Modem-HOWTO may contain more AT commands but the rest of this section is mostly what was in the old Serial-HOWTO. All strings must start with AT. Here's a few Hayes AT codes that should be in the string (if they are not set by using a factory default or by a saved configuration).

E1	command echo ON
Q0	result codes are reported
V1	verbose ON
S0=0	never answer (uugetty does this with the WAITFOR option)

Here's some more codes concerning modem control lines DCD and DSR:

&C1	DCD is on after connect only
&S0	DSR is always on

These affect what your modem does when calls start and end. What DTR does may also be set up but it's more complicated.

If your modem does not support a stored profile, you can set these through the INIT string in a config file (or the like). Some older modems come with DIP switches that affect register settings. Be sure these are set correctly, too.

Greg Hankins has a collection of modem setups for different types of modems. If you would like to send him your working configuration, please do so: <mailto:gregh@cc.gatech.edu>. You can get these setups at <ftp://ftp.cc.gatech.edu/pub/people/gregh/modem-configs>.

Note: to get his USR Courier V.34 modem to reset correctly when DTR drops, Greg Hankins had to set &D2 and S13=1 (this sets bit 0 of register S13). This has been confirmed to work on USR Sportster V.34 modems as well.

Note: some Supra modems treat DCD differently than other modems. If you are using a Supra, try setting &C0 and not &C1. You must also set &D2 to handle DTR correctly.

Serial Port Devices /dev/ttyS2, etc.

For creating devices in the device directory see the Serial-HOWTO: "Creating Devices In the /dev directory".

Serial Port Device Names & Numbers

Devices in Linux have major and minor numbers. Each serial port may have 2 possible names in the /dev directory: ttyS and cua. Their drivers behave slightly differently. The cua device is deprecated and will not be used in the future. See "The cua Device".

DOS/Windows use the COM name while the `setserial` program uses `tty00`, `tty01`, etc. Don't confuse these with `dev/tty0`, `dev/tty1`, etc. which are used for the console (your PC monitor) but are not serial ports. The DOS names (COM1, etc.) and IO address is shown below for the "standard" case (but yours could be different).

dos	set-serial		major	minor		major	minor	IO address
COM1	tty00	/dev/ttyS0	4,	64;	/dev/cua0	5,	64	3F8
COM2	tty01	/dev/ttyS1	4,	65;	/dev/cua1	5,	65	2F8
COM3	tty02	/dev/ttyS2	4,	66;	/dev/cua2	5,	66	3E8
COM4	tty03	/dev/ttyS3	4,	67;	/dev/cua3	5,	67	2E8

Note that all distributions should come with ttyS devices (and cua devices until cua is finally abolished). You can verify this by typing:

```
linux% ls -l /dev/cua*
linux% ls -l /dev/ttyS*
```

Link ttySN to /dev/modem?

On some installations, two extra devices will be created, /dev/modem for your modem and /dev/mouse for your mouse. Both of these are symbolic links to the appropriate device in /dev which you specified during the installation (unless you have a bus mouse, then /dev/mouse will point to the bus mouse device).

There has been some discussion on the merits of /dev/mouse and /dev/modem. The use of these links is discouraged. In particular, if you are planning on using your modem for dialin you may run into problems because the lock files may not work correctly if you use /dev/modem. Use them if you like, but be sure they point to the right device. However, if you change or remove this link, some applications might need reconfiguration.

The cua Device

Each ttyS device has a corresponding cua device. But the cua device is to be abolish so it's best to use ttyS (unless cua is required). There is a difference between cua and ttyS but a savvy programmer can make a ttyS port behave just like a cua port so there is no real need for the cua anymore. Except some older programs may need to use the cua.

What's the difference? The main difference between cua and ttyS has to do with what happens in a C- program when an ordinary open command tries to open the port. If a cua port has been set to check modem control signals, the port can be opened even if the DCD modem control signal says not to. Astute programming (by adding additional lines to the program) can force a ttyS port to behave this way also. But a cua port can be more easily programmed to open for dialing out on a modem even when the modem fails to assert DCD (since no one has called into it and there's no carrier). That's why cua was once used for dial-out and ttyS used for dial-in.

Starting with Linux kernel 2.2, a warning message will be put in the kernel log when one uses cua. This is an omen that cua is on the way out.

Interesting Programs You Should Know About

What is `setserial`?

Introduction Don't ever use `setserial` with Laptops (PCMCIA). `setserial` is a program which allows you to tell the device driver software the I/O address of the serial port, which interrupt (IRQ) is set in the port's hardware, what type of UART you have, etc. It can also show how the driver is currently set. In addition, it can probe the hardware (if certain options are given).

If you only have one or two serial ports, they will usually get set up correctly without using `setserial`. Otherwise (or if there are problems with the serial port) you will likely need to deal with `setserial`. Besides the manual for `setserial`, check out info in `/usr/doc/setserial.../` or the like. It should tell you how setserial is handled in your distribution of Linux.

setserial is often run automatically at boot-time by a start-up shell-script. It will only work if the serial module is loaded. If you should for some reason unload the serial module later on, the changes previously made by setserial will be forgotten by the kernel (but not by /etc/serial.conf). So setserial must be run again to reestablish them. In addition to running via a start-up script, something akin to setserial runs when the serial module is loaded. Thus when you watch the start-up messages on the screen it may look like it ran twice, and in fact it has.

With appropriate options, setserial can probe (at a given I/O address) for a serial port but you must guess the I/O address. If you ask it to probe for /dev/ttyS2 for example, it will only probe at the address it thinks ttyS2 is at. If you tell setserial that ttyS2 is at a different address, then it will probe at that address, etc. See "Probing".

setserial does not set either IRQs nor I/O addresses in the serial port hardware itself. It's set in the hardware either by jumpers or by plug-and-play. You must tell setserial these identical values that have been set in the hardware. Do not just invent some values that you think would be nice to use and then tell them to setserial. However, if you know the I/O address but don't know the IRQ you may command setserial to attempt to determine the IRQ.

You can see a list of possible commands to use (but not the one-letter options such as −v for verbose—which you should normally use when troubleshooting) by just typing setserial with no arguments. Note that setserial calls an I/O address a "port". If you type:

```
setserial-g /dev/ttyS*
```

you'll see some info about how that device driver is configured for your ports. Add a v to the option -g to see more. But this doesn't tell you if the hardware actually has these values set in it. If fact, you can run setserial and assign a purely fictitious I/O address, any IRQ, and whatever uart type you would like to have. Then the next time you type setserial ... it will display these bogus values without complaint. Note that assignments made by setserial are lost when the PC is powered down so it is usually run automatically somewhere each time that Linux is booted.

Probing   In order to try to find out if you have a certain piece of serial hardware you must first know (or guess) its I/O address (or the device driver must have an I/O address for it, likely previously set by setserial). To try to detect the physical hardware use the −v (verbose) and autoconfig command to setserial. If the resulting message shows a uart type such as 16550A, then you're OK. If instead it shows unknown for the uart type, then there is supposedly no serial port at all at that I/O address. Some cheap serial ports don't identify themselves correctly so if you see unknown you still might have a serial port there.

Besides auto-probing for uart type, setserial can auto-probe for IRQs but this doesn't always work right either. In versions of setserial >= 2.15, your last probe test may be saved and put into the configuration file /etc/serial.conf which will be used next time you start Linux. The script that runs setserial at boot-time does not usually probe, but you could change it so that it does. See the next section.

Can Linux Configure The Serial Devices Automagically? Yes, but ... Your distribution may already do this on startup. But you may want to customize it. It's easy to do for setserial < 2.15. Just add some lines to the file that runs setserial on start-up. See "Old Configuration Method: Edit a Script". For example, for ttyS3 you would add:

```
/sbin/setserial /dev/ttyS3 auto_irq skip_test
autoconfig
```

to the file that runs setserial on startup. Do this for every serial port you want to auto configure. Be sure to give a device name that really does exist on your machine. In some cases this will not work right due to the hardware so you may want to assign it an irq and/or a uart type. For example

```
/sbin/setserial /dev/ttyS3 irq 5 uart 16550A skip_test
```

For versions >= 2.15 (provided your distribution implemented the change, Redhat didn't) it's much harder to do since the file that runs setserial on startup, /etc/init.d/setserial or the like was not intended to be edited by the user. There may be no helpful comments in it like there were in earlier versions.

Boot-time Configuration When the kernel loads the serial module (or if the "module" is built into the kernel) then only ttyS{0-3} are auto-detected and the driver is set to IRQs 4 and 3 (regardless of what the hardware is actually set at). You see this as a boot-time message just like as if setserial had been run. If you use 3 or more ports, this may result in IRQ conflicts.

To fix such conflicts by telling setserial the true IRQs (or for other reasons) there may be a file somewhere that runs setserial again. This happens early at boot-time before any process uses the serial port. In fact, your distribution may have set things up so that the `setserial` program runs automatically from a start-up script at boot-time. More info about how to handle this situation should be found in `/usr/doc/setserial.../` or the like.

New Configuration Method Using `/etc/serial.conf`   Prior to `setserial` Version 2.15, the way to configure `setserial` was to manually edit the shell-script that ran `setserial` at boot-time. Starting with Version 2.15 (1999) of `setserial` this shell-script is not edited but instead gets its data from a configuration file: `/etc/serial.conf`. Furthermore not even `serial.conf` is intended to be edited. Instead just use `setserial` on the command line.

Normally, what you changed with the `setserial` command is saved to the configuration file (`serial.conf`) when you shutdown (normally) or reboot. This only works if `###AUTOSAVE###` or the like is on the first line of `serial.conf`. If you should use `setserial` experimentally and it doesn't work out right, then don't forget to redo it so that the experimental settings don't get saved by mistake. The file most commonly used to run `setserial` at boot-time (in conformance with the configuration file) is now `/etc/init.d/setserial` (Debian) or `/etc/init.d/serial` (Redhat), or etc., but it also should not normally be edited.

To disable a port, use `setserial` to set it to `uart none`. The format of `/etc/serial.conf` appears to be just like that of the parameters placed after `setserial` on the command line with one line for each port. If you don't use autosave, you may edit `/etc/serial.conf` manually. For 2.15, the Debian distribution installs the system with autosave enabled, but Redhat 6.0 just had a file `/usr/doc/setserial-2.15/rc.serial` which you have to move to `/etc/init.d/`.

BUG: As of July 1999 there is a bug/problem since with `###AUTOSAVE###` only the `setserial` parameters displayed by `setserial -G /dev/ttyS?` (where `? = 0, 1, 2,...`) get saved but the other parameters don't get saved. This will only affect a small minority of users since the parameters not saved are seldom used anyway. It's been reported as a bug and may be fixed by now.

In order to force the current settings set by `setserial` to be saved to the configuration file (`serial.conf`) without shutting down, do what normally happens when you shutdown: Run the shell-script `/etc/init.d/{set}serial stop`. The `stop` command will save the current configuration but the serial ports still keep working OK.

In some cases you may wind up with both the old and new configuration methods installed but hopefully only one of them runs at boot-time. Debian labeled obsolete files with `... pre-2.15`.

Old Configuration Method: Edit a Script Prior to 2.15 (1999) there was no `/etc/serial.conf` file to configure `setserial`. Thus you need to find the file that runs `setserial` at boot-time and edit it. If it doesn't exist, you need to create one (or place the commands in a file that runs early at boot-time). If such a file is currently being used it's likely somewhere in the `/etc` directory-tree. But Redhat <6.0 has supplied it in `/usr/doc/setserial/` although you need to move it to the `/etc` tree before using it. You might use `locate` to try to find such a file. For example, you could type: `locate "*serial*"`.

What you are looking for could be named `rc.serial`, or `0setserial` (Debian). If such a file is supplied, it should contain a number of commented-out examples. By uncommenting some of these and/or modifying them, you should be able to set things up correctly. Make sure that you are using a valid path for `setserial`, and a valid device name. You could do a test by executing this file manually (just type its name as the super-user) to see if it works right. Testing like this is a lot faster than doing repeated reboots to get it right. Of course you can also test a single `setserial` command by just typing it on the command line.

The script `/etc/rc.d/rc.serial` was commonly used in the past. The Debian distribution used `/etc/rc.boot/0setserial`. Another file once used is `/etc/rc.d/rc.local` but it's not a good idea to use this since it may not be run early enough. It's been reported that other processes may try to open the serial port before rc.local runs resulting in serial communication failure.

IRQs By default, both ttyS0 and ttyS2 share IRQ 4, while `ttyS0` and `ttyS3` share IRQ 3. But sharing serial interrupts is not permitted unless you:

1. Have kernel 2.2 or better, and
2. You've complied in support for this, and
3. Your serial hardware supports it.

See "Interrupt Sharing and Kernels 2.2+". If you only have two serial ports, ttyS0 and ttyS1, you're still OK since IRQ sharing conflicts don't exist for non-existent devices.

If you add an internal modem and retain ttyS0 and ttyS1, then you should attempt to find an unused IRQ and set it both on your serial port (or modem card) and then use `setserial` to assign it to your device driver. If IRQ 5 is not being used for a sound card, this may be one you can use for a modem. To set the IRQ in hardware you may need to use `isapnp`, a

PnP BIOS, or patch Linux to make it PnP. To help you determine which spare IRQs you might have, type `man setserial` and search for say: `IRQ 11`.

What is `isapnp`?

`isapnp` is a program to configure Plug-and-Play (PnP) devices on the ISA bus including internal modems. It comes in a package called `isapnptools` and includes another program, `pnpdump` which finds all your ISA PnP devices and shows you options for configuring them in a format which may be added to the PnP configuration file: `/etc/isapnp.conf`. It may also be used with the –`dumpregs` option to show the current IO address and IRQ of the modem's serial port. The `isapnp` command may be put into a startup file so that it runs each time you start the computer and thus will configure ISA PnP devices. It is able to do this even if your BIOS doesn't support PnP. See Plug-and-Play-HOWTO.

What is `wvdialconf`?

`wvdialconf` will try to find which serial port has a modem on it. It also creates a configuration program for the `wvdial` program. `wvdial` is used for simplified dialing out using the PPP protocol to an ISP. But you don't need to install PPP in order to use `wvdialconf`. It will only find modems which are not in use. It will also automatically devise a "suitable" init strings but sometimes gets it wrong. Since this command has no options, it's simple to use but you must give it the name of a file to put the init string (and other data) into. For example type: `wvdialconf my_file_name`.

What is `stty`?

`stty` is like `setserial` but it sets the baud rate and other parameters of a serial port. Typing `stty -a < /dev/ttyS2` should show you how `ttyS2` is configured. Most of the settings are for things that you never need to use with modems (such as some used only for old terminals of the 1970s). Your communication package should automatically set up all the setting correctly for modems. But `stty` is sometimes useful for troubleshooting.

Two items set by `stty` are:

1. Hardware flow control by `crtscts` and
2. Ignore the DCD signal from the modem: `clocal`.

If the modem is not sending a DCD signal and clocal is disabled (`stty` shows `-clocal`) then a program may not be able to open the serial port. If the port can't open, the program may just hang, waiting (often in vain) for a DCD signal from the modem.

Minicom sets clocal automatically when it starts up so there is no problem. But version 6.0.192 of Kermit hung when I set `-clocal` and tried to `set line...` If `-clocal` is set and there is no DCD signal then even the `stty` command will hang and there is seemingly no way to set `clocal` (except by running minicom). But minicom will restore `-clocal` when it exits. One way to get out of this is to use minicom to send the `AT&C` to the modem (to get the DCD signal) and then exit minicom with no reset so that the DCD signal remains on. Then you may use `stty` again.

Trying Out Your Modem (Dial-Out)

Are You Ready to Dial Out?

Once you've plugged in your modem and know which serial port it's on you're ready to try using it. Before you try to get the Internet on it or have people call in to you, first try something simpler like dialing out to some number to see if your modem is working OK. Find a phone number that is connected to a modem. It you don't know what number to call, ask at computer stores for such phone numbers of bulletin boards, etc. or see if a local library has a phone number for their on-line catalog.

Then make sure you are ready to phone. Do you know what serial port (such as ttyS2) your modem is on? You should have found this out when you io-irq configured your serial ports. Have you decided what speed you are going to use for this port? See "Speed Table" for a quick selection or "What Speed Should I Use" for more details. If you have no idea what speed to set, just set it a few times faster than the advertised speed of your modem. Also remember that if you see a menu where an option is "hardware flow control" and/or "RTS/CTS" or the like, select it. Is a live telephone cable plugged in to your modem? You may want to connect the cable to a real telephone to make sure that it can produce a dial tone.

Now you need to select a communication (dialing) program to use to dial out. Dialing programs include: minicom, seyon (X-window), and kermit. See section "Communications Programs" about some communications programs. Two examples are presented next: "Dialing Out with Minicom" and "Dialing Out with Kermit".

Dial Out with Minicom

Minicom comes with most Linux distributions. To configure it you should be the root user. Type `minicom -s` to configure. This will take you directly to the configuration (set-up) menus. Alternatively you could just run "minicom" and then type ^A to see the bottom status line. This shows to type ^A z for help (you've already typed the ^A so just type z). From the help menu go to the Configuration menu.

Most of the options don't need to be set for just simply dialing out. To configure you have to supply a few basic items: the name of the serial port your modem is on such as `/dev/ttyS2` and the speed such as 115200. These are set at the serial port menu. Go to it and set them. Also (if possible) set hardware flow control (RTS/CTS). Then save them. When typing in the speed, you should also see something like 8N1 which you should leave alone. It means: 8-bit bytes, No parity, 1 stop-bit appended to each byte. If you can't find the speed you want, a lower speed will always work for a test. Exit (hit <return>) when done and save the configuration as default (`dfl`) using the menu. You may want to exit `minicom` and start it again so it can now find the serial port and initialize the modem, or you could go to help and tell `minicom` to initialize the modem.

Now you are ready to dial. But first at the main screen you get after you first type `minicom` make sure there's a modem there by typing AT and then hit the <enter> key. It should display OK. If it doesn't something is wrong and there is no point of trying to dial.

If you got the OK go back to help and select the dialing directory. You may edit it and type in a phone number, etc., into the directory and then select `dial` to dial it. Alternatively, you may just dial manually (by selecting `manual` and then type the number at the keyboard). If it doesn't work, carefully note any error messages and try to figure out what went wrong.

Dial-Out with Kermit

You can find the latest version of kermit at <http://www.columbia.edu/kermit/>. For example, say your modem was on `ttyS3`, and it's speed was 115200 bps. You would do the following:

```
linux# kermit
C-Kermit 6.0.192, 6 Sep 96, for Linux
Copyright (C) 1985, 1996,
Trustees of Columbia University in the City of New
York.
Default file-transfer mode is BINARY
Type ? or HELP for help.
C-Kermit>set line /dev/ttyS3
C-Kermit>set carrier-watch off
C-Kermit>set speed 115200
/dev/ttyS3, 115200 bps
C-Kermit>c Connecting to /dev/ttyS3, speed 115200.
The escape character is Ctrl-\ (ASCII 28, FS)
Type the escape character followed by C to get back,
or followed by ? to see other options.
ATE1Q0V1          ; you type this and then the Enter key
OK                ; modem should respond with this
```

If your modem responds to `AT` commands, you can assume your modem is working correctly on the Linux side. Now try calling another modem by typing:

```
ATDT7654321
```

where 7654321 is a phone number. Use `ATDP` instead of `ATDT` if you have a pulse line. If the call goes through, your modem is working.

To get back to the kermit prompt, hold down the Ctrl key, press the backslash key, then let go of the Ctrl key, then press the C key:

```
Ctrl-\-C
(Back at linux)
C-Kermit>quit
linux#
```

This was just a test using the primitive "by-hand" dialing method. The normal method is to let kermit do the dialing for you with its built-in modem database and automatic dialing features, for example using a US Robotics (USR) modem:

```
linux# kermit C-Kermit 6.0.192, 6 Sep 1997, for Linux
    Copyright (C) 1985, 1996,
Trustees of Columbia University in the City of New York.
Default file-transfer mode is BINARY
Type ? or HELP for help
C-Kermit>set modem type usr      ; Select modem type
C-Kermit>set line /dev/ttyS3     ; Select communication
                                   device
C-Kermit>set speed 115200        ; Set the dialing speed
C-Kermit>dial 7654321            ; Dial
  Number: 7654321
  Device=/dev/ttyS3, modem=usr, speed=115200
  Call completed.<BEEP>
```

Connecting to /dev/ttyS3, speed 115200

The escape character is Ctrl-\ (ASCII 28, FS). Type the escape character followed by C to get back, or followed by ? to see other options.

Welcome to . . .

login:

Dial-In

Overview

Dial-in is where you set up your PC so that others may dial in to your phone number and use your PC. The "point of view" is your PC. When you dial out from your PC you are also dialing in to another computer (but not dialing in to your own computer).

Dial-in works like this. Someone with a modem dials your telephone number. Your modem answers the call and connects. Once the caller is connected, your PC sends a login prompt to the caller. Then the caller logs in and uses your PC. Using your PC may mean that the caller has a shell account and can use your PC just as if they logged in at the console (or text-terminal). It could also mean that they get connected to the Internet. The program that you use at your PC to handle dialin is called getty.

Often, after login, another program is run, including programs to connect the caller to the Internet. This HOWTO doesn't cover such programs that run after your login. For connecting to the internet, the PPP program is usually run (see PPP-HOWTO; a new revision is expected soon). Login may be automated so that the communication program automatically types in a "name" and password each time.

If you expect that people will be able to dial-in to you at 56K, it can't be done unless:

1. You have a digital connection to the telephone company such as a trunkside-T1 or ISDN line. and

2. You use special digital-modems. and

3. You have a "concentrator" or the like to interface your digital-modems to the digital lines of the telephone company. A ". . . concentrator" may be called a "modem concentrator" or a "remote access concentrator" or it could be included in a "remote access server" which includes the modems, etc. If you do all of this you are probably an ISP (Internet Service Provider).

getty

`getty` is the program you run for dial-in. You don't need it for dial-out. In addition to presenting a login prompt, it also answers the telephone. Originally getty was used for logging in to a computer from a dumb terminal. It's currently used for logging in to a Linux console). There are a few different getty programs with slightly different names. Only certain ones work with modems for dialin. This `getty` program is usually started at boot-time. It must be called from the `/etc/inittab` file. You may find an example in this file of a call to `getty` which you will likely need to edit a bit. If you use a different `getty` program than the one shown in such an example, then you will need to edit it quite a bit since the options will have a different format.

There are four different `getty` programs to choose from that may be used with modems for dial-in: `mgetty`, `uugetty`, `getty_em`, and `agetty`. A few details are given in the following subsections. `agetty` is the simplest (and weakest) of the four and some consider it mainly for use with directly connected text-terminals. `mgetty` has support for fax and voice mail but `uugetty` doesn't `mgetty` allegedly lacks a few of the features of `uugetty`. `getty_em` is a simplified version of `uugetty`. Thus `mgetty` is likely your best choice unless you are already familiar with `uugetty` (or find it difficult to get `mgetty`). The syntax for these `getty` programs differs, so be sure to check that you are using the correct syntax in `/etc/inittab` for whichever `getty` you use.

About mgetty   mgetty was written as a replacement for `uugetty` which was in existence long before `mgetty`. Both are for use with modems.

Although mgetty may be also used for directly connected terminals the documentation for this is hard to pinpoint and mgetty will not (as of mid 1999) support software flow control (used on many terminals) without recompiling. This defect is listed as a bug. In addition to allowing dialup logins, mgetty also provides FAX support and auto PPP detection. There is a supplemental program called vgetty which handles voicemail for some modems. mgetty documentation is good (except for voice mail), and does not need supplementing. Please refer to it for installation instructions. You can find the latest information on mgetty at <http://www.leo.org/~doering/mgetty/> and <http://alpha.greenie.net/mgetty>.

About uugetty getty_ps contains two programs: getty is used for console and terminal devices, and uugetty for modems. Greg Hankins (former author of Serial-HOWTO) used uugetty so his writings about it are included here. See uugetty. The other gettys are well covered by the documentation that comes with them.

About getty_em This is a simplified version of uugetty. It was written by Vern Hoxie after he became fully confused with complex support files needed for getty_ps and uugetty.

It is part of the collection of serial port utilities and information by Vern Hoxie available via ftp from <scicom.alphacdc.com/pub/linux>. The name of the collection is serial_suite.tgz. When logging into scicom as anonymous, you must use your full e-mail address as the password. For example: <greg.hankins@cc.gatech.edu>.

About agetty and mingetty agetty is a simple, completely functional implementation of getty which is best suited for virtual consoles or terminals rather than modems. But it works fine with modems under favorable conditions (except you cannot dial out when agetty is running and waiting for a call). agetty in the Debian distribution is just named getty.

mingetty is a small getty that will work only for consoles (monitors) so you can't use it with modems for dial-in.

What Happens When Someone Dials In?

The caller runs some sort of communication program that dials your telephone number and your telephone rings. There are two different ways that your PC can answer the phone. One way is for the modem to automatically answer the call. The other way is for getty to sense the ringing and send a command to the modem to answer the call. Once the call is answered, your modem sends tones to the other modem (and conversely). The two modems negotiate how they will communicate and when this is done your modem sends a CONNECTed message (or the like) to getty. When getty gets this message, it sends a login prompt out the serial port. Sometimes getty just calls on a program named login to handle the logging in. getty usually starts running at boot-time but it must wait until a connection is made before sending out a login prompt.

Now for more details on the two methods of answering the call. By setting the S0 register of the modem to 3, the modem will automatically answer on the 3rd ring. If it's set to 0 then the modem will only answer the call if getty sends it an A (= Answer) command while the phone is ringing. Actually an ATA is sent since all modem commands are prefixed by AT. You might think it best to utilize the ability of the modem to automatically answer the call, but it's actually better if getty answers it. If the modem doesn't automatically answer, it's called manual answer (even though getty automatically handles it).

For the "manual" answer case, getty opens the port at boot-time and listens. When the phone rings, a RING message is sent to the listening getty. Then if getty wants to answer this ring, it sends the modem an ATA command. The modem then makes a connection and sends a CONNECT ... message to getty which then sends a login prompt to the caller.

The automatic answer case uses the CD (Carrier Detect) wire from the modem to the serial port to detect when a connection is made. It works like this. At boot-time getty tries to open the serial port but the attempt fails since there is normally no CD signal from the modem. Then the getty program waits at the open statement in the program until a CD signal appears. When a CD signal arrives (perhaps hours later) then the port is opened and getty sends the login prompt. While getty is waiting (sleeping) at the open statement, other processes can run since Linux is a multiprocessing operating system. What actually wakes getty up is an interrupt which is issued when the CD line from the modem changes state to on.

You may wonder how getty is able to open the serial port in the manual-answer case since there is no CD signal. Well, there's a way to write a program to force the port to open even if there is no CD signal present.

Why Manual Answer is Best

The difference between the two ways of answering will show itself when the computer happens to be down but the modem is still working. For the manual case, the RING message is sent to getty but since the computer is down, `getty` isn't there and the phone never gets answered. There are no telephone charges when there is no answer. For the automatic answer case, the phone is answered but no login message is ever sent since the computer is down. The phone bill runs up as the waiting continues. If the phone call is toll-free, it doesn't make much difference, although it may be frustrating waiting for a login prompt that never arrives. `mgetty` uses manual answer. `uugetty` can do this too using a configuration script.

Callback

Callback is where someone first dials in to your modem. Then, you get a little info from the caller and then call it right back. Why would you want to do this? One reason is to save on telephone bills if you can call the caller cheaper than the caller can call you. Another is to make sure that the caller really is who it claims to be. If a caller calls you and claims to be calling from its usual phone number, then one way to verify this is to actually place a new call to that number.

There's a program for Linux called `callback` that works with `mgetty`. It's at <ftp://ftp.icce.rug.nl/pub/unix/>. Step-by-step instructions on how someone installed it (and PPP) is at <http://www.stokely.com/unix.serial. port.resources/callback.html>.

Voice Mail

Voice mail is like an answering machine run by a computer. To do this you must have a modem that supports "voice" and supporting software. Instead of storing the messages on tape, they are stored in digital format on a disk. When a person phones you, they hear a "greeting" message and can then leave a message for you. More advanced systems would have caller-selectable mail boxes and caller-selectable messages to listen to. Free software is available in Linux for simple answering, but doesn't seem to be available yet for the more advanced stuff.

I know of two different voicemail packages for Linux. One is a very minimal package (see "Voicemail Software"). The other, more advanced, but currently poorly documented, is `vgetty`. It's an optional addition to the well documented and widely distributed mgetty program. It supports ZyXEL-like voice modem commands. In the Debian distribution, you must get the `mgetty-voice` package in addition to the `mgetty` package and `mgetty-doc` package. Obsolete documentation has been removed from `mgetty` but replacement documentation is lacking (except if you use the `-h` (help) option when running certain programs, etc.). But one sees postings about using it on the `mgetty` newsgroup. See "About `mgetty`" and >. It seems that `vgetty` is currently not very stable but it's successfully being used and development of it continues. If this is the latest version of this HOWTO can someone who is familiar with `vgetty` please let me know its current status.

`uugetty` for Dial-In (from the old Serial-HOWTO)

Be aware that you could use `mgetty` as a (better?) alternative to `uugetty`. `mgetty` is newer and more popular than `uugetty`. See "What is `getty`?" for a brief comparison of these 2 `getty`s.

Installing `getty_ps`

Since `uugetty` is part of `getty_ps` you'll first have to install `getty_ps`. If you don't have it, get the latest version from `metalab.unc.edu:/pub/Linux/system/serial`. In particular, if you want to use high speeds (57600 and 115200 bps), you must get version 2.0.7j or later. You must also have libc 5.x or greater.

By default, `getty_ps` will be configured to be Linux FSSTND (File System Standard) compliant, which means that the binaries will be in `/sbin`, and the config files will be named `/etc/conf.{uu}getty.ttySN`. This is not apparent from the documentation! It will also expect lock files to go in `/var/lock`. Make sure you have the `/var/lock` directory.

If you don't want FSSTND compliance, binaries will go in `/etc`, config files will go in `/etc/default/{uu}getty.ttySN`, and lock files will go in `/usr/spool/uucp`. I recommend doing things this way if you are using UUCP, because UUCP will have problems if you move the lock files to where it isn't looking for them.

`getty_ps` can also use `syslogd` to log messages. See the man pages for `syslogd(1)` and `syslog.conf(5)` for setting up `syslogd`, if you don't have it running already. Messages are logged with priority LOG_AUTH, errors use LOG_ERR, and debugging uses LOG_DEBUG. If you don't want to use syslogd you can edit tune.h in the getty_ps source files to use a log file for messages instead, namely /var/adm/getty.log by default.

Decide on if you want FSSTND compliance and syslog capability. You can also choose a combination of the two. Edit the Makefile, tune.h and config.h to reflect your decisions. Then compile and install according to the instructions included with the package.

Setting Up uugetty

With uugetty you may dial out with your modem while uugetty is watching the port for logins. The original author of this HOWTO said to use /dev/cuaN for dial-out (with uugetty running on /dev/ttyN). But others say you must use /dev/ttyN for both dial-in and dial-out ?

uugetty does important lock file checking. Update /etc/gettydefs to include an entry for your modem. When you are done editing /etc/gettydefs, you can verify that the syntax is correct by doing:

```
linux# getty -c /etc/gettydefs
```

Modern Modems If you have a 9600 bps or faster modem with data compression, you can lock your serial port to one speed. For example:

```
# 115200 fixed speed
F115200# B115200 CS8 # B115200 SANE -ISTRIP HUPCL #@S @L @B
   login: #F115200
```

If you have your modem set up to do RTS/CTS hardware flow control, you can add CRTSCTS to the entries:

```
# 115200 fixed speed with hardware flow control
F115200# B115200 CS8 CRTSCTS # B115200 SANE -ISTRIP HUPCL
   CRTSCTS #@S @L @B login: #F115200
```

Old Slow Modems If you have a slow modem (under 9600 bps) Then, instead of one line for a single speed, your need several lines to try a number of speeds. Note the these lines are linked to each other by the last "word" in the line such as #38400. Blank lines are needed between each entry.

```
# Modem entries
115200# B115200 CS8 # B115200 SANE -ISTRIP HUPCL #@S
   @L @B login: #57600
```

```
57600# B57600 CS8 # B57600 SANE -ISTRIP HUPCL #@S @L
   @B login: #38400

38400# B38400 CS8 # B38400 SANE -ISTRIP HUPCL #@S @L
   @B login: #19200

19200# B19200 CS8 # B19200 SANE -ISTRIP HUPCL #@S @L
   @B login: #9600

9600# B9600 CS8 # B9600 SANE -ISTRIP HUPCL #@S @L @B
   login: #2400

2400# B2400 CS8 # B2400 SANE -ISTRIP HUPCL #@S @L @B
   login: #115200
```

Login Banner   If you want, you can make `uugetty` print interesting things in the login banner. In Greg's examples, he has the system name, the serial line, and the current bps rate. You can add other things:

@B The current (evaluated at the time the @B is seen) bps rate.

@D The current date, in MM/DD/YY.

@L The serial line to which `uugetty` is attached.

@S The system name.

@T The current time, in HH:MM:SS (24-hour).

@U The number of currently signed-on users. This is a count of the number of entries in the `/etc/utmp` file that have a non-null `ut_name` field.

@V The value of VERSION, as given in the defaults file.

To display a single @ character, use either \@ or @@.

Customizing uugetty

There are lots of parameters you can tweak for each port you have. These are implemented in separate config files for each port. The file `/etc/conf.uugetty` will be used by all instances of `uugetty`, and `/etc/conf.uugetty.ttySN` will only be used by that one port. Sample default config files can be found with the `getty_ps` source files, which come with most Linux distributions. Due to space concerns, they are not listed here. Note that if you are using older versions of `uugetty` (older than 2.0.7e), or aren't using FSSTND, then the default file will be `/etc/default/uugetty.ttySN`. Greg's `/etc/conf.uugetty.ttyS3` looked like this:

```
# sample uugetty configuration file for a Hayes
  compatible modem to allow
# incoming modem connections
#
# alternate lock file to check... if this lock file
  exists, then uugetty is
# restarted so that the modem is re-initialized
ALTLOCK=cua3
ALTLINE=cua3
# line to initialize
INITLINE=cua3
# timeout to disconnect if idle...
TIMEOUT=60
# modem initialization string...
# format: <expect><send> ... (chat sequence)
INIT="" AT\r OK\r\n WAITFOR=RING CONNECT="" ATA\r
CONNECT\s\A
# this line sets the time to delay before sending the
  login banner DELAY=1
#DEBUG=010
```

Add the following line to your /etc/inittab, so that uugetty is run on your serial port, substituting in the correct information for your environment–run-levels (2345 or 345, etc.) config file location, port, speed, and default terminal type:

```
S3:2345:respawn:/sbin/uugetty -d /etc/default/
uugetty.ttyS3 ttyS3 F115200 vt100
```

Restart init:

```
linux# init q
```

For the speed parameter in your /etc/inittab, you want to use the highest bps rate that your modem supports.

Now Linux will be watching your serial port for connections. Dial in from another machine and login to you Linux system.

uugetty has a lot more options, (see the main page for uugetty) (often just called getty) for a full description. Among other things there is a scheduling feature, and a ringback feature.

What Speed Should I Use with My Modem?

By "speed" we really mean the "data flow rate" but almost everybody incorrectly calls it speed. For all modern modems you have no choice of the speed that the modem uses on the telephone line since it will automatically choose the highest possible speed that is possible under the circumstances. But you do have a choice as to what speed will be used between your modem and your computer. This is sometimes called "DTE speed" where "DTE" stands for Data Terminal Equipment (Your computer is a DTE.) You need to set this speed high enough so this part of the signal path will not be a bottleneck. The setting for the DTE speed is the maximum speed of this link. Most of the time it will likely operate at lower speeds.

For an external modem, DTE speed is the speed (in bits/sec) of the flow over the cable between you modem and PC. For an internal modem, it's the same idea since the modem also emulates a serial port. It may seem ridiculous having a speed limit on communication between a computer and a modem card that is directly connected inside the computer to a much higher speed bus. But it's that way since the modem card probably includes a dedicated serial port which does have speed limits (and settable speeds).

Speed and Data Compression

What speed do you choose? If it were not for "data compression" one might try to choose a DTE speed exactly the same as the modem speed. Data compression takes the bytes sent to the modem from your computer and encodes them into a fewer number of bytes. For example, if the flow (speed) from the PC to the modem was 20,000 bytes/sec (bps) and the compression ratio was 2 to 1, then only 10,000 bytes/sec would flow over the telephone line. Thus for a 2:1 compression ratio you need to set the speed double the maximum modem speed on the phone line. If the compression ratio is 3 to 1 you need to set it 3 times faster.

Where Do I Set Speed?

This DTE speed is normally set by a menu in your communications program or by an option given to the `getty` command if someone is dialing in. You can't set the DCE modem-to-modem speed.

Can't Set a High Enough Speed

You need to find out the highest speed supported by your hardware. As of late 1998 most hardware only supported speeds up to 115.2K bps. A few 56K internal modems support 230.4K bps. Recent Linux kernels support high speeds (over 115.2K) but you might have difficulty using it because of one or both of the following reasons:

1. The application program (or `stty`) will not accept the high speed.

2. `Setserial` has a default speed of 115,200 (but this default is easy to change).

How Speed is Set in Hardware: the Divisor and `baud_base` Here's a list of commonly used divisors and their corresponding speeds (assuming a maximum speed of 115,200): 1 (115.2K), 2 (57.6K), 3 (38.4K), 6 (19.2K), 12 (9.6K), 24 (4.8K), 48 (2.4K), 96 (1.2K), etc. The serial driver sets the speed in the hardware by sending the hardware only a "divisor" (a positive integer). This "divisor" divides the maximum speed of the hardware resulting in a slower speed (except a divisor of 1 obviously tells the hardware to run at maximum speed).

Normally, if you specify a speed of 115.2K (in your communication program or by `stty`) then the serial driver sets the port hardware to divisor 1 which obviously sets the highest speed. If you happen to have hardware with a maximum speed of say 230.4K, then specifying 115.2K will result in divisor 1 and will actually give you 230.4K. This is double the speed that you set. In fact, for any speed you set, the actual speed will be double. If you had hardware that could run at 460.8K then the actual speed would be quadruple what you set.

Work-Arounds for Setting Speed To correct this accounting (but not always fix the problem) you may use `setserial` to change the `baud_base` to the actual maximal speed of your port such as 230.4K. Then if you set the speed (by your application or by `stty`) to 230.4K, a divisor of 1 will be used and you'll get the same speed as you set. PROBLEM: `stty` and many communication programs (as of mid 1999) still have 115.2K as their maximum speed setting and will not let you set 230.4K, etc. So in these cases one solution is not to change anything with setserial but mentally keep in mind that the actual speed is always double what you set.

There's another work-around which is not much better. To use it you set the `baud_base` (with `setserial`) to the maximal speed of your hardware. This corrects the accounting so that if you set say 115.2K you actually get 115.2K. Now you still have to figure out how to set the highest speed if your communication program (or the like) will not let you do it. Fortunately, `setserial` has a way to do this: use the `spd_cust` parameter with `divisor 1`. Then when you set the speed to 38400 in a communication program, the divisor will be set to 1 in the port and it will operate at maximum speed. For example:

`setserial /dev/ttyS2 spd_cust baud_base 230400 divisor 1.` Don't try using "divisor" for any other purpose other than the special use illustrated above (with `spd_cust`).

If there are two or more high speeds that you want to use that your communication program can't set, then it's not quite as easy as above. But the same principles apply. You could just keep the default `baud_base` and understand that when you set a speed you are really only setting a divisor. So your actual speed will always be your maximum speed divided by whatever divisor is set by the serial driver. See "How Speed is Set in Hardware: the Divisor and `baud_base`".

Crystal Frequency is Not `baud_base`   Note that the `baud_base` setting is usually much lower than the frequency of the crystal oscillator in the hardware since the crystal frequency is often divided by 16 in the hardware to get the actual top speed. The reason the crystal frequency needs to be higher is so that this high crystal speed can be used to take a number of samples of each bit to determine if it's a 1 or a 0.

Speed Table

It's best to have at least a 16650 UART for a 56K modem but few modems support it. Second best is a 16550 that has been tweaked to give 230,400 bps. Here are some suggested speeds to set your serial line if your modem speed is:

- 56K (V.90) use 115200 bps or 230400 bps (a few % faster ?)
- UL1-2:28.8K (V.34), 33.6K (V.34) use 115200 bps
- 14400 bps (V.32bis), with V.42bis data compression, use 57600 bps
- 9600 bps (V.32), with V.42bis data compression, use 38400 bps
- slower than a 9600 bps (V.32) modem, set your speed to the highest speed your modem supports.

Communications Programs and Utilities

PPP is by far the most widely used. It's used for Internet access. For dialing out to public libraries, bulletin boards, etc., minicom is the most popular followed by Seyon (X-Window only) and Kermit.

Minicom vs. Kermit

Minicom is only a communications program while Kermit is both a communications program and a file transfer protocol. But one may use the Kermit protocol from within Minicom (provided one has Kermit installed on one's PC). Minicom is menu based while Kermit is command line based (interactive at the special Kermit prompt). While the Kermit program is free software, the documentation is not all free. There is no detailed manual supplied and it is suggested that you purchase a book as the manual. However Kermit has interactive online help which tells all but lacks tutorial explanations for the beginner. Commands may be put in a script file so you don't have to type them over again each time. Kermit (as a communications program) is more powerful than Minicom.

Although all Minicom documentation is free, it's not as extensive as Kermit's. Since permission is required to include Kermit in a commercial distribution, and since the documentation is not entirely free, some distributions don't include Kermit. In my opinion it's easier to set up Minicom and there is less to learn.

Lists of Programs

Here is a list of some communication software you can choose from, available via FTP, if they didn't come with your distribution. I would like comparative comments on the dial-out programs. Are the least popular ones obsolete?

Least Popular Dial-out

- ecu—a communications program
- pcomm—procomm-like communications program with zmodem
- xc—xcomm communication package

Most Popular Dial-out

- `minicom`—telix like communications program. Supports scripts, zmodem, kermit
- C-Kermit <http://www.columbia.edu/kermit/>—portable, scriptable, serial and TCP/IP communications including file transfer, character-set translation, and zmodem support
- `seyon`—X based communication program

Fax

- `efax`—a small fax program
- `hylafax`—a large fax program based on the client-server model.
- `mgetty+fax`—handles fax stuff and login for dial-ins

Voicemail Software

- mvm <http://www-internal.alphabet.ch/~schaefer/mvm/> is a Minimal VoiceMail for Linux
- `vgetty` is an extension to `mgetty` that handles voicemail for some modems. It should come with recent releases of `mgetty`.

Dial-in (Uses `Getty`)

- `mgetty+fax` is for modems and is well documented (except for voicemail as of early 1999). It also handles fax stuff and provides an alternative to `uugetty`. It's incorporating voicemail (using `vgetty`) features. See "About `mgetty`"
- `uugetty` is also for modems. It comes as a part of the `ps_getty` package. See "About `getty_ps`"

Other

- callback is where you dial out to a remote modem and then that modem hangs up and calls you back (to save on phone bills).
- SLiRP and term provide a PPP-like service that you can run in user space on a remote computer with a shell account. See "Term and `SLiRP`" for more details.
- ZyXEL is a control program for ZyXEL U-1496 modems. It handles dial-in, dial-out, dial back security, FAXing, and voice mailbox functions.
- SLIP and PPP software can be found at <ftp://metalab.unc.edu/pub/Linux/system/network/serial>.

■ Other things can be found on <ftp://metalab.unc.edu/pub/Linux/
system/serial> and <ftp://metalab. unc.edu/pub/Linux/apps/
serialcomm> or one of the many mirrors. These are the directories
where serial programs are kept.

SLiRP and Term

SLiRP and term are programs which are of use if you only have a dial-up
shell account on a Unix-like machine and want to get the equivalent of a
PPP account (or the like) without being authorized to have it (possibly
because you don't want to pay extra for it, etc.). SLiRP is more popular
than term which is almost obsolete.

To use SLiRP you install it in your shell account on the remote computer. Then you dial up the account and run SLiRP on the remote and PPP
on your local PC. You now have a PPP connection over which you may run
a web browser on your local PC such as Netscape, etc. There may be some
problems as SLiRP is not as good as a real PPP account. Some accounts
may provide SLiRP since it saves on IP addresses (You have no IP address
while using SLiRP).

term is something like SLiRP only you need to run term on both the local
and remote computer. There is no PPP on the phone line since term uses
its own protocol. To use term from your PC you need to use a term-aware
version of ftp to do ftp, etc. Thus it's easier to use SLiRP since the ordinary version of ftp works fine with SLiRP. There is an unmaintained
Term HOWTO.

What Are UARTs? How Do They Affect Performance?

Introduction to UARTS

(This section is also in the Serial-HOWTO.)

UARTs (Universal Asynchronous Receiver Transmitter) are serial chips
on your PC motherboard (or on an internal modem card). The UART function may also be done on a chip that does other things as well. On older

computers like many 486s, the chips were on the disk IO controller card. Still older computer have dedicated serial boards. The UART's purpose is to convert bytes from the PC's parallel bus to a serial bit-stream. The cable going out of the serial port is serial and has only one wire for each direction of flow. The serial port sends out a stream of bits, one bit at a time. Conversely, the bit stream that enters the serial port via the external cable is converted to parallel bytes that the computer can understand. UARTs deal with data in byte sized pieces, which is conveniently also the size of ASCII characters.

Say you have a terminal hooked up to your PC. When you type a character, the terminal gives that character to it's transmitter (also a UART). The transmitter sends that byte out onto the serial line, one bit at a time, at a specific rate. On the PC end, the receiving UART takes all the bits and rebuilds the (parallel) byte and puts it in a buffer.

Along with converting between serial and parallel, the UART does some other things as a byproduct (side effect) of it's primary task. The voltage used to represent bits is also converted (changed). Extra bits (called start and stop bits) are added to each byte before it is transmitted. See the Serial-HOWTO section, "Voltage Waveshapes" for details. Also, while the flow rate (in bytes/sec) on the parallel bus inside the computer is very high, the flow rate out the UART on the serial port side of it is much lower. The UART has a fixed set of rates (speeds) which it can use at its serial port interface.

Two Types of UARTs

There are two basic types of UARTs: dumb UARTS and FIFO UARTS. Dumb UARTs are the 8250, 16450, early 16550, and early 16650. They are obsolete but if you understand how they work it's easy to understand how the modern ones work with FIFO UARTS (late 16550, 16550A, 16c552, late 16650, 16750, and 16C950).

There is some confusion regarding 16550. Early models had a bug and worked properly only as 16450's (no FIFO). Later models with the bug fixed were named 16550A but many manufacturers did not accept the name change and continued calling it a 16550. Most all 16550's in use today are like 16550A's. Linux will report it as being a 16550A even though your hardware manual (or a label note) says it's a 16550. A similar situation exists for the 16650 (only it's worse since the manufacturer allegedly didn't admit anything was wrong). Linux will report a late 16650 as being a 16650V2. If it reports it as 16650 it is bad news and only is used as if it had a one-byte buffer.

FIFOs

To understand the differences between dumb and FIFO (First In, First Out queue discipline) first let's examine what happens when a UART has sent or received a byte. The UART itself can't do anything with the data passing thru it, it just receives and sends it. For the original dumb UARTS, the CPU gets an interrupt from the serial device every time a byte has been sent or received. The CPU then moves the received byte out of the UART's buffer and into memory somewhere, or gives the UART another byte to send. The 8250 and 16450 UARTs only have a 1 byte buffer. That means, that every time 1 byte is sent or received, the CPU is interrupted. At low transfer rates, this is OK. But, at high transfer rates, the CPU gets so busy dealing with the UART, that is doesn't have time to adequately tend to other tasks. In some cases, the CPU does not get around to servicing the interrupt in time, and the byte is overwritten, because they are coming in so fast. This is called an "overrun" or "overflow".

That's where the FIFO UARTs are useful. The 16550A (or 16550) FIFO chip comes with 16 byte FIFO buffers. This means that it can receive up to 14 bytes (or send 16 bytes) before it has to interrupt the CPU. Not only can it wait for more bytes, but the CPU then can transfer all 14 (or more) bytes at a time. This is a significant advantage over the other UARTs, which only have 1 byte buffers. The CPU receives less interrupts, and is free to do other things. Data is not lost, and everyone is happy. Note that the interrupt threshold of FIFO buffers (trigger level) may be set at less than 14. 1, 4 and 8 are other possible choices.

While most PCs only have a 16550 with 16-byte buffers, better UARTS have even larger buffers. Note that the interrupt is issued slightly before the buffer get full (at say a "trigger level" of 14 bytes for a 16-byte buffer). This allows room for a few more bytes to be received during the time that the interrupt is being serviced. The trigger level may be set to various permitted values by kernel software. A trigger level of 1 will be almost like a dumb UART (except that it still has room for 15 more bytes after it issues the interrupt).

If you type something while visiting a BBS, the characters you type go out thru the serial port. Your typed characters that you see on the screen are what was echoed back thru the telephone line thru your modem and then thru your serial port to the screen. If you had a 16-byte buffer on the serial port which held back characters until it had 14 of them, you would need to type many characters before you could see what you typed (before they appeared on the screen). This would be very confusing but there is a "timeout" to prevent this. Thus you normally see a character on the screen just as soon as you type it.

The "timeout" works like this for the receive UART buffer: If characters arrive one after another, then an interrupt is issued only when say the 14th character reaches the buffer. But if a character arrives and the next character doesn't arrive soon thereafter, then an interrupt is issued. This happens even though there are not 14 characters in the buffer (there may only be one character in it). Thus when what you type goes thru this buffer, it acts almost like a 1-byte buffer even though it is actually a 16-byte buffer (unless your typing speed is a hundred times faster than normal). There is also "timeout" for the transmit buffer as well.

UART Model Numbers

Here's a list of UARTs. TL is Trigger Level

- 8250, 16450, early 16550: Obsolete with 1-byte buffers
- 16550, 16550A, 16c552: 16-byte buffers, TL=1,4,8,14
- 16650: 32-byte buffers. Speed up to 460.8 Kbps
- 16750: 64-byte buffer for send, 56-byte for receive. Speed up to 921.6 Kbps
- Hayes ESP: 1K-byte buffers.

The obsolete ones are only good for modems no higher than 14.4k (DTE speeds up to 38400 bps). For modern modems you need at least a 16550 (and not an early 16550). For V.90 56k modems, it may be a several percent faster with a 16650 (especially if you are downloading uncompressed files). The main advantage of the 16650 is its larger buffer size as the extra speed isn't needed unless the modem compression ratio is high. Some 56k internal modems may come with a 16650 ?? Non-UART, and intelligent multiport boards use DSP chips to do additional buffering and control, thus relieving the CPU even more. For example, the Cyclades Cyclom, and Stallion EasyIO boards use a Cirrus Logic CD1400 RISC UART, and many boards use 80186 CPUs or even special RISC CPUs, to handle the serial IO.

Most newer PCs (486s, Pentiums, or better) come with 16550As (usually called just 16550's). If you have something really old the chip may unplug so that you may be able to upgrade by buying a 16550A chip and replacing your existing 16450 UART. If the functionality has been put on another type of chip, you are out of luck. If the UART is socketed, then upgrading is easy (if you can find a replacement). The new and old are pin-to-pin compatible. It may be more feasible to just buy a new serial board on the Internet (few retail stores stock them today).

Troubleshooting

My Modem is Physically There but Can't Be Found

If you have installed an internal modem or are using an external one and don't know what serial port it's connected to then the problem is to find the serial port. See "My Serial Port is Physically There but Can't Be Found" This section is about finding out which serial port has the modem on it.

There's a program that looks for modems on commonly used serial ports called wvdialconf. Just type wvdialconf <u><a-new-file-name></u>. It will create the new file as a configuration file but you don't need this file unless you are going to use wvdial for dialing. See "What is wvdialconf?"

Your problem could be due to a winmodem (or the like) which can't be used with Linux. See "Avoid Most Software Modems". The setserial program may be used to detect serial ports but will not detect modems on them. Thus wvdialconf is best to try first.

Another way to see if there's a modem on a port is to start "minicom" on the port (go to the setup menus with ^AO). Then type AT and you should see OK (or 0 if it's set for "digit result codes"). If it takes many seconds to get a response (including only the cursor moving down one line) then see "Extremely Slow: Text Appears on the Screen Slowly After Long Delays."

I Can't Get Near 56K on My 56K Modem

There must be very low noise on the line for it to work at even close to 56K. Some phone lines are so bad that the speeds obtainable are much slower than 56K (like 28.8K or even slower). Sometimes extension phones connected to the same line can cause problems. To test this you might connect your modem directly at the point where the telephone line enters the building with the feeds for everything else on that line disconnected (if others can tolerate such a test).

Uploading (Downloading) Files is Broken/Slow

Flow control (both at your PC and/or modem) may not be enabled. If you have set a high DTE speed (like 115.2K) then flow from your modem to your PC may work OK but a lot of flow in the other direction will not all get thru due to the telephone line bottleneck. This will result in many errors and the resending of packets. It may thus take far too long to send a file. In some cases, files don't make it thru at all. If you're downloading long uncompressed files or web pages (and your modem uses data compression) or you've set a low DTE speed, then downloading may also be broken due to no flow control.

For Dial-In I Keep Getting `line NNN of inittab invalid`

Make sure you are using the correct syntax for your version of init. The different inits that are out there use different syntax in the `/etc/inittab` file. Make sure you are using the correct syntax for your version of `getty`.

I Keep Getting: `Id S3 respawning too fast: disabled for 5 minutes`

Id `S3` is just an example. In this case look on the line which starts with `S3` in `/etc/inittab`. This is causing the problem. Make sure the syntax for this line is correct and that the device (`ttyS3`) exists and can be found.

Make sure your modem is configured correctly. Look at registers E and Q. This can occur when your modem is chatting with `getty`.

If you use `uugetty`, verify that your `/etc/gettydefs` syntax is correct by doing the following:

```
linux# getty -c /etc/gettydefs
```

This can also happen when the uugetty initialization is failing. See section "uugetty Still Doesn't Work".

My Modem Is Hosed After Someone Hangs Up, or uugetty Doesn't Respawn

This can happen when your modem doesn't reset when DTR is dropped. Greg Hankins saw his RD and SD LEDs go crazy when this happened. You need to have your modem reset. Most Hayes compatible modems do this with `&D3`, but on his USR Courier, he had to set `&D2` and `S13=1`. Check your modem manual (if you have one).

`uugetty` Still Doesn't Work

There is a DEBUG option that comes with `getty_ps`. Edit your config file `/etc/conf.{uu}getty.ttySN` and add `DEBUG=NNN`. Where `NNN` is one of the following combination of numbers according to what you are trying to debug:

D_OPT	001	option settings
D_DEF	002	defaults file processing
D_UTMP	004	`utmp`/`wtmp` processing
D_INIT	010	line initialization (INIT)
D_GTAB	020	`gettytab` file processing
D_RUN	040	other runtime diagnostics
D_RB	100	ringback debugging
D_LOC	200	`uugetty` lockfile processing
D_SCH	400	schedule processing
D_ALL	777	everything

Setting `DEBUG=010` is a good place to start.

If you are running `syslogd`, debugging info will appear in your log files. If you aren't running `syslogd` info will appear in `/tmp/getty:ttySN` for debugging `getty` and `/tmp/uugetty:ttySN` for `uugetty`, and in `/var/adm/getty.log`. Look at the debugging info and see what is going on. Most likely, you will need to tune some of the parameters in your config file, and reconfigure your modem.

You could also try `mgetty`. Some people have better luck with it.

The Following Subsections Are in Both the Serial and Modem HOW=AD TOs:

My Serial Port is Physically There but Can't be Found

If a device (such as a modem) works on a serial port, then obviously the port has been found. If it doesn't work at all, then you need to make sure your serial port can be found.

Check the BIOS menus and BIOS messages. If it's an ISA bus PnP serial port, try `pnpdump—dumpregs` and/or see Plug-and-Play-HOWTO. For the PCI bus use `lspci`. You may try probing with `setserial`. See "Probing". If nothing seems to get thru the port it may be there but have a bad interrupt. See "Extremely Slow: Text Appears on the Screen Slowly After Long Delays".

Extremely Slow: Text Appears on the Screen Slowly After Long Delays

It's likely mis-set/conflicting interrupts. Here are some of the symptoms which will happen the first time you try to use a modem, terminal, or printer. In some cases you type something but nothing appears on the screen until many seconds later. Only the last character typed may show up. It may be just an invisible <return> character so all you notice is that the cursor jumps down one line. In other cases where a lot of data should appear on the screen, only a batch of about 16 characters appear. Then there is a long wait of many seconds for the next batch of characters. You might also get `input overrun` error messages (or find them in logs).

For more details on the symptoms and why this happens see the Serial-HOWTO section: "Interrupt Problem Details".

If it involves Plug-and-Play devices, see also Plug-and-Play-HOWTO.

As a quick check to see if it really is an interrupt problem, set the IRQ to zero with `setserial`. This will tell the driver to use polling instead of interrupts. If this seems to fix the "slow" problem then you had an interrupt problem. You should still try to solve the problem since polling uses excessive computer resources and sometimes drastically decreases your thruput.

Checking to find the interrupt conflict may not be easy since Linux supposedly doesn't permit any interrupt conflicts and will send you a `/dev/ttyS?: Device or resource busy` error message if it thinks you are attempting to create a conflict. But a real conflict can be created if `setserial` has incorrect information. Thus using `setserial` will not reveal the conflict (nor will looking at `/proc/interrupts` which bases its info on `setserial`). You still need to know what `setserial` thinks so that you can pinpoint where it's wrong and change it when you determine what's really set in the hardware.

What you need to do is to check how the hardware is set by checking jumpers or using PnP software to check how the hardware is actually set. For PnP run either `pnpdump—dumpregs` or run `lspci`. Compare this to how Linux (e.g., `setserial`) thinks the hardware is set.

Somewhat Slow: I Expected It to be a Few Times Times Faster

One reason may be that whatever is on the serial port (such as a modem, terminal, printer) doesn't work as fast as you thought it did. A 56k Modem seldom works at 56k and the Internet often has congestion and bottlenecks that slow things down.

Another possible reason is that the serial driver thinks you have an obsolete serial port (UART 8250,16450 or early 16550). See "What Are UARTs?". Use `setserial -g /dev/ttyS*`. If it shows anything less than a 16550A, this is likely your problem. Then if `setserial` has it wrong, change it. See "What is `setserial`" for more info. Of course if you really do have an obsolete serial port, lying about it to `setserial` will only make things worse.

The Startup Screen Show Wrong IRQs for the Serial Ports

Linux does not do any IRQ detection on startup. When the serial module loads it only does serial device detection. Thus, disregard what it says about the IRQ, because it's just assuming the standard IRQs. This is done, because IRQ detection is unreliable, and can be fooled. But if and when `setserial` runs from a start-up script, it changes the IRQs and displays the new (and hopefully correct) state on on the startup screen. If the wrong IRQ is not corrected by a later display on the screen, then you've got a problem.

So, even though I have my `ttyS2` set at IRQ 5, I still see

```
ttyS02 at 0x03e8 (irq = 4) is a 16550A
```

at first when Linux boots. (Older kernels may show `ttyS02` as `tty02`.) You have to use `setserial` to tell Linux the IRQ you are using.

"Cannot Open /dev/ttyS?: Permission denied"

Check the file permissions on this port with `ls -l /dev/ttyS?_` If you own the `ttyS?` then you need read and write permissions: crw with the c (Character device) in col. 1. It you don't own it then it should show rw- in cols. 8 & 9 which means that everyone has read and write permission on it. Use chmod to change permissions. There are more complicated ways to get access like belonging to a "group" that has group permission.

Operation not supported by device for ttyS?

This means that an operation requested by setserial, stty, etc., couldn't be done because the kernel doesn't support doing it. Formerly this was often due to the "serial" module not being loaded. But with the advent of PnP, it may likely mean that there is no modem (or other serial device) at the address where the driver (and setserial) thinks it is. If there is no modem there, commands (for operations) sent to that address obviously don't get done. See "What is Set in My Serial Port Hardware?".

   If the "serial" module wasn't loaded but lsmod shows you it's now loaded it might be the case that it's loaded now but wasn't loaded when you got the error message. In many cases the module will automatically loaded when needed (if it can be found). To force loading of the "serial" module it may be listed in the file: /etc/modules.conf or /etc/modules. The actual module should reside in: /lib/modules/.../misc/serial.o.

Cannot create lockfile. Sorry

   When a port is "opened" by a program a lockfile is created in /var/lock/. Wrong permissions for the lock directory will not allow a lockfile to be created there. Use ls -ld /var/lock to see if the permissions are OK: usually rwx for everyone (repeated 3 times). If it's wrong, use chmod to fix it. Of course, if there is no "lock" directory no lockfile can be created there. For more info on lockfiles see the Serial-HOWTO subsection: "What Are Lock Files".

Device /dev/ttyS? is locked.

This means that someone else (or some other process) is supposedly using the serial port. There are various ways to try to find out what process is "using" it. One way is to look at the contents of the lockfile (/var/lock/LCK...). It should be the process id. If the process id is say 261 type ps 261 to find out what it is. Then if the process is no longer needed, it may be gracefully killed by `kill 261`. If it refuses to be killed use `kill -9 261` to force it to be killed, but then the lockfile will not be removed and you'll need to delete it manually. Of course if there is no such process as 161 then you may just remove the lockfile but in most cases the lockfile should have been automatically removed if it contained a stale process id (such as 261).

/dev/ttyS?: Device or Resource Busy

This problem can arise when you are trying to dial out with a modem when DCD or DTR are not implemented correctly. DCD should only be on (asserted) when there is an actual connection (ie someone has dialed in), not when getty is watching the port. Check to make sure that your modem is configured to only assert DCD when there is a connection. DTR should be on (asserted) whenever something is using, or watching the line, like `getty`, kermit, or some other comm program.

"resource busy" often means (for the case of `ttyS2`) "You can't use ttyS2 since another device is using ttyS2's interrupt." The potential interrupt conflict is inferred from what `setserial` thinks. A more accurate error message would be "Can't use ttyS2 since the setserial data indicates that another device is using ttyS2's interrupt".

Thus there are two possibilities. There may be a real interrupt conflict that is being avoided. But if `setserial` has it wrong, there may be no reason why `ttyS2` can't be used, except that `setserial` erroneously predicts a conflict. What you need to do is to find the interrupt `setserial` thinks `ttyS2` is using by looking at boot-time messages (using `setserial` will not work since it gives the "device busy" error message). Then check to see if anything else uses this interrupt or if the interrupt reported is the same as set in the hardware.

Troubleshooting Tools

These are some of the programs you might want to use in troubleshooting:

- `lsof /dev/ttyS*` will list serial ports which are open.
- `setserial` shows and sets the low-level hardware configuration of a port (what the driver thinks it is). See "What is `setserial`"
- `stty` shows and sets the configuration of a port (except for that handled by `setserial`). See the Serial-HOWTO section: `Stty`.

- modemstat or statserial will show the current state of various modem signal lines (such as DTR, CTS, etc.)
- irqtune will give serial port interrupts higher priority to improve performance.
- hdparm for hard-disk tuning may help some more.
- lspci shows the actual IRQs, etc., of hardware on the PCI bus.
- pnpdump—dumpregs shows the actual IRQs, etc., of hardware for PnP devices on the ISA bus.
- Some "files" in the /proc tree (such as ioports and interrupts).

Flash Upgrades

Many modems can be upgraded by reprogramming their flash memories with an upgrade program which you get from the Internet. By sending this "program" from the PC via the serial port to the modem, the modem will store this program in its non-volatile memory (it's still there when the power is turned off). The instructions on installing it are usually on how to do in under Windows so you'll need to figure out how to do the equivalent under Linux (unless you want to install the upgrade under Windows). Sending the program to the modem is often called a download.

If the latest version of this HOWTO still contains this request (see "New Versions of this HOWTO") please send me your experiences with installing such upgrades that will be helpful to others.

Here's the general idea of doing an upgrade. First, there may be a command that you need to send your modem to tell it that what follows is a flash ROM upgrade. In one case this was AT** You can do this by starting a communications program (such as minicom) and type. First type AT <enter> to see if your modem is there and answers OK. Next, you need to send a file (sometimes two files) directly to the modem. Communication programs (such as minicom) often use zmodem or kermit to send files to the modem (and beyond) but these put the file into packets which append headers and you want the exact file sent to the modem, not a modified one. But the kermit communications program has a transmit command that will send the file directly (without using the kermit packets) so this is one way to send a file directly. Minicom didn't have this feature in 1998.

Another way to send the file(s) would be to escape from the communications program to the shell (in minicom this is ^AJ) and then: cat upgrade_file_name > /dev/ttyS2 (if your serial port is ttyS2). Then go back to the communication program (type `fg` at the command line prompt in minicom) to see what happened.

Here's an example session for a certain Rockwell modem (C-a is ^A):

Run minicom

Type `AT`** : see "Download initiated . . ."

C-a J

cat FLASH.S37 > `/dev/modem`

fg : see "Download flash code . . ."

C-a J - cat 283P1722.S37 > `/dev/modem`

fg : see "Device successfully programmed"

Other Sources of Information

Miscellaneous

- man pages for: `agetty`(8), `getty`(1m), `gettydefs`(5), `init`(1), `isapnp`(8), `login`(1), `mgetty`(8), `setserial`(8)

- Your modem manual (if it exists). Some modems come without manuals.

- Serial Suite <ftp://scicom.alphadec.com/pub/linux> by Vern Hoxie is a collection of blurbs about the care and feeding of the Linux serial port plus some simple programs.

- The Linux serial mailing list. To join, send email to <majordomo @vger.rutgers.edu>, with `subscribe linux-serial` in the message body. If you send `help` in the message body, you get a help message. The server also serves many other Linux lists. Send the `lists` command for a list of mailing lists.

Books

I've been unable to find a good up-to-date book on modems.

- The Complete Modem Reference by Gilbert Held, 1997. Contains too much info about obsolete topics. More up-to-date info may be found on the Internet.

- Modems For Dummies by Tina Rathbone, 1996. (Have never seen it.)

- Ultimate Modem Handbook by Cass R. Lewart, 1998.

HOWTOs

- Cable-Modem mini-howto
- ISDN Howto (not a LDP Howto)
  <http://www.suse.de/Support/sdb_e/isdn.html>: drivers for ISDN
  "Modems". Much related info on this is in German.
- Modems-HOWTO: In French (Not used in creating this Modem-HOWTO)
- NET-3-HOWTO: all about networking, including SLIP, CSLIP, and PPP
- PPP-HOWTO: help with PPP including modem set-up
- Serial-HOWTO has info on Multiport Serial Cards used for both terminals and banks of modems. Covers the serial port in more detail than in the HOWTO.
- Serial-Programming-HOWTO: for some aspects of serial-port programming
- Text-Terminal-HOWTO: (including connecting up with modems)
- UUCP-HOWTO: for information on setting up UUCP

Usenet Newsgroups

- comp.os.linux.answers FAQs, How-To's, READMEs, etc., about Linux.
- comp.os.linux.hardware Hardware compatibility with the Linux operating system.
- comp.os.linux.setup Linux installation and system administration.
- comp.dcom.modems Modems for all OSs.

Web Sites

- Hayes AT modem commands Technical Reference for Hayes™ Modem Users
  <http://www.hayes.com/TechSupport/techref/>
- Rockwell-based modem commands
  <http://www.rss.rockwell.com/techinfo/>
- Modem FAQs: Navas 28800 Modem FAQ
  <http://web.aimnet.com/~jnavas/modem/faq.html>

- Curt's High Speed Modem Page
  <http://www.teleport.com/~curt/modems.html>

- Much info on 56k modems 56k Modem = v.Unreliable
  <http://808hi.com/56k/>

- Links to modem manufacturers
  <http://www.56k.com/links/Modem_Manufacturers/>

- Identifying modems by FCC ID
  <http://www.sbsdirect.com/fccenter.html>

- Partial list of modems which work/don't_work under Linux
  modem list <http://www.o2.net/~gromitkc/winmodem.html>

Addenda

Addendum A: How Modems Work (Technical) (Unfinished)

Modulation Details

INTRO TO MODULATION This part describes the modulation methods used for conventional modems. It doesn't cover the high speed methods (modulus conversion) sometimes used by "56k Modems (v.90)". But 56k modems also use the modulation methods described here.

Modulation is the conversion of a digital signal represented by binary bits (0 or 1) into an analog signal something like a sine wave. The modulated signal consists pure sine wave "carrier" signal which is modified to convey information. A pure carrier sine wave, unchanging in frequency and voltage, provides no flow of information at all (except that a carrier is present). To make it convey information we modify (or modulate) this carrier. There are 3 basic types of modulation: frequency, amplitude, and phase. They will be explained next.

FREQUENCY MODULATION The simplest modulation method is frequency modulation. Frequency is measured in cycles per second (of a sine wave). It's the count of the number of times the sine wave shape repeats itself in a second. This is the same as the number of times it reaches it peak value during a second. The word "Hertz" (abbreviated Hz) is used to mean "cycles per second".

A simple example of frequency modulation is where one frequency means a binary 0 and another means a 1. For example, for some obsolete 300 baud modems 1070 Hz meant a binary 0 while 1270 Hz meant a binary 1. This was called "frequency shift keying". Instead of just two possible frequencies, more could be used to allow more information to be transmitted. If we had 4 different frequencies (call them A, B, C, and D) then each frequency could stand for a pair of bits. For example, to send 00 one would use frequency A. To send 01, use frequency B; for 10 use C; for 11 use D. In like manner, by using 8 different frequencies we could send 3 bits with each shift in frequency. Each time we double the number of possible frequencies we increase the number of bits it can represent by 1.

AMPLITUDE MODULATION   Once one understands frequency modulation example above including the possibilities of representing a few bits by a single shift in frequency, it's easier to understand both amplitude modulation and phase modulation. For amplitude modulation, one just changes the height (voltage) of the sine wave analogous to changing the frequency of the sine wave. For a simple case there could only be 2 allowed amplitude levels, one representing a 0-bit and another representing a 1-bit. As explained for the case of frequency modulation, having more possible amplitudes will result in more information being transmitted per change in amplitude.

PHASE MODULATION   To change the phase of a sine wave at a certain instant of time, we stop sending this old sine wave and immediately begin sending a new sine wave of the same frequency and amplitude. If we started sending the new sine wave at the same voltage level (and slope) as existed when we stopped sending the old sine wave, there would be no change in phase (and no detectable change at all). But suppose that we started up the new sine wave at a different point on the sine wave curve. Then there would likely be a sudden voltage jump at the point in time where the old sine wave stopped and the new sine wave began. This is a phase shift and it's measured in degrees (deg.) A 0 deg. (or a 360 deg.) phase shift means no change at all while a 180 deg. phase shift just reverses the voltage (and slope) of the sine wave. Put another way, a 180 deg. phase shift just skips over a half-period (180 deg.) at the point of transition. Of course we could just skip over say 90 deg. or 135 deg. etc. As in the example for frequency modulation, the more possible phase shifts, the more bits a single shift in phase can represent.

COMBINATION MODULATION Instead of just selecting either frequency, amplitude, or phase modulation, we may chose to combine modulation methods. Suppose that we have 256 possible frequencies and thus can send a byte (8 bits) for each shift in frequency (since 2 to the 8 power is 256). Suppose also that we have another 256 different amplitudes so that each shift in amplitude represents a byte. Also suppose there are 256 possible phase shifts. Then a certain points in time we may make a shift in all 3 things: frequency, amplitude and phase. This would send out 3 bytes for each such transition.

No modulation method in use today actually does this. It's not practical due to the relatively long time it would take to detect all 3 types of changes. The main problem is that frequent shifts in phase can make it appear that a shift in frequency has happened when it actually didn't.

To avoid this difficulty one may simultaneous change only the phase and amplitude (with no change in frequency). This is called phase-amplitude modulation (sometimes also called quadrature amplitude modulation = QAM). This method is used today for the common modem speeds of 14.4k, 28.8k, and 33.6k. The only significant case where this modulation method is not used today is for 56k modems. But even 56k modems exclusively use QAM (phase-amplitude modulation) in the direction from your PC out the telephone line. Sometimes even the other direction will also fall back to QAM when line conditions are not good enough. Thus QAM (phase-amplitude modulation) still remains the most widely used method on ordinary telephone lines.

56K MODEMS (V.90) The "modulation" method used above 33.6k is entirely different than the common phase-amplitude modulation. Since ordinary telephone calls are converted to digital signals at the local offices of the telephone company, the fastest speed that you can send digital data by an ordinary telephone call is the same speed that the telephone company uses over its digital portion of the phone call transmission. What is this speed? Well, it's close to 64Kbps. It would be 64k but sometimes bits are "stolen" for the purposes of signalling. But if the phone Co. knows that the link is digital, bits may not get stolen. The case of kwill be presented and then it will be explained why the actual speed is lower (56k or less— usually significantly less).

Thus 64k is the absolute top speed possible for an ordinary telephone call using the digital portion of the circuit that was designed to send digital encodings of the human voice. In order to use 64k, the modem must know exactly how the telephone company is doing its digital encoding of the analog signals. This task is far too complicated if both sides of a telephone call have only an analog interface to the telephone company. But if one side has a digital interface, then it's possible (at least in one direction). Thus if your ISP has a digital interface to the phone company, the ISP may send out a certain digital signal over the phone lines toward your PC. The digital signal from the ISP gets converted to analog at the local telephone office near your PC's location (perhaps near your home). Then it's your modem's task to try to figure out exactly what that digital signal was. If it can do this then transmission at 64k (the speed of the telephone company's digital signal) is possible in this direction.

What method does the telephone company use to digitally encode analog signals? It uses a method of sampling the amplitude of the analog signal at a rate of 8000 samples per second. Each sample amplitude is encoded as a 8-bit (ASCII-like) byte. (Note: 8 x 8000 = 64k) This is called "Pulse Code Modulation" = PCM. These bytes are then sent digitally on the telephone company's digital circuits where many calls share a single circuit using a time-sharing scheme known as "time division multiplexing". Then finally at the local telephone office near your home, the digital signal is de-multiplexed resulting in the same digital signal as was originally created by PCM. This signal is then converted back to analog and sent to your home. Each 8-bit byte creates a certain amplitude of the analog signal. Your modem's task is to determine just what that PCM 8-bit byte was based on the amplitude it detects.

This is (sort of) "amplitude demodulation" but not really. It's not amplitude demodulation because there is no carrier. Actually, it's called "modulus conversion" which is the inverse of PCM. In order to determine the digital codes the telephone co. used to create the analog signal, the modem must sample this analog signal amplitude at exactly the same points in time the phone co. used when it created the analog signal. To do this a timing signal is generated from a residual kHz signal on the phone line. The setting of amplitudes to go out to your home/office at 8k settings/sec sort of creates 4k Hz signal. Suppose every other amplitude was of opposite polarity. Then there would be a 4Kk Hz sine-like wave created. Each amplitude is in a sense a 8-bit symbol and when to sample amplitudes is known as "symbol timing".

Now the encoding of amplitudes in PCM is not linear and at low amplitudes the differences between adjacent amplitudes is quite small. So to make the distinction of amplitudes that are close to each other easier, certain amplitudes are not used in the modulation scheme. This give a larger delta between possible amplitudes and makes correct detection of them by your modem easier. If half the amplitude levels were not used by v.90 and it would be tantamount to each symbol (allowed amplitude level) representing

7 bits instead of 8. This is where 56k comes from: 7 bits/symbol x 8k symbols/sec = 56k bps. Of course each symbol is actually generated by 8-bits but only 128 bytes of the possible 256 bytes are actually used. There is a code table mapping these 128 8-bit bytes to 128 7-bit bytes.

But it's a little more complicated that this. If the line conditions are not nearly perfect, then even fewer possible levels (symbols) are used resulting in speeds under 56k. Also due to government rules prohibiting high power levels on phone lines, certain high amplitudes levels can't be used resulting in only about 53.3k at best for "56k" modems.

Note that the digital part of the telephone network is bi-directional. Two such circuits are used for a phone call, one in each direction. The direction from your home/office to the ISP is only a single circuit analog connection. It uses the conventional phase-amplitude modulation scheme with a maximum of 36.6kbps (and not 53.3kbps). Yet due to sophisticated cancellation methods (not explained here) it's able to send simultaneously in both directions.

Addendum B: "baud" vs. "bps"

A Simple Example   "baud" and "bps" are perhaps one of the most misused terms in the computing and telecommunications field. Many people use these terms interchangeably, when in fact they are not! bps is simply the number of bits transmitted per second. The baud rate is a measure of how many times per second a signal changes (or could change). For a typical serial port a 1-bit is -12 volts and a 0-bit is $+12$ v (volts). If the bps is 38,400 a sequence of 010101 . . . would also be 38,400 baud since the voltage shifts back and forth from positive to negative to positive . . . and there are 38,400 shifts per second. For another sequence say 111000111 . . . there will be fewer shifts of voltage since for three 1's in sequence the voltage just stays at -12 volts yet we say that its still 38,400 baud since there is a possibility that the number of changes per second will be that high.

Looked at another way, put an imaginary tic mark separating each bit (even thought the voltage may not change). 38,400 baud then means 38,400 tic marks per second. The tic marks at at the instants of permitted change and are actually marked by a synchronized clock signal generated in the hardware but not sent over the external cable.

Suppose that a "change" may have more than the two possible outcomes of the previous example (of $+/-$ 12 v). Suppose it has 4 possible outcomes, each represented by a unique voltage level. Each level may represent a pair of bits (such as 01). For example, -12v could be 00, -6v 01, $+6$v 10 and +12v 11. Here the bit rate is double the baud rate. For example, 3000 changes per second will generate 2 bits for each change resulting in 6000 bits per second (bps). In other words 3000 baud results in 6000 bps.

Real Examples   The above example is overly simple. Real examples are more complicated but based on the same idea. This explains how a modem running at 2400 baud, can send 14400 bps (or higher). The modem achieves a bps rate greater than baud rate by encoding many bits in each signal change (or transition). Thus, when 2 or more bits are encoded per baud, the bps rate exceeds the baud rate. If your modem- to-modem connection is at 14400 bps, it's going to be sending 6 bits per signal transition (or symbol) at 2400 baud. A speed of 28800 bps is obtained by 3200 baud at 9 bits/baud. When people misuse the word baud, they may mean the modem speed (such as 33.6K).

Common modem bps rates were formerly 50, 75, 110, 300, 1200, 2400, 9600. These were also the bps rates over the serial_port-to-modem cables. Today the bps modem-to-modem rates are 14.4K, 28.8K, 33.6K, and 56K, but the common rates over the serialPort-to-modem cables are not the same but are: 19.2K, 38.4K, 57.6K, 115.2K. Using modems with V.42bis compression (max 4:1 compression), rates up to 115.2K bps are possible for 33.6K modems (230.4K is possible for 56K modems).

Except for the 56k modems, most modems run at 2400, 3000, or 3200 baud. Because of the bandwidth limitations on voice-grade phone lines, baud rates greater than 2400 are harder to achieve, and only work under conditions of pristine phone line quality.

How did this confusion between bps and baud start? Well, back when antique low speed modems were high speed modems, the bps rate actually did equal the baud rate. One bit would be encoded per phase change. People would use bps and baud interchangeably, because they were the same number. For example, a 300 bps modem also had a baud rate of 300. This all changed when faster modems came around, and the bit rate exceeded the baud rate. "baud" is named after Emile Baudot, the inventor of the asynchronous telegraph printer. One way this problem gets resolved is to use the term "symbol rate" instead of "baud" and thus avoid using the term "baud".

Addendum C: Terminal Server Connection

This section was adapted from Text-Terminal-HOWTO.

A terminal server is something like an intelligent switch that can connect many modems (or terminals) to one or more computers. It's not a mechanical switch so it may change the speeds and protocols of the streams of data that go thru it. A number of companies make terminal servers: Xyplex, Cisco, 3Com, Computone, Livingston, etc. There are many different types and capabilities. Another HOWTO is needed to compare and describe them (including the possibility of creating your own terminal server with a Linux PC). Most are used for modem connections rather than directly connected terminals.

One use for them is to connect many modems (or terminals) to a high speed network which connects to host computers. Of course the terminal server must have the computing power and software to run network protocols so it is in some ways like a computer. The terminal server may interact with the user and ask what computer to connect to, etc. or it may connect without asking. One may sometimes send jobs to a printer thru a terminal server.

A PC today has enough computing power to act like a terminal server except that each serial port should have its own hardware interrupt. PCs only have a few spare interrupts for this purpose and since they are hard-wired you can't create more by software. A solution is to use an advanced multiport serial card which has its own system of interrupts (or on lower cost models, shares one of the PC's interrupts between a number of ports). See Serial-HOWTO for more info. If such a PC runs Linux with getty running on many serial ports it might be thought of as a terminal server. It is in effect a terminal server if it's linked to other PC's over a network and if its job is mainly to pass thru data and handle the serial port interrupts every 14 (or so) bytes. Software called "radius" is sometimes used.

Today real terminal servers serve more than just terminals. They also serve PC's which emulate terminals, and are sometimes connected to a bank of modems connected to phone lines. Some even include built-in modems. If a terminal (or PC emulating one) is connected directly to a modem, the modem at the other end of the line could be connected to a terminal server. In some cases the terminal server by default expects the callers to use PPP packets, something that real text terminals don't generate.

Addendum D: Other Types of Modems

This HOWTO currently only deals with the common type of modem used to connect PC's to ordinary analog telephone lines. There are various other types of modems, including devices called modems that are not really modems.

Digital-to-Digital "Modems" The standard definition of a modem is sometimes broadened to include "digital" modems. Today direct digital service is now being provided to many homes and offices so a computer there sends out digital signals directly (well almost) into the telephone lines. But a device is still needed to convert the computer digital signal into type allowed on telephone circuits and this device is sometimes called a modem. This HOWTO doesn't cover such modems but some links to documents that do may be found at the start of this HOWTO. The next 3 sections: ISDN, DSL and 56k, concern digital-to-digital "modems".

ISDN "Modems" The "modem" is really a Terminal Adapter (TA). A Debian package isdnutils is available. There is a ISDN Howto in German with an English translation: <http://www.suse.de/Support/sdb_e/isdn.html>. It's put out by the SuSE distribution of Linux and likely is about drivers available in that distribution. There is an isdn4linux package and a newsgroup: de.alt.comm.isdn4linux. Many of the postings are in German. You might try using a search engine (such as DejaNews) to find isdn4linux.

Digital Subscriber Line (DSL) DSL uses the existing twisted pair line from your home (etc.) to the local telephone office. This can be used if your telephone line can accept higher speeds than an ordinary modem (say 56k) sends over it. It replaces the analog-to-digital converter at the local telephone office with a converter which can accept a much faster flow of data (in a different format of course). The device which converts the digital signals from your computer to the signal used to represent digital data on the local telephone line is also called a modem.

56k Digital-Modems For any 56k modem to work as a 56k modem in your home or office the other end must be connected directly to the digital system of the telephone company. Thus ISPs at the other end of the line must obtain special digital modems to provide customers with 56k service. There's more to it than this since banks of many modems are multiplexed onto a high capacity telephone cable that transports a large number of phone calls simultaneously (such as a T1, E1, ISDN PRI, or better line). This requires a concentrator or "remote access server". This has usually been done by stand-alone units (like PC's but they cost much more and have proprietary OSs). Now there are some cards one may insert into a PC's PCI bus to do this.

Leased Line Modems These are analog and not digital modems. These special modems are used on lines leased from the telephone company or sometimes on just a long direct wire hookup. Ordinary modems for a telephone line will not normally work on such a line. An ordinary telephone line has about 40–50 volts (know as the "battery") on it when not in use and the conventional modem uses this voltage for transmission. Furthermore, the telephone company has special signals indicating a ring, line busy, etc. Conventional modems expect and respond to these signals. Connecting two such modems by a long cable will not provide the telephone signals on the cable and thus the modems will not work.

A common type of leased line used two pairs of wires (one for each direction) using V.29 modulation at 9600 baud. Some brands of leased line modems are incompatible with other brands.

C

Linux-Modem

From the online document "Winmodems are not Modems". Full document title: Linux/Modem Compatibility Knowledge Base 2000-01-19, courtesy of Rob Clark <gromitkc@ o2.net>. Copyright © 1998.

So-called Winmodems, host-based, HCF-, HSP-, HSF-, controllerless, host-controlled, and soft modems require vendor-supplied software to do the work of proper hardware modems. The sale of these devices for x86-based PCs is becoming increasingly popular among retailers and OEMs because of the lower cost. However, Winmodems are only appropriate for use with Microsoft Windows on a fast Pentium. A chart summarizing the hardware differences between traditional modems, controllerless and software modems can be found here.

Key to Column A:

WM = Winmodem, only works with Windows software.

LM = Winmodem, may work with vendor-supplied Linux ('Linmodem') driver.

RP = Rockwell RPI chipset, requires DOS or Windows DSP software, may work with error-correction disabled.

OK = Real modem, reported to work with Linux.

Key	FCC ID or Reg #	Model	PNP	Jumpers	Interface	Thanks to:
1RO		ZyXEL Communications				
?	1ROTAI-18563-MD-E	U-1496	?	?	?	
?	1ROTAI-18518-MD-E I88U1496E	U-1496B	?	?	ISA	
?	1ROTAI-65020-MD-E	U-1496E	-	-	EXT	
?	1ROTAI-27669-M5-E	Omni 56K Plus Modem	?	?	?	
?	1ROTAI-27676-M5-E	Omni 56K Modem	?	?	?	
?	1ROTAI-27700-M5-E	ZyXEL Model U-90E external modem; U336E Plus	?	?	?	
2D7		Smart Modular Technologies				
?	2D7USA-27215-PT-E	Palm V Modem 10401U, Workpad C3 Modem 10414W	?	?	?	
?	2D7USA-27294-PT-E	33.6K GSM/Cellular Modem, Palm V Modem 10401, Workpad C3 Modem 10415W	?	?	?	
WM	2D7USA-25335-M5-E	HP Model 90073 for Pavilion PC, Lucent 1646T00 chipset	Yes	No	PCI	Stephen Davis
?	2D7USA-33303-M5-E	GVC D-1156IVT1/R5, HP Model 90079 for Pavilion PC, modem-audio card MDMSM9098-434, 90079-2 "Chameleon"	?	?	PCI	
?	DK4TAI-27049-M5-E	SMART Rapid Transit K56, Quantex MDM-S56/S, Lucent 1643M48 chipset	Yes	No	ISA	
?	2D7USA-34355-M5-T	Smart Modem DSL-V.90, Model 90079	?	?	PCI	
2EO		Best Communication				
		Best 33614D, *possibly same as*				

Key	FCC ID or Reg #	Model	PNP	Jumpers	Interface	Thanks to:
OK	?	Echo iv336DC , Encore ENF633-IV-DA , Davicom chipset	Yes	No	ISA	Henry Shafiq
WM	2EOTAI-24973-M5-E	Cnet CN5614CH, Cirrus Logic MD5620DT chipset	Yes	No	PCI	Uwe Klein
WM	2EOTAI-25534-M5-E	Best, Prolink, Supermicro, NSL, Encore, Edek, CNet 5614PC	?	?	PCI	
?	2EOTAI-25561-M5-E	Best, Prolink, Supermicro, NSL, Encore, Edek, CNet 5614PH	?	?	?	
WM	2EOTAI-25861-M5-E	Best, Prolink, Supermicro, NSL, Encore, Edek, CNet 5614LP(A) , Lucent LT WinModem chipset	Yes	?	PCI	
WM	2EOTAI-25866-M5-E	CNet Technology CN5614C(P)H , Cirrus Logic CLM chipset	Yes	?	PCI	
OK	2EOTAI-27128-M5-E	Best, Prolink, Supermicro, NSL, Encore, Edek, CNet 5614MX/ 5614XE /5614DE, Cirrus Logic CL-MD5650 chipset	-	-	EXT	Matt Stoodley
2H9		Lectron				
?	2H9TAI-30436-PT-E	CTX 33.6 Deluxe PNP Modem	?	?	?	
OK	-	Accord 33.6K Voice internal. Model H33RFSP-H0, Rockwell chipset Genica/ GCT	Yes	No	ISA	Olivier Vialatte
WM	2H9TAI-25492-M5-E	I56LVP-F0, Lucent chipset	Yes	No	PCI	Brian J McCloud
?	2H9TAI-34597-M5-E	Pragmatic I56LVP-F3	?	?	PCI	
?	2H9TAI-25941-M5-E	Pragmatic O56LVP-FV	?	?	?	

491

This is the Linux/Modem Compatibility Knowledge Base at http://www.o2.net/~gromitkc/winmodem.html

Key	FCC ID or Reg #	Model	PNP	Jumpers	Interface	Thanks to:
?	2H9TAI-27024-M5-E	Pragmatic I56EVP/I56ESP	?	?	?	
?	2H9TAI-27091-M5-E	Pragmatic 156RSP/156RVP	?	?	?	
WM	2H9TAI-27142-M5-E	Pragmatic I56LVP-F1, Lucent 1646T00/1034AH (Mars) chipset	Yes	No	PCI	
?	2H9TAI-27146-M5-E	Pragmatic I56PSP-F1, PCTel chipset	?	?	?	
?	2H9TAI-27632-M5-E	Pragmatic/Accord R56XVP	?	?	?	
?	2H9TAI-27633-M5-E	Pragmatic U56SVP	?	?	USB	
?	2H9TAI-27845-M5-E	Pragmatic C56XVP internal	?	?	?	
?	2H9TAI-32398-M5-E	Pragmatic H56LVP-F0, Lucent chipset	?	?	?	
?	2H9TAI-33009-M5-E	Pragmatic I56PSP-F0/I56PVP, PCTel chipset	?	?	PCI	
?	2H9TAI-40109-M5-E	Pragmatic N56PSP	?	?	?	
2M3		Ardmore Technology				
?	2M3TAI-27540-M5-E	Ardmore Faxboard-4, RASModem-4, ModemBoard-4, Plus-4RAS, PlusRAS-4M, PlusFax-4, MFax-4	?	?	?	
2U6		Xircom				
?	2U6USA-22701-MM-E	28.8 CreditCard Modem	-	-	PCMCIA	
?	2U6USA-22654-MM-E	28.8 CreditCard Modem+Ethernet	-	-	PCMCIA	
OK	2U6USA-24058-M5-E	CreditCard Ethernet+Modem 33.6 Model CEM33	-	-	PCMCIA	Karl Buck

Key	FCC ID or Reg #	Model	PNP	Jumpers	Interface	Thanks to:
?	2U6USA-24769-M5-E	CreditCard Modem CM-56G(MD) GlobalACCESS	-	-	PCMCIA	
?	2U6MLA-25820-M5-E	Realport Modem RM56V1	-	-	PCMCIA	
?	2U6MLA-27849-M5-E	MPCI3A56G-100, Mini PCI type 3A Global Modem + Ethernet	?	?	?	
?	2U6MLA-27852-M5-E	Realport R2M56GA, 2 modem 56G GlobalAccess	?	?	?	
OK	2U6USA-31569-M5-E	CreditCard Ethernet 10/100+Modem 56 CEM56-100	-	-	PCMCIA	Tilo Nitzsche
OK	2U6MLA-32433-M5-E	Creditcard Modem CM56T	-	-	PCMCIA	Dave Looney
OK	2U6MLA-33041-M5-E	RealPort 56-GlobalACCESS RM56G	-	-	PCMCIA	Mark Edwards
OK	2U6MLA-33177-M5-E ANOMLA-33642-M5-E	RealPort CardBus Modem RBM56G, RBEM56G-100 with Ethernet, IBM XWIN/002	-	-	PCMCIA	Atul Chitnis
?	2U6MLA-33657-M5-E EJMMLA-33641-M5-E	Xircom RBEPM56G-100, Intel MBLA3456 cardbus type III integrated PC Card Ethernet 10/100+modem	-	-	PCMCIA	
?	2U6MLA-33742-M5-E	Xircom MPCI2B-56G Mini PCI 56K modem card	?	?	?	
?	2U6MLA-33924-M5-E	Xircom MPCI1B-56G Mini PCI 56K modem card	?	?	?	
?	2U6MLA-34036-M5-E	Xircom MPCI1B56G-100 Mini PCI 56K modem card	?	?	?	

493

Key	FCC ID or Reg #	Model	PNP	Jumpers	Interface	Thanks to:
?	2U6MLA-34086-M5-E	Xircom MPCI2B56G-100 Mini PCI 56K modem card with Ethernet	?	?	?	
?	2U6MLA-34087-M5-E	Xircom CBM56WG	?	-	PCMCIA	
?	2U6MLA-34347-M5-E	Xircom CFM56G	?	-	PCMCIA	
?	2U6MLA-34497-M5-E	Xircom CBM56W	?	-	PCMCIA	
?	2U6MLA-34606-M5-E	Xircom STM56V1	-	-	EXT	
?	2U6MLA-34607-M5-E	Xircom STM56G	-	-	EXT	
?	2U6MLA-34622-M5-E	Xircom M3B56G Mini-PCI 56K	?	?	?	
?	2U6MLA-34623-M5-E	Xircom R2BM56WG 2-line external 56K	-	-	EXT	
3A4		Radicom Research				
?	?	Radicom 560I-ACF	Yes	Yes	ISA	
WM	3A4USA-25857-M5-E	Radicom 560PCI/HSF Soft Modem	Yes	No	PCI	
?	3A4USA-27802-M5-E	Radicom 336I-AC(P)/2, 336I-SVD(P)/2, 560I-AC(P)/2, 560I-SVD(P)/2 K56flex internal modem	?	?	?	
WM	3A4USA-32968-M5-E	Radicom/Bitmaster 560PCI/SP , Harmony 18023-1, V.90/K56Flex , Rockwell HCF chipset	Yes	No	PCI	
?	3A4USA-33618-M5-E	Radicom serial module modem for notebook 560MM-T2M, 336MM-T2	?	?	?	
?	3A4USA-33919-M5-E	Parallel Module Modem 560MM-P, 336MM-P, 240MM-P	?	?	?	

Key	FCC ID or Reg #	Model	PNP	Jumpers	Interface	Thanks to:

Key	FCC ID or Reg #	Model	PNP	Jumpers	Interface	Thanks to:
	4AE	M-G Communication				
?	4AETAI-27680-M5-E	Ablecom AMR001, Kinpo 56MGAMR, Lucky Star 5614ARM, M-G MG56AMR, AMR modem	?	?	?	
	4J2	Aztech Systems				
WM	4J2SNG-25080-M5-E	56K PCI Modem, Model MDP3858-U, MDP3858SP-U, MDP3858V-U, Rockwell HCF chipset	Yes	No	PCI	
?	?	Model MS5000 33.6/56K Soft Modem, PCTel chipset	?	?	?	
WM	4J2SNG-25441-M5-E	Model MDP7800 56K PCI Modem, Lucent Mars II Winmodem chipset	Yes	?	PCI	
WM	4J2SNG-25598-M5-E	Model MSP3880-U(X) , Rockwell RS56-PCI (6795-11) HSF chipset (SoftModem)	?	?	PCI	
WM	4J2SNG-25905-M5-E	Model MF5800, 56K PCI Softmodem, PCTel chipset	?	?	PCI	
?	4J2SNG-27211-M5-E	Model AT3880-U DSP/MMX, AT3880MMX	?	?	PCI	
?	4J2SNG-27505-M5-E	Model MSP3880SP-U(X), MSP3880V-U(X)	?	?	?	
WM	4J2SNG-27506-M5-E	Model MSP5900-U(X), Best Data 56K Mach 2 Model A56FW-PCI, PCTel PCT789T-A chipset	Yes	No	PCI	
?	4J2SNG-27547-M5-E	Model MDP3880-W(X) [X=A-Z optional]	?	?	PCI	
?	4J2SNG-27730-M5-E	Model MDP3900(V)-U(X)	?	?	PCI	
?	4J2SNG-27847-M5-E	Model MDP3930(V)-W(X) [X=A-Z optional]	?	?	?	
?	4J2SNG-27562-M5-E	Model MR8800-U(X), AMR bus PC card V.90/K56flex data modem w/V.17 fax NewCom 56kifxspA v.90 Speakerphone	?	?	?	

Key	FCC ID or Reg #	Model	PNP	Jumpers	Interface	Thanks to:
?	4J2SNG-24732-M5-E	, Aztech MF3850-U(B), Rockwell RCVDL56ACFW/SP R6771-22 chipset	Yes	No	ISA	Matt Thomas
OK	4J2SNG-32038-M5-E	NewCom 56kefxspA v.90 Speakerphone Model EM6800-U(X)	-	-	EXT	Ryan Howell
OK	4J2SNG-33194-M5-E	, TI TMS320x2A chipset 56K PCI Modem, Model MDP3858-UE	-	-	EXT	Kevin Gray
WM	4J2SNG-33392-M5-E	, MDP3858-UE(A), MDP3858SP-UE Model UM9800-U/UM9800(X)	Yes	No	PCI	
	4J2SNG-33497-M5-E	external 56K with USB, SGS Thompson ST7554/ST7550 chipset	-	-	USB	
?	4J2SNG-33739-M5-E	Model MDP3880-U(X)	?	?	PCI	
WM	?	Model MD6802-U, TI chipset	Yes	No	ISA	

Key	FCC ID or Reg #	Model	PNP	Jumpers	Interface	Thanks to:
4N4		C-One Technology				
?	4N4TAI-32956-M5-E	Pretec/TDK Model C2VFM-5614RA	?	-	PCMCIA	
?	4N4TAI-33282-M5-E	Pretec/Compaq Model C2VFM-5614RB, C2VFM-5614RD	?	-	PCMCIA	
4O6		Great Concept Development				
OK	?	Actionwell ActionMedia AC5602 , Cirrus Logic chipset, *possibly same as NewCom 56kifxC*	Yes	Yes	ISA	Actionwell
WM	4O6HKG-33202-M5-E	Actionwell ActionMedia AC5618 Combo Express Modio , Analog Devices (HSP) chipset NewCom 33.6kifxC data/fax , Cirrus Logic CL-MD3450 chipset, *possibly same as Actionwell ActionMedia*	Yes	No	ISA	Rajesh Narayanan NewCom, Nathan Lee

This is the Linux/Modem Compatibility Knowledge Base at http://www.o2.net/~gromitkc/winmodem.html

Key	FCC ID or Reg #	Model	PNP	Jumpers	Interface	Thanks to:
OK	406CHN-31735-PT-E	AC3420	Yes	Yes	ISA	
	409	CIS Technology (Wisecom)				
	L40WS-1414EV1					
?	409TAI-22475-MM-E	Fada WS-1414EV1	?	?	?	
	L40WS-1414EV3					
RP	409TAI-22708-PT-E	Hi-Tech 14400 Fax/Modem Model WS-1414EV3 MaxLink/Wisecom WS-2814IM4, AT&T (Lucent) chipset	-	-	EXT	Rob Clark
OK	?	Wisecom WS-3314JS3, Harmony HM18010-3, chipset	No	Yes	ISA	Kevin Specht
?	?	Wisecom WS-3314JS3, Harmony HM18010-3, Rockwell RCV336ACF/SP chipset	?	No	ISA	
	L40WS-5614JS3					
OK	409TAI-31505-M5-E	Wisecom Accelerator Pro WS-5614JS3, Harmony HM18020-4, Rockwell RCV56DLACF/SP chipset	Yes	Yes	ISA	garv , Brian Reddy
?	?	Wisecom HY-5614WM8, Cardinal 08-0304E, Cardinal 8711US, Practical Peripherals 8601US, Practical Peripherals PM56K HC	?	?	?	
?	?	Wisecom HY-5614JMH, Hayes ACCURA 4702US, Hayes ACCURA ACC56K, Practical Peripherals 4708US, Practical Peripherals PM56KF HC	?	?	?	
OK	409TAI-24727-M5-E	Wisecom Accelerator Pro WS-5614ES3, CIS WS-5614ES3KV, Creative DE5620-2, Actebis/Targa 5614ES3G, Rockwell chipset	-	-	EXT	Alan J. Madler David Morgan
	L40WS-5614ES3					
OK	409TAI-24727-M5-E	Creative ModemBlaster DE5620-2 "Flash 56 II External"	Yes	-	EXT	, Shawn Gu

Key	FCC ID or Reg #	Model	PNP	Jumpers	Interface	Thanks to:
?	409TAI-25583-M5-E	Wisecom WS-5614JS8, TI chipset	Yes	?	ISA	
?	409TAI-25575-M5-E	Wisecom WS-5614ES8, TI chipset	-	-	EXT	Lidong Zhang
WM	L40WS-5614WMC	WS-5614WMC V.90 Flex 56K ISA D/F modem, IBM Aptiva Model 2153 Exx LT Winmodem, Lucent 1641B (Luna) chipset	Yes	No	ISA	Hugo Vanwoerkom
	409TAI-25865-M5-E	WS-5614PVD				
WM	409CHN-25935-M5-E	* , Lucent Mars2 chipset (LT Winmodem)	Yes	No	PCI	Robert MacDougall
?	409TAI-25871-M5-E	OEM/CIS WS-5614BMDG, AC/BM-5614GMDG for notebook	?	?	?	
	409TAI-27093-M5-E	Wisecom WS-5614ES2A , Mitac MDM-56KVR-2, Digicom/Creative DE5620-3, Rockwell ACF-2 chipset	-	-	EXT	
	409TAI-27302-M5-E	WS-5614PM2A(G),				
WM	409CHN-33696-M5-E	WS-5614PS3A / WS-5614PS3A(G) with speakerphone, OEM GM56PCI-R(V), Trust Communicator 56K PCI Winmodem , Rockwell RHP56D R6789-52 (HCF-2) chipset	Yes	No	PCI	
?	409TAI-27349-M5-E	OEM M3-5614PM3	?	?	?	
?	409TAI-27304-M5-E	WS-5614EMF	?	?	?	

Key	FCC ID or Reg #	Model	PNP	Jumpers	Interface	Thanks to:
	409TAI-27383-M5-E	OEM/Wisecom WS-5614PSL, Genius GE56PCI-SM, Pine FM-3721, Motorola chipset				
WM	409CHN-27384-M5-E		Yes	No	PCI	
?	409TAI-27396-M5-E	OEM/Wisecom WS-5614HSM	?	?	?	
?	409TAI-27399-M5-E	OEM/Wisecom WS-LM560	?	?	?	
?	409TAI-27413-M5-E	OEM/				
	409TAI-33925-M5-E	Wisecom WS-5614PM3C PCI SoftModem Card, Genius GM56PCI-SR, Rockwell RS56-PCI R6793-12 (HSF) chipset				
WM			?	No	PCI	
?	409TAI-27446-M5-E	CIS M3-5614PS3	?	?	?	
?	409TAI-27594-M5-E	CIS/Cruiser/Fastsurfr/Prolink/Targa/Wisecom WS-5614PS3D				
?	409CHN-27679-M5-E		?	?	?	
	409TAI-27630-M5-E	CIS/Pine/Trust/Wisecom WS-5614DML, AMR 56K Data/Fax modem card				
?	409CHN-27694-M5-E		?	?	?	
?	409TAI-27631-M5-E	CIS/Pine/Trust/Wisecom WS-5614EV1, 56K External D/F/V modem				
?	409CHN-27691-M5-E		?	?	?	
WM	409TAI-32589-M5-E	OEM Mx/WS-5614PM3, Rockwell RLDL56DPF R6785-68 (HCF) chipset	Yes	No	PCI	
	409TAI-33339-M5-E					

Key	FCC ID or Reg #	Model	PNP	Jumpers	Interface	Thanks to:
?	409CHN-33340-M5-E	WS-5614PME	?	?	ISA	
?	409TAI-33426-M5-E	WS-5614BCJ Notebook modem	?	?	?	
	409TAI-33531-M5-E	Wisecom WS-5614ES2A, Mitac MDM-56KVR-2, Digicom/Creative DE5620-3, Rockwell ACF-2 chipset (manuf. by Plum				
?	409CHN-33531-M5-E	Microsystems)	-	-	EXT	
?	409TAI-33787-M5-E	OEM/Wisecom WS-5614HMM	?	?	PCI	
WM	409TAI-33880-M5-E	OEM/				
?	409CHN-34041-M5-E	Wisecom WS-5614PS3C PCI SoftModem Card with speakerphone, Mitac MDM-56KVR	?	No	PCI	
	409TAI-33881-M5-E	OEM/Wisecom WS-5614PM3D, Genius GM56PCI-R				
?	409CHN-34040-M5-E		?	?	PCI	
	409TAI-33939-M5-E					
?	409TAI-27681-M5-E	OEM/CIS WS-5614ES2B	?	?	EXT	
	409TAI-34274-M5-E					
?	409CHN-27887-M5-E	OEM/CIS WS-5614UVS	?	?	USB	
?	409TAI-34508-M5-E	CIS/Wisecom WS-5614DME	?	?	PCI	

Key	FCC ID or Reg #	Model	PNP	Jumpers	Interface	Thanks to:
?	409TAI-34509-M5-E	OEM WS-5614FMU	?	?	PCI	
	409CHN-40062-M5-E					
?	409CHN-40124-M5-E	CIS FC-5614DML	?	?	?	
4R7		Intellicard Systems				
	L4UICS144-TE01					
?	4R7SNG-22158-MM-E	Model CS14.4TE	-	-	PCMCIA	
4U6		IBM Japan				
?	4U6JPN-27205-MM-E	Mini-PCI Modem I	?	?	?	
	6MMJPN-34526-M5-E					
?	6MMPHL-34527-M5-E	Mini-PCI Modem, Mini-PCI Modem with Voice	?	?	?	

Key	FCC ID or Reg #	Model	PNP	Jumpers	Interface	Thanks to:
	4V4	Diamond Multimedia				
RP	?	SupraExpress 144i RPI	No	Yes	ISA	
?	?	SupraExpress 144i PNP	Yes	?	ISA	
OK	?	SupraExpress 144i Plus	No	Yes	ISA	Jeff Scarbrough
OK	FCZ5D3450125	SupraExpress 288 PnP	-	-	EXT	Jim Gallagher
	FCZ5D3450129i					
OK	FCZUSA-22556-MM-E	SupraExpress 288i PnP	Yes	No	ISA	Michael Patterson
	FCZ5D3450131i					
?	FCZUSA-23030-MM-E	SupraExpress 288i PnP	Yes	?	ISA	
OK	FCZ5D3288FXWJB	SupraExpress 288 External Fax/Modem	-	-	EXT	Enrico Benucci

Key	FCC ID or Reg #	Model	PNP	Jumpers	Interface	Thanks to:
?	?	SupraSonic 336V+, Rockwell RCV228DPi R6682-24 chipset	-	-	EXT	
OK	?	SupraExpress 336i V+	Yes	No	ISA	J M Cabrera
OK	FCZ503450160					
OK	4V4USA-24033-PT-E	SupraExpress 336i Sp	Yes	No	ISA	Paul Momany
?	?	SupraExpress 336i PnP Voice, Quantex MDM-DFV336/D, Rockwell chipset	Yes	No	ISA	
?	?	Model 2084/2480/2490, SupraExpress 56i Sp :(Linux setup	Yes	No	ISA	
OK	4V4USA-24801-M5-E	)	Yes	Yes	ISA	Ipshita and Supratim Sanyal
OK	4V4USA-24801-M5-E	Model 2121/2122/2123/2124/2125, SupraExpress 56i Voice	Yes	No	ISA	C C McPherson
OK	4V4USA-24801-M5-E	Model 2072/2073/2074, SupraExpress 56i	Yes	Yes	ISA	Rain
OK	4V4USA-25283-M5-E	Model 2420, SupraExpress 56e XPR56EPC-XL1S, Rockwell ACF chipset	-	-	EXT	Francis Davidson
?	4V4USA-25573-PT-E	Model 2500/2510/2520/2540, Supra PCI 56i/Sp/Voice	?	?	PCI	
?	4V4USA-27172-M5-E	Model LT2500, Supra 56i PCI	?	?	PCI	
OK	4V4USA-27286-M5-E	Model 2720 SupraExpress 56i Sp V.90, Model 2710 SupraExpress 56i Voice V.90	Yes	Yes	ISA	Jason Smale
WM	4V4USA-25708-M5-E	Model 2380/2390/2560 SupraExpress 56i Pro	?	?	PCI	
OK	4V4USA-40108-M5-E	SupraExpress 56e Pro	-	-	EXT	Ralph Furness
OK	4V4USA-27274-M5-E	Model 2730 SupraExpress 56e V.90, Product number XPR56EPC-XL1S, Rockwell chipset	-	-	EXT	Jimmy Shen
?	4V4USA-25918-M5-E	Model 2640/2660/2670 Supra SST 56	?	?	?	

Key	FCC ID or Reg #	Model	PNP	Jumpers	Interface	Thanks to:
WM	4V4USA-27387-M5-E	Model 2750 SupraMax 56K, Model 2770 Supra SST 56I, Conexant (Rockwell) RS56D-PCI (HCF) chipset	Yes	No	PCI	Beiad Ian Q. Dalton
OK	4V4USA-31098-M5-E	SupraSonic II 2-line	Yes	Yes	ISA	Michael J Surette Dave C.
OK	4V4USA-31098-M5-E	Model 2090/2091 SupraExpress 56e K56	Yes	-	EXT	Carlos Tondreau C.
OK	4V4USA-32453-M5-E	Model 2440 SupraSonic II V.90 2-line	Yes	Yes	ISA	Andrew Robinson
?	4V4USA-25825-PT-E	Model 2620 SupraSonic II PCI dual modem	?	?	PCI	
WM	4V4USA-32554-M5-E	Model 2580 Supra 56i HCF	?	?	?	
WM	4V4USA-32554-M5-E	SupraMax 56K ISA, Model 2300 (SUP2300), Diamond Multimedia controllerless chipset	Yes	No	ISA	
WM	4V4USA-26263-M5-E	SupraMax 56K PCI, Model 2260/2370, SM56IPC-XL1, Rockwell chipset	Yes	No	PCI	Doug Wright
?	4V4USA-25825-PT-E	SupraMax 56K USB	?	?	?	
4W4		First International Computer				
?	4W4TAI-25688-M5-E	NEC LAVTE NX/V1456VQL19M/VERSA NOTE/VERSAPRO NX/ZDS VERSA NOTE, FIC Model 57XXXX internal for notebook	?	?	?	
?	4W4TAI-32933-M5-E	Leo 56MRSF internal modem for notebook	?	?	?	

	FCC ID or Reg #	Model	PNP	Jumpers	Interface	Thanks to:
4X2		3Com/U.S. Robotics				

Key	FCC ID or Reg #	Model	PNP	Jumpers	Interface	Thanks to:
OK	4X2USA-32128-M5-E	Model 5605 (80-5605-00), Model 0525, 56K V90 Pro External USB-ready	-	-	EXT	Clemens Huebner
WM	?	Model 5683-01/5683-03, 56K Winmodem	Yes	?	ISA	Bo Bolinaga
OK	CJEUSA-31214-M5-E	Model 5685-00, Voice Faxmodem (56K, x2, V.90)	Yes	Yes/No	16-bit ISA	Greg Foley, Steven Tsai
OK	?	Model 5685, Voice Faxmodem (56K, x2, V.90)	Yes	No	16-bit ISA	Bill Staehle, Dave Furey
OK	4X2USA-25223-M5-E	Model 5687-00 Faxmodem not 5687-02! Check the barcode carefully!	Yes	Yes	8-bit ISA	Gilles Carrier, Bill Staehle
	4X2USA-25223-M5-E	Model 0584, Model 5687-02 Check the barcode carefully!	Yes	No	16-bit ISA	Bill Staehle
OK	4X2USA-25223-M5-E	Model 5687-03 Check the barcode carefully!: Linux FAQ	Yes	Yes	16-bit ISA	Kurt Savegnago, Jared Smith, The Mighty Mike Master
?	4X2USA-26032-DT-E	Palm Pilot Modem	-	-	Sync	
?	4X2USA-27083-M5-E	Model 3293, Model 3294 Office Connect 56K Business	-	-	EXT/USB	
OK	4X2USA-32034-M5-E	Model 0726, V.90 56K Internal Faxmodem PCI Model 3CP2977-OEM-50	*	No	PCI	Jose Santiago
OK	4X2USA-32034-M5-E	Model 0727, V.90 56K Internal Faxmodem PCI Model 3CP2976-OEM-50	*	No	PCI	Oliver Schulze L.
OK	4X2USA-32034-M5-E	Model 0726, V.90 56K Internal Faxmodem PCI Model 3CP5610, TI "KERMIT" chipset	*	No	PCI	Allan W. Schlaugat, Ron Z

Key	FCC ID or Reg #	Model	PNP	Jumpers	Interface	Thanks to:
?	?	V.90 56K Internal Voice Faxmodem PCI Model 3CP5609	?	?	PCI	
?	?	Model 0787, 56K Fax/Modem Card for PC	?	?	?	
OK	4X2USA-34207-M5-E	Model 0701 (5686-03), Model 0710-D Sportster External	-	-	EXT	Sebastien Nicoud
WM	4X2USA-33236-M5-E	Model 5698-00, PCI Internet Discovery Modem	?	?	PCI	
WM	?	Model 2810, Voice Faxmodem Pro/Plus for Windows	Yes	No	PCI	
WM	?	Model 2974 (66297480) (OEM "Alana") 56K PCI Winmodem D/F/V	Yes	No	PCI	
WM		USR 56k Voice Win RS Rev 1.00.021 (83297400) (Dell OEM) 56K PCI Winmodem D/F/V	Yes	No	PCI	Green Manalishi ,
WM	4X2USA-25314-M5-E	Model 0637 [662974-81] (OEM "Alana") 56K PCI Winmodem	Yes	No	PCI	John Smith
WM	4X2USA-25314-M5-E	Model 0637-D (0421-00, 66297500 R:2) (OEM "Coyote") 56K PCI Winmodem Data/Fax; Model 5690-00 D/F/V; Model 0642	Yes	No	PCI	Steven Tsai , Rob Clark
WM	?	56K PCI Winmodem Model 5699-00	Yes	No	PCI	
?	4X2USA-34111-M5-E	56K PCI Model 0711	?	No	PCI	
?	?	V.90 56K Internal Voice Faxmodem PCI Model 3CP5609	?	?	PCI	
WM	?	IBM 56K Voice Modem Internet Kit V.90, Model 10L7389 (IBM3791)	Yes	No	ISA	
WM	?	Model 1783, Sportster 56K Winmodem	Yes	?	ISA	
OK	?	Model 1785, Sportster 56K Voice Faxmodem, TI chipset	Yes	Yes	ISA	Mel Roth

Key	FCC ID or Reg #	Model	PNP	Jumpers	Interface	Thanks to:
	This is the Linux/Modem Compatibility Knowledge Base at http://www.o2.net/~gromitkc/winmodem.html					
OK	?	Model 1171, Sportster 33.6K Voice Faxmodem	?	Yes	ISA	Ken Draper
?	?	Model 1172, Sportster 33.6K Voice Faxmodem	-	-	EXT	

Key	FCC ID or Reg #	Model	PNP	Jumpers	Interface	Thanks to:
	This is the Linux/Modem Compatibility Knowledge Base at http://www.o2.net/~gromitkc/winmodem.html					
5A4		LASAT Communications				
		LASAT Safire 560 Voice / Web Set Go 56.000V				Karol Kasanicky
?	5A4FRC-25963-M5-E	, Model LC-1891	-	-	EXT	
?	5A4THA-33744-M5-E	LASAT LC-1911	-	-	EXT	
5AK		Sysgration				
	HQX96113-14A					
OK	5AKTAI-30768-PT-E	Sysgration 33.6K external, Model M33 ESF	-	-	EXT	
?		Sysgration SYS-ME56001 Speakerphone modem	-	-	EXT	
?		Sysgration SYS-ME56002 Speakerphone modem	-	-	EXT	
?		Sysgration SYS-ME56003 Speakerphone modem	-	-	EXT	
?		Sysgration SYS-ME56004 Speakerphone modem	-	-	EXT	
?		Sysgration SYS-ME56005 Speakerphone modem	-	-	EXT	
?		Sysgration SYS-MI56001 hardware modem	?	?	ISA	
?		Sysgration SYS-MI56002 hardware modem , Rockwell RC56-D chipset	Yes	Yes	ISA	
WM	5AKTAI-32445-M5-E	SurfRider Technology SurfNet ISA Model SM56VP, Motorola L42005540000 chipset	Yes	No	ISA	
WM	?	Sysgration SYS-MC56001 , Rockwell HCF chipset	Yes	No	PCI	

Key	FCC ID or Reg #	Model	PNP	Jumpers	Interface	Thanks to:
WM	?	Sysgration SYS-MC56003, Rockwell HCF chipset	Yes	No	PCI	
	5AKTAI-33398-PT-E	Amquest AM56Soft				
	5CRKOR-25848-M5-E	, Panacom PM56RS				
WM		, Sysgration SYS-MS56005, Rockwell RS56/SP-PCI11P1 R6793-21 (HSF) chipset	Yes	No	PCI	
WM	5AKTAI-27299-M5-E	Panacom PM56MS, Agiler/Solomon/ Sysgration MS56006, Wintop WIN5606, Motorola HSP chipset	Yes	No	PCI	
?	5AKTAI-33821-M5-E	Sysgration SYS-MC56003, Panacom PM56RH	?	?	PCI	
5BK		Delta Electronics				
?	5BKTAI-27670-M5-E	Delta O56LDP-FB2 56K d/f modem for notebook	?	?	?	
5BQ		Fujitsu				
?	5BQJPN-25675-M5-E	Lifebook E342/E351/E360/E370/E380	?	?	?	
?	5BQJPN-25762-MM-E	Lifebook C360/C352	?	?	?	
?	5BQJPN-31476-M5-E	Lifebook L460	?	?	?	
?	5BQJPN-25762-MM-E	Lifebook L440/L470	?	?	?	
?	5BQUSA-31940-M5-E	Lifebook C325/C340/C350/C332/C342/C353	?	?	?	
?	5BQUSA-34065-M5-E	Lifebook B142	?	?	?	
5C1		Kingmax Technology				

Key	FCC ID or Reg #	Model	PNP	Jumpers	Interface	Thanks to:
?	5C1TAI-32955-PT-E	KFM3360-LF, BFM3360-LF	-	-	PCMCIA	
?	5C1TAI-27320-M5-E	KFM5600-RF, BFM5600-RF	-	-	PCMCIA	
?	5C1TAI-27418-M5-E	KUM5600-LF, BUM5600-LF USB modem	?	?	?	
?	5C1TAI-27740-M5-E	KMM5600-LF, BMM5600-LF Mini-PCI modem Kingmax KFM5600-C,	?	?	?	
OK	5C1USA-32272-M5-E	Hawking Technology V.90/x2 Model 121-PN610-X2 Kingmax KFM5600-L, BFM5602-LF; Hawking Technology Model 121-PN610K-K56-FLEX	-	-	PCMCIA	Bob Martin
OK	5C1TAI-32744-M5-E	(PN610-Flex)	-	-	PCMCIA	Colin Roald
?	5C1TAI-33419-M5-E	KFM5603-LF, BFM5603-LF	-	-	PCMCIA	
?	5C1TAI-33726-M5-E	KFM5600-LF, BFM5600-LF	-	-	PCMCIA	
?	5C1TAI-34371-M5-E	KLM56200LF, BLM5620-LF	-	-	PCMCIA	
?	5C1TAI-34524-M5-E	KFM5605-LF, BFM5605-LF	-	-	PCMCIA	
5CC						
		Jaton				
OK	5CCUSA-25346-M5-E	Modulator V.90, Rockwell RC56D/SP-PnP chipset, Model MORO2C56ISA	Yes	Yes	ISA	Jim
OK	5CCUSA-25691-M5-E	Communicator II, Model MOTI320ISA, TI chipset Traveler 56 ISA , Rockwell RC56D/SP chipset	Yes	Yes	ISA	Maciej Samsel , Jaton
OK	?	Traveler V.90Ex	Yes	Yes	ISA	Jaton
OK	?	Communicator V.90	-	-	EXT	Jaton

Key	FCC ID or Reg #	Model	PNP	Jumpers	Interface	Thanks to:
OK	5CCUSA-31989-M5-E	, Cirrus Logic 5650/5652 chipset	Yes	Yes	ISA	Jaton
WM	5CCUSA-33096-M5-E	WinMOD V.90, Model 6L5WQ43, Lucent L56xMF chipset	?	?	PCI	
WM	5CCUSA-33413-M5-E	WinMOD II, Model 66212	?	?	PCI	
WM	5CCUSA-33289-M5-E	WinCruise V.90-SL, Model 6P5WS	?	?	PCI	
WM	MOCR5620PCI	WinComm V.90, Cirrus Logic CL-MD5620T chipset	Yes	No	PCI	Paul D. López
?	5CCUSA-33735-M5-E	Explorer V.90Ex, Model 63219	-	-	EXT	
?	5CCUSA-40003-M5-E	Model MORORP56DISAEX	?	?	?	
?	5CCUSA-27737-M5-E	USB Communicator				
?	5CCUSA-27797-M5-E	, Model 65218, 56K d/f with voicemail and caller ID	-	-	USB	
5CH		Freetek Technology				
WM	?	GC789, PCTel 789 HSP chipset	Yes	No	PCI	
	5CHCHN-33708-M5-E	56K PCI Modem PCT1789,				
WM	IIAUSA-33260-M5-E	GC1789, PCTel 1789 HSP MicroModem chipset	Yes	No	PCI	
WM	5CHCHN-25904-M5-E	Epic/ Freetek GC560PCT, PC Blvd MD56INFDV, PCTel 388 HSP chipset	Yes	No	ISA	

Key	FCC ID or Reg #	Model	PNP	Jumpers	Interface	Thanks to:
5CN		Bay Networks				

Key	FCC ID or Reg #	Model	PNP	Jumpers	Interface	Thanks to:
?	5CNTAI-34334-M5-E	HomeNet Card Model PA301, 56K fax/10 mbps Ethernet	?	?	PCI	
	5CQ	3J Tech				
?	5CQTAI-34373-M5-E	3J Tech PMIR PM(I)-33600, PM(I)-56000 stand-alone 56k d/f modem with IRDH port for Windows CE, Palmtop & PC	?	?	?	
	5CR	Mac System				
?	5CRKOR-25846-M5-E	Messenger 56K MM560PMW, Amquest AM56PCMCIA	-	-	PCMCIA	
WM	5CRKOR-25847-M5-E	Messenger 56K, Amquest AM56PCT, OEM FM560PT, Messenger 56K HPNA Model EOne, Rockwell chipset (HCF)	?	?	PCI	
WM	5CRKOR-25848-M5-E	Messenger 56K SVM56RI, Micrologic 56K SFM560RI, Amquest AM56HSF(SP-A), Amquest AM56HSF-A, Messenger/Micrologic MW560CI, Baytek AM56HSF, Rockwell RS56/SP-PCI11P1 R6793-21 chipset				
WM	5AKTAI-33398-PT-E	Messenger 56K USB560ST, Amquest AM56USB, Foretech WTC560USB, Micro Logic 56K USB560ST, V.90 USB modem	Yes	No	PCI	Denis Murphy
?	5CRKOR-27334-M5-E	Messenger/Micrologic HD560RI, Amquest AM56H2L, PCI 2-line V.90 D/F/V	?	?	?	
?	5CRKOR-27374-M5-E	Messenger FM560PTMN, Foretech 560PTMN, Sens SFM-1700PW, 56K mini-PCI modem	?	?	PCI	
?	5CRKOR-27891-M5-E	Messenger MR560LPM, Foretech 560MR, Samsung LT560ADW SFM-4100PW, 56K modem riser	?	?	?	
?	5CRKOR-27892-M5-E		?	?	?	
	5DI	Foresson				
?	5DITAI-25977-M5-E	FX2006 internal for Falcon notebook, Rockwell chipset	?	?	?	

Key	FCC ID or Reg #	Model	PNP	Jumpers	Interface	Thanks to:
?	5DITAI-25986-M5-E	FX2021 internal for notebook	?	?	?	
?	5DITAI-34123-M5-E	FX2037 modem module	?	?	?	
?	5DITAI-34124-M5-E	FX2036 modem module	?	?	?	
?	5DITAI-32978-M5-E	FX2052 internal	?	?	?	
?	5DITAI-33315-M5-E	P90 external 56K modem	?	?	?	
?	5DITAI-33512-M5-E	FX2054 internal for notebook	?	?	?	
5DO		Acer Netxus				
?	5DOTAI-27347-M5-E	Acer AMI-PA07P-X/X	?	?	?	
?	5DOTAI-27351-M5-E	Acer AMU-RAXX-X, USB V.90 56K	?	?	?	
?	5DOTAI-27364-M5-E	Acer AME-MAXX-X, AME-MT100	-	-	EXT	
?	5DOTAI-27789-M5-E	Acer AMP-LW08 mini-PCI interface modem card	?	?	?	
?	5DOTAI-27791-M5-E	Acer AMR-LW28M MDC interface modem card	?	?	?	
OK	5DOTAI-32513-M5-E	Acer AME-TS00, V.90 56Kbps External Data/Fax/Voice, TI chipset	-	-	EXT	Saifuladzhar B. Shahbudin
?	5DOTAI-32854-M5-E	?, Rockwell RLDL56DPF chipset	?	?	?	
?	5DOTAI-33008-M5-E	Acer AMI-RJ10PXX	?	?	PCI	
?	5DOTAI-34003-M5-E	Acer AMR-RX56-X, external D/F/V with voice mail and speaker	?	?	EXT	

511

Key	FCC ID or Reg #	Model	PNP	Jumpers	Interface	Thanks to:
?	1X2TAI-34048-M5-E	Acer AMI-RA05P-X	?	?	PCI	
?	1X2TAI-34049-M5-E	Acer AMI-RA20P-X	?	?	PCI	
?	1X2TAI-34050-M5-E	Acer AMI-RA06P-X	?	?	PCI	
?	1X2TAI-34095-M5-E	Acer AMU-AAOO, external USB 56K V.90	?	?	?	
5DT		**Psion Dacom**				
OK	5DTGTB-32316-M5-E	Ericsson K56 CC+ , PSTN, GSM, ISDN modem; IBM International with GSM; Psion Dacom GoldCard Global 56K+Fax/V.34+Fax ; Alcatel One Touch Dual-mode; Hayes Optima 56K Global; Netcom Global; Optegra Global; Freespirit Global; Toshiba Advanced Global, Rockwell chipset	-	-	PCMCIA	Peter Helnwein
?	5DTGTB-32982-M5-E	Gold Card NetGlobal 56K+Fax	?	-	PCMCIA	
?	5DTGTB-32983-M5-E	Gold Card Classic 56K+Fax/V34+Fax	?	-	PCMCIA	
?	5DTGTB-33465-M5-E	Gold Card Netglobal 56K+10/100 Cardbus , Hayes Optima Worldnet 100 Cardbus, Toshiba/IBM/Compaq V.90 + 10/100 Ethernet Cardbus	?	-	PCMCIA	
?	5DTGTB-27848-DT-T	56K Travel Modem with I/R port	?	?	?	
5EM		**Long Well Electronics**				
?	5EMTAI-34217-M5-E	Long Well f/d/v modem Model LW-951	-	-	USB	
5F5		**Shark Multimedia**				

Key	FCC ID or Reg #	Model	PNP	Jumpers	Interface	Thanks to:
		This is the Linux/Modem Compatibility Knowledge Base at http://www.o2.net/~gromitkc/winmodem.html				
	5F5TAI-40032-M5-E	Shark Multimedia Leopard Win 56K-PCI				
WM	5F5USA-40032-M5-E	, Motorola HSP chipset	Yes	No	PCI	
?	5F5TAI-27054-M5-E	Model Leopard Pocket USB	-	-	USB	
?	5F5TAI-27570-M5-E	Model LP USB Int'l	-	-	USB	
?	5F5TAI-31540-PT-E	Shark Multimedia 56K Leopard XT speakerphone, Rockwell RCVDL56ACF/SP chipset	-	-	EXT	Matt Smith
?	5F5TAI-34144-M5-E	Model LPD MR USA, LPD MRB Int'l	?	?	PCI	
5GF		Arescom				
?	5GFUSA-34043-M5-T	EZ Rider, EZ Rider Pro, external 56K D/F modem with Ethernet Router Hub	?	?	?	
5GX		Novaweb Technologies				
?	5GXUSA-33020-M5-E	Novaweb 2001, 56K modem with 4-port ethernet hub	Yes	?	ISA	
?	5GXUSA-33857-M5-E	Novaweb 2021	?	?	PCI	
5HR		Billionton				
WM	5HRUSA-27001-M5-E	HSP Micromodem BM56-SD (PCTel 1789)	Yes	No	PCI	
?	5HRTAI-27109-M5-E	FM56R-BCTV2/FM56R-NCTV2	-	-	PCMCIA	
OK	5HRTAI-25229-M5-E	Billionton FM56R-NFV2, Rockwell chipset	-	-	PCMCIA	Thomas Malcherek
?	?	FM56C-B/FM56C-N	-	-	PCMCIA	
OK	5HRTAI-31904-M5-E	Billionton 56Kbps FAX Modem PC Card, Part Number FM56C-BF	-	-	PCMCIA	Shad Yoakum

This is the Linux/Modem Compatibility Knowledge Base at http://www.o2.net/~gromitkc/winmodem.html

Key	FCC ID or Reg #	Model	PNP	Jumpers	Interface	Thanks to:
OK	5HRTAI-32950-M5-E	Billionton LM5LT-10B, OEM LM5LT-10N, 10LAN+56K Modem	-	-	PCMCIA	Christoph Ganser
?	5HRTAI-32950-M5-E	Billionton FM56RCB	-	-	PCMCIA	
	5HS	Thundercom Holdings				
WM	?	Thundercom 56CV-PCI, Lucent LT Winmodem	Yes	No	PCI	Davide Morando
	5JA	Kye Systems				
?	5JATAI-25617-M5-E	Kye/Genius GM56PCI-R(V)	?	?	PCI	
OK	FSUG7013	Kye/Genius GM56flex-V, Rockwell chipset	Yes	Yes	ISA	Helio Rozenblit
?	5JATAI-25750-M5-E	Kye/Genius GM56flex-V2	?	?	ISA	
WM	5JATAI-25823-M5-E	Kye/Genius GM56PCI-L, Lucent 1646 chipset	Yes	No	PCI	
?	5JATAI-25837-M5-E	Kye/Genius GM56flexE-V2	?	?	?	
?	5JATAI-27524-M5-E	Kye/Genius GM56PCI-SM	?	?	PCI	
?	5JATAI-34378-M5-E	Kye/Genius GM56USB	?	?	USB	
?	5JATAI-34605-M5-E	Kye/Genius GM56E-V	?	?	EXT	
	5JB	Pine Technology				
?	?	FM-3121-312/512, ESS 2820 chipset	Yes	No	ISA	
?	5JBCHN-32170-PT-E	FM-3131-31S/51S, Phoebe CMVP56KCL, Cirrus Logic 3450/5650 chipset	Yes	Yes	ISA	
?	?	FM-3251-412/612, Rockwell R6741/R6761 chipset	?	Yes	ISA	
		Model FM-3611-1				

Key	FCC ID or Reg #	Model	PNP	Jumpers	Interface	Thanks to:
WM	?	, Lucent 1646/1034 chipset	Yes	No	PCI	
WM	5JBCHN-27157-M5-E	Model FM-3621, ESS 2898/2819 chipset	Yes	No	PCI	
WM	5JBCHN-27158-M5-E	Model FM-3631, Cirrus Logic 5620/1724 chipset	Yes	No	PCI	
WM	?	Model FM-3711, Rockwell R6793 chipset	Yes	No	PCI	
5JC		Warpspeed Communications				
?	5JCUSA-32175-PT-E	ESSFMV	?	?	ISA	
?	5JCUSA-33241-M5-E	Onspeed PCTV-1789 (HSP Micromodem)	Yes	No	PCI	
5JT		Ariel				
?	5JTUSA-34311-M5-E	Ariel RSA-400	?	?	?	
5LO		Asian Information Technology				
?	5LOTAI-33175-M5-E	Model I200, Cirrus Logic MD-4450/5650DT chipset	Yes	Yes	ISA	
5MU		Sam Baek Telecom				
?	5MUKOR-32906-M5-E	Ribero-56K, TI chipset	Yes	DIP	ISA	
5N6		Universal Scientific Industrial				
?	5N6TAI-34260-M5-E	Netschools NS2000 internal 56K d/f modem for PC notebook	?	?	?	
5NI		Netronics				
?	5NITAI-25790-M5-E	NW56 56K stand-alone w/voice	-	-	EXT	
?	5NITAI-27452-M5-E	MDX-56KRE	?	?	?	
?	5NITAI-33011-M5-E	TAD-56KRE	?	?	?	
?	5NIUSA-33343-M5-E	V90-IMD	-	-	EXT	

This is the Linux/Modem Compatibility Knowledge Base at http://www.o2.net/~gromitkc/winmodem.html

Key	FCC ID or Reg #	Model	PNP	Jumpers	Interface	Thanks to:
		ACN Technologies				
?	5NJUSA-33022-M5-E	TONGDAL	?	?	?	
		Kasan Electronics				
WM	5NPKOR-33045-M5-E	Kasan Xceed-56K Modio M007-AKS100-XX	Yes	?	ISA	
WM	5NPKOR-33878-M5-E	Kasan Adlas/ Ryng 56K USB modem, HSP chipset	-	-	USB	
?	5NPKOR-27620-FB-E	Kasan Rising Sun	?	?	?	
		Smart Link				
WM	5NUUSA-34149-M5-E	Smart Link HAMR5600	?	?	?	
		Formosa Industrial Computing				
WM	?	Golden Melody FM56PCI , Rockwell RLVDL56DPF/SP 6785-61 (HCF/SP) chipset	Yes	No	PCI	
WM	?	Golden Melody FM56PCIS , Rockwell RS56/SP-PCI 6787-12 (HSP) chipset	Yes	No	PCI	
?	5O6TAI-33795-M5-E	Golden Melody ES56PCI	?	?	PCI	
?	5O6TAI-34372-M5-E	Golden Melody ES56NM-F internal integrated 56K d/f/v modem	?	?	?	
WM	?	Golden Melody GM56PCI , Lucent 1646 controllerless chipset	Yes	No	PCI	
WM	?	Golden Melody MM56PCI , Motorola chipset	Yes	No	PCI	

This is the Linux/Modem Compatibility Knowledge Base at http://www.o2.net/~gromitkc/winmodem.html

	FCC ID or Reg #	Model	PNP	Jumpers	Interface	Thanks to:
	5OV	Hightech Information Systems				

Key	FCC ID or Reg #	Model	PNP	Jumpers	Interface	Thanks to:
WM	5OVCHN-25603-M5-E	Speedcom RW-56VPCI, Rockwell HCF chipset	?	?	PCI	
WM	5OVHKG-25670-M5-E	Speedcom RW-56VPCI	?	?	PCI	
WM	5OVCHN-27013-M5-E	Speedcom RWS56VPCI, Rockwell HCF chipset	?	?	PCI	
WM	5OVHKG-27112-M5-E	HIS-1789 D/F/V	Yes	No	PCI	
WM	5OVUSA-33033-M5-E	Speedcom CL-56VPCI, Cirrus Logic CLM chipset	?	?	PCI	
?	5OVHKG-34277-FB-E	Hightech Information System HIS-SMR1, PCI d/f module (chipless) modem	?	?	PCI	
5OY		Behavior Tech Computer				
WM	?	56IP /C56K, PCTel chipset	Yes	No	ISA	
	E5X1898	Global Connucation Model FB1898, PCTel PCT288-IA chipset				
WM	5OYCHN-32306-PT-E		Yes	No	ISA	
	5OYTAI-27099-M5-E	BTC / GVC / PC/100				
	5OYCHN-33454-M5-E	56IPI				
	5OYCHN-33455-M5-E	/C56K, HSP modem				
	5OYCHN-33456-M5-E					
WM	5OYCHN-27724-M5-E		Yes	No	PCI	
5PH		Pro-Nets Technology				
?	5OYTAI-32944-M5-E	BTC PCM56L	-	-	PCMCIA	
		HPI56M				

Key	FCC ID or Reg #	Model	PNP	Jumpers	Interface	Thanks to:
WM	5PHTAI-33572-M5-E	, Motorola chipset	Yes	No	PCI	
		VPI56SP				
WM	?	, Rockwell chipset (HCF?)	Yes	No	PCI	
		HPI56SP				
WM	?	, Rockwell chipset (HSF?)	Yes	No	PCI	
		VD56SP				
?	?	, Rockwell chipset, horizontal configuration	-	-	EXT	
		VD56SPV				
OK	?	, Rockwell RP56D/SP chipset, vertical configuration	-	-	EXT	Lars Hoel
		VD56SM				
?	?	, Motorola chipset, horizontal configuration	-	-	EXT	
		Multiwave Innovations				
	5QV					
	KLZ1108					
WM	5QVSNG-23653-PT-E	Commwave PCI V.34 PnP	Yes	No	PCI	Sunil Thulasidasan
		CommWave 56K PCI LT Win Modem, Model 56LU-PCI				John J. Cruz
		Genica				; Ivo Johnny Pineda
		GCT				
		CW56LU-PCI,				
		Viking Model RFM56KPCICL				; Bill Huston
WM	5QVSNG-25391-M5-E	, Paradise CW56LTPCIWB-V2	Yes	No	PCI	
		CommWave 56K PCI LT Win Modem, Model 56LU-SPCI				
WM	5QVSNG-25567-M5-E	, Paradise (CW)56(LU)-EXT(S)	Yes	No	PCI	
		WaveCom 56K External Modem PRO				
OK	5QVSNG-25813-M5-E	, Lucent chipset	-	-	EXT	De Geeter Jef
		CommWave 56K PCI Rockwell Modem				
WM	5QVSNG-25892-M5-E	, Paradise CW56ES-DSP	Yes	No	PCI	
WM	?	, ESS chipset	Yes	No	ISA	

This is the Linux/Modem Compatibility Knowledge Base at http://www.o2.net/~gromitkc/winmodem.html

Key	FCC ID or Reg #	Model	PNP	Jumpers	Interface	Thanks to:
WM	?	Paradise CW56KPNP HSP SoftModem, PCTel 388 chipset	Yes	No	ISA	
WM	?	Paradise CW56KPCMCIA HSP SoftModem, PCTel 388 chipset	Yes	-	PCMCIA	
WM	5QVSNG-25384-M5-T	Paradise CW56KPCMCIA-V2 HSP SoftModem	Yes	-	PCMCIA	
WM	5QVSNG-25877-M5-E	Paradise PC Card Modem, CW56K-CB, CW56LU-CB	Yes	-	PCMCIA	Steve Winckelman
5RJ		Amigo Technology				
WM	5RJTAI-32322-M5-E	Model AMI-2010, PCTel 388P-A chipset	?	?	?	
WM	?	Model AMI-2011, PCTel 789 chipset	?	?	PCI	
?	?	Model AMI-2012/AMI-1456L, Lucent chipset	?	?	PCI	
WM	?	Model AMI-2013, Motorola SM56 chipset	?	?	PCI	
WM	5RJTAI-33566-M5-E	Model AMI-2014 /FM56KPMT, PCTel 789 chipset	?	?	PCI	
WM	?	Model AMI-2016, Rockwell HSP chipset	?	?	PCI	
?	5J2TAI-27843-M5-E	Amigo AMI-2018F	?	?	?	
5RX		Viking Components				
OK	5RXUSA-25047-M5-E	56K PC Card Modem, Model RFM56KPA	-	-	PCMCIA	Thomas Nichols
OK	5RXUSA-23967-MM-E	56K External Modem, RFM56KEXT	-	-	EXT	Kevin Snively
OK	5RXUSA-25828-M5-E	56K External Modem, FM56KEXT	-	-	EXT	Jason and Christa Dixon
OK	?	33.6 ISA PnP modem, Model RFM336INC, Rockwell RCV336ACF R6749-23 chipset	Yes	No	ISA	Jim Schlemmer
?	?	56K ISA Speakerphone Modem, Model FM56KISPA/FM56KISPB	Yes	No	ISA	

This is the Linux/Modem Compatibility Knowledge Base at http://www.o2.net/~gromitkc/winmodem.html

Key	FCC ID or Reg #	Model	PNP	Jumpers	Interface	Thanks to:
?	?	56K ISA Modem, Model FM56KIA/FM56KIB	Yes	No	ISA	
WM	5RXUSA-27688-M5-E	56K ISA Windows Modem, Model FM56KICL/RFM56KICLA	Yes	No	ISA	
?	5RXUSA-27693-M5-E	Model FM56KPB/MAC56KPB	?	?	?	
		External USB 56K Modem, Model RFM56KUSB /			USB	
?	5RXUSA-33622-M5-E	FM56KUSB	-	-		
		External 56K Modem, Model RFM56KEXT /				
?	5RXUSA-34080-M5-E	RFMAC56EXT	-	-	EXT	
5SA		NewCom				
?	JDJ-14400EFX/ 28800EFX					
?	JDJUSA-74912-FA-E	33.6EFXN 9747	-	-	EXT	Kavindra , Tesla Coil
OK	5SAHKG-32407-M5-E	56kifxC x2 Data/Fax	Yes	Yes	ISA	
OK	5SAUSA-32354-M5-E	56kefxC x2 Data/Fax	-	-	EXT	NewCom
WM	?	56kifxE X2 Windows95 Data/fax "MediaSurf DSP" , ESS TeleDrive DSP chipset	Yes	No	ISA	
WM	?	56Kpfx PCI Windows Modem	Yes	?	PCI	
OK	?	33.6kifxvC data/fax/voice	Yes	Yes	ISA	NewCom
OK	?	33.6kifxspC speakerphone	Yes	Yes	ISA	NewCom
?	?	33.6kifxR data/fax	No	Yes	ISA	
5WC		Analog & Digital Devices Telecom (ADDTel)				
		ADDTel AD56Kex				

Key	FCC ID or Reg #	Model	PNP	Jumpers	Interface	Thanks to:
OK	5WCUSA-33123-M5-E	, Compaq NC4001	-	-	EXT	Olivier
5WJ		Panacom				
		Amquest AM56IVSP-D				
?	5WJTAI-25894-FB-E	, Panacom PM56DS	Yes	?	ISA	
		Amquest AMQ400				
?	5WJTAI-25897-M5-E	, Panacom PX400 56K PCI Quad Modem	?	?	PCI	
?	5WJTAI-27122-PT-E	Amquest AM56EVSP , Panacom PM56DE	-	-	EXT	
WM	5WJTAI-33174-M5-E	Panacom PM56HC	Yes	No	PCI	
5ZE		TiMedia Technology				
		F560IC				
WM	5ZETAI-25886-M5-E	, Rockwell HCF chipset	Yes	No	PCI	
		F560IC				
WM	5ZETAI-33310-M5-E	, HSP chipset	Yes	No	PCI	
?	?	F560XD	-	-	EXT	

Key	FCC ID or Reg #	Model	PNP	Jumpers	Interface	Thanks to:
6AT		Philips Electronics				
?	6ATTAI-24712-M5-E	Philips EasyCONNECT 56K Video/Voice/Fax/Modem, Rockwell RCDL56ACF R6761-25 chipset	Yes	No	ISA	Francisco Benavides
6BG		InnoMedia				
?	6BGSNG-34248-M5-E	InnoMedia InfoFax IM0700, external 56K	?	?	?	
6BI		Three States Electronics				
		Aeton Webcruiser 56K Voice Model FB R56I,				
OK	6BITAI-24796-M5-E	Rockwell RCVDL56ACF/SP chipset	Yes	Yes	ISA	John Kesa
6BM		Olitec				
		Smart Memory 56000				

Key	FCC ID or Reg #	Model	PNP	Jumpers	Interface	Thanks to:
OK	6BMFRC-27004-M5-E	, Self Memory 2000, Total Office Smart Memory	-	-	EXT	Raphael
OK	?	Speed Voice 56000	-	-	EXT	Carlier Laurent
WM	6BMFRC-27019-M5-E	PCI 56000	?	?	PCI	Francis Montes
?	6BMFRC-33962-M5-E	PCI 56K V2, PCI 56K V3	?	?	PCI	
6BN		Protac International				
?	6BNCHN-25538-M5-E	Web Excel ME120[A..J], ME220[A..J]	?	?	?	
		Web Excel ME201[A..J]				
OK	6BNCHN-25591-M5-E	, Rockwell RP56D/SP chipset	-	-	EXT	Jo Whitby
		Web Excel MD300[A..K]				
WM	6BNCHN-27092-M5-E	, Rockwell RLVDL56DPF/SP chipset	-	No	PCI	Juergen Pierau
		Web Excel MD320[A..J]				
WM	6BNCHN-33153-M5-E	, Cirrus Logic MD5620(X2) chipset	-	No	PCI	
?	6BNCHN-34273-M5-E	Web Excel ME320US	?	?	USB	
?	6BNCHN-34511-M5-E	Web Excel ME322US	?	?	PCI	
		Web Excel MD500[A..K]				
WM	6BNCHN-27338-M5-E	, Rockwell RS56/SP-PCI R6793-11 (HSP) chipset	Yes	No	PCI	Sergio Garcia Reus
?	6BNCHN-33266-M5-E	Web Excel MD510[A..J]	?	?	PCI	
?	6BNCHN-33596-M5-E	Web Excel ME220[A..K]	?	?	EXT	
6BP		Chic Technology				
?	6BPCHN-27858-M5-E	Chic 56SM	?	?	?	
?	6BPCHN-33935-M5-E	Generic/Elda Micro Model 56K EXT.2	?	?	EXT	
6CT		Ambit Microsystems				

522

Key	FCC ID or Reg #	Model	PNP	Jumpers	Interface	Thanks to:
?	6CTTAI-25420-M5-E	Data/Fax/Voice modem for notebook, T62.108.C.00	?	?	?	
?	6CTTAI-27308-FB-E	56K Data/14.4K Fax modem for notebook, T18.019.C.01, HP Omnibook Series, Quanta LFX/LFXX/LTX, Siemens Scenic Mobile Series	?	?	?	
?	6CTTAI-27532-M5-E	Ambit U98.004.C.00, NASCAR P67, Snake P51, Starbucks P64, Boxer P60, 56K Data/14.4K Fax modem for notebook	?	?	?	
?	6CTTAI-27537-M5-E	Ambit U98.003.C.00, NASCAR P67, Snake P51, Starbucks P64, Boxer P60, 56K Data/14.4K Fax modem for notebook	?	?	?	
?	6CTTAI-33024-M5-E	56K/14.4 Fax for PC, T27/006.C.00	?	?	?	
?	6CTTAI-34136-M5-E	Ambit 56K/14.4 Fax for PC, T51.012.C.00; Compal 30T5	?	?	?	
?	6CTTAI-34230-M5-E	HP/Quanta Omnibook, XE2, Pavilion, LT5, LT6, LTL	?	?	?	
?	6CTTAI-32931-M5-E	T42.002.C.00 internal modem for notebook	?	?	?	
?	6CTTAI-33592-M5-E	U01.027.C.00 internal modem for notebook, Apple Power GX, P101	?	?	?	
?	6CTTAI-33822-M5-E	Ambit/Compal T51.004.C.00, 30B2 internal modem for PC notebook	?	?	?	
?	6CTTAI-33822-M5-E	Ambit J07.017.C.01, Acer B-Note/520/730/340	?	?	?	
?	6CTTAI-40000-M5-E	T42.001.C.00	?	?	?	
?	6CTTAI-40048-M5-E	T18.034.C.00, Quanta IA1, Acer XCT310, Inventec AB104	?	?	?	
?	6CTTAI-33025-M5-E	56K/14.4 Fax for PC, 731.015.C.00	?	?	?	

523

This is the Linux/Modem Compatibility Knowledge Base at http://www.o2.net/~gromitkc/winmodem.html

Key	FCC ID or Reg #	Model	PNP	Jumpers	Interface	Thanks to:
?	6CTTAI-25599-DT-E	Data/Fax/Voice modem for notebook, U01.001.C.00	?	?	?	
WM	6CTTAI-25600-DT-E	Data/Fax/Voice modem for Acer Extensa 501T notebook, T62.103.C.00, Lucent 1641B (Luna) LT Winmodem chipset	Yes	No	ISA	Martin Schneebacher
?	6CTTAI-27151-M5-E	Ambit 56K/14.4 for notebook U01.030.C.00, U01.025.C.00, Apple iMac II, Apple P1, Apple P101, Apple Powerbook G4, Apple Powermac G4	?	?	?	
?	6CTTAI-33461-M5-E	Ambit/Vobis Micro/Max Data 56k modem for PC notebook, T31.019.C.00, Highscreen Advanced S1, Artis York	?	?	?	
?	6CTTAI-33516-M5-E	Internal 56K for notebook U01.028.C.00, U01.029.C.00, Apple iMac II, Apple P1, Apple P101, Apple Powerbook G4, Apple Powermac G4	?	?	?	
?	6CTTAI-27175-FB-E	Ambit 56K/14.4 for notebook T31.017.C.00, Twinhead Slimnote GX, Winbook LX2	?	?	?	

This is the Linux/Modem Compatibility Knowledge Base at http://www.o2.net/~gromitkc/winmodem.html

Key	FCC ID or Reg #	Model	PNP	Jumpers	Interface	Thanks to:
6DE		Advanced Digital Industrial				
?	6DECHN-40021-M5-E	Digimate FMDI-RW2V	?	?	?	
6DG		Phoenix Research Group				
WM	6DGUSA-27081-PT-E	Phoenix Research Group 56UVSR-C1, ST soft modem chipset	-	-	USB	
WM	?	Phoenix Research Group 56IVMCR, Motorola controllerless chipset	-	No	PCI	
WM	?	Phoenix Research Group 56IVER, ESS controllerless chipset	Yes	No	ISA	

This is the Linux/Modem Compatibility Knowledge Base at http://www.o2.net/~gromitkc/winmodem.html

Key	FCC ID or Reg #	Model	PNP	Jumpers	Interface	Thanks to:
WM	?	Phoenix Research Group 56ISPR, PCTel soft modem chipset	Yes	No	ISA	
WM	6DGUSA-33729-M5-E	Phoenix Research Group 56IVMSR, Motorola Soft Modem (HSP) chipset	-	No	PCI	
?	6DGUSA-25528-PT-E	Phoenix Research Group 56ILHR	?	?	?	
	6DGUSA-25816-M5-E	Phoenix Research Group 56IXMR-PCI, Motorola				
?	ABZUSA-25799-M5-E	SC143455RDK	?	?	?	
6FW		Maxtech				
WM	6FWTAI-33401-M5-E	56K D/F/V Controllerless Modem, Model XPVS56P/C, Cirrus Logic CLM chipset	Yes	?	PCI	
?	?	56K Speakerphone Modem, Model XPVS-56I NetPacer Pro	Yes	Yes	ISA	
6GA		Allied Data Technologies				
?	6GATAI-33431-M5-E	Great MD-56E, Tornado SFM56E	-	-	EXT	
WM	6GATAI-33432-M5-E	DCS 56RP6, Great MD-56IC, Tornado SFM56H, Rockwell HCF chipset	Yes	No	PCI	
6GD		Option International				
?	5DRBEL-30948-MM-E	GSM-Ready 33.6K PC-Card modem	?	-	PCMCIA	
?	6GDBEL-33439-M5-E	GSM-Ready 56K PC-Card modem	?	-	PCMCIA	
6GL		Westech Korea				
?	6GLKOR-33493-M5-E	QLink WTM-56KUS	?	-	PCMCIA	
6GM		Netron				
?	6GMKOR-33491-M5-E	YES 560 TI/SP V.90 Internal	?	?	ISA	

Key	FCC ID or Reg #	Model	PNP	Jumpers	Interface	Thanks to:
?	6GMKOR-33492-M5-E	YES 560 PCMCIA	?	-	PCMCIA	
		PDMTech				
?	6GOTAI-33542-M5-E	PDM/Acmestar AO-5600E1, MD56ISA-PDM	?	?	PCI	
		Serome Technology				
?	6GQKOR-33540-M5-E	M-CLH-56SP-PCI	?	?	PCI	
?	6GQKOR-34180-M5-E	Serome/Wings/Vivitel/Chaser M-RWS-56SP-PCI	?	?	PCI	
		Whistle Communications				
?	6HHUSA-33644-M5-E	InterJet II external 56K modem Model 2200/2220/2230/2250	-	-	EXT	
		Hsing Tech Enterprise				
		PCChips				
?	6HKCHN-33805-M5-E	M748MR, M741LMR, M741LMRT, P6SE-ML, P6SET-ML motherboards-- on board-modem, PCTel MicroModem chipset?	?	?	MBD	
		Uniwill Computer				
?	6IOTAI-27596-M5-E	Uniwill 5816400012 for notebook	?	?	?	
?	6IOTAI-33909-M5-E	Uniwill WS-5614BAR for PC notebook	?	?	?	
?	6IOTAI-33910-M5-E	Uniwill WS-5614BSDG for PC notebook	?	?	?	
		Zytec				
?	6IQUSA-33903-MM-E	Zytec Mini Modem 33.6 external	?	?	EXT	
		Boca Global				
?	6IVUSA-33954-M5-E	Teleport V.90 56K, Model B103	?	?	EXT	
?	6IVUSA-34227-M5-E	Teleport V.90 56K, Model B105 internal for Apple computer	?	?	?	

This is the Linux/Modem Compatibility Knowledge Base at http://www.o2.net/~gromitkc/winmodem.html

Key	FCC ID or Reg #	Model	PNP	Jumpers	Interface	Thanks to:
		Eiger Labs				
?	6JHUSA-34022-M5-E	Modem Master 8100SW (MM8100SW)	?	?	PCI	
6KG		Biostar Microtech Int'l				
?	6KGTAI-34170-M5-E	Model RB02	?	?	PCI	
6KI		Micro-Star International				
?	6KITAI-34182-M5-E	Micro-Star MS-5966	?	?	PCI	
6KK		CastleNet Technology				
?	6KKTAI-34198-M5-E	CNET CNIM563-SF, CNIM563AF, CTI I800 Series	?	?	PCI	
?	6KKTAI-34510-M5-E	CTI M800 internal notebook modem	?	?	?	
6KM		Omnitronix				
?	6KMUSA-34184-M5-E	Omnitronix OM33699	?	?	PCI	
6KN		Great Microcomputer Technology				
?	6KNTAI-34177-M5-E	Machspeed GTK-MDR56K	?	?	PCI	
6KP		Toshiba TEC				
?	6KPHKG-34174-MM-E	Toshiba 1870	?	?	?	
6KV		Ambient Technology				
?	6KVTAI-34216-M5-E	3Com 3CP5606 56K Faxmodem USB	?	?	?	
6LG		Uplus Technology				
?	6LGTAI-34297-M5-E	Arowana/Ana Conda/Star Web UPM56SU external USB fax modem	?	?	?	
6LP		Digital Integrated System Intelliquis/ StarShip				

This is the Linux/Modem Compatibility Knowledge Base at http://www.o2.net/~gromitkc/winmodem.html

Key	FCC ID or Reg #	Model	PNP	Jumpers	Interface	Thanks to:
?	6LPMLA-34335-M5-E	DIS56CLEXTNL external 56k data/fax modem, Cirrus Logic CL-MD5650DT chipset	-	-	EXT	
?	6LPMLA-34598-M5-E	Intelliquis/Starship DIS56HAM	?	?	PCI	
6LS		Billionton Systems				
?	6LSTAI-34356-M5-E	Billionton Brana FMLA-100B, No Brana FMLA-100N fax modem card with LAN	-	-	PCMCIA	
?	6LSTAI-34528-M5-E	Billionton FM56C-BF, FM56C-NF, Cadmus Micro FM56C-CF, Eagle Tec ET-FM56V, Lapmate FM56C-BK, Rix DC56K, Trigem FM56C-NF-BK, Winward FM56C-NF-HT, internal mini 56K d/f modem	?	?	?	
?	6LSTAI-40081-M5-E	Billionton Brana FM56R-NF-AMV2	?	?	?	
?	6LSTAI-40082-M5-E	Billionton Brana FM56R-CL	?	?	?	
6LX		3Com				
?	6LXUSA-34370-M5-E	3Com Office Connect Dual 56K LAN Modem V.90 Model 3C888	?	?	?	
6MK		Foretech Electronics				
?	6MKKOR-34615-M5-E	Foretech/OEM FS56RC	?	?	PCI	
6MS		Ericsson Radio Systems				
?	6MSUSA-34593-M5-E	EBMODEM ROA 117 9099/1, "external ISA"	?	?	?	

This is the Linux/Modem Compatibility Knowledge Base at http://www.o2.net/~gromitkc/winmodem.html

	FCC ID or Reg #	Model	PNP	Jumpers	Interface	Thanks to:
A11		Amquest				
	A11HKG-25478-M5-E	Hypermodem AM56HCFSP				
	406HKG-33203-M5-E	,				

528

Key	FCC ID or Reg #	Model	PNP	Jumpers	Interface	Thanks to:
WM		Actionwell ActionMedia AC5604 , Rockwell chipset	Yes	No	PCI	
WM	A11KOR-25692-M5-E	Hypermodem AM56HCF	Yes	No	PCI	
A3L		Samsung Electronics				
?	A3LKOR-25631-FB-E	SAM-650R56	?	?	?	
?	A3LKOR-27617-FB-E	StudyPro II	?	?	?	
?	A3LKOR-27251-FB-E	SFM-1400LW	?	?	?	
?	A3LKOR-33131-M5-E	SAM-1000R56 internal 56K modem card for PC notebook	?	?	?	
?	A3LKOR-33263-M5-E	SFM-5660AL ISA 56K modem card	?	?	ISA	
?	A3LKOR-33371-M5-E	SFM-1200L56 internal 56K modem card for PC notebook	?	?	?	
?	A3LKOR-33628-M5-E	SFM-1300KW external 56K modem card for PC notebook	?	?	?	
?	A3LKOR-34332-M5-E	[trade name missing]	?	?	?	
AK3		Motorola				
OK	AK32094219	ModemSURFR 28.8K internal	Yes	Yes	ISA	George Bursha
?	AK3USA-20453-MD-E	V.34R Dial Modem	-	-	EXT	Mr. Fastenow
		Modemsurfr 56K, Model 3456 INT ; Voicesurfr Model 3456, Rockwell RCVDL56ACFW/SP R6761-22 chipset				
OK	AK3USA-24412-M5-E		Yes	No	ISA	Don Moffatt
OK	AK3USA-24411-M5-E	Modemsurfr 56K	Yes	-	EXT	Devin Ferguson
WM	?	SM56 PCI	Yes	?	PCI	

529

This is the Linux/Modem Compatibility Knowledge Base at http://www.o2.net/~gromitkc/winmodem.html

Key	FCC ID or Reg #	Model	PNP	Jumpers	Interface	Thanks to:
?	AK3USA-27762-M5-E	MC143462RDK, 33.6/14.4 Fax modem	?	?	?	
?	AK3USA-32923-M5-E	MC143455RDK	?	?	ISA	
?	5NDTAI-25596-M5-E	Motorola Semi. (HK) MC143450RDK	?	?	EXT	
?	5NDTAI-32980-M5-E	Motorola Semi. (HK) MC143455RDK	?	?	ISA	
?	AK3USA-32924-M5-E	MC143450RDK	-	-	EXT	
AK8		Sony Electronics				
OK	AK8JPN-25704-M5-E	Sony Vaio Notebook Modem, PCG-505F(X)/505G(X)/PCG-505TR	?	?	?	Felix Lam
?	AK8JPN-27432-M5-E	Sony PCG-Z505DXD[1..8], PCG-Z505S(X) Notebook Modem	?	?	?	
	AK8JPN-25980-M5-E	Sony PCG-F1x0 [where x=5-9], PCG-F2x0 [x=0-9], PCG-F3x0 [x=0-9], PCG-F430, PCG-F420, PCG-F490(K), PCG-F480(K), PCG-F450, Rockwell HCF chipset				
WM	AK8JPN-33698-M5-E		Yes	No	PCI	Matt
OK	?	Sony Vaio Notebook Modem, PCG-705/707	?	?	?	Jason Kohles
?	AK8JPN-25738-MM-E	Sony Vaio Notebook Modem, PCG-744/748/812/818	?	?	?	
?	AK8JPN-25987-M5-E	Sony Vaio Notebook Modem, PCG-838	?	?	?	
?	AK8JPN-27432-M5-E	Sony Vaio Notebook Modem, PCG-Z505VR	?	?	?	
?	AK8JPN-27727-MM-E	Sony Notebook Modem, PCG-C1XS	?	?	?	
?	AK8JPN-27659-M5-E	Sony Vaio Notebook Modem, PCG-N505VX, PCG-N505VE, PCG-N505SV, PCG-N505ST	?	?	?	

530

Key	FCC ID or Reg #	Model	PNP	Jumpers	Interface	Thanks to:
?	AK8JPN-32907-M5-E	Sony Vaio Notebook Modem, PCG-505G(X)	?	?	?	
OK	AK8JPN-33453-M5-E	Sony Vaio Notebook Modem, PCG-C1X(D)	?	?	?	Daniel Cunningham
	AK8JPN-34093-M5-E	Sony notebook modem Model IRX-1080, PCG-XG9, PCG-XRG9, PCG-XR1G, PCG-XR7G, PXG-XR3G, PCG-XG18				
?	AK8JPN-40106-M5-E	Sony notebook modem Model PCG-Z505HE, PCG-Z505HS, PCG-Z505HK	?	?	?	
?	AK8JPN-34625-M5-E		?	?	?	
AMV		MediaForte Products				
?	AMVSNG-27084-M5-E	Momenta PCI V.90 Combo, M56-VAP	?	?	PCI	
ANO		IBM				
?	ANOTAI-33638-M5-E	Amigo AMI-2013, 56KPMT	?	?	PCI	
AS5		Lucent Technologies				
?	AS5TAI-27588-M5-T	Wildwire ADSL Client Model 2-12000-1	?	?	?	
ASU		ASUSTeK Computer				
?	ASUTAI-27409-M5-E	ASUS L7000 Series Notebook modem (PCTel HSP?)	?	?	?	
AT9		Motorola Information Systems Group				
?	AT9USA-30836-MD-E	Motorola ISG Model 3460	-	-	EXT	
AU7		Multi-Tech Systems				
?	AU7USA-20673-MM-E	MultimodemZPX MT2834ZPXI	?	?	?	
?	AU7USA-24994-M5-E	Multimodem MTASR3-200	?	?	?	
		MT5634MSV Data/Fax/Voice Messaging Modem				

This is the Linux/Modem Compatibility Knowledge Base at http://www.o2.net/~gromitkc/winmodem.html

Key	FCC ID or Reg #	Model	PNP	Jumpers	Interface	Thanks to:
?	AU7USA-24713-M5-E	, MT5600DSVD2 (w/o ext conn.)	-	-	EXT	
	AU7USA-25814-M5-E	Multimodem MT5634SM, MT5634SMI-NAM, MT4X5634USB, MT3334SMI, Environmental Manager EM-1608				
?	5D9USA-34386-M5-E		?	?	?	Thor Johnson ,
OK	AU7USA-27014-MM-E	MultiModem PCI, Model MT5634ZPX-PCI	*	No	PCI	MultiTech Sales
?	AU7USA-27400-M5-E	Model MT5634MU , Portable USB modem	-	-	USB	
OK	AU7USA-27713-M5-E	Model MT5634MSV	-	-	EXT	Allan W. Martin
?	AU7USA-31089-MM-E	MultiModem Model MT5634ZDX/MY3356ZDX/MT2834ZDX	-	-	EXT	
OK	AU7USA-32234-M5-E	MultiModemZPX, Model MT5634ZPX MultiMobile Model MT5634ZLX(I)/(FE)/(E), MT3400ZLX/E ,	Yes	Yes	ISA	LinuxCyrix
OK	AU7USA-32497-M5-E	Ericsson K56 CC	Yes	-	PCMCIA	David Archer
?	AU7USA-33378-M5-E	MultiModem II, Model MT5600BA, MT5600BL, 56k d/f in chassis	-	-	EXT	
BDN		Zoom Telephonics				
	BDN-VFV32ISB					
?	BDNUSA-75476-MM-E	Zoom Faxmodem 14.4PC, Rockwell chipset	?	Yes	ISA	
?	?	ComStar SVD 33.6 PNP, Model 2800	Yes	No	ISA	
?	?	ComStar SVD 33.6, Model 2802	Yes	?	ISA	
	BDNSPEAKERPHOBE	V.34 Faxmodem w/Speakerphone, Rockwell				
?	BDNUSA-22815-PT-E	RCV288DPi chipset	Yes	No	ISA	

This is the Linux/Modem Compatibility Knowledge Base at http://www.o2.net/~gromitkc/winmodem.html

Key	FCC ID or Reg #	Model	PNP	Jumpers	Interface	Thanks to:
OK	BDNUSA-31000-PT-E	V.34I Faxmodem D/F, Model 2805B/2834	No	Yes	ISA	Rob Clark
?	?	V.34X Plus, Model 2836/2837/2838	-	-	EXT	Ty Mixon
?	?	ComStar 56K, Model 2818 , Rockwell chipset	Yes	Yes	ISA	Bill Staehle
OK	?	56K Model 2819, (PNPID OZO800F) upgradable to V.90	Yes	Yes	ISA	M. G. Backe
OK	-	56K Model 2826 for U.K., (PNPID OZO8047) upgradable to V.90, Rockwell ACF chipset	Yes	Yes	ISA	James Lothian
OK	BDNUSA-31886-M5-E	Dualmode Zoom/FaxModem 56K (internal) Model 2919 , (PNPID OZO9100)	Yes	Yes	ISA	Tim Moore
OK	BDNUSA-25719-CN-E	Dualmode Zoom/FaxModem 56K (internal) Model 2919L , Award Technology A30, Zoom 336 Multi-Function LS PC Card w/Voicemail, Lucent 1673JV7 chipset	Yes	Yes	ISA	Mike Bland
WM	?	Zoom Model 2925 , Rockwell chipset	Yes	?	PCI	D.W.B.
		Genica /OEM Model 1120L, Zoom Model 2925L , ZBP Model 7180L, Pinnacle 910, Award Technology				, Cristi
WM	BDNUSA-33104-M5-E	A10, Lucent chipset Zoom Model 2849A/2949, International 56Kx Model 2869	Yes	No	PCI	James R. Miller , Ronald A. Vazquez
OK	BDNUSA-24481-MM-E		-	-	EXT	, Gonzalo Valencia

Key	FCC ID or Reg #	Model	PNP	Jumpers	Interface	Thanks to:
OK	BDNUSA-33207-M5-E	OEM Model 1144L/1149L, Zoom Model 2945L/2948L/2949L, ZBP Model 7353L, Lucent chipset	-	-	EXT	Rob Clark
	BDNUSA-33450-MM-E	OEM Model 1073L/1074L,				
	AS5USA-31827-MM-E	Zoom Model 2975L/2976L/2875L/2876L				
OK		, dual mode PCMCIA for PC or Mac, Lucent chipset	-	-	PCMCIA	Russ Price
?	BDNUSA-27386-M5-E	OEM Model 1162L/1163L, Zoom Model 2985L/2986L, Zoom XXX-0484-YY, USB 56K in chassis	?	?	?	
BFJ		Hayes Microcomputer Products				
?	BFJUSA-74137-FA-E	ACCURA 144B+FAX Model 5109AM V.32	?	Yes	ISA	
?	BFJ5201AM	ACCURA 28800 V.34/V.FC+Fax Model 5242AM	-	-	EXT	
	BFJ5201AM					
OK	BFJUSA-75692-MM-E	OPTIMA 28800 V.FC FAX Model 5201AM	-	-	EXT	Rob Clark
	JFJ0337H	ACCURA 144+FAX Model 5302AM (made by Practical Peripherals/J&M)				
OK	1B5USA-20230-MM-E		No	DIP	ISA	Rob Clark
	BFJ636US	ACCURA 336 Internal PnP Fax Modem, Model 5636US, P/N 08-0275, Rockwell chipset				
OK	BFJUSA-23929-MM-E		Yes	Yes	ISA	Rob Clark
?		ACCURA External Speakerphone, Part Number 08-02889	-	-	EXT	
?		ACCURA Internal Speakerphone, Part Number 08-02890	?	?	ISA	
OK	?	ACCURA 56K Internal Speakerphone, Part Number 08-2989	Yes	Yes	ISA	Jeremy Shervell

534

Key	FCC ID or Reg #	Model	PNP	Jumpers	Interface	Thanks to:
OK	?	ACCURA 56K V.90 4704, Part Number 08-03304	Yes	Yes	ISA	Robert J. Hansen
?		ACCURA K56flex/V.90 External, Part Number 08-03328	-	-	EXT	
?		Model 5669US, ACCURA 56k internal DFV	Yes	?	ISA	
?		Model 5670US, ACCURA 56k external DFV	-	-	EXT	
?		Model 5670UK, ACCURA 56k external DFV	-	-	EXT	Steve McGarrity
OK	?	ACCURA K56flex/V.90 Internal, Part Number 08-03329	Yes	Yes	ISA	
OK	BFJUSA-24459-M5-E	Model 5674US, ACCURA 56k external D/F modem	-	-	EXT	Pete Ritter
OK	BFJCHN-31922-MM-E	Model 5675US, ACCURA 56k internal D/F modem	Yes	Yes	ISA	Paul Abendroth
OK	BFJUSA-24458-M5-E	ACCURA 56K, Part Number 09-00458	Yes	Yes	ISA	David Lautenschlager
	BFJUSA-25621-M5-E	56K PCI dual-mode 4725				
	G2MUSA-32838-M5-E	Part Number 08-03357 ; Digitan DS560-548				
WM		DS560-552	Yes	?	PCI	

Key	FCC ID or Reg #	Model	PNP	Jumpers	Interface	Thanks to:
	CGG	MiTAC Technology Corp.				
?	CGGTAI-27095-M5-E	MTC FM20-APU1	?	?	?	
?	CGGTAI-33511-M5-E	33-APSU1 internal for notebook	?	?	?	
?	CJ6	Toshiba				

Key	FCC ID or Reg #	Model	PNP	Jumpers	Interface	Thanks to:
?	CJ6JPN-27783-M5-E	Model MJMDMUS1	?	?	?	
?	CJ6JPN-34016-M5-E	Model ARMDMWW1 for Toshiba PC notebook	?	?	?	
?	CJ6JPN-34291-M5-E	Model SMMDMWW1 for Toshiba PC notebook	?	?	?	
?	CJ6JPN-34292-M5-E	Model SMMDMUS1 for Toshiba PC notebook	?	?	?	
?	CJ6JPN-27657-M5-E	Model GSMDMUS1, 33.6K/14.4K Fax Modem board	?	?	?	
?	CJ6JPN-27805-M5-E	Model ATMDMWW1, 33.6K/14.4K Fax Modem board	?	?	?	
?	CJ6JPN-40071-M5-E	Model GSMDMWW1, 56K modem board	?	?	?	
?	CJ6JPN-40072-M5-E	Model GSMDMUS2, 56K modem board	?	?	?	
CJE		**U.S. Robotics Access Corp.**				
	CJE-0320					
RP	CJEUSA-22184-MM-E	Sportster 14.4 V32b RPI Fax, Model 0921 (00092100), Rockwell RC144ATF-P chipset	No	Yes	ISA	Jacob Poon
RP	?	Sportster 14.4 V32b RPI Fax, Model 0922	-	-	EXT	
OK	CJEUSA-20778-MM-E	US Robotics Sportster VI 33600 fax/voice modem	Yes	Yes	ISA	Vildenei Negrao Pereira
OK	CJEUSA-20778-MM-E	56K Voice Internal, OEM Model 0484 X2,V90 56K Sportster, OEM Model 0484 (831749-01 R:2)	Yes	Yes	ISA	John Mock , George Andrews
OK	CJEUSA-20778-MM-E	56k Sportster Flash Internal Voice Modem (Italian Model) (81-131742-00)	Yes	Yes	ISA	Armando Duarte
OK	?	Model 1749 (66174981), OEM "Python"	Yes	Yes	ISA	Giovanni Carboni
OK	CJEUSA-20778-MM-E	Fax/Data/Voice	Yes	Yes	ISA	Donald Yee

Key	FCC ID or Reg #	Model	PNP	Jumpers	Interface	Thanks to:
	CJE-0411					Itamar Almeida de Carvalho
WM	CJEUSA-23364-MM-E	Model 1125 Sportster Winmodem 33.6	Yes	No	8-bit ISA	
WM	CJE-0418	Sportster Winmodem [00162200]	Yes	No	ISA	
	CJE-0420					
WM	CJEUSA-23364-MM-E	Sportster Winmodem 28.8	Yes	No	ISA	
	CJE-0423	Gateway Telepath 28.8 for Windows, Model				
WM	CJEUSA-23364-MM-E	Model MODISA007AAUS	Yes	No	ISA	Jalesh Dikshit
OK	CJEUSA-24161-M5-E	Model 2806 (0396F) Courier V. Everything 56K, Model 1124 (0396F) Courier V.34	No	Yes	EXT	Eric S. Raymond
WM	CJEUSA-24178-M5-E	Model 0478 [87173100] (OEM "Greyhound") 56K Sportster Winmodem with speaker, Gateway TelePath for Windows with X2, TI TL16CFM600APJM chipset	Yes	No	ISA	Rob Clark
WM	CJEUSA-24178-M5-E	Model 0481 [52191701]	Yes	No	ISA	Fred M. Philip
OK	CJEUSA-24375-M5-E	Model 0839-07 (0459), Model 0839-08 (0648), 33.6K External	-	-	EXT	Paul Thorsted , Rob Clark
OK	CJEUSA-24375-M5-E	Model 5686-00 (0459), 56K V.90 External	-	-	EXT	Manoj Bhatti , Fang Yuan
WM	CJEUSA-24425-M5-E	Model 1750 (66175001 R:2), OEM Model 0467 (83175001 R:2), Sportster 56K Winmodem Voice, TI TL16CFM600APJM chipset	Yes	No	ISA	
OK	CJEUSA-24497-M5-E	Model 1784, Sportster 56K Voice Faxmodem	-	-	EXT	Nameless Hero
OK	CJEUSA-24629-M5-E	Model 0460-D (1787-81 R:2) (OEM "Akita") 56K V.90 Sportster, P/N 1.028.0512-00	Yes	Yes	ISA	Bob Dryden
OK	CJEUSA-30429-MM-E	Model 0460-C, TI chipset	Yes	Yes	ISA	Arkady Andrukonis

Key	FCC ID or Reg #	Model	PNP	Jumpers	Interface	Thanks to:
OK	CJEUSA-30429-MM-E CJE-0269	Model 0460-D (1787-02) (OEM "Akita") 56K x2 Sportster, TI chipset	Yes	Yes	ISA	Rob Clark
OK	CJEUSA-65828-FA-E CJE-0335	Model 840-00 (000840-00) Sportster 28.8, TI chipset	No	Yes	ISA	Jeff Cullen
OK	CJEUSA-65828-FA-E	Model 840-01 (000840-01) Sportster 33.6 (1.012.0335-C), TI chipset	Yes	Yes	ISA	Jeff Cullen
OK	CJEUSA-65828-FA-E	Model 0640 (000840-04 R:2) Sportster 33600 Fax V10.0.23 (1.012.0335-C), TI chipset	Yes	Yes	ISA	Rob Clark
?	CJE-0223	33.6K Sportster (00027600), TI chipset	?	Yes	ISA	?
OK	CJE-0297 CJEUSA-65828-FA-E	Model 0276-05 Sportster 14400 FAX RS Rev 1.5 (1.012.0297 E), TI chipset	Yes	Yes	ISA	Rob Clark
OK	CJE-0297 CJEUSA-65828-FA-E CJE-0374	Model 0276-06 Sportster 14400 FAX RS Rev 1.7, TI chipset	Yes	Yes	ISA	Rob Clark
OK	CJEUSA-65828-FA-E CJE-0265	Model 0839, 28.8K Sportster Faxmodem	-	-	EXT	Claudio Miranda
?	CJEUSA-65828-FA-E CJE-0268	14.4K Sportster Faxmodem (0268-02)	-	-	EXT	
?	CJE-0340	Model 0839-00, 28.8K Sportster Faxmodem	-	-	EXT	
OK	CJEUSA-65828-FA-E	Model 0839-01, 28.8K Sportster Faxmodem	-	-	EXT	Dave Rennie
	CJE-0374C	Model 0840 [87117101], Sportster 33.6 V.34/V42b				stegre

Key	FCC ID or Reg #	Model	PNP	Jumpers	Interface	Thanks to:
OK	CJEUSA-65828-FA-E	Fax Voice Speakerphone; Gateway Telepath 33.6, TI TL16CFM504PJM chipset	Yes	Yes	ISA	, Rob Clark
OK	CJEUSA-65828-FA-E	Model 1786, Sportster 56K Faxmodem	-	-	EXT	marty
OK		Model 5630 (81-135630-01), 56K Faxmodem (Europe)	-	-	EXT	Antonio Maschio
OK	CJEUSA-65828-FA-E	Model 1787-00, Sportster 56K Faxmodem, TI chipset	Yes	Yes	ISA	Howard Mann
OK	CJEUSA-65828-FA-E	Model 0460 (001787-01), Sportster 56K Faxmodem, P/N 1.012.0460-C, TI chipset, *same as Cardinal Connecta 3440*	Yes	Yes	ISA	August Pamplona
?	CJE-0149 / CJEUSA-73130-FA-E	Sportster 14,400	-	-	EXT	
OK	CJE-0280 / CJEUSA-75811-MM-E	US Robotics Courier V.Everything PCMCIA 33,600	-	-	PCMCIA	Dave Croal
OK	CJE-0263 / CJEUSA-73130-FA-E	Courier v.34 external, Courier V.Everything external	-	-	EXT	Mike Loewen
?	CJE-0269 / CJEUSA-73130-FA-E	Courier v.34 internal	No	Yes	ISA	
?	CJE-0295	Sportster Vi 28.8 Faxmodem, Model 0279-00	-	-	EXT	

Key	FCC ID or Reg #	Model	PNP	Jumpers	Interface	Thanks to:
CNT		Compaq Computer				
	CNT75MPSBD7	CO-2819IVD, 221500-001, Series PSB215, (				
	CNTTAI-30032-PT-E	Presario 4100/4400), AT&T chipset	Yes	No	ISA	
WM		CO-5614WVDA, 292256-003, Series PSB225, (				

This is the Linux/Modem Compatibility Knowledge Base at http://www.o2.net/~gromitkc/winmodem.html

Key	FCC ID or Reg #	Model	PNP	Jumpers	Interface	Thanks to:
WM	CNTTAI-31396-M5-E	Presario 4880), Lucent Luna chipset	Yes	No	ISA	
WM	CNTTAI-31396-M5-E	CO-5614WMD, 293057-001, Series PSB228, (Presario 4500)	Yes	No	ISA	
WM	CNTTAI-24639-TT-E	Presario 56K-VSC	?	?	?	Chris Ediger
WM	?	Presario 336-VSCi	?	?	?	
WM	?	Presario 336-DF(i)	?	?	?	
?	CNTTAI-27290-M5-T	Compaq Aero 8000 Series PE2006A	?	?	?	
?	CNTSNG-32813-DT-E	Compaq Series 577/2585/2896 33.6/19.2 Data fax modem for portable PC	?	?	?	
?	CNTSNG-32813-PT-E					
?	CNTCHN-32987-PT-E	Compaq Officeporte Voice Series NCM 105	?	?	?	
?	CNTSNG-25900-M5-E	Compaq Series NC4008	?	?	?	
WM	CNTTAI-32206-DT-E	Compaq Armada 1500 Series 560CL Telephony Modem, Compaq Series NC1000 internal notebook modem, Lucent 1643 (Apollo FDSP) chipset	Yes	No	ISA	Rojer J. Allen
?	CNTSNG-25911-M5-E	Compaq Series NC1004	?	?	?	
?	CNTSNG-25912-M5-E	Compaq Series NC1006	?	?	?	
?	CNTSNG-33039-M5-E	Compaq Series EVB100/NC2002	?	-	PCMCIA	
?	CNTSNG-33489-M5-E	Compaq Deskporte P 56K, Series 585	?	?	?	

540

This is the Linux/Modem Compatibility Knowledge Base at http://www.o2.net/~gromitkc/winmodem.html

Key	FCC ID or Reg #	Model	PNP	Jumpers	Interface	Thanks to:
	CNTSNG-33490-M5-E					
	CLBCHN-21430-MM-E					
	CLBCHN-21805-MM-E					
?	CLBCHN-23504-MM-E	Compaq Deskporte S Internal, Deskporte Fast, Deskporte S	?	?	?	

This is the Linux/Modem Compatibility Knowledge Base at http://www.o2.net/~gromitkc/winmodem.html

Key	FCC ID or Reg #	Model	PNP	Jumpers	Interface	Thanks to:
DK4		GVC				
	DK4SF1114HVC2					
?	DK4TAI-23008-PT-E	GVC SF-1114HV/C2, Cirrus Logic chipset	?	Yes	ISA	
OK	DK4F1114PVC1	GVC F-1114PV1, Cirrus Logic CL-MD1414AT/EC chipset	-	-	PCMCIA	Dave Croal
OK	DK4TAI-30391-PT-E	GVC, Rockwell RCV336DPF/SP chipset	Yes	No	ISA	Edgar Itokazu
?	DK4CHN-30962-PT-E	Maxtech XPV336I/C, Cirrus Logic chipset	?	Yes	ISA	
	DK4SF1133VR16	Model SF-1133V/R16				
?	DK4TAI-31565-PT-E	, Rockwell chipset	-	-	EXT	
	DK4FM9648HR					
?	DK4TAI-18703-FA-E	Model FM-9648HR/I, Rockwell chipset	?	DIP	ISA	
	DK4FM144VR1					
?	DK4TAI-74516-FA-E	Model FM-144VR/1, Intel 14.4 Model PCFM7600	-	-	EXT	
?	DK4VF1128HVR9					

This is the Linux/Modem Compatibility Knowledge Base at http://www.o2.net/~gromitkc/winmodem.html

Key	FCC ID or Reg #	Model	PNP	Jumpers	Interface	Thanks to:
?	DK4TAI-22919-PT-E	Model VF-1128HV/R9, Rockwell RCV288DPi R6682-24 chipset	?	Yes	ISA	
	DK4F1156IVA2A	GCT				
	DK4TAI-25249-M5-E	, Gateway Telepath/LT Win Modem, Maxtech XPV56P				
WM		, Model (D)F-1156IV/A2(A), Lucent HV90P-T/1034AH-J chipset	Yes	No	PCI	Steve Sanfratello
WM	?	KTX FM-56K-PCII V90/56KFlex, GVC Model F-1156IV+/A2A , Lucent LT Winmodem chipset	Yes	?	PCI	Richard Close
WM	DK4DF1156HVA2B	Model DF-1156HV/A2B, IBM Aptiva modem Model 2139-SE7, Lucent 1643 chipset	Yes	No	ISA	Gene
WM	DK4TAI-24427-M5-E	Model DF-1156HV/R2B, IBM Aptiva modem Model 2140-L61, Lucent 1643 chipset	?	?	?	
?	DK4TAI-25552-M5-E	GVC/OEM Model (S)F-1156HV/R21 , Rockwell ACF chipset	Yes	?	ISA	
?	?	(S)F-1156(H)V/T3, Maxtech XPVS56I/F, TI chipset	Yes	?	ISA	
?	?	SF-1156V/T4, Maxtech XPVS56E, TI chipset	Yes	-	EXT	
?	?	SF-1156HV/C3, Maxtech XPVS56I/C, Cirrus Logic CL-MD5650/T chipset	Yes	Yes	ISA	
?	DK4TAI-25613-M5-E	Model D-1156HVA1/R19	?	?	ISA	
?	DK4TAI-25614-M5-E	Model (S)F-1156HV/R21 , Rockwell ACF chipset	Yes	?	ISA	
?	DK4TAI-25615-M5-E	GVC/OEM Model (S)F-1156V/R21 , Rockwell ACF chipset	-	-	EXT	
?	DK4TAI-27287-M5-E	OEM Model (S)F-1156V/R6	?	?	?	

Key	FCC ID or Reg #	Model	PNP	Jumpers	Interface	Thanks to:
	DK4CHN-27169-M5-E					
	DK4TAI-33728-M5-E					
?	DK4CHN-27725-M5-E	Model (D)F-1156IV/R2	?	?	?	
?	DK4TAI-27335-M5-E	Model D-1156NVX+/A2A	?	?	?	
?	DK4TAI-27865-M5-E	GVC/Sony Model D-1156IVY1/A3	?	?	?	
?	DK4TAI-27391-M5-E	GVC/Kye/Maxtech/Boca/OEM Model F-1156IV/R9(A), Conexant (Rockwell) RH56D-PCI R6795-18 chipset	Yes	No	PCI	
OK	DK4DF1156HVR19 DK4TAI-31895-M5-E	Model SF-1156HV/R19, (PNPID GVC0505) Rockwell chipset	Yes	No	ISA	Igor Sorsak
WM	DK4TAI-32210-M5-E	Model F-1156HV/A5, Lucent Luna chipset	Yes	No	ISA	Barnaby DiAnni
WM	DK4TAI-33273-M5-E	Model DF-1156IV/R3, Kye GM56PCI-RV, Rockwell HCF chipset	?	?	PCI	
?	DK4TAI-33599-M5-E	GVC, Clevo, Hitachi D-1156NVX+/A2B internal for notebook	?	?	?	
?	DK4TAI-33719-M5-E	GVC/OEM MR-001(+)/R1	-	-	PCMCIA	
?	DK4TAI-33867-M5-E	GVC/Acer/OEM D-1156IVY1/A2	?	?	PCI	
?	DK4TAI-34187-M5-E	GVC/Acer/Boca/OEM MR-001/X1, MR-001/A1, MR-001/P1, MR0991/M1, MR-002/X1, MR-002/A1, MR-002/P1	?	?		
?	DK4CHN-34188-M5-E		?	?	PCI	
?	DK4TAI-34225-M5-E	GVC/Acer/Boca/OEM F-1156IV/P1	?	?	PCI	

Key	FCC ID or Reg #	Model	PNP	Jumpers	Interface	Thanks to:
?	DK4TAI-34551-M5-E	GVC/Compaq/PCTel F-1156IV/P2	?	?	PCI	
?	DK4TAI-34263-M5-E	GVC/Acer/Boca/OEM PF-56IMH/R2	?	?	PCI	
?	DK4TAI-34379-M5-E	GVC/OEM 1156NV(+)/A3B internal 56K d/f mountable modem	?	?	?	
?	DK4TAI-34512-M5-E	GVC/OEM (D)F-1156IV/A3	?	?	PCI	
DUP		Practical Peripherals				
?	DUP0336S					
?	DUPUSA-20231-MM-E	MC144MT II	-	-	EXT	
?		Model 4705US, Practical 56K PC Card	-	-	PCMCIA	
?		Model 4709US, PM K56Flex MT	-	-	EXT	
?		Model 4718US, Practical 336 Flash HC	?	?	?	
?		Model 4719US, PM 336 Flash MT	?	?	?	
?		Model 4720US, Practical 336 Flash PC Card	-	-	PCMCIA	
?		Model 4721US, PM K56Flex MT	-	-	EXT	
?		Model 4722US, Practical K56 Flash HC	?	?	?	
OK	DUPUSA-23918-PT-E	Model 5652US, 33.6Kbps	No	Yes	ISA	Rob Clark
OK	DUP5624US					
OK	DUPCHN-30493-PT-E	Model 5652US	?	Yes	ISA	Silviu
?		Model 5672US, PM K56Flex HC Voice, PM V.90 HC Voice	Yes	Yes	ISA	
OK		Model 5676, PM K56Flex HC	Yes	Yes	ISA	R. A. Wilson
?		Model 5677, PM K56Flex MT MiniTower	-	-	EXT	
?		Model 5688, Practical 56K PC Card	-	-	PCMCIA	
?		Model 86001, PM56K MT	-	-	EXT	
?		Model 86003, PM56K MT	?	?	?	
DWE		Xecom				

Key	FCC ID or Reg #	Model	PNP	Jumpers	Interface	Thanks to:
?	DWEUSA-21473-MD-E	XE2400,XE2496L	?	?	?	
DXZ						
	In-Jet Electronics					
WM	?	IJ-5614RPS/RPV , Rockwell HCF Data Fax	Yes	?	PCI	
WM	DXZTAI-25751-M5-E	IJ-5614CPS , Cirrus CLM Data/Fax/Voice	Yes	No	PCI	Michael Douglass
?	DXZTAI-25836-M5-E	IJ-5614RDS, Cirrus CLM Data/Fax/Voice	?	?	?	

Key	FCC ID or Reg #	Model	PNP	Jumpers	Interface	Thanks to:
E2O						
	Datatronics Technology					
?	E2OTAI-27435-M5-E	Datasystem/Discovery 5614MI	?	?	PCI	
?	E2OTAI-27478-M5-T	Data System 5614M14/20/99	?	?	PCI	
?	E2OTAI-27602-M5-E	Discovery 5614UB, 5614SB	?	?	?	
E8H						
	Chicony Electronics					
?	E8HTAI-27662-M5-E	FM993 Fax modem card for notebook	?	?	?	
?	E8HTAI-32916-M5-E	FM983 Internal	?	?	?	
?	E8HTAI-33514-M5-E	Chicony FM982, Micron internal V.90 56K for Transport NX	?	?	?	
?	E8HTAI-34051-M5-E	Chicony FM995 internal for PC notebook	?	?	?	
EBZ						
	Dialogic					
?	EBZUSA-27244-M5-E	CPI/400 PCI, CPI/200 PCI	?	?	PCI	
EJM						
	Intel					

Key	FCC ID or Reg #	Model	PNP	Jumpers	Interface	Thanks to:
?	EJMUSA-18144-MD-E EJM-28PSVD	PCEM72144 14.4 External	-	-	EXT	
?	EJMUSA-22745-PT-E	MDM28PSPKR	?	No	PCI	
?	EJMMLA-33467-M5-E	Intel Pro/100 LAN+Modem56 Cardbus II MBLA3356	?	?	PCMCIA	
?	EJMUSA-27678-M5-E	BP810 Model BEBPGCNHO/BEBPGFEHOM/BEBPSCEHOM, Black Pine motherboard with integrated modem and home networking	?	?		MBD
EUD		**Boca Research**				
?	EUD5U5BRI4815					
?	EUDUSA-22968-PT-E EUD5U9BRI4545	?, Rockwell RCV288DPi R6682-24 chipset	?	?	?	
?	EUDUSA-21494-MM-E EUD5U9BRI4466	?	?	?	ISA	
?	EUDUSA-24032-MM-E EUD5U9BRI4925	33.6 Speakerphone Model FDSP34xxx GD/FV336E	-	-	EXT	
WM	EUDUSA-23524-MM-E	On-Line EXPRESS MV34.AI, Lucent UART-less chipset, DOS or Windows software required	No	Yes	8-bit ISA	Alexsander da Rosa
WM	?	On-Line EXPRESS FDSP34AI, Lucent UART-less chipset, DOS or Windows software required	No	Yes	8-bit ISA	
?	?	Tidalwave 56K internal, Model M(D)56IV, pre-10/98	Yes	No	ISA	Tim C.
		Tidalwave 56K internal, Model M(D)56IV, post-10/98, BRI 4140, Compaq "Netelligent" 56k internal ISA				, Tim Mann

Key	FCC ID or Reg #	Model	PNP	Jumpers	Interface	Thanks to:
		This is the Linux/Modem Compatibility Knowledge Base at http://www.o2.net/~gromitkc/winmodem.html				
OK	EUDUSA-31497-PT-E	, Rockwell R6761-25	Yes	Yes	ISA	
OK	?	Tidalwave 56K external, Model M(D)56EV	-	-	EXT	Jim B Batchelor
WM	EUDUSA-25432-M5-E	WinStorm 56K, Model M(D)56HI / , Rockwell RLVDL56DPF/SP R6785-61 chipset	Yes	No	PCI	
?	EUDUSA-33545-M5-E	Model M56AI	?	?	PCI	
?	EUDUSA-33561-M5-E	Tidal Wave Model M56INTLI	?	?	ISA	
OK	?	External 56K Multimedia Modem Model M56INTLE	-	-	EXT	Luis Larmand Cardoso
EVZ		Data Race				
?	EVZUSA-27417-MM-E	Data Race Lamprey	?	?	?	

Key	FCC ID or Reg #	Model	PNP	Jumpers	Interface	Thanks to:
		This is the Linux/Modem Compatibility Knowledge Base at http://www.o2.net/~gromitkc/winmodem.html				
F2M	F2M9510021	Megahertz				
OK	F2MUSA-23064-MM-E	XJ4288, cellular-capable	-	-	PCMCIA	Dave Brink
OK	5QPUSA-24210-MM-E	XJ1560	-	-	PCMCIA	Mel Roth
WM	?	XJ2560, CC2560 PC Card	-	-	PCMCIA	
WM	4X2IRL-25604-M5-E	CCSPWM WinModem PC Card				
WM	5QPIRL-31517-M5-E	IBM Model 10L7393	-	-	PCMCIA	
WM	?	Megahertz 3CXM356/3CCM356, 3013, 3014 WinModem PC Card	-	-	PCMCIA	
WM	4X2USA-25317-MM-E					
WM	4X2IRL-27040-MM-E	, IBM Model 10L7394	-	-	PCMCIA	Mike Kompar

Key	FCC ID or Reg #	Model	PNP	Jumpers	Interface	Thanks to:
	4X2USA-34153-M5-E					
	4X2SNG-34154-MM-E					
?	4X2IRL-34155-MM-E	3Com Model 3CXM356B/3CCM356B, 3CXM756/3CCM756, USR Model 3056/3057	-	-	PCMCIA	
WM	?	3Com/USRobotics 3014A WinModem PC Card	-	-	PCMCIA	
	4X2USA-26031-M5-E					
?	4X2SNG-27037-M5-E	3CCM156 (CC1560i) 56K Global Modem	-	-	PCMCIA	
OK	5QPUSA-24948-M5-E	3CCM156B-US 56K Global Modem	-	-	PCMCIA	Susie Arnold
	4X2USA-25318-M5-E					
?	4X2IRL-27070-M5-E	3CXM556/3CCM556	-	-	PCMCIA	
?	4X2USA-25547-M5-E	Model 3CCFEM556B, 10/100 LAN + 56K Global	-	-	PCMCIA	
OK	5QPUSA-31362-M5-E	3Com Megahertz 56K Cellular Modem PC Card, Model 3CXM556	-	-	PCMCIA	Chris Ediger, Kevin Snively
	4X2USA-25622-M5-E					
?	4X2IRL-27039-M5-E	3CXM056B/3CXM556B/3CCM156B 56K Global Modem	-	-	PCMCIA	
	4X2USA-25454-M5-E	3CXM656/3CCM656/3014 56K Global GSM WinModem PC Card	-	-		
WM	4X2IRL-27069-M5-E	Megahertz PC383/3, 3CI1BM556, 3CN1BMX56	-	-	PCMCIA	
WM	4X2USA-33324-M5-E	56K WinModem MiniPCI Card	?	?	?	

Key	FCC ID or Reg #	Model	PNP	Jumpers	Interface	Thanks to:
		This is the Linux/Modem Compatibility Knowledge Base at http://www.o2.net/~gromitkc/winmodem.html				
?	4X2USA-32908-M5-E	3CCFEM656 10/100 LAN+56K	-	-	PCMCIA	
?	4X2USA-34233-M5-E	3CXFEM656 10/100 LAN+56K modem Cardbus Global	-	-	PCMCIA	
WM	4X2USA-27196-M5-E	3CCFEM656B 10/100 LAN+56K	-	-	PCMCIA	Matt
	4X2USA-33602-MM-E					
	4X2IRL-33603-MM-E					
?	4X2SNG-33604-MM-E	3CXM756, 3CCM756 33.6K modem	-	-	PCMCIA	
?	4X2USA-33858-MM-E	3C1BC556 Mini PCI 33.6K modem	?	?	?	
	4X2USA-33859-MM-E					
	4X2SNG-27792-MM-E					
?	4X2IRL-27797-MM-E	3CN3BM556 Mini PCI 33.6K modem	?	?	?	
	4X2USA-27606-MM-E					
	4X2SNG-27798-MM-E	3CN3ACX556 33.6K/14.4 modem/fax board, 3CN3ACX556B				
?	4X2IRL-27800-MM-E		?	?	?	
	4X2USA-27793-MM-E					
	4X2SNG-34344-MM-E					
?	4X2IRL-34346-MM-E	3CN3BM1556B fax/data/voice modem board	?	?	?	

Key	FCC ID or Reg #	Model	PNP	Jumpers	Interface	Thanks to:
	4X2USA-27796-MM-E					
	4X2SNG-34345-MM-E					
?	4X2IRL-27799-MM-E	3CN1BM556B fax/data/voice board	?	?	?	
EHX		Multi-Tech Systems				
	EHXUSA-27463-MM-E	Black Box MD1625A, Multimodem MT5634ZBA-USB, USB modem				
?	AU7USA-25665-MM-E		?	?	?	
FEL		Taicom Data Systems				
	FEL MR56S	AOpen FM56-EX(/2)				
OK	FELTAI-31984-M5-E	, Atrie 56K Explore, Patton 2190(-230), Taicom MR56SVS, Rockwell RCVDL56ACF/SP chipset	Yes	-	EXT	Simon South
		AOpen FM56-RS				
?	?	, Rockwell RCVDL56ACF/SP chipset	No	Yes	ISA	
?	FELTAI-27144-M5-E	Taicom MR56PVS-SOFT	?	?	?	
		AOpen FM56-RU				
?	FELTAI-27489-M5-E	, Taicom MR56SVS-RU, USB/RS232 standalone modem, Rockwell RD56D/SP chipset	-	-	USB/EXT	
?	FELTAI-34235-M5-E	AOpen FM56-USB, Taicom MST56U, External USB modem	-	-	?	
?	FELTAI-27593-M5-E	AOpen FM56-MR; Taicom MS56A, MP56A	?	?	?	
		AOpen FM56PVS				
?	?	, Rockwell RCVDL56ACF/SP chipset	No	Yes	ISA	
		AOpen FM56PVS-DL				
OK	?	, Rockwell RCVDL56ACF/SP chipset	No	Yes	ISA	Jon
		AOpen F56				

Key	FCC ID or Reg #	Model	PNP	Jumpers	Interface	Thanks to:
OK	?	export modem, Rockwell RCVDL56ACF/SP chipset	Yes	No	ISA	Bengal
	FELMR56PVS	AOpen FM56PVS-T				
OK	FELTAI-31280-PT-E	, TI TMS320X2APJ chipset	Yes	Yes	ISA	Mike Werner
	FELMR56PVS	AOpen FM56-ITU/2				Andrew Comech
OK	FELTAI-31280-PT-E	, Rockwell RP56D/SP R6764-61 chipset	No	Yes	ISA	, Mike Jing
		AOpen FM56-ITU				
OK	?	, Rockwell RCVDL56ACFW/SP R6771-22 chipset	No	Yes	ISA	Bill Staehle
	FELMR56PVS-HI	AOpen FM56-P				
	FELTAI-32698-M5-E	, Acer/ AOpen FM56-H , Acer FM56PVS(P)-HI, Wintec Powmem P56KDFV, Rockwell RLVDL56DPF/SP chipset				
WM		AOpen FM56-PM , Rockwell chipset	Yes	No	PCI	
WM	?	AOpen FM56-S , Rockwell RS56/SP-PCI chipset	Yes	No	PCI	
WM	?		Yes	?	PCI	
	?	MP56 SRS 3D Audio & 56Kbps F/M/Sp combo, Rockwell RCVDL56ACF/SP chipset	?	?	ISA	
?	?	MR56PVS-COMBO	?	?	PCI	
?	FELTAI-33615-M5-E	MP56PVS	?	?	?	
?	FELTAI-33623-M5-E	AOpen FM56-RM, Taicom MR56PVS-RSI, AOpen FM56-SM	?	?		
WM	FELTAI-33947-M5-E	, Rockwell RS56/SP-PCI R6793-11 (HSF) chipset	Yes	No	PCI	

Key	FCC ID or Reg #	Model	PNP	Jumpers	Interface	Thanks to:
WM	FELTAI-33947-M5-E	Taicom MR56PVS-RHI, AOpen FM56-PM, Rockwell RS56D/SP-PCI (HCF) chipset	Yes	No	PCI	Steve Sanfratello

Key	FCC ID or Reg #	Model	PNP	Jumpers	Interface	Thanks to:
FI7		Archtek Telecom				
OK	FI7TAI-25018-M5-E	SmartLink 5634BTS * V.90/K56Flex Flashable Voice Faxmodem, Powercom M56VI-ST1, TI chipset	Yes	Yes	ISA	Michael Shell
?		SmartLink 5634TS , External Speakerphone Video Ready Modem, TI chipset	-	-	EXT	
?		SmartLink 5634BRS , 5634BRV-1 V.90/K56Flex Speakerphone Modem, Rockwell chipset	Yes	Yes	ISA	
?		SmartLink 5634RS , V.90/K56Flex FDSP Modem, Rockwell chipset	-	-	EXT	
?		SmartLink 5634PCA, K56Flex Fax Modem, Lucent chipset	?	-	PCMCIA	
?		SmartLink 5634PCC, X2 Fax Modem, Cirrus Logic chipset	?	-	PCMCIA	
?		SmartLink 5634BTV * - X2 Speakerphone Modem, Powercom M56VI-STP, TI chipset	Yes	Yes	ISA	
?		SmartLink 5634BT X2 Modem	Yes	Yes	ISA	
WM		SmartLink 5634BEW Win Modem, ESS chipset	Yes	No	ISA	
?		SmartLink 56PCI-R,				

Key	FCC ID or Reg #	Model	PNP	Jumpers	Interface	Thanks to:
WM	?	SmartLink 5634PRW Win Modem, Rockwell chipset	Yes	No	PCI	
WM	?	SmartLink 56PCI-C V.90 Data/Fax/FDSP Modem, Cirrus Logic CLM chipset	Yes	No	PCI	
WM	?	SmartLink 56PCI-L V.90 Voice/Data/Fax, Lucent LT Winmodem chipset	Yes	No	PCI	
WM	?	SmartLink 5634PRS Software Modem, Rockwell HSP chipset	Yes	No	PCI	
?	FI7TAI-25875-FB-E	SmartLink 5634BIF	?	?	?	
?	FI7TAI-25743-PT-E	SmartLink 5634IF * -, 4 Dimension Modem	-	-	EXT	
OK	FI7TAI-27209-PT-E	SmartLink 5634RCS FDSP external	-	-	EXT	John Cooper
WM	FI7TAI-33176-M5-E	SmartLink 5634PEW Win Modem, ESS chipset	Yes	No	PCI	
?	FI7TAI-33869-M5-E	Smartlink Model T 56UST, external mini 56K USB modem	-	-	USB	
?	FI7TAI-27527-M5-E	Smartlink Model MRS /MRM/MRP 56K/14.4 AMR fax modem	?	?	AMR	
?	FI7TAI-34596-M5-E	Smartlink 5634PCV	?	?	PCI	
FJE		Packard Bell/NEC				
?	FJEUSA-40066-M5-E	Versa Lite FX, 56K LS modem in laptop	?	?	?	
FKG		Twinhead International				
?	FKGTAI-27526-M5-E	Twinhead Model V1456VQL14P for notebook	?	?	?	
?	FKGTAI-27550-M5-E	Twinhead Model V1456VQL14N	?	?	?	

Key	FCC ID or Reg #	Model	PNP	Jumpers	Interface	Thanks to:
?	FKGTAI-34164-M5-E	Twinhead Sliimnote XVE, Mirable TE Model V1456VQL14Q(INT)	?	?	?	
	FN6	Best Data Products				
	FN6-1442F					
OK	FN6USA-74372-FA-E	Newcom 14400ifx, Rockwell chipset	No	Yes	ISA	Carlos Tondreau C.
OK	FN6USA-30412-PT-E	Model 336F, Smart One 33.6K data/fax	Yes	Yes	ISA	Roger Liu
WM	FN6USA-32761-M5-E	Model 56FW, Smart One 56K int. win modem, ISA, Rockwell chipset	Yes	No	ISA	Brad Erickson
WM	?	Model 56FW-PCI, Smart One 56K int. win modem, PCI	Yes	?	PCI	Donald I. Brown
OK	FN6USA-31385-M5-E	Model 56SPS/SF/SVF, Smart One 56K	Yes	Yes	ISA	Gus Palandri
OK	FN6USA-31385-M5-E	Model 56SX/56X/56 SPX/56 SPMAC/56 MAC, Smart One 56K	-	-	EXT	Sean Azelton
?	FN6USA-32462-M5-E	SmartOne 56SPC, Rockwell chipset	-	-	PCMCIA	Tim McLarnan
?	FN6USA-33445-M5-E	SmartOne 56USB(-Mac)/G56USB(-Mac)/56USB Mach 2	?	?	?	
OK	FN6USA-33838-M5-E	SmartOne 56SPSX(-Mac), 56SX-2(-Mac)	-	-	EXT	Stuart A. Hall
	FQU	Computer Peripherals Inc.				
	FQU-DFV-502770					
?	FQUUSA-20961-MM-E	ViVa 14.4i FAX Voice, Cirrus Logic chipset	?	?	ISA	
	FQU-228-03035	ViVa28.8i DSVD PnP Speakerphone modem (PNPID ROK4920), Rockwell chipset				
OK	FQUUSA-23430-PT-E	Maxtech N-XPVS336I/R NetPacer	Yes	No	ISA	Greg Gershowitz
	FQU-336-04040					

This is the Linux/Modem Compatibility Knowledge Base at http://www.o2.net/~gromitkc/winmodem.html

Key	FCC ID or Reg #	Model	PNP	Jumpers	Interface	Thanks to:
?	FQUUSA-30442-PT-E	, Rockwell RCV336ACF/SP chipset	Yes	No	ISA	D.W.B.
?		ViVa CommCenter, Quantex MDM-DFVS336/C , Rockwell chipset	Yes	No	ISA	
?		ViVa CommCenter, Quantex MDM-DFVS336-1/C , Rockwell RCV336ACF/SP R6749-21 chipset	Yes	No	ISA	
?	FQUUSA-25674-M5-E	ViVa RAS/56 Model 500-XXX, 4-modem 56K PCI card	?	?	PCI	
?	FQUUSA-40014-M5-E	ViVa/56R-SX/SM/S/V/XX, Rockwell ACF chipset	Yes	?	ISA	
WM	?	ViVa/56LC-V , Lucent 1641B chipset	Yes	No	ISA	

This is the Linux/Modem Compatibility Knowledge Base at http://www.o2.net/~gromitkc/winmodem.html

Key	FCC ID or Reg #	Model	PNP	Jumpers	Interface	Thanks to:
G2M		Digitan Systems				
	G2MUSA-33611-M5-E	56K Data/Fax with USB, Digitan Model DS560-600(D),				
?	4V4USA-27376-M5-E	Diamond SupraExpress 56E USB V.90 Model 2780	?	-	USB	
?	G2MUSA-33941-M5-E	56K PCI Data/Fax Modem Model DS560-558	?	?	PCI	
?	G2MUSA-40099-M5-E	56K PCI Data/Fax Modem Model DS560-558-WW	?	?	PCI	
G9T		E-Tech Research				
?		E56RX	-	-	EXT	
OK		E56KRVP (*) , Rockwell RP56D/SP chipset	-	-	EXT	Martijn van den Burg
?	G9TTAI-25564-M5-E	E56D [E56KRVP-D]	-	-	EXT	

This is the Linux/Modem Compatibility Knowledge Base at http://www.o2.net/~gromitkc/winmodem.html

Key	FCC ID or Reg #	Model	PNP	Jumpers	Interface	Thanks to:
WM	?	PC56PVP	Yes	No	ISA	
WM	G9TTAI-25851-M5-E	PCI56PVP, HSP chipset	-	No	PCI	Stuart Butterfield
WM	G9TTAI-25852-M5-E	PCI56SRXV	-	No	PCI	
?	?	PC56RX (*)	Yes	Yes	ISA	
WM	?	PCI56RX	Yes	No	PCI	
	G9TPC56EX-V					
WM	G9TTAI-25067-M5-E	PC56EXV	Yes	No	ISA	Ed Griffin
OK	?	PC56RVP	Yes	Yes	ISA	Bill Brower
?	?	PC56RVP/29	Yes	Yes	ISA	
WM	G9TTAI-27127-M5-E	PCI56RVP+, Rockwell HSF chipset	Yes	No	PCI	
WM	G9TTAI-27154-M5-E	PCI56PVP+, HSP chipset, Bullet	Yes	No	PCI	
WM	G9TPCI56RVP	PCI56RVP, Rockwell RLVDL56DPF/SP chipset	Yes	No	PCI	Boudewijn Visser
?	G9TTAI-32469-M5-E	MR56P 56k/14.4k AMR d/f modem	?	?	AMR	
?	G9TTAI-27672-M5-E	MR56S 56k/14.4k AMR d/f modem	?	?	AMR	
?	G9TTAI-27673-M5-E	PCI56CX	?	?	PCI	
?	G9TTAI-33010-M5-E	USB56L	-	-	USB	
?	?	USB56S	-	-	USB	
GDE	GDE	Cardinal Technologies				
OK	GDE0203	MVPV34I, (PNPID CRD0030) V.34 + Class 1 & 2 Fax	Yes	No	ISA	Rob Clark

Key	FCC ID or Reg #	Model	PNP	Jumpers	Interface	Thanks to:
?	?	MVPV34IV, (PNPID CRD0031) V.34 + Class 1 & 2 Fax + Voice	Yes	?	ISA	
?	?	MVPV34IS, (PNPID CRD0032) V.34 + Class 1 & 2 Fax + Voice + Speakerphone	Yes	?	ISA	
?	?	MVPV34XF, (PNPID CRD1030) V.34 + Class 1 & 2 Fax	-	-	EXT	
?	?	MVPV34XV, (PNPID CRD1031) V.34 + Class 1 & 2 Fax + Voice	-	-	EXT	
?	?	MVPV34XV, (PNPID CRD1032) V.34 + Class 1 & 2 Fax + Voice + Speakerphone	-	-	EXT	
WM	?	Model 3250 56K Windows Fax Modem	Yes	?	?	
OK	GDEUSA-31032-MM-E CJEUSA-65828-FA-E	Model 3440 (310-0025) 56K Fax Modem, *same as* USR 1787-01	Yes	Yes	ISA	John E. Jardine
?	?	Model 3480 56K Fax Modem	-	-	EXT	
?		Connecta Model 3640 56K Speakerphone Modem	Yes	?	?	
?		Connecta Model 3680 56K Speakerphone Modem	-	-	EXT	
?		Connecta (PNPID CRD5103) 56k External D/F	-	-	EXT	
?		Connecta (PNPID CRD5003) 56k Internal D/F	Yes	?	ISA	
?		Connecta (PNPID CRD5102) 336 External D/F	-	-	EXT	
?		Connecta (PNPID CRD5002) 336 Internal D/F	Yes	?	ISA	
?		Connecta (PNPID CRD5004) 56k External Spk	-	-	EXT	
?		Connecta (PNPID CRD5203) 56k Internal Spk	Yes	?	ISA	
	Metricom					
OK	GNW21062	Ricochet Wireless Modem, Model 21062	-	-	EXT	Kevin Snively
	GX5	Digicom Systems				
?	GX5USA-27717-MM-E	Creative ModemBlaster DE5625, external modem	?	?	?	
OK	GX5USA-31644-M5-E	Creative ModemBlaster DI5601	Yes	Yes	ISA	Ian Burry

557

Key	FCC ID or Reg #	Model	PNP	Jumpers	Interface	Thanks to:
?	GX5USA-34024-M5-E	Creative ModemBlaster DI5601-1	?	?	PCI	
WM	GX5USA-33051-M5-E	Creative ModemBlaster DI5630(-3), Rockwell RLVDL56DPF/SP chipset	Yes	No	PCI	Tom Hodges
WM	GX5USA-27261-PT-E	Creative ModemBlaster DI3635-1; DI5655	Yes	No	PCI	Greg Moody
?	?	Creative ModemBlaster DI5610 Cellular Ready	-	-	PCMCIA	
		DSI DI3660				
WM	GX5USA-33277-M5-E	(PNPID DMB2002), Creative ModemBlaster DI5660 (PNPID DMB2001), ESS ES336/ES56 chipset	Yes	No	ISA	Murat Saygili
WM	GX5USA-33278-M5-E	Creative ModemBlaster DI5635, Rockwell HCF chipset	Yes	No	PCI	
?	?	Creative ModemBlaster DI5665	Yes	?	8-bit ISA	

Key	FCC ID or Reg #	Model	PNP	Jumpers	Interface	Thanks to:
H4T		Zoltrix				
?	H4TFZX1848A	?	?	Yes	ISA	
?	1B9ZMB-60334-MD-E	FM144ATi, Rockwell 14,400 RPI chipset (RC144DPi & C39R/U-AT)	No	DIP	ISA	Rob Clark
RP	H4TFM-9696 1B9USA-73793-FA-E	Zoltrix Platinum Series 14.4,	No	DIP	ISA	Rob Clark
OK	H4TFM-9696 1B9USA-73793-FA-E	FMVOC1414, Rockwell ACi 14,400 chipset (RC144DPi & C39R/U)	No	DIP	ISA	Rob Clark
	H4TFM-RIA3X	FM-VSP336i				Francisco Dominguez-Adame

Key	FCC ID or Reg #	Model	PNP	Jumpers	Interface	Thanks to:
	This is the Linux/Modem Compatibility Knowledge Base at http://www.o2.net/~gromitkc/winmodem.html					
OK	1B9USA-24358-PT-E	, Rockwell RCV336ACF/SP R6749-21 chipset, not upgradable	No	Yes	ISA	Marcio H. Parreiras
	H4TFM-E-144-288V	FM-VSP336e	-	-	EXT	
?	1B9USA-22636-MM-E	, not upgradable	-	-	EXT	
?	H4TFM-VSP56I	FMVSP56e, Rockwell ACF chipset / FMVSP56i, FMVSP56i2				
OK	1B9USA-25111-M5-E	, Rockwell RCVDL56ACF/SP R6761-21 chipset	No	Yes	ISA	Lou
	H4TFM-VSP56I	FMVSP56i3				
OK	1B9USA-25111-MT-E	, Rockwell RCVDL56ACFW/SP R6771-22 chipset	No	Yes	ISA	Steven Clarke
	H4TFM-REB3X	FMVSP56e2 "Rainbow"				
OK	1B9USA-25422-M5-E	, Rockwell ACF chipset	-	-	EXT	Alexandre Ferluc
WM	?	FMHSP56p, PCTel 388P chipset	Yes	No	ISA	
WM	H4TFM-HSP336I	FMHSP366p, PCTel 288PNP chipset	Yes	No	ISA	
WM	H4TFM-PIB3C	Model FM-PIB3PC,				
WM	1B9USA-25853-M5-E	Zoltrix Phantom 56K FM-HSP56PCI, PCTel 1789 (HSP) chipset	Yes	No	PCI	Dariusz Goiński
WM	?	FMHCF56i Spirit 56K Model FM-5668 Rev 1.3, Rockwell HCF chipset	Yes	No	PCI	
WM	H4TFM-RIB3HC					
WM	1B9USA-33032-M5-E	FMHCF56i Spirit 56K Model FM-5668 Rev 3.1, Rockwell RCVDL56DPGL/SP R6776-33 (HCF) chipset	Yes	No	PCI	
	H4TFM-RIB3HC	Model FM-RIB3HC,				

Key	FCC ID or Reg #	Model	PNP	Jumpers	Interface	Thanks to:
WM	1B9USA-33032-M5-E	Cobra 56K Model FM-5668/FMSFT56i, Rockwell (two-chip) HSF chipset	Yes	No	PCI	
WM	1B9USA-27236-M5-E	Cobra 56K Model FM-5687/FMSFT56i, Rockwell RS56/SP-PCI R6793-11P1 (single-chip HSF) chipset	Yes	No	PCI	
?	1B9USA-33347-M5-E	Model FM-RIB3HSF	?	?	PCI	
H52		**Puretek Industrial**				
?	H52PT-3011	Model PT-3011, K56Flex Hardware Modem, Rockwell RCVDL56ACF/SP R6761-21 chipset	?	Yes	ISA	
OK	H52PT-3012	Model PT-3012, External K56Flex/V90 Data/Fax/Voice	Yes	-	EXT	Thomas Dagonnier
WM	H52PT-3017	Maxsenger, Motorola SM56 ISA ; Puretek Model PT-3017 Software Modem, Motorola chipset	Yes	No	ISA	
?	H52PT-3023	Model PT-3023, PCI 56K Modem	?	?	PCI	
?	5OITAI-33328-M5-E	Generic/Phanta Link/Macrex Model PT-3027, PCI 56K Software Modem	?	?	PCI	
	H52PT-3027					
WM	5OITAI-33330-M5-E	, Motorola chipset	Yes	No	PCI	
?	5OITAI-34600-M5-E	Model PT-3037, PCI 56K D/F/V Modem	?	?	PCI	
?	5OITAI-34569-M5-E	Model PT-3050, External USB 56K D/F/V Modem	?	?	?	
WM	H52PT-3511	Model PT-3511, V.90 Win Modem, Archtek SmartLink 5634 PCI (56PCI-R), Rockwell RLVDL56DPF/SP R6785-61 (HCF) chipset	Yes	No	PCI	Brian W. Johnson

This is the Linux/Modem Compatibility Knowledge Base at http://www.o2.net/~gromitkc/winmodem.html

Key	FCC ID or Reg #	Model	PNP	Jumpers	Interface	Thanks to:
	H52PT-3515					
WM	5OITAI-33329-M5-E	Model PT-3515, V.90 Software Modem	Yes	No	PCI	Antti Aaltonen
OK	H52PT-3911	Model PT-3911 , K56Flex, v.90 Hardware Modem, Rockwell RCVDL56ACF/SP R6761-21 chipset	Yes	Yes	ISA	
?	5OITAI-33793-M5-E	Model PT-3026 D/F/V USB modem	-	-	USB	
?	5OITAI-33794-M5-E	Model PT-3022 D/F/V USB modem	-	-	USB	
?	5OITAI-33942-M5-E	Model PT-3060 External D/F/V USB hub modem	-	-	USB	
?	5OITAI-33986-M5-E	Model PT-3517	?	?	PCI	

This is the Linux/Modem Compatibility Knowledge Base at http://www.o2.net/~gromitkc/winmodem.html

Key	FCC ID or Reg #	Model	PNP	Jumpers	Interface	Thanks to:
	H8N	Askey Computer Corp.				
RP	H8N1414H	Fax/Data Modem	-	-	EXT	David Lawyer
	H8N96144VH					
OK	H8NTAI-74209-FA-E	14.4 Fax/Modem	No	Yes	ISA	Rob Clark
	H8N9624SH					
?	H8NTAI-73003-MD-E	?	?	Yes	ISA	
OK	H8N1428VQHV34	Phoebe 1428VQH-R1, Rockwell RC288DPi chipset	No	Yes	ISA	Martin Maney
	H8NV1428VQE					
?	H8NTAI-22674-PT-E	Dynamode 33.6 bps V1428VQE	?	?	PCI	
?	H8NV1428VQH	Askey V1428VQH-S, Sierra SQ3465 chipset	?	?	ISA	
?	?	Thundermax V1433VQH-L, Cirrus Logic CL-MD3450 chipset	Yes	?	ISA	

Key	FCC ID or Reg #	Model	PNP	Jumpers	Interface	Thanks to:
?	?	V1433VQE-L, Cirrus Logic CL-MD3450 chipset	-	-	EXT	
	H8NV1433VQH-R	V1433VQH-R , DSI/Creative Modem Blaster 33.6, Harmony HM18010-4, Rockwell RCV336ACF/SVD R6759-21 chipset				
OK	H8NTAI-30603-PT-E		Yes	Yes	ISA	Rob Clark
	H8N1433VQH-X	Askey				
	H8NTAI-23598-PT-E	/ AmJet 1433VQH-X, Dynalink				
OK	H8NV1433VQH-X	FastCard +, TI chipset Dynalink Voicecard33 / Askey	Yes	Yes	ISA	Dave Slusky
OK	H8NTAI-30357-PT-E	V1433VQH-X , Harmony HM18008-2, TI chipset	Yes	Yes	ISA	Blair George
		V1433VQH-U				
OK	H8NTAI-31760-PT-E	, MagicExpress MX33V-U, Davicom (UMC) chipset	Yes	Yes	ISA	JR Putnam
?	H8NTAI-32454-MM-E	V1433VQE-U, MagicExpress MX33VX-U	?	?	?	
		MagicXpress MX56-R, Max-Link/OEM/ AmJet 1456VQH-R, Dynalink PCI Card56				
WM	H8NTAI-25712-M5-E	, Rockwell RLDL56DPF (HCF) chipset	Yes	No	PCI	Vardan Akopian
	H8NTAI-25862-M5-E	MagicXpress MX56V-R1, Phoebe Micro/OEM V1456VQE-R1,				Silviu
	3T4SNG-27090-M5-E	ZyXEL Comet 3356				, Wolfgang Schneider
		Dynalink VoiceDesk56 Pro				

This is the Linux/Modem Compatibility Knowledge Base at http://www.o2.net/~gromitkc/winmodem.html

Key	FCC ID or Reg #	Model	PNP	Jumpers	Interface	Thanks to:
OK		, Rockwell ACF2 chipset	-	-	EXT	Walter Coole
WM	H8NTAI-25618-M5-E	1456VQH-T1, 1456VQH-T2, MagicXpress MX56-T2, Lucent 1646T00 (Mars) chipset	Yes	No	PCI	
?	H8NTAI-27611-M5-E	Generic/Askey 1456VQH-R1, MagicXpress MX56-R1, IBM 1456VQH75A, 1456VQH20C, 1456VQH-R2, MX56-R2	?	?	?	
?	H8NTAI-27582-M5-E	Generic/Askey V1456VQH-T6, MagicXpress MX56-T6	?	?	?	
OK	H8NTAI-25919-M5-E	MagicXpress MX56VX-T1, OEM V1456VQE-T1, Digicom/ModemBlaster DE5670, USB w/speakerphone, *requires kernel USB modem support*	-	-	USB	Douglas Straub
OK	H8NTAI-26018-M5-E	OEM/ AmJet V1456VQH-R5, MagicXpress SF MX56V-R5, Dynalink VoiceCard56 Pro ISA, Rockwell RP56D/SP chipset	Yes	Yes	ISA	Geir Agdesteen
OK	?	Phoebe CMV1456VQH-2MRA (R5), 56K V.90 dual-mode Voice/Speakerphone modem	Yes	Yes	ISA	Doug Wright
WM	H8NTAI-34139-M5-E	Askey/ AmJet V1456VQH-R6, Rockwell HSF chipset	Yes	No	PCI	
?	H8NTAI-34354-M5-E	Askey/OEM V1456VHQ-R6(NP(1)), MagicXpress MX56-R6(NP(1))	?	?	PCI	
?	H8NTAI-27123-M5-E	MagicXpress MX56VX-R2, OEM/ AmJet V1456VQE-R2	-	-	USB	
?	H8NTAI-34543-M5-E	MagicXpress MIX56X-R3, OEM V1456VQE-R3	-	-	USB	
?	H8NTAI-27709-M5-E	Askey/OEM HNH010-D75, home LAN with d/f modem	?	?	?	

Key	FCC ID or Reg #	Model	PNP	Jumpers	Interface	Thanks to:
?	H8NTAI-27731-M5-E	Askey/OEM 1456VQL1Q-2	?	?	?	
?	H8NTAI-27733-M5-E	Askey/OEM 1456VQC-T3	?	?	?	
?	H8NTAI-27784-M5-E	Askey/OEM ALH010	?	?	?	
?	H8NTAI-34271-M5-E	Askey 1456VQH-P, 1456VQH-S	?	?	?	
?		Phoebe Micro Rocket USB Deluxe	-	-	USB	
?	H8NTAI-27397-M5-E	Askey 1456VQL10H (INT), 1456VQL10J (INT)	?	?	?	
WM	H8NTAI-27454-M5-E	OEM/Askey V1456VQH-P2, Acer V1456VQH2OB, MagicXpress MX56V-P2, PCTel PCT789T chipset	Yes	No	PCI	
?	H8NTAI-27564-M5-E	Askey 1456VQH-R1, 56K data/14.4 fax/6.3k voice modem card	?	?	?	
?	H8NTAI-27539-M5-E	Askey 1414VQL60, GI Starphone SFT2	?	?	?	
?	H8NTAI-27842-M5-E	OEM 1456VQC-T5, MagicXpress MX56C-T5	?	?	?	
?	H8NTAI-27850-M5-E	Askey/DSI/Dynalink/Phoebe 1456VQE-C, MagicXpress MX56X-C	?	?	?	
?	H8NTAI-32298-PT-E	Digicom DI5615, Phoebe 1456VQC-T4, Lucent chipset	-	-	PCMCIA	
?	H8NTAI-32855-M5-E	OEM 1456VQC-T(INT), MagicExpress MX56PCM-T(INT)	-	-	PCMCIA	
?	H8NTAI-32857-M5-E	V.90 Speakerphone				
?	RYNTAI-25967-M5-E	OEM /				

Key	FCC ID or Reg #	Model	PNP	Jumpers	Interface	Thanks to:
WM		AmJet V1456VQH-R3, Phoebe CMV1456VQHRPCI/ROCKET DELUXE , MagicXpress MX56VX-R3, Rockwell RLVDL56DPF/SP R6785-61 chipset	Yes	No	PCI	
?	?	Thundermax /OEM V1456VQH-R4, Phoebe CMV1456VQH-PLUS/RV90, Rockwell chipset	Yes	?	ISA	
?	H8NV1456VQH-R	MagicXpress MX56V-R				
OK	H8NTAI-31661-M5-E	, Philips PCA 561 IS, ZyXEL Comet 3356B, OEM V1456VQH-R ; Quantex MDM-S56/A ; Rockwell RCVDL56ACF/SVD R6761-27 chipset	Yes	Yes	ISA	Benjamin Hendricks
WM	H8NTAI-27108-M5-E	OEM 1456VQLIN, Compaq Presario 56K V.90 PCI DF for notebook, Lucent chipset	Yes	No	PCI	John Christopher
WM	H8NTAI-32446-M5-E	V.90 Speakerphone, OEM V1456VQH-P , PC-Tel (HSP) chipset	Yes	Yes	ISA	Keith Anderson
OK	H8NTAI-32590-M5-E	Digicom DI3658, Philips PCA561 IS/US	Yes	Yes	ISA	Phil Burke
WM	H8NTAI-33182-M5-E	MagicXpress MX56V-P1, OEM/ AmJet / Dynamode V1456VQH-P1, Phoebe Micro CMV1456VQH-P1 , PC-Tel HSP chipset	Yes	No	PCI	
?	?	OEM V1456VQH-T , Lucent Venus chipset	?	?	ISA	
		Askey				

Key	FCC ID or Reg #	Model	PNP	Jumpers	Interface	Thanks to:
?	H8NTAI-31758-M5-E	AmJet / V1456VQE-R, MagicXpress MX56VX-R, Philips PCA 561EM, ZyXEL Comet 3356, Rockwell chipset	-	-	EXT	Joey Smith ; Frederic van Hoof
		MagicXpress MX56V-X , Phoebe Micro CMV1456VQH-XV.90				
OK	H8NTAI-31778-M5-E	AmJet / Askey /Thunderlink/OEM V1456VQH-X, Harmony HM18022-1, TI chipset	Yes	Yes	ISA	
?	?	MagicXpress MX56VX-X , Phoebe/ Askey / AmJet / V1456VQE-X, TI chipset	-	-	EXT	
?	H8NTAI-33943-M5-E	Askey V1456VQH-R7	?	?	PCI	
?	?	Askey / MagicXpress MX56VXU, USB D/F/V 56K V.90	-	-	USB	
?	H8NTAI-34052-M5-E	FIC V1456VQL19M internal for notebook	?	?	?	
?	H8NTAI-34309-M5-E	OEM 1456CQL19Q, 1456VQL82, V1456VQL1R PCI internal module modem	?	?	?	
?	H8NTAI-40125-M5-E	OEM 1456VQL84 internal modem	?	?	?	

This is the Linux/Modem Compatibility Knowledge Base at http://www.o2.net/~gromitkc/winmodem.html

Key	FCC ID or Reg #	Model	PNP	Jumpers	Interface	Thanks to:
?	H8NTAI-34262-M5-E	Askey/OEM 1456VQH-C	?	?	PCI	
?	H8NTAI-34329-M5-E	Askey/OEM HNH030	?	?	PCI	
	H8NTAI-40049-M5-E	Askey/OEM 1456VQL42P(JAPAN), MagicXpress MX56L-P1(INT)	?	?	?	
?	H8NTAI-40050-M5-E	Askey/OEM 1456VQL-P2(INT), MagicXpress MX56L-P2(INT)	?	?	?	
?	H8NTAI-34552-M5-E	Askey/OEM 1456VQH87	?	?	?	
?	H8NTAI-34615-M5-E	Askey/OEM 1456VQH87	?	?	PCI	
?	H8NTAI-34557-M5-E	MagicXpress MX56-P1, mini PCI modem	?	?	?	
HHR		Paradise Innovations				
?	HHRSNG-27020-M5-E	Paradise/CW/Multiwave Innovation (CW)56RS-PCI	?	?	?	
?	HHRSNG-27025-M5-E	Paradise/CW/Multiwave Innovation (CW)56PT-PCI	?	?	?	

This is the Linux/Modem Compatibility Knowledge Base at http://www.o2.net/~gromitkc/winmodem.html

Key	FCC ID or Reg #	Model	PNP	Jumpers	Interface	Thanks to:
I38		Aztech Systems				
	I38-MMSN843					
OK	4J2SNG-22647-PT-E	14.4 Modem & sound okay, joystick?, Rockwell chipset	?	No	ISA	Rob Clark
?	I38-SN96109	Model MF3850, K56Flex Voice/Data/Fax Modem	?	?	ISA	
?	?	Model EM3850 , K56Flex Voice/Data/Fax Modem, Rockwell RCVDL56ACFW/SP chipset	-	-	EXT	
IEJ		Global Village Communication				

567

Key	FCC ID or Reg #	Model	PNP	Jumpers	Interface	Thanks to:
OK	IEJA824	Global Village Model A824, Boca Research Tidalwave Model MD56AE	-	-	EXT	Richard Wenzel
	IFA	Acex				
	IFAXDM2400H					
?	1JBTAI-61338-MD-E	?	?	DIP	ISA	
	IFAXDM2814H					
?	1JBTAI-20553-MM-E	DM-2814VH 33.6K	No	Yes	ISA	
	IFAXDM33V14H					
?	1JBTAI-23995-PT-E	DM-33V14H Voice 33.6K	No	Yes	ISA	
	IFAXDM33V14					
?	1JBTAI-30605-PT-E	DM-33V14 Voice 33.6K	-	-	EXT	
	IFAXDM56V14H					
WM	1JBTAI-25959-M5-E	DM-56V14/PCI, DM-56V14HSF, Motorola 62412-51 chipset	Yes	No	PCI	Aristide Aragon Jeff
	IFAXDM56V14H	DM-56V14/PCI,				
WM	1JBTAI-25959-M5-E	DM-56V14HSF/2 , Rockwell RS56/SP-PCI (HSF) chipset	Yes	No	PCI	Gerard Lanois
?	1JBTAI-27664-M5-E	DM-56V14/USB V.90 56K fax modem	?	?	?	
	IFAXDM56V14H	DM-56V14H K56flex Voice				
OK	1JBTAI-31412-M5-E	, Rockwell ACF/SP chipset	No	Yes	ISA	Javier Bolaños Molina
	IFAXDM56V14					
?	1JBTAI-32587-M5-E	DM-56V14 K56flex Voice	-	-	EXT	
		DM-56V14HCF , Rockwell chipset				
WM	?		Yes	No	PCI	

Key	FCC ID or Reg #	Model	PNP	Jumpers	Interface	Thanks to:
		This is the Linux/Modem Compatibility Knowledge Base at http://www.o2.net/~gromitkc/winmodem.html				
WM	?	DM-56V14HSF/5, Motorola chipset	Yes	No	PCI	
	IIA	**PCtel**				
?	5ZXUSA-27655-MM-E	HSP56 Modemriser 2303N	?	?	?	
?	5ZXUSA-27656-MM-E	HSP56 World Modemriser 2303W	?	?	?	
?	5ZXUSA-40128-M5-E	HSP56 World Modemriser 2303W Rev 3.5	?	?	?	
?	IIAUSA-25537-M5-E	PCT789	?	?	?	
WM		HSP Micromodem PCT1789, Zoltrix FMHSP56PCI Phantom 56K, PCTel 1789 chipset				
WM	IIAUSA-33240-M5-E	HSP56 World Micromodem PCT1789W	Yes	No	PCI	
?	5ZXUSA-33606-M5-E		?	?	ISA	
?	5ZXUSA-33607-M5-E	HSP56 Micromodem PCT1789N, IISP56 Micromodem 1789N-C, Wisecom WS-5614PMEA				
?	409TAI-34113-M5-E		?	?	ISA	
?	5ZXUSA-34494-M5-E	HSP Micromodem 1789N Rev. 5.0, Wisecom CO-5614PMEB, WS-5614PMEB				
?	409TAI-40134-M5-E		?	?	PCI	
	J4I	**Sierra Semiconductor**				
	J4I-SQ3465V34P	Wisecom WS-2814JS6,				
?	409TAI-23357-PT-E	Quantex MDM-DFVS2828/W, Sierra SQ3465 chipset	Yes	No	ISA	
		Motorola VoiceSURFR 28.8, Sierra SQ3465 chipset				
OK	J4I-SQ3465V34P	**Well Communication**	Yes	Yes	ISA	Allen Peluso
	JCH	**Acorp**				

Key	FCC ID or Reg #	Model	PNP	Jumpers	Interface	Thanks to:
OK	?	336EMS, Rockwell RCV336DPFSP chipset	-	-	EXT	Vasil Tonev
?	?	Acorp A-56EMR	-	-	EXT	
?	?	Acorp A-56EMS	-	-	EXT	
?	1YYTAI-25791-M5-E	Well/Origo/PC-Link/NSP/WellLink/Xtrun FM-56xx-RWD	?	?	?	
OK	?	US Sertek DCS 56RP1, version ACF-UK, part number 1630.5RP11.301	-	-	EXT	Karl
?	?	FM-56PC-CL , Cirrus Logic chipset	?	Yes	ISA	
WM	JCH-FM56PCI	FM-56PCI-CL , Cirrus Logic CL-MD5620T chipset	?	No	PCI	
WM	1YYTAI-32421-M5-E	FM-56PCI-ML, Motorola soft modem chipset	Yes	No	PCI	
WM	?	Well / US Sertek FM-56PC-PT, PCtel PCT388 chipset	Yes	No	ISA	
?	?	FM-56PC-RW , Rockwell ACF chipset	?	Yes	ISA	
?	?	FM-56PC-RWD , Rockwell RC56D chipset	?	Yes	ISA	
WM	?	Origo FM-56PCI-RW , US Sertek DCS 56PR6-PCI , Rockwell RCV56HCF chipset	Yes	No	PCI	Hashi
OK	1YYTAI-32455-M5-E	FM-56PC-TI , V.90 x2 D/F/V, TI chipset ACorp A56PIM-RWS	Yes	Yes	ISA	John Klar
		, Add ADD56K-PCIW, Maxtech/PowerCom/Well/Origo/WellLink/Archtek/ US Sertek				

Key	FCC ID or Reg #	Model	PNP	Jumpers	Interface	Thanks to:
WM	1YYTAI-27061-M5-E	FM-56PCI-RWS, Rockwell Soft K56 (HSF) chipset	?	-	PCI	
?	1YYTAI-27549-M5-E	Well/Origo FM-56AMR	?	?	?	
WM	?	ACorp A-56PIM , Rockwell RCV56HCF chipset	?	-	PCI	
WM	?	ACorp A-56PML , Lucent Mars2 chipset	Yes	-	PCI	
		ACorp M-56EMU, EA/Prestige FM-56PK-ST, Well /Origo RM56USB-ST, Addtel AD56K-EU, possibly Dynamode FM-56USB-ST				
?	1YYTAI-27363-M5-E	, USB V.90 56K modem, SGS-Thompson chipset	-	-	USB	
?	1YYTAI-25868-MD-E	Well GI-14400, SFT2-B	-	-	EXT	
?	1YYTAI-27336-M5-E	Well/Origo/Prestige FM-56PCI-SL	?	?	?	
WM	1YYTAI-27337-M5-E	Acorp M-56PMS, Encore RNF656-PCI-MO, Maxtech XPV(S)56P/MSW, Sertek DCS 56MP8-PCI-S11, Well/Origo/Prestige FM-56PCI-MT , Motorola soft modem chipset	Yes	No	PCI	
WM	1YYTAI-33513-M5-E	Well FM-56PCI-RWSB, Formosa A-56SIM, Micronet SP3000S, US Sertek 56RP8-PCI-S21, Well FM-56PCI-HSF, Encore FM-56PCI-HSF, Maxtech XPVS56P/RS/WL, Addtel AD56K-IP-HSF, Rockwell HSF chipset	?	?	PCI	
?	1YYTAI-33543-M5-E	Well/Origo/Archtek/US Sertek FM-56PCI-PT	?	?	PCI	
?	1YYTAI-33936-M5-E	Well/Origo/Titan/ICC/Sunroute FM-56PC-RWD	?	?	PCI	

Key	FCC ID or Reg #	Model	PNP	Jumpers	Interface	Thanks to:
?	1YYTAI-33937-M5-E	ACorp M56PIM, Micronet SP3OOOL, Well/Origo/Titan/ICC/Sunroute FM-56CI-RWM, Addtel AD56K-IP	?	?	PCI	
?	1YYTAI-34353-M5-E	Well/Origo/Well-Link Topic FM-56PCI-TP, TOPIC TP560i/9922S14 chipset	Yes	No	PCI	Well Communications
JJR		HTC Corp.				
?	JJRTAI-27514-M5-E	Everex Stingray notebook modem	?	?	?	
JYB		Alaris				
?	JYBUSA-27060-M5-E	56IFXC	?	?	?	

Key	FCC ID or Reg #	Model	PNP	Jumpers	Interface	Thanks to:
K89		Novalink Technologies (Novaweb)				
OK	K89CELLDATAFAX	Eiger Labs EFX-2880P Cellular-Ready, Rockwell RC288DPi chipset	-	-	PCMCIA	Dave Croal
?	?	Eiger Labs EFX-2880PL(-92CF), Fujitsu chipset	-	-	PCMCIA	
?	?	Eiger Labs EFX-2880PL, AT&T chipset	-	-	PCMCIA	
?	?	Eiger Labs EFX-2880PL, Rockwell chipset	-	-	PCMCIA	
?	?	Eiger Labs EFX-2880, Lucent chipset	-	-	PCMCIA	
KBC		Itronix				
?	KBCUSA-33722-PT-E	Itronix X-C 6250+ internal 33.6K modem for laptop	?	?	?	
KIW		TDK Systems				
	KIWDF2814C-07A	TDK Global Class 2814 Model DF2814C-07A, IBM PC Card 33.6 Kbps International Data/FAX Modem 42H4326 (MOD 319)				
?	1Y5JPN-22219-MM-E		-		PCMCIA	
	KIWDFV3400					

Key	FCC ID or Reg #	Model	PNP	Jumpers	Interface	Thanks to:
OK	1Y5JPN-23278-MM-E	TDK DataVoice 3400, PCMCIA	-	-	PCMCIA	Peter Englmaier
?	1Y5JPN-23632-MM-E	TDK Global Networker 3410	?	?	?	
	1Y5JPN-30910-MM-E	TDK Global Pro 3600 Model DFI 3600 V.90, Eicon				
?	E3SJPN-33327-M5-E	Diva Mobile V.90 Model 800-332	?	?	?	
?	1Y5USA-32187-M5-E	TDK Global Freedom Model DF5660, Motorola 56K Global Modem, Cellular Companion 5630CE	?	?	?	
LBY		**Apache Micro Peripherals**				
OK	?	Sevel V34i-V+ /C	?	Yes	ISA	Augusto
?	?	A56-R controller-based modem	?	?	ISA	
?	?	A56SP-R controller-based modem	?	?	ISA	
?	?	A56SP-RA controller-based modem	?	DIP	ISA	
?	P5JUSA-27252-M5-E	A56SP-RA/2	?	?	?	
WM	P5JUSA-27504-M5-E	Sevel A56SP-RS internal, Rockwell SoftK56 chipset	Yes	No	PCI	Augusto
WM	?	A56-HCF host-based modem	Yes	No	PCI	
WM	?	A56SP-HCF host-based modem	Yes	No	PCI	
LEM		**Garnet Systems**				
?	?	GTM-56KPC1	No	Yes	ISA	
?	?	GTM-56KSPC1	Yes	Yes	ISA	
?	?	GTM-56KSPC4, Rockwell ACF/SP chipset	No	Yes	ISA	
?	?	GTM-56KM1	?	Yes	ISA	
?	LEMKOR-33170-M5-E	GTM-56KM2	No	Yes	ISA	
?	LEMKOR-33523-M5-E	GTM-56KSH1	Yes	?	PCI	

Key	FCC ID or Reg #	Model	PNP	Jumpers	Interface	Thanks to:
?	LEMKOR-33524-M5-E	GTM-56KPCM2	Yes	-	PCMCIA	
?	LEMKOR-33613-M5-E	GTM-56KSH3	?	?	ISA	
?	LEMKOR-33614-M5-E	GTM-56KKH3	?	?	ISA	
?	LEMKOR-33627-M5-E	ITM-56KPCI	?	?	PCI	
WM	?	GTM-56KM3	Yes	No	PCI	
WM	LEMKOR-33662-M5-E	GTM-56KM4	Yes	No	PCI	
LNI		Blatzheim Datensysteme				
?	LNIGER-27247-MM-E	BMPC1 internal 28.8/14.4 fax	?	?	?	

Key	FCC ID or Reg #	Model	PNP	Jumpers	Interface	Thanks to:
LNQ		ActionTec				
?	LNQUSA-25518-MM-E	MD56017, LF560LKI	?	-	PCMCIA	
?	LNQUSA-25551-PT-E	LF560LHC	?	?	?	
?	LNQUSA-25774-M5-E	LF560LHC-03	?	?	?	
?	LNQUSA-27421-M5-E	MP560LH internal	?	?	?	
?	LNQUSA-27592-M5-E	Actiontec USB56012 Model UM100	?	?	?	
?	LNQUSA-27741-M5-E	Actiontec LF560LKQ	?	?	?	
?	LNQUSA-27830-M5-E	Actiontec HPP 00160, HP2000C	?	?	PCI	

Key	FCC ID or Reg #	Model	PNP	Jumpers	Interface	Thanks to:
OK	LNQUSA-31455-MM-E 2HMUSA-33200-MM-E	MD56002/FM560SK DataLink 56K x2 , DataLink 56K PC Card , Pora ProLink 1456CS , Cirrus Logic chipset	Yes	-	PCMCIA	Neil Zanella
OK	LNQUSA-31455-MM-E 2HMUSA-33200-MM-E	MD56002/FM560LK Datalink 56K , MDV9012-01 (retail box), MDV9012-02 (white box), DataLink 56K PC Card , Pora ProLink 1456C , Lucent Venus chipset	Yes	-	PCMCIA	Glenn K. Beer , Norman Yarvin
?	2HMUSA-33200-MM-E LNQUSA-31455-MM-E	Pora ProLink 1456C , (Rockwell chipset?)	Yes	-	PCMCIA	
OK	LNQUSA-31996-M5-E	Actiontec External; Pora ProLink 1456VE	-	-	EXT	Maksim Zaritskiy
OK	LNQUSA-31600-M5-E	DeskTalk 56K x2 Model DT56000 , Model IS560SKV, Cirrus Logic CL-MD54xx chipset	Yes	Yes	ISA	Green Manalishi Silviu
LM	LNQUSA-32756-M5-E	Phoebe Micro PCI v.90, ASMAX Internal PCI V.90 , Lucent chipset DeskTalk Master v.90	Yes	No	PCI	Pawel Sakowski

Key	FCC ID or Reg #	Model	PNP	Jumpers	Interface	Thanks to:
OK	LNQUSA-32913-M5-E	Model DT56010-01 (retail box), DT56010-02 (white box), IS560LKV, Lucent Venus chipset	Yes	Yes	ISA	Joe Cendrowski
WM	LNQUSA-32558-M5-E	DeskLink Advantage Model DT56016-01 (retail box), DT56016-02 (white box), DT56018, IS560LH, Lucent Luna chipset	Yes	No	ISA	Steve Flock
WM	LNQUSA-33112-M5-E	DeskVoice Pro PCI Model DT560SHV, PCI56019-01 (retail box), PCI56019-02 (white box), PM560LH, Lucent Mars chipset	Yes	No	PCI	
?	LNQUSA-33206-M5-E	LF560LHQ-02 Notebook Modem	?	?	?	
?	LNQUSA-33290-M5-E	LF560LHQ-03(l)	?	-	PCMCIA	
?	LNQUSA-33291-M5-E	CM560LH Notebook Modem	?	?	?	
OK	LNQUSA-33437-M5-E	Actiontec Model PCI56012/PM560LKi ; Telepath 600/022; IBM Model 33L4618 , PCI V.90 56 D/F Controller-based Modem, Lucent Venus chipset	*	No	PCI	Bill Pier
?	LNQUSA-27507-M5-E	Model PCI56012/PM560LKC	?	?	?	Marisa
OK	LNQUSA-33895-M5-E	Model PCI56012-01CW/PM560LKC Call-Waiting modem, Lucent Venus chipset	*	No	PCI	; Gus Palandri
OK	LNQUSA-27509-M5-E	Model EX56012/EX560LKC Call-Waiting modem, Lucent Venus chipset	-	-	EXT	Actiontec
?	LNQUSA-33876-M5-E	Actiontec, HPP CO/01-01 Model HP2000A PCI D/F modem/LAN card	?	?	PCI	

This is the Linux/Modem Compatibility Knowledge Base at http://www.o2.net/~gromitkc/winmodem.html

Key	FCC ID or Reg #	Model	PNP	Jumpers	Interface	Thanks to:
?	LNQUSA-33953-M5-E	Actiontec LF560LHC-06(U) module modem for notebook	?	?	?	
?	LNQUSA-34023-M5-E	ASUS F7400 Model NB-F7PR001 modem for PC notebook	?	?	?	
?	LNQUSA-34266-M5-E	Actiontec LF560LHQ-07 with RPX, modem module for PC notebook	?	?	?	
?	LNQUSA-34293-M5-E	Actiontec LF560LHQ-041, modem module for Sharp PC notebook	?	?	?	
?	LNQUSA-34522-M5-E	Actiontec LF560ED1 internal 56K d/f modem for PC notebook	?	?	?	
?	LNQTAI-34542-M5-E	Actiontec HSP56	?	?	PCI	
?	LNQUSA-40033-M5-E	LF560LHS	?	-	PCMCIA	
?	LNQUSA-34145-M5-E	LF560LHS-02 internal for PC notebook	?	?	?	
?	?	MD56020-01 (retail box), MD56020-02 (white box), FM560RK, DataLink 56K PC Card Windows-only Cellular, Rockwell chipset	?	-	PCMCIA	
?	LNQUSA-40064-M5-E	MP100IM mini PCI 10/100BASE-T Ethernet & modem combo card	?	?	?	

This is the Linux/Modem Compatibility Knowledge Base at http://www.o2.net/~gromitkc/winmodem.html

Key	FCC ID or Reg #	Model	PNP	Jumpers	Interface	Thanks to:
M4T		Silicom Multimedia Systems				
?	M4TUSA-25690-M5-E	Modem Master 550/56K	?	?	?	
WM	M4TUSA-33142-M5-E	Modem Master 9050/56K; EigerCom 56K PCI WinModem EFX-56KPCI, PCTel 789T-A chipset	Yes	No	PCI	Matt Derbyshire
MEI		Imecom Group				

Key	FCC ID or Reg #	Model	PNP	Jumpers	Interface	Thanks to:
?	MEIFRC-27528-FB-T	Imecom FAXPASS[1,2,4]	?	?	?	
	MF6	Motorola PCMCIA Products Division				
	MF62074235					
OK	ABZUSA-23472-MM-E	Montana 33.6 Modem/Fax PC Card, Part Number 62075007-01	-		PCMCIA	Elmo Recio
?		Mariner 33.6 Kbps PC Card	-	-	PCMCIA	
	MGA	King Max Technology				
?	MGAKFM5600-L	FM566L_Lucent Venus chipset		-	PCMCIA	
	NIG	Davicom Semiconductor				
?	NIG-EAGLE-1-V1	Model 3334BDV	?	No	ISA	
	OMD	Movita Technologies				
?	OMDTAI-27475-M5-E	Movita FM200, 56/14.4 D/F/V for notebook	?	?	?	
	OOA	Fujitsu Personal Systems				
?	OOAJPN-25625-M5-E	Stylistic 2300 internal, FMW2901F, Stylistic LT, FM2901T	?	?	?	
?	OOAJPN-25675-M5-E	Lifebook E330/E335/E340/E350	?	?	?	
?	OOAUSA-27385-MM-E	Pen Centra Model 130	?	?	?	
	PCC	D-Com Technology				
?	PCCTAI-27218-M5-E	Great MD-56IS, Lacom DM-56IS, Tornado SFM56HS	?	?	?	

Key	FCC ID or Reg #	Model	PNP	Jumpers	Interface	Thanks to:
	RIG	TurboComm Tech				
		OEM (Mx-)E210				
		CNet 5614XE				
		Cirrus Logic chipset				
?	RIGTAI-25870-M5-E	OEM (Mx-)l301,	-	-	EXT	

578

Key	FCC ID or Reg #	Model	PNP	Jumpers	Interface	Thanks to:
WM	RIGTAI-25896-M5-E	CNet 5614LPA, Cirrus Logic MD-5620DT chipset	Yes	No	PCI	
WM	RIGTAI-25942-M5-E	OEM (Mx-)I601, CNet 5614MH, 56K v.90, Motorola SM56 chipset	Yes	No	PCI	Daniel Bremer
WM	RIGTAI-33503-M5-E	OEM (Mx-)I101, Conexant (Rockwell) HSF chipset	?	?	PCI	
WM	?	OEM (Mx-)I101H, Conexant (Rockwell) HCF chipset	?	?	PCI	
?	RIGTAI-33504-FB-E	OEM (Mx-)E110, Conexant (Rockwell) chipset	-	-	EXT	
?	RIGTAI-33505-FB-E	OEM (Mx-)E500, Paradise/CNET WC7550(U)/UM561-SF, OEM				
?	RIGTAI-34541-M5-E	5614UB, Trendware TFM-560U, ST chipset	?	-	USB	
?	RIGTAI-33571-M5-E	OEM P100, Conexant (Rockwell) chipset	?	-	PCMCIA	
?	RIGTAI-33860-M5-E	Turbocomm/Gigatech/Castlenet M111, 5500, 7500, internal for notebook	?	?	?	
?	RIGTAI-33861-M5-E	Turbocomm/OEM (Mx-)E300, CNet T-UM560, USB modem, Lucent chipset	?	?	USB	
?	RIGTAI-33921-M5-E	Turbocomm/OEM M161 soft modem	?	?	?	
?	RIGTAI-34231-M5-E	CNet IM561-RF, OEM (Mx-)I101(C), Trendware	?	?	?	
?	RIGCHN-34565-M5-E	TFM-561PCI	?	?	PCI	
?	RIGTAI-27210-FB-E	M710 for notebook	?	?	?	
?	RIGTAI-27761-M5-E	(Mx-)I102, CNet/TFM/ADI IM561-RF, Trendware	?	?	?	
?	RIGTAI-34540-M5-E	TFM-560PCI	?	?	?	

This is the Linux/Modem Compatibility Knowledge Base at http://www.o2.net/~gromitkc/winmodem.html

Key	FCC ID or Reg #	Model	PNP	Jumpers	Interface	Thanks to:
	RIGTAI-40045-M5-E					
?	RIGTAI-34604-M5-E	OEM (Mx-)J201, CNet 5614CH	?	?	?	
?	RIGTAI-40086-M5-E	Turbocomm/Clevo/TBC M191	?	?	?	
?	RIGTAI-34377-M5-E	OEM M801 internal 56K d/f modem for PC notebook	?	?	?	
TLC		Aureal Semiconductor				
?	TLCUSA-27474-M5-E	VCom/8810 Vortex Modem Model BA88MO10AD-01, 33.6 Data/14.4 Fax modem	?	?	?	
?	TLCUSA-34295-M5-E	Model 8810 SoundCom V90	?	?	PCI	
UVN		Point Multimedia Systems				
?	UVNKOR-27803-M5-E	Modem Master MM9250 internal 56K/14.4 data/fax	?	?	?	
VOL		S.A. Banksys				
?	VOLBEL-27880-M5-E	Smash Desktop	?	?	?	
WPE		AboCom Systems				
?	WPETAI-27303-M5-E	D-Link/ UFM560 USB V.90 56K fax modem	?	-	USB	Peter J. Weyers
OK	MQ4FM560	Fiberline PCM-FM560	-	-	PCMCIA	, AboCom
OK	MQ4LF560TX	LF560TX , Linksys PCMLM56 , 56k modem + 10/100 Ethernet	-	-	PCMCIA	Glenn K. Beer , AboCom
?	WPETAI-27457-M5-E	Multitech MT5634ZLX/FE; Linksys/Link Mate/D-Link LF560MX, DMF560TXK, PCMLM56	?	-	PCMCIA	

Key	FCC ID or Reg #	Model	PNP	Jumpers	Interface	Thanks to:
?	WPETAI-27861-M5-E	Abocom Model FM560CB, FM560B, FM560AB, FM560JB, FM560MB	?	?	?	
?	WPETAI-27874-M5-E	Abocom/Dlink Model USM560	?	?	?	
?	WPETAI-34169-M5-E	Abocom Model MR560	?	?	PCI	
?	WPETAI-34303-M5-E	Abocom Model MR560, MR56IM, MR560M soft modem	?	?	PCI	
XXA		Moreton Bay				
OK	XXAAUS-27237-M5-E	RAStel8 PCI, Model RA8002, Chase Research PCI-RAS 8, 8 modem PCI adapter card, w/Linux drivers	Yes	No	PCI	Doug DeJulio at Hell's Kitchen Systems, Moreton Bay
OK	XXAAUS-25673-M5-E	RAStel4 PCI, Model RA4002, Chase Research PCI-RAS 4, 4 modem PCI adapter card, w/Linux drivers	Yes	No	PCI	Doug DeJulio at Hell's Kitchen Systems, Moreton Bay
?	?	RAStel2+2 PCI, Model RA2022, 2 modem PCI + 2 serial port adapter card, w/Linux drivers	Yes	?	PCI	Moreton Bay
?	?	RAStel8 ISA, Model RA8001, 8 modem ISA adapter card, w/Linux drivers	?	?	ISA	Moreton Bay
?	?	RAStel8 ISA, Model RA4001, 4 modem ISA adapter card, w/Linux drivers	?	?	ISA	Moreton Bay
?	?	RAStel2+2 ISA, Model RA2021, 2 modem + 2 serial port ISA adapter card, w/Linux drivers	?	?	ISA	Moreton Bay

Key	FCC ID or Reg #	Model	PNP	Jumpers	Interface	Thanks to:
KJG		ELSA (DE)				

This is the Linux/Modem Compatibility Knowledge Base at http://www.o2.net/~gromitkc/winmodem.html

Key	FCC ID or Reg #	Model	PNP	Jumpers	Interface	Thanks to:
OK	?	ELSA MicroLink 28.8TQV	-	-	EXT	Peter Reinhart
?	?	ELSA MicroLink 33.6TQV	-	-	EXT	
?	?	ELSA MicroLink Office	-	-	EXT	
?	?	ELSA MicroLink 56K Pro	-	-	EXT	
OK	?	ELSA MicroLink 56k Internet / Basic	-	-	EXT	Ralf Kleineisel
?	?	ELSA MicroLink 56k USB	-	-	USB	
WM	?	ELSA MicroLink 56k-PCI, Rockwell HCF chipset	Yes	No	PCI	
		Digicom (IT)				
OK	?	Digicom Tiziano 33.6	-	-	EXT	Davide Morando
?	?	Digicom Tiziano 56 Memory	-	-	EXT	
?	?	Digicom Giotto	-	-	EXT	
		Ericsson				
?	?	K56 DTV, V.90 Desktop Voice Modem	-	-	EXT	
?	?	V34 DT, V.34 Desktop Modem	-	-	EXT	
?	?	V34 HE, V.34 High-Security Modem	-	-	EXT	
		Hamlet (IT)				
?	?	56K Voice external	-	-	EXT	
?	?	56K Voice internal HAM56PCI	?	?	PCI	
?	?	56K PCMCIA FM560 (*)	-	-	PCMCIA	
		Harmony USA				
?	?	Model 18008, Rockwell RCV288DPi chipset	No	DIP	ISA	
?	?	Model 18008-1, Rockwell RCV288DPi chipset	?	Yes	ISA	
?	?	Model 18008-3, Cirrus Logic chipset	Yes	Yes	ISA	
?	?	Model 18008-4, Rockwell RCV336ACF/SVD chipset	Yes	No	ISA	
?	?	Model 18008-5, Cirrus Logic chipset	Yes	Yes	ISA	
?	?	Model 18008-6, Davicom chipset	Yes	No	ISA	
?	?	Model 18009, Rockwell RCV336ACF chipset	No	Yes	ISA	

This is the Linux/Modem Compatibility Knowledge Base at http://www.o2.net/~gromitkc/winmodem.html

Key	FCC ID or Reg #	Model	PNP	Jumpers	Interface	Thanks to:
OK	?	Model 18009-1 , Rockwell RCV336ACF chipset	No	Yes	ISA	Brian Kieslich
?	?	Model 18010, Rockwell RCV336ACF/SP chipset	No	Yes	ISA	
?	?	Model 18010-1, Rockwell RCV336ACF/SP chipset	?	No	ISA	
?	?	Model 18010-2, Rockwell RCV336ACF/SP chipset	Yes	Yes	ISA	
?	?	Model 18026-1, Lucent PCI	Yes	?	PCI	
?	?	Model 18026, Lucent ISA	Yes	Yes	ISA	
?	?	Model 18023 , K56Flex PCI, Rockwell RLDL56DPF (HSF Softmodem) chipset	Yes	No	PCI	
WM	?	Model 18022-2, Cirrus Logic X2	Yes	Yes	ISA	
?	?	Model 18022, X2 TI Chipset	Yes	Yes	ISA	
?	?	Model 18021-1, PCtel Chipset	Yes	?	PCI	
WM	?	Model 18021, K56Flex HSP , PCT338P chipset	Yes	No	PCI	
WM	?	Model 18020A , Rockwell ACF/SP Chipset	-	-	EXT	
?	?	Model 18020-1 , Rockwell RCVDL56ACF/SP R6761-21 chipset	Yes	Yes	ISA	
?	?	Model 18020-2 , Rockwell RCVDL56ACF/SP R6761-21 chipset	Yes	Yes	ISA	
?	?	Model 18020-3 , Rockwell RCVDL56ACF R6761-23 chipset	?	Yes	ISA	
		Jetway				
?	?	Model 1456ESP-R , Rockwell chipset	-	-	EXT	
WM	?	Model 1456PCI-R , Rockwell RCV56HCF chipset	Yes	No	PCI	
WM	?	Model 1456HSP-R (FM-56PCI V:RWHS-B), Rockwell RS56/SP-PCI R6793-11 chipset	Yes	No	PCI	
		Legato				

This is the Linux/Modem Compatibility Knowledge Base at http://www.o2.net/~gromitkc/winmodem.html

Key	FCC ID or Reg #	Model	PNP	Jumpers	Interface	Thanks to:
WM	?	CV56 PCI Fax Modem	Yes	?	PCI	
		Microcomputer Research (UK)				
		MRi 1456PCI				
		, GVC				
		F-1156IV+/A2A				
WM	?	, Lucent DSP 1646 controllerless chipset	Yes	No	PCI	Jo Whitby
OK	?	MRi-IVS/IVSD "Mr. Modem" Internal 56K V.90	Yes	Yes	ISA	David Mullin
		, Rockwell RC56D chipset				
		Modular Technology (UK)				
OK	(BABT ID:608461)	HW 56k/V.90 PCV Internal modem	No	Yes	ISA	Donald Page
		HW560PCVC 56k D/F/V/Video PnP Internal Camera-ready modem				
OK	(BABT ID:6007480)	, Rockwell RCVDL56ACFW/SP R6771-22 chipset	Yes	No	ISA	Neal Cartwright
?	(BABT ID:608462)	Superhighway 56 DTV D/F/V desktop modem	-	-	EXT	
		SuperHighway 56PCI Internal modem, Model				
WM	(BABT ID: 60848)	560HCF	Yes	No	PCI	jp-morris
		NetComm (AU)				
		InPlus SVD				
OK	(AusTel A96/0433)	, Model IN3420	Yes	Yes	ISA	Karl J. Ots
		InPlus 56				
?	?	, Model IN3424	?	?	?	
?	?	InModem 56, Model IN5600	?	?	?	
?	?	SmartModem56, Model SM5600	-	-	EXT	NetComm
OK	?	"Simple Modem", Model AM5675	-	-	EXT	Stephen Barratt
?	?	Roadster II 56 ULTRA, Model AM5692	-	-	EXT	
?	?	Roadster II 56 USB, Model AM5050	-	-	?	
		Pace (PMC Consumer Electronics, UK)				
		Pace 56 Solo				
?	?	V1.00 self-memory modem (PNPID PMC1461)	-	-	EXT	
		Pace 56 Solo				
?	?	V2.00 self-memory modem (PNPID PMC1471)	-	-	EXT	
		Pace 56 Voice External				

This is the Linux/Modem Compatibility Knowledge Base at http://www.o2.net/~gromitkc/winmodem.html

Key	FCC ID or Reg #	Model	PNP	Jumpers	Interface	Thanks to:
?	?	(PNPID PMC0430) Pace 56 Voice Internal	-	-	EXT	
?	?	(PNPID PMC2430)	Yes	?	ISA	
?	?	Pace NB 56 Voice	-	-	PCMCIA	
		Trust (NL)				
OK	?	Communicator 56K ESP-2 , Rockwell chipset	-	-	EXT	Col Wilson
OK	?	Communicator 56K PC-Card , Lucent chipset	Yes	-	PCMCIA	Peter Weyers
		Xtreama				
OK	?	Twister SFM336E, Rockwell RCV336ACF/SP chipset	-	-	EXT	Martijn van den Burg

585

Sound-HOWTO

This document describes sound support for Linux. It lists the supported sound hardware, describes how to configure the kernel drivers, and answers frequently asked questions. The intent is to bring new users up to speed more quickly and reduce the amount of traffic in the Usenet news groups and mailing lists.

Introduction

This is the Linux Sound-HOWTO. It is intended as a quick reference covering everything you need to know to install and configure sound support under Linux. Frequently asked questions about sound under Linux are answered, and references are given to some other sources of information on a variety of topics related to computer generated sound and music.

The scope is limited to the aspects of sound cards pertaining to Linux. See the other documents listed in the References section for more general information on sound cards and computer sound and music generation.

Acknowledgments

Much of this information came from the documentation provided with the sound driver source code, by Hannu Savolainen (<hannu@opensound.com>). Thanks go to Hannu, Alan Cox, and the many other people who developed the Linux kernel sound drivers and utilities.

Thanks to the SGML Tools package, this HOWTO is available in several formats, all generated from a common source file.

New Versions of This Document

New versions of this document will be periodically posted to the comp.os.linux.answers newsgroup. They will also be uploaded to various anonymous ftp sites that archive such information including <ftp://metalab.unc.edu/pub/Linux/docs/HOWTO/>.

Hypertext versions of this and other Linux HOWTOs are available on many world-wide web sites, including <http://metalab.unc.edu/LDP/>. Most Linux CD-ROM distributions include the HOWTOs, often under the /usr/doc directory, and you can also buy printed copies from several vendors. Sometimes the HOWTOs available from CD-ROM vendors, ftp sites, and printed format are out of date. If the date on this HOWTO is more than six months in the past, then a newer copy is probably available on the Internet.

Please note that, due to the dynamic nature of the Internet, all web and ftp links listed in this document are subject to change.

Translations of this document are available in several languages:

Chinese: <http://www.linux.org.tw/CLDP/Sound-HOWTO.html>
French: <http://www.freenix.org/unix/linux/HOWTO/>
Japanese: <http://yebisu.ics.es.osaka-u.ac.jp/linux/>
Korean: <http://kldp.linux-kr.org/HOWTO/html/Sound/Sound-HOWTO.
    html>
Russian: <http://www.phtd.tpu.edu.ru/~ott/russian/linux/howto-rus/
    Sound-HOWTO.html>
Spanish: <ftp://ftp.insflug.org/es>

Most translations of this and other Linux HOWTOs can also be found at <http://metalab.unc.edu/pub/Linux/docs/HOWTO/translations/> and <ftp://metalab.unc.edu/pub/Linux/docs/HOWTO/translations/>. If you make a translation of this document into another language, let me know and I'll include a reference to it here.

Feedback

I rely on you, the reader, to make this HOWTO useful. If you have any suggestions, corrections, or comments, please send them to me, <tranter@pobox.com>, and I will try to incorporate them in the next revision.

I am also willing to answer general questions on sound cards under Linux, as best I can. Before doing so, please read all of the information in this HOWTO, and send me detailed information about the problem. Please do not ask me about using sound cards under operating systems other than Linux.

If you publish this document on a CD-ROM or in hardcopy form, a complimentary copy would be appreciated. Mail me for my postal address. Also consider making a donation to the Linux Documentation Project to help support free documentation for Linux. Contact the Linux HOWTO coordinator, Tim Bynum <mailto:linux- howto@metalab.unc.edu>, for more information.

Distribution Policy

Copyright © 1995–1999 by Jeff Tranter. This document may be distributed under the terms set forth in the LDP license at <http://metalab.unc.edu/LDP/COPYRIGHT.html>.

Sound Card Technology

This section gives a very cursory overview of computer audio technology, in order to help you understand the concepts used later in the document. You should consult a book on digital audio or digital signal processing in order to learn more.

Sound is an analog property; it can take on any value over a continuous range. Computers are digital; they like to work with discrete values. Sound cards use a device known as an Analog to Digital Converter (A/D or ADC) to convert voltages corresponding to analog sound waves into digital or numeric values which can be stored in memory. Similarly, a Digital to Analog Converter (D/A or DAC) converts numeric values back to an analog voltage which can in turn drive a loudspeaker, producing sound.

The process of analog to digital conversion, known as sampling, introduces some error. Two factors are key in determining how well the sampled signal represents the original. Sampling rate is the number of samples made per unit of time (usually expresses as samples per second or Hertz). A low sampling rate will provide a less accurate representation of the analog signal. Sample size is the range of values used to represent each sample, usually expressed in bits. The larger the sample size, the more accurate the digitized signal will be.

Sound cards commonly use 8 or 16 bit samples at sampling rates from about 4000 to 44,000 samples per second. The samples may also be contain one channel (mono) or two (stereo).

FM Synthesis is an older technique for producing sound. It is based on combining different waveforms (e.g., sine, triangle, square). FM synthesis is simpler to implement in hardware that D/A conversion, but is more difficult to program and less flexible. Many sound cards provide FM synthesis for backward compatibility with older cards and software. Several independent sound generators or voices are usually provided.

Wavetable Synthesis combines the flexibility of D/A conversion with the multiple channel capability of FM synthesis. With this scheme digitized voices can be downloaded into dedicated memory, and then played, combined, and modified with little CPU overhead. State of the art sound cards all support wavetable synthesis.

Most sound cards provide the capability of mixing, combining signals from different input sources and controlling gain levels.

MIDI stands for Musical Instrument Digital Interface, and is a standard hardware and software protocol for allowing musical instruments to communicate with each other. The events sent over a MIDI bus can also be stored as MIDI files for later editing and playback. Many sound cards provide a MIDI interface. Those that do not can still play MIDI files using the on-board capabilities of the sound card.

MOD files are a common format for computer generated songs. As well as information about the musical notes to be played, the files contain digitized samples for the instruments (or voices). MOD files originated on the Amiga computer, but can be played on other systems, including Linux, with suitable software.

Supported Hardware

This section lists the sound cards and interfaces that are currently supported under Linux. The information here is based on the latest Linux kernel, which at time of writing was version 2.2.4. This document only applies to the sound drivers included with the standard Linux kernel source distribution. There are other sound drivers available for Linux (see the later section entitled Alternate Sound Drivers).

For the latest information on supported sound cards and features see the files included with the Linux kernel source code, usually installed in the directory /usr/src/linux/Documentation/sound.

The information in this HOWTO is valid for Linux on the Intel platform.

The sound driver should also work with most sound cards on the Alpha platform. However, some cards may conflict with I/O ports of other devices on Alpha systems even though they work perfectly on i386 machines, so in general it's not possible to tell if a given card will work or not without actually trying it.

Users have reported that the sound driver was not yet working on the PowerPC version of Linux, but it should be supported in future.

Sound can be configured into the kernel under the MIPs port of Linux, and some MIPs machines have EISA slots and/or built in sound hardware. I'm told the Linux-MIPs group is interested in adding sound support in the future.

The Linux kernel includes a separate driver for the Atari and Amiga versions of Linux that implements a compatible subset of the sound driver on the Intel platform using the built-in sound hardware on these machines.

The SPARC port of Linux currently has sound support for some models of Sun workstations. I've been told that the on-board sound hardware works but the external DSP audio box is not supported because Sun has not released the specifications for it.

Sound Cards

The following sound cards are supported by the Linux kernel sound driver. Some of the items listed are audio chip sets rather than models of sound cards. The list is incomplete because there are many sound cards compatible with these that will work under Linux. To add further to the confusion, some manufacturers periodically change the design of their cards causing incompatibilities and continue to sell them as the same model.

- 6850 UART MIDI Interface
- AD1816/AD1816A based cards
- ADSP-2115
- ALS-007 based cards (Avance Logic)
- ATI Stereo F/X (no longer manufactured)
- Acer FX-3D
- AdLib (no longer manufactured)
- Audio Excel DSP 16
- AudioDrive
- CMI8330 sound chip
- Compaq Deskpro XL onboard sound
- Corel Netwinder WaveArtist
- Crystal CS423x
- ESC614
- ESS1688 sound chip
- ESS1788 sound chip
- ESS1868 sound chip
- ESS1869 sound chip
- ESS1887 sound chip
- ESS1888 sound chip
- ESS688 sound chip
- ES1370 sound chip
- ES1371 sound chip
- Ensoniq AudioPCI (ES1370)
- Ensoniq AudioPCI 97 (ES1371)
- Ensoniq SoundScape (and compatibles made by Reveal and Spea)
- Gallant SC-6000
- Gallant SC-6600

- Gravis Ultrasound
- Gravis Ultrasound ACE
- Gravis Ultrasound Max
- Gravis Ultrasound with 16 bit sampling option
- HP Kayak
- Highscreen Sound-Booster 32 Wave 3D
- IBM MWAVE
- Logitech Sound Man 16
- Logitech SoundMan Games
- Logitech SoundMan Wave
- MAD16 Pro (OPTi 82C928, 82C929, 82C930, 82C924 chipsets)
- Media Vision Jazz16
- MediaTriX AudioTriX Pro
- Microsoft Windows Sound System (MSS/WSS)
- MiroSOUND PCM12
- Mozart (OAK OTI-601)
- OPTi 82C931
- Orchid SW32
- Personal Sound System (PSS)
- Pinnacle MultiSound
- Pro Audio Spectrum 16
- Pro Audio Studio 16
- Pro Sonic 16
- Roland MPU-401 MIDI interface
- S3 SonicVibes
- SY-1816
- Sound Blaster 1.0
- Sound Blaster 2.0
- Sound Blaster 16
- Sound Blaster 16ASP
- Sound Blaster 32
- Sound Blaster 64
- Sound Blaster AWE32
- Sound Blaster AWE64
- Sound Blaster PCI 128
- Sound Blaster Pro
- Sound Blaster Vibra16
- Sound Blaster Vibra16X
- TI TM4000M notebook
- Terratec Base 1
- Terratec Base 64

- ThunderBoard
- Turtle Beach Maui
- Turtle Beach MultiSound Classic
- Turtle Beach MultiSound Fiji
- Turtle Beach MultiSound Hurricane
- Turtle Beach MultiSound Monterey
- Turtle Beach MultiSound Pinnacle
- Turtle Beach MultiSound Tahiti
- Turtle Beach WaveFront Maui
- Turtle Beach WaveFront Tropez
- Turtle Beach WaveFront Tropez+
- VIA chip set
- VIDC 16-bit sound
- Yamaha OPL2 sound chip
- Yamaha OPL3 sound chip
- Yamaha OPL3-SA1 sound chip
- Yamaha OPL3-SA2 sound chip
- Yamaha OPL3-SA3 sound chip
- Yamaha OPL3-SAx sound chip
- Yamaha OPL4 sound chip

A word about compatibility: even though most sound cards are claimed to be SoundBlaster compatible, very few currently sold cards are compatible enough to work with the Linux SoundBlaster driver. These cards usually work better using the MSS/WSS or MAD16 driver. Only real SoundBlaster cards made by Creative Labs, which use Creative's custom chips (e.g., SoundBlaster16 Vibra), MV Jazz16 and ESS688/1688 based cards generally work with the SoundBlaster driver. Trying to use a SoundBlaster Pro compatible 16 bit sound card with the SoundBlaster driver is usually just a waste of time.

The Linux kernel supports the SCSI port provided on some sound cards (e.g., ProAudioSpectrum 16) and the proprietary interface for some CD-ROM drives (e.g., Soundblaster Pro). See the Linux SCSI HOWTO and CDROM HOWTO documents for more information.

A kernel driver to support joystick ports, including those provided on some sound cards, is included as part of the 2.2 kernels.

Note that the kernel SCSI, CD-ROM, joystick, and sound drivers are completely independent of each other.

Alternate Sound Drivers

Sound support in the Linux kernel was originally written by Hannu Savolainen. Hannu then went on to develop the Open Sound system, a commercial set of sound drivers sold by 4Front Technologies that is supported on a number of Unix systems. Red Hat Software sponsored Alan Cox to enhance the kernel sound drivers to make them fully modular. Various other people also contributed bug fixes and developed additional drivers for new sound cards. These modified drivers were shipped by Red Hat in their 5.0 through 5.2 releases. These changes have now been integrated into the standard kernel as of version 2.0. Alan Cox is now the maintainer of the standard kernel sound drivers, although Hannu still periodically contributes code taken from the commercial driver.

The commercial Open Sound System driver from 4Front Technologies tends to be easier to configure and support more sound cards, particularly the newer models. It is also compatible with applications written for the standard kernel sound drivers. The disadvantage is that you need to pay for it, and you do not get source code. You can download a free evaluation copy of the product before deciding whether to purchase it. For more information see the 4Front Technologies web page at <http://www.opensound.com>.

Jaroslav Kysela and others started writing an alternate sound driver for the Gravis UltraSound Card. The project was renamed Advanced Linux Sound Architecture (ALSA) and has resulted in what they believe is a more generally usable sound driver that can be used as a replacement for the built-in kernel drivers. The ALSA drivers support a number of popular sound cards, are full duplex, fully modularized, and compatible with the sound architecture in the kernel. The main web site of the ALSA project is <http://www.alsa-project.org>. A separate "Alsa-sound-mini-HOWTO" is available which deals with compiling and installing these drivers.

Markus Mummert (mum@mmk.e-technik.tu-muenchen.de) has written a driver package for the Turtle Beach MultiSound (classic), Tahiti, and Monterey sound cards. The documentation states:

> It is designed for high quality hard disk recording/playback without losing sync even on a busy system. Other features such as wave synthesis, MIDI and digital signal processor (DSP) cannot be used. Also, recording and playback at the same time is not possible. It currently replaces VoxWare and was tested on several kernel versions ranging from 1.0.9 to 1.2.1. Also, it is installable on UN*X SysV386R3.2 systems.

It can be found at <http://www.cs.colorado.edu/~mccreary/tbeach>.

Kim Burgaard (burgaard@daimi.aau.dk) has written a device driver and utilities for the Roland MPU-401 MIDI interface. The Linux software map entry gives this description:

> A device driver for true Roland MPU-401 compatible MIDI interfaces (including Roland SCC-1 and RAP-10/ATW-10). Comes with a useful collection of utilities including a Standard MIDI File player and recorder.
>
> Numerous improvements have been made since version 0.11a. Among other things, the driver now features IRQ sharing policy and complies with the new kernel module interface. Metronome functionality, possibility for synchronizing e.g. graphics on a per beat basis without losing precision, advanced replay/record/overdub interface and much, much more.

It can be found at <ftp://metalab.unc.edu/pub/Linux/kernel/sound/mpu401-0.2.tar.gz>.

Another novel use for a sound card under Linux is as a modem for amateur packet radio. The 2.1 and later kernels include a driver that works with SoundBlaster and Windows Sound System compatible sound cards to implement 1200 bps AFSK and 9600 bps FSK packet protocols. See the Linux AX25 HOWTO for details (I'm a ham myself, by the way—callsign VE3ICH).

PC Speaker

An alternate sound driver is available that requires no additional sound hardware; it uses the internal PC speaker. It is mostly software compatible with the sound card driver, but, as might be expected, provides much lower quality output and has much more CPU overhead.

The results seem to vary, being dependent on the characteristics of the individual loudspeaker. For more information, see the documentation provided with the release. The software, which has not been updated for some time, can be found at <ftp://ftp.informatik.hu-berlin.de/pub/Linux/hu-sound/>.

Parallel Port

Another option is to build a digital to analog converter using a parallel printer port and some additional components. This provides better sound quality than the PC speaker but still has a lot of CPU overhead. The PC sound driver package mentioned above supports this, and includes instructions for building the necessary hardware.

Installation

Configuring Linux to support sound involves the following steps:

1. Installing the sound card.
2. Configuring Plug and Play (if applicable).
3. Configuring and building the kernel for sound support.
4. Creating the device files.
5. Booting the Linux kernel and testing the installation.

If you are running Red Hat Linux there is a utility called sndconfig that in most cases will detect your sound card and set up all of the necessary configuration files to load the appropriate sound drivers for your card. If you are running Red Hat I suggest you try using it. If it works for you then you can skip the rest of the instructions in this section.

If `sndconfig` fails, you are using another Linux distribution, or you want to follow the manual method in order to better understand what you are doing, then the next sections will cover each of these steps in detail.

Installing the Sound Card

Follow the manufacturer's instructions for installing the hardware or have your dealer perform the installation.

Older sound cards usually have switch or jumper settings for IRQ, DMA channel, etc; note down the values used. If you are unsure, use the factory defaults. Try to avoid conflicts with other devices (e.g., ethernet cards, SCSI host adaptors, serial and parallel ports) if possible.

Usually you should use the same I/O port, IRQ, and DMA settings that work under DOS. In some cases though (particularly with PnP cards) you may need to use different settings to get things to work under Linux. Some experimentation may be needed.

Configuring Plug and Play

Most sound cards now use the Plug and Play protocol to configure settings for i/o addresses, interrupts, and DMA channels. If you have one of the older sound cards that uses fixed settings or jumpers, then you can skip this section.

As of version 2.2 Linux does not yet have full Plug and Play support in the kernel. The preferred solution is to use the isapnp tools which ship with most Linux distributions (or you can download them from Red Hat's web site <http://www.redhat.com/>).

First check the documentation for your Linux distribution. It may already have Plug and Play support set up for you or it may work slightly differently than described here. If you need to configure it yourself, the details can be found in the man pages for the isapnp tools. Briefly the process you would normally follow is:

- Use pnpdump to capture the possible settings for all your Plug and Play devices, saving the result to the file /etc/isapnp.conf.

- Choose settings for the sound card that do not conflict with any other devices in your system and uncomment the appropriate lines in /etc/isapnp.conf. Don't forget to uncomment the (ACT Y) command near the end.

- Make sure that isapnp is run when your system boots up, normally done by one of the startup scripts. Reboot your system or run isapnp manually.

If for some reason you cannot or do not wish to use the isapnp tools, there are a couple of other options. If you use the card under Microsoft Windows 95 or 98, you can use the device manager to set up the card, then soft boot into Linux using the LOADLIN program. Make sure Windows and Linux use the same card setup parameters.

If you use the card under DOS, you can use the icu utility that comes with SoundBlaster16 PnP cards to configure it under DOS, then soft boot into Linux using the LOADLIN program. Again, make sure DOS and Linux use the same card setup parameters.

A few of the sound card drivers include the necessary software to initialize Plug and Play for the card. Check the documentation for that card's driver for details.

Configuring the Kernel

When initially installing Linux you likely used a precompiled kernel. These kernels often do not provide sound support. It is best to recompile the kernel yourself with the drivers you need. You may also want to recompile the kernel in order to upgrade to a newer version or to free up memory resources by minimizing the size of the kernel. Later, when your sound card is working, you may wish to rebuild the kernel sound drivers as modules.

The Linux Kernel HOWTO <u>http://metalab.unc.edu/LDP/HOWTO/ Kernel-HOWTO.html</u>> should be consulted for the details of building a kernel. I will just mention here some issues that are specific to sound cards.

If you have never configured the kernel for sound support before it is a good idea to read the relevant documentation included with the kernel sound drivers, particularly information specific to your card type. The files can be found in the kernel documentation directory, usually installed in `/usr/src/linux/Documentation/sound`. If this directory is missing you likely either have a very old kernel version or you have not installed the kernel source code.

Follow the usual procedure for building the kernel. There are currently three interfaces to the configuration process. A graphical user interface that runs under X11 can be invoked using `make xconfig`. A menu-based system that only requires text displays is available as `make menuconfig`. The original method, using `make config`, offers a simple text-based interface.

When configuring the kernel there will be many choices for selecting the type of sound card you have and the driver options to use. The on-line help within the configuration tool should provide an explanation of what each option is for. Select the appropriate options to the best of your knowledge.

After configuring the options you should compile and install the new kernel as per the Kernel HOWTO.

Creating the Device Files

For proper operation, device file entries must be created for the sound devices. These are normally created for you during installation of your Linux system. A quick check can be made using the command listed below. If the output is as shown (the date stamp will vary) then the device files are almost certainly okay.

```
% ls -l /dev/sndstat
crw-rw-rw-  1 root     root     14,   6 Apr 25  1995 =
  /dev/sndstat
```

Note that having the right device files there doesn't guarantee anything on its own. The kernel driver must also be loaded or compiled in before the devices will work (more on that later).

In rare cases, if you believe the device files are wrong, you can recreate them. Most Linux distributions have a /dev/MAKEDEV script which can be used for this purpose.

Booting Linux and Testing the Installation

You should now be ready to boot the new kernel and test the sound drivers. Follow your usual procedure for installing and rebooting the new kernel (keep the old kernel around in case of problems, of course).

During booting, check for a message such as the following on powerup (if they scroll by too quickly to read, you may be able to retrieve them with the dmesg command):

```
Sound initialization started
<Sound Blaster 16 (4.13)> at 0x220 irq 5 dma 1,5
<Sound Blaster 16> at 0x330 irq 5 dma 0
<Yamaha OPL3 FM> at 0x388
Sound initialization complete
```

This should match your sound card type and jumper settings (if any).

Note that the above messages are not displayed when using loadable sound driver module (unless you enable it, e.g., using insmod sound trace_init=1).

When the sound driver is linked into the kernel, the Sound initialization started and Sound initialization complete messages should be displayed. If they are not printed, it means that there is no sound driver present in the kernel. In this case you should check that you actually installed the kernel you compiled when enabling the sound driver.

If nothing is printed between the Sound initialization started and the Sound initialization complete lines, it means that no sound devices were detected. Most probably it means that you don't have the correct driver enabled, the card is not supported, the I/O port is bad or that you have a PnP card that has not been configured.

The driver may also display some error messages and warnings during boot. Watch for these when booting the first time after configuring the sound driver.

Next you should check the device file /dev/sndstat. Reading the sound driver status device file should provide additional information on whether the sound card driver initialized properly. Sample output should look something like this:

```
% cat /dev/sndstat
Sound Driver:3.5.4-960630 (Sat Jan 4 23:56:57 EST 1997
root, Linux fizzbin 2.0.27 #48 Thu Dec 5 18:24:45 EST
1996 i586) Kernel: Linux fizzbin 2.0.27 #48 Thu Dec 5
18:24:45 EST 1996 i586

Config options: 0

Installed drivers:
Type 1: OPL-2/OPL-3 FM
Type 2: Sound Blaster
Type 7: SB MPU-401

Card config:
Sound Blaster at 0x220 irq 5 drq 1,5
SB MPU-401 at 0x330 irq 5 drq 0
OPL-2/OPL-3 FM at 0x388 drq 0

Audio devices:
0: Sound Blaster 16 (4.13)

Synth devices:
0: Yamaha OPL-3

Midi devices:
0: Sound Blaster 16

Timers:
0: System clock

Mixers:
0: Sound Blaster
```

The command above can report some error messages. No such file or directory indicates that you need to create the device files (see section 4.3). No such device means that sound driver is not loaded or linked into kernel. Go back to section 4.2 to correct this.

If lines in the "Card config:" section of /dev/sndstat are listed inside parentheses [such as (SoundBlaster at 0x220 irq 5 drq 1,5)], it means that this device was configured but not detected.

Now you should be ready to play a simple sound file. Get hold of a sound sample file, and send it to the sound device as a basic check of sound output, e.g.

```
% cat endoftheworld >/dev/dsp
% cat crash.au >/dev/audio
```

(Make sure you don't omit the > in the commands above).

Note that, in general, using `cat` is not the proper way to play audio files, it's just a quick check. You'll want to get a proper sound player program (described later) that will do a better job.

This command will work only if there is at least one device listed in the audio devices section of `/dev/sndstat`. If the audio devices section is empty you should check why the device was not detected.

If the above commands return `I/O error`, you should look at the end of the kernel messages listed using the "`dmesg`" command. It's likely that an error message is printed there. Very often the message is `Sound: DMA (output) timed out - IRQ/DRQ config error?`. The above message means that the driver didn't get the expected interrupt from the sound card. In most cases it means that the IRQ or the DMA channel configured to the driver doesn't work. The best way to get it working is to try with all possible DMAs and IRQs supported by the device.

Another possible reason is that the device is not compatible with the device the driver is configured for. This is almost certainly the case when a supposedly `SoundBlaster (Pro/16) compatible` sound card doesn't work with the SoundBlaster driver. In this case you should try to find out the device your sound card is compatible with (by posting to the comp.os.linux.hardware newsgroup, for example).

Some sample sound files can be obtained from <ftp://tsx-11.mit.edu/pub/linux/packages/sound/snd-data-0.1.tar.Z>

Now you can verify sound recording. If you have sound input capability, you can do a quick test of this using commands such as the following:

```
# record 4 seconds of audio from microphone
EDT% dd bs=8k count=4 </dev/audio >sample.au
4+0 records in
4+0 records out
# play back sound
% cat sample.au >/dev/audio
```

Obviously for this to work you need a microphone connected to the sound card and you should speak into it. You may also need to obtain a mixer program to set the microphone as the input device and adjust the recording gain level.

If these tests pass, you can be reasonably confident that the sound D/A and A/D hardware and software are working. If you experience problems, refer to the next section of this document.

Troubleshooting

If you still encounter problems after following the instructions in the HOWTO, here are some things to check. The checks are listed in increasing order of complexity. If a check fails, solve the problem before moving to the next stage.

Step 1: Make Sure You are Really Running the Kernel You Compiled   You can check the date stamp on the kernel to see if you are running the one that you compiled with sound support. You can do this with the uname command:

```
% uname -a
Linux fizzbin 2.2.4 #1 Tue Mar 23 11:23:21 EST 1999
i586 unknown
```

or by displaying the file /proc/version:

```
% cat /proc/version
Linux version 2.2.4 (root@fizzbin) (gcc version
2.7.2.3) #1 Tue Mar 23 11:23:21 EST 1999
```

If the date stamp doesn't seem to match when you compiled the kernel, then you are running an old kernel. Did you really reboot? If you use LILO, did you re-install it (typically by running lilo)? If booting from floppy, did you create a new boot floppy and use it when booting?

Step 2: Make Sure the Kernel Sound Drivers Are Compiled In
The easiest way to do this is to check the output of dev/sndstat as described earlier. If the output is not as expected then something went wrong with the kernel configuration or build. Start the installation process again, beginning with configuration and building of the kernel.

Step 3: Did the Kernel Detect Your Sound Card During Booting?
Make sure that the sound card was detected when the kernel booted. You should have seen a message on bootup. If the messages scrolled off the screen, you can usually recall them using the dmesg command:

```
% dmesg
```

or

```
% tail /var/log/messages
```

If your sound card was not found then something is wrong. Make sure it really is installed. If the sound card works under DOS then you can be reasonably confident that the hardware is working, so it is likely a problem with the kernel configuration. Either you configured your sound card as the wrong type or wrong parameters, or your sound card is not compatible with any of the Linux kernel sound card drivers.

One possibility is that your sound card is one of the compatible type that requires initialization by the DOS driver. Try booting DOS and loading the vendor supplied sound card driver. Then soft boot Linux using Control-Alt-Delete. Make sure that card I/O address, DMA, and IRQ settings for Linux are the same as used under DOS. Read the Readme.cards file from the sound driver source distribution for hints on configuring your card type.

If your sound card is not listed in this document, it is possible that the Linux drivers do not support it. You can check with some of the references listed at the end of this document for assistance.

Step 4: Can You Read Data From the `dsp` Device? Try reading from the `/dev/audio` device using the `dd` command listed earlier in this document. The command should run without errors.

If it doesn't work, then chances are that the problem is an IRQ or DMA conflict or some kind of hardware incompatibility (the device is not supported by Linux or the driver is configured for a wrong device).

A remote possibility is broken hardware. Try testing the sound card under DOS, if possible, to eliminate that as a possibility.

When All Else Fails If you still have problems, here are some final suggestions for things to try:

- carefully re-read this HOWTO document
- read the references listed at the end of this document and the relevant kernel source documentation files
- post a question to one of the `comp.os.linux` or other Usenet newsgroups (`comp.os.linux.hardware` is a good choice; because of the high level of traffic in these groups it helps to put the string "sound" in the subject header for the article so the right experts will see it)
- Using a `web/Usenet` search engine with an intelligently selected search criteria can give very good results quickly. One such choice is <http://www.altavista.digital.com>
- try using the latest Linux kernel (but only as a last resort, the latest development kernels can be unstable)
- send mail to the author of the sound driver
- send mail to the author of the Sound-HOWTO
- fire up emacs and type `Esc-x doctor` :-)

Applications Supporting Sound

I give here a sample of the types of applications that you likely want if you have a sound card under Linux. You can check the Linux Software Map, Internet archive sites, and/or files on your Linux CD-ROM for more up to date information.

As a minimum, you will likely want to obtain the following sound applications:

- audio file format conversion utility (e.g., sox)
- mixer utility (e.g., aumix or xmix)
- digitized file player/recorder (e.g., play or wavplay)
- MOD file player (e.g., tracker)
- MIDI file player (e.g., playmidi)

There are text-based as well as GUI-based versions of most of these tools. There are also some more esoteric applications (e.g., speech synthesis and recognition) that you may wish to try.

Answers to Frequently Asked Questions

This section answers some of the questions that have been commonly asked on the Usenet news groups and mailing lists.

Answers to more questions can also be found at the OSS sound driver web page.

What Are the Various Sound Device Files?

These are the most standard device file names, some Linux distributions may use slightly different names.

```
/dev/audio
```
> normally a link to /dev/audio0

```
/dev/audio0
```
> Sun workstation compatible audio device (only a partial

> implementation, does not support Sun `ioctl` interface, just u-law encoding)

`/dev/audio1`
> second audio device (if supported by sound card or if more than one sound card installed)

`/dev/dsp`
> normally a link to `/dev/dsp0`

`/dev/dsp0`
> first digital sampling device

`/dev/dsp1`
> second digital sampling device

`/dev/mixer`
> normally a link to `/dev/mixer0`

`/dev/mixer0`
> first sound mixer

`/dev/mixer1`
> second sound mixer

`/dev/music`
> high-level sequencer interface

`/dev/sequencer`
> low level MIDI, FM, and GUS access

`/dev/sequencer2`
> normally a link to /dev/music

`/dev/midi00`
> 1st raw MIDI port

`/dev/midi01`
> 2nd raw MIDI port

`/dev/midi02`
> 3rd raw MIDI port

`/dev/midi03`
> 4th raw MIDI port

`/dev/sndstat`
> displays sound driver status when read (also available as `/proc/sound`)

The PC speaker driver provides the following devices:

`/dev/pcaudio`
> equivalent to `/dev/audio`

`/dev/pcsp`
> equivalent to `/dev/dsp`

`/dev/pcmixer`
> equivalent to `/dev/mixer`

How Can I Play a Sound Sample?

Sun workstation (.au) sound files can be played by sending them to the /dev/audio device. Raw samples can be sent to /dev/dsp. This will generally give poor results though, and using a program such as play is preferable, as it will recognize most file types and set the sound card to the correct sampling rate, etc.

Programs like wavplay or vplay (in the snd-util package) will give best results with WAV files. However they don't recognize Microsoft ADPCM compressed WAV files. Also older versions of play (from the Lsox package) doesn't work well with 16 bit WAV files.

The splay command included in the snd-util package can be used to play most sound files if proper parameters are entered manually in the command line.

How Can I Record a Sample?

Reading /dev/audio or /dev/dsp will return sampled data that can be redirected to a file. A program such as vrec makes it easier to control the sampling rate, duration, etc. You may also need a mixer program to select the appropriate input device.

Can I Have More Than One Sound Card?

With the current sound driver it's possible to have several SoundBlaster, SoundBlaster/Pro, SoundBlaster16, MPU-401 or MSS cards at the same time on the system. Installing two SoundBlasters is possible but requires defining the macros SB2_BASE, SB2_IRQ, SB2_DMA and (in some cases) SB2_DMA2 by editing local.h manually. It's also possible to have a SoundBlaster at the same time as a PAS16.

With the 2.0 and newer kernels that configure sound using make config, instead of local.h, you need to edit the file /usr/include/linux/autoconf.h. After the section containing the lines:

```
#define SBC_BASE 0x220
#define SBC_IRQ (5)
#define SBC_DMA (1)
#define SB_DMA2 (5)
#define SB_MPU_BASE 0x0
#define SB_MPU_IRQ (-1)
```

add these lines (with values appropriate for your system):

```
#define SB2_BASE 0x330
#define SB2_IRQ (7)
#define SB2_DMA (2)
#define SB2_DMA2 (2)
```

The following drivers don't permit multiple instances:

- GUS (driver limitation)
- MAD16 (hardware limitation)
- AudioTrix Pro (hardware limitation)
- CS4232 (hardware limitation)

Error: No Such File or Directory For Sound Devices

You need to create the sound driver device files. See the section on creating device files. If you do have the device files, ensure that they have the correct major and minor device numbers (some older CD-ROM distributions of Linux may not create the correct device files during installation).

Error: No Such Device For Sound Devices

You have not booted with a kernel containing the sound driver or the I/O address configuration doesn't match your hardware. Check that you are running the newly compiled kernel and verify that the settings entered when configuring the sound driver match your hardware setup.

Error: No Space Left on Device For Sound Devices

This can happen if you tried to record data to /dev/audio or /dev/dsp without creating the necessary device file. The sound device is now a regular file, and has filled up your disk partition. You need to run the script described in the Creating the Device Files section of this document.

This may also happen with Linux 2.0 and later if there is not enough free RAM on the system when the device is opened. The audio driver requires at least two pages (8k) of contiguous physical RAM for each DMA channel. This happens sometimes in machines with less than 16M of RAM or which have been running for very long time. It may be possible to free some RAM by compiling and running the following C program before trying to open the device again:

```
main() {
    int i;
    char mem[500000];
    for (i = 0; i < 500000; i++)
      mem[i] = 0;
    exit(0);
}
```

Error: Device Busy For Sound Devices

Only one process can open a given sound device at one time. Most likely some other process is using the device in question. One way to determine this is to use the fuser command:

```
% fuser -v /dev/dsp
/dev/dsp:                   USER        PID ACCESS COMMAND
                            tranter     265 f.... tracker
```

In the above example, the fuser command showed that process 265 had the device open. Waiting for the process to complete or killing it will allow the sound device to be accessed once again. You should run the fuser command as root in order to report usage by users other than yourself.

On some systems you may need to be root when running the fuser command in order to see the processes of other users.

I Still Get Device Busy Errors!

According to Brian Gough, for the SoundBlaster cards which use DMA channel 1 there is a potential conflict with the QIC-02 tape driver, which also uses DMA 1, causing device busy errors. If you are using FTAPE, you may have this driver enabled. According to the FTAPE-HOWTO the QIC-02 driver is not essential for the use of FTAPE; only the QIC-117 driver is required. Reconfiguring the kernel to use QIC-117 but not QIC-02 allows FTAPE and the sound-driver to coexist.

Partial Playback of Digitized Sound File

The symptom is usually that a sound sample plays for about a second and then stops completely or reports an error message about "missing IRQ" or "DMA timeout". Most likely you have incorrect IRQ or DMA channel settings. Verify that the kernel configuration matches the sound card jumper settings and that they do not conflict with some other card.

Another symptom is sound samples that loop. This is usually caused by an IRQ conflict.

There Are Pauses When Playing MOD Files

Playing MOD files requires considerable CPU power. You may have too many processes running or your computer may be too slow to play in real time. Your options are to:

- try playing with a lower sampling rate or in mono mode
- eliminate other processes
- buy a faster computer
- buy a more powerful sound card (e.g., Gravis UltraSound)

If you have a Gravis UltraSound card, you should use one of the mod file players written specifically for the GUS (e.g., gmod).

Compile Errors When Compiling Sound Applications

The version 1.0c and earlier sound driver used a different and incompatible ioctl() scheme. Obtain newer source code or make the necessary changes to adapt it to the new sound driver. See the sound driver Readme file for details.

Also ensure that you have used the latest version of soundcard.h and ultrasound.h when compiling the application. See the installation instructions at beginning of this text.

SEGV When Running Sound Binaries That Worked Previously

This is probably the same problem described in the previous question.

What Known Bugs or Limitations Are There in the Sound Driver?

See the files included with the sound driver kernel source.

Where Are the Sound Driver `ioctls()` etc. Documented?

Currently the best documentation, other than the source code, is available at the 4Front Technologies web site, <http://www.opensound.com>. Another source of information is the Linux Multimedia Guide, described in the references section.

What CPU Resources Are Needed to Play or Record Without Pauses?

There is no easy answer to this question, as it depends on:

- whether using PCM sampling or FM synthesis
- sampling rate and sample size
- which application is used to play or record
- Sound Card hardware
- disk I/O rate, CPU clock speed, cache size, etc.

In general, any 386 machine or better should be able to play samples or FM synthesized music on an 8 bit sound card with ease.

Playing MOD files, however, requires considerable CPU resources. Some experimental measurements have shown that playing at 44kHz requires more than 40% of the speed of a 486/50 and a 386/25 can hardly play faster than 22 kHz (these are with an 8 bit card sound such as a SoundBlaster). A card such as the Gravis UltraSound card performs more functions in hardware, and will require less CPU resources.

These statements assume the computer is not performing any other CPU intensive tasks.

Converting sound files or adding effects using a utility such as sox is also much faster if you have a math coprocessor (or CPU with on board FPU). The kernel driver itself does not do any floating point calculations, though.

Problems With a PAS16 and an Adaptec 1542 SCSI Host Adaptor

(The following explanation was supplied by <seeker@indirect.com>)

Linux only recognizes the 1542 at address 330 (default) or 334, and the PAS only allows the MPU-401 emulation at 330. Even when you disable the MPU-401 under software, something still wants to conflict with the 1542 if it's at its preferred default address. Moving the 1542 to 334 makes everyone happy.

Additionally, both the 1542 and the PAS-16 do 16-bit DMA, so if you sample at 16-bit 44 KHz stereo and save the file to a SCSI drive hung on the 1542, you're about to have trouble. The DMAs overlap and there isn't enough time for RAM refresh, so you get the dread PARITY ERROR - SYSTEM HALTED message, with no clue to what caused it. It's made worse because a few second-party vendors with QIC-117 tape drives recommend setting the bus on/off times such that the 1542 is on even longer than normal. Get the SCSISEL.EXE program from Adaptec's BBS or several places on the internet, and reduce the BUS ON time or increase the BUS OFF time until the problem goes away, then move it one notch or more further. SCSISEL changes the EEPROM settings, so it's more permanent than a patch to the DOS driver line in CONFIG.SYS, and will work if you boot right into Linux (unlike the DOS patch). Next problem solved.

Last problem—the older Symphony chipsets drastically reduced the timing of the I/O cycles to speed up bus accesses. None of various boards I've played with had any problem with the reduced timing except for the PAS-16. Media Vision's BBS has SYMPFIX.EXE that's supposed to cure the problem by twiddling a diagnostic bit in Symphony's bus controller, but it's not a hard guarantee. You may need to:

- get the motherboard distributor to replace the older version bus chip,
- replace the motherboard, or
- buy a different brand of sound card.

Young Microsystems will upgrade the boards they import for around $30 (US); other vendors may be similar if you can figure out who made or imported the motherboard (good luck). The problem is in ProAudio's bus interface chip as far as I'm concerned; nobody buys a $120 sound card and sticks it in a 6MHz AT. Most of them wind up in 25-40MHz 386/486 boxes, and should be able to handle at least 12MHz bus rates if the chips are designed right. Exit soapbox (stage left).

The first problem depends on the chipset used on your motherboard, what bus speed and other BIOS settings, and the phase of the moon. The second problem depends on your refresh option setting (hidden or synchronous), the 1542 DMA rate and (possibly) the bus I/O rate. The third can be determined by calling Media Vision and asking which flavor of Symphony chip is incompatible with their slow design. Be warned, though —3 of 4 techs I talked to were brain damaged. I would be very leery of trusting anything they said about someone else's hardware, since they didn't even know their own very well.

Is It Possible to Read and Write Samples Simultaneously?

The drivers for some sound cards support full duplex mode. Check the documentation available from 4Front Technologies for information on how to use it.

My SB16 is Set to IRQ 2, But Configure Does Not Allow This Value

On '286 and later machines, the IRQ 2 interrupt is cascaded to the second interrupt controller. It is equivalent to IRQ 9.

If I Run Linux, Then Boot DOS, I Get Errors and/or Sound Applications Do Not Work Properly

This happens after a soft reboot to DOS. Sometimes the error message misleadingly refers to a bad CONFIG.SYS file.

Most of the current sound cards have software programmable IRQ and DMA settings. If you use different settings between Linux and MS-DOS/Windows, this may cause problems. Some sound cards don't accept new parameters without a complete reset (i.e., cycle the power or use the hardware reset button).

The quick solution to this problem it to perform a full reboot using the reset button or power cycle rather than a soft reboot (e.g., Ctrl- Alt-Del).

The correct solution is to ensure that you use the same IRQ and DMA settings with MS-DOS and Linux (or not to use DOS :-).

Problems Running DOOM Under Linux

Users of the port of ID software's game DOOM for Linux may be interested in these notes.

For correct sound output you need version 2.90 or later of the sound driver; it has support for the real-time DOOM mode.

The sound samples are 16-bit. If you have an 8-bit sound card you can still get sound to work using one of several programs available in <ftp://metalab.unc.edu/pub/Linux/games/doom>.

If performance of DOOM is poor on your system, disabling sound (by renaming the file sndserver) may improve it.

By default DOOM does not support music (as in the DOS version). The program musserver will add support for music to DOOM under Linux. It can be found at <ftp://pandora.st.hmc.edu/pub/linux/musserver.tgz>.

How Can I Reduce Noise Picked Up By My Sound Card?

Using good quality shielded cables and trying the sound card in different slots may help reduce noise. If the sound card has a volume control, you can try different settings (maximum is probably best). Using a mixer program you can make sure that undesired inputs (e.g., microphone) are set to zero gain. Philipp Braunbeck reported that on his ESS-1868 sound card there was a jumper to turn off the built-in amplifier which helped reduce noise when enabled.

On one 386 system I found that the kernel command line option no-hlt reduced the noise level. This tells the kernel not to use the halt instruction when running the idle process loop. You can try this manually when booting, or set it up using the command `append="no-hlt"` in your LILO configuration file.

Some sound cards are simply not designed with good shielding and grounding and are prone to noise pickup.

I Can Play Sounds, But Not Record

If you can play sound but not record, try these steps:

- use a mixer program to select the appropriate device (e.g., microphone)
- use the mixer to set the input gains to maximum
- If you can, try to test sound card recording under MS-DOS to determine if there is a hardware problem

Sometimes a different DMA channel is used for recording than for playback. In this case the most probable reason is that the recording DMA is set up incorrectly.

My "Compatible" Sound Card Only Works If I First Initialize Under MS-DOS

In most cases a "SoundBlaster compatible" card will work better under Linux if configured with a driver other than the SoundBlaster one. Most sound cards claim to be compatible (e.g., "16 bit SB Pro compatible" or "SB compatible 16 bit") but usually this SoundBlaster mode is just a hack provided for DOS games compatibility. Most cards have a 16 bit native mode which is likely to be supported by recent Linux versions (2.0.1 and later).

Only with some (usually rather old) cards is it necessary to try to get them to work in the SoundBlaster mode. The only newer cards that are the exception to this rule are the Mwave-based cards.

My 16-bit SoundBlaster "Compatible" Sound Card Only Works in 8-bit Mode Under Linux

16-bit sound cards described as SoundBlaster compatible are really only compatible with the 8-bit SoundBlaster Pro. They typically have a 16-bit mode which is not compatible with the SoundBlaster 16 and not compatible with the Linux sound driver.

You may be able to get the card to work in 16-bit mode by using the MAD16 or MSS/WSS driver.

Where Can I Find Sound Applications for Linux?

Here are some good archive sites to search for Linux specific sound applications:

- <ftp://metalab.unc.edu/pub/Linux/kernel/sound/>
- <ftp://metalab.unc.edu/pub/Linux/apps/sound/>
- <ftp://tsx-11.mit.edu/pub/linux/packages/sound/>
- <ftp://nic.funet.fi/pub/Linux/util/sound/>
- <ftp://nic.funet.fi/pub/Linux/xtra/snd-kit/>
- <ftp://nic.funet.fi/pub/Linux/ALPHA/sound/>

Also see the References section of this document.

Can the Sound Driver be Compiled as a Loadable Module?

With recent kernels the sound driver is supported as several kernel loadable modules.

See the files in `/usr/src/linux/Documentation/sound`, especially the files Introduction and `README.modules`.

Can I Use a Sound Card to Replace the System Console Beep?

Try the `oplbeep` program, found at
<ftp://metalab.unc.edu/pub/Linux/apps/sound/oplbeep-2.3.tar.gz>.

Another variant is the beep program found at
<ftp://metalab.unc.edu/pub/Linux/kernel/patches/misc/modreq_beep.tgz>.

The modutils package has an example program and kernel patch that supports calling an arbitrary external program to generate sounds when requested by the kernel.

Alternatively, with some sound cards you can connect the PC speaker output to the sound card so that all sounds come from the sound card speakers.

What is VoxWare?

The commercial version of the sound drivers sold by 4Front Technologies was previously known by other names such as VoxWare, USS (Unix Sound System), and even TASD (Temporarily Anonymous Sound Driver). It is now marketed as OSS (Open Sound System). The version included in the Linux kernel is sometimes referred to as OSS/Free.

For more information see the 4Front Technologies web page at <http://www.opensound.com/>. I wrote a review of OSS/Linux in the June 1997 issue of Linux Journal.

`Sox/Play/Vplay` reports invalid block size 1024

A change to the sound driver in version 1.3.67 broke some sound player programs which (incorrectly) checked that the result from the SNDCTL _DSP_GETBLKSIZE ioctl was greater than 4096. The latest sound driver versions have been fixed to avoid allocating fragments shorter than 4096 bytes which solves this problem with old utilities.

The Mixer Settings Are Reset Whenever I Load the Sound Driver Module

You can build the sound driver as a loadable module and use kerneld to automatically load and unload it. This can present one problem—whenever the module is reloaded the mixer settings go back to their default values. For some sound cards this can be too loud (e.g., SoundBlaster16) or too quiet. Markus Gutschke (gutschk@uni- muenster.de) found this solution. Use a line in your /etc/conf.modules file such as the following:

```
options sound dma_buffsize=65536 &&
     /usr/bin/setmixer igain 0 ogain 0 vol 75
```

This causes your mixer program (in this case `setmixer`) to be run immediately after the sound driver is loaded. The `dma_buffsize` parameter is just a dummy value needed because the option command requires a command line option. Change the line as needed to match your mixer program and gain settings.

If you have compiled the sound driver into your kernel and you want to set the mixer gains at boot time you can put a call to your mixer program in a system startup file such as `/etc/rc.d/rc.local`.

Only User Root Can Record Sound

By default the script in `Readme.linux` that creates the sound device files only allows the devices to be read by user root. This is to plug a potential security hole. In a networked environment, external users could conceivably log in remotely to a Linux PC with a sound card and microphone and eavesdrop. If you are not worried about this, you can change the permissions used in the script.

With the default setup, users can still play sound files. This is not a security risk but is a potential for nuisance.

Is the Sound Hardware on the IBM ThinkPad Supported?

Information on how to use the `mwave` sound card on an IBM ThinkPad laptop computer can be found in the file `/usr/src/linux/Documentation/sound/mwave`, which is part of the kernel source distribution.

Applications Fail Because My Sound Card Has No Mixer

Some old 8-bit SoundBlaster cards have no mixer circuitry. Some sound applications insist on being able to open the mixer device, and fail with these cards. Jens Werner (<<u>werner@bert.emv.ing.tu-bs.de</u>>) reports a workaround for this is to link /dev/mixer to /dev/null and everything should work fine.

Problems with a SB16 CT4170

From Scott Manley (spm@star.arm.ac.uk):

> There seems to be a new type of Soundblaster—it was sold to us as a SB16—the Model no. on the Card is CT4170. These Beasties only have one DMA channel so when you try to set them up then the kernel will have trouble accessing the 16 bit DMA. The solution is to set the second DMA to 1 so that the card will behave as advertised.

How to Connect a MIDI Keyboard to a Sound Card

From Kim G. S. OEyhus (kim@pvv.ntnu.no):

> I looked all around the internet and in sound documentation on how to do something as simple as connecting the MIDI output from a master keyboard to the MIDI input on a sound card. I found nothing. The problem is that they both use the same device, /dev/midi, at least when using the OSS sound system. So I found a way to do it, which I want to share. This makes for a very simple synthesizer, with full MIDI support:
>
> CONNECTING A MIDI MASTER-KEYBOARD DIRECTLY TO A SOUNDCARD WITH MIDI
>
> A MIDI master-keyboard is a keyboard without any synthesizer, and with only a MIDI-out plug. This can be connected to the 15-pin D-SUB port on most sound-cards with a suitable cable.
>
> Such a keyboard can be used to control the MIDI synthesizer device for the card, thus making a simple keyboard controlled synthesizer.
>
> Compile the following program, say with 'gcc -o prog prog.c' and run it:

```
#include <fcntl.h>
main()
{
    int fil, a;
    char b[256];
```

```
fil=open("/dev/midi", O_RDWR);
 for(;;)
   {
     a=read(fil, b, 256);
     write(fil, b, a);
   }
}
```

Problems with IRQ 15 and Ensoniq PCI 128

From Matthew Inger (<<u>mattinger@mindless.com</u>>):

Information on getting an Ensoniq PCI 128 card to work.

The problem that it was exhibiting was that it was trying to use interrupt 15 by default (Plug and Pray was responsible for this one). This interrupt is used by the secondary ide controller, and cannot be shared by other devices. You need to somehow force the es1370 to use another interrupt (should use interrupt 11 like it does under windows).

I figured this one out for myself believe it or not.

What I had to do was:

a) in the BIOS, you have to tell the computer that you don't have a Plug and Play OS. I believe this is under advanced options in my BIOS.

b) in the PCI settings in the BIOS, tell the computer to reserve interrupt 15 for legacy ISA devices. In my bios, under advanced options, there is a section for PCI settings. Under there, there is a Resource Exclusion area, and that's where to do this.

When you reboot into linux you will be able to use sound. (I don't remember if it shows up in the boot messages or not like it used to). To be safe, I ran sndconfig again so that it would play the test message, which sounded not great, but it was there. When I played a CD however, it sounded perfect. Don't worry about windows, I tried both my cards: ISA Modem, and the Sound Card out, and they work without any hitches.

The odds are your BIOS will be different from mine, but you just have to figure out where the settings are for the above two items. Good luck.

Where Can I Get Freely Available MIDI Patches to Run SoftOSS?

SoftOSS is a software-based wavetable synthesizer included with the kernel sound driver that is compatible with the Gravis Utrasound card. To operate the driver needs GUS compatible MIDI patch files. The documentation mentions the "public domain MIDIA patchset available from several ftp sites".

As explained on the 4Front Technologies web page <http://www.opensound. com/softoss.html> they can be downloaded from <ftp://archive.cs.umbc.edu/ pub/midia/instruments.tar.gz>.

References

If you have a sound card that supports a CD-ROM or SCSI interface, the Linux SCSI HOWTO and the Linux CD-ROM HOWTO have additional information that may be useful to you.

The Sound Playing HOWTO describes how to play various types of sound and music files under Linux.

The Linux SoundBlaster AWE32/64 Mini-HOWTO describes how to get a SoundBlaster 32 or 64 card working under Linux.

Programming information is available from the 4Front Technologies web site at <http://www.opensound.com/pguide>.

The following FAQs are regularly posted to the Usenet newsgroup news.announce as well as being archived at <ftp://rtfm.mit.edu/pub/usenet/news.answers>:

- PCsoundcards/generic-faq (Generic PC Soundcard FAQ)
- PCsoundcards/soundcard-faq (comp.sys.ibm.pc.soundcard FAQ)
- PCsoundcards/gravis-ultrasound/faq (Gravis UltraSound FAQ)
- audio-fmts/part1 (Audio file format descriptions)
- audio-fmts/part2 (Audio file format descriptions)

The FAQs also list several product specific mailing lists and archive sites. The following Usenet news groups discuss sound and/or music related issues:

- alt.binaries.sounds.* (various groups for posting sound files)
- alt.binaries.multimedia (for posting Multimedia files)
- alt.sb.programmer (Soundblaster programming topics)
- comp.multimedia (Multimedia topics)
- comp.music (Computer music theory and research)
- comp.sys.ibm.pc.soundcard.* (various IBM PC sound card groups)

A web site dedicated to multimedia can be found at <http://viswiz. gmd.de/MultimediaInfo/>. Another good site for Linux MIDI and sound applications is <http://sound.condorow.net/>. Creative Labs has a web site at <http://www.creaf.com/>. MediaTrix has a web site at <http://www.mediatrix.com/>.

The Linux mailing list has a number of "channels" dedicated to different topics, including sound. To find out how to join, send a mail message with the word "help" as the message body to <majordomo@vger.rutgers.edu.> These mailing lists are not recommended for questions on sound card setup etc., they are intended for development related discussion.

As mentioned several times before, the kernel sound driver includes a number of Readme files containing useful information about the sound card driver. These can typically be found in the directory /usr/src/linux/drivers/sound.

Information on OSS, the commercial sound driver for Linux and other Unix compatible operating systems, can be found at the 4Front Technologies web page at <http://www.opensound.com/>.

The Linux Software Map (LSM) is an invaluable reference for locating Linux software. Searching the LSM for keywords such as sound is a good way to identify applications related to sound hardware. The LSM can be found on various anonymous FTP sites, including <ftp://metalab.unc.edu/pub/Linux/docs/LSM/> (formerly known as sunsite). There are also various web sites that maintain databases of Linux applications. One such site is <http://www.freshmeat.net>.

The Linux Documentation Project has produced several books on Linux, including Linux Installation and Getting Started. These are freely available by anonymous FTP from major Linux archive sites or can be purchased in hardcopy format.

Finally, a shameless plug: If you want to learn a lot more about multimedia under Linux (especially CD-ROM and sound card applications and programming), check out my book Linux Multimedia Guide, ISBN 1-56592-219-0, published by O'Reilly and Associates. As well as the original English version, French and Japanese translations are now in print. For details, call 800-998-9938 in North America or check the web page <http://www.ora.com/catalog/multilinux/noframes.html> or my home page <http://www.pobox.com/~tranter>.

E

NET3-4-HOWTO

The Linux Operating System boasts kernel based networking support written almost entirely from scratch. The performance of the tcp/ip implementation in recent kernels makes it a worthy alternative to even the best of its peers. This document aims to describe how to install and configure the Linux networking software and associated tools.

Introduction

This is the first release since LinuxPorts has become the author of this document. First let me say that we hope that over the next few months you will find this document to be of use and that we are able to provide accurate and timely information in regards to networking issues with Linux.

This document like the other HOWTO's that we manage is going to become very different, this document will shortly become the Networking-HOWTO not just the Net-3(4)-HOWTO. We will cover such items as PPP, VPN, and others.

Document History

The original NET-FAQ was written by Matt Welsh and Terry Dawson to answer frequently asked questions about networking for Linux at a time before the Linux Documentation Project had formally started. It covered the very early development versions of the Linux Networking Kernel. The NET-2-HOWTO superceded the NET-FAQ and was one of the original LDP HOWTO documents; it covered what was called version 2 and later version 3 of the Linux kernel Networking software. This document in turn supercedes it and relates only to version 4 of the Linux Networking Kernel or more specifically kernel releases 2.x and 2.2.x.

Previous versions of this document became quite large because of the enormous amount of material that fell within its scope. To help reduce this problem a number of HOWTO's dealing with specific networking topics have been produced. This document will provide pointers to them where relevant and cover those areas not yet covered by other documents.

Feedback

We are always interested in feedback. Please contact us at: <poet@linuxports. com>.

Again, if you find anything erroneous or anything you would like to see added, please contact us.

How To Use This HOWTO

This document is organized top-down. The first sections include informative material and can be skipped if you are not interested; what follows is a generic discussion of networking issues, and you must ensure you understand this before proceeding to more specific parts. The rest, "technology specific" information is grouped in three main sections: Ethernet and IP-related information, technologies pertaining to widespread PC hardware and seldom-used technologies.

The suggested path through the document is thus the following:

Read the generic sections.
> These sections apply to every, or nearly every, technology described later and so are very important for you to understand. On the other hand, I expect many of the readers to be already confident with this material.

Consider your network.
> You should know how your network is, or will be, designed and exactly what hardware and technology types you will be implementing.

Read the "Ethernet and IP" section if you are directly connected a LAN or the Internet.
> This section describes basic Ethernet configuration and the various features that Linux offers for IP networks, like firewalling, advanced routing and so on.

Read the next section if you are interested in low-cost local networks or dial-up connections.
> The section describes PLIP, PPP, SLIP and ISDN, the widespread technologies used on personal workstations.

Read the technology specific sections related to your requirements.
> If your needs differ from IP and/or common hardware, the final section covers details specific to non-IP protocols and peculiar communication hardware.

Do the configuration work.
> You should actually try to configure your network and take careful note of any problems you have.

Look for further help if needed.
> If you experience problems that this document does not help you to resolve then read the section related to where to get help or where to report bugs.

Have fun!
> Networking is fun, enjoy it.

Conventions Used in This Document

No special convention is used here, but you must be warned about the way commands are shown. Following the classic Unix documentation, any command you should type to your shell is prefixed by a prompt. This HOWTO shows user% as the prompt for commands that do not require superuser privileges, and root# as the prompt for commands that need to run as root. I chose to use root# instead of a plain # to prevent confusion with snapshots from shell scripts, where the hash mark is used to define comment lines.

When kernel compile options are shown, they are represented in the format used by menuconfig. They should be understandable even if you (like me) are not used to menuconfig. If you are in doubt about the options' nesting, running the program once can't but help.

Note that any link to other HOWTOs is local to help you browsing your local copy of the LDP documents, in case you are using the html version of this document. If you don't have a complete set of documents, every HOWTO can be retrieved from metalab.unc.edu (directory /pub/Linux/HOWTO) and its countless mirrors.

Generic Network Configuration Information

The following subsections you will pretty much need to know and understand before you actually try to configure your network. They are fundamental principles that apply regardless of the exact nature of the network you wish to deploy.

What Do I Need to Start ?

Before you start building or configuring your network you will need some things. The most important of these are:

Current Kernel Source (Optional) Please note: The majority of current distributions come with networking enabled, therefore it may not be required to recompile the kernel. If you are running well known hardware you should be just fine. For example: 3COM NIC, NE2000 NIC, or a Intel NIC. However if you find yourself in the position that you do need to update the kernel, the following information is provided.

Because the kernel you are running now might not yet have support for the network types or cards that you wish to use you will probably need the kernel source so that you can recompile the kernel with the appropriate options.

For users of the major distributions such as Red Hat, Caldera, Debian, or Suse this no longer holds true. As long as you stay within the mainstream of hardware there should be no need to recompile your kernel unless there is a very specific feature that you need.

You can always obtain the latest kernel source from <ftp.cdrom.com>. This is not the official site but they have LOTS of bandwidth and ALOT of users allowed. The official site is kernel.org but please use the above if you can. Please remember that <ftp.kernel.org> is seriously overloaded. Use a mirror.

Normally the kernel source will be untarred into the `/usr/src/linux` directory. For information on how to apply patches and build the kernel you should read the Kernel-HOWTO. For information on how to configure kernel modules you should read the "Modules mini-HOWTO". Also, the README file found in the kernel sources and the Documentation directory are very informative for the brave reader.

Unless specifically stated otherwise, I recommend you stick with the standard kernel release (the one with the even number as the second digit in the version number). Development release kernels (the ones with the odd second digit) may have structural or other changes that may cause problems working with the other software on your system. If you are uncertain that you could resolve those sorts of problems in addition to the potential for there being other software errors, then don't use them.

On the other hand, some of the features described here have been introduced during the development of 2.1 kernels, so you must take your choice: you can stick to 2.0 while wait for 2.2 and an updated distribution with every new tool, or you can get 2.1 and look around for the various support programs needed to exploit the new features. As I write this paragraph, in August 1998, 2.1.115 is current and 2.2 is expected to appear pretty soon.

Current Network Tools   The network tools are the programs that you use to configure Linux network devices. These tools allow you to assign addresses to devices and configure routes for example.

Most modern Linux distributions are supplied with the network tools, so if you have installed from a distribution and haven't yet installed the network tools then you should do so.

If you haven't installed from a distribution then you will need to source and compile the tools yourself. This isn't difficult.

The network tools are now maintained by Bernd Eckenfels and are available at: <ftp.inka.de> and are mirrored at: <ftp.uk.linux.org>.

You can also get the latest Red Hat packages from net- tools-1.51-3.i386.rpm.

Be sure to choose the version that is most appropriate for the kernel you wish to use and follow the instructions in the package to install.

To install and configure the version current at the time of the writing you need do the following:

```
user% tar xvfz net-tools-1.33.tar.gz
user% cd net-tools-1.33
user% make config
user% make
root# make install
```

Or to use the Red Hat packages:

```
root# rpm -U net-tools-1.51-3.i386.rpm
```

Additionally, if you intend configuring a firewall or using the IP masquerade feature you will require the ipfwadm command. The latest version of it may be obtained from: <ftp.xos.nl>. Again there are a number of versions available. Be sure to pick the version that most closely matches your kernel. Note that the firewalling features of Linux changed during 2.1 development and has been superceded by ipchains in v2.2 of the kernel. ipfwadm only applies to version 2.0 of the kernel. The following are known to be distributions with version 2.0 or below of the kernel.

Redhat 5.2 or below

Caldera pre version 2.2

Slackware pre version 4.x

Debian pre version 2.x

To install and configure the version current at the time of this writing you need to read the IPChains HOWTO located at The Linux Documentation Project.

Note that if you run version 2.2 (or late 2.1) of the kernel, ipfwadm is not the right tool to configure firewalling. This version of the NET-3-HOWTO currently doesn't deal with the new firewalling setup. If you need more detailed information on ipchains please refer to the above.

Network Application Programs   The network application programs are programs such as telnet and ftp and their respective server programs.

David Holland has been managing a distribution of the most common of these, which is now maintained by `netbug@ftp.uk.linux.org`. You may obtain the distribution from: <ftp.uk.linux.org>.

IP Addresses, an Explanation Internet Protocol Addresses are composed of four bytes. The convention is to write addresses in what is called 'dotted decimal notation'. In this form each byte is converted to a decimal number (0-255) dropping any leading zeroes unless the number is zero and written with each byte separated by a '.' character. By convention each interface of a host or router has an IP address. It is legal for the same IP address to be used on each interface of a single machine in some circumstances but usually each interface will have its own address.

Internet Protocol Networks are contiguous sequences of IP addresses. All addresses within a network have a number of digits within the address in common. The portion of the address that is common amongst all addresses within the network is called the 'network portion' of the address. The remaining digits are called the 'host portion'. The number of bits that are shared by all addresses within a network is called the netmask and it is role of the netmask to determine which addresses belong to the network it is applied to and which don't. For example, consider the following:

```
----------------------       ----------------------
Host Address                  192.168.110.23
Network Mask                  255.255.255.0
Network Portion               192.168.110.
----------------------       ----------------------
Host portion                  .23
Network Address               192.168.110.0
Broadcast Address             192.168.110.255
----------------------       ----------------------
```

Any address that is 'bitwise anded' with its netmask will reveal the address of the network it belongs to. The network address is therefore always the lowest numbered address within the range of addresses on the network and always has the host portion of the address coded all zeroes.

The broadcast address is a special address that every host on the network listens to in addition to its own unique address. This address is the one that datagrams are sent to if every host on the network is meant to receive it. Certain types of data like routing information and warning messages are transmitted to the broadcast address so that every host on the network can receive it simultaneously. There are two commonly used standards for what the broadcast address should be. The most widely accepted one is to use the highest possible address on the network as the broadcast address. In the example above this would be 192.168.110.255. For some reason other sites have adopted the convention of using the network address as the broadcast address. In practice it doesn't matter very much which you use but you must make sure that every host on the network is configured with the same broadcast address.

For administrative reasons some time early in the development of the IP protocol some arbitrary groups of addresses were formed into networks and these networks were grouped into what are called classes. These classes provide a number of standard size networks that could be allocated. The ranges allocated are:

Network Class	Netmask	Network Addresses	
A	255.0.0.0	0.0.0.0 - 127.255.255.255	
B	255.255.0.0	128.0.0.0 - 191.255.255.255	
C	255.255.255.0	192.0.0.0 - 223.255.255.255	
Multicast	240.0.0.0	224.0.0.0 - 239.255.255.255	

What addresses you should use depends on exactly what it is that you are doing. You may have to use a combination of the following activities to get all the addresses you need:

Installing a linux machine on an existing IP network. If you wish to install a linux machine onto an existing IP network then you should contact whoever administers the network and ask them for the following information:

- Host IP Address
- IP network address
- IP broadcast address
- IP netmask
- Router address
- Domain Name Server Address

You should then configure your linux network device with those details. You can not make them up and expect your configuration to work.

Building a brand new network that will never connect to the Internet: If you are building a private network and you never intend that network to be connected to the Internet then you can choose whatever addresses you like. However, for safety and consistency reasons there have been some IP network addresses that have been reserved specifically for this purpose. These are specified in RFC1597 and are as follows:

```
---------------------------------------------------------------------------
|          RESERVED PRIVATE NETWORK ALLOCATIONS                           |
---------------------------------------------------------------------------
|     | Network | Netmask        | Network Addresses                      |
|     | Class   |                |                                        |
---------------------------------------------------------------------------
|     | A       | 255.0.0.0      | 10.0.0.0    - 10.255.255.255           |
|     | B       | 255.255.0.0    | 172.16.0.0  - 172.31.255.255          |
|     | C       | 255.255.255.0  | 192.168.0.0 - 192.168.255.255         |
---------------------------------------------------------------------------
```

You should first decide how large you want your network to be and then choose as many of the addresses as you require.

Where Should I Put the Configuration Commands ?

There are a few different approaches to Linux system boot procedures. After the kernel boots, it always executes a program called init. The init program then reads its configuration file called /etc/inittab and commences the boot process. There are a few different flavours of init around, although everyone is now converging to the System V (Five) flavor, developed by Miguel van Smoorenburg.

Despite the fact that the init program is always the same, the setup of system boot is organized in a different way by each distribution.

Usually the /etc/inittab file contains an entry looking something like:

```
si::sysinit:/etc/init.d/boot
```

This line specifies the name of the shell script file that actually manages the boot sequence. This file is somewhat equivalent to the AUTOEXEC.BAT file in MS-DOS.

There are usually other scripts that are called by the boot script and often the network is configured within one of many of these.

The following table may be used as a guide for your system:

```
------------------------------------------------------------------------
 Distrib.    | Interface Config/Routing   | Server Initialization
------------------------------------------------------------------------
 Debian      | /etc/init.d/network        | /etc/rc2.d/*
------------------------------------------------------------------------
 Slackware   | /etc/rc.d/rc.inet1         | /etc/rc.d/rc.inet2
------------------------------------------------------------------------
 Red Hat     | /etc/rc.d/init.d/network   | /etc/rc.d/rc3.d/*
------------------------------------------------------------------------
```

Note that Debian and Red Hat use a whole directory to host scripts that fire up system services (and usually information does not lie within these files, for example Red Hat systems store all of system configuration in files under /etc/sysconfig, whence it is retrieved by boot scripts). If you want to grasp the details of the boot process, my suggestion is to check /etc/inittab and the documentation that accompanies init. Linux Journal is also going to publish an article about system initialization, and this document will point to it as soon as it is available on the web.

Most modern distributions include a program that will allow you to configure many of the common sorts of network interfaces. If you have one of these then you should see if it will do what you want before attempting a manual configuration.

```
--------------------------------------------------------------
 Distrib       |   Network configuration program
--------------------------------------------------------------
 Red Hat       |   /usr/bin/netcfg
 Slackware     |   /sbin/netconfig
--------------------------------------------------------------
```

Creating Your Network Interfaces

In many Unix operating systems the network devices have appearances in the /dev directory. This is not so in Linux. In Linux the network devices are created dynamically in software and do not require device files to be present.

In the majority of cases the network device is automatically created by the device driver while it is initializing and has located your hardware. For example, the ethernet device driver creates eth[0..n] interfaces sequentially as it locates your ethernet hardware. The first ethernet card found becomes eth0, the second eth1 etc.

In some cases though, notably slip and ppp, the network devices are created through the action of some user program. The same sequential device numbering applies, but the devices are not created automatically at boot time. The reason for this is that unlike ethernet devices, the number of active slip or ppp devices may vary during the uptime of the machine. These cases will be covered in more detail in later sections.

Configuring a Network Interface

When you have all of the programs you need and your address and network information you can configure your network interfaces. When we talk about configuring a network interface we are talking about the process of assigning appropriate addresses to a network device and to setting appropriate values for other configurable parameters of a network device. The program most commonly used to do this is the ifconfig (interface configure) command.

Typically you would use a command similar to the following:

```
root# ifconfig eth0 192.168.0.1 netmask 255.255.255.0 up
```

In this case I'm configuring an ethernet interface eth0 with the IP address '192.168.0.1' and a network mask of '255.255.255.0'. The 'up' that trails the command tells the interface that it should become active, but can usually be omitted, as it is the default. To shutdown an interface, you can just call ifconfig eth0 down.

The kernel assumes certain defaults when configuring interfaces. For example, you may specify the network address and broadcast address for an interface, but if you don't, as in my example above, then the kernel will make reasonable guesses as to what they should be based on the netmask you supply and if you don't supply a netmask then on the network class of the IP address configured. In my example the kernel would assume that it is a class-C network being configured on the interface and configure a network address of '192.168.0.0' and a broadcast address of '192.168.0.255' for the interface.

There are many other options to the ifconfig command. The most important of these are:

up   this option activates an interface (and is the default).

down   this option deactivates an interface.

[-]arp   this option enables or disables use of the address resolution protocol on this interface.

`[-]allmulti` this option enables or disables the reception of all hardware multicast packets. Hardware multicast enables groups of hosts to receive packets addressed to special destinations. This may be of importance if you are using applications like desktop video-conferencing but is normally not used.

`mtu N` this parameter allows you to set the MTU of this device.

`netmask <addr>` this parameter allows you to set the network mask of the network this device belongs to.

`irq <addr>` this parameter only works on certain types of hardware and allows you to set the IRQ of the hardware of this device.

`[-]broadcast [addr]` this parameter allows you to enable and set the accepting of datagrams destined to the broadcast address, or to disable reception of these datagrams.

`[-]pointopoint [addr]` this parameter allows you to set the address of the machine at the remote end of a point to point link such as for slip or ppp.

`hw <type> <addr>` this parameter allows you to set the hardware address of certain types of network devices. This is not often useful for ethernet, but is useful for other network types such as AX.25.

You may use the `ifconfig` command on any network interface. Some user programs such as `pppd` and `dip` automatically configure the network devices as they create them, so manual use of `ifconfig` is unnecessary.

Configuring Your Name Resolver

The 'Name Resolver' is a part of the linux standard library. Its prime function is to provide a service to convert human-friendly hostnames like `ftp.funet.fi` into machine friendly IP addresses such as 128.214.248.6.

What's In a Name ? You will probably be familiar with the appearance of Internet host names, but may not understand how they are constructed, or deconstructed. Internet domain names are hierarchical in nature, that is, they have a tree-like structure. A 'domain' is a family, or group of names. A 'domain' may be broken down into 'subdomain'. A 'toplevel domain' is a domain that is not a subdomain. The Top Level Domains are specified in RFC-920. Some examples of the most common top level domains are:

COM   Commercial Organizations

EDU   Educational Organizations

GOV   Government Organizations

MIL   Military Organizations

ORG   Other organizations

NET   Internet-Related Organizations

Country Designator   These are two letters codes that represent a particular country.

For historical reasons most domains belonging to one of the non-country based top level domains were used by organizations within the United States, although the United States also has its own country code `.us`. This is not true any more for `.com` and `.org` domains, which are commonly used by non-us companies.

Each of these top level domains has subdomains. The top level domains based on country name are often next broken down into subdomains based on the `com`, `edu`, `gov`, `mil` and `org` domains. So for example you end up with: `com.au` and `gov.au` for commercial and government organizations in Australia; note that this is not a general rule, as actual policies depend on the naming authority for each domain.

The next level of division usually represents the name of the organization. Further subdomains vary in nature, often the next level of subdomain is based on the departmental structure of the organization but it may be based on any criterion considered reasonable and meaningful by the network administrators for the organization.

The very left-most portion of the name is always the unique name assigned to the host machine and is called the 'hostname', the portion of the name to the right of the hostname is called the 'domainname' and the complete name is called the 'Fully Qualified Domain Name'.

To use Terry's host as an example, the fully qualified domain name is `perf.no.itg.telstra.com.au`. This means that the host name is `perf` and the domain name is `no.itg.telstra.com.au`. The domain name is based on a top level domain based on his country, Australia and as his email address belongs to a commercial organization, `.com` is there as the next level domain. The name of the company is (was) `telstra` and their internal naming structure is based on organizational structure, in this case the machine belongs to the Information Technology Group, Network Operations section.

Usually, the names are fairly shorter; for example, my ISP is called `sys-temy.it` and my non-profit organization is called `linux.it`, without any com and org subdomain, so that my own host is just called `"morgana.sys-temy.it"` and `rubini@linux.it` is a valid email address. Note that the owner of a domain has the rights to register hostnames as well as subdomains; for example, the LUG I belong to uses the domain `pluto.linux.it`, because the owners of `linux.it` agreed to open a subdomain for the LUG.

What Information You Will Need   You will need to know what domain your hosts name will belong to. The name resolver software provides this name translation service by making requests to a 'Domain Name Server', so you will need to know the IP address of a local nameserver that you can use.

There are three files you need to edit; I'll cover each of these in turn.

/etc/resolv.conf   The `/etc/resolv.conf` is the main configuration file for the name resolver code. Its format is quite simple. It is a text file with one keyword per line. There are three keywords typically used, they are:

`domain`   this keyword specifies the local domain name.

`search`   this keyword specifies a list of alternate domain names to search for a hostname

`nameserver`   this keyword, which may be used many times, specifies an IP address of a domain name server to query when resolving names

An example `/etc/resolv.conf` might look something like:

```
domain maths.wu.edu.au
search maths.wu.edu.au wu.edu.au
nameserver 192.168.10.1
nameserver 192.168.12.1
```

This example specifies that the default domain name to append to unqualified names (ie hostnames supplied without a domain) is `maths.wu.edu.au` and that if the host is not found in that domain to also try the `wu.edu.au` domain directly. Two nameservers entry are supplied, each of which may be called upon by the name resolver code to resolve the name.

/etc/host.conf   The `/etc/host.conf` file is where you configure some items that govern the behaviour of the name resolver code. The format of this file is described in detail in the `resolv+` man page. In nearly all circumstances the following example will work for you:

```
order hosts,bind
multi on
```

This configuration tells the name resolver to check the `/etc/hosts` file before attempting to query a nameserver and to return all valid addresses for a host found in the `/etc/hosts` file instead of just the first.

/etc/hosts   The `/etc/hosts` file is where you put the name and IP address of local hosts. If you place a host in this file then you do not need to query the domain name server to get its IP Address. The disadvantage of doing this is that you must keep this file up to date yourself if the IP address for that host changes. In a well managed system the only hostnames that usually appear in this file are an entry for the loopback interface and the local hosts name.

```
# /etc/hosts
127.0.0.1 localhost loopback
192.168.0.1 this.host.name
```

You may specify more than one host name per line as demonstrated by the first entry, which is a standard entry for the loopback interface.

F

Linux IP Masquerade HOWTO

This document describes how to enable the Linux IP Masquerade feature on a given Linux host. IP Masq is a form of Network Address Translation or NAT that allows internally connected computers that do not have one or more registered Internet IP addresses to have the ability to communicate to the Internet via your Linux box's single Internet IP address. This excerpt is based on the official Linux IP Masquerade HOWTO.

Introduction

Introduction to IP Masquerading (IP MASQ)

It is possible to connect your internal machines to the Linux host with LAN technologies like Ethernet, TokenRing, FDDI, as well as other kinds of connections such as dialup PPP or SLIP links. This document uses Ethernet for the primary example since it is the most common scenario.

This document is intended for users using either of the stable Linux kernels: 2.0.36+ and 2.2.9+ on a IBM-compatible PC. Older kernels such as 1.2.x, 1.3.x, and 2.1.x are NOT covered in this document and, in some kernel versions, can be considered broken. Please upgrade to one of the stable Linux kernels before using IP Masquerading. The new 2.3 and 2.4 kernels with the new NetFilter code aren't covered yet but URLs are provided below. Once the feature set for Netfilter is final, the new code will be covered in this HOWTO.

If you are configuring IP Masq for use on a Macintosh, please email Taro Fukunaga, <htmlurl url="mail:tarozax@earthlink.net"name="tarozax @earthlink.net"> for a copy of his short MkLinux version of this HOWTO.

Foreword, Feedback & Credits

As a new user, I found it very confusing to setup IP masquerade on Linux kernel, (1.2.x kernel back then). Although there is a FAQ and a mailing list, there was no document that was dedicated to it. There were also some requests on the mailing list for such a HOWTO. So, I decided to write this HOWTO as a starting point for new users and possibly create a building block for other knowledgeable users to add to in the future. If you have any ideas for this document, corrections, etc., feel free to tell us so that we can make it better.

This document was originally based on the original FAQ by Ken Eves and numerous helpful messages from the IP Masquerade mailing list. A special thanks to Mr. Matthew Driver whose mailing list message inspired me to set up IP Masquerade and eventually writing this. Recently, David Ranch re-wrote the HOWTO and added a substantial number of sections to the HOWTO to make this document as complete as possible.

Please feel free to send any feedback or comments to <htmlurl url= "mailto:ambrose@writeme.com" name="ambrose@writeme.com"> and <htmlurl url="mailto:dranch@trinnet.net" name="dranch@trinnet.net"> if you have any corrections or if any information/URLs/etc., is missing. Your invaluable feedback will certainly influence the future of this HOWTO!

This HOWTO is meant to be a fairly comprehensive guide on getting your Linux IP Masquerading network working in the shortest time possible. As neither Ambrose nor David are technical writers, you might find the information in this document not as general and/or objective as it could be. The latest news and information regarding this HOWTO and other IP MASQ details can be found at the <url url="http://ipmasq.cjb.net/" name="IP Masquerade Resource"> web page that we actively maintain. If you have any technical questions on IP Masquerade, please join the IP Masquerade Mailing List instead of sending email to either Ambrose or David. Most MASQ problems are common for ALL MASQ users and can be easily solved by someone on the list. In addition to this, the response time of the IP MASQ email list will be much faster than a reply from either Ambrose or David.

The latest version of this document can be found at the following sites which also contains HTML and postscript versions

- <htmlurl url="http://ipmasq.cjb.net/"name="http:// ipmasq.cjb.net/: The IP Masquerade Resources">
- <htmlurl url="http://ipmasq2.cjb.net/"name="http:// ipmasq2.cjb.net/: The IP Masquerade Resources MIRROR">
- <htmlurl url="http://metalab.unc.edu/LDP" name="The Linux Documentation Project">
- <htmlurl url="http://www.ecst.csuchico.edu/~dranch/LINUX/ index-linux.html#ipmas=q" name="Dranch's Linux page">
- Also refer to <url url="http://imasq.cjb.net/index.html# mirror" name="IP=Masquerade Resource Mirror Sites Listing"> for other local mirror sites.

Copyright & Disclaimer

The information herein this document is, to the best of Ambrose's and David's knowledge, correct. However, the Linux IP Masquerade feature is written by humans and thus, there is the chance that mistakes, bugs, etc. might happen from time to time.

No person, group, or other body is responsible for any damage on your computer(s) and any other losses by using the information on this document, i.e.

THE AUTHORS AND ALL MAINTAINERS ARE NOT RESPONSIBLE FOR ANY DAMAGES INCURRED DUE TO ACTIONS TAKEN BASED ON THE INFORMATION IN THIS DOCUMENT.

Background Knowledge

What is IP Masquerade?

IP Masquerade is a networking function in Linux similar to one-to-many NAT (Network Address Translation) found in many commercial firewalls and network routers. For example, if a Linux host is connected to the Internet via PPP, Ethernet, etc., the IP Masquerade feature allows other "internal" computers connected to this Linux box (via PPP, Ethernet, etc.) to also reach the Internet as well. Linux IP Masquerading allows for this functionality even though these internal machines don't have *an officially assigned IP addresses*.

MASQ allows a set of machines to *invisibly* access the Internet via the MASQ gateway. To other machines on the Internet, all this outgoing traffic will appear to be from the IP MASQ Linux server itself. In addition to the added functionality, IP Masquerade provides the foundation to create a VERY secure networking environment. With a well built firewall, breaking the security of a well configured masquerading system and internal LAN should be considerably difficult.

Current Status

IP Masquerade has been out for several years now and is fairly mature as Linux enters the 2.2.x kernel stage. Kernels since Linux 1.3.x have had

MASQ support built-in. Today many individuals and commercial businesses are using it with excellent results.

Common network uses like Web browsing, TELNET, FTP, PING, TRACEROUTE, etc., work well over IP Masquerade. Other communications such as FTP, IRC, and Real Audio work well with the appropriate IP MASQ modules loaded. Other network-specific programs like streaming audio (MP3s, True Speech, etc.) work too. Some fellow users on the mailing list have even had good results with video conferencing software.

Please refer to <ref id="Supported Client Software"> section for a more complete listing of software supported.

IP Masquerade works well as a server to other 'client machines' running various different OS and hardware platforms. There are successful cases with internal MASQed systems using :

- Unix: Sun Solaris, *BSD, Linux, Digital UNIX, etc.
- Microsoft Windows 95/98, Windows NT, and Windows for Workgroups (with the TCP/IP package)
- IBM OS/2
- Apple Macintosh MacOS machines running either MacTCP or Open Transport
- DOS-based systems with packet drivers and the NCSA Telnet package
- VAXen
- Compaq/Digital Alpha running Linux and NT
- even Amiga computers with AmiTCP or AS225-stack.

The list goes on and on but the point is, if your OS platform talks TCP/IP, it should work with IP Masquerade!

Who Can Benefit From IP Masquerade?

- If you have a Linux host connected to the Internet and
- if you have some computers running TCP/IP connected to a Linux box on a local subnet, and/or
- if your Linux host has more than one modem and acts as a PPP or SLIP server connecting other computers, which

■ those **OTHER** machines do not have official or public assigned IP addresses (i.e., addressed with private TCP/IP numbers).

■ And, of course, if you want those **OTHER** machines to communicate to the Internet without spending extra money to get additional Public/Official TCP/IP addresses from your ISP and either configure Linux to be a router or purchase an external router.

Who Doesn't Need IP Masquerade?

■ If your machine is a stand-alone Linux host connected to the Internet (though setting up a firewall is a good idea), or

■ if you already have multiple assigned public addresses for your **OTHER** machines, and

■ of course, if you don't like the idea of a 'free ride' using Linux and feel more comfortable using expensive commercial tools to do the exact same thing.

How Does IP Masquerade Work?

From the original IP Masquerade FAQ by Ken Eves:
Here is a drawing of the most simple setup:

```
SLIP/PPP          +------------+                        +-------------+
to ISP provider   | Linux      |      SLIP/PPP          | Anybox      |
<---------- modem1|    #1      |modem2 ----------- modem3|             |
  111.222.333.444 |            |        192.168.0.100   |             |
                  +------------+                        +-------------+
```

In the above drawing, a Linux box with IP_MASQUERADING is installed as Linux #1 and is connected to the Internet via SLIP/or/PPP using modem1. It has an assigned public IP address of 111.222.333.444. It also has modem2 connected to allow callers to dial-in and start a SLIP/or/PPP connection.

The second system (which doesn't have to be running Linux) calls into the Linux #1 box and starts a SLIP/or/PPP connection. It does NOT have a publicly assigned IP address from the Internet so it uses the private address 192.168.0.100. (See below for more information.)

With IP Masquerade and the routing configured properly, the machine "ANYBOX" can interact with the Internet as if it was directly connected to the Internet (with a few small exceptions).

Quoting Pauline Middelink:

> Do not forget to mention that the "ANYBOX" machine should have the Linux #1 box configured as its gateway (whether is be the default route or just a subnet is no matter). If the "ANYBOX" machine can not do this, the Linux machine should be configured to support proxy arp for all routed addresses. But, the setup and configuration of proxy arp is beyond the scope of the document.

The following is an excerpt from a previous post on comp.os.linux.networking which has been edited to match the names used in the above example:

- I tell machine ANYBOX that my PPP or SLIPed Linux box is its gateway.

- When a packet comes into the Linux box from ANYBOX, it will assign it a new TCP/IP source port number and slap its own IP address in the packet header, saving the originals. The MASQ server will then send the modified packet out over the SLIP/PPP interface to the Internet.

- When a packet returns from the Internet to the Linux box, Linux examines if the port number is one of those ports that was assigned above. If so, the MASQ server will get the original port and IP address, put them back in the returned packet header, and send the packet to ANYBOX.

- The host that sent the packet will never know the difference.

Another IP Masquerading Example:

A typical example is given in the diagram following.

In this example, there are (4) computer systems that we are concerned about. There is also presumably something on the far right that your PPP connection to the Internet comes through (terminal server, etc.) and that there is some remote host (very far off to the right of the page) out on the Internet that you are interested communicating with). The Linux system

```
+----------+
|          |  Ethernet
| A-box    |::::::
|          |.2    : 192.168.0.x
+----------+      :
                  :       +----------+  PPP
+----------+      :    .1 |  Linux   |  link
|          |      :       | Masq-Gate|:::::::::::::::::::::// Internet
| B-box    |::::::        |          |  111.222.333.444
|          |.3   :        +----------+
+----------+     :
                 :
+----------+     :
|          |     :
| C-box    |::::::
|          |.4
+----------+


|                        |        |
| <-Internal Network--> |        | <- External Network ---->
|                        |        |
```

Masq-Gate is the IP Masquerading gateway for ALL the internal network
of machines **A-box**, **B-box** and **C-box** to get to the Internet. The internal
network uses one of the <htmlurl url="http://www.cis.ohio-state.edu/htbin/
rfc/rfc1918.html"name="several RFC-1918 assigned private network
addresses"> where in this case, the Class-C network 192.168.0.0. The
Linux box having the TCP/IP address 192.168.0.1 while the other systems
having the addresses:

- A-Box: 192.168.0.2
- B-Box: 192.168.0.3
- C-Box: 192.168.0.4

The three machines, A-box, B-box and C-box, can be running any operating system as long as they can speak TCP/IP. OSes such as **Windows 95**,
Macintosh MacTCP or OpenTransport or even another **Linux box** can
connect to other machines on the Internet. When running, the masquerading system or MASQ-gate converts all of these internal connections so that
they appear to originate from masq-gate itself. MASQ then arranges so
that data coming back in to a masqueraded connection is relayed back to
the proper originating system. Because of this, the systems on the internal

network see a direct route to the internet and are unaware that their data is being masqueraded. This is called a "Transparent" connection.
NOTE: Please see the <ref id="FAQ"> for more details on topics such as:

- The differences between NAT, MASQ, and Proxy servers.
- How packet firewalls work

Requirements for IP Masquerade on Linux 2.2.x

** Please refer to <url url="http://ipmasq.cjb.net/" name="IP Masquerade Resource"> for the latest information. **

- Kernel 2.2.x source available from <htmlurlurl="http://www.kernel.org/" name="http://www.kernel.org/">

  NOTE #1: Linux 2.2.x kernels less than 2.2.11 have a <htmlurl url "ftp://ftp.rustcorp.com/ipchains/ipchains-patch-2.2.desc" name="IPCHAINS fragmentation bug">. Because of this, people running strong IPCHAINS rulesets are open to attack. Please upgrade your kernel to a fixed version. NOTE #2: Most newer <ref id="MASQ-supported-Distributions"> such as Redhat 5.2 might not be Linux 2.2.x ready for your setup. Tools like DHCP, NetUtils, etc., will need to be upgraded. More details can be found in the HOWTO.

- Loadable kernel modules, preferably 2.1.121 or newer available from <htmlurl url="http://www.pi.se/blox/modutils/index.html" name="http://www.pi.se/blox/modutils/index.html"> or <htmlurl url="ftp://ftp.ocs.com.au/pub/modutils/"name="ftp://ftp.ocs.com. au/pub/modutils/">

- A running TCP/IP network or LAN covered in <url url="http://metalab.unc.edu/mdw/HOWTO/NET-3-HOWTO.html" name="Linux NET-3HOWTO"> and the <url url="http://metalab.unc.edu/mdw/LDP/nag/nag.html" name="Network Administrator's Guide">. (Also check out the <url url="http://www.ecst.csuchico.edu/~dranch/LINUX/TrinityOS.wri "name="TrinityOS"> document. TrinityOS is a very comprehensive guide on Linux networking. Including topics like IP MASQ, security, DNS, DHCP, Sendmail, PPP, Diald, NFS, IPSEC-based

VPNs, and performance sections to name a few. Over Fifty sections in all!

■ Connectivity to Internet for your Linux host covered in <url url="http://metalab.unc.edu/mdw/HOWTO/ISP Hookup HOWTO.html"name="Linux ISP Hookup HOWTO">, <url url="http://metalab.unc.edu/mdw/HOWTO/PPPHOWTO.html"name="Linux PPP HOWTO">, <url url="http://www.ecst.csuchico.edu/~dranch/LINUX/TrinityOS. wri name ="TrinityOS">, <url url="http://metalab.unc.edu/mdw/HOWTO/mini/DHCP.html" name="Linux DHCP mini-HOWTO"> and <url url="http://metalab.unc.edu/mdw/HOWTO/mini/Cable Modem.html"name="Linux Cable Modem mini-HOWTO">

■ IP Chains 1.3.9 or newer available from <htmlurl url="http://www.rustcorp.com/linux/ipchains/"name="http://www.rustcorp.com/linux/ipchains/"> (Additional information on version requirements is at the <url url="http://www.rustcorp.com/linux/ipchains/" name="Linux IP Firewalling Chains page">

■ Know how to configure, compile, and install a new Linux kernel as described in the <url url="http://metalab.unc.edu/mdw/HOWTO/Kernel-HOWTO.html"name="Linux Kernel HOWTO">

■ You can download and use various optional IP Masquerade tools to enable other functionality such as:

— TCP/IP port-forwarders or re-directors:

• <url url="http://juanjox.kernelnotes.org/" name="IP PortForwarding (IPMASQADM) - RECOMMENDED"> or his old <htmlurl l="http://www.geocities.com/Silicon Valley/Campus/4869/" name="mirror">.

ICQ MASQ module

— <htmlurl url="http://members.tripod.com/~djsf/masq-icq/" name="Andrew Deryabin's ICQ MASQ module ">

Please see the <url url="http://ipmasq.cjb.net/" name="IP Masquerade Resource"> page for more information available on these patches and possibly others as well.

Requirements for IP Masquerade on Linux 2.3.x and 2.4.x

** Please refer to <url url="http://ipmasq.cjb.net/" name="IP Masquerade Resource"> for the latest information. **

■ The newest 2.3.x and 2.4.x kernels are now using a completely new system called NetFilter (much like the 2.2.x kernels went to IPCHAINS). Many architectual changes have gone into this new code that will give the user a lot more flexibility, future features, etc.

As of this version of the HOWTO, Netfilter is NOT covered. Once the feature set of NetFilter is set, it will be decided if it will be added to -this- HOWTO or a new HOWTO. Until then, please see the following links for the available NetFilter documentation.

<htmlurl url="http://netfilter.kernelnotes.org/iptables-HOWTO.html" name="http://netfilter.kernelnotes.org/iptables-HOWTO.html"> and more specifically

<htmlurl url="http://netfilter.kernelnotes.org/ipnatctl-HOWTO.html" name="http://netfilter.kernelnotes.org/ipnatctl-HOWTO.html">

Setting Up IP Masquerade

If your private network contains any vital information, think carefully in terms of SECURITY before implementing IP Masquerade. By default, IP MASQ becomes a GATEWAY for you to get to the Internet but it also can allow someone on the Internet to possibly get into your internal network. Once you have IP MASQ functioning, it is HIGHLY recommended for the user to implement a STRONG IPFWADM/IPCHAINS firewall ruleset. Please see the <ref id="Strong-IPFWADM-Rulesets"> and <ref id="Strong-IPCHAINS-Rulesets"> sections below for more details.

Compiling the Kernel for IP Masquerade Support

If your Linux distribution already has all the required feature support compiled such as:

■ IPFWADM/IPCHAINS

■ IP forwarding

- IP masquerading
- IP Firewalling
- etc.

and all MASQ-related modules compiled (most modular kernels will have all you need), then you will NOT need to re-compile the kernel. If you aren't sure if you Linux distribution is MASQ ready, see the <ref id="MASQ-supported-Distributionsn"> section or the <url url="http://ipmasq.cjb.net/" name="IP Masquerade Resource"> for more details. If you can't find out if your distribution does support IP Masquerading by default, ASSUME IT DOESN'T.

Regardless of native support or not, reading this section is still highly recommended as it contains other useful information.

Linux 2.2.x Kernels

Please see the <ref id="2.2.x-Requirements"> section for any required software, patches, etc.

- First of all, you need the kernel source for 2.2.x (preferably the latest kernel version 2.2.11 or above)

NOTE #1: Linux 2.2.x kernels less than 2.2.11 have a <htmlurl url="ftp://ftp.rustcorp.com/ipchains/ipchains-patch-2.2desc" name=" IPCHAINS fragmentation bug">. Because of this, people running strong IPCHAINS rulesets are open to attack. Please upgrade your kernel to a fixed version.

- If this is your first time compiling the kernel, don't be scared. In fact, it's rather easy and it's covered in several URLs found in the <ref id="2.2.x-Requirements"> section.
- Unpack the kernel source to `/usr/src/` with a command: `tar xvzf linux-2.2.x.tar.gz -C /usr/src`, where the `x` in `2.2.x` is the current Linux 2.2 kernel. Once finished, make sure there is a directory or symbolic link to `/usr/src/linux/`
- Apply any appropriate or optional patches to the kernel source code. As of 2.2.1, IP Masq does not require any specific patching to get everything working. Features like PPTP and X Window forwarders are optional. Please refer to the <ref id="2.2.x-Requirements"> section for URLs and the <htmlurl url="http://ipmasq.cjb.net/" name="IP Masquerade Resources"> for up-to-date information and patch URLs.

■ Here are the MINIMUM options that are needed to be compiled into the kernel. You will also need to configure the kernel to use your installed network interfaces as well. Refer to the <url url="http://metalab.unc.edu/mdw/HOWTO/Kernel-HOWTO.html" name="Linux Kernel HOWTO"> and the README file in the kernel source directory for further instructions on compiling a kernel.

Please note the **YES or NO ANSWERS** to the following. Not all options will be available without the proper kernel patches described later in this HOWTO:

- Prompt for development and/or incomplete code/drivers (CONFIG_EXPERIMENTAL) [Y/n/?]
    — YES: though not required for IP MASQ, this option allows the kernel to create the MASQ modules and enable the option for port forwarding

- Enable loadable module support (CONFIG_MODULES) [Y/n/?]
    — YES: allows you to load kernel IP MASQ modules

- Networking support (CONFIG_NET) [Y/n/?]
    — YES: Enables the network subsystem

- Packet socket (CONFIG_PACKET) [Y/m/n/?]
    — YES: Though this is OPTIONAL, this recommended feature will allow you to use TCPDUMP to debug any problems with IP MASQ

- Kernel/User netlink socket (CONFIG_NETLINK) [Y/n/?]
    — YES: Though this is OPTIONAL, this feature will allow the logging of firewall hits

- Routing messages (CONFIG_RTNETLINK) [Y/n/?]
    — NO: This option does not have anything to do with packet firewall logging

- Network firewalls (CONFIG_FIREWALL) [Y/n/?]
    — YES: Enables the IPCHAINS firewall tool

- TCP/IP networking (CONFIG_INET) [Y/n/?]
    — YES: Enables the TCP/IP protocol

- IP: advanced router (CONFIG_IP_ADVANCED_ROUTER) [Y/n/?]
    — NO: This is only required for CONFIG_IP_ROUTE_VERBOSE and fancy routing (independent of ipchains/masq).

- IP: verbose route monitoring (CONFIG_IP_ROUTE_VERBOSE) [Y/n/?]
  - YES: This is useful if you use the routing code to drop IP spoofed packets (highly recommended) and you want to log them.

- IP: firewalling (CONFIG_IP_FIREWALL) [Y/n/?]
  - YES: Enable the firewalling feature

- IP: firewall packet netlink device (CONFIG_IP_FIREWALL_NETLINK) [Y/n/?]
  - YES: Though this is OPTIONAL, this feature will enhance the logging of firewall hits

- IP: always defragment (required for masquerading) (CONFIG_IP_ALWAYS_DEFRAG) [Y/n/?]
  - YES: This feature is REQUIRED to get asked about enabling the IP Masquerade and/or Transparent Proxying features. This feature also optimizes IP MASQ connections.

- IP: masquerading (CONFIG_IP_MASQUERADE) [Y/n/?]
  - YES: Enable IP MASQ to re-address specific internal to external TCP/IP packets

- IP: ICMP masquerading (CONFIG_IP_MASQUERADE_ICMP) [Y/n/?]
  - YES: Enable support for masquerading ICMP ping packets (ICMP error codes will be MASQed regardless). This is an important feature for troubleshooting connections.

- IP: masquerading special modules support (CONFIG_IP_ MASQUERADE_MOD) [Y/n/?]
  - YES: Though OPTIONAL, this enables the OPTION to later enable the TCP/IP Port forwarding system to allow external computers to directly connect to specified internal MASQed machines.

- IP: ipautofw masq support (EXPERIMENTAL) (CONFIG_IP_MASQUERADE_IPAUTOFW) [N/y/m/?]
  - NO: IPautofw is a legacy method of port forwarding. It is mainly a hack which is better handled by per-protocol modules. NOT recommended.

- IP: ipportfw masq support (EXPERIMENTAL) (CONFIG_IP_MASQUERADE_IPPORTFW) [Y/m/n/?]

— YES: Enables `IPPORTFW`.

> With this option, external computers on the Internet can directly communicate to specified internal MASQed machines. This feature is typically used to access internal SMTP, TELNET, and WWW servers. FTP port forwarding will need an additional patch as described in the FAQ section. Additional information on port forwarding is available in the Forwards section of this HOWTO.

- IP: `ip fwmark` masq-forwarding support (EXPERIMENTAL) (`CONFIG_IP_MASQUERADE_MFW`) `[Y/m/n/?]`
  — NO: This allows to do IP forwarding from IPCHAINS directly. Currently, this code is EXPERIMENTAL and the recommended method is to use `IPMASQADM` and `IPPORTFW`.
- IP: optimize as router not host (`CONFIG_IP_ROUTER`) `[Y/n/?]`
  — YES: This optimizes the kernel for the network subsystem though it isn't known if it makes a siginificant performance difference.
- IP: GRE tunnels over IP (`CONFIG_NET_IPGRE`) `[N/y/m/?]`
  — NO: This OPTIONAL selection is to enable PPTP and GRE tunnels through the IP MASQ box
- IP: `TCP` syncookie support (not enabled per default) (`CONFIG_SYN_COOKIES`) `[Y/n/?]`
  — YES: HIGHLY recommended for basic network security
- Network device support (`CONFIG_NETDEVICES`) `[Y/n/?]`
  — YES: Enables the Linux Network sublayer
- Dummy net driver support (`CONFIG_DUMMY`) `[M/n/y/?]`
  — YES: Though OPTIONAL, this option can help when debugging problems
- `/proc` filesystem support (`CONFIG_PROC_FS`) `[Y/n/?]`
  — YES: Required to enable the Linux network forwarding system

NOTE: These are just the components you need for IP Masquerade, select whatever other options you need for your specific setup.

- ■ After compiling the kernel, you should compile and install the IP MASQ modules by doing:

```
make modules; make modules_install
```

- Then you should add a few lines into your `/etc/rc.d/rc.local` file to load the IP Masquerade modules and enable IP MASQ automatically after each reboot:

```
.
.
.
#rc.firewall script - Start IPMASQ and the firewall
/etc/rc.d/rc.firewall
.
.
.
```

Linux 2.3.x / 2.4.x Kernels   The 2.3.x and 2.4.x kernels are NOT covered in this HOWTO yet. Please see the <ref id="2.3.x/2.4.x-Requirements"> section for URLs, etc., until it is covered by this or a NEW HOWTO.

Assigning Private Network IP Addresses to the Internal LAN

Since all **INTERNAL MASQed** machines should NOT have official Internet assigned addressees, there must be specific and accepted way to allocate address to those machines without conflicting with anyone else's Internet addresses.

From the original IP Masquerade FAQ:

<htmlurl url="http://www.cis.ohio-state.edu/htbin/rfc/INDEX.rfc.html:" name="RFC 1918"> is the official document on which IP addresses are to be used on a non-connected or "private" network. There are 3 blocks of numbers set aside specifically for this purpose.

Section 3: Private Address Space

The Internet Assigned Numbers Authority (IANA) has reserved the following three blocks of the IP address space for private networks:

```
10.0.0.0     - 10.255.255.255
172.16.0.0   - 172.31.255.255
192.168.0.0  - 192.168.255.255
```

We will refer to the first block as "24-bit block", the second as "20-bit block", and to the third as "16-bit" block". Note that the first block is nothing but a single class A network number, while the second block is a set of 16 contiguous class B network numbers, and third block is a set of 255 contiguous class C network numbers.

For the record, my preference is to use the 192.168.0.0 network with a 255.255.255.0 Class-C subnet mask and this HOWTO reflects this. But, any of the above private networks are valid but just be SURE to use the correct subnet-mask.

So, if you're using a Class-C network, you should number your TCP/IP enabled machines as 192.168.0.1, 192.168.0.2, 192.168.0.3, . . ., 192.168.0.x

192.168.0.1 is usually the internal gateway or Linux MASQ machine to get out to the external network. Please note that 192.168.0.0 and 192.168.0.255 are the Network and Broadcast address respectively (these addresses are RESERVED). Avoid using these addresses on your machines or your network will not work properly.

Configuring IP Forwarding Policies

At this point, you should have your kernel and other required packages installed. All network IP addresses, gateway, and DNS addresses should be configured on your Linux MASQ server as well. If you don't know how to configure your Linux network cards, please consult the HOWTOs listed in either the <ref id="2.0.x-Requirements"> or <ref id="2.2.x-Requirements"> sections.

Now, the only thing left to do is to configure the IP firewalling tools to both FORWARD and MASQUERADE the appropriate packets to the appropriate machine:

    ** This can be accomplished in many different ways. The following suggestions and examples worked for me, but you may have different ideas or needs.

    ** This section ONLY provides you with the bare minimum firewall ruleset to get the IP Masquerade feature working. Once IP MASQ has been successfully tested (as described later in this HOWTO), please refer to the <ref id="Strong-IPFWADM-Rulesets"> and <ref id="Strong-IPCHAINS-Rulesets"> sections for more secure firewall rulesets. In addition, check out the IPFWADM (2.0.x) and/or IPCHAINS(2.2.x) man pages for more details.

Linux 2.2.x Kernels   Please note that **IPFWADM is no longer the firewall tool** for manipulating IP Masquerading rules for both the 2.1.x and 2.2.x kernels. These new kernels now use the IPCHAINS tool. For a more detailed reason for this change, please see the <ref id="FAQ"> section.

Create the file /etc/rc.d/rc.firewall with the following initial SIMPLE ruleset:

```
#!/bin/sh
#
# rc.firewall - Initial SIMPLE IP Masquerade test for 2.1.x and
#               2.2.x kernels using IPCHAINS
#
#
# Load all required IP MASQ modules
#
# NOTE: Only load the IP MASQ modules you need. All current IP MASQ
#       modules are shown below but are commented out from loading.
```

```
# Needed to initially load modules
#
/sbin/depmod -a

# Supports the proper masquerading of FTP file transfers using the
#          PORT method
#
/sbin/modprobe ip_masq_ftp

# Supports the masquerading of RealAudio over UDP. Without this
#          module, RealAudio WILL function but in TCP mode. This
#          can cause a reduction in sound quality
#
# /sbin/modprobe ip_masq_raudio

# Supports the masquerading of IRC DCC file transfers
#
#/sbin/modprobe ip_masq_irc

# Supports the masquerading of Quake and QuakeWorld by default.
#          This modules is for for multiple users behind the Linux
#          MASQ server. If you are going to play Quake I, II, and
#          III, use the second example.
#
# NOTE: If you get ERRORs loading the QUAKE module, you are running
#       an old kernel that has bugs in it. Please upgrade to the
#       newest kernel.
#
#Quake I / QuakeWorld (ports 26000 and 27000)
#/sbin/modprobe ip_masq_quake
#
#Quake I/II/III / QuakeWorld (ports 26000, 27000, 27910, 27960)
#/sbin/modprobe ip_masq_quake 26000,27000,27910,27960

# Supports the masquerading of the CuSeeme video conferencing
# software
#
#/sbin/modprobe ip_masq_cuseeme

# Supports the masquerading of the VDO-live video conferencing
#          software
#
# /sbin/modprobe ip_masq_vdolive

# CRITICAL: Enable IP forwarding since it is disabled by default
#          since
#
#          Redhat Users: you may try changing the options in
#                        /etc/sysconfig/network from:
#
#      FORWARD_IPV4=false
#              to
#      FORWARD_IPV4=true
#
echo "1" > /proc/sys/net/ipv4/ip_forward

# Dynamic IP users:
#
```

```
# If you get your IP address dynamically from SLIP, PPP, or DHCP,
#    enable this following option. This enables dynamic-ip address
#    hacking in IP MASQ, making the life with Diald and similar
#    programs much easier.
#
#echo "1" > /proc/sys/net/ipv4/ip_dynaddr

# MASQ timeouts
#
#  2 hrs timeout for TCP session timeouts
# 10 sec timeout for traffic after the TCP/IP "FIN" packet is
#         received
# 160 sec timeout for UDP traffic (Important for MASQ'ed ICQ users)
#
/sbin/ipchains -M -S 7200 10 160

# DHCP:  For people who receive their external IP address from
#        either DHCP or BOOTP such as ADSL or Cablemodem users, it
#        is necessary to use the following before the deny command.
#        The "bootp_client_net_if_name" should be replaced the
#        name of the link that the DHCP/BOOTP server will put an
#        address on to?
#        This will be something like "eth0", "eth1", etc.
#
#        This example is currently commented out.
#
#
#/sbin/ipchains -A input -j ACCEPT -i bootp_clients_net_if_name
                 -s 0/0 67 -d 0/0 68 -p udp

# Enable simple IP forwarding and Masquerading
#
# NOTE: The following is an example for an internal LAN address in
#        the 192.168.0.x network with a 255.255.255.0 or a "24" bit
#        subnet mask.
#
#        Please change this network number and subnet mask to match
#        your internal LAN setup
#
/sbin/ipchains -P forward DENY
/sbin/ipchains -A forward -s 192.168.0.0/24 -j MASQ
```

Once you are finished with editing the /etc/rc.d/rc.firewall rule-set, make it executable by typing in chmod 700 /etc/rc.d/rc.firewall

You could have also enabled IP Masquerading on a PER MACHINE basis instead of the above method enabling an ENTIRE TCP/IP network. For example, say if I wanted only the 192.168.0.2 and 192.168.0.8 hosts to have access to the Internet and NOT any of the other internal machines. I would change the in the "Enable simple IP forwarding and Masquerading" section (shown above) of the /etc/rc.d/rc.firewall ruleset.

```
#!/bin/sh
#
# Enable simple IP forwarding and Masquerading
#
```

```
# NOTE: The following is an example to only allow IP Masquerading
#        for the 192.168.0.2 and 192.168.0.8 machines with a
#        255.255.255.0 or a "24" bit subnet mask.
#
#   Please change this network number and subnet mask to match your
#            internal LAN setup
#
/sbin/ipchains -P forward DENY
/sbin/ipchains -A forward -s 192.168.0.2/32 -j MASQ
/sbin/ipchains -A forward -s 192.168.0.8/32 -j MASQ
```

What appears to be a common mistake with new IP Masq users is to make the first command:

```
/sbin/ipchains -P forward masquerade
```

Do **NOT** make your default policy be MASQUERADING. Otherwise someone who can manipulate their routing tables will be able to tunnel straight back through your gateway, using it to masquerade their OWN identity!

Again, you can add these lines to the `/etc/rc.d/rc.firewall` file, one of the other rc files you prefer, or do it manually every time you need IP Masquerade.

Please see the <ref id="Strong-IPFWADM-Rulesets"> and <ref id="Strong-IPCHAINS-Rulesets"> sections for a detailed guide on IPCHAINS and a strong IPCHAINS ruleset example. For additional details on IPCHAINS usage, please refer to the <htmlurl url="http://meta-lab.unc.edu/mdw/HOWTO/IPCHAINS-HOWTO.html" name="Linux IP CHAINS HOWTO">

Configuring the Other Internal To-Be MASQed Machines

Besides setting the appropriate IP address for each internal MASQed machine, you should also set each internal machine with the appropriate gateway IP address of the Linux MASQ server and required DNS servers. In general, this is rather straight forward. You simply enter the address of your Linux host (usually 192.168.0.1) as the machine's gateway address.

For the Domain Name Service, you can add in any DNS servers that are available. The most apparent one should be the one that your Linux server is using. You can optionally add any "domain search" suffix as well.

After you have properly reconfigured the internal MASQed machines, remember to restart their appropriate network services or reboot them.

The following configuration instructions assume that you are using a Class C network with 192.168.0.1 as your Linux MASQ server's address. Please note that 192.168.0.0 and 192.168.0.255 are reserved TCP/IP address.

As it stands, the following Platforms have been tested as internal MASQed machines:

- Linux 1.2.x, 1.3.x, 2.0.x, 2.1.x, 2.2.x
- Solaris 2.51, 2.6, 7
- Windows 95, OSR2, 98
- Windows NT 3.51, 4.0, 2000 (both workstation and server)
- Windows For Workgroup 3.11 (with TCP/IP package)
- Windows 3.1 (with the Netmanage Chameleon package)
- Novell 4.01 Server with the TCP/IP service
- OS/2 (including Warp v3)
- Macintosh OS (with MacTCP or Open Transport)
- DOS (with NCSA Telnet package, DOS Trumpet works partially)
- Amiga (with AmiTCP or AS225-stack)
- VAX Stations 3520 and 3100 with UCX (TCP/IP stack for VMS)
- Alpha/AXP with Linux/Redhat
- SCO Openserver (v3.2.4.2 and 5)
- IBM RS/6000 running AIX

Configuring Microsoft Windows 95

1. If you haven't installed your network card and adapter driver, do so now. Description of this is beyond the scope of this document.

2. Go to the *Control Panel —> Network*.

3. Click on *Add —> Protocol —> Manufacture: Microsoft —> Protocol: TCP/IP protocol* if you don't already have it.

4. Highlight the TCP/IP item bound to your Windows95 network card and select *Properties*. Now go to the *IP Address* tab and set IP Address to 192.168.0.x, (1 < x < 255), and then set the Subnet Mask to 255.255.255.0

5. Now select the *Gateway* tab and add 192.168.0.1 as your gateway under *Gateway* and hit *Add*.

6. Under the *DNS Configuration* tab, make sure to put in a name for this machine and enter in your official domain name. If you don't have your own domain, put in the domain of your ISP. Now, add all of the DNS server that your Linux host uses (usually found in /etc/resolv.conf). Usually these DNS servers are located at your ISP though you can be running either your own CACHING or Authoritative DNS server on your Linux MASQ server as well. Optionally, you can add any appropriate domain search suffixes as well.

7. Leave all the other settings as they are unless you know what you're doing.

8. Click *OK* on all dialog boxes and restart system.

9. Ping the linux box to test the network connection: *Start/Run*, type: ping 192.168.0.1 (This is only an INTERNAL LAN connection test, you can't ping the outside world yet.) If you don't see "replies" to your PINGs, please verify your network configuration.

10. You can optionally create a HOSTS file in the C:\Windows directory so that you can ping the "hostname" of the machines on your LAN without the need for a DNS server. There is an example called HOSTS.SAM in the C:\windows directory.

Configuring Windows NT

1. If you haven't installed your network card and adapter driver, do so now. Description of this is beyond the scope of this document.

2. Go to *Control Panel —> Network —> Protocols*

3. Add the TCP/IP Protocol and related Components from the *Add Software* menu if you don't have TCP/IP service installed already.

4. Under *Network Software and Adapter Cards* section, highlight the *TCP/IP Protocol* in the *Installed Network Software* selection box.

5. In *TCP/IP Configuration*, select the appropriate adapter, e.g., [1]Novell NE2000 Adapter. Then set the IP Address to 192.168.0.x (1 < x < 255), then set Subnet Mask to 255.255.255.0 and Default Gateway to 192.168.0.1

6. Do not enable *Automatic DHCP Configuration*, put anything in those *WINS Server* input areas, and *Enable IP Forwardings* unless you're either in a Windows NT domain and you know EXACTLY what you're doing.

7. Click *DNS*, fill in the appropriate information that your Linux host uses (usually found in `/etc/resolv.conf`) and then click '*OK*' when you're done.

8. Click *Advanced*, be sure to DISABLE *DNS for Windows Name Resolution* and *Enable LMHOSTS lookup* unless you known what these options do. If you want to use a `LMHOSTS` file, it is stored in `C:\winnt\system32\drivers\etc`.

9. Click *OK* on all dialog boxes and restart system.

10. `Ping` the linux box to test the network connection: *File / Run*, type: `ping 192.168.0.1` (This is only an INTERNAL LAN connection test, you can't `ping` the outside world yet.) If you don't see "replies" to your PINGs, please verify your network configuration.

Configuring Windows for Workgroup 3.11

1. If you haven't installed your network card and adapter driver, do so now. Description of this is beyond the scope of this document.

2. Install the TCP/IP 32b package if you don't have it already.

3. In *Main / Windows Setup / Network Setup*, click on *Drivers*.

4. Highlight *Microsoft TCP / IP-32 3.11b* in the *Network Drivers* section, click *Setup*.

5. Set the IP Address to 192.168.0.x (1 < x < 255), then set the Subnet Mask to 255.255.255.0 and Default Gateway to 192.168.0.1

6. Do not enable *Automatic DHCP Configuration* or put anything in those *WINS Server* input areas unless you're in a Windows NT domain and you know what you're doing.

7. Click *DNS*, fill in the appropriate information your Linux host uses (usually found in `/etc/resolv.conf`). Then click *OK* when you're done with it.

8. Click *Advanced*, check *Enable DNS for Windows Name Resolution* and *Enable LMHOSTS lookup* found in `c:\windows`.

9. Click *OK* on all dialog boxes and restart system.

10. `Ping` the linux box to test the network connection: *File / Run*, type: `ping 192.168.0.1` (This is only an INTERNAL LAN connection test, you can't `ping` the outside world yet.) If you don't see "replies" to your PINGs, please verify your network configuration.

Configuring UNIX Based Systems

1. If you haven't installed your network card and recompile your kernel with the appropriate adapter driver, do so now. Description of this is beyond the scope of this document.

2. Install TCP/IP networking, such as the net-tools package, if you don't have it already.

3. Set IPADDR to 192.168.0.x ($1 < x < 255$), then set *NETMASK* to 255.255.255.0, *GATEWAY* to 192.168.0.1, and *BROADCAST* to 192.168.0.255. For example with Redhat Linux systems, you can edit the `/etc/sysconfig/network-scripts/ifcfg-eth0` file, or simply do it through the Control Panel. These changes are different for other UNIXes such as SunOS, BSDi, Slackware Linux, Solaris, SuSe, Debian, etc . . .). Please refer to your UNIX documentation for more information.

4. Add your domain name service (DNS) and domain search suffix in `/etc/resolv.conf` and for the appropriate UNIX versions, edit the `/etc/nsswitch.conf` file to enable DNS services.

5. You may want to update your `/etc/networks` file depending on your settings.

6. Restart the appropriate services, or simply restart your system.

7. Issue a `ping` command: `ping 192.168.0.1` to test the connection to your gateway machine. (This is only an INTERNAL LAN connection test, you can't `ping` the outside world yet.) If you don't see "replies" to your PINGs, please verify your network configuration.

Testing IP Masquerade

Finally, it's time to give IP Masquerading an official try after all this hard work. If you haven't already rebooted your Linux box, do so to make sure the machines boots ok, executes the `/etc/rc.d/rc.firewall` ruleset, etc. Next, make sure that both the internal LAN connection and connection of your Linux hosts to the Internet is okay.

Now do the following:

- One: From an internal MASQed computer, try pinging your local IP address (i.e., `ping 192.168.0.10`). This will verify that TCP/IP is correctly working on the local machine. If this doesn't work, make sure that TCP/IP is correctly configured on the MASQed PC as described earlier in this HOWTO.

- Two: On the MASQ server itself, ping then internal IP address of the MASQ network (i.e., `ping 192.168.0.1`). Now then `ping` the external IP address connected to the Internet. This address might be your PPP, Ethernet, etc. address connected to your ISP. If you don't know what this IP address is, run the Linux command `/sbin/ifconfig` on the MASQ server to get the Internet address. This will confirm that the MASQ server has full network connectivity.

- Three: Back on a internal MASQed computer, try pinging the IP address of the Masquerading Linux box's internal Ethernet card, (i.e., `ping 192.168.0.1`). This will prove that your internal network and routing is OK. If this fails, make sure Ethernet cards of the MASQ server and the MASQed computer have `link`. This is usually a LED light on either the back of each Ethernet card and also on the Ethernet hub/switch (if you are using one).

- Four: From an internal MASQed computer, ping the IP address of the MASQ server's external TCP/IP address obtained in item TWO above. This address might be your PPP, Ethernet, etc. address connected to your ISP. This ping test will prove that masquerading is working (ICMP Masquerading specifically). If it doesn't work, make sure that you enabled "ICMP Masquerading" in the kernel and "IP Forwarding" in your `/etc/rc.d/rc.firewall` script. Also make sure that the `/etc/rc.d/rc.firewall` ruleset loaded ok. Try run the `/etc/rc.d/rc.firewall` script manually for now to see if it runs ok.

If you still can't get things to work, take a look at the output from

- `ifconfig` : Make sure your Internet connection is UP and you have the correct IP address for the Internet connection

- `netstat -rn` : Make sure your default gateway (the column one with the IP address in the Gateway column) is set

- `cat /proc/sys/net/ipv4/ip_forward` : Make sure it says "1" so that Linux forwarding is enabled

- `/sbin/ipfwadm -F -l` for 2.0.x or `/sbin/ipchains -F -L` for 2.2.x users : Make sure you have MASQ enabled

- Five: From an internal MASQed computer, now ping a static TCP/IP address out on the Internet [i.e., `ping 152.19.254.81` (this is <http://metalab.unc.edu>—home of the LDP)]. If this works, that means that ICMP Masquerading is working over the Internet. If it didn't work, again check your Internet connection. If this still doesn't work, make sure you are using the simple `rc.firewall` ruleset and that you have ICMP Masqurading compiled into the Linux kernel.

- Six: Now try TELNETing to a remote IP address [i.e., `telnet 152.2.254.81` (`metalab.unc.edu`—Note that this might take a while to get a login prompt since this is a VERY busy server)]. Did you get a login prompt after a while? If that worked, that means that TCP Masquerading is running ok. If not, try TELNETing to some other hosts you think will support TELNET like 198.182. 196.55 (www.linux.org). If this still doesn't work, make sure you are using the simple `rc.firewall` ruleset for now.

- Seven: Now try TELNETing to a remote HOSTNAME [i.e., `telnet metalab.unc.edu` (152.2.254.81)]. If this works, this means that DNS is working fine as well. If this didn't work but step FOUR did work, make sure that you have valid DNS servers configured on your MASQed computer.

- Eight: As a last test, try browsing some *INTERNET* WWW sites on one of your MASQed machines, and see if you can reach them. For example, access the <htmlurl url="http://metalab.unc. edu/LDP" name="Linux Documentation Project site">. If this works, you can be fairly certain that everything is working FINE!

If you see The Linux Documentation Project homepage, then **CONGRATULATIONS! It's working!** If that WWW site comes up correctly, then all other standard network tolls such as PING, TELNET, SSH, and with their related IP MASQ modules loaded: FTP, Real Audio, IRC DCCs, Quake I/II/III, CuSeeme, VDOLive, etc. should work fine! If FTP, IRC, RealAudio, Quake I/II/III, etc. aren't working or are performing poorly, make sure their associated Masquerading modules are loaded by running `lsmod` and also be sure you are loading the module with any non-default server ports. If you don't see your needed module, make sure your `/etc/rc.d/rc. firewall` script is loading them (i.e., remove the # character for a give IP MASQ module).

Other IP Masquerade Issues and Software Support

Problems with IP Masquerade

Some TCP/IP application protocols will not currently work with Linux IP Masquerading because they either assume things about port numbers or encode TCP/IP addresses and/or port numbers in their data stream. These latter protocols need specific proxies or IP MASQ modules built into the masquerading code to make them work.

Incoming Services

By default, Linux IP Masquerading cannot handle incoming services at all but there are a few ways of allowing them.

If you do not require high levels of security then you can simply forward or redirect IP ports. There are various ways of doing this though the most stable method is to use IPPORTFW. For more information, please see the <ref id="Forwarders"> section.

If you wish to have some level of authorization on incoming connections then you will need to either configure TCP-wrappers or Xinetd to then allow only specific IP addresses through. The TIS Firewall Toolkit is a good place to look for tools and information.

More details on incoming security can be found in the <url url="http://www.ecst.csuchico.edu/~dranch/LINUX/TrinityOS.wri"name= "TrinityOS"> document and at <url url="http://ipmasq.cjb.net" name="IP Masquerade Resource">.

Supported Client Software and Other Setup Notes

**The <url url="http://www.tsmservices.com/masq"name="Linux Masquerade Application list"> has a lot of good information regarding applications that work through Linux IP masquerading. This site was recently taken over by Steve Grevemeyer who implemented it with a full database backend. Its a great resource!

Generally, any application that uses standard TCP and UDP should work. If you have any suggestion, hints, etc., please see the <url url="http://ipmasq.cjb.net/" name="IP Masquerade Resource"> for more details.

Network Clients That -Work- with IP Masquerade   General Clients:

Archie   all supported platforms, file searching client (not all Archie clients are supported)

FTP   all supported platforms, with the `ip_masq_ftp.o` kernel module for active FTP connections.

Gopher client   all supported platforms

HTTP   all supported platforms, WWW surfing

IRC   all IRC clients on various supported platforms, DCC is supported via the `ip_masq_irc.o` module

NNTP (USENET)   all supported platforms, USENET news client

PING   all platforms, with ICMP Masquerading kernel option

POP3   all supported platforms, email clients

SSH   all supported platforms, Secure TELNET/FTP clients

SMTP   all supported platforms, email servers like Sendmail, Qmail, PostFix, etc.

TELNET   all supported platforms, remote session

TRACEROUTE   UNIX and Windows based platforms, some variations may not work

VRML   Windows (possibly all supported platforms), virtual reality surfing

WAIS client   all supported platforms

Multimedia and Communication Clients:

Alpha Worlds   Windows, Client-Server 3D chat program

CU-SeeMe   All supported platforms, with the `ip_masq_cuseeme` module loaded, please see the <ref id="CuSeeme"> section for more details.

ICQ   all supported clients. Requires the Linux kernel to be compiled with `IPPORTFW` support and ICQ is configured to be behind a NON-SOCKS proxy. A full description of this configuration is in the <ref id="ICQ"> section.

Internet Phone 3.2   Windows, Peer-to-peer audio communications, people can reach you only if you initiate the call, but people cannot call you without a specific port forwarding setup. See the <ref id="Forwarders"> section for more details.

Internet Wave Player   Windows, network streaming audio

Powwow   Windows, Peer-to-peer Text audio whiteboard communications, people can reach you only if you initiate the call, but people cannot call you without a specific port forwarding setup. See the <ref id="Forwarders"> section for more details.

Real Audio Player   Windows, network streaming audio, higher quality available with the `ip_masq_raudio` UDP module

True Speech Player 1.1b   Windows, network streaming audio

VDOLive   Windows, with the `ip_masq_vdolive` patch

Worlds Chat 0.9a   Windows, Client-Server 3D chat program

Games–See the <ref id="LooseUDP"> section for more details on the LooseUDP patch.

Battle.net   Works but requires TCP ports 116 and 118 and UDP port 6112 IPPORTFWed to the game machine. See the id="Forwarders"> section for more details. Please note that FSGS and Bnetd servers still require IPPORTFW since they haven't been re-written to be NAT-friendly.

BattleZone 1.4   Works with LooseUDP patch and new NAT-friendly <htmlurl url="http://us4.alink.activision.com/tmp/nat/"name=".DLLS from Activision">

Dark Reign 1.4   Works with LooseUDP patch or requires TCP ports 116 and 118 and UDP port 6112 IPPORTFWed to the game machine. See the <ref id="Forwarders"> section for more details.

Diablo   Works with LooseUDP patch or requires TCP ports 116 and 118 and UDP port 6112 IPPORTFWed to the game machine. Newer versions of Diablo use only TCP port 6112 and UDP port 6112. See the <ref id="Forwarders"> section for more details.

Heavy Gear 2   Works with LooseUDP patch or requires TCP ports 116 and 118 and UDP port 6112 IPPORTFWed to the game machine. See the <ref id="Forwarders"> section for more details.

Quake I/II/III   Works right out of the box but requires the `ip_masq_quake` module if there are more than one Quake I/II/III player behind a MASQ box. Also, this module only supports Quake I and QuakeWorld by default. If you need to support Quake II or non-default server ports, please see the module install section of the <ref id="rc.firewall-2.0.x"> and <ref id="rc.firewall-2.2.x"> rulesets.

StarCraft   Works with the LooseUDP patch and IPPORTFWing TCP and UDP ports 6112 to the internal MASQed game machine. See the <ref id="Forwarders"> section for more details.

WorldCraft   Works with LooseUDP patch

Other Clients:

Linux net-acct package   Linux, network administration-account package

NCSA Telnet 2.3.08   DOS, a suite containing telnet, ftp, ping, etc.

PC-anywhere for Windows   MS-Windows, Remotely controls a PC over TCP/IP, only work if it is a client but not a host without a specific port forwarding setup. See the <ref id="Forwarders"> section for more details.

Socket Watch   uses NTP—network time protocol

Clients That Do Not Work:

All H.323 programs

MS Netmeeting, Intel Internet Phone Beta 2—Connects but voice travels one way (out). Check out <url url="http://www.equival. com.au/phonepatch/index.html" name="Equivalence's PhonePatch"> H.323 gateway for one possible solution.

UPDATE: There is now BETA code on the MASQ WWW site to work with Microsoft Netmeeting v2.x code on 2.0.x kernels. There is NO modules as of yet for NetMeeting v3.x and/or 2.2.x kernels.

Intel Streaming Media Viewer Beta 1   Cannot connect to server

Netscape CoolTalk   Cannot connect to opposite side

WebPhone   Cannot work at present (it makes invalid assumptions about addresses).

Diagnosing Your Samba Server

This file contains a list of tests you can perform to validate your Samba server. It also tells you what the likely cause of the problem is if it fails any one of these steps. If it passes all these tests then it is probably working fine.

You should do ALL the tests, in the order shown. I have tried to carefully choose them so later tests only use capabilities verified in the earlier tests.

I would welcome additions to this set of tests. Please mail them to <samba-bugs@samba.org>.

If you send me an email saying "it doesn't work" and you have not followed this test procedure then you should not be surprised if I ignore your email.

Assumptions

In all of the tests I assume you have a Samba server called `BIGSERVER` and a PC called `ACLIENT`. I also assume the PC is running windows for workgroups with a recent copy of the microsoft `tcp/ip stack`. Alternatively, your PC may be running Windows 95 or Windows NT (Workstation or Server).

The procedure is similar for other types of clients.

I also assume you know the name of an available share in your `smb.conf`. I will assume this share is called `tmp`. You can add a `tmp` share like by adding the following to `smb.conf`:

```
[tmp]
 comment = temporary files=20
 path = /tmp
 read only = yes
```

THESE TESTS ASSUME VERSION 1.9.16 OR LATER OF THE SAMBA SUITE. SOME COMMANDS SHOWN DID NOT EXIST IN EARLIER VERSIONS

Please pay attention to the error messages you receive. If any error message reports that your server is being unfriendly you should first check that your IP name resolution is correctly set up, eg.: Make sure your `/etc/resolv.conf` file points to name servers that really do exist.

Also, if you do not have DNS server access for name resolution please check that the settings for your `smb.conf` file results in `dns proxy = no`. The best way to check this is with `testparm smb.conf`.

Test 1

In the directory in which you store your `smb.conf` file, run the command `testparm smb.conf`. If it reports any errors then your `smb.conf` configuration file is faulty.

    Note: Your `smb.conf` file may be located in: `/etc`
               Or in: `/usr/local/samba/lib`

Test 2

run the command `ping BIGSERVER` from the PC and `ping ACLIENT` from the unix box. If you don't get a valid response then your `TCP/IP` software is not correctly installed.

Note: You will need to start a dos prompt window on the PC to run ping.

If you get a message saying host not found or similar then your DNS software or /etc/hosts file is not correctly setup. It is possible to run samba without DNS entries for the server and client, but I assume you do have correct entries for the remainder of these tests.

Another reason why ping might fail is if your host is running firewall software. You will need to relax the rules to let in the workstation in question, perhaps by allowing access from another subnet (on Linux this is done via the ipfwadm program.)

Test 3

Run the command smbclient -L BIGSERVER on the unix box. You should get a list of available shares back. If you get a error message containing the string Bad password then you probably have either an incorrect hosts allow, hosts deny or valid users line in your smb.conf, or your guest account is not valid. Check what your guest account is using testparm and temporarily remove any hosts allow, hosts deny, valid users or invalid users lines.

If you get a connection refused response then the smbd server could not be running. If you installed it in inetd.conf then you probably edited that file incorrectly. If you installed it as a daemon then check that it is running, and check that the netbios-ssn port is in a LISTEN state using netstat -a.

If you get a session request failed then the server refused the connection. If it says Your server software is being unfriendly then it's probably because you have invalid command line parameters to smbd, or a similar fatal problem with the initial startup of smbd. Also check your config file (smb.conf) for syntax errors with testparm and that the various directories where samba keeps its log and lock files exist.

There are a number of reasons for which smbd may refuse or decline a session request. The most common of these involve one or more of the following smb.conf file entries:

```
hosts deny = ALL
hosts allow = xxx.xxx.xxx.xxx/yy
bind interfaces only = Yes
```

In the above, no allowance has been made for any session requests that will automatically translate to the loopback adaptor address 127.0.0.1. To solve this problem change these lines to:

```
hosts deny = ALL

hosts allow = xxx.xxx.xxx.xxx/yy 127.
```

Do NOT use the `bind interfaces only` parameter where you may wish to use the samba password change facility, or where smbclient may need to access local service for name resolution or for local resource connections. (Note: the "bind interfaces only" parameter deficiency where it will not allow connections to the loopback address will be fixed soon).

Another common cause of these two errors is having something already running on port 139, such as Samba (ie: `smbd` is running from `inetd` already) or something like Digital's Pathworks. Check your `inetd.conf` file before trying to start `smbd` as a `daemon`, it can avoid a lot of frustration!

And yet another possible cause for failure of Test 3 is when the subnet mask and / or broadcast address settings are incorrect. Please check that the network interface IP Address / Broadcast Address / Subnet Mask settings are correct and that Samba has correctly noted these in the `log.nmb` file.

Test 4

Run the command `nmblookup -B BIGSERVER _SAMBA_`. You should get the IP address of your Samba server back.

If you don't then `nmbd` is incorrectly installed. Check your `inetd.conf` if you run it from there, or that the `daemon` is running and listening to `udp port 137`.

One common problem is that many `inetd` implementations can't take many parameters on the command line. If this is the case then create a one-line script that contains the right parameters and run that from `inetd`.

Test 5

Run the command `nmblookup -B ACLIENT '*'`

You should get the PCs IP address back. If you don't then the client software on the PC isn't installed correctly, or isn't started, or you got the name of the PC wrong.

Test 6

Run the command `nmblookup -d 2 '*'`

This time we are trying the same as the previous test but are trying it via a broadcast to the default broadcast address. A number of `Netbios/`

`TCPIP` hosts on the network should respond, although Samba may not catch all of the responses in the short time it listens. You should see `got a positive name query response` messages from several hosts.

If this doesn't give a similar result to the previous test then nmblookup isn't correctly getting your broadcast address through its automatic mechanism. In this case you should experiment use the `interfaces` option in `smb.conf` to manually configure your IP address, broadcast and netmask.

If your PC and server aren't on the same subnet then you will need to use the `-B` option to set the broadcast address to the that of the PCs subnet.

This test will probably fail if your subnet mask and broadcast address are not correct. (Refer to Test 3 notes above).

Test 7

Run the command `smbclient '\\BIGSERVER\TMP'`. You should then be prompted for a password. You should use the password of the account you are logged into the unix box with. If you want to test with another account then add the `-U <accountname>` option to the end of the command line. e.g.: `smbclient //bigserver/tmp -Ujohndoe`.

> Note: It is possible to specify the password along with the username as follows:

`smbclient //bigserver/tmp -Ujohndoe%secret`

Once you enter the password you should get the `smb>` prompt. If you don't then look at the error message. If it says `invalid network name` then the service `tmp` not correctly setup in your `smb.conf`.

If it says `bad password` then the likely causes are:

- you have shadow passwords (or some other password system) but didn't compile in support for them in `smbd`
- your `valid users` configuration is incorrect
- you have a mixed case password and you haven't enabled the `password level` option at a high enough level
- the `path =` line in `smb.conf` is incorrect. Check it with `testparm`
- you enabled password encryption but didn't create the `SMB` encrypted password file

Once connected you should be able to use the commands `dir get put` etc. Type `help <command>` for instructions. You should especially check that the amount of free disk space shown is correct when you type `dir`.

Test 8

On the PC type the command `net view \\BIGSERVER`. You will need to do this from within a `dos prompt` window. You should get back a list of available shares on the server.

If you get a `network name not found` or similar error then net-bios name resolution is not working. This is usually caused by a problem in `nmbd`. To overcome it you could do one of the following (you only need to choose one of them):

- fixup the `nmbd` installation
- add the IP address of `BIGSERVER` to the `wins server` box in the advanced `tcp/ip` setup on the PC.
- enable windows name resolution via `DNS` in the advanced section of the `tcp/ip setup`
- add `BIGSERVER` to your `lmhosts` file on the PC.

If you get an `invalid network name` or `bad password error` then the same fixes apply as they did for the `smbclient -L` test above. In particular, make sure your `hosts allow` line is correct (see the man pages).

Also, do not overlook that fact that when the workstation requests the connection to the samba server it will attempt to connect using the =20 name with which you logged onto your Windows machine. You need to make sure that an account exists on your Samba server with that exact same name and password.

If you get `specified computer is not receiving requests` or similar it probably means that the host is not contactable via `tcp` services. Check to see if the host is running `tcp wrappers`, and if so add an entry in the hosts.allow file for your client (or subnet, etc.)

Test 9

Run the command `net use x: \\BIGSERVER\TMP`. You should be prompted for a password then you should get a `command completed successfully` message. If not then your PC software is incorrectly installed or your `smb.conf` is incorrect. make sure your `hosts allow` and other config lines in `smb.conf` are correct.

It's also possible that the server can't work out what user name to connect you as. To see if this is the problem add the line `user = USERNAME` to the `[tmp]` section of `smb.conf` where USERNAME is the username corresponding to the password you typed. If you find this fixes things you may need the username mapping option.

Test 10

From file manager try to browse the server. Your samba server should appear in the browse list of your local workgroup (or the one you specified in smb.conf). You should be able to double click on the name of the server and get a list of shares. If you get an invalid password error when you do then you are probably running WinNT and it is refusing to browse a server that has no encrypted password capability and is in user level security mode. In this case either set security = server AND password server = Windows_NT_Machine in your smb.conf file, or enable encrypted passwords AFTER compiling in support for encrypted passwords (refer to the Makefile).

Still Having Troubles?

Try the mailing list or newsgroup, or use the tcpdump-smb utility to sniff the problem. The official samba mailing list can be reached at <samba@samba.org>. To find out more about samba and how to subscribe to the mailing list check out the samba web page at

<http://samba.org/samba>

Also look at the other docs in the Samba package!

Index

K

N